W9-BXL-808

WORKING CAPITAL BUDGET

BUDGETING FOR LONG-TERM FUNDS

ADMINISTRATIVE AND OTHER ASPECTS OF BUDGETING

Budgeting and Profit Planning Manual

James D. Willson, CPA
Senior Vice-President — Finance (retired)
Northrop Corporation

Simonoff Accounting Series

WARREN, GORHAM & LAMONT
Boston • New York

Copyright © 1983 by

WARREN, GORHAM & LAMONT, INC.
210 SOUTH STREET
BOSTON, MASSACHUSETTS 02111

ALL RIGHTS RESERVED

No part of this book may be reproduced in any form, by photo-
stat, microfilm, xerography, or any means, or incorporated into
any information retrieval system, electronic or mechanical, without the written permission of the copyright owner.

ISBN 0-88712-000-8

Library of Congress Catalog Card No. 83-50499

PRINTED IN THE UNITED STATES OF AMERICA

Preface

THE ROLE OF FINANCIAL officers has expanded during the past two decades, corresponding to the growth in complexity of managing a business. The transformation of the financial executive from historian to participant in important decision-making has come about as a result of several pervasive forces: government regulations, volatile economic conditions, greater internationalism, changes in the capital markets, increased competition, and changing rates of inflation.

It is now necessary to be more sensitive to product, market, and cost trends. Added to those external forces are changes within business itself, including a tendency toward decentralized management, the greater relative significance of internal cash flow, increased computerization, and improved methods of communication.

All of these external and internal forces make it more feasible and desirable — in fact, imperative — to allocate capital resources to their highest and best uses. With a greater premium being placed on sound financial planning and effective efforts to bring actual performance in line with plan, there is a growing demand for more knowledgeable financial officers. Improved budgeting, involving the participation of all of management, and the use of the computer to quickly test alternative courses of action, is more vital than ever before to the success of the enterprise.

While businesses have long budgeted sales, costs, and operating expenses, the increased sophistication of financial and other kinds of management is now causing a review of the propriety of the financial goals and objectives, and the techniques used in evaluating resources and the expected return. Thus, better answers are being demanded and generated to questions such as:

- Should the corporate profit objective be an increase in earnings per share or in shareholders' equity? Which is more appropriate and why?
- How can major projects requiring differing resources and providing vastly dissimilar patterns of cash return be compared?
- What is the best measure of return on capital expenditures? Payback period? Average return on total investment? Internal rate of return?
- What return on assets should a company achieve?

More attention is required — and is being paid — to the wise management of assets and liabilities.

This book focuses on every aspect of effective budgeting. Practical examples of simple and effective techniques, forms, analyses, and reports are discussed in nontechnical language. The basic concepts and conditions necessary to make budgeting work more effectively are discussed; cost behavior, cost-volume-profit analysis, and the cost of capital as related to planning are reviewed. Budgets for every operating function, including sales, marketing, manufacturing, research, and advertising, are considered in detail. Techniques to improve the return on assets through planning and control of working capital — cash, accounts receivable, inventories, current liabilities — are covered intensively. Up-to-date capital budgeting techniques are discussed in detail, as are the planning and control of long-term liabilities and shareholders' equity.

Critically important but often-ignored phases of budget management are covered. These include securing approval of the board of directors; corporate planning models; profit improvement programs; budget procedures and manuals; and the human relations aspects.

Budgeting and Profit Planning Manual is a complete, practical working guide that provides nearly 250 illustrative budgets, checklists, forms, budget manuals, reports, presentations, and analyses for daily use. This book will be updated through the issuance of yearly supplements, so that readers will have easy access to the latest budgeting computer applications and new developments in budgeting techniques.

Acknowledgments

The publication of any good book reflects not merely the ideas and experience of the author, but also the efforts and thoughts of the many individuals who have worked with him. In this context, a special commendation is due to the staff of Warren, Gorham & Lamont, but especially to Martha Jewett, senior editor, for her significant contributions toward layout and format, and suggestions regarding writing style. I should also like to acknowledge the assistance of some of the financial staff at Northrop Corporation with whom I have worked for several years — particularly John B. Campbell, Vice-President and Controller, Jack Wear, Director–Corporate Accounting, and Ken Mars, Manager–Financial Accounting — for their contribution and assistance regarding corporate planning models, labor budgets, and general and administrative budget material. Particular thanks is due to Nelson F. Gibbs, Jr., Partner, Touche Ross & Co., and William G. Dudley, Partner, Ernst & Whinney, for assistance in researching current financial and accounting data. Hugo Standing, Chairman of Alexander &

Alexander of California, provided suggestions in connection with budgeting for service companies. Sherry du Roy, Librarian, Ernst & Whinney, Los Angeles, made significant contributions in computer research and retrieval of current data.

Any of the opinions expressed in this text are those of the author, and not necessarily those of any company or institution with which the author has been or is associated.

JAMES D. WILLSON

Los Angeles, California
September 1983

Contents

PART IV — BUDGETING FOR LONG-TERM FUNDS

PART V — ADMINISTRATIVE AND OTHER ASPECTS OF BUDGETING

PART I

Foundation for an Effective Planning and Control System

1

Budgeting as a Tool for Effective Management

INTRODUCTION

A business is an economic entity whose objective is providing needed or desired goods or services in an economical manner. In so doing, management achieves its mission or purpose through several interrelated functions: planning, organizing, directing, and measuring. Basically, given the risks and opportunities, the chief executive and the staff select certain business objectives for the company. Supporting these overall objectives are the profit goals and other objectives of each segment of the business as developed by a coordinated management.

The budget, being the annual profit plan expressed in financial terms consistent with the long-term strategic plan, is a management tool which should assist in meeting the business objectives.

THE BUSINESS OBJECTIVE: TO MAXIMIZE RETURN TO SHAREHOLDERS

The purpose of a business organization, under the private enterprise system as it operates in the United States, has long been characterized by the business sector as the earning of the highest possible return over an extended period of time. In more sophisticated terms, the business objective has been defined as optimizing the return on assets or return on shareholders' equity, as the case may be, over the longer term. Hence, the enlightened business person looks to *continuity* of the enterprise and the efficient allocation of the firm's resources.

To be sure, the profit motive must remain dominant, but, in a larger sense, a business organization is an economic institution. Its purpose is to economically provide its customers with those goods and/or services they desire. There is no other principle reason for its existence. If it can efficiently and effectively supply this service on an economical basis, it will survive and prosper.

There may be other collateral or supplemental objectives a business may pursue as its social responsibility. It may use corporate resources to further national goals or community welfare, or to improve employee benefits, or to better environmental conditions. Yet, any such purposes will be supported only if the business achieves its principal objective — the economical satisfaction of customer needs or desires.

MANAGEMENT'S LEADERSHIP TASK

It is the task of management to guide or lead the business enterprise in meeting its principal objective; to earn the highest possible return over time for the owners. This is not a simple undertaking. Management must take the broad objective, refine it, and carry it out by setting specific goals in a constantly changing environment. To begin with, management must perceive or determine what the needs and desires of the prospective customers are. Within its managerial and financial capabilities, it must assemble and organize the financial, technical, production, and distribution agencies to satisfy those needs. It must coordinate and direct the activities to meet the overall objective: the goals must be intelligently conceived, the activities efficiently planned, and properly executed.

The task is continuous and challenging because what the customer wants and needs usually changes frequently. Further, the environmental constraints ebb and flow — whether they be governmental restrictions, competitive retaliation, economic pressures, or other factors. Management must successfully meet these challenges. New products, services, or processes must be developed continuously. All the business functions of management, production, marketing, research, finance, and administration must be constantly reviewed and improved to effectively and efficiently meet the customer's needs and desires.

"BUDGETING" DEFINED

A budget is often thought of as a financial plan, but this alone is an inadequate definition. There are several names for the planning process that focuses on the near-term (usually one or two years into the future): annual profit plan, short-term profit plan, tactical plan, operating plan or budget. While "budgeting" is the commonly used term, some executives feel it has negative connotations of restraint. Of course, if certain expenditures must be limited, there usually would be good management reasons for this — all directed to meeting a short-term profit objective.

The word "budget" and the term "budgeting," as used in this text, mean the short-term or annual profit plan and its development, expressed largely in financial terms, consistent with the long-range, or ("strategic") plan, together with the actions taken to meet the goals of the plan. It includes quantifying the operating plans and expectations. The process involves converting, usually month-by-month, the sales and revenue plans, the costs and expenses of doing business, the capital expenditures, and planned changes in financial position into an integrated financial model of the company. Finally, it involves taking those corrective actions necessary to bring sub-standard actual performance into line with the plan.

Thus, budgeting is composed of two parts: (1) the *planning* phase of determining what is to be done, and when, where, and how it is to be done and (2) the *control* phase of bringing actual performance into line with the plan. The following four-fold segregation of management functions emphasizes the differences in related activities. However, the processes are interdependent, intertwined, and overlap to the degree that one cannot be discussed without the other in considering the total management process. Planning must involve organization. Coordination ties in continuously with planning, organizing, directing, and measuring (controlling). In fact, some authorities conceive of the management process as planning, coordination, and control. These interrelated management functions of which the management process is comprised are inevitably tied to budgeting, and vice versa.

INTERRELATED MANAGEMENT AND BUDGETING FUNCTIONS

Effective budgeting and the business management process are intricately entwined. If a successful budgetary system is to be implemented or operated, the following elements of the management process must be recognized and taken into account. The task of the professional business manager can be divided into four functions or activities, which relate intimately with the budgeting process:

1. Planning
2. Organizing
3. Directing
4. Measuring and Controlling

Each function has several aspects, and the process, when conducted through the proper organization structure, might be depicted as in Figure 1-1. Thus, tentative objectives and goals are set for the enterprise, tested and evaluated, and finally, perhaps with adjustments, become the approved ones. Plans are then developed by each department or function to achieve these goals and objectives. When the plans are analyzed, consolidated, and found acceptable, they are approved. They must then be executed. In so doing, actual performance is measured against plan, and any necessary corrective action is taken to bring the operations back on course. In a very definite sense, the management function and budgeting are much the same process.

Budgeting is a continuous cycle, with information constantly being fed into the system for further action and reaction. Each stage in the process is described separately in the following text. However, it should be recognized that in actuality the functions are interrelated and are not necessarily completely separable in a time sequence: Several activities may proceed simultaneously.

Planning

In a general sense, planning might be described simply as determining *what* should be done, *how* it should be done, and *when* it should be done.

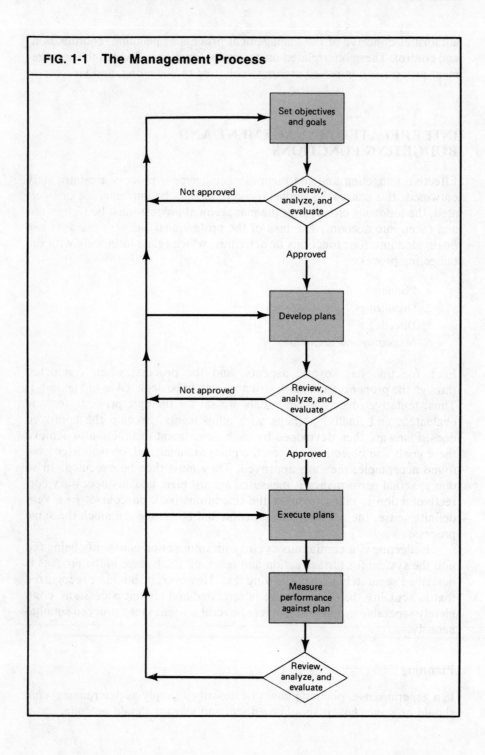

FIG. 1-1   The Management Process

Set objectives
and goals

Review,
analyze, and
evaluate

Not approved

Approved

Develop plans

Review,
analyze, and
evaluate

Not approved

Approved

Execute plans

Measure
performance
against plan

Review,
analyze, and
evaluate

From a total company or corporate viewpoint, the planning function involves two aspects:

1. Establishing the goals and objectives of the enterprise; and
2. Developing the plan or plans to achieve them.

Actually, planning is a very complex procedure. The setting of goals and objectives involves judgments and decision-making related to both the future environment and the future resources of the company. Conditions change, and the objectives of the management may change. Hence, planning is by necessity an iterative process, as reflected in Figure 1-1, requiring constant, repeated communication on present environment and resources, prospective changes in these factors, and progress towards meeting the objectives. Planning is the continuous process of making judgments about the events and activities essential to attaining the stated goals and objectives and, as such, is closely linked to management's leadership task.

Coordinating

For practical purposes, coordinating, or organizing, may be defined as securing the necessary personnel, plant and equipment, and materials, and arranging them so as to cause them to function to meet the business objectives. This involves coordination of the various subdivisions of the firm so that each is working in unity towards the accepted goals. An organization has been defined as a system of consciously coordinated activities, relationships, and people attempting to meet a common objective. The planning and budgeting process is an integral part in this coordinating activity. The management information system — the communication process — through which the business operates, should recognize these common characteristics of an effective organization:

1. The willingness or desire to achieve a common objective or goal which a single individual cannot accomplish alone.
2. The division or segregation of the various elements of the total task according to the skills, knowledge, or facilities required.
3. Assignment of responsibility to specific organizational units for accomplishing specified functions.
4. Coordination of personnel, resources, and facilities in an effective, smoothly working manner.
5. A sensitivity to the need for change, as circumstances change, in organization, procedures, or objectives.

Directing

The third basic management function is directing. Directing involves seeing that the tasks involved in the implementation or execution of the plan or activity — the doing — are performed efficiently and economically. Work must be carried out under time and cost constraints. Obviously, directing or implementing implicitly assumes that the plans have been communicated to all levels of management and that the results expected are known.

Measuring and Controlling

Measuring, sometimes referred to as the control function, is the last of the business management functions. It is an evaluative activity, which involves a comparison of actual activity with planned performance. It seeks to compare actual results with a standard or expected performance. This comparison may be in monetary terms, manhours, quantity, or value. The process involves making such a comparison and then taking action to bring substandard performance into line with expectations. Decisions are made concerning the unacceptable results, and the information is fed back into the management cycle.

Differences between plan and actual performance may occur for either of these two reasons or a combination of both:

1. Execution or implementation of the plan was faulty.
2. The plan was inadequate or not suitable to the conditions that came to exist.

Consequently, as a result of the differences reported, new plans or strategies must be pursued, or new actions taken to bring actual performance up to the plan.

BUDGETING AS A TOOL FOR EFFECTIVE MANAGEMENT

Planning Advantages

Budgeting is, first of all, a planning procedure. As such, it serves as a communicating mechanism that permits a full exchange of ideas to the end that the best near-term plan is selected. In its planning role, budgeting has the following important advantages when properly executed.

Improved Decision-Making. Budgeting tends to force management to base its actions on adequate consideration of study. The budgeting procedure tends to instill the practice of careful study before decisions are made.

There are fewer opportunistic or "seat-of-the-pants" decisions. If the entire management staff, from president to foreman, knows that their plans are to be formally expressed, and their execution judged, then the possible alternative actions will be more carefully thought out.

Increased Management Motivation. Budgeting assists in motivating management to meet the objectives of the business or department. When the individual members of management know that a plan exists, and understand what the objectives are for each subdivision, then in all probability they will make a greater attempt to achieve that objective. People respond to leadership if they know where the leadership is taking them. Nothing is so disruptive to effective performance in the middle and lower echelon of management as being "in the dark" about where the company is heading.

Full Involvement of Management. Budgeting enlists the aid of the entire organization in selecting the most profitable (or optimal) course of action. When the annual budgeting or profit planning process is undertaken in sufficient time, it enables all members of management — foremen, supervisors, department managers, sales people, branch or division heads, and members of top management — to consider (under proper guidance) and give assistance in selecting the most profitable actions. The interacting of the various functions tends to result in a better profit plan.

There are other related advantages to the company when a proper budgeting procedure is in place. Among them may be (1) a related written statement of company policies; (2) more stable employment; (3) more effective use of plant and equipment; and (4) better coordination with government agencies, where applicable.

Coordinating Advantages

Budgeting assists in *coordination* of the business. Coordination has been defined as the process by which each subdivision of a business or concern works towards a common objective, giving consideration to the decisions of the other subdivisions — thus maintaining a unit of effort. Several aspects of coordination should be addressed.

Coordinated Response to Change. The budget assists in correlating and coordinating human effort in each function of the business to that of the whole. This is accomplished in several ways. When the plan is originally prepared, it serves as a coordinating device between functions. Thus, for example, the production manager's plan must coordinate with the sales manager's plan so that adequate product is available, and both must coordinate with the advertising manager's plan for what products should be promoted. A properly prepared operating plan will be coordinated to take into account the objectives, activity level, and problems of each subdivision, and of the business as a whole.

The budget further coordinates various functions when operations are underway, and allows the various heads of different functions to know what progress is being made in the other areas to meet the plan — daily, weekly, or monthly. Hence, when a major dislocation occurs in one function, the communications are such that changes in other functions can be made, if necessary. For example, if sales are not up to expectation, and inventories are getting too high, the production executive will be informed and, based on economic analyses, will make the most prudent adjustment: either reducing the manufacturing rate or preparing to handle higher inventory levels — costs and other pertinent factors considered. Or, if conditions unexpectedly change, so that financing is difficult, or there is a question about the long-term need for plant expansion, capital expenditure plans can be modified. The point is, plans must be reviewed continuously and changed when deemed necessary. If unforeseen or uncontrollable conditions arise that materially affect the activities of one division, the mechanism must be available to make necessary and quick changes in the other divisions or subsidiaries. Inflation, wars, foreign disruptions, collapse of markets, major product failures, destruction of plant or facilities, whatever, may require a change in plans. And the budgeting process is a means to accomplish this.

Anticipation of Future Trends. The budget assists in relating the planned activities to the expected general level of business. As previously stated, the budgeting process more or less forces management to study the probable future economic conditions and business environment. Business management must be alert to changes in those factors or conditions that have the greatest impact on its operations. There is some evidence that success in business may relate as much to a firm's ability to adapt to changing conditions or fortuitous circumstances, as it does to efficiently meeting the more normal competitive forces of the marketplace. While there may be disagreement as to exactly what economic trends may be at a given time, the fact remains that businesses do move through cycles of low or high activity, and that the ability to detect or forecast these trends is important. The signals must be observed and business plans made accordingly.

Productive Allocation of Resources. The budgeting process assists in the allocation of capital and human resources into the more productive areas or channels. One of the tasks of business management, as stewards for the shareholders, is to optimize the return on shareholders' equity. This, in turn, is accomplished by securing a proper return on the assets entrusted to the management, and by increasing such return through proper leverage achieved by prudent borrowing. This is discussed in Chapters 25, 26, and 27. Suffice it to say here that capital projects should not be undertaken without the reasonable assurance of an adequate return. Of the many alternatives available, management must select those that offer the best prospects. Funds should be directed into plant and equipment or receivables and inventory only after knowing: (1) what is required; (2) what the return is reasonably expected to be; and (3) where such funds will come from. Activities must be planned within available resources, and must be coordinated. Production should not be planned for those items that cannot be sold and inventory levels should be considered. Receivables must be held within financeable and economic limits.

The same approach holds with the allocation of human resources. The abilities and talents of the company personnel should be directed to those fields of greatest promise. Perhaps the brightest and most capable staff, assuming they have adequate knowledge, should be employed in the areas offering the greatest growth or profit opportunities.

In summary, where a company operates on a day-to-day basis — where the efforts of the management are directed largely to "putting out fires" — the final profit results are less than optimum. A well-conceived, coordinated program for the balanced allocation of resources, based on study and analysis, is necessary for the most productive results. Coordination on such a basis lifts unwanted restraints, removes uncertainty, and permits the organization to function fully.

Organizational Weaknesses Revealed. The budgeting process reveals weaknesses in organization structure, authority, and responsibility, and permits their correction. As budgets or plans are prepared for each segment the plan for that segment will correspond with or relate to the activities of that part. The costs or revenues budgeted, or funds committed or profits planned, will, or should also be, under the control of the budgeted segment. If the executive does not have the authority or responsibility for the control of the funds, this should come to light and should be corrected. Weakness in the delegation of authority will be revealed because, ordinarily, a person will not accept responsibility for activities he cannot control. Proper budgeting will force a proper segregation of costs and expenses, or of revenues, commensurate with the authority of the executive involved.

Control Advantages

Control, the means of assuring that performance will be as specified by plan or standard, may be considered in the context of budgeting as the systematized effort in keeping management informed of how actual results compare with the plan or predetermined results. As a *control* (or *measuring*) device, a budget system offers the following advantages or benefits.

Prompt Reporting on Performance. A sound budgeting procedure provides the mechanism for prompt reporting of actual versus planned performance, and the taking of corrective action. The annual profit plan is prepared in rather extensive detail, closely paralleling the organization structure of the company. For example, the sales budget broken down by salesperson for each month and for the year may be known. The manhours and cost by department or cost center are known. The plan is, in effect, constructed from the bottom up, so that what is expected of each activity and individual is known, with provision at some level for a certain amount of slippage.

In its control function, the reporting or communicating system inherent in a budget provides for the following information to be made available as fast as is practical:

1. Actual performance by operator (manhours, units or costs);
2. Expected (planned or standard) performance;
3. The difference or variance between (1) and (2); and
4. The cause of the departure from plan.

With this information, the supervisor is in a position to take corrective action quickly. The cause of the variance is corrected, if possible, and the operation gets on plan.

Prevention of Unplanned Expenditures. The budgeting system provides the means of preventing expenditures over plan (preventive control) in many circumstances. Some expenditures involve direct disbursements or commitments to third parties outside the business. Expenditures for advertising, purchase of supplies, and for plant and equipment are examples. In such cases, budgetary procedures can be established so that expenditures are held to a predetermined level. Thus, through a commitment ledger, purchases for advertising or selected supplies are held within limits. The executive is not informed *after the fact,* but can exercise preventive control to avoid an over budget commitment.

Accurate Cost Evaluation. Budgetary procedures tend to provide better standards for control. In many companies without good budgeting procedures, a usual practice is to attempt to judge costs or expenses by past performance. This usually is inadequate. Performance should be measured by what must be done in a coordinated plan to attain a certain profit goal or level of performance. It is much better to compare performance to a standard that is a segment of an acceptable plan. Such a comparison basis causes a review of expense levels and tends to eliminate waste.

EVALUATION OF ALTERNATIVE PLANS

Much has been said about basing plans on study and analysis. Effective management involves a careful study of alternatives and their impact, direct and indirect, long-term as well as short-term, on the business. The essence of good planning is the appraisal of the different alternative actions possible. Planning attempts to select the most profitable course of action for the business, and keep the ship on course to meet the target. As is discussed in later chapters, there are a variety of devices available for the analysis and selection of the best plan: break-even analysis; marginal cost analysis; return on assets; and return on shareholders' equity.

Modern computers may facilitate analysis that management can use in its deliberations and in reaching judgments. This consideration of alternatives is an iterative process, for changes in one factor can influence or cause changes in other factors. It is worth repeating that effective budgeting involves the continuous analysis or review of plans and modification thereof when necessary.

THE SYSTEM OF BUSINESS PLANS

The short-term plan is but one type of plan, and bears a defined relationship to other plans. It might be well to first define a plan, before discussing the relationship among various business plans. A plan is a *predetermined course of action*. It involves thinking ahead, giving consideration to the alternative course of action available, and making a business decision on what one should be selected. A plan, by implication, has these elements:

1. It deals with the future.
2. It implies or directs actions to be taken.
3. It operates through the company organization structure, recognizing the authority and responsibility of the various segments.

The short-term plan, of course, does not stand by itself. It is a segment or part of a system of business plans that many successful companies have adopted, or are adopting. A structure of plans is illustrated in Figure 1-2.[1]

Basically, a comprehensive planning system may be composed of two major segments with several sub-plan categories:

1. *The strategic or long-range plan:*
   □ The related development plans:
     • Research and development plans
     • Acquisition plan
     • Divestment plan
2. *The annual profit plan:*
   □ Marketing plan
   □ Production plan — By project, if applicable
   □ Research and development plan
   □ Financial plan
   □ Administrative plan

The strategic plan is to guide the company to its mission, or objective, and goals. It reaches far into the future — as far as practical or useful. Typically, this is for five or ten years, but, as in a forest products company, for example, it might be fifty years. The strategic plan must relate not only to existing products, but also to new products and markets. Hence, development plans for these new products and markets play a large role in the strategic plan.

From the strategic plan comes the short-term profit plan, which deals more with *existing* products and markets, and which might be said to be the near-year part or the first step of the strategic plan. The relationship of the strategic plan and the short-term profit plan or budget is illustrated in Figure 1-3.

Some, especially those schooled in the financial discipline, conceive of planning, whether strategic or near-term, as the preparation of a mass of schedules — sales volumes, sales and revenue levels, related costs and expenses, cash income and expenditures, and the related statement of financial position. To be sure, the plans will be given expression finally in financial-type statements. However, planning is an organized process of conceptualizing the business, establishing objectives and goals, setting priorities, agree-

---

[1] Business Intelligence Programs, "A Framework for Business Planning," Research Report No. 162, page 4 (Menlo Park: SRI International, 1963). Copyright © 1963 by SRI International. Reprinted with permission.

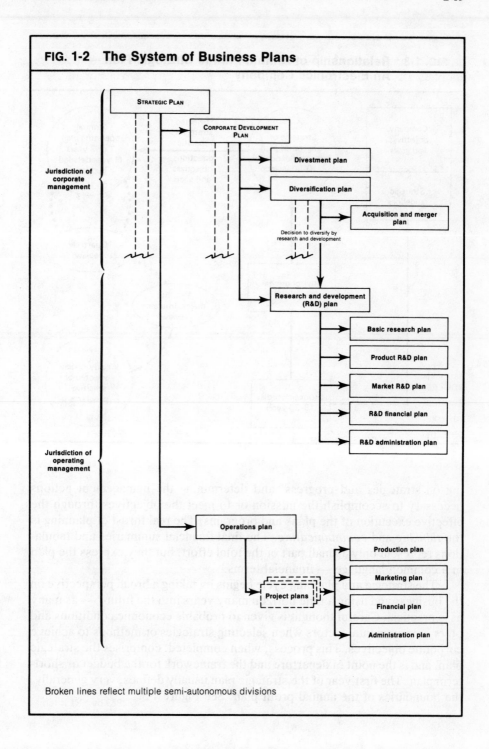

FIG. 1-2 The System of Business Plans

Broken lines reflect multiple semi-autonomous divisions

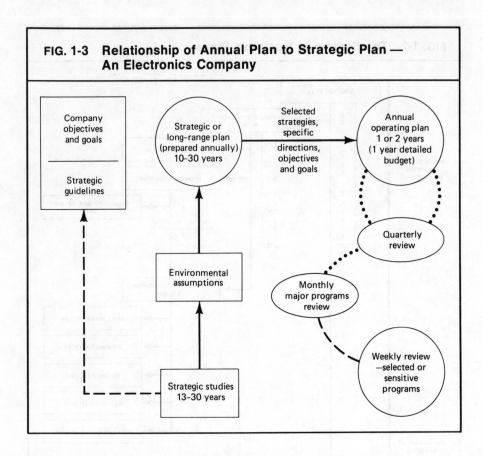

**FIG. 1-3   Relationship of Annual Plan to Strategic Plan —
An Electronics Company**

ing on strategies and progress, and determining the management actions necessary to accomplish the mission or to meet the objectives through the effective execution of the plans and programs. The real thrust of planning is the *thinking* and *communicating*. The final financial summaries and tabulations represent only a small part of the total effort, but they express the plan in a common language — financial terms.

The strategic and planning cycle begins by taking a broad perspective on the business and using a time horizon many years into the future — as many as is practical. Careful thought is given to probable economic conditions and other environmental factors when selecting strategies or methods to achieve corporate objectives. This process, when completed, comprises the strategic plan, and is the point of departure and the framework for the budget or short-term plan. The first year of the strategic plan usually defines, very generally, the boundaries of the annual profit plan. See Figure 1-3.

The Strategic Plan

Given the strategic plan as a point of departure for the budgeting process, some comments are in order before the discussion is restricted to the short-term plan.

The strategic planning process should be continuous, with frequent interaction and reiteration among the parties. See Figure 1-1. While such continuous planning is desirable, in the real world at present the strategic plan is prepared annually and completed some three to six months before the annual profit plan cycle commences. The strategic plan may, however, be prepared at the same time. A graphic depiction of the long-range planning process is shown in Figure 1-4, and is a somewhat more detailed disclosure of the many facets of this important planning procedure, which is directly related to the short-term budget. The steps in the process might be outlined in more detail as follows:

Assessment of the Environment and Business. This phase also is described as "situation analysis," and is intended to provide a picture of the business status or relative condition. Included are subjects such as these:

1. *Description of the future environment:*
   □ Governmental actions
   □ Price inflation
   □ Competitive product status
   □ Product trends

2. *Identification of the attributes of success for each business segment (product line). This may involve a study of the "winners" and "losers" in each industry segment of interest.*

3. *Identification of the present status of the company as to each of its business segments.* This might involve classifying the business segments according to the Boston Consulting Group matrix,[2] which involves industry growth rate as a measure of attractiveness, and market share as an indicator of competitive strength, as follows:
   □ A *star* — high share, high growth. Perhaps the client company should increase market strength.
   □ A *cash cow* — high share, low growth. The low growth signifies less of a cash need; and the business segment should generate significant cash for investment in more opportune areas or markets.

---

[2] For more details, see H.W. Allen Sweeny and Robert Rachlin, *Handbook of Budgeting* (New York: John Wiley & Sons, 1981), Chapter 2. This chapter also makes reference to the McKinsey/General Electric Company matrix.

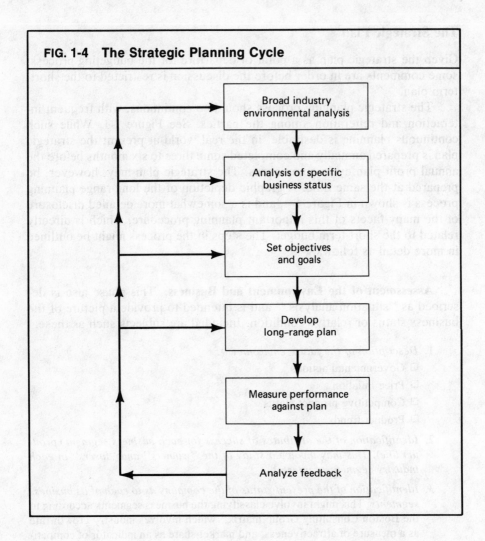

FIG. 1-4   The Strategic Planning Cycle

Broad industry environmental analysis

Analysis of specific business status

Set objectives and goals

Develop long-range plan

Measure performance against plan

Analyze feedback

☐ A *wildcat* — low share, high growth. Adequate investment and proper strategy should be used, perhaps, to develop this product line until it moves into the "star" category.

☐ A *dog* — low share, low growth. Because prospects are poor, plans perhaps should be made to divest the line.

4. *Identification of the company strengths and weaknesses.* Analysis of strengths and weaknesses involves (1) an understanding of where the company performs well; (2) how its strengths compare to those of its competitors; (3) whether or not its competitive strengths can be maintained or improved. The following factors should be considered:

☐ Market share
☐ Product acceptability
☐ Quality control
☐ Marketing posture
☐ Relative manufacturing costs
☐ Proprietary product status
☐ Patent status

Basically, in strategic planning, management should take advantage of company strengths, and should correct weaknesses.

After developing this background and perspective, the next step is to analyze the direction of the business, which requires great perception and intuitive thinking.

Analysis of the Direction of the Business. The first phase of this deeper analysis involves a definition of the opportunities or threats to each business segment and an understanding of the direction the company is taking. An *opportunity* may be defined as a combination of circumstances, including time and place, that offers potential benefits for the business. It may arise by reason of changes in the marketplace, government action, or other developments. It provides a condition to be exploited by the company if it takes proper action. Obviously, if the company cannot take the needed steps, then it is not a true opportunity; or, if nothing must be done, it is a part of the environment to be recognized in the planning. A *threat* is the exact opposite of an opportunity. It, too, represents a combination of circumstances — but those that could have a negative impact on the business if not repulsed.

Since a company is subjected to many opportunities and threats, it is important to classify or identify the important ones and give priority to necessary actions. Degree of impact, probability of occurrence, and timing are factors to be weighed in setting priorities to deal with opportunities and threats.

The second phase of the analysis is to identify the critical issues — the more important opportunities or threats. These are the issues that must be addressed in the strategic planning process. The higher levels of management should agree on the critical issues, and on the degree of further analysis needed, before the strategic plan is completed. Having agreed on the critical issues to be resolved, the third phase is to reach conclusions on the desired strategy. This involves considering alternative plans (or strategies) so that the plan will withstand scrutiny as to completeness and usefulness.

Concurrent with studying the alternatives, suggested strategies are decided upon.

Setting the Objectives and Goals. Through the interaction of various segments of the business with its top management and corporate top management, objectives and goals will be set for the segment and for the business as a whole.

Examples of some company objectives might be to:

- Capture a major portion of the engine market for private plane business
- Secure a dominant position in the minicomputer field

Examples of some objectives for the business segment might be to:

- Procure the . . . . contract on an economically acceptable basis
- Penetrate the countermeasure market to a level of 10 percent

Some goals — being quantified objectives — for the company might be expressed as:

		198X	199X
1.	Sales level	$980MM	$1,870MM
2.	Rate of return:		
	• On shareholder equity	18.00%	23.00%
	• On assets employed	10.00%	13.00%
	• As percentage of net sales	6.40%	7.50%
3.	Earnings per share	$6.50	$14.90
4.	Price/earnings ratio	8 to 1	10 to 1

The budget officer will be particularly concerned with these quantified goals in connection with the detailed project planning.

Preparation of the Long-Range Plan. The first step is to prepare the long range operating plan and related financial statements. This involves the same steps as in the annual profit plan, but in less detail. It is discussed in the context of the annual plan.

Measurement of Performance Against Plan. This is the "feedback" phase in a very broad or gross sense. Perhaps there is nothing so foolish as continuing on a planned course when such a plan is no longer feasible. To know this it is necessary to have a feedback system to advise management of *major* deviations from plan. Some of this channel of communication will be through short-term performance. Other elements will be direct to the director of long-range planning and relate to specific major environmental changes. In any event, the measurement system is in less frequent use than the annual plan, and is less related to financial statements. A sound strategic planning procedure is highly desirable as a condition precedent to the most effective short-term planning, and has been dealt with at some length because it should be a significant business function. The reader is referred to some of the excellent books on long-range planning for further details of the process. See Selected References at the end of the chapter.

The remainder of this book relates principally to the annual profit plan.

The Annual Profit Plan

In order to implement effective short-term planning, the budgeting executive obviously must be familiar with the assumptions of the strategic plan, and changes that have taken place in the environment since the long-range plan was completed, as well as changes in the company posture, whether in product lines, in financial strength, or in operating capabilities. In the process of preparing an annual profit plan, it is necessary to:

1. Ascertain — as a point of departure — that the assumptions and expectations for the first year of the strategic plan are valid and reasonable.
2. Develop, as necessary, the supporting plans envisioned in the strategic plan, in minute detail on a month-to-month basis, department by department, profit center by profit center, program by program, and product by product.
3. Prepare the consolidated annual profit plan, and provide the means of monitoring and measuring progress of the plan — the managerial control function — as frequently as necessary, usually monthly, by means of monthly budgets. This review process is illustrated in Figure 1-3.

The short-term planning procedure is discussed at length in Chapter 4.

MANAGEMENT BY OBJECTIVES

The overall budgeting process, or annual profit planning process, is a coordinating, communicating, and motivating device. However, there are several ways in which this process can take place.

One approach in developing a profit plan, which might be described as a "top-down" budgeting approach, is to involve only the top echelon of management, perhaps with staff assistance. Middle and lower levels of management are not active in the process. Yet it is precisely the middle and lower levels of management that are most involved in carrying out the plans, and in meeting the various departmental objectives. It is less than productive not to use the knowledge and experience of these groups and, in fact, involvement by the entire management staff can prove a motivating force.

In effect, a budget must be a combination of a top-down approach — in order to provide goals, certain constraints, and to allocate a given share of resources by the top management — and a "building up" approach by the middle and lower management echelons. By participating in the iterative planning process, managers contribute their know-how and experience in developing the cost center or departmental objectives, and essentially commit themselves to achieving the goals and objectives. In turn, the various departmental goals and objectives are melded into the divisional and company goals and objectives. Such an approach, of permitting all members of management to participate in setting goals and objectives, is much more effective than imposing them from the top down. This participative process is often called management by objectives.

One other facet of management by objectives deserves mention. In many types of business, such as construction or aerospace, the management objectives are achieved through proper performance on programs or projects (building a B-1 bomber, for example) which endure for several years and which cut across departmental lines. Under such circumstances, it is not enough to focus attention on the budgetary performance in a given department. This may cause a department manager to over-emphasize solely meeting the departmental budget objectives and to disregard key interdepartmental relationships. Hence, management by objectives seeks to concentrate on managing opportunities in a coordinated effort. More is said on this important subject in Chapter 30.

LIMITATIONS OF BUDGETING

Planning and control are basic necessary functions of business management and every successful business, large or small, must effectively perform these activities. Budgeting is a systematic method of planning and control that is applicable to all types and sizes of business. The size or type of business merely influences the methodology, not the need for the function.

Yet, there are many instances where a budgetary system has not been effective. To be sure, there are numerous advantages in budgeting, but a budget does not run the business. Rather, it is only a management tool. It may be that some business managers have expected too much from the budgeting process. Some may have assumed that the institution of a budgeting process and plan automatically guaranteed profit results. Yet, a budget, being merely a tool, has limitations that must be recognized and provided for.

Continual Updating Needed

A budgetary program must be modified at fairly frequent intervals to meet changing conditions. A budgeting program cannot be installed in a company and forgotten. Rather, it must be modified to correct imperfections in the system; that is, to begin with, it must be adapted to the needs of the particular company. Then, as circumstances change, it must be modified. If certain parts are not effective, then changes should be made with the help of those using the system to improve it. As techniques or technology change, the system should be changed. For example, the development of small computers, may mean it would be advantageous to install them for use in speeding up slower manual operations. Where feedback information is inadequate, modification should be made. Where changes in organization and responsibilities occur, budgeting procedures must recognize them. In a sense, the budget process must be dynamic or flexible to serve the management needs.

Management Motivation

The entire management must be motivated to meet the budget. An annual operating plan is not self-executing. Experience shows that the various levels of management periodically must be motivated by the CEO and their superiors to achieve the plan. The department head must appreciate the need for meeting departmental goals so that the company will achieve its target and must be convinced that the system and program are sound and will work to benefit his own interests. In other words, the department head must be "sold" on the process.

Budgets Are Estimates

Budgets or plans consist of a series of estimates. Because the profit plan is based on estimates, there are bound to be differences between planned and actual performances. Humans are unable to predict an exact outcome or forecast a specific condition in many instances. These estimates, of course, should be based on available facts and the exercise of good judgment. In most cases, actual results will come close to plan; but circumstances will arise where there are significant or major differences. In fact, there will be occasional circumstances where the plan must be revised. The test of a good budgeting process should not be solely how close actual performance was to plan, although this is a consideration; a more important test is whether or not the process contributed to a coordinated attempt to reach an optimum profit result more so than would have occurred without such a system.

2

Conditions Essential for Planning

OVERVIEW OF ESSENTIAL ELEMENTS

The role of planning and control in achieving the business objective has been discussed in Chapter 1. Yet, successful implementation of these functions depends on the existence of several essential conditions. Based on years of experience with the budgeting process, the author believes certain circumstances are indispensable. The relative importance of each may be debated; but the following elements are essential to successful planning and control:

- Support of the chief executive officer (CEO)
- Support of the major functional and staff executives
- Satisfactory organization, including assignment of responsibility and designation of a budget coordinator
- An adequate management information system
- Sound budget procedures

Without these basic provisions, the annual planning process is just another ineffective procedure.

Supporting the basic conditions necessary to good budgeting are some related subjects that warrant explanation:

- Reasonable objectives
- A proper planning cycle
- A practical and sufficient planning period.

SUPPORT OF THE CHIEF EXECUTIVE

In an effective budgeting procedure, attention must be secured, direction must be given, and leadership must be provided. The chief motivator in this process is the CEO. He should be a major player in the budgeting process. In fact, the success or failure of planning may well depend on his degree of involvement. This does not, of course, mean that he must participate in every phase. It does signify, however, that he should actively support the procedure and objectives. He ought to demonstrate interest in the outcome of the plan and need for the planning process; he should be consulted on the more important assumptions. He should concur in the basic guidelines — perhaps sign or approve the directive that initiates the annual planning process. He must communicate his personal concern with the planning. When the attitude of the CEO is made known, the necessary cooperation usually will be forthcoming.

SUPPORT OF MAJOR EXECUTIVES

Most practitioners would list as a necessary condition for effective budgeting the support of the chief executive or perhaps "top management." In smaller companies the participation of the CEO in the budget process will usually insure its success. Yet, in the larger corporation, where great delegation is necessary, such support will be more meaningful if the entire upper echelon of executives provides active and enthusiastic sustenance. Without such rather broad-based corroboration, there is the danger of mere compliance with the procedure — perhaps a nuisance process in some minds — without stimulating that extra effort or thinking which results in a better plan. While the impetus must come from the top, every major functional executive should eagerly lend his effort to the planning process and actively contribute to it. It must not become another routine procedure or a financial exercise. Each executive must be made aware, perhaps through incentive payments, of the need and advantages of the profit planning and control procedure to him personally and to the business.

To be sure, much of the planning detail and coordination may be delegated to the budget director, or the executive's functional executive staff. But the CEO and the major executives should review the plan, modify proposals, examine alternatives, and finally support a soundly conceived plan by which they are willing to be measured.

SOUND ORGANIZATION

As previously stated, one of the advantages of budgeting is that it will reveal weaknesses in organization. The converse is equally true. A budget program cannot be effectively implemented without proper organization. A sound or satisfactory organization is a prime essential. Reduced to its simplest terms, a sound organization consists of an intelligent grouping of tasks, the coordination of the efforts of the various groups, the establishment of definite line of authority and responsibility, and a procedure for enforcing the implementation of the group objectives.

Assignment of Responsibility

There are two aspects of sound organization. First, responsibility and authority must be established for all operating departments and all functions. In the absence of proper organization of those who must do the planning and the subsequent execution, it is not possible to place responsibility for performance in achieving the plan or standard. Indeed, in the first instance, without such organization, it would not be possible to construct the initial plan or budget.

Designation of a Budget Coordinator

Second, the procedure applies to those responsible for establishing and supervising the budgeting function itself. Someone must serve as the budget coordinator, executive, or director and cause the pieces to be assembled, reviewed, and evaluated as an integrated plan for presentation to the major executives and the CEO. This coordinating task is usually assigned to a financial executive, perhaps the controller or the budget director. Comments on this function are made later in this chapter.

AN ADEQUATE MANAGEMENT INFORMATION SYSTEM

Definition

Another major requisite for sound planning or budgeting is the establishment and continuing use of an adequate management information system (MIS). Technically, an MIS encompasses all information available to executives. It may be from internal or external sources, and be formal as well as informal, and may include all types of operational or accounting information. Especially of concern are those reports prepared from accounting records or operational records together with the analytical reports which seek to analyze the available information for use in the management process. It may involve the output from high-speed computers or merely hand-prepared data. Basically, we are concerned with the formal MIS, which is defined simply as an organized method of providing each business executive or manager with all the data he needs, and hopefully *only* that data that he needs for decision-making. In an effective MIS, such data will be provided when he needs it, and in a form that he accepts and understands, in order that he may act upon it.

Responsibility Reporting

The accounting system is an integral part of the management information system, and, of course, must meet the needs of the executives. Basically, the chart of accounts must conform to the organization chart and to cost and revenue behavior, as is explained in Chapter 5. The accounting system must embrace more than historical facts. Principally, it must conform to the concept of "responsibility accounting" or reporting: transactions or events are recorded in a manner such that they are identified with the supervisor or individual in the organization who controls the activity and is held accountable for it.

Under responsibility reporting, the dissemination of facts and figures concerning revenues and costs relates to the segment of the organization being reported upon. The communication concerns costs and/or revenues that can be controlled by the person being reported upon, or that are attributable to his efforts. Such a system avoids allocation of costs for *control* purposes to any organizational unit that does not control them and cannot be held accountable for them.

The principle is illustrated in Figure 2-1 relative to a simplified *expense* structure wherein the reporting follows the organizational chart. Since the president is accountable for the *entire* business, he would receive an expense summary segregated by the functions incurring such expenses, and assignable to the individual whom he holds responsible — Item A in the illustration. In this case, his own departmental expenses are compared with budget, as are those of each vice-president who reports to him.

The vice-president for manufacturing receives a summary of expense performance for each organizational segment reporting to him — shown as Item B in the figure. In turn, the production superintendent receives a summary on the three cost centers — Item C — for which he is accountable. Finally, the departmental foreman is informed on his cost performance in detail by type of expense, as reflected in Item D.

Each manager may secure such further detailed reports as he desires on each area for which he is assigned responsibility, authority, or accountability.

Of course, in the first instance, the business plan is developed by these responsibility centers. Accordingly, actual performance is recorded in a parallel structure so as to permit comparison of actual and planned perfor-

FIG. 2-1   Responsibility Reporting — Flow of Information

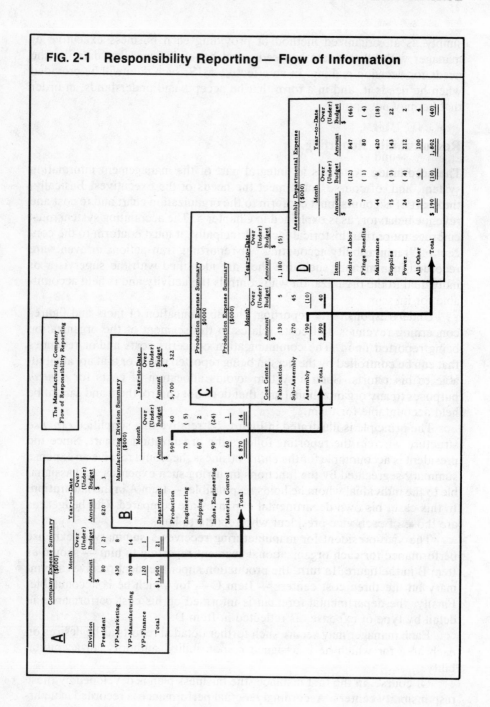

mance. The quality of the reporting system, embracing responsibility accounting and "exception reporting" (reporting only significant departures from plan) will have much to do with the acceptance of the system.

SOUND BUDGET PROCEDURES

Finally, sound budget procedures and the related proper administration thereof are necessary requisites for successful budgeting. As most financial executives are aware, the objectives may seem desirable, and the concepts and principles may be understood. Needless obstacles impede success, however, when the specific procedures, routines, or systems by which proper budgets are created and actual performance is measured are viewed as cumbersome, impractical, or too "accounting oriented." The procedures must be seen as simple, effective, efficient and easy to follow, and not as useless, distasteful, detailed "bookkeeping" routines.

Business managers need fairly specific guides to explain how their budgets are to be prepared. Procedures should be simple and specific in explaining what is to be done, and when. Certain data should be provided and explained, e.g., inflation rates, compensation increase rates, tax rates, and rate of return objectives, if applicable. The procedural aspects for different budgeting situations are covered in appropriate chapters and in Chapter 33 on budget procedures and manuals.

Setting Reasonable Objectives

A word of caution is in order about the objectives of the plan, whether for a cost center, department, profit center, or, indeed, for the entire company. Sometimes there is a tendency to set objectives that are simply unattainable, which might represent wishful or hoped-for results. Especially in the "top-down" approach, some executives may set goals that are too high, or that may be regarded as unreachable targets. In the integrated approach, where a "bottom-up" procedure is in use, on the other extreme, lesser executives may attempt to set goals that are easily attainable. For example, the amount by which the plan is exceeded might help determine the incentive payment. Hence, the objective must be to set "tight" objectives in order to secure better performance, but not so high that all incentive to attain them is discouraged.

Deciding on the Time Span of the Budget

In preparing the short-term profit plan or budget, a matter to be resolved is the period to be covered by the budget. Is it to be one year, two years, or some other time span? And in preparing the plan, in what time segments should it be constructed? By weeks, months, or quarters, or by the entire period budgeted?

There are several considerations that should guide the decision:

- Nature of the industry
- Reliability of the information
- Use to be made of the data

Nature of the Industry. The nature of the business or industry obviously will be an important factor. If the business is of the contract type, with the typical contract lasting perhaps 12 to 18 months or so, it may be desirable to plan two years ahead. Under such circumstances, a two-year period may be required to make significant changes in the operation and it may not be practical to plan for a shorter period. On the other hand, a small retail business may find a one-year period is adequate in planning for future change. A look at industry practice may provide some helpful guidelines.

Reliability of the Data. A great many companies find that a one-year time span is practical, and the data are reasonably reliable for such a period. When the period is longer than one year, the data may be largely guesswork and not dependable.

Use Made of the Data. In selecting the time segments for data accumulation and presentation of the profit plan, the building blocks of the plan should provide for the the shortest time segment likely to be used. The data bank should contain the segments in the smallest time units likely to be called upon or needed. Computer applications permit the easy build-up of the information and its ready retrieval.

What time segment is selected for review will (of course) depend on the use. The most extensive or fullest available detail need not be presented at all times.

For internal operating or financial planning purposes, most companies review plans, and conformance to plan, monthly, and consequently, build up data on such a basis. Certain circumstances require a more frequent review either in total or for certain segments of the business: seasonal income, requirement of banks or other creditors, low margin businesses, businesses in financial difficulty, and government contract discussions. Certain situations require less frequent review. Thus, the board of directors may be interested in the plan by calendar quarters only, so the plan should be summarized by quarters.

Other combinations may be found necessary: perhaps by weeks for the first three-month period, and by months or quarters thereafter.

If the purposes of budgeting are clear there will be little difficulty in determining the length of the budget periods. Such matters as normal turnover periods, seasons, length of production period must be considered, but the length of the budget periods need not be rigidly established. Plans may vary in length of time for different types of operations within the same concern; for example, program or contract activities may be planned for two or three years, but bid-type small metal fabrication jobs may be planned for only one year. Moreover, the periods may be shorter in times of marked uncertainty than under more stabilized conditions.

Frequency of the Planning Cycle

A related question is the frequency of the planning cycle; that is, how often the profit plan or budget should be prepared. This planning cycle is not necessarily the same as the period covered by the plan.

For example, a company may prepare a budget covering a two-year period, but may go through this procedure every six months. Most companies that prepare budgets do this for the coming year, and revise the estimates each quarter. Companies whose business is subject to a marked seasonal influence may use the natural business year, starting at the time when inventories and accounts receivable are at their lowest point.

There is much to be said in favor of a continuous, as opposed to a periodic, program of budgeting. If definite plans can be made one-quarter year in advance, they may be revised monthly, progressively dropping and adding a month, thereby always keeping a three months' program ahead. If a tentative program can be made for one year, this may also be revised monthly or quarterly by the same progressive procedure. This is particularly advantageous in a seasonal business. As one month ends, plans can be laid for the corresponding month one year hence while seasonal conditions are fresh in the minds of the executives and subordinates. A further advantage of continuous budgeting is that it keeps the problems constantly before the organization with a continuous process of examination and revision. Moreover, budgets that are continuously revised are more useful as control tools because plans can be revised to more closely conform to actual external conditions. In fact, when the budget serves in an effective way as a control mechanism, frequent revisions are mandatory in all but the most stable companies.

The advent of the computer is making economically feasible very frequent testing and revision of plans, and competitive conditions often require it.

BUDGET COORDINATION

The designation of a budget coordinator has been mentioned as an essential condition for effective short-term planning. The question may be raised as to who should put together or coordinate the final plan for approval. An effective budget usually is the result of joint and coordinated thinking of the functional or line executives. But, because accounting is the language of business, the budget is finally consolidated in financial statement format, and is generally prepared by financial personnel under the direction of the chief financial executive or the controller. It is a mistake to regard the plan as that of the chief financial executive, or any other individual since it is, after all, the *company* plan, supported and approved by the chief executive officer.

Yet, someone must be assigned the responsibility of establishing and revising procedures, securing and coordinating the data, checking and verifying the information, analyzing and interpreting the data, and expressing the final answer in financial terms. In most companies this is the function of the chief financial official or the controller. The reasons for this selection may be stated as follows:

- His purview extends to all functions of the business.
- Since he is primarily a staff officer, he is detached from functional responsibility, and therefore he is best able to maintain a neutral, unprejudiced, and unbiased attitude.
- Budgets are based largely on past experience. One of the chief tasks of the financial officer or controller is to collect, analyze, and interpret data relative to past performance, and to translate this information into useful signals for the future.
- He is, or at least by the nature of his training and experience should be, the best analyst in the company.
- He is in a position to translate proposed plans into their effect upon operating results and financial position.
- Effective budgetary control requires that budget allowances and actual charges be on a parallel basis — that the same accounts be used for the same purpose. When both the budgeting activity and accounting activity are controlled by the same official, the coordination and correlation on this point is likely to be more positive.

The exact organizational structure depends upon many factors, some of the more important being the personality and knowledge of the executives. In some circumstances the controller is of sufficient stature that the function can be placed under his jurisdiction. In other situations, the pressures of the day-to-day tasks are such that the controller simply cannot devote enough time to the planning function, and it is entirely separated from the report preparation activity. Under these conditions the budget director may report to the financial vice-president through whose office the necessary coordination is secured with the controller and other planning executives. There are occasions, of course, when the responsibility for planning development and coordination is placed under a separate officer reporting directly to the CEO.

The need, especially in the larger companies, for a full-time planning and control activity usually results in a separate department, which is usually under the jurisdiction of the controller. A typical organizational chart is shown in Figure 2-2.

Budget Committee

In some concerns, particularly larger ones, it is desirable to create a budget committee. Such a committee, usually consisting of the heads or representatives of major departments, should serve in an advisory capacity to the budget official. The chief executive or budget officer should serve as chairman of the budget committee. While such committees are useful and in some cases essential, they are not a substitute for the budget executive. Their function consists mainly in offering advice and suggestions and in interpreting the program to the organization at large.

Budget Coordinator's Role

It should be emphasized that the budget director does not *make* the budget — this is the responsibility of the chief executive, supported by the entire executive group — but the budget director should be in charge of the *procedure* by which the budget is developed. Specifically, the duties of the budget director in relation to budgeting may be stated as follows:

☐ Prepare all necessary forms, schedules, and manuals of instruction required for carrying forth the budgeting procedure. This should cover all procedures relating to preliminary suggestions, review, revision, adoption, and transmittal.

☐ Supply all executives, major and minor, with such analysis of past operations as may be useful in determining future plans and assist in the interpretation of these data.

☐ Translate proposed policies and plans into their detailed requirements and their probable effect upon operating results and financial condition.

☐ Receive preliminary estimates, transmit them through the proper channels for review and revision, and transmit final plans to those concerned.

☐ Keep all executives informed as to the execution of the budget. Analyze the variances between the budgeted and actual results and, insofar as possible, interpret these variances in relation to cause and effect.

☐ Initiate prompt revision of the budget, as circumstances require, in order to maintain a coordinated program.

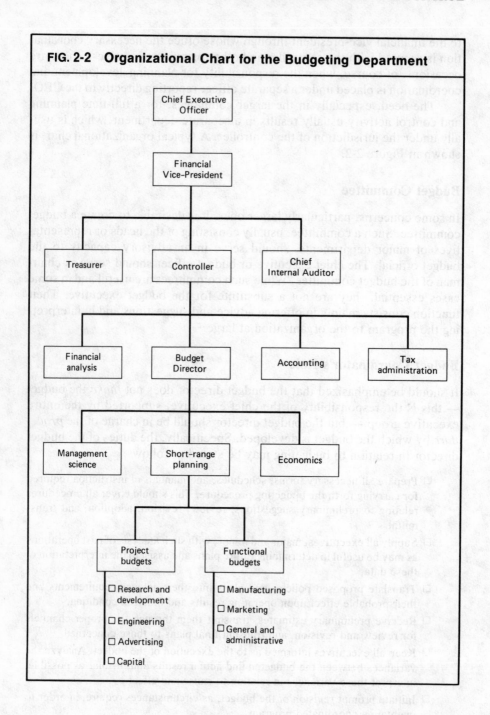

FIG. 2-2   Organizational Chart for the Budgeting Department

To perform these duties efficiently, the budget director must be an accurate analyst, a sympathetic counselor, and a good communicator.

In a decentralized company, counterparts of the corporate budget officer, reporting to the profit center executive, would perform these coordinating procedures. They would, however, be working closely with the corporate staff.

APPLICATION OF BUDGETING TO MOST BUSINESSES

Having reviewed the management process in relationship to profit-planning and those conditions essential to effective budgeting, the question can still arise: "Does it apply to my business?" The answer is that the budgeting process should, and can, apply to most businesses.

While the basic idea of budgeting is applicable to most types and sizes of business undertakings, the method of application does vary. In a company manufacturing steel railroad cars it is difficult to make immediate future plans because of the uncertainty of volume. The company may have made bids on 1,000 cars. It may receive all or none of this business. In the latter case operations will consist merely of minor repair work. If a quarter-year is under consideration, the volume may vary from $500,000 to $10 million, depending upon the acceptance of bids. Here the plans for the immediate future must wait until the result of bids is known. Looking over a longer period, however, the problems are normal. Does the outlook for the industry and for the company at hand justify more or less capital? What changes should be made in plant facilities? Into what pattern should the asset and equity relationships be directed? What changes should be developed in sales, production, and engineering methods? Should new products be developed? These questions suggest the need of study and plans for the longer period. When volume is known for the immediate future, detailed plans must be developed also for the shorter term.

At the other extreme is a company operating a chain of large public parking garages in numerous cities. Volume arises from thousands of small transactions daily. The margin of profit on each transaction is small; operations must be highly efficient; fixed charges and labor costs are high. To a certain extent volume can be predetermined by price policies and sales promotion effort, but, except for general business conditions and seasonal fluctuations, volume is fairly stable. Here the plans for the immediate future can be developed regularly and translated into expected operating results. Moreover, the long-term plans are fully as important as in the company mentioned above.

The difference in the problem of budgeting for the two concerns is mainly in the regularity of the short-term plans. While such variations of application will be met, the basic purpose of budgeting remains the same for all types of concerns.

Likewise, the size of the concern has little bearing upon the necessity for budgeting. Many smaller concerns fear that a formal budget procedure involves too much red tape. Any intelligent planning and control of business requires extensive study, be the company large or small, but there is no substitute. The small concern has the advantage of close personal supervision and direction, but this is not a substitute for intensive study as to what has been done, what should be done, and how best to do it. The procedure is easier in the small company but no less important.

The small concern is likely to view with alarm the multiplicity of forms used by the larger concern in building up its program. These suggest an expensive procedure. While forms as such have nothing to do with the basic purpose of budgeting, certain records and clerical work usually accompany any intensive business analysis. If in the development of the budget weaknesses are revealed, dangerous roads avoided, and profitable courses found, the clerical cost will be of little consequence.

REVEALING INFORMATION TO SUBORDINATES

Finally, one of the problems certain to be met in the work of budgeting is the objection to revealing information to subordinates. The objection is usually based on the fear that operations will slow down if it appears that work is to be scarce; that the information may reach competitors; or, if profits are running high, that subordinates will insist on higher pay. The force of these objections varies with the nature of the facts to be revealed and with the size of the concern. The objections arise more in small concerns than in large ones. While no one can deny the fact that individual circumstances arise in which it seems best not to reveal certain facts to subordinates, it is a poor organization where this is the general policy. Such a policy invariably indicates executive weakness and in due time breeds distrust, dissension, and disloyalty. The strong executives are the ones who do not fear their subordinates but boldly demand their interest, counsel, and intelligent support in both making and executing plans, and who recognize that such subordinates must to a considerable degree be given the facts upon which plans and operations are based. This is the only policy by which loyalty, cooperation, and strength of organization can ultimately be developed.

A positive approach to the problem requires that each echelon be given the information for its area of activity. It does not mean that everyone be given all the information. Each individual should be given the data he needs to properly perform his job. In the parlance of the aerospace business, information should be made available on a "need-to-know" basis. When the opinion of the subordinate is welcomed, and when he is given the data related to his activity, he will usually exert his best efforts to improve the operation.

KNOWLEDGE OF THE BUSINESS

In this chapter the author has discussed those essential conditions upon which effective planning depends. It has not been mentioned, but it has been implicit, that those responsible for the planning process must possess an intimate, yet broad, knowledge of the business. This is especially true of the financial discipline, which plays a key role in the budgetary system. The budgetary process, especially including those key points which make for successful plans, will be influenced by the perception and breadth of knowledge of the executives as to the special quirks or key factors involved in the business.

An intelligent attack upon the problems of business budgeting and control should begin with a careful analysis and understanding of the present status of the company. This procedure is not a prerequisite to the study of the mechanics or techniques of budgetary control in their more limited applications. However, such a review should give the proper perspective to business problems. It cannot help but assist in a deeper understanding of the managerial viewpoint, and, therefore, in the longer run contribute to a more effective system of budgetary control.

Any one of several classifications of business factors may be useful in diagnosing business problems. The following appears to be logical and simple:

Products or services — are the means of satisfying customer needs or desires. Upon them depends the development of the other factors.

Market — has to do with the customers, their location, and the nature and extent of their wants.

Distribution system — relates to the means of getting the product to the market and into the hands of the customers.

Production plan — relates to the facilities and processes used to manufacture the product.

Research and development program — relates to the efforts and effectiveness in creating new products or improving existing products or product applications, or manufacturing processes.

Organization — has to do with the employees in the organization, and their duties, responsibilities, and relationships — the organization structure and the track record of the management.

Finances — includes acquisition and use of capital needed in the enterprise, and factors making for a sound financial condition in the industry.

Control system — relates to the techniques used to guide the functions so as to achieve the business objective.

3

Profit Goals and Profit Planning

PLANS AND PROFIT GOALS

A "plan" can be defined as a predetermined course of action. A plan must involve the future and must involve action. Action is what distinguishes planning from forecasting, which involves the future but does not contemplate action by the planner or the company. A forecast is a necessary adjunct to planning in that the prediction of future conditions, such as the environment, state of the art, or government action, may be useful input in selecting alternative courses of action. Yet, the chief planner of the company, the chief executive officer, usually will possess, whether well documented or only in his/her mind, some idea of the actions the company should take to reach its objectives. Here, we will examine the planning process with respect to these objectives — especially the profit objectives or profit goals. Profit planning is the function of examining the various business alternatives and, considering the cost-volume-profit relationships, arriving at an acceptable financial plan.

ESSENTIAL ELEMENTS OF A PLAN

Business plans may differ in the time period covered (long-range or short-term) or the subject area covered (e.g., total company, a profit center, or a department), but certain elements are common to each. These are well described in Figure 3-1.[1] Note that they apply to each function or activity in the company. The elements in the plan answer these four questions:

1. Why is the action required?
2. What action must be taken and with what resources?
3. What are the goals of this action and when will they be reached?
4. What conditions or events must exist to reach the goal?

---

[1] Adapted from Business Intelligence Programs, "A Framework for Business Planning," Research Report No. 162, p. 11 (SRI International 1963). Copyright © 1963, by SRI International. Reprinted with permission.

The "why" question relates to the purpose of each segment, or echelon, or line item of the organization. At the corporate or top echelon level, the purpose is stated in rather broad terms, such as "to maintain the existing share of market in the home computer area," or "to improve company profit levels by developing new business in the fixed-wing aircraft market." These are rather general purposes at the highest echelon. But, as planning purposes are set in lower levels, they become more and more specific.

What actions are to be taken and what resources to be deployed also become more specific as one descends the organization ladder. Thus, corporate strategy will involve in very general terms the manner in which the corporate resources of funds, people, and facilities will be deployed against competitors. Projects are rather broad segments of functional activities, often involving many departments, deployed to achieve a given purpose. Programs relate to smaller segments, often of the normal or existing business.

The end result of the action, or what is to be accomplished, is the goal. A goal may be defined as quantified or measurable results which are expected at a stated point in time. They are so defined and stated so that they can be measured in terms of amount and time. Thus, a strategic goal may be "to achieve a sales level of $350 million of product X by the year 198X." This general corporate goal will be supported by sub-goals for each function and/or department.

Finally, the conditions to be met to achieve the purpose and the goals encompass all those matters which must come to exist. It probably will involve actions by third parties or probable environmental status, as well as actions controllable by the company.

THE STRATEGIC PLAN

The annual profit plan should be consistent with the long-range plan. Thus, it ordinarily makes no economic sense in the short-term plan to expand activities of a construction arm of a company when the strategic plan calls for divestment, unless expansion of the segment will facilitate sale — thus supporting a corporate strategy. The near-term budgeting process must be aware of the strategic plan as a starting point. Therefore, a discussion of the short-term profit plan must begin with the strategic profit plan.

The strategic plan usually begins with the present status and extends to that most remote period in the future which is considered useful for planning purposes. It may be fifty years in the forest products business, ten years in the aerospace business, and perhaps only three years in the garment business.

FIG. 3-1   **The Essential Elements of Plans by Corporate Jurisdiction and Function**

JURISDICTION OF CORPORATE MANAGEMENT

Plan	Targeted Area	Action and Resources	Goals	Conditions Necessary to Meet Goals
STRATEGIC				
Corporate	Corporate purposes	Corporate strategy	Corporate goals	Forecasts Policy Decision guidelines
Corporate Development	Corporate development purposes	Corporate development projects	Corporate development goals	Forecasts Policy Schedules and budgets
Divestment	Divestment purposes	Divestment projects	Divestment goals	Goal feasibility Criteria for decision
Diversification	Diversification purposes	Diversification projects	Diversification goals	Forecasts Criteria for decision
• Acquisition and Merger	Acquisition and merger purposes	Acquisition and merger projects	Acquisition and merger goals	Availability of candidates Criteria for decision

JURISDICTION OF OPERATING MANAGEMENT

Plan	Targeted Area	Action and Resources	Goals	Conditions Necessary to Meet Goals
Research and Development (R&D)	R&D Purposes	R&D Projects	R&D Goals	Policy Decision guidelines Schedules and budgets
• Basic Research	Basic research purposes	Basic research projects	Basic research goals	Goal feasibility Criteria for decision

• Product R&D	Product R&D purposes	Product R&D projects	Product R&D goals	Technical feasibility Cost feasibility Schedules and budgets
• Market R&D	Market R&D purposes	Market R&D projects	Market R&D goals	Forecasts Competition Schedules and budgets
• R&D Financial	R&D financial purposes	R&D financial projects	R&D financial goals	Technical feasibility Market forecasts Cost performance
• R&D Administration	R&D administration purposes	R&D administration projects	R&D administration goals	Business feasibility Managerial availability Other resource availability
OPERATIONS	Operations purposes	Operations program	Operations goals	Business forecasts Organization and procedures Schedules and budgets
Production	Production purposes	Production program	Production goals	Workload forecasts Methods and standards Schedules and budgets
Marketing	Marketing purposes	Marketing program	Marketing goals	Sales forecasts Competition Schedules and budgets
Financial	Financial operations purposes	Financial operations program	Financial operations goals	Financial performance Schedules and budgets
Administration	Administration operations purposes	Administration operations program	Administration operations goals	Managerial performance

As stated in Chapter 1, the strategic plan focuses on those unique factors which make the business a success, and on the threats and opportunities perceived to exist in the future. The strategic plan involves these components, all of which are also germane to the annual plan.

Statement of Basic Purpose

A clear and understandable statement of the company's *basic purpose* is necessary. Some typical examples could include these: to sustain and improve the company's existing product and marketing strengths; to develop new products related to our existing electronic capability, which will permit the company to grow faster than the industry.

The Strategy

A *strategy* indicates the ways by which the firm, reacting to its environment and threats and opportunities, will deploy its resources in the most advantageous way to achieve its basic purposes. Some illustrations include these actions: Discontinue employment of further resources in the architectural design business; sell Division *W*; accelerate research on product *Y* derivative; program a gradual entry into the tactical missile business.

Specific Goals

An expression should be included of *specific goals* or milestones to be reached under the strategy. Some examples could include these: Complete all necessary research into product *R*; construct new facilities at Houston, and complete the move of Division *P* by September 30, 198X. Financially expressed goals could include these:

	198R	199P
1. *Sales:*		
Attain a sales level of:	$400MM	$800MM
with present product component of:	50%	30%
2. *Rate of return:*		
Achieve these returns on:		
Assets employed:	15%	17%
Shareholders' equity:	18%	24%
3. *Per share earnings* — Attain:	$6.50	$10.00

Basic Assumptions

A statement of the basic assumptions is necessary in the strategic plan. These ground rules are important in that the board of directors and management must be aware of them. These could include:

- Inflation will continue at about 8 percent annually.
- The U.S. government will discontinue support of research in field *L*.
- Borrowed funds will not be available at less than 15 percent per annum.
- Foreign competition probably will dominate the commercial market for silicone chips.

All of these elements of the long-range plan must be taken into account in developing the annual profit plan. It may well be that circumstances have changed to such a degree that a goal contemplated in the long-range plan is no longer feasible — with a consequent impact on a short-term goal. Conversely, the reasonable goal for the annual plan will not permit reaching a goal expected in the strategic plan. The long-range plan usually is broad and general; and the specific analysis made in the annual profit planning procedure may cause a re-thinking of the corporate goals and objectives. The two planning processes, long-range and short-term, are intricately mixed, and iteration is often necessary.

FINANCIALLY EXPRESSED GOALS

A corporation may have any number of financially expressed goals applicable to both long-range and short-term plans. The following are commonly used:

1. *Measures of growth:*
   - Percent increase in sales per annum
   - Percent increase in net income over the prior year
   - Increase in earnings per share
2. *Measures of financial condition:*
   - Debt to equity ratio
   - Current ratio
   - Increase in working capital
   - Increase in book value per share
3. *Measures of profitability:*
   - Percent return on sales
   - Percent operating margin to sales
   - Percent return on assets employed in the business
   - Percent return on capital employed (long-term debt plus equity)
   - Percent return on shareholders' equity

In addition to these commonly used goals, a substantial number of other financial ratios (e.g., long-term debt to equity), or financial-operating ratios (e.g., net sales to receivables), operating ratios (e.g., sales deductions to gross sales or salaries and wages to net sales), or miscellaneous relationships (e.g., amount of fixed assets per employee) may be used as internal goals for the business in total or for segments or divisions of the entity. While each serves a useful purpose, the emphasis in this chapter is on profitability goals. It should be stated that some of these other goals may be used as guides in reaching the profit goals, primarily because they relate to a measurement factor that should be controlled in attaining the corporate goals, though they do not directly relate to measurements of profit.

PRINCIPAL PROFIT GOALS

As discussed above, a principal purpose of business, as an economic institution, is the earning of a profit. Profit is the catalyst, the incentive, the carrot in the American private enterprise system. Therefore, the basic question in the planning process is, What profit objective should be selected as a goal? The proper goal, as you will see, can be important to the continuity and well-being of the firm. A choice of an improper goal could be a disservice to the owners of the business and all stake holders who have an interest in the enterprise. The profit goal selected does make a difference! What profit goal, then, should be selected?

Very often, in discussions among the top executives prior to the start of the formal annual planning process, the chief executive officer may say, "I think we ought to earn $25 million this next year," or, "Maybe we should aim for a 15 percent increase in earnings per share." How the profit goal for a single year is expressed may not be as important as selecting the right measure. That is to say, for political or motivational or other reasons, a corporate goal may be described or explained in one way (increase in earnings per share) while the true objective may be some more appropriate measure (such as return on shareholders' equity). The stated goal must be supportive of the real goal. Further, it should be recognized that business management has a responsibility to provide an adequate return to the owners of the risk capital — the shareholders. Moreover, not only present owners should be considered. Ordinarily, a well-managed business will grow; and additional capital will be needed for expansion from new owners as well as new creditors. Therefore, mindful of the business objective and future capital needs, the author will discuss these profitability goals and the relationship between them:

- Net income as a percentage of sales
- Return on assets employed
- Return on shareholders' equity
- Growth in earnings per share

It should be noted that all these profit goals are expressed, not in the absolute, but in relationship to some base.

Net Income as a Percentage of Sales

One of the most common profit goals and measures of profitability of a business is the relationship of net income to net sales, also called the earnings ratio. Publication of quarterly and annual results of the income-to-sales ratio is widespread. *Fortune, Forbes, Business Week,* and other private sources, as well as the Securities and Exchange Commission and Federal Trade Commission, periodically issue comparative figures. This ratio, and its trend over time — for both the entire business and segments (product lines or profit centers) of the business — should indeed be considered in profit planning. But net income as related to sales is, however, only one factor in the profit equation. Net income as a percentage of sales, used alone, is not a sufficient goal for annual planning or indeed for long-range planning. That enterprise which produces the highest ratio of net income to sales may not be providing the best return on the financial resources devoted to the business. For example, consider this simple tabulation:

	Company	
Item	A	B
Net sales	$100,000,000	$100,000,000
Net income	$6,000,000	$6,100,000
Net income — Percentage of sales	6.0%	6.1%
Assets employed	$50,000,000	$55,000,000
Percent return on assets employed	12.0%	11.09%

Although the company *B* ratio of net income to net sales is higher than *A*, and both are in the same industry, company A has a higher profit ratio on the resources used in the business.

The same relative comments can be made about using the ratio of operating margin to net sales as a profit goal.

The relationship of return on assets employed and net income as a percentage of sales is covered in the following text. In any event, standing alone, the return on net sales is not considered the best profit goal for planning purposes.

Net Income as Related to Assets Employed

Another measure of profitability is the percent return on assets employed (ROAE). In fact, this is highly useful in measuring segments of a business, such as a division or profit center, as well as the company as a whole. It may be said that the objective of management is to optimize the return on assets entrusted to its care. The company should earn an acceptable rate of return on those assets, regardless of who provided the funds (i.e., the creditors or the owners).

Management should be interested in increasing its return on presently employed assets, to say nothing about the rate of return on future assets. This return is composed of two elements, as shown in Figure 3-2. In their combined use (often called the duPont formula, since it has been widely used by E.I. duPont de Nemours and Company), they constitute an important management tool.

As the illustration shows, the return on assets employed is composed of two principal factors: (a) the earnings ratio, or relationship of net income to net sales and (b) the utilization of assets in the production of the net income, or the net sales as related to assets employed, otherwise known as turnover. The return on assets is calculated by multiplying (a) by (b), as in the following steps.

1. *Assume a division with these typical results:*

Net sales	$10,000,000
Assets employed	2,500,000
Net income	500,000

2. *Basic formula for ROAE:*

$$\text{ROAE} = \frac{\text{Net income}}{\text{Sales}} \times \frac{\text{Sales}}{\text{Assets employed}}$$

3. *Cancel out sales:*

$$\text{ROAE} = \frac{\text{Net income}}{\cancel{\text{Sales}}} \times \frac{\cancel{\text{Sales}}}{\text{Assets employed}}$$

4. *Net income to sales (a) is 5%, as follows:*

$$\frac{\text{Net income}}{\text{Net sales}} = \% \text{ profit on sales} = \frac{\$500,000}{10,000,000} = 5\%$$

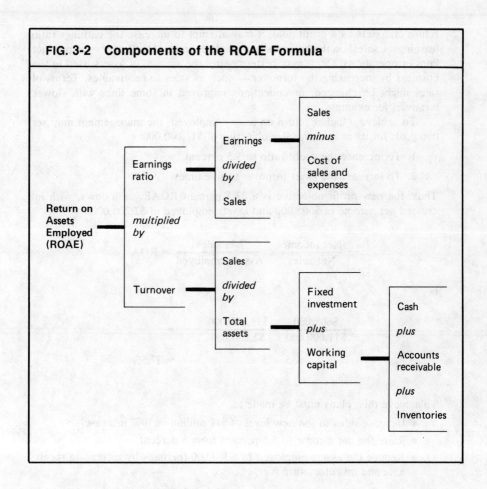

FIG. 3-2 Components of the ROAE Formula

5. *Turnover of assets is four times, as follows:*

$$\frac{\text{Net sales}}{\text{Assets employed}} = \text{Turnover} = \frac{\$10,000,000}{2,500,000} = 4$$

6. *ROAE is 20 percent:*

$$\text{Earnings ratio} \times \text{Turnover} = 5\% \times 4 = 20\%$$

Sensitivity to the resources (assets) needed to produce net income, in addition to the net income ratio to sales, are legitimate management concerns. The relationship of income to assets may be changed, or improved, by better performance on each, or both, factors. Hence, if management seeks a higher return on assets as a profit goal, it may attempt to increase the earnings ratio (earnings ÷ sales) on the business as a whole or some of the lower ratio product lines or operations. Or, it may better control the amount of assets used in the business by increasing the turnover — such as sales to receivables. Terms of sales might be changed, or collections improved in some lines with slower turnover, for example.

To achieve a higher return on assets employed, the management may set two goals for its near-term sales objective of $11,000,000:

1. To increase the profit ratio to 5.5 percent

2. To increase the asset turnover to five times

Thus, the new profit objective is a 27.5 percent ROAE, as follows, with increased net income of $605,000 and assets employed of $2,200,000:

$$\frac{\text{Net income}}{\text{Net sales}} \times \frac{\text{Net sales}}{\text{Assets employed}} = \text{ROA}$$

or

$$\frac{\$605,000}{\$11,000,000} \times \frac{\$11,000,000}{\$2,200,000} =$$
$$.055 \times 5 \qquad = 27.5\%$$

To achieve this, plans must be made to:
- Increase sales to the new level of $11 million (a 10% increase)
- Raise the net income to 5.5 percent from 5 percent
- Reduce the assets employed by $300,000 (perhaps by increasing receivable and inventory turnover)

The released assets, in the nature of unused cash perhaps, can be returned to the parent for employment elsewhere. Or, perhaps the funds may be needed in the division to finance further expected increase in sales. In any event, through improved asset utilization, resources have been released for expansion, or new, more profitable uses. An emphasis solely on the net income-to-sales ratio might not have stimulated the more productive use of assets.

Limitations on Return on Assets Employed

The ROAE (or the related concept of net assets employed, being total assets less current liabilities) is useful for management. It may compare itself with other companies in the same business, where the divisions are supplied capital by the corporate management, and a division has no responsibility regarding equity. It is an important device to compare the rate of return among the divisions — since the management task could be to allocate resources relative to future potential. It can be a profit objective for the entire company in terms of how well the assets are used.

It should be noted that ROAE is not quite the same as return on assets (ROA). There will be instances where assets are owned by the company, such as idle land, but not used in the business. As an internal planning device, it may be found desirable to eliminate such nonbusiness assets in calculating target rates of return. Likewise, refinements in the treatment of leased property may be found practical.

Return on Shareholders' Equity

Mature reflection might result in the conclusion that management must not only secure an acceptable return on assets, or assets employed, but must also optimize the return to the shareholders. This return is composed of the dividend yield and the appreciation in the share value. It will grow as the return on equity of the corporation increases. This return on equity is influenced by two factors: (1) the return on assets and (2) the method of financing the corporation. This latter factor includes leveraging, or degree of use of borrowed funds, as well as the terms on which such funds are secured (interest rate, loan period, etc.). Hence, in a sense, the return to shareholders represents the operating efficiency (use of assets) as well as the "financing" efficiency — the skill and judgment used in obtaining capital.

The return on shareholders' equity simply adds another factor to the formula for ROAE: the relationship of assets to shareholders' equity.

1. *ROAE calculation:*

$$\text{ROAE} = \frac{\text{Net income}}{\text{Net sales}} \times \frac{\text{Net sales}}{\text{Assets employed}}$$

2. *Cancel out sales:*

$$\text{ROAE} = \frac{\text{Net income}}{\text{Net sales}} \times \frac{\text{Net sales}}{\text{Assets employed}} = \frac{\text{Net income}}{\text{Assets employed}}$$

3. *Return on shareholders' equity introduces the third factor:*

Return on shareholders' equity =

$$\frac{\text{Net income}}{\text{Net sales}} \times \frac{\text{Net sales}}{\text{Assets employed}} \times \frac{\text{Assets employed}}{\text{Shareholders' equity}}$$

4. *Cancel out sales and assets:*

$$= \frac{\text{Net income}}{\text{Net sales}} \times \frac{\text{Net sales}}{\text{Assets employed}} \times \frac{\text{Assets employed}}{\text{Shareholders' equity}}$$

$$= \frac{\text{Net income}}{\text{Shareholders' equity}}$$

5. *Assume a company with these expected results for the current year:*

Net sales	$250,000,000
Net income	12,500,000
Assets employed (average)	100,000,000
Shareholders' equity (average)	75,000,000

6. *Ratios may be determined as follows:*

Net income to sales ($12,500,000 ÷ $250,000,000) = 5.0%

ROAE ($12,500,000 ÷ $100,000,000) = 12.5%

Return on shareholders' equity ($12,500,000 ÷ $75,000,000) = 16.67%

7. *Assume further the following industry upper quartile and average results in comparison:*

	Industry		Company
	Upper Quartile	Average	
Percent return on sales	5.25%	4.73%	5.00%
Percent return on assets employed	17.40	13.50	12.50
Percent return on shareholders' equity	25.23	17.00	16.67

Given these performance figures, the management well might further analyze its performance as against its competitors by component (profit rate, turnover of assets, and methods of financing), to arrive at realistic profit goals for the next year. Thus, while the profit ratio is quite good, turnover of 2.5 times ($250 million ÷ $100 million) is lower than the industry average of 2.8 times. Given the reasonable expected growth in sales to a level of about $200 million, the management, through analysis, might set a profit objective of 20.0 percent on shareholders' equity for the coming year. Detailed analysis of the possibilities, based on a review of the best and worst performing divisions in the company might result in objectives such as this:

	Present Year	Objective
Return on shareholders' equity	16.67%	20.00%
Return on sales	5.00	5.25
Turnover of assets	2.50	3.00

Applying these factors (for convenience) to beginning shareholders' equity produces a sales goal and assets employed target as follows:

	Plan Objective
Beginning shareholders' equity	$75,000,000
Rate of return objective	20%
Profit objective ($75,000,000 × .20)	15,000,000
Net profit ratio considered attainable	5.25%
Realizable sales volume ($15,000,000 ÷ .0525)	$285,715,000
Asset turnover (average)	3.00 times
Average assets to be employed ($285,715,000 ÷ 3.00)	$95,240,000

Thus, emphasis would be on securing the slightly higher margin (to net after taxes) on the sales volume and an increase in turnover to reduce assets employed. Borrowed funds thus could be lowered and by all measures the company would be approaching the performance of its closest competitors. This illustration has been grossly simplified to express an approach. The point to be made is that return on shareholders' equity probably is *the best* measure of management's total performance. Further, it bears a direct relationship to the earnings per share factor that Wall Street watches so closely.

Earnings per Share

In directing the business, most managements, and the financial community as well, pay great attention to the earnings per share (total net income

FIG. 3-3   Increase in EPS With a Constant ROE

THE STABLE COMPANY

ROE VS. GROWTH IN EPS

(dollars in thousands except per share)

Year	Beginning Shareholders' Equity	Net Income	Dividends Paid	Ending Shareholders' Equity	Return on Beginning Equity	Dividend Payout Percentage	Dividends per Share	Earnings per Share	Growth in EPS (%)
19X1	$100,000	$10,000.00	$4,000.00	$106,000	10%	40%	$4.00	$10.00	—
19X2	106,000	10,600.00	4,240.00	112,360	10	40	4.24	10.60	6%
19X3	112,360	11,236.00	4,496.00	119,100	10	40	4.50	11.24	6
19X4	119,100	11,910.00	4,764.00	126,246	10	40	4.76	11.91	6
19X5	126,246	12,624.60	5,049.84	133,821	10	40	5.05	12.63	6
19X6	133,821	13,382.10	5,352.84	141,850	10	40	5.35	13.38	6

applicable to common shares ÷ number of common shares outstanding) or more specifically to the *growth* in earnings per share. Many business people would consider growth in earnings per share a sound goal. The author concurs that this is an important figure, and even that growth in per share earnings is desirable. For simplicity, it may be useful to refer to the per share earnings trend, and even express it as a goal to some of the less sophisticated. But, again, it is important to understand the relationship between growth in earnings per share (EPS) and return on shareholders' equity (ROE). A growth in the EPS does not necessarily signify an increasingly profitable return on the shareholders' interest or the return on long-term capital. In fact, a company may well show an increase in the EPS but a decrease in return on total capital. And there are many other caveats.

Consider the relationship of ROE and growth in EPS. If a company earns a *constant* (flat) rate on shareholders' equity, the EPS will increase. And if the dividend payout ratio remains constant, the per share dividends will increase. Witness the simple example in Figure 3-3. In this illustration, the rate of return on (beginning) shareholders' equity is a constant 10 percent; the dividend payout is kept at 40 percent of earnings. The resulting annual growth rate in the EPS is 6 percent, being the plowback or retained earnings rate multiplied by the return on shareholders' equity (100% − 40% = 60% retention rate × 10% = 6% annual growth rate in the EPS). Even if the rate of return on the retained earnings, the "new" capital, is very low, — unacceptably low — the EPS will rise. But this incremental rate of return is important in capital formation — in securing additional capital.

Growth in Earnings per Share

Management often considers it has done a good job when the EPS increases. But, if a company earns a constant rate on the shareholders' equity, and retains *some* earnings, then the EPS should increase. Conversely, if the business paid out all earnings, the EPS would not increase. It is desirable to recognize the various factors that can influence the EPS, and equally important, to examine the incremental rate on the new retained earnings (new capital) versus the rate of return needed on new projects to attract additional capital.

Without getting into excessive detail, a summary overview on EPS changes may be helpful, especially given the disposition of management and the financial community to equate growth in EPS as an indicator of real growth:

FIG. 3-4   Impact of EPS of Selling Shares Above Book Value

	Presently Outstanding Shares	New Shares	Total
Number of shares	100,000	50,000	150,000
Total equity	$2,000,000	$1,500,000	$3,500,000
Book value per share	$20.00	$30.00	$23.33
Return on book value	10%	10%	10%
Net Income:			
Total	$200,000	$150,000	$350,000
Per share	$20.00	$30.00	$23.33

□ EPS in most companies is heavily influenced by the normal plowback of earnings. Whether or not the increase is adequate depends, among other things, on what is required to bring new capital into the company. Given the risks, what is the investor demanding? And how does this compare with the return on the newly retained earnings (and the return on new capital projects?)

□ EPS is altered by events including, but not limited to

• Retirement of common shares through purchases of treasury shares with excess or available cash.

• Impact of changes in the capital structure, such as increased leverage through the use of long-term debt.

• Acquisition of companies for cash or stock wherein the acquired has a lower price to earnings ratio than the acquiring company.

□ An increase in the EPS does not necessarily denote an increasing rate of return on either the shareholders' equity, or that related measure, return on long-term capital employed (ROI) (company capitalization of long-term debt and equity). Sale of new stock above the book value of the existing stock will increase the EPS if the rate of return realized on the new capital is the same as on the prior retained earnings.

For example, see Figure 3-4. If the company continues to earn the same 10 percent rate on shareholders' equity for both old and new shares, the EPS increases from $20.00 to $23.33 with no increase in efficiency of use of the shareholders' funds. This is not to say that a company should not sell shares above book value, but merely to indicate that management should be sensitive to the impact the value received on new shares has on the EPS.

RETURN ON SHAREHOLDERS' EQUITY PROFIT GOAL

The introduction of a new profit goal into a company must be done with care. The management, of course, finally must be made aware of the weaknesses of certain former profit goals and the strengths of the ROE as an objective. However, some of those less involved with the financial implications may be better served by translating, for a time, the profit goal based on return on shareholders' equity into an EPS, or percent income on sales, or ROAE.

Applying a ROE goal may begin by using somewhat less analysis or refinement, as long as reasonable judgment is applied. An examination of the company's recent history, coupled with a review of competitive results in the ROE area, may provide a guide as to a starting goal. A convenient reference may be the *Forbes* annual profit results, as illustrated for the drug industry in Figure 3-5.[2]

As the process is refined, the management should consider a goal somewhat higher than the existing cost of capital for the enterprise, that is, higher than the return on present equity. What is key in planning is not the historical rate of return on equity, but that deemed acceptable in the future — by the marketplace. See Chapter 7.

OTHER PROFIT GOALS

In addition to the more popular, and perhaps more useful, profit goals which can be helpful in planning — whether short- or long-term — there are, of course, other profit goals, including:

- Interest rate on long-term debt (which assumes that this rate measures the cost of equity capital as is *not* often the case)
- Interest on long-term debt, plus dividends paid to shareholders, plus some margin (this also does not recognize the cost of equity capital, and might perpetuate a given dividend rate)
- Percentage increase in net earnings, unrelated to sales, equity, or assets (which tends to perpetuate historical performance as distinguished from a more objective or required rate of return)
- The historical or experienced rate of return on capital. (While this may be a consideration, recognition must be given to the capital marketplace requirements. It leaves largely unresolved the minimum rate of return.)

---

[2] From *Forbes* (January 3, 1983), p. 192. Copyright © 1983, by Forbes, Inc. Reprinted with permission.

FIG. 3-5   Yardsticks of Management Performance

Company	Profitability										Growth				
	Return on Equity			Debt/ Equity Ratio	Return on Total Capital			Net Profit Margin			Sales			Earnings Per Share	
	5-Year Rank	5-Year Average	Latest 12 Months		5-Year Rank	5-Year Average	Latest 12 Months		5-Year Rank	5-Year Average		5-Year Rank	5-Year Average	5-Year Rank	5-Year Average
SmithKline Beckman	1	37.5%	28.5%	0.2	2	33.1%	24.8%	15.4%			1	24.7%	1	31.5%
American Home Products	2	33.5	32.9	0.0	1	33.5	32.6	12.2			10	10.9	6	12.4
Merck	3	23.5	20.4	0.1	5	20.2	17.1	13.5			6	12.3	8	10.6
Bristol-Myers	4	22.4	21.9	0.1	4	20.7	20.7	9.5			8	11.5	5	13.4
Eli Lilly	5	21.9	21.1	0.0	3	20.9	19.2	13.5			3	14.9	7	11.3
Upjohn	6	21.2	15.3	0.4	7	15.5	10.9	8.2			5	13.1	2	15.5
G D Searle	7	20.2	25.0	0.3	8	14.9	19.9	14.5			13	7.6	3	14.4
Schering-Plough	8	19.8	13.9	0.2	6	18.7	11.7	10.1			2	15.0	10	8.0
Pfizer	9	17.3	18.1	0.4	10	13.6	14.1	9.3			7	12.0	9	9.6
Sterling Drug	10	16.2	15.5	0.1	9	14.5	13.8	7.2			11	10.4	12	7.3
A H Robins	11	14.6	14.9	0.1	11	12.7	13.4	9.7			9	11.2	11	7.4
Squibb	12	13.3	13.4	0.4	12	10.5	10.5	8.7			14	7.0	13	3.6
Warner-Lambert	13	11.5	13.8	0.4	13	8.7	9.7	5.2			12	8.9	14	-2.8
Richardson-Vicks		**	13.4	0.1		**	13.2	5.9			4	14.2‡	4	13.5‡
Industry medians		20.2	16.8	0.2		15.5	14.0	9.6				11.8		11.0
All-industry medians		15.9	12.7	0.4		11.0	9.3	3.4				13.3		12.3

‡ Four-year growth.
** Not available; not ranked.

SUMMARY

A company may have several goals or objectives for different purposes. For budgeting or planning purposes, the discussion has centered on profit-related goals. A profit-oriented goal probably is more closely related to a principal corporate objective of optimizing the return to the shareholder — the ultimate risk-taker. We have attempted to explain the inadequacy of certain profit goals — percent return on sales or earnings per share increase — when considered solely by themselves. Perhaps the most useful profit goal is return on equity. And this, in turn, must bear a relationship to the cost of attracting funds into the business. This return on capital must be high enough, over the longer term, to adequately compensate the risk-takers and provide the incentive to make necessary investments.

4

Overview of the Short-Term Planning Process

THE STRUCTURE OF BUSINESS PLANS

Business plans are, or should be, interrelated. The short-term plan should relate to the long-range plan, which should be "built up" from detailed budgets, based on guidelines set by management. The relationship of the long-range plan and short-term plan is illustrated in Figure 1-2 in Chapter 1. Corporate plans are of two basic types, long-range and short-term, which differ substantially in level of detail gathered and the time span covered. The long-range or strategic plan sets the general course over a longer period of time and summarizes in financial terms the overall expected results.

Strategic Plan

The strategic plan sets out in very broad terms where the company expects to go, and the strategy it will use to get there. The plan is divided into two broad categories, development and operations, each covering the longest period deemed practical to plan — perhaps five or ten years in a typical business. The development plan relates basically to new products and markets. The operations plan covers the continuous long-term activity that relates mostly to present products and markets. The segments of each plan are denoted as follows:

1. *Development plan:*
   ☐ Diversification plan
   ☐ Divestment plan
   ☐ Research and development plans

2. *Operations plan:*
   ☐ Manufacturing
   ☐ Marketing
   ☐ Finance
   ☐ Administration

Short-Term Profit Plan

The detailed short-term profit plan, usually constructed along departmental lines, for one or two years, encompasses all corporate functions:

- Sales plan
- Marketing plan
- Manufacturing plan
- Research plan
- Plans of related staff functions (finance and administration)
- Consolidated plan

The short-term plan, once approved, becomes a commitment by those responsible, each for his own segment, and hence translates to a control device. Thus, the short-term management task involves these three functions:

1. Development of the short-term plan,
2. Measurement of actual performance against plan, and
3. Initiation of corrective action to bring actual results into line with expectations.

THE SHORT-TERM PLANNING CYCLE

The annual plan cycle for most companies is illustrated in Figures 4-1 and 4-2. For a decentralized company with separate divisions, each with a profit

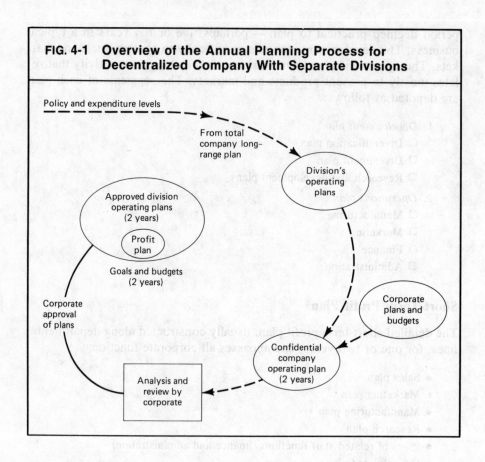

FIG. 4-1   Overview of the Annual Planning Process for Decentralized Company With Separate Divisions

responsibility, the overall development process of the short-term plan is described in Figure 4-1. The more detailed process that occurs at the division level is illustrated in Figure 4-2. If a company has a centralized structure, then the process at the central level closely follows that shown in Figure 4-2.

STEPS IN THE SHORT-TERM PLANNING PROCESS

The integrated plan, i.e., one that is consolidated and covers all operations, is formally developed at least once a year. The process is an iterative one, with changes in one segment or department often causing adjustments in other departments. The comprehensive procedure is diagrammed in Figure 4-3, and is summarized in these six steps:

FIG. 4-2 Division-Level View of the Annual Planning Process for a Decentralized Company

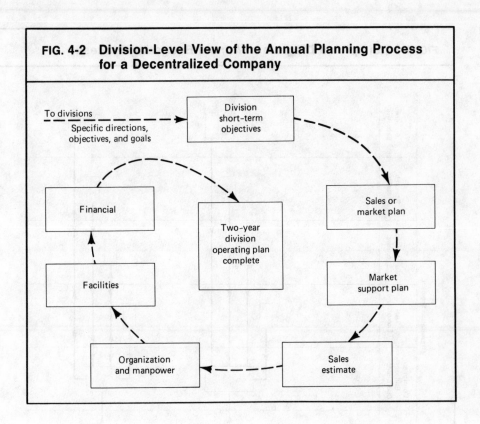

Prior to budget preparation:

1. Based on a review of the current environment, recent company performance, and the strategic plan, in consultation with the financial officer and other involved executives, the chief executive officer (CEO) issues the company/division annual plan guidelines and objectives. See Action A(1,2,3) in Figure 4-3.

Budget preparation:

2. Each profit center and/or other related segment prepares its detailed plan based on the annual plan guidelines. See B(1,2,3,4).

3. The plans are consolidated, reviewed, and adjusted as necessary to coordinate efforts by all departments. See B(5,6,7).

4. When the final plan for the year or two years has been agreed to by the CEO, it is presented to the board of directors for approval. See B(8).

5. Upon approval by the board, each operating segment is notified. See B(9).

Control phase:

6. The necessary comparison of budget and actual results is made throughout the period, and corrective action is taken. See C(1,2,3).

(*text continues on page 4-10*)

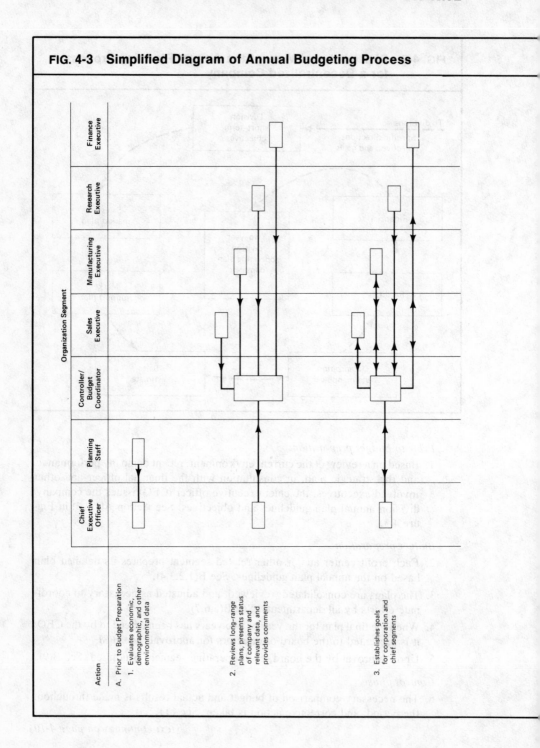

FIG. 4-3 Simplified Diagram of Annual Budgeting Process

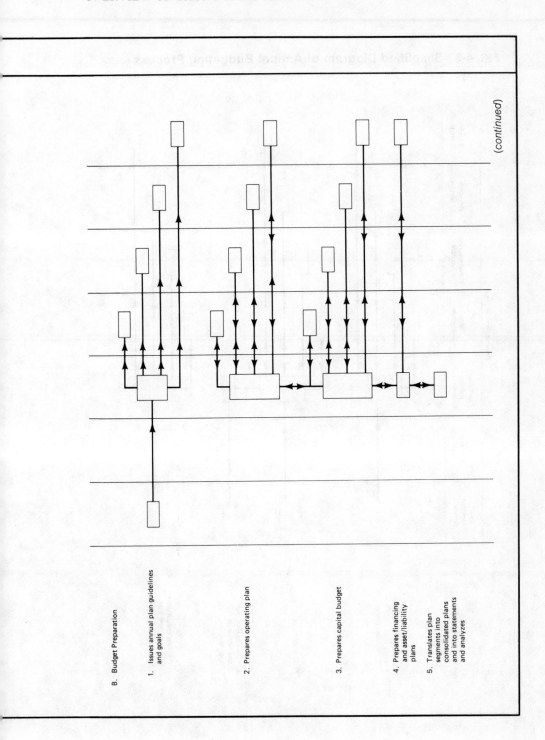

(continued)

FIG. 4-3 Simplified Diagram of Annual Budgeting Process (cont'd)

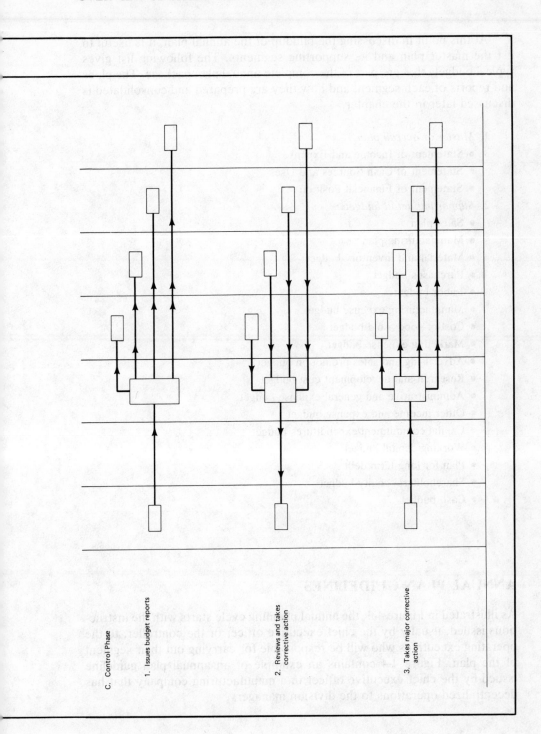

C. Control Phase

1. Issues budget reports

2. Reviews and takes corrective action

3. Takes major corrective action

At this point in discussing the buildup of the annual plan, it is useful to list the master plan and its supporting segments. The following list gives typical budgets that are part of the complete annual plan package. The plans and reports of each segment and how they are prepared and consolidated is discussed later in the chapter.

1. *Master or overall plan:*
   - Statement of Income and Expense
   - Statement of Cash Sources and Uses
   - Statement of Financial Position
2. *Supporting detail budgets:*
   - Sales plan
   - Manufacturing plan
   - Material and inventory budget
   - Purchases budget
   - Labor budget
   - Manufacturing expense budget
   - Cost-of-goods-sold budget
   - Marketing expense budget
   - Advertising and sales promotion budget
   - Research and development cost budget
   - Administrative and general expense budget
   - Other income and expense budget
   - Capital commitment/expenditures budget
   - Working capital budget
   - Plan for long-term debt
   - Shareholders' equity budget
   - Cash budget

ANNUAL PLAN GUIDELINES

As illustrated in Figure 4-3, the annual planning cycle starts with the instructions issued, usually by the chief executive officer or the controller, to the operating executives who will be responsible for carrying out their segment of the plan. Figure 4-4 contains an example of an annual plan guideline issued by the chief executive officer in a manufacturing company that has decentralized operations to the division managers.

FIG. 4-4   Guidelines for Business Plans

TO: Division General Managers   FROM: T. R. Atkins
SUBJECT: Business Plan Guidelines — 19X1/19X2

To enhance our financial planning process, and in recognition of the fact that most of the company contracts are performed over a period greater than one year, the business plan financial data will be presented for a two-year period, 19X1 and 19X2. The business plan for 19X1/X2 should be submitted to the corporate office by 30 September 19X0. The data provided should be in consonance with long-range considerations and represent the most realistic and probable level of business for the period.

SUBMISSION OF PLANS:

The schedule for preparation, submission, review, and approval of the plan is as follows:

- Submission to the corporate office (Controller's Department) of complete plan (including monthly detail)   30 September 19X0

- Business plans review/analysis and approval by the corporate office   12 November 19X0

- Corporate business plan consolidated and approved by executive office   8 December 19X0

- Review and approval by the Board of Directors   21 December 19X0

FINANCIAL OBJECTIVES:

For your information, as major executives of the company, the corporate or overall financial objectives are set forth below. These have been developed, giving consideration to the most recent strategic plan, adjusted for the major contract awards made last month. Your planning and financial staffs have been consulted on certain relevant details. I am advised that you have been kept fully informed on our thinking.

The corporate financial objectives are outlined below ($ in millions):

	19X1	19X2
Return on beginning shareholders' equity	22.3%	22.4%
Net sales	$580	$630
Operating margin	9.1%	9.2%
Return on average assets	10.6%	10.6%

Given the heavy capital expenditures for 19X1, no change has been made in the ROA objectives. We believe the sales, margin, and return on asset targets are consistent with the return on shareholders' equity (ROA) objective.

The objectives for each of your divisions are outlined on attachment A [omitted]. If, in your planning process, you conclude that any of the objectives for your division are unrealistic, or are inconsistent with the expected near-term environment in any material way, please contact me.

(continued)

FIG. 4-4   Guidelines for Business Plans (cont'd)

PERIOD OF BUSINESS PLAN:

The plan should be prepared by months for each of the two years. Monthly details of the approved plan will be used to compare and measure actuals against plan monthly on a cumulative basis. The data will also be used to prepare the periodic reports for management and the Board of Directors. However, as you know, in the presentations to the Board, as well as to our bankers, the monthly data for the two years will be consolidated into quarterly information.

OPERATING CENTER IDENTIFICATION:

Separate detailed business plans will be required for each of the operating centers reporting to you, per the attached schedule [*omitted*].

PLAN OBJECTIVES AND ASSUMPTIONS:

The plan *must* establish realistic but "tight" and attainable goals. In the past some operating center plans have not been based on the *most* probable case, resulting in significant variances and less than optimum use of the company's cash resources. In monitoring and measuring performance, consideration will be given to the degree of difficulty in achieving the planned goals.

As you know, financial planning for the entire corporation is based on individual operating center plans. It is important that the consolidated financial data, which includes your projection, represent the most probable financial results of your operations.

The plan will be evaluated using various financial ratios and factors, as well as by appraising its adequacy to meet operating center and overall short-term and long-term corporate objectives.

Consideration should be given to any critical assumption or unusual conditions which could have a significant impact, whether positive or negative, on the plan. An assessment of these factors should be included in the narrative portion of the plan.

It is the responsibility of a division or subsidiary considered the prime contractor to ensure that the inter/intracompany data are consistent with performing organizations. It is essential that this coordination be accomplished prior to the submittal of the plans so that inter/intracompany transactions can be reconciled and properly eliminated in the consolidated business plan.

OVERHEAD TECHNICAL ACTIVITY:

The Overall Technical Activity (OTA) Plan will be prepared in accordance with Policy Directive 26. Among other things, we must be certain that any planned "investments" in research and development, which should not be capitalized under current accounting practices, are, in fact, handled as period costs.

FEDERAL AND FOREIGN INCOME TAXES:

The basic provision for federal and foreign income taxes should be computed at 48 percent of the planned income before taxes. Any special situation which would result in a requirement for additional taxes or tax credits should be discussed with and authorized by the Corporate Director of Tax Administration prior to being included in the plan.

Divisions and subsidiaries using the completed contract method for reporting taxable income must update their calculation of deferred income taxes and submit revised computations with the business plan if the projected deferrals have changed from the amounts previously used in the long-range plan.

STATE INCOME TAXES/PROPERTY TAXES/FRINGE BENEFITS:

The estimated provisions for state income and/or franchise taxes are set forth on the attached schedule. [*Schedule omitted.*] Given the range of conditions in each profit center, guidelines are provided on attachment B for these items [*attachment B omitted*]:

- Property taxes
- FICA taxes
- Other local taxes
- Fringe benefits
  a. Health care benefits
  b. Life insurance
  c. Long-term disability insurance
  d. Retirement plan costs
- Corporate expense allocation

WAGE RATES:

Each operating center should include realistic estimates of its expected wage rates, considering geographic location, union agreements, rate of inflation, and so forth. The narrative should include assumptions that have been made in developing the plan.

CAPITAL ASSET BUDGET:

The vice-president–facilities has provided a tentative budget for capital asset *commitments* based on that information contained in your strategic plan, and recent discussions with your facilities staff. You are aware of the cut-off rate of return required for all additions to plant and equipment not essential to the continuance of the business. Given the high borrowing cost and the recent buildup in inventories, we must restrict capital expenditures to our internal cash generation for 19X1.

Any plans you may have for divestment of unused facilities, or alternate use of plant and equipment, should be explained in the narrative section of the plan.

The various schedules should be prepared as outlined in Policy Directive 8. As you are well aware, your written commentary on the plan highlights, special circumstances, and critical assumptions are vital to our understanding and evaluation of the two-year plan.

When the preliminary analysis of the consolidated plan has been completed, I will look forward to your oral presentation, with emphasis on the actions you will take to meet your various profit and manpower objectives.

SEGMENTS OF THE ANNUAL PLAN OR BUDGET

After the general guidelines and time schedules are issued, the operating management commences the budget preparation. Meanwhile, much thinking and discussion of alternatives has already taken place in anticipation of the plan requirements. In fact, with the aid of computers, several "what if" scenarios have probably already been prepared.

While the operating executives, in fact, must develop the plan and be responsible for its implementation, much of the detail work to prepare the plan is done by the financial and accounting groups. Since both operating and nonoperating areas are covered in the plan, it is helpful to survey the various budget segments and review their functions and conditions as they relate to the budget.

In this overly simplified example, the budget will be shown for the year as a whole. In actual practice, the data usually is compiled by month. For simplification, the many complications, the interplay, and other considerations are omitted.

The Sales Plan

The usual starting point in budget preparation is with the sales plan. Based on knowledge of economic conditions, industry trends, and market conditions, the vice-president–sales arrives at a sales plan. This, in fact, may be based on an evaluation of the individual estimates of the sales people concerning their knowledge of the territory. In our illustration, the company manufactures only three products. The preliminary sales plan or estimate is shown in Figure 4-5.

The Production Plan

When the sales plan has been more or less finalized, such information is provided to the vice-president–manufacturing, who then is able to establish a tentative schedule for the production of the finished product to meet both the sales and related inventory requirements. The production plan is illustrated in Figure 4-6.

The Purchases Budget

With the level of production set, the next task is that of determining what raw materials and purchased parts will be required to fill the production and related inventory needs. The result of this usually laborious job, now made easier with the help of computers, is illustrated in Figure 4-7 as to quantities to be purchased, and in Figure 4-8 as to the investment levels.

FIG. 4-5   Sales Plan

THE MANUFACTURING COMPANY

PRELIMINARY SALES PLAN

For the Year Ending December 31, 19X1

Product	Number of Units	Unit Selling Price	Total Sales
B	50,000	$ 47.50	$2,375,000
C	17,000	106.00	1,802,000
D	9,000	210.00	1,890,000
		Total	$6,067,000

FIG. 4-6   Planned Production

THE MANUFACTURING COMPANY

PRODUCTION BUDGET

For the Year Ending December 31, 19X1

Description	Products B	C	D
Quantity needed for sale	50,000	17,000	9,000
Desired ending inventory	10,000	4,000	1,500
Total Requirements	60,000	21,000	10,500
Deduct: Beginning inventory	7,000	6,000	1,500
Required production quantity	53,000	15,000	9,000

As is discussed in Chapter 21, expensive elements of raw materials or purchased parts may be controlled on a per-piece basis, but other items may be purchased and controlled on a class or dollar-value basis.

The Labor Budget

Once the quantity of production is known, the manpower requirements can be determined. Whether the labor is classified as direct or indirect labor in

FIG. 4-7   Quantity Purchases

THE MANUFACTURING COMPANY

MATERIAL REQUIREMENTS

For the Year Ending December 31, 19X1

Raw Materials and Purchased Parts	Quantity Needed for Production Budget — Finished Product Totals						Total Unit Requirements
	B		C		D		
	Units Req'd	Total	Units Req'd	Total	Units Req'd	Total	
MM	10	530,000	2	30,000	1	9,000	569,000
NN	4	212,000	3	45,000	1	9,000	266,000
PP	2	106,000	1	15,000	4	36,000	157,000
QQ	—	—	1	15,000	3	27,000	42,000

the traditional sense may be irrelevant. The proper staffing must be in place. A method of calculating the labor budget is illustrated in Figure 4-9.

This figure illustrates the labor budget for manufacturing only. Usually, each department supplements its expense budget with detailed personnel plans.

The Manufacturing Expense Budget

The manufacturing budget is an important segment of cost for a company engaged in this type of activity. Given the production level in total, the requirements of each department must be determined. Based on the cost structure in each center — the share of expenses that are variable with volume, and those that are fixed — the vice-president–manufacturing is able to determine the required budget. This is summarized by type of expense in Figure 4-10. Incidentally, the trend to heavy automation results in less of the costs being related directly to manufacturing the product, with a relatively larger share being in the nature of indirect labor and machinery-related expense (e.g., depreciation).

Other Operating Expenses Budget

The various functional executives must determine the needed budgets for expenses under their jurisdiction on a department-by-department basis. A summary by type of expense, for general and administrative, sales, and research and development functions, is reflected in Figure 4-11.

FIG. 4-8 Purchases Budget

THE MANUFACTURING COMPANY

PURCHASES BUDGET

For the Year Ending December 31, 19X1

Raw Materials and Purchased Parts	Production	Ending Inventory	Unit Requirements Total	Less: Beginning Inventory	Quantity to Be Purchased	Estimated Unit Price	Purchases Budget
MM	569,000	100,000	669,000	169,000	500,000	$ .50	$ 250,000
NN	266,000	50,000	316,000	40,000	276,000	1.00	276,000
PP	157,000	10,000	167,000	9,000	158,000	2.00	316,000
QQ	42,000	2,000	44,000	2,000	42,000	10.00	420,000
						Total	$1,262,000

FIG. 4-9   Labor Budget

THE MANUFACTURING COMPANY

MANUFACTURING LABOR BUDGET

For the Year Ending December 31, 19X1

Product	Quantity to Be Produced	Standard Labor Hours Per Unit	Total Standard Hours	Labor Budget*
B	53,000	1.00	53,000	$397,500
C	15,000	2.00	30,000	60,000
D	9,000	3.00	27,000	51,000
		Total	110,000	$508,500
		Allowance for over-standard hours		41,250
		Total Labor Budget		$549,750

* At $7.50 per hour

FIG. 4-10   Manufacturing Expense Budget

THE MANUFACTURING COMPANY

MANUFACTURING EXPENSE BUDGET

For the Year Ending December 31, 19X1

Item	Amount
Indirect labor	$ 510,000
Payroll taxes and insurance	34,000
Retirement plan expense	152,000
Supplies	32,000
Repairs and maintenance	40,000
Power	72,000
Rent expense	72,000
Property taxes	10,000
Insurance — Property	3,000
Depreciation	175,000
Total	$1,100,000

FIG. 4-11 Summary of Budgets for Operating Expenses

THE MANUFACTURING COMPANY

SUMMARY OF BUDGETED OPERATING EXPENSES

For the Year Ending December 31, 19X1

Expense Item	General and Administrative	Selling	Research and Development
Salaries	$320,000	$ 210,000	$120,000
Commissions	—	250,000	—
Payroll taxes and insurance	32,000	46,000	12,000
Retirement plan expense	64,000	92,000	24,000
Advertising and sales promotion	—	290,000	—
Travel and entertainment	70,000	150,000	20,000
Rent	40,000	35,000	30,000
Supplies	20,000	30,000	50,000
Occupancy	80,000	60,000	50,000
Purchased services	43,000	15,000	61,000
Repairs and maintenance	15,000	12,000	18,000
Depreciation	17,000	24,000	34,000
	$701,000	$1,214,000	$419,000

The Inventory Budget

While a simplified version of the expense budgets of the company have been presented in sequence, in actual practice other asset-type budgets are being developed simultaneously with such plans. Hence, the budget for investment in inventory would be determined when all prospective manufacturing costs have been calculated. The finished inventory budget, based on unit standard costs, would be figured. As an example, the unit costs of the three products can be set as follows:

Product	Material	Labor	Mfg. Expense*	Total
		Unit Cost		
B	$10.00	$ 7.50	$16.22	$ 33.72
C	18.00	15.00	32.45	65.45
D	39.50	22.50	48.67	110.67

* For simplification, calculated at 216.30 percent of labor

FIG. 4-12   Computation of Finished Goods Inventory

THE MANUFACTURING COMPANY

FINISHED GOODS BUDGET
For the Year Ending December 31, 19X1

Product	Quantity	Unit Price	Aggregate Budget
B	10,000	$ 33.72	$337,200
C	4,000	65.45	261,800
D	1,500	110.67	166,005
		Total	$765,005

FIG. 4-13   Summary of Planned Inventories

THE MANUFACTURING COMPANY

STATEMENT OF PLANNED INVENTORIES
For the Year Ending December 31, 19X1

Item	Amount
Raw materials and purchased parts	$ 140,000
Supplies	5,000
Work-in-process	240,000
Finished goods	765,005
Total	$1,150,005

Based on the standard unit costs, the finished goods inventory budget would be set at $765,005, as shown in Figure 4-12. All other inventory investments would be calculated by a similar procedure.

A summary of the expected or planned investment in inventory at year-end is disclosed in Figure 4-13. In the real world, inventory levels will be reviewed and tested as to acceptable turnover rate in an effort to keep the funds tied up in these assets to a minimum.

FIG. 4-14   Capital Expenditures Budget

THE MANUFACTURING COMPANY

CAPITAL EXPENDITURES BUDGET

For the Year Ending December 31, 19X1

Item	For Continuance of Present Business	For Expansion	Total
Land	—	$ 100,000	$ 100,000
Buildings	$220,000	700,000	920,000
Machinery and equipment	310,000	980,000	1,290,000
Total	$530,000	$1,780,000	$2,310,000

FIG. 4-15   Calculation of Estimated Cost of Goods Sold

THE MANUFACTURING COMPANY

STATEMENT OF COST OF GOODS SOLD (STANDARD)

For the Year Ending December 31, 19X1

Item	Amount
Raw Materials	
Beginning inventory	$ 162,500
Add: Purchases [Fig. 4-8]	1,262,000
Total available	1,424,500
Deduct: Ending inventory [Fig. 4-13]	140,000
Transfers to work-in-process	1,284,500
Direct Labor (Standard) [Fig. 4-9]	508,500
Manufacturing Expense [Fig. 4-10]	1,100,000
Total charges to work-in-process	2,893,000
Add: Beginning inventory work-in-process	270,000
Total available	3,163,000
Less: Ending work-in-process [Fig. 4-13]	240,000
Total transfers to finished goods (F.G.)	2,923,000
Add: Beginning inventory (F.G.)	720,000
Total available	3,643,000
Less: Ending inventory (F.G.) [Fig. 4-12]	765,005
Estimated Cost of Goods Sold (Standard)	$2,877,995

FIG. 4-16   Statement of Planned Income and Expense

THE MANUFACTURING COMPANY

STATEMENT OF PLANNED INCOME AND EXPENSE

(Iteration No. 1)

For the Year Ending December 31, 19X1

	Amount
Gross sales [Fig. 4-5]	$6,067,000
Less: Returns and allowances	67,000
Net sales	$6,000,000
Cost of goods sold	
Standard [Fig. 4-15]	$2,877,995
Over-standard [Fig. 4-9]	41,250
Total	$2,919,245
Operating margin	$3,080,755
Operating expenses [Fig. 4-11]	
General and administrative	$ 701,000
Selling	1,214,000
Research and development	419,000
Total operating expenses	$2,334,000
Other income and expense	
Investment income	460,000
Interest expense	74,000
Net other income	386,000
Income before income taxes	$1,132,755
Federal income taxes (38%)	430,447
Net Income	$ 702,308

The Capital Budget

A detailed review of the budgeting process for investment in fixed assets is made in Chapter 25. Suffice it to state, now, that consideration must be given to both commitments and expenditures. It is important that these long-term investments be consistent with the long-range plan and related to the expected rate of return that must be earned by the company.

A capital budget is prepared after giving proper weight to future prospects of the company, the cash and borrowing capacity available, and relative present investment in plant and equipment. A simple summary capital expenditures budget is shown in Figure 4-14.

FIG. 4-17 Statement of Estimated Sources and Uses of Cash

THE MANUFACTURING COMPANY

STATEMENT OF ESTIMATED SOURCES AND USES OF CASH

For the Year Ending December 31, 19X1

	Amount
Sources of Funds	
Net income	$ 702,308
Depreciation and amortization	250,000
Deferred income taxes	80,000
Internal cash generation	$1,032,308
Decrease in non-cash working capital	170,000
Proceeds from notes payable — Long-term	1,600,000
Sale of common stock	800,000
Total sources of funds	$3,602,308
Uses of Cash	
Increases in land, plant and equipment	$2,310,000
Dividends to common shareholders	320,000
Increases in long-term investments	460,000
Total uses of cash	$3,090,000
Net increase in cash	$ 512,308
Cash and cash items — Beginning of year	710,000
Cash and cash items — End of year	$1,222,308

Statement of Estimated Income and Expense

When the operating budgets have been completed, as well as those asset budgets that directly affect, or are affected by, the manufacturing process, the statement of planned income and expense can be prepared.

First, the statement of cost of goods sold must be calculated. A comprehensive statement, including the change in principal inventories, is shown in Figure 4-15.

With this information and related income and expense data, the preliminary statement of planned income and expense may be prepared, as reflected in Figure 4-16. While Figure 4-16 is a consolidated statement, under normal circumstances, it would be summarized in any one of several ways: by profit center, by product line, by geographical area — or such other manner as necessary to convey the significant facts to the management.

FIG. 4-18   Comparative Statement of Estimated Financial Position

THE MANUFACTURING COMPANY

COMPARATIVE STATEMENT OF ESTIMATED FINANCIAL POSITION

As at December 31, 19XX and 19X1

ASSETS	Indicated Final 19XX	Estimated 19X1	Increase (Decrease)
Current Assets			
Cash and cash items	$ 710,000	$1,222,308	$ 512,308
Accounts receivable	540,000	520,000	(20,000)
Inventories	1,157,000	1,150,005	(6,995)
Prepaid items	11,000	12,000	1,000
Total current assets	$2,418,000	$2,904,313	$ 486,313
Property, Plant and Equipment			
Land & land improvements	$ 76,000	$ 176,000	$ 100,000
Buildings	440,000	1,360,000	920,000
Machinery & equipment	810,000	2,100,000	1,290,000
Total	$1,326,000	$3,636,000	$2,310,000
Less: Accumulated depreciation & amortization	610,000	860,000	250,000
Net property, plant & equipment	716,000	2,776,000	2,060,000
Other Assets			
Notes and accounts receivable	$ 84,000	$ 84,000	—
Investments — Other	810,000	1,270,000	$ 460,000
Total	894,000	1,254,000	460,000
Total Assets	$4,028,000	$7,034,313	$3,006,313

Statement of Estimated Sources and Uses of Cash

Ordinarily, when the various operating statements and required assets are known, the next step in budget preparation is completing the estimated cash picture. One form of such a statement is illustrated in Figure 4-17.

Statement of Estimated Financial Position

The results of the year's transactions are reflected in the statement of financial position. Given the results of the year's operations and cash changes, a

LIABILITIES AND SHAREHOLDERS' EQUITY			
	Indicated Final 19XX	Estimated 19X1	Increase (Decrease)
Current Liabilities			
Trade accounts payable	$ 205,000	$ 200,000	$ (5,000)
Notes payable	420,000	592,990	172,990
Accrued employees' compensation	107,000	120,000	13,000
Income taxes payable	110,000	80,000	(30,000)
Deferred income taxes	40,000	41,000	1,000
Other current liabilities	135,000	127,015	(7,985)
Total current liabilities	$1,017,000	$1,161,005	$ 144,005
Long-Term Obligations	$ 120,000	$1,720,000	$1,600,000
Deferred Income Taxes	70,000	150,000	80,000
	$1,207,000	$3,031,005	$1,824,005
Shareholders' Equity			
Paid-in capital	$ 482,000	$1,282,000	$ 800,000
Retained earnings	2,339,000	2,721,308	382,308
Total shareholders' equity	$2,821,000	$4,003,308	$1,182,308
Total Liabilities and Shareholders' Equity	$4,028,000	$7,034,313	$3,006,313

test of the acceptability of the plan lies in the financial condition at the year-end.

A simplified statement is shown in comparative form in Figure 4-18. The related statement of shareholders' equity is presented in Figure 4-19.

These statements should be tested against criteria such as management objectives of acceptable financial condition, earnings on shareholders' equity, industry data, credit agreement requirements, and such other standards as may be warranted.

FIG. 4-19 Statement of Shareholders' Equity

THE MANUFACTURING COMPANY

STATEMENT OF SHAREHOLDERS' EQUITY

For the Years Ending at December 31, 19XX and 19X1

	Indicated Final 12/31/XX	Estimated 12/31/X1
Paid-in Capital		
At beginning of year	$ 482,000	$ 482,000
Sale of shares	—	800,000
At end of year	$ 482,000	$1,282,000
Retained Earnings		
At beginning of year	$1,979,000	$2,339,000
Net income	520,000	702,308
Cash dividends	(160,000)	(320,000)
At end of year	$2,339,000	$2,721,308

BUDGET APPROVAL

As initially consolidated, the preparation of the various budget segments results in an integrated business plan for the year — iteration number one. As the overall results are tested, further consideration may reveal that certain phases are unacceptable to the management, or are not deemed reasonable. If so, the segments must be modified until the plan is considered do-able, and until it meets the corporate objectives.

In this iterative process, much of the analysis will be done by the budgeting staff — a part of the financial group.

When the budget is finalized, usually it is presented to the chief executive officer and the senior executives, along with detailed commentary on assumptions, highlights, and the critical issues. Upon approval by this management group, the next step is review and approval by the board of directors. Once approved by the board of directors, the budget in fact passes from the planning phase to the control phase. Submission of the budget constitutes a commitment by the entire management to meet or exceed the plan, and board approval binds this commitment. The responsible managers are notified that the annual plan has been approved, and they know they are responsible for meeting their segment.

THE CONTROL PHASE

In the control phase, actual results are compared with plan results for the week, month, or such other time period as is deemed necessary — cost and revenue item by item, department by department, profit center by profit center. For some critical programs, the computer permits a review of real time data on a daily basis.

When these actual to plan comparisons are made, the causes for the variances are analyzed and corrective action is taken. To use a maritime metaphor, the ship must be kept on course. The shoals and rocks are charted and steps are taken to get the ship safely to harbor.

Use of the plan as a control device does not eliminate other tools. For example, alternative or supplemental standards may be employed in judging actual performance — but there would be a relationship between such a guide and the plan. From the management viewpoint, the plan specifies the profit goal to be achieved.

ROLE OF THE BUDGET OFFICER

The annual plan has been described as a communication device in the planning and control of the business. While each organization segment, within established guidelines or limits, does its planning and takes later corrective action, there is an enormous amount of calculating and analysis necessary in the process — much of it in financial terms. Accordingly, those knowledgeable in the financial discipline must play a major role in assisting line management to prepare a coordinated plan, and in measuring actual results. For ease of discussion, the term "budget officer" will describe the individual supervising the process. In decentralized operations, the budget officer at the corporate level will coordinate activities with his/her counterpart in the profit center — the assistant to the manager of the profit center. The role of this individual — perhaps on the controller's staff — may be described as carrying out these duties:

1. *Preplanning:*
   □ Establish, and revise as necessary, the *procedures* by which the annual plan is developed.
   □ Work with management to develop and revise the *format* in which the various organization elements should prepare and submit the plan. Formats would designate the degree of detail necessary for proper analyses and consolidation and method of summarization.
   □ Ascertain that the management information system for reporting plan performance is in place, and that it reports results by organization (i.e., responsibility reporting).

2. *The planning process:*

☐ In conjunction with the cognizant officers, assemble the environmental and other data needed as a basis for plan preparation.

☐ Prepare the necessary *analyses* to enable top management to set the current year *objectives*.

☐ Assure that the annual plan *guidelines* are distributed to the line management, and that they are *understood*. This would include, as to financial guidelines, items such as:

• Overall and segment goals

• Accounting principles to be used

• Definitions for the accumulation of data

• Required financial constraints, such as
  a. Tax rates
  b. Interest expense rates
  c. Turnover rates
  d. Selected ratios
  e. Capital expenditure
  f. Contingent liability limits

☐ Review the planning data as submitted for conformance to instructions, completeness, and consistency.

☐ Analyze the various segment plans for reasonableness, acceptability, and possible alternatives for improvement. Such analysis by profit center or product line is desirable to assure compatability *before* consolidation. (Suggestions for changes are provided to the plan originator or his representative.)

☐ Consolidate the data for the overall company plan. This will include the usual financial statements:

• Consolidated Statement of Income and Expense

• Consolidated Statement of Sources and Uses of Cash

• Consolidated Statement of Financial Position

☐ Test or evaluate the plan for acceptability according to predetermined criteria: return on shareholders' equity, return on assets, earnings per share, inventory turnover, and means of achieving certain milestones.

☐ Provide the summarized data, together with any recommendations or interpretive commentary, to the chief executive officer for his approval or concurrence.

☐ Work with the line and staff to finalize the plan for presentation to the board of directors.

☐ Upon approval by the board, assure that the responsible executives who must carry out the plan are advised of the board action and comments. The role of the budget officer is to ascertain this step is done — not to do it himself.

3. *The control phase:*
   - ☐ Determine that actual and planned results are compared and reported to the appropriate management levels.
   - ☐ Ascertain that analysis of the causes of variances are promptly and correctly reported, and that corrective action is taken.
   - ☐ Where necessary, assist in plan revision.

5

Cost Behavior and Flexible Budgeting

INTRODUCTION

Someone has epitomized the purpose of budgeting by saying it is undertaken to see what we should do, and to see that we do what we should. Of course, we must chart the course and lay the plans by which it is to be followed; but we must also plan what must be done in the event we are blown off course. The crew must know its responsibilities both on and off course. The business budget, if it possesses adequate flexibility, will provide an important instrument for the planning and control of operations, costs, assets, and liabilities. In this context, cost behavior is key.

COST CLASSIFICATIONS

Knowledge of the various classifications of costs and the distinctions between them is most helpful in business planning and control. As is true in many situations, the way costs should be classified in particular instances depends on the use or application of the data.

Full and Incremental for Planning Purposes

In *planning*-type business decisions, many alternative choices of action may be possible. In this environment it is often necessary to distinguish between

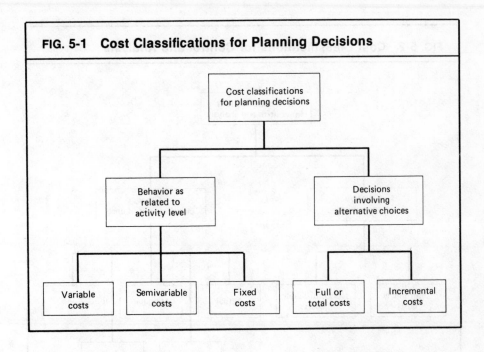

FIG. 5-1 Cost Classifications for Planning Decisions

total or *full* costs on the one hand, and, on the other, those additional, incremental, or marginal costs that a given activity may produce. In other planning situations, the relation of the cost to the activity level is important. A segregation of costs often needed for planning decisions is illustrated in Figure 5-1.

By Responsibility for Control Purposes

In the context of cost *control* decisions, costs must be segregated according to those responsible for the levels. In general discussions of types of costs, any number of other definitions or classifications will prove useful. Some of these are shown in Figure 5-2.

DEFINITIONS OF TYPES OF COSTS

In any effective planning and control activity, knowledge of how costs and expenses and income should behave or react under various circumstances is essential to proper direction. Only when this type of information is known is an executive in a position to plan properly or to judge actual performance.

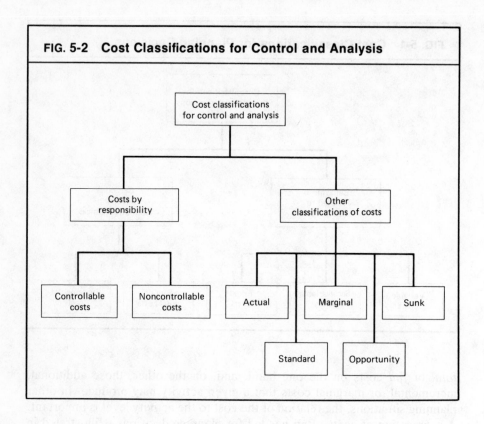

FIG. 5-2   Cost Classifications for Control and Analysis

Moreover, it is only by such knowledge that costs or expenses can be properly segregated, classified, or utilized for sound management decisions.

To this end, then, a few definitions in the cost-expense area are necessary. These definitions are clarified or refined as necessary elsewhere in this book. These segregations of costs are particularly germane to the discussion of the planning and control of the business.

Variable costs — those costs or expenses that vary in total more or less in direct proportion to production or sales volumes. (E.g., direct labor, direct material.)

Fixed costs — those that do not change in the aggregate as the level of output varies. (E.g., depreciation, rent, property taxes.)

Semivariable costs — those that change as volume changes, but not in direct proportion. (E.g., power, maintenance.)

Direct costs — those incurred by or resulting from, and specifically traceable to, the segment of the business being analyzed (i.e., a particular unit of output).

They represent costs that would not have been incurred without the existence of the segment (e.g., direct labor, direct material, direct expenses).

Indirect costs — costs that cannot be clearly identified with a cost objective such as a specific product. Since they cannot be directly associated with a specific cost objective, such costs must be allocated among the various objectives to which they apply. (E.g., occupancy costs, power.)

Period costs — costs associated with the passage of time, but not directly related to changes in activity level. Such costs are substantially similar to fixed costs. *Programmed* costs are closely related to period costs. They are based on a definite program, such as research or advertising. Once established by management policy, they are fixed, but can be changed if management so wishes.

Opportunity costs — those costs associated with an alternative course of action.

Sunk costs — those investments already made in plant and equipment or intangible assets (and on which recovery may be limited if the process or product is discontinued).

Replacement costs — those costs associated with replacing existing facilities such as machinery and equipment.

Marginal or incremental costs — term used to describe the increase in total costs resulting from the production of one more unit.

COSTS IN RELATION TO VOLUME

The relationship of costs to volume may be illustrated graphically as shown in Figure 5-3. Thus, variable costs are directly proportionate to volume, as in (*a*). An example is the direct material content of a product. Fixed costs, or period costs, bear no immediate relationship to volume output, as reflected by the horizontal line in (*b*). Illustrative of this expense is depreciation expense, which is not determined on a unit-of-output basis. Semivariable costs may be graphically depicted as in (*c*); or, if the movement is somewhat inclined to be in a series of steps, then (*d*) is representative. The supervisory costs in a factory are one category which may be considered in this classification.

As a practical matter, costs may not behave in the ways illustrated. Rather, the real pattern may be as shown by the curved line in Figure 5-4, caused, for example, by overtime penalties above a given amount. Within reasonable limits, the solution to this situation is to recognize the costs as variable or fixed within the limited range for the period of budgeted activity. See line *rt*.

With this background, the appropriate question to consider next is the

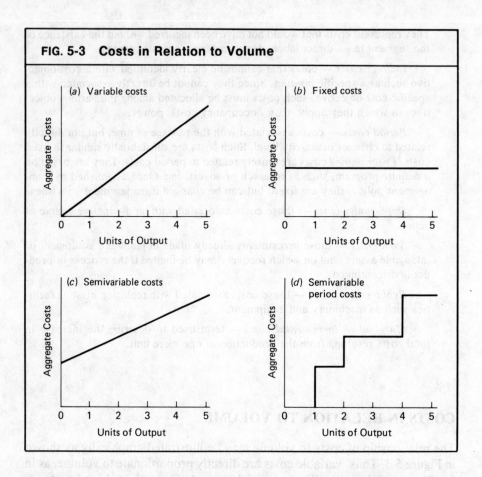

FIG. 5-3   Costs in Relation to Volume

technique. Just how are costs segregated into their elements (e.g., fixed costs, variable costs, and semivariable costs)?

The undertaking of any such determination in a business organization requires, first of all, an understanding of the various processes and functions in the business. With such a background, a review of the cost history and the application of common sense will help establish the cost behavior pattern.

The steps in the process may be outlined as follows:

1. A general review of costs by type of item, by department, and in total.
2. The selection of the activity measure or factor of variability for each function and/or cost.
3. The review of costs in relation to the measure of activity, and determination of the cost segments and rate of variability, if applicable.

In classifying costs into the variable, fixed, and semivariable segments, such classification should be made within restricted volume ranges. For

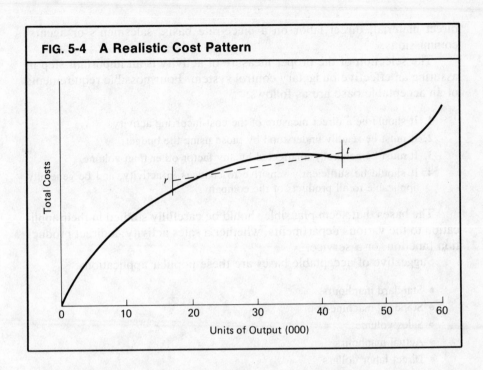

FIG. 5-4   A Realistic Cost Pattern

example, if the sales volume is not more than $1.5 million nor less than $1 million, certain costs will be fixed. The same costs might increase, however, were the volume to be extended beyond $1.5 million. As a rule, the volume ranges under consideration in any one budget period are sufficiently restricted to occasion no difficulty in setting such limits.

While few costs are entirely fixed or 100 percent variable within a given volume range, a considerable number are so nearly so that, for all practical purposes, they can be thus classified. All others must be assigned to the semivariable group.

As a general statement, fixed costs occasion no difficulty as they will be the same at each level of volume under consideration. Illustrative of fixed costs are bond interest, property taxes on plant and equipment, depreciation charged on a time basis, fixed executive salaries, and rent.

VARIABLE COSTS AND MEASURES OF ACTIVITY

As the name implies, variable costs are those that vary in direct ratio to volume. This volume factor may be any one of several measures discussed in this section. Some illustrative variable costs under certain conditions are direct material, direct labor on a piece-rate basis, salesmen's or agents' commissions.

The selection of the proper measure of activity is an important step in assuring an effective budgetary control system. Four possible requirements of an acceptable base are as follows:

1. It should be a direct measure of the cost-incurring activity.
2. It must be readily understood by those using the budget.
3. It must be generally unaffected by any factor other than volume.
4. It should be sufficiently sensitive to changes in activity, and be generally applicable to all products of the company.

The bases that seem plausible should be carefully studied in their application to the various departments, whether a sales activity, a direct production function, or a service.

Suggestive of acceptable bases are these popular applications:

- Standard manhours
- Standard machine-hours
- Sales volume
- Actual manhours
- Direct labor dollars
- Pounds of material consumed
- Units of output (i.e., finished product)
- Number of orders filled
- Number of deliveries

Many different measurements of volume must be used for the various functions and operations of the business. The characteristics of the industry or activity will determine the bases, and special volume factors often must be used. For example, in hotels, the percentage of room occupancy is used; in office buildings, the floor-space occupancy; and in parking garages, the units handled.

The measures of activity selected for the variable costs very often will be applicable to the semivariable costs.

DETERMINING SEMIVARIABLE COSTS

Semivariable costs are those that vary with volume but do not vary in *direct* relationship to the volume changes. It is with this group that the chief difficulty arises in determining what the costs should be at different volume levels. As in the case of the variable costs, these items must first be classified according to their relationship to various production or sales volume factors.

Next, some methods must be found for determining what the relationship is between these cost items and the respective volume factors to which they are related.

There are at least three methods available for determining the expected cost at different volume levels:

1. Direct estimate or synthesis of the semivariable costs
2. Calculation of fixed and variable elements of costs, based on the minimum and maximum expected volume
3. Graphic determination of fixed and variable costs.

Direct Estimate

One method of budgeting the semivariable costs for different volume levels is to make individual estimates and calculations of every semivariable cost item at each of several volume levels falling within the range of volume expectancy. The steps involved are:

1. Measurement factors of production or sales volume are selected for the cost items under consideration.
2. Maximum and minimum limits of volume expectancy are established.
3. Various production or sales volume levels or brackets are established within the range of volume expectancy as a basis for the cost estimates.
4. Estimates and calculations are made for each cost item for each of the volume levels or brackets.

To illustrate this procedure, it may be assumed that production volume for any one month is not expected to be less than 600 units or more than 1,200 units, and that sales are not expected to be less than $1,200 or more than $2,400. Here the measure of production volume is physical units and the measure of sales volume is dollar sales. It may be further assumed that it is desirable to know what costs should be expected at each of the following volume levels:

Production Volume in Units	Sales Volume in Dollars
600	$1,200
800	1,600
1,000	2,000
1,200	2,400

It is further assumed that the semivariable costs relating to production volume include only supervision, and those relating to sales volume include only sales salaries and accounting department salaries. The next step is to determine the amount of each of these semivariable costs that is justified at each volume level. Such calculations must be based upon estimates made by the various executives concerned. Once the calculations are made, they need not be changed until there is some change in conditions or circumstances affecting the cost items.

It may be assumed in this case that the estimates and calculations indicate that the semivariable costs should be as follows:

SEMIVARIABLE COSTS

Relating to Production Volume		Relating to Sales Volume			
Production Volume in Units	Supervision Cost	Sales Volume in Dollars	Sales Salaries	Accounting Department Salaries	Total
600	$245	$1,200	$160	$ 80	$240
800	280	1,600	190	90	280
1,000	300	2,000	200	100	300
1,200	320	2,400	220	110	330

This procedure is the same regardless of the factors used for volume measurement. If direct labor hours were used for production volume, then the estimates and calculations of supervision would be made for different numbers of direct labor hours. Different measures can be used in different departments and for different operations; for example, labor hours can be used in some departments, while machine hours are used in other departments.

One objection to this method is that it does not indicate what costs should be expected at every volume point but only at certain points established as a basis for calculation. For example, in the illustration at hand, the production volume in January was actually 720 units. What should the supervision cost have been? In the figures above, it is shown that a supervision cost of $245 may be expected at a volume of 600 units and $280 at a volume of 800 units, but no cost is shown for 720 units. Between the established points, costs can be determined by interpolation. In this case the calculation would be as follows:

$$\left(\frac{\$280 - \$245}{800 - 600}\right) \times (720 - 600) + \$245 = \text{Expected cost at 720 units}$$

or

$$\frac{\$35}{200} \times 120 + 245 =$$

$$\$26 + 245 = \$266$$

Another method is to make calculations for a sufficient number of volume levels so that any actual volume would be closely approximated by one of the calculations. This plan is illustrated in Figure 5-5. In this example, expenses were calculated for selected volumes ranging from 5,100,000 standard labor hours (60 percent of normal activity) to 11,050,000 standard labor hours (130 percent of normal activity). It is to be noted that depreciation, property taxes, insurance, and the salaries of foremen (all fixed expenses in this case) were included in calculating the cost levels at the specified volumes. This chart was prepared for one production department; similar charts can be prepared for all other departments. Costs at actual production levels are compared with the nearest volume calculation on the chart.

This method would seem to involve a vast amount of calculation. It will be found in practice, however, that once a method of calculating individual cost items is established, much less work is involved than might appear. Moreover, it will be found that many semivariable costs will bear a similar relationship to volume changes and can be grouped for purposes of calculation.

Calculation of Fixed and Variable Elements

Another method of budgeting semivariable costs at different volume levels is based on the theory that every semivariable cost item consists of a fixed and variable element, that between certain volume limits a cost item can be separated into these two elements, that the fixed element remains the same between these two limits, and that the variable element bears a constant relationship to volume between the two limits.

Under this method, an estimate is made of each semivariable cost at the maximum and minimum volume levels expected. A calculation is then made of the fixed and variable elements of these costs and the two are separated. By this procedure it is then possible to ascertain the cost justified at any volume level lying between the maximum and minimum volume limits.

Reverting to the previous figures, this method, sometimes called the high-low method, may be illustrated as follows:

Costs Relating to Production Volume

	Minimum	Maximum
Production volume limits	600 units	1,200 units
Estimated costs:		
Supervision	$245	$320

(continues on page 5-14)

FIG. 5-5   Manufacturing Expense Budget at Selected Levels of Activity

THE CONSOLIDATED CORPORATION
AIRCRAFT DIVISION

MANUFACTURING EXPENSE BUDGET
(dollars in thousands)

Department: Subassembly
Department Head: Ship

Year: ___
Normal Activity: ___
Base: Standard Labor Hours   8,500,000

Account	Percentage of Normal Activity							
	60%	70%	80%	90%	100% (N.A.)	110%	120%	130%
Salaries								
General Foremen	$ 700	$ 700	$ 700	$ 700	$ 700	$ 700	$ 700	$ 700
Foremen	1,100	1,500	1,900	2,200	2,200	2,200	2,600	2,600
Clerks, etc.	700	700	950	950	950	950	950	1,200
Subtotal	$ 2,500	$ 2,900	$ 3,550	$ 3,850	$ 3,850	$ 3,850	$ 4,250	$ 4,500
Hourly labor — Indirect	$ 1,500	$ 1,750	$ 2,000	$ 2,250	$ 2,500	$ 2,500	$ 2,750	$ 3,000
Fuel	350	400	430	470	510	530	570	620

Power	2,620	3,020	3,430	3,870	4,300	4,740	5,140	5,320
Water	210	220	230	240	250	260	270	280
Maintenance and repairs	1,630	1,875	2,050	2,250	2,500	2,790	3,070	3,660
Supplies	270	315	360	405	450	495	540	585
Mule expense	140	180	190	200	210	230	260	270
Traveling	70	70	100	100	100	100	120	120
Telephone and telegraph	70	80	90	100	100	100	110	120
Cartons and containers	150	175	200	225	250	275	300	325
Recreation and welfare	30	40	50	50	50	60	60	60
Miscellaneous	120	130	150	160	175	190	200	210
Subtotal	$ 9,660	$11,155	$12,830	$14,170	$15,245	$16,120	$17,640	$19,070
Depreciation — Building	$ 900	$ 900	$ 900	$ 900	$ 900	$ 900	$ 900	$ 900
Depreciation — Machinery and equipment	1,800	1,800	1,800	1,800	1,800	1,800	1,800	1,800
Property taxes	1,200	1,200	1,200	1,200	1,200	1,200	1,200	1,200
Insurance	350	350	400	400	400	400	400	450
Total	$13,910	$15,405	$17,130	$18,470	$19,545	$20,420	$21,940	$23,420

COSTS RELATING TO SALES VOLUME

	Minimum	Maximum
Sales volume limits	$1,200	$2,400
Estimated costs:		
Sales salaries	160	220
Accounting department salaries	80	110

The first problem is to find for each of these cost items (1) the percentage relationship between the variable portion and volume, and (2) the portion that is fixed. Taking supervision cost, for example, a difference of 600 units in volume makes a difference of $75 in supervision cost. This gives a variable relationship of 12.5 percent (75 ÷ 600), or 12.5 cents per unit. The fixed portion can be determined as follows:

	Minimum Volume	Maximum Volume
Total supervision cost	$245	$320
Variable portion of cost (12.5% of 600 and 1,200, respectively)	75	150
Fixed portion of cost	$170	$170

The variable percentage and the fixed portion of every semivariable cost item can be determined in this manner. For example, the calculations for the remaining costs in this illustration would be as follows:

	Variable Percentage	Fixed Portion of Cost
Sales salaries:		
$\dfrac{\$220 - \$160}{\$2,400 - \$1,200} =$	5.0%	
$160 - (5\% \text{ of } \$1,200) =$		$100
Accounting department salaries:		
$\dfrac{\$110 - \$80}{\$2,400 - \$1,200} =$	2.5%	
$80 - (2.5\% \text{ of } \$1,200) =$		$50

Assume that the actual volume for January consisted of production of 720 units and sales of $1,600. What costs should be expected at these volumes? These may be shown as follows:

Actual production volume = 720 units
Actual sales volume   = $1,600

Costs	Fixed Portion	Variable Portion		Total Expected Cost	Actual Cost	Gain (Loss)
		Per-centage	Amount			
Supervision	$170	12.5	$90[a]	$260	$270	($10)
Sales salaries	100	5.0	80[b]	180	190	(10)
Accounting department salaries	50	2.5	40[c]	90	90	None

(a) 12.5% of 720 (or actual production volume) = $90
(b) 5% of $1,600 (or actual sales volume) = $80
(c) 2.5% of $1,600 (or actual sales volume) = $40

By this method it can readily be determined what costs should be expected at any volume, and such costs can then be compared with the actual costs to signal failure or success in adjusting costs to changes in volume. In this case the production department used $10 more supervision, or 3.86 percent ($10 ÷ $260) more, than was justified by the production volume; the sales department used $10 more sales salaries, or 5.55 percent ($10 ÷ $180) more, than was justified by the sales volume. The accounting department, on the other hand, kept its salaries in line with the changes in sales volume.

This method may be criticized in that it assumes a constant relationship between the variable element of the costs and volume, within the volume range under consideration; but the error is usually slight and not sufficient to affect the usefulness of the method.

It should be noted that this method can be applied to groups of costs as well as to individual cost items.

Graphic Determination. The use of only two or a few points, such as only minimum and maximum limits, to determine the fixed and variable cost segments is sometimes subject to a wider degree of error than may be desirable because only a limited number of activity levels are considered. If more accuracy is desired, another convenient approach is the use of a scatter chart. Assume, for illustrative purposes, that the following data on production control department costs are available, adjusted for wage differences and similar factors.

Month	Reference	Factory Standard Manhours	Total Departmental Costs
January	1	20,000	$6,100
February	2	16,000	5,300
March	3	13,000	4,700
April	4	14,000	4,900

(continued)

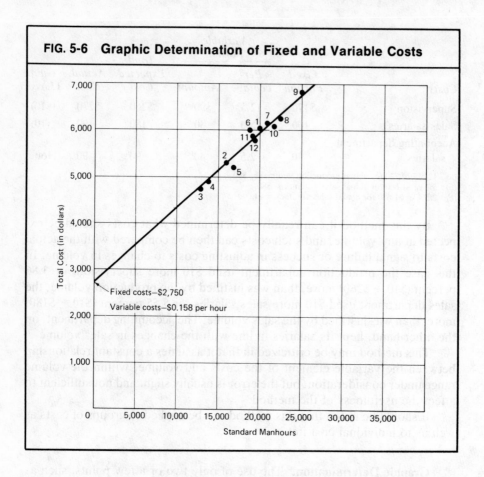

FIG. 5-6   Graphic Determination of Fixed and Variable Costs

		Factory Standard	Total Departmental
Month	Reference	Manhours	Costs
May	5	17,000	5,200
June	6	19,000	6,000
July	7	21,000	6,200
August	8	23,000	6,300
September	9	25,000	6,800
October	10	22,000	6,100
November	11	18,000	5,900
December	12	19,000	5,800

These points are then plotted on a chart as shown in Figure 5-6, each point
being numbered for reference purposes. The vertical axis represents the

dollar costs, while the horizontal axis represents the factor of variability (standard manhours in the illustration). After the points are plotted, a line of best fit may be drawn by inspection in such a manner that about one half of the points are above it and the other half below. Any highly variant items should be disregarded. For a higher degree of refinement, the method of least squares may be used instead of inspection.

The point at which the line of best fit intersects the vertical axis indicates the fixed cost that might be expected if the plant were in an operating condition, but producing nothing. The total cost at any level of activity is determined by reading the chart. For example, at a level of 25,000 standard manhours, the budgeted expense would be $6,700. This is made up of $2,750 fixed and $3,950 variable elements. The variable rate is $0.158 per standard manhour.

In reviewing the chart it can be seen that the slope of the line indicates the degree of variability. Thus a horizontal line would represent a fixed cost, whereas a line that goes through the point of origin indicates a completely variable cost. Sometimes in constructing a chart the points show no tendency to arrange themselves along a line. If this situation does exist, then either the control of costs has been absent or a poor choice has been made as to the factor of variability. Use of another factor should be tested to ascertain the cause. Incidentally, the chart may be used as a tool in illustrating the degree of success in controlling costs, the extent of accomplishment being measured by the closeness of actual expense to the line of budgeted expense.

The Least Squares Method. The previous graphic determination will be recognized by statisticians or those familiar with computer applications in this area as a rough approximation of the least squares method. A more accurate method of determining the regression line (the line of best fit) is by this statistical technique. It involves the use of two simultaneous equations:

$$\Sigma XY = a(\Sigma X) + b(\Sigma X^2)$$

and

$$\Sigma Y = Na + b(\Sigma X)$$

where:

N = Number of observations
X = Units of volume
Y = Total costs
a = Total fixed costs
b = Variable cost per unit
Σ = Sum of

The readers are referred to a book on statistical methods for an understanding of this now commonly used procedure. Use of a computer, of course, permits accurate calculations rather quickly, using substantially larger samples.

Allowing for Extraordinary Costs

The preceding discussion of the methods of classifying costs into fixed, variable, and semivariable related to the normally expected costs. Often, however, extraordinary or unanticipated expenditures of a manufacturing expense nature must be made. These may fall well outside the scope of the usual budget, even when the cumulative yearly condition is considered. In such instances, and if the expenditure is considered necessary and advisable, a special budget allowance may be made over and above the usual budget — something superimposed on the regular flexible budget structure.

It is to be emphasized that the important consideration is not necessarily *how* flexibility is introduced into the budget plan, but rather that it *is* made a part of the planning, coordinating, and control technique.

Procedure Applicable to All Departments

In order to reveal clearly the principles involved, the illustrations in this chapter have been reduced to the simplest possible terms. Only a few cost items relating to production and sales have been considered. It should be emphasized, however, that the procedure must be extended throughout the full range of operations and to all departments and cost items involved. Many different measures of volume may be in use at the same time in different divisions or departments. Since volume does not necessarily run uniformly in different divisions, the maximum and minimum limits may differ in the various divisions. For example, the measures and volume limits for the purchasing department may be entirely different and independent of those applicable to the maintenance or accounting departments.

STANDARD COSTS IN RELATION TO PLAN OR BUDGET

Most readers are familiar with the standard cost concept, that is, a predetermined cost or a determination of what a cost *should be*. A basic point to be clarified is the relationship of this "standard cost" to the operating plan or budget.

In line with the previous discussion, it is perhaps evident that the so-called standard cost must be segregated into its variable and fixed elements.

The standard variable cost can be used to determine what the aggregate variable cost for the planned volume should be. Additionally, if experience indicates that the standard variable cost will not be attained, then the business plans must include a factor for this inefficiency.

The fixed element of the standard cost will, of course, be recognized in arriving at the planned level of the total fixed expense.

RESPONSIBILITY COSTING

All costs should be further classified according to executive responsibility. If, for example, it is found that the actual volume justifies the use of $100 of supplies in a certain production department but the supplies actually used amount to $125, then it must be possible to point the finger of responsibility definitely to the foreman or department head under whose jurisdiction the waste occurred.

This implies, on the other hand, that an executive will be held responsible for only those costs over which he has control. The analysis of costs for control purposes must be made independently of any accounting method used in the distribution of burden or overhead. The control of power costs, for example, must be directed toward the executives responsible for power production insofar as the cost per unit of power is concerned; but the foremen or department heads of the production and service departments that consume the power must be held responsible for the number of units consumed.

This segregation of costs and revenues by responsibility should be reflected in the management information system, and hence in the accounting system. Costs and revenues must, in effect, be segregated not only by element, but also according to the organizational chart.

TYPES OF BUDGETS

With the background of the importance of cost behavior, it is possible to evaluate better the type of budget needed for a given application.

Budgets may be classified into three principal types:

1. Appropriation
2. Fixed or planning
3. Flexible or variable

The appropriation-type budget, though common in governmental budgeting, has rather restricted usage in business. Essentially, a particular sum is established as the limit to be spent on a given activity, and is formalized by the board of directors through approval of an appropriation of this specified amount. Appropriation-type budgets are sometimes used in connection with advertising expenses, charitable contributions, or research and development expense. (See Chapters 16 and 17.)

Fixed or planning budgets involve a plan that is unchanging. As the sales or production volume varies with actual conditions, the standard of measurement is *not* changed.

A flexible budget, on the other hand, is one that permits revision of estimates of operating costs and profits with changes in the sales or production volume. It refines the static or fixed-type of budget by adjusting for variations in the output rate.

Budgets of each type will be discussed later. However, the principle of variability is so fundamental that it should be understood before proceeding to a detailed review of the various income and expense elements. The principle of variability is the key to an effective budgetary control system.

THE NEED FOR BUDGET FLEXIBILITY

A business program for the future must be predicated upon conditions that are *expected* to exist during the period under consideration. Since economic currents shift quickly as a result of changes in physical, political, and social forces, the future of business can never be certain. Therefore, in the planning and control of operations some consideration must be given to *unexpected* circumstances.

The degree of flexibility that should be injected into the program depends upon the particular purpose of budgeting given major emphasis. For some purposes little or no flexibility is desirable; for others a high degree of flexibility is required.

The basic purposes of budgeting, as previously stated, are:

1. To find the most profitable direction the operations can take.
2. To develop in detail a balanced and coordinated program in that direction.
3. To assist in controlling the operations in the execution of the program.

The degree of flexibility required in relation to each of these basic purposes is illustrated below.

In Planning

As a simple illustration, assume that a concern has adopted the following program for the first quarter of the year.

SUMMARY BUDGET FOR QUARTER

Sales of 3,000 units at a price of $2 each	$6,000
Production of 3,000 units at a cost of $1.20 each	3,600
Selling and general costs amounting to 30% of sales	1,800
Profit amounting to 10% of sales	600

This is an extremely simplified expression of the accomplishment of the first basic purpose of budgeting. To be sure, such a program requires a vast amount of refinement, but the principle involved should be clear: A definite program has been set, which, all things considered, is believed to be the most profitable one that could be found.

There can be only one best program, and insofar as the work of budgeting is done to find this program, there would seem to be no need of flexibility in the plans. Indeed, it would seem that there should be no flexibility, that the program should be rigidly followed. Actually, however, the program is predicated upon so many uncertain factors that alternative plans may be given consideration for use in case external conditions or internal operations do not develop as expected.

In the illustration at hand, for example, the program calls for the expenditure of $3,600 for manufacturing costs and $1,800 for selling and general costs; however, if the orders do not develop at such a rate as to provide the 3,000 units of sales, some timely revision of the program will be necessary. Fewer units may be produced and the expenditures for labor and material may be reduced accordingly. Also, expenditures for selling and general costs may be adjusted.

The program cannot always be entirely rigid and inflexible. There will usually be some "ifs" connected with it. Indeed, it may be *expressed* to a certain extent in flexible terms. For example, the production department may be told that the program calls for 3,600 units, which will require 1,500 labor hours. If, however, the volume of production is reduced, the relationship of one labor hour to two units of product should be maintained. Again, the allowance for supplies may be set at $150, but with the further provision that the quantity of supplies used should not exceed $0.10 for each labor hour used.

Hence, it should be apparent that a certain degree of flexibility may be necessary (1) in the sense that provision should be made for a revised program when conditions do not permit the developments as expected, and (2) in the method of presenting the plan so as to facilitate changes when necessary for the other purposes budgeting serves.

In Coordinating

To continue the illustration, assume next that all executives, major and minor, have been given full details of their respective parts in the program, definite methods of execution, definite time schedules of performance, and the detailed components constituting their costs (it being understood that such executives have had a full share in the development of their respective parts in the program). These details are assumed to be as follows:

SALES VOLUME

Month	Units	Dollars
January	1,000	$2,000
February	800	1,600
March	1,200	2,400
Total	3,000	$6,000

PRODUCTION VOLUME

Month	Units
January	800
February	1,000
March	1,200
Total	3,000

Note that the number of units to be produced in the respective months varies from those to be sold. This is the usual situation, the variation being reflected in the inventories. While sales and production cannot always be expressed in uniform units, they are so expressed here for the sake of simplicity. The situation in which they cannot be so expressed is discussed later.

Production Costs. For the sake of simplicity, assume that there are no production costs other than the following:

			Costs		
Month	Production Volume in Units	Direct Labor and Material	Fixed Property Taxes	Super-vision	Total Production Costs
January	800	$ 640	$100	$280	$1,020
February	1,000	800	100	300	1,200
March	1,200	960	100	320	1,380
Total	3,000	$2,400	$300	$900	$3,600

Note here that three types of production costs are illustrated. Direct labor and material may be taken as representing those costs that vary in direct ratio to the physical volume of production. These are designated as *variable* costs. Fixed property taxes may be taken as representing those costs that are entirely fixed, regardless of physical volume, at least within certain limits. These are designated as *fixed* costs. Supervision may be taken as representing those costs that vary with physical volume, but not in direct ratio to physical volume. These are designated as *semivariable* costs. Thus, in January, with a production of 800 units, direct labor and material cost is 80 cents per unit, taxes are a fixed amount of $100, and supervision is $280 or 35 cents per unit; in February, with a production of 1,000 units, the direct labor and material cost is still 80 cents per unit, taxes are $100, and supervision is $300 or 30 cents per unit. With an increase in volume from 800 to 1,000 units, or 25 percent, supervision increases from $280 to $300, or only 7.14 percent. Likewise in March, with an increase in volume of 20 percent over February, supervision increases only $20 or 6.67 percent.

The determination of what the variable and fixed production costs should be for different physical volumes is comparatively simple. The methods of determining what the semivariable production costs should be were discussed above. For the moment it may be assumed that a satisfactory way has been found to predetermine the semivariable costs and that they will be as shown above.

Selling and General Costs. For the sake of simplicity, assume that there are no selling and general costs other than the following:

						Costs
Month	Sales Volume in Dollars	Sales Commis- sions	Rent	Sales Salaries	Accounting Department Salaries	Total Selling and General Costs
January	$2,000	$200	$100	$200	$100	$ 600
February	1,600	160	100	190	90	540
March	2,400	240	100	210	110	660
Total	$6,000	$600	$300	$600	$300	$1,800

Note again that the three types of costs, variable, fixed, and semivariable, are illustrated. The variability here, however, relates to sales rather than production volume. Sales commissions are 100 percent variable and amount to 10 percent of sales at each volume level. Rent is fixed regardless of the volume of sales. (Rent in this instance pertains to sales facilities.) Sales salaries vary with sales volume but not in direct ratio thereto. Accounting department salaries may be taken as representing semivariable administrative and general costs. These may be affected by either production or sales volume but they are assumed here to relate more closely to sales volume. Note also that the degree of variability differs as between sales salaries and accounting department salaries. For example, in February, the sales volume is 20 percent less than in January, whereas sales salaries are 5 percent less while accounting department salaries are 10 percent less. This illustrates the fact that the degree of variability may differ with different semivariable costs — whether production, sales, or general.

The foregoing illustration indicates the accomplishment of the second basic purpose of planning — that is, the development in detail of a unified, balanced, and properly coordinated program.

Note that the above detailed program is a definite one. The production department is told to proceed with the expenditure of $3,600, of which $1,020 is to be made in January; and with the production of 3,000 units, of which 800 are to be made in January. Moreover, these expenditures are broken down into their component parts. January expenditures for direct material and labor are to be $640, supervision $280, and so on. Likewise, the sales department is told to proceed with a program of $1,200 for direct sales effort (sales commissions of $600 and sales salaries of $600) in an effort to secure a sales volume of $6,000. Expenditure for direct sales effort in January is to be $400 in an effort to develop a sales volume of $2,000.

Such programs must be definite if the full coordinated power of the organization is to be applied. It is usually ineffective to say to the production department that *if* the sales department develops sales of $6,000, then 3,000 units should be produced. By the time the sales are known, it will be too late to make the production plans. It is, in reality, necessary to say that the sales plans are such that they call for a production program of 800 units in January, 1,000 units in February, and 1,200 units in March, and that production plans should be made accordingly. Contracts should be made for materials, a labor force should be acquired, and plant facilities should be ready for the expected production. If it develops later that the sales plans miscarry, then adjustments to the production program will have to be made as quickly and effectively as possible. In the meantime, the production department should apply full power toward the program as planned.

Likewise, it would be equally ineffective to say to the sales department that *if* the production department maintains a production schedule of 3,000 units, then sales effort should be applied toward securing a sales volume of $6,000.

This emphasizes the point that the initial program must be definite insofar as it serves as a basis for coordinated departmental action. On the other hand, the operations must be closely watched, and as variances from the original program occur in one department or in particular operations, revisions must be made in other departments and operations. To a certain extent such plans may be self-revising. For example, as sales operations proceed, it may develop that they are running 10 percent above or below the expectations. This may automatically signal other departments to enlarge or curtail their operations by corresponding, though not necessarily identical, degrees. Since programs are seldom executed exactly as planned, such flexibility is necessary.

In Control

To achieve this necessary coordination and to permit those responsible for the program to make the required adjustment to the revised activity level, it is essential that (1) the costs be properly segregated by their behavior in relation to volume, and (2) that such costs be *expressed* in relation to the unit of variability.

To continue the illustration, it may be assumed next that the actual operations for January result as follows:

Sales of 800 units at a price of $2 each		$1,600
Production of 720 units at the following costs:		
Direct labor and material	$630	
Taxes	100	
Supervision	270	
Total production costs		$1,000
Selling and general costs:		
Sales commissions	$160	
Rent	110	
Sales salaries	190	
Accounting department salaries	90	
Total selling and general costs		$ 550

These figures show a wide variance from the original program for January. The comparison may be shown as follows:

	Program	Actual	Increase (Decrease) Amount	Increase (Decrease) Percentage
Production (units)	800	720	(80)	(10.00)
Production costs:				
Direct labor and material	$ 640	$ 630	($ 10)	(1.56)
Taxes	100	100	None	
Supervision	280	270	(10)	(3.57)
Total production costs	$1,020	$1,000	($ 20)	(1.96)
Sales	$2,000	$1,600	($400)	(20.00)

(continued)

	Program	Actual	Increase (Decrease) Amount	Increase (Decrease) Percentage
Selling and general costs:				
Sales commissions	$ 200	$ 160	($40)	(20.00)
Rent	100	110	10	10.00
Sales salaries	200	190	(10)	(5.00)
Accounting department salaries	100	90	(10)	(10.00)
Total selling and general costs	$ 600	$ 550	($50)	(8.33)

Production volume is 10 percent below the original program and sales volume is 20 percent below. Costs, however, have not been reduced in proportion to volume. Production costs have been reduced only 1.96 percent, and selling and general costs only 8.33 percent. This situation illustrates three points:

1. That costs do not, as a rule, rise and fall in direct ratio to changes in volume. This is due to the fact that fixed costs remain the same regardless of volume; and that semivariable costs, while increasing or decreasing with volume, do not change in direct ratio thereto.
2. That changes in costs are the result of two major factors (eliminating price factors): volume and operating efficiency.
3. That, in any comparison of actual results with estimates, allowance must be made for the effect of the volume factor before any conclusions can be drawn relative to operating efficiency.

In the case at hand, the question naturally arises as to whether or not the production department should have reduced its costs more than 1.96 percent when production volume was being reduced by 10 percent. It is not to be expected that costs could be reduced by 10 percent, but the question still remains as to how much reduction should have been effected. This principle applies to all divisions of the business and to all departments and sections whose general efficiency is subject to measurement.

FLEXIBLE BUDGETING REVEALS COSTS AT VARIOUS VOLUME LEVELS

It is seldom, indeed, that the volume will be exactly as planned; hence, it is seldom that costs as planned can be compared with actual costs for the purpose of indicating operating efficiency. In this case, supervision cost was planned at $280 for a volume of 800 units. If the volume had been 800 units in January, then the actual supervision cost could be compared with the estimate of $280 as a signal of operating efficiency. With an actual volume of 720 units, the facts are not at hand as to what the supervision cost should be.

To the extent, then, that the budget is to serve for the purpose of controlling operations, and particularly for the purpose of controlling costs, it must show what the costs should be at various levels of production and sales volume. *This is the primary reason for injecting flexibility into the budget.*

To continue the illustration, assume in this case that the drop in sales of 20 percent below the expected amount has been caused by unexpected developments in the industry to which the concern sells a major part of its product. These could not be foreseen. Production was checked as rapidly as possible but the total reduction amounted to only 10 percent. The question now is: Were operating costs reduced to the extent they should have been in January and, assuming that such conditions are now expected to prevail throughout February and March, what reductions in operating costs should be planned for those months in order to bring them in line with the 20 percent decrease in volume over the original plans?

The various types of costs may be considered in detail as follows.

PRODUCTION COSTS

Variable. Since the physical volume of production was cut 10 percent, the variable production costs, represented by direct labor and material, should have been cut 10 percent, or $64. Actually, these costs were cut only 1.56 percent or $10; hence, this provides a signal of production inefficiency amounting to $54.

Fixed. The fixed costs, as represented by taxes, were the same as planned.

Semivariable. The method of determining what the semivariable costs should be at different volume levels has been discussed. Assume here that the semivariable production costs, as represented by supervision, should have been only $260 at a volume of 720 units. Since these costs were actually $270, they were $10 or 3.85 percent ($10 ÷ $260) higher than should have been the case. Here again is a signal of production inefficiency.

SELLING AND GENERAL COSTS

Variable. Since the sales volume was reduced 20 percent, the variable selling and general costs, as represented by sales commissions, should have been cut 20 percent, or from $200 to $160. Since these costs were exactly $160, the results in this respect appear satisfactory.

Fixed. The fixed selling and general costs, as represented by rent, are $10 more than the amount estimated. This suggests either an error in the preparation of the budget or a change in circumstances which could not have been foreseen, and calls for investigation.

Semivariable. It may be assumed that the semivariable selling and general costs, for a volume of $1,600, should be:

Sales salaries	$180
Accounting department salaries	90

It is apparent from these figures that the actual sales salaries were $10 more than they should have been even for a volume of $1,600. Here again there is a signal of inefficiency. Accounting department salaries, while not reduced proportionately, were in line with the reduced volume.

The foregoing analysis presents a simplified illustration of the use of the budget for the accomplishment of its third basic purpose: the control of operations and costs.

It should be stated that the budget figures do not serve in their entirety as measures of performances. The figures must, first of all, express actual expectation, good or bad; but in a very large measure such expectation is based upon satisfactory performance. This is especially true in regard to controllable costs of distribution and production. The budget therefore serves as an important tool of control. *Such control is possible only if the budget reveals what the costs should be at various volume levels.* The need for such flexibility is apparent from the comparisons for January (continuing the illustration as above):

SALES AND PRODUCTION VOLUME

	Original Program	Actual Operations in January	Percentage Decrease
Sales volume	$2,000	$1,600	20
Production volume (units)	800	720	10

COSTS

	Budgeted Costs for Original Program	Budgeted Costs for Actual Volume	Actual Costs at Actual Volume	Variance Between Budgeted Costs and Actual Costs at Actual Volume
Production costs:				
Variable	$ 640	$576	$ 630	$54
Fixed	100	100	100	None
Semivariable	280	260	270	10
Total production costs	$1,020	$936	$1,000	$64

	Budgeted Costs for Original Program	Budgeted Costs for Actual Volume	Actual Costs at Actual Volume	Variance Between Budgeted Costs and Actual Costs at Actual Volume
Selling and general costs:				
Variable	$ 200	$160	$ 160	None
Fixed	100	100	110	$10
Semivariable	300	270	280	10
Total selling and general costs	$ 600	$530	$ 550	$20

The figures in the last column of the above comparison signal the following facts:

- The production department is failing to keep its variable and semivariable costs in line with volume.
- The sales and administrative departments are keeping their variable but not their semivariable costs in line with volume.
- The fixed selling and general costs are in excess of those planned and should be investigated.

It should be apparent that such information would not be available unless it were known what the costs should be at the actual production and sales volumes for January.

If the actual variable production cost ($630) is compared with the amount originally budgeted ($640), it shows a decrease of $10. That is, the production department used less direct labor and material than the original program called for. At first thought, this might appear to indicate favorable operation. Actually, the production department used $54 more than was justified.

The figures presented are extremely simple and are intended only to illustrate the principle involved. Once this is understood, there is no particular difficulty in the refinement of the process. It is also assumed throughout the foregoing illustrations that factors other than volume and operating efficiency remain approximately the same. Other factors which may influence the situation are changes in price, type of goods made and sold, and methods of production, selling, and financing. When such changes come quickly enough to alter the relationships, adjustments must be made to give effect to the changes, or the entire budget figures must be revised.

LIMITS TO VARIABLE BUDGET APPLICATIONS

There are two trends occurring in U.S. industry that may limit the flexible budget concept in its application. The first is increased automation. As investments in plant and equipment, including robots, grow in size, a smaller and smaller portion of the costs remain as variable. Manpower-related costs are replaced by depreciation and become fixed in nature. Secondly, with the need for greater and greater technical knowledge, it is no longer wise to layoff the workers, because their skills will be lost to the company. Hence, such persons will be "inventoried" so as to be available when needed. They must be temporarily placed in other assignments. Hence, an element of flexibility or variability is lost, and different reporting or control techniques to foster maximum alternate use of the skills in temporary over-supply will be required. Even so, these trends do not invalidate the principle of flexible or variable budgets, only the extent of the principle's application.

6

The Profit Structure

IMPORTANCE OF THE PROFIT STRUCTURE

The relationship of costs, volume, and profit makes up what is known as the profit structure of a company. Through the use of this relationship, it is quite easy to predict the effect of many business decisions. The profit structure is therefore of substantial assistance in reaching better judgments.

This chapter applies to business planning what was covered in the previous chapter: cost behavior and the process by which costs are separated into useful categories, particularly as related to the volume of business done. It should be clear by now that an accurate description of cost behavior is fundamental to proper use. Management is usually faced with uncertainties concerning the future, and unless knowledge of probable trends of both costs and revenues is reasonably accurate, business decisions may be incorrect and will produce unfavorable results. Given certain alternatives, the expected outcome should be quantified in an effort to select the most appropriate course.

THE CONTRIBUTION MARGIN

Before dealing with the entire cost-volume-profit (C-V-P) relationship, it may be helpful first to discuss the contribution margin. This concept is the key to answering, with ease, many of the typical business questions involving changes in sales price, quantities to be sold, and the impact on operating income. The contribution margin, simply stated, is the difference between the selling price and the variable costs. It is the contribution made by the particular segment being measured to cover all fixed or period costs and the profit margin, if any. The higher the sales volume, the greater the contribution margin, as long as the variable costs for the marginal addition are less than the net sales revenue added. Thus, assume a product with these unit characteristics:

Sales price	$100
Manufacturing costs	
Variable	43
Fixed	24
Total	67
Manufacturing margin	33
Selling and administrative expenses	
Variable	4
Fixed	6
Total	10
Income before taxes	$ 23

The contribution that this product makes towards fixed manufacturing costs (the difference between the selling price and the variable costs), as well as fixed selling and administrative expense and profit before income taxes is $53 per unit. The contribution margin (difference between selling price and the variable costs) is calculated as follows:

Sales price		$100
Less:		
Variable costs		
Manufacturing	43	
Selling, etc.	4	47
Contribution margin		$53

The marginal income ratio is the relationship of the contribution margin to the sales price; or, it may be stated as

$$\text{Marginal income ratio} = \frac{\text{Sales less Variable costs}}{\text{Sales}}$$

The marginal income ratio of this product would be stated as $\frac{(\$100 - \$47)}{\$100}$ = 53 percent. In other words, 53 percent of the sales price is available to cover all costs and expenses that do not vary with the sales volume (viz., the fixed costs) plus profit. Even limited changes in sales volume of a product with a high marginal income ratio produce a substantially greater profit contribution than one with a low ratio.

FIG. 6-1 Break-Even Chart

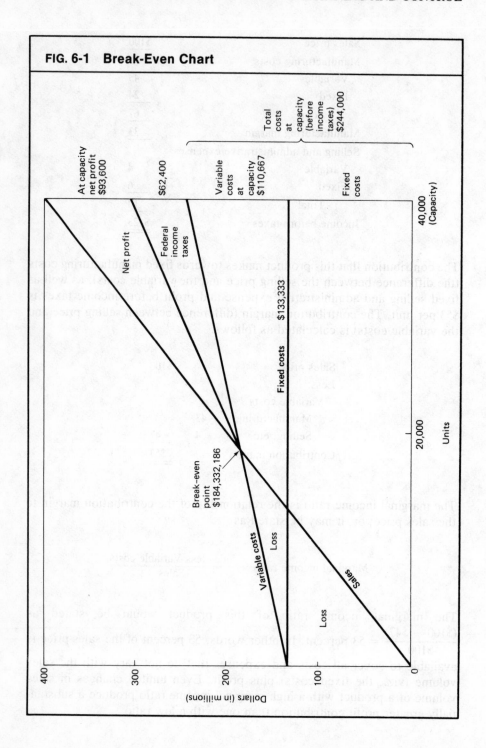

THE BREAK-EVEN CHART

The profit structure of a business may be presented in what is called a break-even chart or break-even analysis. The term is unfortunate in that the relationships are used mostly to determine the profit impact of decisions and very seldom just to calculate the break-even point of a business or a business segment. After all, who is interested in just "breaking even"? But the interplay is shown in Figure 6-1.

This diagram and background data provide several bits of useful planning information:

1. *Sales* in the graph may range from zero to $400 million. They are represented by a straight line extending from zero on the left and diagonally to the maximum potential on the right.

2. The *fixed costs* aggregate $133,333,000. They include the fixed elements of manufacturing, selling, research, and administrative expense. Such types of cost are represented on the break-even chart by a horizontal line.

3. The *variable costs* begin at unit point zero and reach a level of $110,667,000. Variable costs commence just above the fixed cost line at zero sales volume and continue diagonally upward to the maximum cost level corresponding to the sales volume of $400 million. The marginal income, or variable income ratio, may be calculated as follows:

$$\text{Marginal income ratio} = 1 - \frac{\text{Variable costs}}{\text{Sales}}$$

$$= 1 - \frac{\$110,667,000}{400,000,000}$$

$$= 1 - .27667$$

$$= .72333$$

4. With *federal income taxes* at a 40 percent rate, total federal income taxes at capacity are $62,400,000.

5. The *volume of sales* required to just break even with the cost structure — the point where the sales line crosses the total cost line (fixed plus variable) — is $184,332,186 or 46.1 percent of capacity. As these cost or revenue factors are changed by management decisions or market conditions, or whatever, the break-even point and/or marginal income ratio also change.

6. The net loss is calibrated by the vertical line, at any point of measurement desired (unit sales) between sales and variable costs. By the same token, profit before federal income taxes is measured by a vertical line, at point of measurement, from the total cost line to the total sales line; and net profit is measured by a vertical line from the federal income tax line to the sales line.

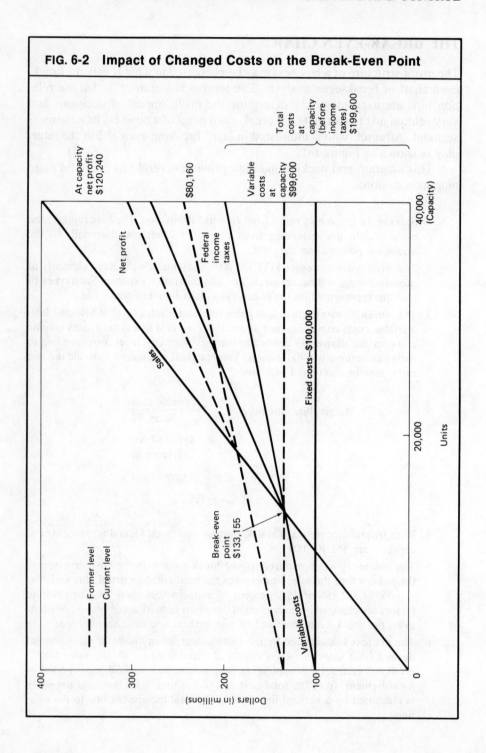

FIG. 6-2 Impact of Changed Costs on the Break-Even Point

Assume that by a judicious review of the fixed costs, reductions of $33,333,000 can be made. Assume further that variable costs can be reduced by 10 percent. The new profit structure may be illustrated as in Figure 6-2. Given the new level of fixed costs and new marginal income, the break-even point has been reduced to $133,155,000. Of more importance, each sales dollar contributes more toward fixed costs and profit, with the new marginal income ratio of $.751; and the profit potential of the company increases to $120,240,000.

Changes in the sales level also have an impact on the profit structure and the break-even point. Perhaps it should be pointed out that a change in sales price will affect the slope of the sales line.

THE BREAK-EVEN FORMULA

It is not necessary, of course, to construct a break-even chart to determine the break-even point. It can be calculated by this equation:

$$\text{Break-even point} = \frac{\text{Total fixed costs}}{1 - \left(\dfrac{\text{Total variable costs}}{\text{Total sales}}\right)}$$

Applying the data from Figure 6-1, the break-even sales volume is determined to be:

$$= \frac{\$133,333,000}{1 - \left(\dfrac{\$110,667,000}{400,000,000}\right)}$$

$$= \frac{\$133,333,000}{.72333}$$

$$= \$184,332,186$$

COMMON MANAGEMENT QUESTIONS

In analyzing the business picture, during a search for the best combination of sales volume, price, or sales mix for use in business planning, the impact of changing each of the factors is ordinarily weighed. And the break-even formula, or parts of it, can be useful in providing some of the answers. Typical questions members of management might ask in business planning sessions are these:

- If prices are raised 10 percent, what is the impact on profit before taxes?
- If unit prices are reduced 5 percent and sales unit volume increases 15 percent, how does this affect operating profit?
- How will a reduction of $x in fixed costs affect the estimated 19x1 net income and the break-even point?
- In a multiproduct chemical plant, what mix of product will produce the maximum operating margin?
- How will the proposed plant expansion affect net income next year, and at capacity operation?
- What additional sales volume is needed to offset the higher fixed charges resulting from the plant X addition?
- What profit will result from adding a second shift?
- Is it better to add two shifts in plant C or expand the plant at location D?
- If sales increase by 15 percent, what will the unit cost be?
- How do we know that the proposed annual plan is continuing an acceptable C-V-P relationship for the longer term?

APPLICATION OF THE PROFIT STRUCTURE TO MANAGEMENT QUESTIONS

Suffice it to say that knowledge of the C-V-P structure for company products, profit segments, or the entire business, will permit the rapid calculation of answers to a wide variety of sales and pricing policy questions, as well as certain production and financial questions. Some are illustrated in the following commentary.

Unit Costs at Selected Volume Levels

Management is often concerned with unit costs at differing volume levels. This information would be matched against the possibility of price changes. Segregation of costs into the fixed and variable elements permits easy computation of unit costs.

Assume these facts for the product:

Selling price per unit	$5.00
Present monthly volume	150,000 units
Present unit costs:	
Variable	$2.00
Fixed	1.00
Total	$3.00

The proposed volume levels to be discussed are:

$$
\begin{array}{l}
\textit{Units} \\
200,000 \\
250,000 \\
325,000 \quad \text{(plant capacity)}
\end{array}
$$

What are the respective unit costs? The formula is simple. The unit cost is:

$$
\text{Unit cost} = \frac{\text{Fixed costs}}{\text{Proposed unit volume}} + \text{Variable unit cost}
$$

For a volume of 200,000 units, the unit cost would be:

$$
\begin{aligned}
\text{Unit cost} &= \frac{\$150,000}{200,000} &+ \$2.00 \\
&= \quad \$\,.75 &+ \$2.00 \\
&= \quad \$2.75 &
\end{aligned}
$$

The total fixed costs were determined from the data given ($1.00 × 150,000). In the real world, the aggregate fixed costs would be known by the analyst. The unit costs for the other two proposed volumes would be:

		Unit Costs	
Volume	Fixed	Variable	Total
250,000	$.60	$2.00	$2.60
325,000	$.46	$2.00	$2.46

Maximizing the Use of Scarce Resources

Most companies manufacture several products, each using at least some of the same production facilities or departments. Usually there are critical department or bottleneck areas, which determine or limit how much of several products may be produced, or there may be usage of a scarce material that has a similar impact. One of management's tasks is to maximize profits by the correct allocation of the critical item or departmental time to the products manufactured.

Assume this information for three products based on known cost behavior:

		Product	
Item	*A*	*B*	*C*
Sales price per unit	$1.00	$2.00	$3.00
Variable costs per unit	.50	1.00	1.50
Contribution margin	$ .50	$1.00	$1.50

Assume, further, that period fixed costs for all departments, which are common, are $100,000 and that such costs are fairly allocated to an operating hour basis as follows:

Product	*Hours*	*Fixed Costs*
A	3,000	$ 15,000
B	7,000	35,000
C	10,000	50,000
Total	20,000	$100,000

A simplified income statement would be:

Product	*Unit Sales*	*Net Sales*	*Variable Costs*	*Contribution Margin*	*Fixed Costs*	*Operating Margins*
A	39,000	$ 39,000	$ 19,500	$ 19,500	$ 15,000	$ 4,500
B	49,000	98,000	49,000	49,000	35,000	14,000
C	30,000	90,000	45,000	45,000	50,000	(5,000)
Total		$227,000	$113,500	$113,500	$100,000	$13,500

It might be concluded that because the unit contribution margin of Product *C* is $1.50 and that of product *A* is only $.50, more operating hours should be devoted to Product *C* to eliminate the loss. However, since the plant is operating at practical capacity, the critical factor is not contribution margin per *unit* of product, but per *operating hour*. Given these further facts:

	Product		
	A	*B*	*C*
Production per hour (units)	13	7	3
and the practical maximum market demand of (units)	75,000	56,000	31,000

The contribution margin per operating hour can be calculated:

		Contribution
Product		Margin
A	(13 × $ .50)	$6.50
B	(7 × $1.00)	7.00
C	(3 × $1.50)	4.50

For an income statement that shifts emphasis to Product *B*, with its $7 per operating hour contribution margin, secondly to Product *A*, with an hourly contribution margin of $6.50, and lastly to Product *C*, the revised production schedule to maximize income is as follows:

Product	Unit Sales	Net Sales	Variable Costs	Contri-bution Margin	Fixed Costs	Operating Margin (Loss)
A	75,000	$ 75,000	$ 37,500	$ 37,500	$28,845	$ 8,655
B	56,000	112,000	56,000	56,000	40,000	16,000
C	18,693	56,079	28,040	28,039	31,155	(3,116)
Total		$243,079	$121,540	$121,539	$100,000	$21,539

The redistribution of factory hours on which operating margin by product line is calculated is:

Product	Unit Sales	Factory Hours Consumed
A	75,000	5,769
B	56,000	8,000
C	18,693	6,231
Total		20,000

Product *C* provides a loss after allocation of all fixed costs; however, it still furnishes a contribution, after variable costs, in the amount of $28,039. This is available to cover *most* of the fixed costs. Since Product *C* is contributing to operating profit some value in excess of the variable costs, the line should not be dropped unless a more profitable (higher contribution margin) item can be found to replace it.

To illustrate another case of resource allocation, assume that limited availability of a material component restricts production. Then, calculations for marginal profit per pound of scarce *S* material should be made. An example of the allocation of a limited or rationed element in several drug products is shown below. Assume the use of *S* material as follows:

Pharmaceutical Product	Unit Selling Price	Unit Variable Cost	Contri- bution Margin	Pounds of S Consumed per Unit Product	Contri- bution Margin per Pound of S
A	$19.70	$15.10	$4.60	.2	$23.00
B	22.40	14.30	8.10	.3	27.00
C	11.70	9.30	2.40	.1	24.00
D	28.70	21.60	7.10	.4	17.75
E	32.10	26.50	5.60	.1	56.00

Other factors being equal, since Product *E* produces the greatest margin per material *S* content, it should be given priority; Product *B* should be given the next highest priority, and so forth.

Sales Volume Required to Offset Unit Price Reduction

It is not uncommon for the sales manager to complain that sales were under plan because "the price is too high." So management must weigh the impact of lower prices on both sales volume and income. A typical question is, what is the impact on income before taxes if the sales price is reduced 10 percent; or under given conditions, what sales volume is needed to reach the present income level?

Assume these facts:

1. Present unit sales price	$ 5.00
2. Present unit variable cost	2.00
3. Present fixed costs	$150,000
4. Unit sales volume	150,000
5. Estimate of unit sales with a 10 percent price reduction	170,000

The present profit picture is:

Net sales ($5.00 × 150,000)	$750,000
Less: Variable costs ($2.00 × 150,000)	300,000
Contribution margin	$450,000
Fixed costs	150,000
Operating margin	$300,000

To answer the questions raised: If the sales price is reduced 10 percent, the operating margin will be correspondingly reduced by $75,000 (10 percent of $750,000) to a level of $225,000. This assumes no change in sales volume. If, however, unit sales can be increased to the 170,000 units estimated with no change in unit variable costs or total fixed expenses, then the income statement would look like this:

Net sales (170,000 units × $5.00 − 10% = $4.50)	$765,000
Variable costs (170,000 × $2.00)	340,000
Contribution margin	$425,000
Less: Fixed costs	150,000
Operating margin	$275,000

Given the suggested reduction of 10 percent in the unit sales price and the sales manager's estimate of volume attainable, operating margin would be reduced by $25,000 to a level of $275,000.

The answer to the last question — the sales volume required, given a 10 percent price reduction, to equal the present profit of $300,000, is easily calculated.

Sales volume needed to offset reduced price is calculated as:

$$= \frac{\text{Profit desired} + \text{fixed costs}}{1 - \left(\dfrac{\text{Present variable cost ratio}}{1 - \text{Proposed percentage reduction in sales price}}\right)}$$

$$= \frac{\$300,000 + \$150,000}{1 - \dfrac{\$300,000 \div \$750,000}{1 - .10}}$$

$$= \frac{\$450,000}{1 - \dfrac{.40}{1 - .10}}$$

$$= \frac{\$450,000}{1 - .4444}$$

$$= \frac{\$450,000}{.55556}$$

$$= \$810,000, \text{ or } 180,000 \text{ units (rounded)}$$

The proof is as follows:

Net sales ($4.50 × 180,000 units)	$810,000
Variable costs ($2.00 × 180,000 units)	360,000
Contribution margin	$450,000
Less: Fixed costs	150,000
Income before income taxes	$300,000

In essence, the desired profit is treated as a fixed cost, and the adjusted (after price reduction) contribution margin ratio is calculated. This latter profit factor, divided into the required "cost" level, produces the necessary sales volume.

Impact of Plant Expansion

Sooner or later many companies must consider whether or not to acquire new manufacturing facilities. Adding a significant amount of new plant increases the cost level and, of course, impinges on — at least in the early stages of expansion — earnings. In weighing such a capital addition, management should be cognizant of several economic results that flow from the higher investment:

1. Change in the break-even point
2. Added sales volume necessary to retain the existing profit level
3. A different sales volume required to provide an adequate return on the investment
4. A greater maximum profit potential

Assume that the present company status and the plant expansion under consideration are as follows for any given year:

Present maximum operation:	
Net sales	$50,000,000
Costs and expenses	
Variable (50% of sales)	25,000,000
Fixed	16,666,667
Total	41,666,667
Income before income taxes	8,333,333
Federal income taxes (40%)	3,333,333
Net income	$ 5,000,000
Plant expansion under consideration:	
Estimated cost	$ 8,000,000
Estimated higher sales	30,000,000
Estimated additional fixed costs	
Depreciation	$ 1,900,000
Taxes and insurance	190,000
Other fixed expenses	2,410,000
Total	$ 4,500,000

Variable costs to continue at 50% of sales.

The following calculations can now be made for the changes as a result of the new plant:

1. *Change in break-even point:*

a. Break-even point of present facilities:

$$= \frac{\text{Fixed costs}}{\text{Marginal income ratio}}$$

$$= \frac{\$16,666,667}{.50}$$

$$= \$33,333,334$$

b. Break-even point with proposed new facility:

$$= \frac{\$16,666,667 + \$4,500,000}{.50}$$

$$= \frac{\$22,166,667}{.50}$$

$$= \$44,333,334$$

Thus, the break-even point moves up by $10,000,000, or 33⅓ percent.

2. *Added sales volume required to earn existing net income.* This can be calculated in this manner:

$$= \frac{\begin{array}{c}\text{Existing income before taxes} \\ + \text{ Present fixed costs} + \text{Additional fixed costs}\end{array}}{\text{Marginal income ratio}}$$

$$= \frac{\$8,333,333 + \$16,666,667 + \$4,500,000}{.50}$$

$$= \frac{\$29,500,000}{.50}$$

$$= \$59,000,000 \text{ sales volume}$$

Thus, additional sales of $9,000,000 will be needed to maintain existing net income, with no consideration having been given to an acceptable return on the assets acquired.

3. *Different sales volume required to return 10 percent on new assets employed* (*16.67 percent before income taxes*):

$$= \frac{\begin{array}{c}\text{Required return on assets} \\ + \text{ Existing income before income taxes} \\ + \text{ Additional fixed costs} \\ + \text{ Present fixed costs}\end{array}}{\text{Marginal income ratio}}$$

$$= \frac{(\$8,000,000 \times .1667) + \$8,333,333 \\ + \$4,500,000 + \$16,666,667}{.50}$$

$$= \frac{\$30,833,600}{.50}$$

$$= \$61,667,200$$

Net sales of $61,667,200 are needed, at the assumed variable income ratio, to provide a 10 percent net return on the new assets employed.

4. *Greater maximum potential earnings.* This may be determined as follows:

Net sales		
Present		$50,000,000
New plant capacity		30,000,000
Total		$80,000,000
Costs		
Variable (50% of sales)		40,000,000
Contribution margin		$40,000,000
Fixed costs		
Present	$16,666,667	
New plant	4,500,000	21,166,667
Income before federal income taxes		$18,833,333
Federal income taxes (40%)		7,533,333
Net income — Maximum		$11,300,000

Thus, the increase in maximum potential earnings, assuming no change in the variable income ratio, is $6,300,000 or 126 percent.

5. *Summary of the economic impact of the proposed plant.* The economic impact of the proposed plant expansion may be summarized for management in this fashion:

	Present	*With Plant Addition*	*Increase*
Annual break-even sales volume	$33,333,333	$44,333,333	$11,000,000
Sales volume to earn present net income	50,000,000	59,000,000	9,000,000

	Present	With Plant Addition	Increase
Sales volume to earn 16.67% before taxes on new plant investment	—	61,667,200	—
Sales volume at capacity	50,000,000	80,000,000	30,000,000
Net income at capacity	5,000,000	11,300,000	6,300,000

ANALYSIS BY PRODUCT LINE

The illustrative break-even charts presented earlier were for the company as a whole; but the other illustrative specific analyses in many instances were by product line. By and large, most businesses are multiproduct, and alternative choices in many cases will relate to a specific product or product line. Practically speaking, it is highly desirable that the C-V-P analysis be applied to specific products so that the management can more clearly understand the impact of volume and sales price or other policy changes.

The same techniques applicable to the business as a whole may be applied to specific product lines. It is necessary, of course, that the costs be segregated properly by product line. In most instances, the variable costs will be identified by product. Direct materials are usually "called out" by product; and the direct labor is ascertainable from product specifications or job tickets, among other factors. Ordinarily, the variable expenses, whether manufacturing or selling expense, for example, can be determined. A problem might arise with respect to fixed costs. Segment analyses will separate certain fixed costs as direct, but much of the fixed costs, especially manufacturing, will need allocation. And the allocation of fixed costs can be important in setting selling prices. After all, over a period of time, the business must recover not only the variable costs and direct fixed costs, but also a proper share of the fixed costs that should be borne by the product when full costs are considered.

There are perhaps four points to be kept in mind in allocating costs to product lines:

1. There are fair or logical bases on which to allocate fixed costs, fundamentally relating to the amount of usage. Examples are given in Figure 6-3. The base considered most applicable in the circumstances should be used.
2. Changes in sales volume or product mix will, of course, have an impact on the allocation.
3. A test of fair allocation may be the impact of product elimination. Will most costs disappear (e.g., depreciation, maintenance, rent, and insurance)?
4. It is desirable to isolate the direct fixed expenses from the allocated so that managment will realize the effect of its decision on the total business.

FIG. 6-3   Bases for Allocating Fixed Costs

Cost	Base
Personnel department expenses	▪ Number of employees (head count) ▪ Hours worked
Production control department expenses	▪ Amount of direct labor ▪ Head count or direct labor hours ▪ Total direct costs
Heat, light, and power	▪ Number of machine hours ▪ Machine hours weighted by power consumption
Occupancy costs	▪ Square feet occupied ▪ Space occupied
Stores department expenses	▪ Number of requisitions ▪ Cost of materials used
Depreciation — Building	▪ Space occupied
Depreciation — Machinery and equipment	▪ Machine hours ▪ Manhours
Insurance	▪ Space occupied
Maintenance and repairs	▪ Manhours ▪ Machine hours ▪ Space occupied

An example of a helpful product analysis that can be used in C-V-P decisions is illustrated in Figure 6-4.

In preparing product break-even analyses, the reader should be aware that the sum of sales, contribution margin, and net income from each product line should equal the total for the company. However, it will often be found that the sum of the break-even points by product line is not necessarily the same as the overall company break-even point. The condition may not be significant; however, it should be known that this condition arises because of the sales mix. The sales figures for each product line must bear the same relationship to total sales as the individual break-even sales bear to the total break-even point sales.[1]

---

[1] James D. Willson and John B. Campbell, *Controllership* (New York: John Wiley & Sons, 1981), p. 213.

FIG. 6-4   Product Statement With Cost Elements

PRODUCT INCOME STATEMENT
(dollars in thousands, except unit)

	Product					
	A			**B**		
	Amount	Per Unit	Percent Sales	Amount	Per Unit	Percent Sales
Net Sales	$22,900	$10.00	100.0%	$64,830	$22.00	100%
Variable Costs						
Manufacturing	8,244	3.60	36.0	12,966	4.40	20
Sales	5,496	2.40	24.0	20,746	7.04	32
Total variable costs	13,740	6.00	60.0	33,712	11.44	52
Contribution Margin	$ 9,160	4.00	40.0	31,118	10.56	48
Fixed Costs						
Manufacturing						
Direct	2,290	1.00	10.0	1,297	.44	2
Allocated	1,603	.70	7.0	3,241	1.10	5
Total	3,893	1.70	17.0	4,538	1.54	7
Selling						
Direct	1,374	.60	6.0	6,483	2.20	10
Allocated	229	.10	1.0	648	.22	1
Total fixed costs	5,496	2.40	24.0	11,669	3.96	18
Income Before Taxes	3,664	1.60	16.0	19,449	6.60	30
Federal Income Taxes (40%)	1,466	.64	6.4	7,780	2.64	12
Net Income	$ 2,198	$ .96	9.6%	$11,669	$ 3.96	18%

CHANGES IN SALES MIX

Earlier in this chapter, an example is given of adjusting sales mix to reflect
the marginal income per (critical) operating hour. But aside from maximizing
use of scarce resources, management may wish to consider changes in sales
mix even when common departments are not used and a bottleneck condition is not a critical factor. Changes in sales mix may be desirable to increase
or maximize the operating profit. A knowledge of marginal income by product line may prove useful in such a planning exercise.

Assume the following product mix, variable costs, and fixed costs:

Product	Sales Percent	Sales Amount	Variable Costs	Contribution Margin Amount	Contribution Margin Percentage of Net Sales
X	20.0%	$ 20,000,000	$12,000,000	$ 8,000,000	40.00%
Y	70.0	70,000,000	52,500,000	17,500,000	25.00
Z	10.0	10,000,000	8,800,000	1,200,000	12.00
Total or average	100.0%	$100,000,000	$73,300,000	$26,700,000	26.70%
Fixed costs				13,000,000	
Operating profit				$13,700,000	

The *average* contribution margin rate, or variable income rate, is 26.70 percent. The break-even point, incidentally, is $48,689,139, calculated as follows:

$$\frac{\text{Fixed costs}}{\text{Marginal income ratio}} = \frac{\$13,000,000}{.2670} = \$48,689,139$$

Assuming that the sales manager believes the market can absorb a 200 percent increase in the volume of the highest margin Product X, with a corresponding dollar decrease in the volume of competitive Product Y, and assuming the production manager can handle the change at no increase in costs or no sacrifice of volume, what is the profit impact?
The change in sales mix produces this picture:

Product	Sales Percent	Sales Amount	Variable Costs	Contribution Margin Amount	Contribution Margin Percentage of Net Sales
X	60.0%	$ 60,000,000	$36,000,000	$24,000,000	40.00%
Y	30.0	30,000,000	22,500,000	7,500,000	25.00
Z	10.0	10,000,000	8,800,000	1,200,000	12.00
Total or average	100.0%	$100,000,000	$67,300,000	$32,700,000	32.70%
Fixed costs				13,000,000	
Operating profit				$19,700,000	

By the change in sales emphasis to the higher margin item, the operating profit can be increased by $6,000,000 or 43.80 percent. (The break-even point is reduced to a sales volume of $39,755,351.) Use of the variable income ratio approach, with due care to influences on costs — both production and marketing — can provide interesting business choices to consider.

CHANGES IN SELLING PRICES

One of the most vexing problems in business planning is the selection of the sales price that provides the maximum profit. A decrease in price will ordinarily cause an increase in volume. What is the impact of alternative pricing? Use of the variable cost concept and the judgment of the marketing department as to elasticity of demand should produce useful pricing information. A summary of four alternatives is shown in Figure 6-5. Assuming the volume estimates are proper, a reduction of 10 percent in price would produce the highest contribution margin and operating margin. Of course, more calculations by a computer, using more alternative choices, would assist in locating the optimum price.

CHANGES IN COSTS

Management must continually battle rising costs, and much of the cost reduction effort in business is devoted to reducing total costs, whether fixed or variable. With increased automation, there is a tendency to increase fixed costs (depreciation and maintenance) in an effort to reduce the variable costs (direct labor, direct material, and variable overhead). Interesting cost studies can be made on the trade-offs. An increase in fixed costs of 20 percent, with a reduction in variable costs of 20 percent, might be reflected on a break-even chart as shown in Figure 6-6. In tabular form, the results appear as follows (dollars in millions):

	Present Sales Level		At Capacity	
	Present Cost Structure	Changed Cost Structure	Present Cost Structure	Changed Cost Structure
Net sales	$170,000	$170,000	$250,000	$250,000
Variable costs	102,000	81,600	150,000	120,000
Contribution margin	68,000	88,400	100,000	130,000
Fixed costs	53,833	64,600	53,833	64,600
Profit before income taxes	14,167	23,800	46,167	65,400
Federal income taxes (40%)	5,667	9,520	18,467	26,160
Net income	$ 8,500	$ 14,280	$ 27,500	$ 39,240
Break-even sales volume	$134,583	$124,231		

FIG. 6-5 Price Impact on Margin

PRICE-VOLUME CHANGES

Item	Present Policy	Increase Price 10%	Increase Price 5%	Decrease Price 5%	Decrease Price 10%
Unit sales price	$ 1.00	$ 1.10	$ 1.05	$ .95	$ .90
Variable unit cost	.40	.40	.40	.40	.40
Estimate of sales volume (units)	2,000,000	1,600,000	1,900,000	2,200,000	2,400,000
Income Statement					
Net sales	$2,000,000	$1,760,000	$1,995,000	$2,090,000	$2,160,000
Variable costs	800,000	640,000	760,000	880,000	960,000
Contribution margin	1,200,000	1,120,000	1,235,000	1,210,000	2,200,000
Fixed costs	400,000	400,000	400,000	400,000	400,000
Operating margin	$ 800,000	$ 720,000	$ 835,000	$ 810,000	$1,800,000

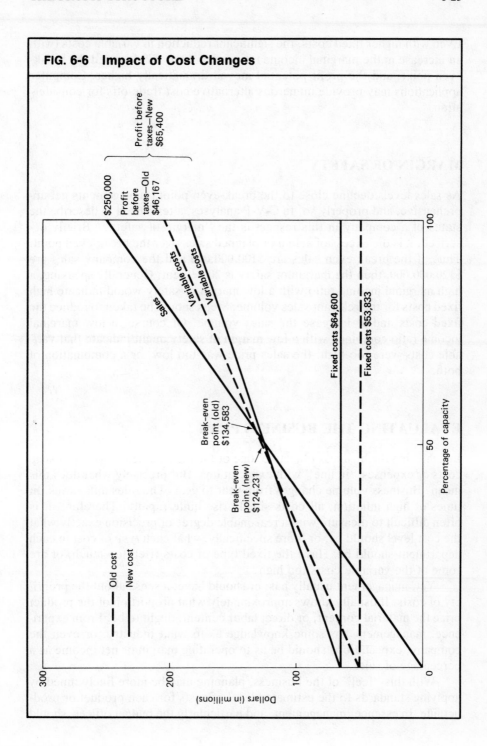

FIG. 6-6 Impact of Cost Changes

Profit before
taxes—New
$65,400

Profit
before
taxes—Old
$46,167

$250,000

Sales

Variable costs

Variable costs

Fixed costs $64,600

Fixed costs $53,833

Break-even
point (old)
$134,583

Break-even
point (new)
$124,231

--- Old cost

—— New cost

300

200

100

0

Dollars (in millions)

0

50

100

Percentage of capacity

Even with higher fixed costs, the significant reduction in variable costs (with an increase in the marginal income ratio from .40 to .52) lowered the break-even point; and the profit potential moved dramatically higher. Computer applications may provide numerous alternative cost trade-offs for consideration.

MARGIN OF SAFETY

As sales levels decline close to the break-even point, managements get apprehensive, and properly so. In C-V-P analyses, a term used to describe the status of a company in this respect is the "margin of safety." Briefly described, it is the excess of actual or planned sales over the break-even point. Thus, if the break-even sales are $100,000,000 and the company sales are $120,000,000, then the margin of safety is 20 percent. Generally speaking, a high marginal income ratio with a low margin of safety would indicate high fixed costs for the relevant sales volume. Steps should be taken to reduce the fixed costs and/or increase the sales volume. Of course, a low marginal income ratio combined with a low margin of safety might indicate that variable costs were too high, the sales price was too low, or a combination of both.

EVALUATING THE BUSINESS PLAN

In achieving the business objective, one of the management tasks is to keep costs or expenses "in line" with expectations. But precisely what does this mean? Business volume changes from year to year. The sales mix varies. In times of high inflation, all costs simply rise quite rapidly. Therefore, it is often difficult to measure with a reasonable degree of precision exactly what the cost level should be, or more specifically, what each *type* of cost in each department should be. Have the fixed type of costs risen too much, or are some of the variable costs too high?

Yet, management usually has, or should have, a sense about the propriety of costs. It usually knows approximately what proportion of the product price the material content, or direct labor content, ought to be. From experience, management has some knowledge as to what industry, or even the company, expectations should be as to operating margin or net income as a percentage of sales.

With this "feel" of the business, planning may be more finely tuned by applying standards to the estimated level of costs for each product or product line. In essence, management, and particularly the budget officer, should

FIG. 6-7   An Acceptable Profit Structure

THE SPEEDY MACHINE SHOP
PROFILER LINE

COST-VOLUME-PROFIT STRUCTURE
(dollars in thousands)

| Item | Fixed Costs | Variable Costs | | Total |
		Amount	Percent Net Sales	
Net Sales				$120,000
Costs and Expenses				
Direct material	—	$20,000	16.67	
Direct labor	—	20,000	16.67	
Manufacturing expense	$10,000	10,000	8.33	
Engineering expense	10,000	10,000	8.33	
Marketing expense	6,000	2,400	2.00	
Research & development expense	3,000	1,000	.83	
General & administrative expense	3,000	500	.42	
Total	$32,000	$63,900	53.25%	95,900
Income Before Income Taxes				$ 24,100
Federal Income Taxes (40%)				9,640
Net Income				$ 14,460
Net Income as Percentage of Net Sales				12.05%

develop an acceptable cost-volume-profit structure and test the business plan against it. For example, assume as a matter of experience that the management of the company concurs that the profit structure shown in Figure 6-7, properly segregated by fixed and variable elements, is acceptable. Then, when a business plan is submitted, it might be enlightening to test the plan against this standard, as is illustrated in Figure 6-8. This analysis pinpoints the over or under "standard" condition by type of cost or expense and, further, determines whether it is in the variable or fixed category. Relatively small cost overruns in the cost of sales categories account for a significant amount of dollars percentage-wise. The other major area of

FIG. 6-8 Measurement of Business Plan Against Standard Profit Structure

The Speedy Machine Shop
Profiler Lines

MEASUREMENT OF BUSINESS PLAN
For the year ending December 31, 19XX
(dollars in thousands)

Item	Proposed Plan	Application of Standard Structure	Plan Over (Under) Standard Amount	Plan Over (Under) Standard Percentage
Net Sales	$168,000	$168,000	—	—
Cost of Sales				
Direct material	28,840	28,000	$ 840	3.00%
Direct labor	29,000	28,000	1,000	3.57
Engineering expense				
Variable	14,694	13,994	700	5.00
Fixed	10,000	10,000	—	—
Total	24,694	23,994	700	2.92
Manufacturing expense				
Variable	14,554	13,994	560	4.00
Fixed	10,750	10,000	750	7.50
Total	25,304	23,994	1,310	5.46
Total cost of sales	107,838	103,988	3,850	3.70
Gross Margin	60,162	64,012	(3,850)	(6.01)
Operating Expenses				
Marketing				
Variable	5,409	3,360	2,049	60.98
Fixed	7,200	6,000	1,200	20.00
Total	12,609	9,360	3,249	34.71
Research & development				
Variable	1,760	1,399	361	25.80
Fixed	2,900	3,000	(100)	(3.33)
Total	4,660	4,399	261	5.93
General & administrative				
Variable	710	706	4	.57
Fixed	3,400	3,000	400	13.33
Total	4,110	3,706	404	10.90
Total Operating Expenses	21,379	17,465	3,914	22.41
Income Before Income Taxes	38,783	46,547	(7,764)	(16.68)
Federal Income Taxes (40%)	15,513	18,619	(3,106)	(16.68)
Net Income	$ 23,270	$ 27,928	$(4,658)	(16.68)%

excess costs lies in the marketing operation. Those who analyze the costs must seek out the causes and determine whether the plan needs adjusting or whether the measuring stick is not applicable.

On the whole subject of planned income and expenses, management has a tendency to accept the new plan if the income is somewhat higher than the preceding year — either in total, or as a percentage of sales. Yet, in instances where there are major changes in sales volume, the test of apparent reasonableness of change in planned profits might not be sufficient. A sharper tool — the use of the cost-volume-profit analysis just illustrated — is necessary.

SOME GENERAL OBSERVATIONS ON THE COST-VOLUME-PROFIT RELATIONSHIP

Perhaps one of the best ways to truly understand the profit structure is to construct a break-even chart of a product or division, or the total company, and then modify some of the conditions or assumptions and observe the impact. The same results also can be obtained by simple arithmetic, of course. The following are some of the general observations on the influence of such changes:

□ A change in the amount of fixed costs will impact profit before taxes by the same amount and will not affect the variable, or marginal, income ratio. The break-even point will move by the same percentage that fixed costs are modified.

□ A change in selling price will modify the marginal income ratio and the break-even point. If variable costs are changed, they too will modify the marginal income ratio and break-even point. A given percentage change in the sales price will not equate to the same percentage change in variable costs.

□ A high variable income ratio will cause a significant change in the operating income level with relatively small changes in sales volume.

COST-VOLUME-PROFIT ANALYSIS AND PLANNING

In this chapter, the impact of costs, volume, and sales price changes on the profit structure of the company has been explored. Each of these factors are interrelated, and changes in one will can cause changes in another. Price and volume changes in one product line may well impact other product lines (e.g., allocation of fixed manufacturing costs). In a multiproduct environment, the number of calculations may literally be astronomical. Yet analysis is highly desirable in selecting alternative strategies. Accordingly, in most situations it is suggested that computer modeling techniques are the most effective means of dealing with the problem.

A number of ready-made software computer programs are available to help those doing the analysis. And, of course, the data processing or financial groups may develop their own programs. The many alternatives will require numerous iterative steps to arrive at combinations that, for example, will satisfy the vice-president–marketing. Moreover, the various choices will have an impact on inventory/receivable levels with associated financing costs. Computer applications on a time-shared basis with access to a terminal and a large computer, if needed, ought to be most helpful. But the results will be no better than the assumptions used, including the proper segregation of fixed and variable costs, direct versus indirect costs, relationship to volume changes, ad infinitum.

7

The Cost of Capital

THE "COST OF CAPITAL" DEFINED

Individuals and companies are willing to place funds at risk in the expectation of not only recouping such capital at some time in the future, but also of making a reasonable return. Some might invest in a practically risk-free vehicle such as short-term U.S. Government securities; but others assume greater risks for an expected higher rate of return. Private investors in the aggregate who are willing to commit huge amounts of capital have produced in the United States the highest standard of living in the world.

Cost of capital is that rate of return that must be paid to investors to induce them to supply the necessary funds. Capital will flow to those markets where the investor expects to receive a rate of return consistent with his perception of the business and financial risks and the rate available elsewhere in the marketplace. Interest payments and possible capital gains to the bondholder may be clearly recognized as a "cost." But the common shareholder, also, must secure a return; and, as will be seen, this is not necessarily measured by the dividend rate. The "cost" in cost of capital, as is apparent from the ensuing discussion, goes beyond any accounting concept to an economic definition.

SIGNIFICANCE OF THE COST OF CAPITAL

The cost of capital is important to the business manager for two reasons: First, of course, in planning company expansion, or in securing funds for continuance of the business, he should be aware of the cost of capital. It must be recognized in the short- and long-range business plans. Second, and more important than this general application, the cost of capital is basic to any decision to invest in plant and equipment and the related long-term working capital needed for a project. Obviously, a manager will not commit capital funds when the likelihood of payback is nil. Nor is it likely that an investor would invest if it were known that the rate of return would be less than the cost. A commitment of funds is made by the prudent businessperson only if after the recovery of the investment something is left over. That is to say, the amount of profit must be sufficient to justify making the investment in the first place. Hence, cost of capital sets the *floor* under normal circumstances as the minimum rate of return required before the investment should even be considered. It is the cutoff point, the minimum acceptable rate of return for capital expenditures, as discussed in Chapter 25.

Knowing the cost of capital, within reasonable limits, is essential to any business management that expects to make investment decisions on a prudent basis. If the management underestimates the cost, it may make either less profitable or relatively unprofitable investments. If it overestimates the cost, the business manager may miss some profitable opportunities.

Further, cost of capital should be considered the overall cost, a blended cost of all sources to be used. From the long-run viewpoint, the cost of specific financing or funds should *not* be the criterion. For example, if a building is financed completely by a corporate bond obligation at 10 percent, the cost of capital is not 10 percent. The *equity* of the company made the financing possible and must be considered. The cost of funds from all sources or probable sources should be used to evaluate investment opportunities.

STEPS IN DETERMINING THE COST OF CAPITAL

From the standpoint of the planning process, we are not greatly concerned with the cost of capital in industry as a whole. We are concerned about the cost of capital for a particular company in a particular industry and within a limited time period. The industry is mentioned because securing funds in one industry may require a different inducement rate (cost) than some other. Moreover, the process is easy to outline but sometimes is more difficult to accomplish. The steps in determining the cost of capital are outlined below, with subsequent text discussing the many ramifications. The steps are:

1. Select the appropriate capital structure for the company.
2. Determine the appropriate rate of return to investors (the cost of capital) for each segment of the capital structure.
3. Properly weight each segment and calculate the overall cost to the company.

In an overly simplified manner, the cost of capital in a given company might be determined as follows:

Type of Security	Capitalization	Investor Required Rate (before taxes)	After-Tax Rate to Company*	Company Cost of Capital
Senior obligation	$ 60,000,000	12%	7.2%	$ 4,320,000
Common stock	140,000,000	20	20.0	28,000,000
Total	$200,000,000			
Cost of capital				$32,320,000
Rate required				16.16%

* 40% income tax rate assumed

For this particular company, the after-tax cost of capital is 16.16 percent, or ($32,320,000 ÷ $200,000,000).

Having briefly discussed the basic principle, let us consider some of the questions to be answered in addressing cost of capital decisions in a specific corporation.

WHICH CAPITAL STRUCTURE?

The capital structure of the company is that proportion of long-term debt and equity that is required to provide the necessary funds for the operation and growth of the enterprise. Each security type has a different cost, and the mix or proportion of each in a particular company must be known to calculate the cost of each segment.

But which capital structure should be used? The present one? One giving effect to near-term, expected financing? Or, should a long-term view be taken?

Basically, the capital structure in most companies must command respect from investors far into the future. Only by following such a policy will the requisite funds be secured at all or obtained on an economical basis. Therefore, it is usually unwise to use spot figures (i.e., figures at any instant in time). Because structures may change as financings are undertaken from year to year, it is preferable to select an average structure over a period of years — one that conforms to the nature of the capital structure chosen. This will vary by industry and company inasmuch as the investor-perceived amount of risk varies, and therefore relative cost may be different.

In selecting the structure, what guidelines may be used? How much senior debt, for example, may prudently be assumed? There are several suggested sources that will give the financial executive some assistance in selecting an optimum capital structure, as outlined below.

Advice of Investment Bankers

The better known and reputable investment bankers usually have a good knowledge of the financial marketplace and the current thinking of institutional or other large investors. Such firms will be able to give advice on an acceptable structure for the industry under discussion, as well as for the specific company. This source also will have opinions on maximum debt capacity, as well as the terms of recent financings.

Advice of Commercial Bankers

The commercial banking arm is often well-informed on the industry outlook and conditions, especially where such financial institutions are organized primarily on an industry basis, such as in the petroleum industry, aerospace, or retailing. Because commercial banks are a major source of working capital, their views on total debt capacity, long-term debt levels, and, of course, capital structure and other debt-limiting factors should be carefully weighed.

Competitive Action

An analysis of the financial statements and credit agreements of competitors in the industry will usually provide some clues or guidelines on acceptable capital structure and tests of debt capacity. Such analyses also will be helpful in discussions with investment and commercial bankers while exploring ranges and ratios related to capital structure.

Analysis of Company History

Another useful source of data about capital structure is an analysis of past practice and conditions in the specific company seeking answers. A review of debt-coverage ratios and other related factors in "normal" times and in adversity may provide some insight. Such analysis is necessary when examining probable future ranges of activity and ratios — all in an effort to secure funds on the most advantageous basis and to avoid severe financial difficulties.

COST OF SENIOR CAPITAL

For business-planning purposes, securities may be categorized as either (1) senior securities (all securities that are senior to, or rank ahead of, common equity) or (2) common equity. A listing of the principal types of senior issues is as follows.

1. Debt instruments:
   - Long-term notes — Unsecured obligations
   - Debentures — Unsecured debt obligations
   - Mortgages
   - Mortgage bonds — Bonds that possess, as security, a lien on certain property
   - Capitalized leases
   - Subordinated debentures — Unsecured obligations that are junior to certain other indebtedness (but ahead of stock)
   - Convertible debentures
   - Income bonds — Bonds on which interest payments are dependent on earnings
2. Preferred stock:
   - Preferred (regular) — Preferred in some way over the common equity (i.e., dividend and in liquidation)
   - Convertible preferred

In today's principles of accounting terms, a convertible may be treated as debt or equity depending on several factors, including nearness to conversion. However, for our purposes, convertibles should be treated as equities, which bear a higher cost than do other senior securities, and hence will result in a somewhat higher cost of capital.

In calculating the cost of senior capital, two practical observations may be made:

1. In most industrial companies, as distinguished from utilities, the proportion of senior capital is relatively small as compared with equity. Therefore, its cost is relatively less important.
2. Great accuracy in calculating the cost of senior securities is not critical; hence, reasonable approximations may be used. As mentioned earlier, judgment must be exercised in arriving at an average cost expected to prevail over several years in the future.

CALCULATING THE SENIOR DEBT COST

If the cost of most senior debt is comparable, then a single base figure and a single rate for senior debt may be used, as is discussed earlier in this chapter. However, where there are significant differences in the marketplace, then each segment of the debt structure should be weighted, and separate calculations made. Further, if the financing costs, including both the underwriting commission and the financing expenses (legal fees, accounting fees, printing costs, and mailing costs) are significant, then these should be taken into account in arriving at the cost of the net proceeds to the company. If applicable, bond value tables may be used to calculate the yield to maturity.

An illustrative summary of the cost of senior debt, where substantially different costs attach to each segment, is shown below. Financing costs are ignored for simplicity purposes. The senior debt segment, which is expected to equal 30 percent of the capitalization, is as follows, reflecting the probable sources of capital:

Type of Instrument	Principal Amount	Investor Required Rate	Company After-Tax Rate	Company Cost
Term notes	$ 30,000,000	19%	11.4%	$3,420,000
Mortgage bonds	15,000,000	11	6.6	990,000
Debentures	25,000,000	15	9.0	2,250,000
Capitalized leases	30,000,000	16	9.6	2,880,000
Total	$100,000,000			$9,540,000
Rate				9.54%

COST OF EQUITY CAPITAL

As previously stated, an investor will purchase common stock if he thinks the anticipated return is adequate to reward him for the perceived risk. This reward is in the form of both dividends and price appreciation. Some may argue that common stock does not have a "cost" but does have an "earnings requirement"; however, this is mere semantics. The economic cost, call it what you will, must be recognized in the capital structure of a company.

In most industrial companies, the common equity portion of long-term capital is significantly larger than the senior capital share. Typically, it is between 50 percent and 70 percent of the total capitalization. Of course, in conservative financial enterprises it is 90 percent or 100 percent.

Because it is such a large segment, and because common equity capital is the more expensive since it commands a higher rate of return than senior debt due to the greater risk, the impact on total cost is most significant. For these same reasons, it has the greatest impact on the capital cost as related to plant and equipment expenditures and new projects requiring both capital assets and working capital.

In calculating the cost of common equity for a particular company, several matters should be addressed:

- What earnings level should be used?
- Is the cost of equity capital to be applied against book value or market value in weighting the segment?
- Is the same rate to be applied against the capital stock segment and the retained earnings segment?
- What securities should be treated as common equity — Straight preferred, convertible preferred, or convertible debt?

The following text comments on these questions. It should be recognized that determining the cost of common equity capital cannot be done with great mathematical precision; it has a large element of subjectivity.

The Earnings Level

The relationship of the market price to earnings is, of course, a key element in determining the cost of common equity. And the question arises, which earnings level is most appropriate?

There are at least three different per share earnings levels available to the management representative who seeks to determine the cost of equity capital:

1. Historical earnings, including the recent level as well as the trend of several years
2. The management estimate of future earnings per share
3. The investors perceived or expected future earnings per share

Suffice it to say that historical earnings in some instances may be a guide to future earnings — but not necessarily so. Benefits to the shareowner must come from *future* earnings, and the cost of common equity is the relationship of market price to the future earnings.

Management, of course, probably will possess a good estimate of expected future per share earnings based on the strategic planning and annual business plans prepared by the company. However, such estimates are not usually known publicly.

This leaves us with the future earnings expected by the investor. Security analysts and others rather constantly estimate earnings per share for one, two, three years, and longer. The cost of common stock relates to the market price the investor is willing to pay, based on the earnings he expects in the future. If the earnings do not materialize and he is disappointed — for example, if earnings were in line with the management estimate and not the prevailing public expectation — then ordinarily the price of the stock will decline.

As a further refinement, where it is significant, the market price of the stock should be adjusted for financing costs. In summary, the cost of common equity is determined in this manner:

$$\text{Cost of common equity} = \frac{\text{Expected future earnings as perceived by investors}}{\substack{\text{Market price of the shares,}\\ \text{perhaps adjusted for financing costs}}}$$

Assume these facts:

1. Market price of the stock $52
2. Estimated financing costs for new issue   15%
3. Net proceeds to company ($52 less $7.80) $44.20
4. Perceived earnings per share, by investors $6.50

The cost of common equity is, then:

$$\text{Cost of common equity} = \frac{\$6.50}{\$44.20} = 14.71\%$$

It should be mentioned, finally, that the investors' expected rate of return gives effect to the tax impact of the investment. Hence, this factor need not be directly considered.

The Price-Earnings Ratio

Before dealing with the remaining questions in applying the cost of equity capital, some comments should be made on the price-earnings (P/E) ratio. This, of course, is a key factor in evaluating the price an investor is willing to pay. In testing the applicability or reasonableness of the P/E ratio, consideration should be given to the growth in earnings per share. If investors expect that earnings will be static and therefore the average earnings of the past will be repeated, then an average of past ratios of earnings per share to market price will approximate the common equity cost. The analyst who develops a cost of common equity may check the average relationships for perhaps the past five or ten years, comparing these trends and the average, to reach a judgment:

1. Earnings per share
2. Average market price
3. Market price reduced by financing costs
4. P/E ratio of common equity to average equity costs

5. Return on average or year-end equity
6. Dividend yield

Where probable growth is involved, such expectation is reflected in the P/E ratio. Thus, the perceived yield to the common shareholder might be calculated as:

Dividend yield	5.5%
Expected growth in earnings per share	9.0
Total return	14.5%

In any event, the company analyst should explore the growth rate in earnings per share and the P/E ratio of the company and some of its competitors in arriving at a judgment on a realistic P/E ratio and related cost of capital. Some relate the future stream of dividends, plus expected market appreciation, on a time-value basis to estimate investor expectations.[1]

Role of Book Value

The cost of common equity is determined on the basis of an investor's expected return on the market value of the stock. The marketplace sets the required rate of return. A perceptive reviewer might ask, in figuring the composite cost of capital, whether or not the market value of existing shares should be substituted for book value in the calculation. The question may be answered by indicating that a company can earn only on the capital it possesses. What it has is the book value of the stock, and not market value. Therefore, this base should be employed, plus other indicated financing, to meet the desired capital structure in determining the cost of capital.

Treatment of Retained Earnings

In calculating cost of equity capital, some supposedly knowledgeable analysts argue that the retained earnings segment of equity capital should be treated in a different fashion than that raised from the sale of shares. However, there should be no distinction in handling any part of common shareholders' equity. Whether paid-in capital, capital stock, or retained earnings, each represents a part of the common shareholders' equity and should be treated the same. With the exception of financing costs, it makes no difference whether a company retains some earnings for reinvestment or pays out all earnings as dividends and then sells new shares.

---

[1] See Chapter 25 for a discussion of the discounted cash-flow rate of return.

Elements of Common Equity Capital

Technically, equity capital includes any type of ownership interest: straight preferred stock, convertible preferred stock, and common stock (and, under some rules, convertible debt if it is apt to be converted).

For purposes of cost-of-capital calculations, the convertible instrument should be treated as common equity, and straight preferred issues should be handled on their own base (i.e., similar to bonds).

Cost of Equity Capital Calculation

The cost of *equity capital* in an illustrative company may be calculated as follows:

Segment	Principal Amount	Investor Required Rate	Company After-Tax Cost	Total Cost
Preferred stock	$ 30,000,000	14%	14%	$ 4,200,000
Convertible preferred	30,000,000	22	22	6,600,000
Common stock				
Present	100,000,000	22	22	22,000,000
Future	40,000,000	22	22	8,800,000
Total	$200,000,000			
Cost of Equity Capital				$41,600,000
Rate				20.8%

The composite cost of long-term capital, using the senior debt structure shown earlier, may be determined in this fashion:

Segment	Capitalization	Cost
Senior debt	$100,000,000	$ 9,540,000
Equity capital	200,000,000	41,600,000
Total	$300,000,000	$51,140,000
Rate		17.000

TREATMENT OF DEFERRED TAXES

An increasingly important element in the balance sheet of many companies is deferred taxes, whether carried as a current liability under certain accounting concepts, in the statement of financial position as a part of long-term liabilities, or between long-term liabilities and equity.

In a general sense, deferred taxes are a liability that must be paid sometime in the future — in portions over a period of years as, for example, when contracts are completed or when the business terminates. On the other hand, because of the continuing existence of long-term contracts or other financial arrangements, it might be argued that some companies will not pay such taxes in the foreseeable future. Be that as it may, deferred taxes provide a source of cash — usually at no cost.

The basic question is whether or not this segment of the balance sheet should be given any weight in the cost of capital or in analyzing capital structure ratios. Perhaps the treatment should be determined on an individual basis in the light of circumstances and probable disposition as seen by the financial executives of the company involved. To avoid *understating* the cost of capital, consideration should be given to omitting deferred taxes from the capital structure. (One reason for this is that tax laws may change.)

PROFIT GOALS FOR CAPITAL PROJECTS

When the return is sufficient, funds will be attracted to a company. It is obvious that over a longer term, a company must earn, at a minimum, its cost of capital. Hence, should a management invest at *less* than the cost of capital floor, then the requisite rate of return will not be met and necessary external capital will not be forthcoming — if this condition exists over a period of time. If the rate of return is not achieved, the management is detracting from the values owned by the shareholders.

While the cost of capital may be considered the *floor* for the rate of return on major capital expenditures, the fact remains that a company should have a *profit goal* that is higher than the cost of capital for any one of several reasons:

- Some capital expenditures and projects will be undertaken and fail to produce the objective return, for whatever reason. Hence, these deficient projects must be made up by higher rates of return on other projects.
- Certain capital expenditures must be undertaken, with a low rate of return or no return, simply to remain in business. Examples could include pollution abatement installations, employee's parking lot or lunch facilities, or obsolete painting equipment. Here, again, some returns above the cost of capital on selected proposals would be necessary to secure an *average* return on shareholder equity equivalent to the cost of capital.
- Finally, certain undertakings will entail substantially more risk than, for example, the present products or markets, and this risk must be compensated for. Diversification, for example, usually will require more risk than a known business.

Given actual results that often do not meet plan, and other failures in human judgment, how much above the cost of capital should a profit goal be set? This is a matter of management judgment, taking into account the risks involved, the competitive strength, and position of the company, among other factors. Too low a profit goal will finally erode the earnings on shareholders' equity. Too high a goal may mean lost opportunity or increased competition in the field. Some companies may seek a goal perhaps 5 percent above the cost of capital:

Cost of capital	12.0%
Allowance above cost	5.0
Profit goal	17.0%

Depending on circumstances, some companies use a goal of providing 25 percent return on the equity portion of capital.

Project Costs

Long-term investments such as plant and equipment usually should be financed by long-term capital sources — hence the need to know the floor rate (the cost of capital). Very often, however, expansion projects require (1) long-term capital for the fixed assets and the more or less permanent investment in receivables and inventory, and (2) short-term capital for start-up phases (e.g., peak inventories). Hence, project costs should recognize the profit goal objective for long-term capital and the current cost for working capital components. A summary of the cost rates to be considered in recovering project investment opportunities is summarized in Figure 7-1.

Profit Goals for the Company or for Capital Projects?

In Chapter 3, the proper profit goal for the company as a whole is discussed. It was suggested that the appropriate profit goal for business planning (short- and long-term) is one representing a stipulated return on shareholders' equity. This section reviews the profit goal, based on something above the cost of capital, as applied to major capital expenditures, and indeed, with proper consideration of working capital, as applied to major new expansion projects.

It prudently might be asked what the relationship is between these two goals. The profit goal for planning purposes — especially near-term planning — gives recognition to the *present* capital structure; present operating efficiency, including the impact of research and development programs that may be in a cycle diluting earnings; businesses that are being phased out; the short-term bank or other financing; and the present tax laws. In short, there

FIG. 7-1   Cost Rates for Capital Segments*

Security Item	Cost Data
Current Liabilities	
▪ Those requiring no interest	None
▪ Short-term notes	Interest cost
Long-Term Debt	
▪ Term loans	
▪ Mortgages	Interest cost
▪ Mortgage bonds	experience
▪ Debentures	or
▪ Capitalized leases	anticipated
Convertibles	
▪ Debentures	Cost of common
▪ Preferred stock	equity
Common Equity	
▪ Stated value	
▪ Paid-in capital	Cost of common
▪ Retained earnings	equity

Note: To be adjusted for before and after taxes, as appropriate.

may exist a host of short-term or cyclical factors that the industry, and companies in it, must consider, together with special and undesirable circumstances. While these must be recognized in setting planning goals, it would seem that often they are extraneous to a given capital project, or the likely conditions expected to exist in, for example, five years. Hence, the two profit goals, in the opinion of the author, usually will not be the same. Perhaps the profit goals for capital expenditures and projects should be higher, giving proper weight to the long-term capital involved, since these projects will presumably not be burdened with known past errors. Here, again, the management must exercise judgment in setting each of the two types of goals.

PART II

The Operating Budget

8

Standards as a Planning and Control Device

A "STANDARD" DEFINED

A standard may be described as a measuring stick by which something is judged. Webster's *New Collegiate Dictionary* defines a standard as "something set up and established by authority as a rule for the measure of quantity, weight, extent, value, or quality."

A standard for accomplishing a task might be described as the best method or process devised at the time the standard is established, by those who are qualified to know what constitutes good performance. A standard may or may not be expressed in monetary units. But a standard cost is the amount that should be expended under normal operating conditions. It may be described as a predetermined cost, determined scientifically. It is not necessarily an actual or average cost, although past experience in most instances is a factor in setting a standard.

A budget itself is one type of standard, although this chapter will discuss standards that are not necessarily a part of a budgetary planning and control system. Certainly, in the planning and control of a business there is a need for something other than historical costs or levels of performance. Management should know what performance or cost should be expected that is not distorted by avoidable excess cost, defective material, poor worker performance, or other factors not ordinarily present.

TYPES OF STANDARDS NEEDED

Managerial planning and control extends, or should extend, to every function in business: manufacturing, marketing, research and development, administration, and finance. It would seem beneficial, therefore, to have standards to measure performance in each of these areas, as well as standards to measure relationships and conditions. And there are, in fact, measuring sticks for many activities and results.

To be sure, standards are thought of mostly in connection with manufacturing activities, but they do exist for a vast range of nonmanufacturing functions and conditions or relationships. Some specific standards to be briefly reviewed include:

1. Manufacturing standards:
   - Direct material price standards
   - Direct material quantity standards
   - Direct labor rate standards
   - Direct labor quantity standards
   - Manufacturing expense standards
2. Marketing activity:
   - Sales standards
   - Marketing expense standards
   - Marketing cost/result standards
3. Administrative activity:
   - Functional standards
   - Expense level standards
4. Research and development activity:
   - Expense standards
   - Result standards
5. Financial activities:
   - Activity expense standards
   - Expense level standards
   - Financial condition standards

Activities and costs are planned and controlled by individuals. It is through the action of a specific person directed to a specific condition that results are brought into line with plan. Thus, it is largely due to a departmental foreman that labor or expense performance is maintained within acceptable limits. By motivating and spurring on the efforts of an individual salesperson, the budgeted sales or the sales quota are achieved. The point to be made is that standards must relate to *specific* points rather than to *general* results to be most effective.

RELATIONSHIP OF STANDARDS TO THE BUDGET

It was stated earlier that a budget, in itself, is a standard for measuring actual results. This is true, but there are relationships between the types of standards enumerated in the prior section and the budgetary process that bear explanation.

1. *Preparation of the budget.* Certain standards facilitate the preparation of the annual planning budget and revisions of plans. In some functional areas, the unit standards developed may serve to develop the planning budget. This is particularly true with respect to manufacturing standards. Thus, material usage standards would normally be used in developing the materials usage budget and the related purchases budget. See Chapter 12. By the same token, labor usage standards and rate standards would facilitate developing the direct labor or indirect labor budget. See Chapter 11. The budget structure developed for flexible budgeting would be applied in developing the manufacturing expense budget. Also, in other functions where flexible budgets are applied, the expense standards may be helpful.

    Standards also may be valuable in testing plans or budgets. Thus, the current ratio, a type of standard, may be checked, or the relationship of selected expenses to sales may be tested.

2. *Control phase.* Standards may facilitate the control phase of budgeting. Aside from the plan itself, the flexible budget standards should be useful in controlling costs or comparable expenses. Additionally, the direct labor and direct material standards should be the basis, in most instances, for measuring actual costs against what the costs should have been.

3. *Standards to measure and control costs.* There are standards that are not part of the budgetary procedure but that nevertheless are useful in measuring results or controlling costs. Thus, it may not be practical to develop the distribution cost budget for automobile expense to be incurred by salesperson *A* in territory *Y* through the extension of miles to be traveled by a standard cost per mile. But this standard may be helpful in checking the reasonableness of auto expenses. It may not be feasible to develop the billing department clerical expense through multiplying the standard cost per invoice rendered by the expected volume of invoices for the planning period. The clerical task might be enormous (but some concerns may develop the budget in this manner). However, the standard could prove helpful in measuring the efficiency of the billing department on an after-the-fact basis.

PROCEDURES IN SETTING STANDARDS

It is not within the scope of a basically financially oriented book to describe in great detail the methodology in setting standards. In manufacturing, for example, the setting of labor usage standards, or material usage standards, requires a specialized knowledge of the production processes and the product; and tasks of this nature are best left to the skills and experience of the engineers. However, there are a number of functional areas, where the same precision is not necessary or applicable, and where somewhat less technical standards may be of assistance. Some of the routine activities in marketing, administration, and finance fit this category, and a nonengineer with reasonable analytical ability may help in establishing some standards. Of course, it should be recognized that a great many functions in the nonmanufacturing area do not lend themselves to standard applications. Thus, few of the activities in developing and implementing an advertising program or testing its effectiveness would fit into the standard category. Devising schemes of financing for an enterprise or its customers would also fit the nonstandard category. Conducting financial relations might be difficult, indeed, to test by performance standards.

But, for those areas where standards might be applicable, this generalized procedure is suggested:

1. Select those functions where performance or cost standards might apply.
2. In a preliminary sense, observe and study the area to get an idea of the operation, the problems, and the activities.
3. Take steps to be sure the function is properly segregated in terms of the activity and responsibility; and that a proper departmentalization of costs, by logical breakdown as to nature of expense, exists.
4. Select the unit of measure to which the activity should respond and in which the standard should be expressed.
5. Review past experience and observe the various processes to select the "best" method. This may involve making changes in layout and working conditions. It may require some time and motion study or assistance by those skilled in office methods.
6. Using the best method, unit of measure, and costs, determine a preliminary standard.
7. Test the standard in several applications, perhaps with different people, and see that it meets the requirements. Perhaps some changes and compromises will be necessary to reach a satisfactory solution.
8. Apply the standard to the operation and examine the results. Only when the standard has been tested for a period of time, and the judgment of the people involved and of the supervisors has been secured, can it be concluded that the standard is fair and reasonable.

LEVEL OF THE STANDARD

A standard is a device to assist in the planning and control of the enterprise; and perhaps the emphasis in this chapter should be placed on its role in control. Its purpose is to assist in holding performance to where it should be.

But there is some confusion as to just how "tight" or "tough" a standard should be. Experience shows that standards have been set on three distinct levels:

- An ideal standard
- An average of past "good" performance
- The attainable and maintainable standard of good performance

A few clarifying statements for guidance in setting or selecting standards are necessary.

An ideal standard is one that represents the best performance under the most favorable set of circumstances. In a sense it sets a goal that seldom can be achieved. The variances are almost continuously unfavorable simply because the level of performance can rarely be achieved. If the standard is set at a usually unattainable level, the cost level sought will not be reached without changes in design or layout, or different equipment. Hence, serious doubt should exist as to its effectiveness as a control tool.

Standards are often simply an average of page performance, with perhaps the very worst performance episodes eliminated. Basically, the measuring stick reflects only what was done in the past, without the improvements in the process that could rather easily be instituted. It inherently contains the waste reflected in poor operations.

The last of the three levels is that representing good and efficient, but attainable, performance. This method includes spoilage, lost time, or other inefficiencies, but only to the extent that they cannot be practically eliminated. This standard can be met regularly or bettered, by efficient performance. This is the standard that the author believes is the most practical for planning and control where standards should be set with precision.

RESPONSIBILITY FOR SETTING STANDARDS

Who should set the standards? The correct answer is those who are qualified by training and experience to judge exactly what good or acceptable performance should be. It should be remembered that the standards must be achievable under particular circumstances. The ability to develop standards may come from experience, training, education, or expert knowledge of the operations. In most cases it takes the effort of more than one individual or department. To consider all aspects such as historical performance, competitive developments, value engineering inputs, and "should cost" analyses takes a coordinated effort. The budget department, for example, may have voluminous analyses and statistical data that can be used; however, the staff may not be familiar with current environment.

The industrial engineers may have a thorough knowledge of the operations and processes but may lack some realism when it comes to actual performance. Obviously, the production force can contribute actual experience to the evaluation process and determination of standards. In any event, it takes a detailed review and analysis of the operations to be performed if the standards are to be useful.

Standards should be set by someone without a bias who is independent of those whose performance is to be measured. The industrial engineering function and the budget department probably have the broadest background and knowledge, as well as a great deal of independence. Management must accept the responsibility for those organizations that can develop and set the most realistic standards for performance measurement. Of course, the type of standard being developed should be considered. Standards must be fair, reasonable, attainable, and acceptable to those being measured. In setting standards, a great deal of dependence is placed on the informed judgment of experienced people who are qualified, based on their experience, to make a proper determination.

ROLE OF THE FINANCIAL EXECUTIVE

The financial executive, usually the controller, is responsible for providing adequate cost performance reports for the company to management. In this role, he has a trained group of financial analysts experienced in collecting and analyzing data. With the historical cost records and the established standards, the financial executive is in an excellent position to provide management with reports noting where actual cost performance has deviated from standard. He is also able to point out performance trends so that corrective actions can be taken in a timely manner.

With the broad knowledge of all activities of the company and responsibility for total financial reporting, the financial executive is in a unique position to contribute significantly to the use of standards for performance measurement. The independence from operational responsibility provides an unbiased viewpoint that is invaluable in measuring cost performance; it contributes to the integrity of the reporting system. In addition, with the broad perspective, interrelationships can be evaluated and the standards for cost control become a more integrated management tool.

Broad knowledge of the company's operations, independence, control of the historical performance records, and a well-qualified analytical staff provide the financial executive with a unique opportunity to use standards in the financial reporting of the cost performance of the business.

MANUFACTURING ACTIVITY STANDARDS

It is beyond the scope of this book to describe how standards should be set. But some comments on the characteristics of some of the standards, as well as identifying some specific standards in use, may be helpful. For purposes of discussion, manufacturing activity standards are discussed here and are then followed by administrative, research and development, and financial standards.

Direct Material Quantity Standards

Direct material costs represent some of the most significant expenditures in many manufacturing operations. They have two variables: the quantity used and the price.

A primary source for quantity standards is the bill of material or the specifications developed by the engineering or production planning department. These documents list in detail the individual quantities for each type of material or part that will be used to manufacture the specific product. In determining the quantities, engineering will have taken into account the best kind and quality of material with due consideration to the production methods and processes. Some other factors to be evaluated and considered in setting quantity standards for material are:

- Scrap or waste of materials
- Shrinkage due to theft or lost parts
- Shelf life
- Spoilage
- Damage in handling
- Rework or remake
- Rejections due to poor quality of material or workmanship
- Salvage

An analysis of the inventory and production control records will provide data that should be helpful in establishing standard quantities in the standard cost of the finished article. Examples of reports using material quantity standards are given in Chapter 12.

Direct Material Price Standards

The planning and control of material costs require a segregation of usage variance from price variance. The former is under the control of the using department supervisor, while prices and price variance usually are the responsibility of the purchasing department. Thus, when a quantity of material in excess of standard is used, it should be costed at the standard price, so as not to mix responsibilities.

The material price usually is set by the purchasing department, since it has historical prices on the direct material, is knowledgeable as to prospective price changes in the marketplace, and is familiar with the sources of supply, delivery routes, and vendor reliability. Usually the price standard will take into account the most economical ordering quantities, the most competitive and reliable sources, and the proper timing.

Normally, price standards are set for a period of about one year. However, when major changes take place, they must be changed. This is especially true when finished product prices are sensitive to changes in direct material costs. Examples of reports relating to material price standards are provided in Chapter 12.

Direct Labor Rate Standards

Labor standards expressed in monetary terms (cost standards) are the result of multiplying the standard quantity of labor in the product by the standard labor rate. Hence, when standard costs are used to calculate product costs for pricing purposes, or to measure performance and control costs, a standard labor rate is needed.

The price of labor for a particular skill, in a specific geographical area, may lie outside the control of the individual company. It may be determined by union negotiations, or simply may be the prevailing wage rate in the area. In any event, the standard or expected wage rate for each job or skill is usually available from the industrial relations department. This standard rate would be used in the standard cost applications.

Where standard costs are used, there will usually be some labor rate variances, arising from such causes as:

- Assignment of wrong classification or skill
- Overtime
- Temporary use of a higher skill
- Improper mix of crew

When the actual labor rate in a department exceeds the standard rate, an analysis of the causes may be necessary.

Direct Labor Quantity Standards

The labor content in a product or part is usually identified as standard labor hours. Budgeting labor (planning and scheduling production) is discussed in

Chapter 11. It basically involves multiplying the labor quantity standard per part by the expected or planned level of production. In addition, the control of labor costs may involve a measurement of actual hours consumed in a department as compared to standard hours. There are any number of reasons why labor quantity variances may develop:

- Poor workmanship
- Improper tooling
- Inoperative or poorly operating machinery and equipment
- Substandard or improper material

The labor hours content of a product usually is developed by the industrial engineers, who will have a thorough knowledge of the method of production, the sequence of operations, and the skills required to properly manufacture the product. The technical data sheets provide the time-study results for each phase of the operation, together with related set-up time and personal time. This is the source of the technical labor quantity standards used in planning and control.

Chapter 11, dealing with the direct labor budget, provides examples of labor reports comparing actual and standard labor hours.

Manufacturing Expense Standards

The third area for application of standards in the production function is that of manufacturing overhead or expenses. The most widely used standard is the flexible budget (see Chapter 13), with its segregation into fixed and variable components. This approach facilitates the segregation of above-standard expenses for the experienced production level into the three causes of excess costs: (1) volume, (2) rate of expenditure (per hour), and (3) efficiency.

However, standards may be set to measure efficiency that are independent of a flexible budgeting system, for example:

- Supply expense per manhour
- Kilowatts consumed per production hour
- Repair expense per operating hour
- Perishable tools expense per operating hour
- Indirect labor per direct producing hour

Chapter 13 illustrates reports using flexible budget standards to measure expenditures in the manufacturing overhead area.

MARKETING ACTIVITY STANDARDS

Standards for marketing activity relate basically to (1) sales and (2) marketing expense.

Sales Standards

Sales standards may be set for measuring sales effectiveness and for controlling and directing selling effort. The sales budget, of course, is one standard. But other standards, which generally are independent of the budget, may be expressed either in terms of effort, or results, or the relationship of effort and result. For example, a salesperson might be required to make four calls a day — a standard of effort. Further, in a given territory, for every six calls made, four orders are expected to be received — a standard of effort and result. Or, even more simple, the salesperson is expected to achieve a sales quota of $4 million for the month — a standard of results.

These standards might be regarded as supplemental to the sales budget in that they provide information on substandard performance that, if corrected, will aid in meeting the company sales budget. Any sales executive or financial manager can devise simple reports comparing actual and standard performance. Some illustrative sales standards are these:

1. Standards of results:
   - A sales quota to be met
   - Amount of dollar volume to be secured
   - Number of units to be sold
   - Dollar volume to be sold to particular (large) customers
   - Percentage of standard gross margin to be secured
   - Amount of gross margin to be secured
   - Percentage of new product to be sold in relation to other sales
   - Average size of order to be sold
   - Number of new customers to be secured
2. Standards of effort:
   - Number of calls to be made per month
   - Number of new potential customers to be contacted per month
   - Number of demonstrations to be made in the period
3. Standards of effort related to results:
   - Number or value of orders to be secured per call
   - Amount of selling expense incurred as related to sales
   - Average amount per order for each telephone call made
   - Number of new customers per call on prospects

Marketing Expense or Distribution Cost Standards

Marketing expense standards may relate to individual performance or to group performance. By and large, many of these standards are independent of the budgetary system and may be considered supplementary control devices. Depending on local circumstances, however, some may be factors of variability in a flexible budget. See Chapter 15.

Illustrative of standards that may be applied in judging individual performance, such as that of a specific salesperson, are:

- Cost per day for traveling expense
- Cost per mile traveled for automobile expense
- Entertainment expense as a percentage of sales
- Direct selling expenses per dollar of sales

Illustrative of standards that may measure the cost effectiveness of a group activity, such as a warehouse, are:

- Cost per pound handled
- Cost per item handled
- Cost per order filled

Typical of standards that may be used to compare costs per sales territory, per product, or other similar distribution segments are:

- Cost per order received
- Cost per call
- Selling expense as a percentage of sales
- Advertising and sales promotion as a percentage of sales
- Cost per customer account
- Comparative cost per unit of differing channels of distribution

As a general statement, which control methods would be applicable to each type of cost and in each situation should be studied. Standard measures of the type discussed may supplement budgetary control.

ADMINISTRATIVE ACTIVITIES STANDARDS

To be sure, the costs of general and administrative activities must be kept within reasonable limits for the type and size of business. However, the nature of many expenses do not lend themselves directly to volume-related control. See Chapter 18. Therefore, performance-type standards are not applicable. The best standard probably is keeping such expenses at an acceptable level as related to sales or gross income. There may be some functions, involving high volumes of repetitive actions — similar to certain accounting procedures — where performance standards can be employed. These are reviewed below in "Financial Standards" of this chapter.

STANDARDS FOR RESEARCH AND DEVELOPMENT ACTIVITIES

As set forth in Chapter 17, research and development cost ordinarily is planned and controlled on a project basis. There are, however, some instances where performance standards may be helpful, although there is no substitute for the watchful eye of the supervisor.

Some applications of performance or cost standards, most largely independent of the project budget, but perhaps of some value, are these:

- Number of supply requisitions filled — supply room
- Number of tests performed per month
- Number of pages of patent applications written per day
- Number of formulas developed per quarter
- Costs per manhour per project
- Cost per patent application
- Cost per operating hour for research
- Percentage of sales spent on research and development — in total and per product line
- Cost per test (routine tests)

FINANCIAL STANDARDS

Activity Standards

In many concerns, there are a vast number of accounting and clerical functions that are voluminous and repetitive. For these, activity standards can be set and cost standards can be established to assist in controlling costs. Volume handled may be the factor of variability, in some cases, such as the billing activity. The estimated number of invoices to be handled in a planning period might be the basis for staffing the activity. Whether used in setting the flexible budget or as supplemental aids, some control can be exercised on certain operations through departmental or individual performance standards.

Examples of some routine functions, and activity standards by which they might be measured, are:

Function	Activity Measure — Number of:
Payroll	Checks written
	Employees
Billing and accounts receivable	Postings
	Invoices
	Statements prepared
Purchasing	Purchase orders handled
Typing pool	Letters typed
	Lines typed
Mail	Pieces handled
Filing	Items filed

Closely related to performance standards are cost standards. They may be applied to individual functions or to the overall activity. Most financially trained executives could review the various activities and develop or select cost standards that could be employed to measure the activity. Typical examples applicable to the accounts receivable function are these:

Activity	Unit Cost Standard — Cost Per:
Posting charges	Invoice or per posting
Preparing invoices	Invoice
	Invoice line
Preparing customer statements	Statement
	Active account
Accounts receivable correspondence	Letter
	Active account
Posting credits	Remittance
	Active account

It is to be emphasized that financial expenses must be kept to reasonable levels, and standards may assist in the effort. However, they cannot apply to all accounting/financial activities (e.g., the "thinking" activities); nor can they be applied with the same precision as in the factory.

Financial Ratios

The final category of useful standards relates not directly to human performance, but to conditions — especially to financial conditions. These are financial ratios: a type of standard found helpful in testing the profit plan, financial condition, or certain aspects of financial capability.

The financial officer of the company, and indeed, financial analysts for the industry, or the company's bankers, usually have in mind certain financial standards that should exist and by which an enterprise should be judged. They may be categorized as:

- Accepted ratios of the industry of which the company is a member
- Ratios of competing companies, particularly the leaders
- Ratios developed from the past experience of the company itself
- Ratios developed through computer models

Be that as it may, the planners and financial executives should be cognizant of certain financial ratios that may be useful in measuring the financial performance or condition of the company. Included are these:

- Current ratio
- Quick ratio
- Net sales to receivables
- Inventory turnover
- Debt to equity
- Long-term debt to equity
- Return on assets

- Return on shareholders' equity
- Selected operating ratios:
  a. Operating expenses to net sales
  b. Gross margin to net sales
  c. Net income to net sales
  d. Indirect labor to direct labor

The list is quite extensive, and the reader is referred to some of the writings on ratio analysis.[1]

REVISION OF STANDARDS

If standards are to be useful in planning and control — in measuring actual performance — then it is important they be kept up to date. Little is gained when costs or performance is compared with a standard that does not represent the "should cost" in those areas calling for precision such as labor and material usage standards.

Revision of the standards is necessary when *significant* changes take place in methods or processes, or in the prices paid for direct labor, direct material, or expenses of any type. The competitive necessity for controlling costs requires that the tools be sharpened continuously and that management not be furnished with wrong or misleading information.

---

[1] For example, see James D. Willson and John B. Campbell, *Controllership, The Work of the Managerial Accountant*, Chapter 8 (New York: John Wiley & Sons, 1981).

INCORPORATION OF STANDARDS
IN THE ACCOUNTS

This chapter has dealt with the use of standards as a planning and control device. The question might be raised as to whether the costs related to the standards should be incorporated into the financial accounting records. Basically, many companies use standards and standard costs as statistical tools without their being made a part of the cost accounting system.

By and large, the author does not recommend the use of standards in the accounting system for the nonmanufacturing-related activities or costs. However, much can be said for the adoption of standard costs in accounting for the direct material, direct labor, and manufacturing expenses in an industrial concern. A system tied into the manufacturing accounts might offer the chance of better coordination and cohesiveness in the planning and control of inventories and overall measurement of operating effectiveness.

9

Sales

INTRODUCTION

The sales plan is the foundation for the entire operating plan, and has a direct influence on the capital expenditure working capital budgets. Developing the sales plan is a complex process involving interplay between market potential and sales effort, impact of pricing policy, costs, and the other primary business functions.

A BUDGET VS. A FORECAST

In the planning and control of a business, a distinction must be made between the "sales forecast" and the "sales budget," or "sales revenue plan." A sales forecast is an estimate or projection of future sales demand. It is an extrapolation of what might happen by more or less continuing present activities or conditions. In a sense, it is rather passive. A sales plan, on the other hand, is a planning and control document that indicates what the management intends to accomplish. It represents acceptable future results that are, in part, brought about by actions the company intends to take to achieve its sales objective. It involves decision-making and action. This distinction is also important in how the business is run. A sound budgetary procedure implies aggressive management activity. If, for example, the sales budget is not met, what happens? If no corrective measures are taken, or if the sales budget is revised downward simply because actual sales were less than plan, then perhaps the sales "budget" is really only a forecast — a statistical tool of less value than a sales plan.

In most companies, a forecast has a function or place in the setting of the sales budget; but in most cases, the sales forecast is *not* the sales plan.

SALES PLAN AS BASIS FOR ENTIRE BUSINESS PLAN

The sales budget must usually be formulated before the production, purchasing, research, and financial plans can be developed or finalized.

The ultimate goal of an individual business is to make profit consistent with its social objectives; but profit can be made only by selling goods and services at a price in excess of the cost to make (or buy) and sell them. The problem is then one of determining, first, what goods and services can be sold and at what price; and next, what costs will be entailed in making and selling them. Unless a program can be clearly defined that indicates that the proceeds of the sales will exceed the costs by an amount sufficient to reward the necessary investment and compensate for the risk of uncertainty (for no program of future action can be certain), the venture should not be made; or, if already started, it should be modified or stopped and the remaining investment salvaged.

This obvious truth is so elementary that it seems foolish to state it; yet its violation constitutes one of the greatest single causes of economic waste. Securities are sold, buildings are built, machinery is purchased, material is acquired, and workers are hired to make and sell products or services in the vain hope that profit will result, when the hope has no foundation in experience and fact. Indeed, no painstaking examination is made of the facts bearing upon the venture. Every close observer of business has seen many such instances. He sees them constantly in the organization of new concerns, in new ventures within going concerns, and in the continuation of old projects in going concerns.

In summary, then, the more realistic and accurate the sales plan, the more accurate are all plans based on it — the advertising program, the manufacturing plan, the inventory, the manpower requirements, and the research activity, to name a few.

THE SALES BUDGET VS. THE STRATEGIC SALES PLAN

The sales budget may be regarded as the short-term tactical sales plan, coupled with the necessary control action. It should, therefore, closely relate to the long-term or strategic sales plan. While the long-term plan is broad in nature, the sales budget is quite specific. In many companies, the long-

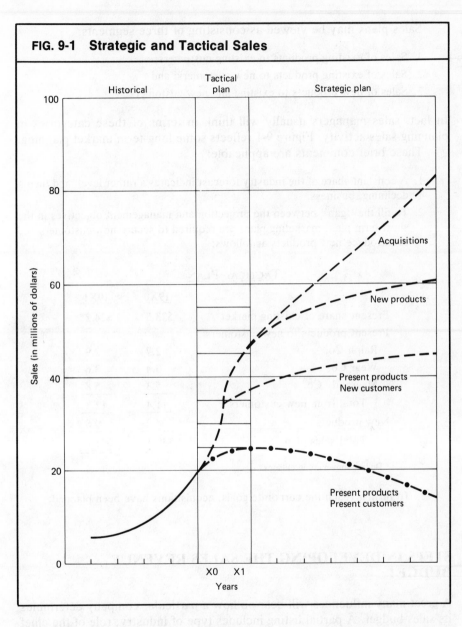

FIG. 9-1 Strategic and Tactical Sales

term plan is developed or completed prior to the annual plan. Hence, the short-term plan uses the first year of the long-term plan and expands or modifies it to transform it into a very specific plan of action. The relationship of historical sales, the short-term sales plan or budget, and the stragetic plan is illustrated in Figure 9-1. The cycle of the present product lines is also charted.

Sales plans may be viewed as consisting of three segments:

1. Sales of existing products to existing customers;
2. Sales of existing products to new customers; and
3. Sales of new products to existing and new customers.

In fact, sales managers usually will think in terms of these categories in planning sales activity. Figure 9-1 reflects some long-term market planning. These brief comments are applicable:

1. A constant share of the industry forecast indicates a rather level, and then a declining, business.
2. To fill the "gap" between the projection and management objectives in the short-term plan, marketing plans are required to secure new customers and to introduce new products as follows:

TACTICAL PLAN

	19X0	19X1
Present share of existing market	$23.5*	$24.2*
Present products to new customers:		
Ralph Co.	2.7	2.9
Wear Co.	3.4	3.6
Magraudy Co.	5.3	5.8
Total from new customers	11.4	12.3
New products	4.2	9.6
Total sales plan	$39.1	$46.1

* Dollars shown are in millions.

3. To further reach the corporate goals, acquisitions have been planned.

STEPS IN DEVELOPING THE SALES REVENUE BUDGET

A great many influences will bear on how a particular company determines its sales budget. A partial listing includes type of industry; role of the chief executive; management style of the top sales executive; size of company; availability of information; and magnitude of the marketing effort.

Outlined below are steps that might be taken in a medium-sized company selling consumer products, and where industry data is available, combined with the means to quickly analyze past internal sales activity.

Responsibility for developing the sales budget rests with the chief marketing officer. Some of the actions will be taken by him or his staff. Other actions will be of an assisting nature, performed for him by the accounting department, or the economics department, if one exists, or by the budget director.

Preplanning and Planning

Preplanning and planning involve the following steps:

1. Obtain and analyze industry data on market trends and market share.
2. Secure other data, including external and internal data bearing on general business conditions, cyclical trends, and seasonal sales variations.
3. Develop, secure, and analyze internal marketing information, such as sales by customer, territory, product, or such other segment as may be useful.
4. Perform such subanalyses as may be useful in determining profit contribution margins of products and/or customers and of territories.
5. Provide the information requested or that may be helpful to the sales executive and individual salespersons in securing sales estimates of the individual salespersons, by customer.
6. Examine matters such as sales policies, pricing practices, marketing effort, advertising and sales promotion effort, and product changes, where it appears changes may be necessary in maximizing sales of particular products.
7. Based on the data gathered and the judgment of sales executives and salespersons, arrive at a tentative sales budget in such detail as may be appropriate, such as by customer, by product, by territory, and by appropriate time period, such as month, for the planning period. The planning period may be a year to two-year time span.

   The format and method of expressing the plan, whether in physical units or monetary units, is discussed later.
8. Summarize data received from the sales manager, and analyze it in relation to corporate objectives and goals, including share of market, profit goals, compatability with other activities (production capability, research activity, physical distribution, and facilities).
9. Provide the tentative sales budget to all other functions needing such data to complete their budgets.
10. When the program appears satisfactory to the sales executive and others who must pass judgment, consolidate the data with other budgets, both operating and asset, to arrive at the overall plan.
11. Present the completed plan and relevant analyses to the chief executive for approval, and then to the board of directors.
12. Advise the sales executives that the budget has been approved and provide any necessary details.

Control

When the company short-term plan has been approved by the board of directors, which constitutes a commitment, the implementing control procedures should be followed:

1. Compare actual performance with plan, for the week, month, or such time period as may be appropriate.
2. Analyze the activity as to cause of subplan performance, if applicable.
3. Institute corrective action, if needed, by the sales executive.
4. Institute such other supplemental control or motivational tools as deemed advisable by sales management:
   - Comparisons with standards
   - Adoption of special incentives
   - Institution of new short-term promotional efforts

It can be seen that developing and implementing the sales budget requires much analysis, planning, and integrating of marketing and other effort.

METHODS OF DETERMINING SALES LEVEL

Germane to developing a sound sales plan are the methods of forecasting, and subsequently planning, sales.

The development of a sound sales program or budget finally rests with the knowledge and judgment of the sales executives. However, in putting the plan together, consideration usually will be given to both external and internal factors. External factors relate to competitive actions, market potential, industry trends, and general business conditions. They are beyond the control of the company, but they largely prescribe the sales possibilities. Internal factors include past sales experience, changes in sales methods or effort, product development, and impact of advertising and market research, to name a few. A combination of estimating methods and the use of judgment probably will be needed to arrive at a suitable sales plan. Forecasting or planning techniques might be segregated into "macro," dealing with an overall demand approach, and "micro," relating to internal demand buildup. For our purposes, some of the methods used in forecasting market demand and assisting in preparing a satisfactory sales plan may be classified as follows:

1. Mathematical/statistical methods:
   - Trend analysis
   - Correlation analysis

2. Judgmental methods (nonstatistical):
   - Sales department estimate
   - Customer surveys
   - Executive opinion composite
3. Other methods:
   - Share of the market
   - Product line analysis
   - End-use analysis
   - Combination of methods

In a certain way, all these methods are or may be related.

Mathematical/Statistical Methods

These methods require the services of a person trained in statistical techniques — a statistician, economist, or perhaps an accountant. The activity might be regarded as a staff function. Basically, the approach is one of developing a *forecast* for the company. This projection then must be converted to a plan, by superimposing management judgment. The impact of new products, additional sales efforts, an advertising program, and other influences must be weighed, and adjustments made. Basically, industry data may be used to project expected industry sales, which are then provided to the sales executives as a guide in developing the company plan. In other instances, the methods may be used directly to create a detailed forecast for the company. Or both may be prepared.

Trend Analysis.   Trend analysis involves several determinations:

1. *Long-term trend.* A long-term trend is developed using a computer, although it may be done with a calculator. The well-known least squares method may be utilized. Several less accurate, and more simple, techniques, such as moving averages or semi-averages, may be employed.

2. *Cyclical movement.*   After the long-term trend has been determined, it may be desirable to isolate the cyclical movement to measure the effect of the business cycle on sales, if this is a consideration.

3. *Seasonal pattern.* If the industry or company sales are seasonal, then this pattern may be isolated. To complete the statistical analysis, the random fluctuations must be estimated. Hence, we have the four elements to be determined:
   - ☐ Secular or long-term trend
   - ☐ Cyclical movements

☐ Seasonal patterns
☐ Random fluctuations

There are many good statistical texts for a discussion of the techniques.[1]

Correlation Analysis.   Another statistical method is correlation analysis. As the name implies, the system is founded on the correlation of some basic series with the sales of the particular company involved. For example, sales might relatively correspond with the Federal Reserve Index of Industrial Production, or an index of bank deposits. The basic series selected, in addition to moving sympathetically with company sales, should be available and reliable and, it is hoped, be one that leads the company products in its movement. An example of the correlation of product sales of one company with Federal Reserve Index of Industrial Production is shown in Figure 9-2. The dots are the annual product sales for each year plotted against the index. If the index activity has been forecasted several months or years ahead, then the company has a basis for projecting its own product sales.

Judgmental Methods

Sales Department Estimates.   The use of estimates by sales department personnel is a rather common means of arriving at a preliminary sales volume. This is especially true in smaller companies and for products where the "feel" of the market is key. In applying the technique, there are several alternatives. One plan commences with the securing of estimates from *each salesperson* as to the probable future sales in his territory. This estimate is usually by class of product, and very often is detailed by customer. Quite frequently, the salesperson is provided with a record of past sales as a guide. He may make the estimates himself on forms provided specifically for the purpose, or he may prepare the estimates in consultation with the area or branch manager. In this latter case, the manager has a better opportunity to evaluate in detail the reasons for any abnormal changes. In any event, as the estimate progresses from the salesperson upward through the supervisory force to the chief sales executive, it is subjected to more or less careful scrutiny. The division managers and sales managers examine the estimates in the light of past performance and their own ideas as to future demand. The

---

[1] See, for example, an explanation of time series analysis in Frederick E. Croxton, Dudley J. Cowden, and Ben W. Bolch, *Practical Business Statistics* (Englewood Cliffs, N.J.: Prentice-Hall, Inc., 1969), Chapters 19–21; or Spyros Makridakis and Steven C. Wheelwright, *The Handbook of Forecasting,* (New York: John Wiley & Sons, Inc., 1982).

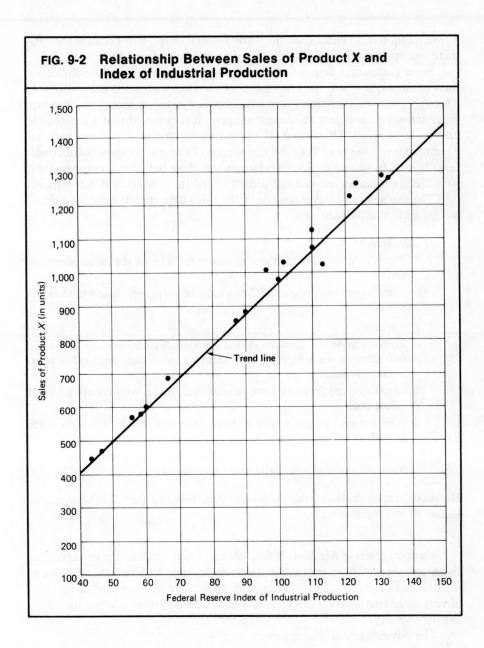

FIG. 9-2   Relationship Between Sales of Product X and
Index of Industrial Production

above method has been called the "grass-roots" approach because the estimate originates with the representative on the sales firing line.

Some companies do not feel that it is necessary to ask the sales force for their opinions. Instead, the knowledge of the sales executive group is used. Through checking and cross-checking between division managers, product sales managers, and general sales managers, it is believed that a reasonable answer is secured. Of course, if the estimates are made at too high an executive level, the benefit of the knowledge of those who know local conditions is lost. In instances where relations are close between a company and its outlets, estimates are secured directly from the jobbers and distributors.

The use solely of the estimates of the sales department may have these advantages or disadvantages:

1. *Advantages:*
   □ Places responsibility for the plan with those who must produce the sales results.
   □ Uses to the utmost the entire knowledge of the people closest to the sales picture.

2. *Disadvantages:*
   □ Risks using biased opinions in that estimates by salespersons tend to be too optimistic when the level of business activity is high, and too low when business is poor.
   □ Sometimes requires extensive time of sales force, with resulting loss of selling time.
   □ Does not give proper weight to broad economic trends which the sales force does not recognize or fails to evaluate.
   □ Results in low estimates, so as to permit a record of good performance, when the same data are used to set sales quotas.

However, recognition of the disadvantages permits the development of means to minimize them.

Customer Survey Method. The customer survey method may be used in those instances where sufficient data are lacking with which to make a realistic sales estimate, and where the manufacturer serves a limited number of very large customers. An example would be a company serving the automotive industry.

The advantages of this approach are:

• The information is obtained directly from the user whose actions will determine the sales volume.
• It provides the planner with the thinking or reasons behind the intention of the major buyers.

- It probably facilitates securing the data in the form and detail required.
- It is the only adequate manner of planning in many instances, such as an entirely new industrial product.

On the other hand, there are some obvious disadvantages:

- Dependence is almost entirely on the cooperation and judgment of the user — who may not cooperate, or who may, in fact, be ill-informed.
- It is difficult to employ where the users are numerous or not easily located.
- It may require much time and effort to secure the data.

Survey of Executive Opinion. Another common and simple method of developing a sales plan is that obtained through a weighting or combining of the views of the top executives. Under such a system, the company brings together the sales, production, research, financial, and administrative executives to secure broad coverage of experience and opinion. Each executive may make his own independent estimate by means known to himself, or the group may meet and discuss the prospects and test the reasons behind each opinion.

The sales estimates may be averaged, or the president may review each and make the final estimate. A presidential review may take into account his experience as to the relative accuracy of each executive in making sales estimates.

It can be seen that such a procedure has the advantages of wide coverage of viewpoint and perhaps of simplicity. However, unless the executives are inclined to be analytical, the answers tend to be based largely on general guesses or opinions and somewhat less on facts. Moreover, in many cases the breakdown by product lines or areas is either nonexistent or rather sketchy.

Other Methods

Remaining procedures for developing forecasts or a sales plan have been grouped together under this heading for lack of a better name. They may be applied in conjunction with some of the statistical or judgmental approaches.

Share of the Market. Under this system, the total historical industry sales are tabulated and the growth rate determined, along with the projected sales, if possible. The market share of sales obtained by the company is then calculated, and such a percentage is modified, if applicable (for impact of sales effort), and applied to projected sales to arrive at the company expected sales volume (in units or prices).

Product Line Analysis. This system might be used where differing major items are sold through different channels of distribution, where sales must be managed by product line.

Basically, it involves analysis by each product line in such way and detail as deemed useful.[2] It may be employed in conjunction with either sophisticated statistical procedures or more simple techniques.

End-Uses Analysis. This system is based on analysis of product sales by end use. For example, suppliers to the automotive industry may secure estimates of product need, such as windshield glass, from the auto company. This would be combined with other end-use (replacement market) estimates to arrive at total demand.

Obviously, information provided by a car manufacturer as to production schedules, possible new products, and sales promotion efforts is sensitive; without the manufacturer's complete confidence in a supplier, it would be hard for the supplier to secure this information.

Statistical and nonstatistical techniques may be used in developing sales estimates.

This approach is a somewhat specialized one in arriving at probable demand and closely parallels the customer survey method.

Market Simulation. Given the progress in market research, and the development of computers, some of the larger companies are creating models of their product market. With the input of marketing management, market simulation is being performed to measure the influence of, for example, different advertising programs, sales promotion efforts, or other marketing strategy changes. This is another aid in arriving at an acceptable sales plan.

Combined Method. A sound approach to sales planning is through the use of several methods. If answers developed by statistical techniques, by the estimates of the sales department, and by a survey of executive opinion are individually in somewhat the same area, then there is some reason to be more confident of the figures. Certainly, knowledge that statistical methods or careful analysis of past sales performance is to be brought into play will tend to force the executives to be more careful in their estimates. It is in this area that the chief accounting official can be of great value in seeing that the necessary analyses are made, and that the estimates are subjected to a

---

[2] See the earlier discussion as to types of analyses or subanalyses that might be appropriate.

critical review. This approach is fundamental because the sales budget is usually the basis of all other budgets.

It is to be further noted that the approach to sales estimating can begin in one of two ways: It may begin through estimating the sales of each customer, territory, and salesperson, and integrating these individual figures into a composite program for the company as a whole; or it may begin by a determination of the total planned sales volume and the subsequent apportionment to individual territories, products, and salespersons.

Illustration of Combined Method. The results obtained by one method may be checked against those of another, with a final estimate based on further study. To reduce this to a very simple illustration, the following figures may be assumed:

Sales of last period	$1,000,000
Executives' decision as to volume to be secured for next period (8% increase)	1,080,000

In contrast, the following salespersons' estimates are more optimistic than appear justified by the expected trend of general conditions. Assume now that *A*'s situation is reviewed and found to be entirely too optimistic.

SALESPERSONS' ESTIMATES

Salesperson	Sales of Last Period	Estimate for Next Period	Percent Increase
A	$ 500,000	$ 575,000	15.0%
B	300,000	336,000	12.0
C	200,000	220,000	10.0
Total	$1,000,000	$1,131,000	13.1%

His sales are already large, his territory is fully exploited, and the outlook for some of his largest industrial customers is not as favorable as for business generally. It is not at all likely that his volume can come up to even the increase expected in business generally. Instead of a 15 percent increase, he will do well, in the face of this situation, to secure a 5 or 6 percent increase. To a lesser degree, the same situation obtains for salesperson *B*. Here, however, there are certain products that have been neglected, and, with proper emphasis on these, his increase should reach 10 percent. Salesperson *C*, on the other hand, has failed to cover his customers thoroughly and to push all products. His sales are low and with proper effort can be increased by 14 percent instead of the 10 percent which he estimates.

As a result of combining the judgment of both executives and salespersons, and bringing to bear all statistical aid, the following estimates are developed:

Salesperson	Percent Increase	Estimate for Next Period
A	6.0%	$ 530,000
B	10.0	330,000
C	14.0	228,000
Total	8.8%	$1,088,000

Here it is apparent that both salespersons and executives were wrong in their original estimates. The illustration is perhaps oversimple. The analysis must usually extend to individual products and customers, but the basic idea of harmonizing the two views is sound.

SOURCES OF INFORMATION USEFUL IN FORECASTING

In an attempt to determine probable future trends in economic activity, a great deal of time and effort has been spent in developing comprehensive measures of individual segments. For example, the Bureau of Economic Analysis (BEA) of the U.S. Department of Commerce publishes certain indicators. A partial listing of graphs and charts from a recent issue of *Business Conditions Digest* is as follows:

Part I. *Cyclical Indicators:*
    A. Composite Indexes and Their Components
        A1 Composite Indexes
        A2 Leading Index Components
        A3 Coincident Index Components
        A4 Lagging Index Components
    B. Cyclical Indicators by Economic Process
        B1 Employment and Unemployment
        B2 Production and Income
        B3 Consumption, Trade, Orders, and Deliveries
        B4 Fixed Capital Investment
        B5 Inventories and Inventory Investment
        B6 Prices, Costs, and Profits
        B7 Money and Credit
    C. Diffusion Indexes and Rates of Change
        C1 Diffusion Indexes
        C2 Selected Diffusion Index Components
        C3 Rates of Change

Part II. *Other Important Economic Measures:*

   A. National Income and Product

      A1 GNP and Personal Income

      A2 Personal Consumption Expenditures

      A3 Gross Private Domestic Investment

      A4 Government Purchases of Goods and Services

      A5 Foreign Trade

      A6 National Income and Its Components

      A7 Saving

      A8 Shares of GNP and National Income

   B. Prices, Wages, and Productivity

      B1 Price Movements

      B2 Wages and Productivity

   C. Labor Force, Employment, and Unemployment

      C1 Civilian Labor Force and Major Components

   D. Government Activities

      D1 Receipts and Expenditures

      D2 Defense Indicators

   E. U.S. International Transactions

      E1 Merchandise Trade

      E2 Goods and Services Movements

   F. International Comparisons

      F1 Industrial Production

      F2 Consumer Prices

      F3 Stock Prices

Part III. *Appendixes:*

   A. MCD and Related Measures of Variability (*January 1981 issue*)

      QCD and Related Measures of Variability (*January 1981 issue*)

   B. Current Adjustment Factors

   C. Historical Data for Selected Series

   D. Descriptions and Sources of Series (*See "Alphabetical Index — Series Finding Guide"*)

   E. Business Cycle Expansions and Contractions (*July 1981 issue*)

   F. Specific Peak and Trough Dates for Selected Indicators (*April 1981 issue*)

   G. Experimental Data and Analyses

   Alphabetical Index — Series Finding Guide

   Titles and Sources of Series

Of particular value to some businesses are the composite indexes, which are listed in A1 above: one composite leading index, developed from the specific leading indicators, one composite coincident index, developed from the coincident components, and one composite lagging index. A particular business may find close correlation with certain indices. Of particular interest are three groups of indicators:

1. Twelve *leading* indicators, or series that usually reach peaks or troughs before general economic activity;
2. Four roughly *coincident* indicators, or series that tend to move with aggregate economic activity (more or less);
3. Six *lagging* indicators, or series that usually reach turning points after the aggregate economic activity has.

The components of each classification (from the *Business Conditions Digest*) are as follows.

TWELVE LEADING INDICATORS SERIES

Series No.

1. Average workweek, production workers, manufacturing (hours)
3. Layoff rate, manufacturing (per 100 employees), inverted scale
8. New orders for consumer goods and materials (1972 dollars)
12. Net business formation (index: 1967 = 100)
19. Stock prices, 500 common stocks (index: 1941–1943 = 10)
20. Contracts and orders for plant and equipment, 1972 dollars (billions of dollars)
29. New building permits, private housing units (index: 1967 = 100)
32. Vendor performance, percent of companies receiving slower deliveries (percent)
36. Net change in inventories on hand and on order, 1972 dollars, smoothed (annual rate, billions of dollars)
92. Change in sensitive crude materials, prices, smoothed
104. Change in total liquid assets, smoothed (percent)
106. Money supply — M2 — in 1973 dollars (billions of dollars)

FOUR COINCIDENT INDICATORS

Series No.

41. Employees on nonagricultural payrolls (millions)
47. Industrial production, total (index: 1967 = 100)
51. Personal income less transfer payments, 1972 dollars (annual rate, billions of dollars)
57. Manufacturing and trade sales, 1972 dollars (billions of dollars)

Six Lagging Indicators

Series No.

62. Labor cost per unit of output, manufacturers (index: 1967 = 100)
70. Manufacturing and trade inventories, 1972 dollars (billions of dollars)
72. Commercial and industrial loans outstanding, weekly reporting large commercial banks (billions of dollars)
91. Average duration of unemployment (weeks — inverted scale)
95. Ratio, consumer installment credit to personal income (percent)
109. Average prime rate charged by banks (percent)

Data available from the BEA for use in economic analysis includes such publications as:

1. *Business Conditions Digest* — previously mentioned, which is a monthly report for analyzing economic fluctuations over a short span of years.
2. *Survey of Current Business* — a monthly report for analyzing current economic developments.
3. *Business Statistics* — a biennial reference volume (currently back to 1947) containing the statistical series reported currently in the Survey of Current Business — some 2500 time series.

In addition to data published by the Department of Commerce, other federal departments regularly issue useful information. Some sources are:

- Department of Labor
- Department of Agriculture
- Bureau of Mines
- U.S. Government Printing Office

Finally, state governments, trade associations, universities, banks, the Federal Reserve Board, and financial services such as Standard & Poor's or Moody's may provide helpful data.

Clearly, there is a host of information sources that financial executives or business people will find useful in sales projection analysis. In addition, the public libraries, and the libraries of those institutions mentioned above, usually are very cooperative in giving assistance.

SALES ANALYSIS — THE STARTING POINT OF THE SALES BUDGET

Usually, the first step in the development of the sales budget is a thorough analysis of past sales performance. What have been the sales, the cost to sell, and the resulting profits or losses of each salesperson or other segment being analyzed, and how do they compare with respect to one another? A study of what has been done does not supply the answer to the question as to what can and should be done, but it affords a starting point and supplies valuable signals as to the directions in which further investigation should proceed. To illustrate, assume that Salespersons A and B have territories of approximately the same potentialities and that a comparison of their performance reveals the following:

	Salesperson A		Salesperson B		Combinations of Best Performance	
	Amount	Per-centage	Amount	Per-centage	Amount	Per-centage
Sales	$1,000,000	100	$2,000,000	100	$2,000,000	100
Gross profit	400,000	40	600,000	30	800,000	40
Selling cost	300,000	30	500,000	25	500,000	25
Profit	$ 100,000	10	$ 100,000	5	$ 300,000	15

Signals for investigation are available here. If the territories possess the same potentialities and other conditions are similar, then:

A should produce sales of $2 million instead of $1 million.

B should produce a gross profit of 40 percent instead of 30 percent.

A's sales should require a selling cost of 25 percent instead of 30 percent.

Total profit for the two salesmen should be $600,000 instead of $200,000.

Before making the budget for the coming period, investigation should be made of the cause of A's low volume, B's low gross profit percentage, and A's high selling costs.

Analysis of Past Performance Not Enough

Analysis of past performance, while valuable in itself, is not enough. It is easily conceivable that a still more profitable program for each salesperson would be:

	Amount	Percentage
Sales	$1,800,000	100
Gross profit	720,000	40
Selling cost	360,000	20
Profit	$ 360,000	20

This program would result in a total profit of $720,000 instead of the present $200,000.

For clarity, this illustration has been oversimplified. The practical complexities are great. It is difficult to measure exactly the potentialities of territories; many items with different gross profit margins may enter into the line; selling costs consist of many items, some within and some beyond the control of salespersons, many of the selling costs are joint costs and are difficult to separate and analyze. Every executive who has attempted this type of analysis has met discouraging obstacles. He has been faced with a hundred reasons (many in the nature of alibis), given by salespersons, department heads, and branch managers, why the analyses are unreliable; but the principle involved is sound, workable, and of the greatest importance. The concern which examines its past sales performance, proceeds from that point to a study of its future sales possibilities, and enforces a program based upon such possibilities is the one most likely to outdistance its competitors.

Numerous Analyses Required

In the study of past sales performance there are, in most concerns, numerous analyses and cross-analyses which can and should be made. It is necessary for the controller and sales executives to select from these the ones that are significant and useful in guiding the future course of the sales program. Some analyses must be made continuously, others only periodically as a test of the efficacy of the program. For example, the records may be designed so as to signal continuously the cessation of orders from any customer or a significant decrease in sales to any customer or class of customers. In fact, such records may be refined to the point of continuously signaling a decrease in sales of each of several classes of commodities to any customer. On the other hand, only periodic studies may be necessary to test the profitableness of orders of varying sizes or of customers whose annual purchases fall within certain limits.

The nature of the analyses of sales and selling cost naturally varies with the type of business; however, the following are illustrative.

Analysis by Commodities. Such an analysis should reveal which commodities:

- Are being neglected and offer promise of increased volume.
- Are returning insufficient gross profit and whether this is due to competitive conditions, unsatisfactory price policy, or excessive production cost.
- Move too slowly and what adjustments are necessary in production and inventory policies.
- Require excessive distribution cost and what items of cost are excessive.

- Do not return sufficient net profit, the reasons why, and the changes necessary to make them profitable.
- Offer no promise of profit; would result in indirect losses if dropped; and should be dropped.

In order to answer such questions, it may be necessary to cross-analyze the sales of various commodities by customers, channels of distribution, terms, methods of sale, sizes of orders, territories, salespersons, and methods of delivery and service.

These analyses may be extended to individual commodities or to classes of homogeneous items. Where thousands of items are carried, such analyses as suggested above would appear to involve a vast amount of work. However, it is not always necessary to include every item. It frequently happens that the bulk of the sales are in a comparatively few items. In one concrete case, for example, a concern carries over 30,000 items in stock ready for shipment. Eighty percent of the money volume, however, is in some 300 items, another 15 percent of the money volume is represented by items which fall in natural classifications of some 40 groups, leaving not more than 5 percent of the money volume in a miscellaneous unclassified group. This is a fairly typical situation. While the task of analyzing the sales and selling cost of 30,000 items appears somewhat formidable, it seems far less so when reduced to 340 items and groups.

Analysis by Customers. Such an analysis should reveal which customers:

- Offer promise of more volume and in what lines it may be secured.
- Return insufficient gross profit margin and whether this is due to low prices, terms, or purchases restricted to low-profit lines.
- Require excessive distribution cost and what items are excessive.
- Are unprofitable, why, and what adjustments are required to make them profitable.
- Offer no promise of profit and should be dropped.

In order to answer such questions, it may be necessary to cross-analyze the sales to customers by commodities, channels of distribution, terms, methods of sale, sizes of orders, and methods of delivery and service.

The analysis may be directed either to individual customers or to classes of customers. In the latter case, the classification of customers may be based upon the average volume of purchases or the nature of the service rendered.

The study may be directed not only to present customers but also to those who have been lost. A study of the causes of loss of customers may contribute valuable information for future plans.

Analysis by Territories. Territories usually consist of natural market areas, states, counties, towns, or prescribed sales routes. An analysis according to such territories should reveal which territories:

- Offer promise of more volume and in what lines it should be secured.
- Return insufficient gross profit and whether this is due to competitive conditions, improper price policy, or neglect of high-profit lines.
- Entail excessive distribution costs and which cost items are excessive.
- Are not sufficiently profitable, why, and what changes in selling and service methods would be necessary to make them profitable.
- Offer no promise of adequate profit, what indirect losses would be suffered by the abandonment of such territories, and which of such territories should be wholly or partially abandoned.

In order to answer such questions, it may be necessary to cross-analyze the business done in each territory by channels of distribution, methods of sale, commodities, customers, sizes of orders, salespersons, and methods of delivery and service.

Analysis by Salespersons. An analysis of the work of each salesperson should reveal which salespersons:

- Are securing inadequate volume and on which commodities, and to which customers the sales are unsatisfactory.
- Are returning inadequate gross profit and why.
- Have excessive distribution costs including their own expenses, and what cost items are excessive.
- Are returning inadequate profit, and what corrections are necessary to make their work profitable.

Here, also, other cross-analyses may be required.

Other Analyses. Many other analyses and cross-analyses of sales and distribution costs will be found useful in particular concerns. For example, analysis may be made by channels of distribution, such as through wholesalers or directly to the consumer; by method of sale, such as mail order, or through company-owned stores; by organization division — branches or districts; by method of delivery; by size of order; by terms of sale — cash, open account, installment, and C.O.D.; by time of sales — seasons, quarters, months, weeks, and hours of the day; by the size of units of product sold — dozens, half-dozens, full cases, and broken cases; and by the quality of products — brands, first, seconds, and mill run.

Another type of analysis of past sales performance is that which attempts to find the cause of weakness in performance. For example, analyses may be made to determine the cause of losing customers, the causes of returns and adjustments, the responsibility for unsatisfactory service, and stock shortage.

Extent of Analysis

It is not to be inferred that all the analyses and cross-analyses suggested above are necessary in the same concern, but rather that from many possible analyses, the useful ones must be selected.

Generally speaking, the analysis of past sales performance must be extended to gross sales, sales deductions, cost of goods sold, gross profit, and distribution cost in order to provide the information needed. Moreover, often it will be found necessary to distinguish between *direct* and *out-of-pocket* costs or expenses on the one hand, and *continuing* or *period* costs on the other. For example, a given territory may reflect a slight operating loss. Yet, included in the charges may be a substantial amount of allocated general selling expenses which would not be reduced if the territory were abandoned. Such costs must be known in formulating decisions on territorial coverage.

Finally, and in summary, the accountant making the analyses should realize that the various studies are being made to search out weaknesses and improve the sales program and the related direction of sales effort. The planning is for *profits,* not merely sales volume.

Sales in Physical Units

Wherever practicable, the analysis of past sales performance should be made in terms of physical units, of goods or services, as well as dollars. This eliminates the element of price fluctuation. Where this is not practicable, a price index should be developed and maintained whereby the money volume of different periods can be converted into physical volume for comparative purposes.

Data Must Be Interpreted

The possible analysis of past performance relative to sales and selling costs is almost limitless, and a word of warning is in point. No amount of analysis is valuable in itself. A hundred pages of sales statistics revealing what has been sold, to whom, how, when, and at what cost will neither increase sales nor reduce selling costs. Only the intelligent interpretation of such data and the translation of their signals into future action justify their cost. This warning should be directed somewhat more to controllers, whose duty it is to gather the data, than to sales and general executives, whose duty it is to act upon them.

Some budget officers, in their enthusiasm to supply information, rate higher when tested by quantity than by quality. They supply raw material rather than finished product. Most of such material is wasted. It is one thing to supply a wealth of information to sales executives relative to the sales to every customer or of every product, in the expectation that such executives will pore through this material for important deductions; and quite another to say that the sales made to Customer *A* by Method *Y* have been subjected to the light of investigation, and for reasons given, it appears that the sales department should consider the desirability of shifting more effort to Customer *B* or to Method *X*. If to this are appended the specific data which will be needed by the sales executives in making the decisions, the effort will be fruitful. If such information is not coming through to the sales executives, the deficiency is in the controller's department.

In many instances the investigation must be a joint effort of the controller and sales executive; in others, the budget officer can do no more than suggest the desirability of further investigation of such nature that it must be undertaken by the sales department.

PERSONAL FACTORS IN SALES BUDGETING

It is, of course, fine to make sales analyses. Yet, the final sales program, to be of practical use, must represent a compromise between sales possibilities — as indicated by statistical analysis — and individual capacities of salespersons and sales executives. Individual capacities are limited and the sales program must be adjusted to such limitations. It is one thing to ascertain statistically what a territory should produce in sales volume and quite another to estimate what a given salesman or district manager, if placed on that territory, will immediately produce. The former is an impersonal factor, the latter a personal factor. Both factors are important and the two must be combined in the development of the final program. Time is required for the training and development of personnel, weaknesses are constantly being revealed and must be corrected, and temporary adjustments are often necessary. There is seldom a time when the sales organization is operating as desired in every quarter. The standardization of operations is more difficult with sales than with production.

Not only must the personal element be duly considered in sales planning, but also the intimate knowledge of salespersons and sales executives must be fully utilized. The relative importance of these factors in an individual concern largely determines the precise method to be followed in formulating the final program.

EXPRESSION OF THE SALES BUDGET

Terms

The sales budget should be developed and expressed in terms of physical units, such as tons, pieces, and yards, as well as in dollar amount. This is necessary in order fully to coordinate the sales program with the purchasing and production programs, which must be expressed chiefly in terms of physical units. Moreover, this makes possible the separation of the price and physical volume factors. This separation assists later in the analysis of variations between the budget and the actual results.

There is an exception to this rule in certain concerns, particularly merchandising, where the lines are so varied and numerous as to make the expression in units virtually impossible. Here the entire program — sales and purchases — may be expressed in monetary units. This is true, for example, in drug sundries. Even in such cases, it is often possible to use physical units for a considerable number of items of major importance.

Even in some manufacturing concerns, the number of items made and sold (when different styles and sizes are considered) runs into the thousands. While a large number of items complicates the problem of sales budgeting, it will often be found that the bulk of the money volume is in a comparatively few items. These major items can be grouped separately and resolved into physical units. Minor items can then be expressed in terms of money volume only. For example, a certain manufacturer of small tools makes and sells over 6,000 items. Detailed plans in terms of physical units are made for only 400 of these items, but these 400 items constitute more than 80 percent of the total money volume of the business. A program of this type usually extends itself gradually to more and more items until it covers the major part of the business and often serves to eliminate many slow-moving and unprofitable items.

Classifications

No general statement can be made as to the extent to which sales should be classified and subclassified in developing the sales budget. In one case, it may be necessary to plan the sales of each salesperson to each of his customers and to show the volume of each of several classes of goods which he is expected to sell to each customer. Again, it may be necessary only to plan the volume of each class of goods to be sold in each territory. Obviously, the extent to which such classification should go depends entirely upon the circumstances of the individual case. Classifications commonly useful are by:

- Products or commodities
- Territories

- Customers
- Channels of distribution
- Organization division (i.e., branches, stores, departments)
- Salespersons
- Terms of sale
- Method of sale
- Method of delivery
- Size of units of product (e.g., full cases, broken lots)
- Size of orders

Each of these classifications lends itself to numerous subclassifications. For example, the sales of each product may be further classified by territories, customers, channels of distribution, and so forth.

The sales and accounting executives must strike a balance between the value of refining the information relative to past and potential sales and the cost of securing the information.

Budgeting Orders Received as Well as Shipments. In many concerns, there is a considerable lapse of time between the date of receiving orders and making shipments. Sales are usually recorded at the time of shipment or delivery. Since the sales budget usually serves as a basis for financial, purchasing, and production plans, and since these are more directly related in point of time to orders received than to shipments, it is frequently desirable to extend the detailed estimates to cover orders received as well as shipments. Provision should be made for cancellation of orders.

Sales Deductions. The detailed sales budget should cover all major sales deductions common to the business, such as returns, allowances, freight allowances, extra discounts which are not considered as price adjustments, and special service allowances. Each of these should be carefully estimated on the basis of past experience and special studies as to future expectations. This is desirable not only for the purpose of determining net sales, but also as a means of exercising control over these deductions.

Length of Sales Budget Period

The length of the period in advance for which the budget generally should be made is discussed in Chapter 2. The sales budget should be projected only so far as it is possible, with intensive analysis and study, reasonably to predict what can and will be sold with a given amount of sales effort. The periods most usually selected are the quarter, half-year, year, or two years. These are then broken down into months or corresponding periods such as the four weeks' period. This permits a closer coordination with buying, production, and finance.

The length of the sales planning period may vary for different products and territories in the same concern. Moreover, tentative programs may be developed for a year, then revised and definitely established for shorter periods. In some cases as, for example, with utilities, the general sales program must be projected for quite long periods as a basis for planning important capital expenditures.

The fact that the future and related conditions can never be foretold with 100 percent accuracy does not remove the value of the planning effort. A concern must seek the one program which offers the most promise, and this can be found only as effort is made to predict the results of alternative methods. The planning effort loses its value, however, when it is projected to a point where probable conditions become too uncertain to serve as a basis for intelligent action. The factors which usually determine the length of the sales budget period are:

☐ *Seasonal nature of production, sales, or products.* Here, the budget period usually conforms to the season. Christmas cards, ice skates, and electric fans serve as illustrations.

☐ *Style.* Where style is a major factor, the sales program may be timed to the period of normal style change. Women's clothing and shoes are illustrative.

☐ *Manufacturing and buying customs.* The custom of producing new automobile models annually and of presenting new furniture semiannually illustrates the influence of manufacturing and buying customs on sales plans.

☐ *Stability of markets.* Established and stabilized markets permit longer sales planning periods than those in which there are frequent changes in products and frequent fluctuations in volume and price. Baking soda and paper clips illustrate products of stability.

☐ *Length of production period.* If the normal production period is long and if the product is stored following production, then the sales program must cover a period from the time of acquiring raw materials to sale of finished product.

☐ *Extent of past experience.* If the products are new or if data on past experience are meager, the sales program may be developed for short periods until more information is available.

☐ *Views or outlook of executives.* The sales program must at times be made to conform to the views or outlook of major executives. If, for example, by custom they think in terms of quarters, it may be desirable to develop the sales program accordingly.

☐ *Stability of general economic conditions.* As with all budgeting, the sales program can be projected further in times of comparative stability of economic conditions than in times of marked uncertainty.

Revision of Sales Program

When unforeseen and unexpected conditions arise which indicate that the sales program cannot be executed as planned, the program must be promptly revised; otherwise it will not serve either as a basis for coordination or as a means of control of sales operations. Since other operations such as production, purchasing, and finance are based largely upon the sales budget, it is particularly important that the sales program be promptly revised to accord with changed conditions.

ASSEMBLING THE SALES PLAN AND MONITORING PERFORMANCE

The preliminary sales estimates or plans for the short-term budget probably will be modified by successive echelons of sales management and top management until the short-term sales plan represents a suitable and reasonable objective. It will, of course, be influenced strongly by the planned marketing effort and competitor activity. Thus, the sales plan must be closely coordinated with the distribution cost budget; the two are meshed together, one dependent upon the other.

The total sales revenue plan must be assembled on a responsibility basis — so that each segment of the sales organization knows what its part of the total sales plan is. And, since financial statements must be prepared by predetermined time periods, the data must be available in the smallest denominator or time period needed for control, but presented or analyzed by the time frame most appropriate for the viewing entity — for example, weekly or monthly for the sales force, and by quarters or annually for the board of directors. An overall summarized sales revenue plan, by division, for a decentralized company is illustrated in Figure 9-3. The subsegment for a branch is shown in Figure 9-4. Both presentations are simple; but the thought that went into the plan was extensive.

Role of Budget Officer

The responsibility for the development of the sales plan, and its subsequent implementation, of course, is that of the chief sales executive. However, the budget officer and his related financial associates can, or should, offer assistance in interpreting sales in financial terms and communicating their findings to the sales executive. They are, or should be, the skilled financial analysts of the company. They are presumed to understand the significance of the figures, including the cost-volume-profit relationships and the contri-

FIG. 9-3   Consolidated Annual Sales Plan

THE JOHNSON COMPANY
CONSOLIDATED SALES REVENUE PLAN
For the Year Ending 12/31/X1
(dollars in thousands)

Division	1st Quarter	2d Quarter	Second Half	19X1 Yearly Total	19XX Indicated Total	Increase/(Decrease) Amount	Percentage
Home appliances	$ 6,000	$ 7,000	$ 14,000	$ 27,000	$ 25,000	$ 2,000	8.0%
Steel products	13,500	17,900	43,600	75,000	47,000	28,000	59.6
Military products	14,800	19,900	47,300	82,000	60,000	22,000	36.7
Automotive products	16,100	14,300	25,600	56,000	74,000	(18,000)	(24.3)
Total	$50,400	$59,100	$130,500	$240,000	$206,000	$34,000	16.5%

FIG. 9-4 Branch Office Sales Budget

THE JOHNSON COMPANY
LOS ANGELES BRANCH
STEEL PRODUCTS DIVISION

SALES BUDGET — 19X1
(dollars in thousands)

Salesperson	January	February	March	1st Qtr. Total	Year 19X1	Year 19XX	Increase Amount	Increase Percentage
Campbell	$ 810	$ 830	$ 860	$ 2,500	$10,100	$ 6,500	$ 3,600	55.4%
Root	700	760	790	2,250	9,400	4,300	5,100	118.6
Buck	690	700	700	2,090	9,100	3,100	6,000	193.4
Wear	600	650	710	1,960	8,700	2,700	6,000	222.2
Johns	250	270	290	810	3,700	1,300	2,400	184.6
Rodriguez	190	200	210	600	3,000	1,100	1,900	172.7
Total	$3,240	$3,410	$3,560	$10,210	$44,000	$19,000	$25,000	131.6%

Note to branch manager:
Budgeted gross margin, less branch expenses:

First quarter $2,040,000
Year $10,700,000

bution margins of the product lines. They should be able to ferret out significant trends and relationships that ought to be communicated to the sales executives.

In assisting in the preparation of a sound sales revenue plan and marketing plan, the budget director is responsible for the following.

1. *Planning phase:*
   - ☐ Assure that there exists, in writing, a practical procedure for developing the sales plan. This should include:
     - Specific steps to be followed in developing the sales plan, with responsibility assigned for each.
     - The required format in submitting the sales data.
     - The scheduled due date of the various kinds of data.
     - Provision for securing the necessary statistical and other related data needed by those of the sales staff developing the forecasts and plan.
   - ☐ Make analyses of past sales performance and provide it to the sales executive and staff for use in developing the sales plan, including significant trends, relationships, and interpretation, if warranted.
   - ☐ Upon receipt of the sales plan from the sales executive, analyze it for consistency, completeness, proper format, and any other significant observations that should be brought to the attention of the sales executive.
   - ☐ Ascertain that those other organizational units who need the sales plan data for their budget preparation have it, and in acceptable form for their own use.
   - ☐ Prepare any related supplemental data to be derived from the sales plan for inclusion in the final plan for net sales revenues, such as a plan for sales deductions, returns and allowances, and cash discounts.
   - ☐ As requested, assist the sales staff in preparing the tentative sales revenue budget. This might include computer applications in developing dollar volume from estimates of physical units and trend analyses.
   - ☐ Incorporate the sales plan into the consolidated short-term plan (or long-term), and advise responsible executives of apparent inconsistencies or weak areas, if any. When the iteration is complete, prepare the final consolidated plan.

2. *Control phase:*
   - ☐ Ascertain that the periodic control reports needed by the sales executive are issued — and in a format desired by him — and are properly interpreted or understood.
   - ☐ Check to assure that follow-up action, if needed, has been taken (the written procedure should provide what type of correction is required).

☐ As appropriate, incorporate comparison of budget and actual performance, by responsibility, in the reports going to top management, with interpretive commentary if required.

☐ See that the various sales executives receive other supplemental control reports, or subanalyses requested by them.

☐ Where applicable, arrange for budget revisions.

Sales Budget Reports

The success of any budgetary program depends in part on whether there is sufficient control after the plans are made, and this often depends upon the adequacy of the reporting system. Those responsible for controlling sales and meeting budget must be receptive to the report and must be motivated to take remedial action, if called for.

Kind of Reporting Reflected. Sales budget reports should, of course, follow the principles of good communication. They ought to reflect four kinds of reporting:

1. *Responsibility reporting.* The data presented basically should relate to the responsibilities of the person reported upon. The organization chart and position description responsibilities are reflected in the document. The items reported should be those largely controllable by the reportee.

2. *Exception reporting.* Preferably, a sales report should avoid a mass of non-significant detail, and present only that data which reflects out-of-line performance — better than budget or plan performance or under-budget results.

3. *Interpretive reporting.* Where useful, the figures should be interpreted. Thus, the reasons a division, branch, or salesperson failed to achieve budget could be given. Explanations that might be helpful to the recipient in correcting performance should be made. Perhaps the financial representative explains *what* happened, and the sales supervisor states *why,* and suggests *remedial* action.

4. *Person-oriented reporting.* Especially in presenting sales information to the extent practicable, the reporting should be adopted to the management style of the user. For example, graphs may be more effective than tables. Brief, to-the-point, summarized reports may be more useful than longer reports. The written report might be supplemented with a brief oral review.

Content of Reports. In general, every attempt should be made to have the sales budget report fit a real need. The content of the sales report, whether incorporating the budget, or other control data, will vary from company to company, depending on the industry, management style, nature of the problem, and background and training of the recipient. Some suggested contents are these:

- Comparison of budgeted and actual sales, by month and year-to-date
- Comparison of quota and actual sales for period and year-to-date
- Tabulation of sales orders received and on hand, compared to plan
- Analysis of variances between budget and actual sales
- Comparison of actual sales and percent change from base, with industry data
- Provision of sales to expense relationships
- Presentation of sales to gross profit or contribution margin, compared to plan or standard
- Provision of standards comparison — sales to the selected standard

The report must be designed to the need and fit the requirements of the sales executive or salesperson involved.

Sales Budget Reports — Illustrated. Sales budget reports usually compare actual and budgeted performance of the segment being reported upon. An example of an overall sales report, by division, is shown in Figure 9-5. A graphic report on actual and budgeted sales by months, compared with the prior year, is illustrated in Figure 9-6. This three-way measurement is popular among many top managers and chief sales executives. An exception report, emphasizing those salespersons substantially above budget and those not achieving plan is presented in Figure 9-7. Finally, a report for an individual salesperson — his or her own record — is shown in Figure 9-8.

The reports illustrated follow the "responsibility" principle. Of course, a wide variety of actual-budget comparisons for information or planning purposes may be made by other segments such as product, method of sale, size of order, territory, or channel of distributions. And any number of subanalyses can be made available.

Frequency of Reports. The frequency in which a sales budget report, or any sales report, is issued should depend upon its usefulness or the need of the reader. Depending on the industry, management style, condition of performance, and other factors, a sales report may be published daily, weekly, or monthly. It is not uncommon for the chief executive or the top sales officer to want to see the daily sales report as the top priority item each business morning. Or the executive may want to see a daily report of orders received and on hand, in physical units by product or in monetary terms. Unsatisfactory conditions may require a daily report until normal performance exists; thereafter, a weekly report might suffice.

FIG. 9-5 Summary Sales Performance Report by Division

THE JOHNSON COMPANY

COMPARISON OF ACTUAL AND PLANNED SALES

Month and Year to Date

(dollars in thousands)

Division	Month of April			Year-to-Date		
	Actual	Planned	Over (Under) Plan	Actual	Planned	Over (Under) Plan
Adhesives	$10,320	$ 9,100	$1,220[1]	$ 32,400	$ 35,400	($3,000)[1]
Plastics	9,210	9,010	200[2]	33,900	32,800	1,100
Resins	7,300	7,460	(160)	34,500	29,000	5,500
Molding compounds	6,200	6,100	100	25,700	24,400	1,300
Subtotal divisions	33,030	31,670	1,360	126,500	121,600	4,900
Intercompany	(2,000)	(600)	(1,400)[2]	(7,000)	(6,000)	(1,000)
Consolidated sales	$31,030	$31,070	($ 40)	$119,500	$115,600	$3,900

(1) Adhesives made a special sales effort in the Southwest, which was successful, in an effort to get closer to plan.

(2) The Plastics Division is better than plan solely because of purchases by the Molding Compounds Division of $1,900,000 over plan. The under-budget condition of $1,700,000 results from the Sharen flats fire and plant closedown.

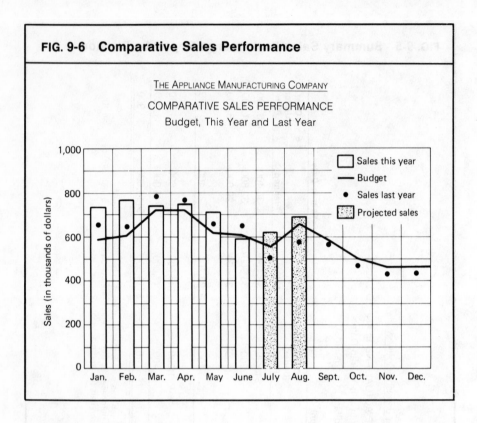

FIG. 9-6 Comparative Sales Performance

THE APPLIANCE MANUFACTURING COMPANY

COMPARATIVE SALES PERFORMANCE
Budget, This Year and Last Year

Where data are gathered from remote areas by computer and stored in the machine, data may be made available on a visual display unit on a real-time basis.

Perhaps the test as to frequency and content is, What information is needed, and when, to control sales?

SALES STANDARDS

A standard has been defined as a measure by which performance is judged. In a sense, a sales budget is a standard. But there are other measurements that are useful in the control of sales. Further, it ought to be kept in mind that effective control of the marketing function requires that both attaining sales volume and monitoring marketing or distribution effort and costs must be viewed as one, or a closely related, management task. The marketing executive must plan and control both the sales revenues and the costs of securing them. Indeed, often it is desirable to measure what constitutes satisfactory

FIG. 9-7 Sales Budget Performance by Salesperson — Exception Report

THE WEST COAST COMPANY
Los Angeles District
SALES BUDGET PERFORMANCE BY SALESPERSON
Month of March 19XX and Year-to-Date
(dollars in thousands)

	Month			Year-to-Date		
		Over (Under) Budget			Over (Under) Budget	
Salesperson	Actual	Amount	Percentage	Actual	Amount	Percentage
Performance Better Than Budget[1]						
Andersen	$ 21,600	$ 6,100	28.2%	$ 60,000	$14,100	23.5%
Crawford	12,100	1,490	12.3	31,700	3,300	10.4
Nomura	13,700	1,300	9.5	42,800	4,280	10.0
O'Brien	33,400	4,760	14.3	109,300	16,300	14.9
All others	41,600	600	1.4	120,100	3,080	2.6
Total	$122,400	$14,250	11.6%	$363,900	$41,060	11.3
Performance Under Budget[1]						
Antonio	$ 9,200	($ 900)	(9.8%)	$ 28,200	($ 1,130)	(4.0%)
Callahan	7,400	(490)	(6.6)	21,100	(500)	(2.4)
Douglas	8,600	(960)	(11.2)	27,400	(274)	(1.0)
Martinez	9,400	(1,100)	(11.7)	35,900	3,490	9.7
Owens	10,100	(570)	(5.6)	27,800	(3,100)	11.2
All others	70,200	(1,060)	(1.5)	206,700	(1,010)	(.5)
Total	114,900	(5,080)	(4.4%)	347,100	(2,524)	(.7)
Grand Total	$237,300	$9,170	3.9%	$711,000	$38,536	5.4%

(1) 2 percent or more for month

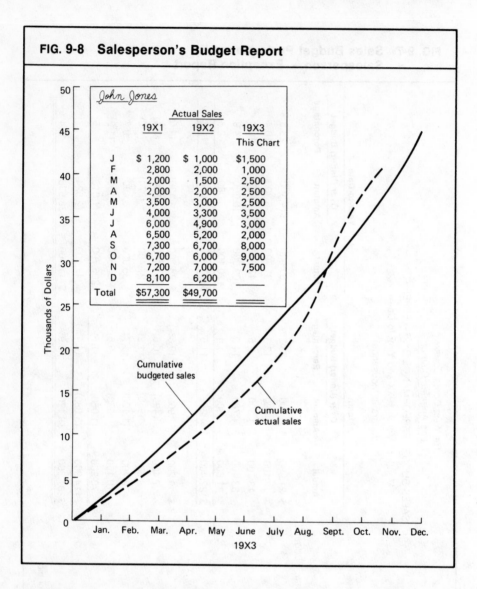

FIG. 9-8   Salesperson's Budget Report

John Jones

	Actual Sales		
	19X1	19X2	19X3
			This Chart
J	$ 1,200	$ 1,000	$1,500
F	2,800	2,000	1,000
M	2,000	1,500	2,500
A	2,000	2,000	2,500
M	3,500	3,000	2,500
J	4,000	3,300	3,500
J	6,000	4,900	3,000
A	6,500	5,200	2,000
S	7,300	6,700	8,000
O	6,700	6,000	9,000
N	7,200	7,000	7,500
D	8,100	6,200	
Total	$57,300	$49,700	

performance (the standard) against what is actually expected under certain conditions.

While this text is not a treatise on standards, it may be helpful to:

- Distinguish between the sales budget as a coordinating device and standard performance; and
- Provide some examples of sales standards useful in the control of the sales effort.

Distinction Between Sales Standards and Sales Budget

In the establishment of individual tasks as a part of the general sales program, there is sometimes a conflict between what should be done — that is, what represents satisfactory performance — and what it is actually expected will be done. This problem is discussed in Chapter 1, relative to budgeting generally. It has particular significance in relation to sales budgeting where operations are not fully controllable. It frequently happens that two figures are necessary: one expressing a standard by which to measure the quality of performance; the other expressing actual expectation for the immediate period under consideration, and serving as a basis for a unified and coordinated program.

To illustrate, let us assume that the company under consideration has budgeted a total sales volume of $10 million, has three sales districts with a manager over each, and three salespersons in each district. The figures representing satisfactory performance (standards) and actual expectation (sales budget) are as follows:

	Satisfactory Performance (Standards)	Actual Expectation (Budget)	Percentage of Expectation to Standard
District A:			
Salesperson A 1	$ 2,000,000	$ 2,000,000	100.0
A 2	2,000,000	2,000,000	100.0
A 3	1,200,000	1,000,000	83.3
Total for District A	$ 5,200,000	$ 5,000,000	96.2
District B:			
Salesperson B 1	$ 1,200,000	$ 1,200,000	100.0
B 2	1,000,000	1,000,000	90.9
B 3	1,000,000	800,000	80.0
Total for District B	$ 3,300,000	$ 3,000,000	90.9
District C:			
Salesperson C 1	$ 900,000	$ 800,000	88.9
C 2	800,000	700,000	87.5
C 3	800,000	500,000	62.5
Total for District C	$ 2,500,000	$ 2,000,000	80.0
Grand Total for Company	$11,000,000	$10,000,000	90.9

Here, it is assumed that if the performance of every salesperson and district manager were to be 100 percent satisfactory, a volume of $11 million would be secured. This, however, is hardly to be expected. It is rarely the case that everyone in the organization is doing all that he could and should do. There are always weak spots and, in developing the plans, allowance must be made for them. In the case at hand, actual sales of only $10 million are expected, or 90.9 percent of standard. No district as a whole is expected to reach the level of entirely satisfactory performance, and only salespersons *A 1, A 2,* and *B 1* are expected fully to measure up to this standard. The expectations for District *C* and for salespersons *C 3, B 3, A 3, C 2,* and *C 1* are all well below standard. Corrective effort must be directed to these points. When hope is abandoned for particular persons, new personnel must be secured and trained; but this requires time. By the time Districts *C* and *B* are brought nearer to satisfactory performance, District *A* may have slipped back. While the illustration exaggerates the typical case, it serves to emphasize the fact that one set of figures will not always serve the dual purpose of measuring performance and providing a basis for a coordinated program. Actual experience in budgeting soon demonstrates this fact.

The development of individual sales standards is extremely important as a basis for measuring individual performance, rewarding merit, and strengthening the organization; but this procedure must not be confused with the necessity of developing a sales program that will serve as a basis for a coordinated program of purchasing, production, and finance. In the case at hand, such a program will be based upon a sales volume of $10 million.

Types of Sales Standards

Proper use of sales standards may be of assistance in identifying weak performance, or contributory causes thereto, in planning sales effort, or otherwise of value in meeting the sales plan. Sales standards may be standards of effort, standards of result, or those expressing the relationship of effort to result. While such standards will differ by industry and types of management or operations, illustrated below are some sales standards that frequently are found useful:

1. Standards of effort:
   - Number of calls to be made per day or month
   - Number of new prospects to be contacted per month
   - Number of catalogs to be mailed
   - Number of sales promotion items to be distributed per quarter
   - Number of foreign agents to be established
2. Standards of results:
   - Percentage of sales from new customer or new territories
   - Share of sales from new product
   - Number of new customers secured
   - Dollar volume of sales achieved

- Sales volume secured from a given sales promotion
- Increase in average size of order per month
- Percentage of sales in product X (higher margin) achieved
- Largest amount of product X sold to a single customer
- Sales volume achieved per call
- Percentage of sales in product X (higher margin) achieved
- Dollar contribution margin after selling expense attained

3. Standards of results to effort:
   - Sales secured per dollar of sales effort
   - Number of new customers per prospect calls
   - Sales per dollar of sales promotion
   - Sales expense per dollar of sales

Such measurements as the above may be useful in stimulating sales effort, rewarding merit, and in meeting the sales plan or ferreting out areas for improvement. They are not a substitute for sales management. They must be used with care, revised when necessary, and abandoned when they interfere with effective selling.

COST INFORMATION AND PRICING POLICY

Pricing Policy and the Sales Budget

Pricing policy and pricing strategy have an impact on the sales budget. Sales prices and physical sales volume are interdependent. Changes in sales price can influence the quantity of product sold; and the volume sold directly affects the cost to manufacture and distribute. Hence, the cost-volume-profit structure, discussed in Chapter 6, is germane to the corporate strategy and the sales plan.

To be sure, prices must be in line with the market. And the reader is referred to texts on the elasticity of demand and other influences on price setting. However, our concern here will be principally with costs.[3]

While every experienced executive in a competitive field knows that prices cannot be rigidly keyed to costs, it should be strongly emphasized that detailed cost information is essential both in establishing price policies and in making intelligent deviations from such policies. This extends to the costs of both production and distribution. Such costs must be thoroughly analyzed as to their fixed and variable elements and it must be known when such costs are excessive. Also, the analysis of costs of distribution must frequently be

---

[3] For a more full discussion of profit structure and price-cost changes, see Chapters 5 and 6.

extended to different territories, customers, channels, and methods before price policies can be intelligently determined.

Over the longer term, no business can consistently sell all or most of its products at less than cost — cost meaning the cost to manufacture and distribute, together with the cost of related administrative and other services. In a sense, it is desirable to make a profit on every product, in every territory, and from every customer. Yet, this ordinarily is not possible, given the action of competitors. Nevertheless, tactics can be developed, prices can be set, and sales policies can be implemented, which may increase earnings over the budget period.

One of the major determinants in pricing strategy is costs. The budget director and his financial associates should be intimately familiar with the product costs — all costs — and their behavior. The sales manager should be provided with relevant cost data for use in contemplating pricing policy. The concern, of course, is with the costs likely to prevail in the budgeting period — not necessarily historical costs — and should include manufacturing costs, distribution costs, and all other related costs. And, of course, in some circumstances, the cost of capital or return on assets must be considered.

For pricing purposes, the costing techniques to be discussed include:

- Full cost method
- Direct (or marginal or contribution) margin costing
- Return on assets employed
- Conversion costs method

Full Cost Method

As the name implies, under this method, total, all, or full costs are considered. Normally, when full costs are used for pricing purposes, the total costs are determined (using certain assumptions) and to these is added a markup, to arrive at the selling price.

The unit cost and proposed selling price of two different products might be calculated as follows:

	Product	
	X	Y
Costs		
Direct materials (quantities × expected cost)	$22.50	$ 4.10
Direct labor (hours × expected rate)	7.90	8.40
Manufacturing expense (200 percent of direct labor)	15.80	16.80
Total manufacturing cost	$46.20	$29.30

	Product	
	X	Y
Costs		
Distribution costs — Direct (total distribution costs for channel ÷ units)	7.00	11.50
Selling and marketing overhead (percentage of direct costs)	5.95	9.77
Research and development expense (7 percent direct manufacturing cost)	2.13	.88
Subtotal	61.28	51.45
General and administrative expense (10 percent of above costs)	6.13	5.15
Total cost	67.41	56.60
Margin		
Desired margin (30 percent of total cost)	20.22	16.98
Proposed selling price	$87.63	$73.58

Certainly, the sales management should be aware of the total costs in setting selling prices. These comments apply to the example:

1. Indirect costs have been calculated on the specified basis. There are other methods of allocation that can be used, such as costs per direct labor hour, or a refinement of departmental overhead rates times the direct labor or direct cost component consumed in each department.
2. All indirect costs assume a selected physical volume. Departures from this level change unit costs.
3. The margin is calculated as a percentage of total cost. It could be determined as a percentage of sales. Thus, the 30 percent of cost margin equates to 23.2 percent of the selling price.

These comments apply to the full cost method:

1. It does not distinguish between out-of-pocket costs and total costs. Yet, there will be times when product may be sold at less than full cost, and provide a net gain to the company — as long as capacity exists and the price is higher than the out-of-pocket unit cost.
2. It lacks flexibility in that the fixed costs at a specified volume level are not identified. These could be adjusted for differing volume to reflect more clearly the expected costs at the anticipated level, with adjustments made in the selling price.
3. Although differing profit rates could be applied to different product lines on a specific product, usually a tendency exists to apply one rate to a broad variety of product, even though market conditions make this practice unreal-

istic. Further, full costing may assume the same profit markup on differing elements of cost, despite the fact that it is not feasible. Thus, should the same rate of profit be secured on a heavy material content product as contrasted to one with low material element but heavy conversion costs?

Variable/Direct Cost Method

This cost technique identifies the following:

1. Those costs which would not be incurred if the product is not manufactured and sold (the variable costs).
2. Those costs *direct* as to the product, as long as the line is in production, but fixed in nature and not variable.
3. The allocated share of all costs — costs that may rightfully be chargeable to the product on the basis of services available or used, but which would continue even if no production existed.

A cost buildup on this system is reflected below:

	Unit Cost
Direct Costs	
Variable:	
Direct labor	$17.20
Direct material	10.50
Manufacturing expense	8.60
Total Variable Manufacturing Cost	$36.30
Marketing expense	12.70
Total Variable Costs	$49.00
Fixed:	
Manufacturing (normal activity level)	$ 2.90
Marketing (normal activity level)	1.40
Total Fixed Costs	$ 4.30
Total Direct Costs	$53.30
Allocated Costs	
Manufacturing expense (25 percent of direct manufacturing cost)	$ 9.80
Selling expense (10 percent of direct marketing cost)	1.41
General and administrative expense (15 percent of total costs)	9.68
Total Allocated Costs	$20.89
Total Costs	$74.19

Given this information, and to the extent that costs are an important factor in the selling effort, the following is true:

1. Some business may be planned which recovers all costs, plus an acceptable margin.
2. A share of business for this product may be taken at a lower price as long as it is higher than the direct *variable* costs of $49.00 per unit. It might cover all *direct* costs of $53.30, thus increasing earnings by $4.30 per unit; or provide for recouping some allocated costs if above the $53.30 level.

Management should weigh the impact of selling certain customers (such as private brand outlets) at less than the "normal" price.

Marginal costs should be used for tactical or short-term decisions only. Over the longer term, the selling price should provide for recovery of total costs, plus an adequate return on assets employed, or shareholders' equity. Thus, recovery of direct costs or variable direct costs, with no share of allocated costs being recouped, might be justified in these circumstances:

1. If idle plant capacity will exist for some period and can be utilized only at the lower price level, and perhaps only in special sales outlets.
2. If sales to other classes of customers, or through all channels of distribution, or as private brands, will provide a sustained level of production — at above the variable direct cost level — so as to reduce the costs allocated to the "regular" business, and will not adversely impact the chief product line.

Covering the market through dissimilar outlets or brand names may enhance the total marketing effort.

Return on Assets Employed (or on Shareholders' Equity)

An obviously desirable costing method would be one that permits a return on the assets employed (ROAE) in the product line. Circumstances may exist, as in capital intensive industries or monopoly situations, where such pricing is workable. It will be noted that the costing methods just discussed make no direct provision for return on the assets employed. Indirectly, depreciation on the assets employed is a cost factor. But this is not the full measure of the cost of the fixed assets used in the product. And working capital is not covered.

If the business objective is to provide an acceptable return on shareholders' equity, and therefore the factored impact of assets employed, then pricing policy should at least be sensitive to the assets utilized in the manufacture and distribution of the product. The assets employed are fixed in nature as to plant and equipment, but usually are variable as to receivables and inventory, these being a function of physical volume and selling price.

Accounts receivable will be greater as sales volume and sales prices are higher. Investment in inventory will increase or decrease as volume changes and as manufacturing costs and raw material prices fluctuate. In view of the variables, a formula may be employed to calculate the unit sales price required to produce a planned return on assets employed:

$$\text{Unit price} = \frac{\dfrac{\text{Cost} + (\text{Desired percent return} \times \text{Fixed assets})}{\text{Annual sales volume in units}}}{1 - \left(\dfrac{\text{Desired percent}}{\text{return}}\right)\left(\dfrac{\text{Variable assets expressed}}{\text{as percent of sales volume}}\right)}$$

where:

Cost = Total cost of manufacturing, selling, administrative, and research

Percent return = Rate desired on assets employed (before income taxes)

Fixed capital = Machinery, plant, and equipment although some of the current assets might be placed in this category

Variable capital = The current assets which are a function of volume and prices — receivables and inventory

The total costs of Product X, may be incorporated into a cost-volume-profit formula to return 25 percent before income taxes on the assets employed. Other assumptions are these:

1. Planned annual sales volume is 4,800,000 units.
2. The fixed assets aggregate $3,100,000.
3. Inventory and receivables, the current or variable assets, are expected to average 33⅓ percent of sales — a turnover of three times per year.

Applying these inputs to the above formula, the unit price is determined as follows:

$$\text{Unit price} = \frac{\dfrac{(4,800,000 \times \$67.40) + (.25 \times \$3,100,000)}{4,800,000}}{1 - (.25)(.333)}$$

$$= \frac{\dfrac{\$323,568,000 + \$775,000}{4,800,000}}{1 - .083325}$$

$$= \frac{\$67.57}{.916675}$$

$$= \$73.712$$

Proof of the calculation is as follows:

Income

Net sales (4,800,000 units × $73.72)	$353,820,000
Costs	323,568,000
Income before income taxes	$ 30,252,000

Assets Employed

Fixed Assets	$ 3,100,000
Variable (receivables and inventory) (33⅓ percent of $353,808,000)	117,924,200
Total Assets Employed	$121,024,200

Return (ROAE)

25 percent of $121,024,200	$ 30,252,000

Applying Assets to Product Lines. The following comment may be useful in applying assets employed to a particular price calculation.

Assets employed are considered to include all assets used in manufacturing and selling the product (including related services). It is immaterial how the funds were provided — whether by debt or equity. The management of a company should effectively use all capital, whether owner supplied or creditor supplied.

Questions may arise regarding the basis of valuation of assets. Should replacement value be considered? Should fixed assets be included on a gross or depreciated basis? Essentially, policies of valuation will have no appreciable effect on price determination. Recognition can be provided directly or indirectly in the rate of return objective. Consistency is the objective.

In a multiproduct company, a problem to be solved is the allocation of capital employed to the various product lines. Upon reflection, this need not be a major stumbling block. Just as accountants have been allocating costs to products for years, so also can they allocate capital on a reasonable basis consistent with the facts of the particular business. Some suggested methods of prorating capital to product lines are these:

Item	*In Ratio to:*
Cash	Total product cost
Accounts receivable	Sales, adjusted for significant differences in terms of sale
Raw material	Actual or expected usage
Work in process	Actual or expected usage
Finished goods	Cost of manufacture
Fixed assets	Conversion costs (labor and variable manufacturing overhead) or labor hours — either actual, normal, or standard

Conversion Costs for Pricing Purposes. Still another economic concept useful in pricing is termed the "conversion cost theory of value." In essence, this view holds that profits are, or should be, earned commensurate with the effort and risk inherent in converting raw materials into finished products. This approach has merit, particularly in situations where relative material content varies widely by product. For example, if one product is largely an assembly of purchased parts, and another requires extensive processing in expensive facilities, application of the same markup to each probably would result in a price too high on the assembly item and too low on the fabricated product. Differences in types of costs may therefore need to be recognized. A combined use of the return on capital concept and direct costs may be illustrative.

Assume the following is a typical pricing and profit planning problem:

1. A given product line R is made up of products of varying material content.
2. $24 million are the gross assets employed for the line.
3. Management desires a 20 percent return (before taxes) on the assets employed.
4. The pertinent profit data are as follows:
   a. Period (fixed or continuing) expenses are $6 million.
   b. The P/V (profit to volume, or contribution margin) ratio is 30 percent.
   c. Direct materials and conversion expenses are, on the average, in a 4-to-3 ratio.
   d. Material turnover is twice a year.

With these premises it is necessary to calculate:

1. The sales volume needed to produce the desired rate of return.
2. The markup to be applied on each of the direct cost factors in the product line

Net sales and aggregate costs by element may be determined in this manner:

Required operating profit (20% of $24,000,000)		$ 4,800,000
Add: Continuing or period expenses		6,000,000
Required margin over direct costs		10,800,000
Required Sales [$10,800,000 ÷ 30% (P/V ratio)]		36,000,000
Deduct: Margin		10,800,000
Direct costs		25,200,000
Segregated on a 4-to-3 ratio as follows:		
Direct material	$14,400,000	
Conversion	10,800,000	$24,200,000

Inasmuch as the material turnover is two times per year, the investment is $7,200,000 ($14,400,000 ÷ 2). Twenty percent of this figure is $1,440,000. Consequently, the additive factor is 10 percent ($1,400,000 ÷ $14,400,000), and the portion of sales revenue needed to provide a 20 percent return is $15,840,000 ($14,400,000 + $1,440,000).

The additive factor on conversion costs may be determined by the difference method as follows:

Total required income (Sales)	$36,000,000
Less: Direct material and related profit additive	15,840,000
Balance attributable to conversion factor	$20,160,000

Therefore, 1.867 ($20,160,000 ÷ $10,800,000) is the conversion markup.

If the direct costs of product *R162* in the line are known, the target or "ideal" selling price is then determined in this fashion:

	Unit Direct Cost	Factor	Unit Selling Price
Direct material	$16.10	1.100	$17.71
Conversion	20.30	2.867	58.20
Total	$36.40		$75.91

Such proposed prices are a starting point only — they must be considered in relation to competitive prices.

Obviously, costs are only one factor in determining sales prices, and, in fact, in setting sales policies. But they are an important consideration in the planning effort. In developing sales plans, the appropriate costs should always be examined.

10

Production

WHAT IS THE PRODUCTION BUDGET?

Succinctly stated, the production budget is the plan for the quantity of goods to be manufactured during the budget period. In any company the sales plan is basic to the entire budgeting process. That segment of the sales plan or budget having to do with manufactured goods, as distinguished from services or purchased goods, must be converted into the production or manufacturing requirements. In so doing, recognition must be given to the finished goods inventory and work-in-process. The entire sequence of relationships in the manufacturing process — stemming from the sales plan — is illustrated in Figure 10-1. The sales plan, adjusted for applicable inventory levels, is converted into production quantities needed. The production volume requirements, in turn, are the basis for the direct labor budget, the direct material budgets, and the manufacturing expense budget.

Production cannot be planned independently of sales — or, for that matter, independently of the financial resources of the enterprise; the programs must be coordinated. For example, the production department may suggest the desirability of a greater degree of standardization of products — fewer styles, sizes, and so forth. Such elimination of items may have a distinct bearing on sales plans. Again, the production department may desire to level out its program in order to utilize its facilities to better advantage and to provide regularity of employment. But this may necessitate increased or redistributed sales effort, larger inventories, and greater financial demands. The problem is one of coordinating all factors in the direction of the most effective utilization of the total resources available.

The problem of budgeting production differs somewhat as between concerns that manufacture standard commodities for stock in anticipation of sales demand and those that produce to customers' specifications upon receipt of orders. In the former case the problem is to have the goods available when orders are received; in the latter case the problem is to be prepared to produce goods promptly after the orders are received. The basic principles and methods are the same in both cases, but in the latter case the plans cannot be projected as far in the future, and more frequent revision is required. In summary, the production plan must represent a balancing between sales, inventory levels and production volume. Some of these interrelationships are addressed in this chapter.

RESPONSIBILITY FOR THE PRODUCTION PLAN

It is the chief manufacturing executive who has the responsibility for developing an efficient production plan. To be sure, he must operate within the perimeters set by the chief executive officer. However, it is the manufacturing or production executive who has first-hand knowledge of the production

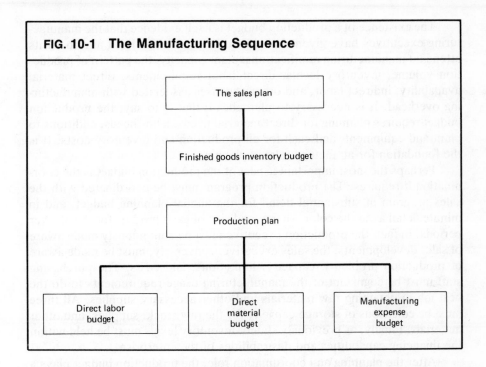

FIG. 10-1   The Manufacturing Sequence

The sales plan

Finished goods inventory budget

Production plan

Direct labor budget

Direct material budget

Manufacturing expense budget

processes, plant capacity, availability of required personnel, and the status of required materials, supplies, and services. It is he who must decide the *how, what, when* and *where* of production.

The financial staff, including the budget coordinator, will provide as much assistance as is reasonable. They will review financial implications of the production plan and related facets, but the final responsibility for the production plan rests with the chief manufacturing executive. The responsibility will cover, at least in most companies, these directly related segments:

- Production volume (plan) — The quantity of units
- Inventory levels
- Direct labor planning and control
- Direct materials planning and control — Purchases and usage
- Manufacturing expense budget — Both the annual planning budget and the flexible control budgets

ROLE OF THE PRODUCTION BUDGET

The production budget should be viewed as a tool to assist in the planning, coordination, and control of the manufacturing operations.

The existence of a production budget is itself evidence that the manufacturing executives have given thought to the production level and to all its attendant manufacturing ramifications: plant capacity, the pattern of production volume, inventory levels, direct labor requirements, direct material availability, indirect labor, and other expenses associated with manufacturing overhead. It is necessary to plan ahead; that is to say, the production budget requires planning for direct material needs, labor needs, additions to plant and equipment, and cash for all production and inventory costs. It is the foundation for all factory-related planning.

Perhaps the most important aspect of the production budget is the coordination it requires. The production program must be coordinated with the sales program in substantial detail for the annual planning budget, and in minute detail as to the color, shape, and size of each product for the shorter periods. In fact, the production executive must be continuously made aware of sales developments; the sales executive, conversely, must be made aware of production problems, capacity, limitations, and costs. The purchasing staff must be cognizant of the manufacturing usage requirements to do the best job in obtaining raw materials and other necessary supplies. All three must be conscious of storage capacity for the raw stock, supplies, and other materials. Finally, as previously stated, inventory levels must be held within the financing capabilities and desirabilities of the enterprise.

After the planning and coordination role, the production budget plays a part in cost control. Obviously, rates, times, and places of production have a bearing on the cost components of labor, materials, and overhead. The production budget must be known to establish the proper unit costs. Then, too, actual unit costs must be compared with the budget-based standard, or planned, unit costs to signal departures from acceptable cost levels. The techniques involved in cost control are reviewed in detail in Chapters 11, 12, and 13.

FACTORS IN DEVELOPING THE PRODUCTION PLAN

The development of the annual production budget or the plan for somewhat shorter periods does not contemplate the day-to-day planning and scheduling of production. This is the task of the production planning and scheduling department. But the basic or general production program first must be established. Then, within this perimeter, the daily and weekly production is set as the time approaches.

The production budget contemplates the balancing of sales, inventory, and production to produce the lowest overall cost results consistent with meeting customer needs, as well as other factors which are beyond the scope of this book. Because of its ramifications, development of the production budget is a complicated process, and only principal budgetary issues can be illustrated and commented on in this chapter. Computer techniques are useful in solving many of these complex problems.

The development of the production budget involves the consideration of these basic factors:

- Selection of the budget period
- Total production (quantity) requirements, by product or groups of product, for the budget period
- Allocation of production within the budget period
- Availability of raw material and purchased parts
- Availability of labor
- Inventory policy relative to work-in-process and finished goods
- Standards of performance for each function, by product
- Plant capacity and best method of utilization
- Determination of which plant is to manufacture the various products
- Consideration of plant expansion or contraction
- Labor policy — as related to stability of employment, for example
- Economical quantities to manufacture
- Financial resources of the enterprise

The integration of these factors will depend on items such as the nature of the manufacturing process, the size of the company, and the nature of the product and distribution system. The intent of the author is to make the reader aware of the complexities, for the production budget is not simply a matter of determining the sales requirements and then saying, "Produce it." These matters must be resolved largely by the manufacturing executives, but comments may assist the budget executives to understand some of the matters that must be dealt with. To the extent these matters are reviewed in this volume, some are discussed in this chapter, and others in Chapters 11, 12, 13, and 21.

Production Budget Period

In general, the production budget period should conform in length to the sales budget period; however, special circumstances may dictate a longer or shorter period. Since sales can never be projected with absolute certainty, the production budget period should be as short as possible, consistent with reasonable efficiency in the production program. If, for example, goods are being manufactured for stock, if no special equipment is required, and if labor, materials, and supplies are readily available, the production budget period may be comparatively short. If, on the other hand, models and pat- ·

terns are being changed yearly, if annual equipment modifications are necessary, if yearly material contracts must be placed, or if stability of employment is a paramount factor, the period must be longer.

Undoubtedly, the commonest practice of concerns manufacturing for stock is to prepare a tentative production program for one year, with a definite budget for a shorter period — usually one to three months. Where goods are made to order, no definite period can be set. Here the budgeting of production must be a continuous process. As orders are received they must be merged with the existing program by a process of progressively dropping completed orders and adding new ones. Many concerns, producing both for stock and to order, are compelled to employ both methods.

Factors of particular consequence in selecting the production budget period may be summarized as follows:

- Length of the sales budget period
- Length of the normal production cycle
- Necessity for changing patterns, models, fixtures, and equipment; and the length of time involved in making such changes
- Time necessary to secure materials and supplies
- Difficulty of securing and maintaining a skilled labor force
- Importance of stability of employment
- Extent of the dangers attendant upon inventory accumulation
- Stability of general business conditions

Physical Quantities to Be Produced

When the sales budget is expressed in physical units, only a simple computation is necessary to reveal the physical quantities that must be produced to supply the customers and to provide adequate inventories. For example, if it is expected that 60 units of product A will be on hand at the beginning of the production budget period, 100 are to be sold during the period, and 40 are to be in the inventory at the end of the period, then the production budget must provide for the delivery to stock of 80 units. If this procedure is followed for each product, the total physical production requirements will be known.

If the sales budget is developed only in terms of dollars, then the translation into physical units must be based on past experience. Thus, if product A has in the past represented 5 percent of the sales volume and the current sales budget is $1 million, then an output amounting to $50,000 of product A is called for. This must then be converted into physical units on the basis of budgeted prices. In rare instances, the conversion to production requirement must be expressed in such terms as labor hours, machine hours, or plant operating hours; usually, however, the final expression should be in terms of units of specific products or classes of products.

The quantities may be tentatively set for the full budget period, as, for example, the season or year, with more definite determination for a shorter period, such as the month or quarter.

Before computing the quantities to be produced, it is necessary to decide upon the quantities that are to be in the inventory at the close of the production budget period. This decision must be based upon factors such as:

- Margin of safety necessary to insure proper service to customers
- Necessary protection against material and labor shortage and labor trouble
- Cost of maintaining inventories
- Danger of obsolescence
- Expected price trends
- Financial strength of the company

The consideration of quantities in inventory concerns not only finished goods but also work-in-process, parts, and partially assembled goods. It frequently happens that quick service can be given to customers if goods are processed up to a certain point and stocked at that point; then, when orders are received, completing operations can be performed quickly and goods shipped on schedule. While final operations may be short in point of time, they may represent considerable cost, and this plan of holding back the inventories may result in substantial savings in inventory investment. To illustrate, assume that product A is made up as follows:

Parts Included	Days Required to Produce	Number of Parts Used in the Finished Product	Unit Cost of Parts	Total Cost
A1	60	1	$ 5	$ 5
A2	30	3	10	30
A3	2	5	15	75
Assembly	1			10
		Total cost of finished product		$120

It is obvious here that customers can be supplied if a relatively small number of finished units are on hand, provided an adequate supply of parts A1 and A2 is available. One thousand units of part A1 would represent an investment of only $5,000, whereas 1,000 finished units require an investment of $120,000. While the illustration is an exaggeration of the usual situation, it emphasizes the importance of giving consideration to such possibilities.

Where goods are manufactured to order, the physical quantities to be produced can be definitely ascertained only as orders are received. Some estimate is usually possible on the basis of past experience, expected general business conditions, and sales representatives' current reports, but definite determination must await the receipt of the orders. The budgeting of quantities in this case is based on a combination of orders actually received and contemplated orders.

Timing the Production

Having determined the length of the production budget period and having ascertained the quantities to be produced within that period, there arises next the question of the distribution of the work throughout the period. This does not contemplate the day-to-day planning and scheduling. Such work must be done by the production planning department; but it can be done only after a basic production program has been established. If, for example, a six months' production program is being developed and it has been decided to produce, in that time, 100,000 units of product A, 200,000 of product B, and 300,000 of product C, the question remains as to when and at what rate the goods should be produced. Should all of the A goods be made in January, the B goods in February, and C goods in March, and then the plant be closed for April, May, and June? While this is unlikely, it is conceivable that such a program might be desirable. Obviously, the production planning department cannot proceed to schedule the work until the general program is established.

This program applies particularly to stock goods. With special orders the concern must prepare itself as best it can to produce the orders as they are received.

The ultimate goal is to ensure the production of goods in quantities sufficient to meet the requirements of the sales budget without the accumulation of excessive inventories, without creating excessive costs through uneconomical lots, and without waste of labor and equipment.

The best service is provided to customers when the production program is timed well ahead of sales budget requirements. Thus, if orders for the delivery of 1,000 units of product A are expected to be received during the month of February, the entire production might be timed for January in order to be sure that the goods are available immediately should the orders be unexpectedly heavy during the first few days of February. This plan may have the serious disadvantage, however, of tying up excessive working capital in inventories, of creating heavy storage and handling charges, and of risking price declines and obsolescence. Inventory accumulation, on the other hand, presents opportunities for reducing costs through level production and economical runs. All factors must be properly balanced.

In determining the time of production and the size of the inventory to be carried, the following factors must be considered:

1. *Available plant facilities.* The production program must obviously conform to plant facilities and should contemplate the most effective and economical use of such facilities. Any additions contemplated should be subjected to the most exacting tests of ultimate profitability. Far too often equipment has been added to meet temporary demands and then left idle. On the other hand, the fact that expensive equipment will otherwise be idle and that large underabsorbed overhead will thereby develop often leads to the budgeting of standard items for stock in excess of current demands.

2. *Adequacy of storage facilities.* Where the goods are bulky in nature, it may be impractical to provide storage facilities greatly in excess of current requirements. The cost of such storage must be weighed against the gains of level production.

3. *Stability of employment.* Where the demand is seasonal and production follows the sales budget, workers must be frequently added and laid off with resulting instability of employment. This is costly to the producer and demoralizing to the worker. This may be avoided in some instances by carefully planning the production and building up inventories during slack seasons. This factor has gained added importance through the merit rating provisions of unemployment insurance acts of the federal and state governments. These acts, as presently constituted, contemplate a lower tax rate on employers who provide regularity of employment. Some concerns have developed a remarkable degree of stability of employment, insofar as seasonal factors are concerned, by carefully planning the year's production; with many others, there is still much to be accomplished in this direction.

4. *Economical runs and efficiency of operation.* In some instances the quantities of a particular item provided in the sales budget are not sufficient for efficient production operations. They do not constitute an economical run. Here, larger quantities may be run and placed in the inventory on the theory that carrying costs will be more than offset by lower production costs. Extreme caution is necessary in such a procedure as actual carrying costs and obsolescence are frequently higher than estimated.

   Moreover, in considering the efficiency of operations, the accountant will sometimes find it desirable to prepare preliminary estimates of the financial results of stabilized production. It is a vital part of the planning function — the consideration of alternatives. Such computations permit management to see the relative merits of the two plans.

5. *Economies in purchasing.* In some instances the production program may be influenced by possible economies in large-scale purchases of materials. Here again, the gain must be carefully weighed against the cost of carrying such inventories.

6. *Adequacy of capital.* Limitations of capital may prevent the accumulation of large inventories, no matter how desirable from other standpoints. The production must be so timed as to result in a balanced financial program.

All such factors must be taken into account in planning the production program.

The planning and control of inventories is discussed in Chapter 21. However, for a better understanding of the interrelationship of inventory and the production schedule, a simplified commentary on inventory control is made here.

Frequently, the best way to proceed is to set minimum limits below which the inventory of each item is not permitted to fall, as a matter of ensuring reasonable service to customers; and maximum limits above which the inventory should not go, as a protection against excessive carrying costs, dangers of inventory losses, and excessive demands on capital. The next step is to schedule the production between these limits at as level a rate as possible consistent with economical operation.

To illustrate, assume the following data relative to product A:

Minimum inventory, 50 units
Maximum inventory, 150 units
Budget period, 6 months
Expected inventory as of January 1, 50 units
Required inventory as of June 30, 110 units

Month	Production Schedule	Budgeted Shipments	Inventory at Close of Month
Inventory January 1			50
January	75	20	105
February	75	30	150
March	100	100	150
April	150	150	150
May	70	100	120
June	70	80	110

Here the production schedule is fairly even for four of the six months but it rises sharply in March and April. If, however, the maximum inventory is raised from 150 to 180 units, a level schedule of production can be developed as follows:

Month	Production Schedule	Budgeted Shipments	Inventory at Close of Month
Inventory January 1			50
January	90	20	120
February	90	30	180
March	90	100	170
April	90	150	110
May	90	100	100
June	90	80	110

Under the former plan the average inventory is 119.3 units, whereas under the second plan it is only 120 units; thus it would appear that the second plan is desirable.

Initial inventory limits may be developed by means of turnover rates that experience indicates to be practicable, or by applying selected factors to the sales budget. Thus, the maximum may be set as one-third of the period's expected sales and the minimum as one-sixth. Resulting figures can then be modified as indicated by the above illustration.

In summary, a company may select a stable production budget or a stable inventory level — or, better yet, some slight flexibility in both inventory levels and production levels.

Place of Production

Where there is more than one plant adapted to the same product, the production budget must indicate where the goods are to be produced. This involves such considerations as:

1. Relative cost of operations
2. The obligation felt by management to local communities
3. Distribution of employment desired
4. Dangers of labor trouble and consequent advantage of decentralizing operations

Manufacturing Operations Required

Where there is a varied line of products, it is frequently necessary that the physical quantities budgeted be resolved into production operations and machine capacity required. In such cases records must be kept for each product showing the manufacturing operations necessary; and a record of each machine should be maintained showing the operations performed by the machine together with its capacity. Figure 10-2 illustrates the adaptation of such information to a cigar manufacturing concern.

Standards of Production Performance

Standards of production performance are necessary to reveal the quantities of material, the number of hours of labor, the machine hours, and quantities of service (e.g., power or steam) necessary to perform the various production operations. The establishment of such standards is an engineering rather than an accounting task, but it should be emphasized that such standards are essential to the development of the budgetary procedure — at least insofar as the budget is to serve as a tool of control. Such standards serve not only in

FIG. 10-2   Record of Machine Capacity

MACHINE CAPACITY — NORMAL SCHEDULE

Kind of Cigar	Number of Machines	Production per Hour	Machine Hours on Schedule of 2,179 Hours* per Year	Annual Production (in thousands)
Brand A	130	457	283,270	129,454
Brand B	30	400	65,370	26,148
Brand C	20	514	43,580	22,400
Brand D	50	457	108,950	49,790
Brand E	10	457	21,790	9,958
				237,750

* Each machine is expected to operate 2,179 hours during the year after making proper allowance for Sundays, holidays, inventory, adjustments, and repairs.

the development of the budget and in measuring efficiency of production performance, but also in developing purchase requirements and in estimating costs.

MATERIAL, LABOR, SERVICE, AND EQUIPMENT REQUIREMENTS

Once it is known what quantities are to be produced during the budget period, how the production is to be distributed in point of time and place, what manufacturing operations are entailed, and the standards of production performance, it is possible to develop the detailed programs of material, labor, service, and equipment purchases. These phases of production budgeting are discussed in Chapters 11 through 13, and 24.

It should be noted that these requirements can be determined definitely only where goods are manufactured for stock and where special orders can be estimated with reasonable accuracy. Some concerns manufacturing to order must continually revise the production program by progressively adding the requirements for new orders received and dropping completed orders.

TRANSLATION OF PRODUCTION PROGRAM INTO COSTS

Before reviewing in detail the manufacturing cost elements, the relationship of the production program to manufacturing costs and cost control may be better understood by a bird's-eye view of the translation of the *volume* budget into values.

After the production program has been developed in terms of physical quantities to be produced, manufacturing operations involved, and material, labor, and equipment required, the entire program must be expressed in terms of cost. Insofar as practicable, standard costs should be established and the planned production translated into such costs in the following manner:

1. Direct material cost (varying directly with volume):
   a. At standard quantities
   b. At standard or estimated prices
2. Direct labor cost (varying directly with volume):
   a. At standard hours
   b. At standard or estimated rates
3. Burden cost:
   a. Variable directly with volume — at standard amounts or rates
   b. Semivariable with volume — at standard amounts or rates for each volume bracket within the probable volume range
   c. Fixed — at standard amounts to be charged to production and remaining amounts to be charged to idle capacity

The procedure may be illustrated very simply. Assume that a concern has a normal plant capacity of 100 units of product and that the current production budget calls for 80 units. Only one product is made and its production requires two operations, *A* and *B*. For the sake of simplicity, assume further that all costs can be resolved into variable and fixed classifications. Standard costs are:

Variable costs per unit of product:

1 unit of direct material at $2.00	$ 2.00
Operation *A* (variable labor and burden)	3.00
Operation *B* (variable labor and burden)	5.00
Total	$10.00

Fixed production costs for the budget period are $500, or $5.00 per unit, based on normal capacity. The production cost budget would then be expressed as follows:

BUDGET

Variable costs (80 units at $10.00)	$ 800
Fixed costs (80 units at $5.00)	400
Costs chargeable to production	$1,200
Cost of idle capacity	100
Total budgeted costs	$1,300

In this manner the physical production program is translated into terms of cost to be projected ultimately into the financial program and expressed in the budgeted statements of operations and financial position.

BUDGETED COSTS AS BASIS FOR COST CONTROL

A continuation of the above illustration will serve to indicate the value of budgeted costs as a basis for cost control. Assume, for example, that actual results are as follows:

Units produced	72
Material used (units)	74

Actual costs are:

Material cost (74 units at $1.80)	$ 133.20
Operation *A* — Variable costs (72 units at $3.00)	216.00
Operation *B* — Variable costs (72 units at $5.2416)	377.40
Fixed costs — Charged to production	400.00
Costs charged to production	$1,126.60
Cost of idle capacity	100.00
Total actual costs	$1,226.60

It is apparent from these figures that total production costs are less than the budget by $73.40 ($1,300 − $1,226.60). This figure is not particularly significant, however, as the actual production was 8 units less than the quantity budgeted. Carrying the analysis further, the following results may be obtained:

	Flexible Budget Restated for 72 Units	Actual Costs	Favorable Variance	Unfavorable Variance
Material	$ 144	$ 133.20	$10.80	
Operation A	216	216.00		
Operation B	360	377.40		$17.40
Fixed costs	360	400.00		40.00
Total	$1,080	$1,126.60	$10.80	$57.40
				10.80
Net unfavorable variance				$46.60

A more detailed review of variances would provide this breakdown:

	Favorable	Unfavorable
Excessive material usage (2 units at $1.80)		$ 3.60
Material price below standard (72 units at 20 cents)	$14.40	
Excessive operation B cost		17.40
Idle capacity cost in excess of budget		40.00
	$14.40	$61.00
		14.40
Net unfavorable variance		$46.60

Here it is apparent that production operations were not as efficient as planned. Excessive material was used and operation B was costly. The only reduction in costs arose from a reduction in the price of material over which the production department had no control. The increase in idle-capacity cost may be assumed to lie with management rather than with the production department.

It should be noted that such results are available only when the budgeted costs are flexible. Such flexibility is secured by resolving the costs into their variable and fixed elements; in fact, it is usually necessary to extend the analysis to semivariable elements.

While an actual case is considerably more involved than the illustration and the analyses of variances and their causes must be greatly refined, the example as shown should serve to demonstrate the value of the budget as a cost control device.

SUBSTITUTION OF ESTIMATES FOR STANDARDS

Where standard costs are not available or their use is impracticable due to uncertainty of prices, estimates of the costs must be made on the basis of past experience and expected conditions. Failure to use standards largely eliminates the use of the budget for purposes of control of costs but its value remains for purposes of coordination of the program with purchases and finance.

COST STANDARDS FACILITATE CONTROL

The manufacture of goods is a complicated process. It results from the combined effort of many individuals in many different departments, performing numerous functions and operations; and it frequently involves many different products. No one executive can directly supervise all of the activities. Innumerable opportunities exist for the waste of time and materials. The budgetary procedure constitutes perhaps the greatest single aid to the executives who must assume the responsibility for efficient direction and control of the production operations. This procedure, if fully developed, presents an organized plan of operations with predetermined standards by which to measure and control the cost of such operations. This control is exercised by means of prompt reports to major and minor executives that reveal the failure or success of effort as related to individuals, operations, departments, and products. While it is seldom possible that to provide standard measurements continuously for every operation and the performance of every individual, the principle is widely applicable and the extent of its use is generally a fair measure of the degree of efficiency of central management.

The budgetary control reports are discussed in the chapter dealing with the relevant cost item: thus, the budget related to direct labor is reviewed in Chapter 11. It should be noted, however, that a difference between planned production volume and actual volume, or between "standard capacity" and actual volume in any month, will give rise to a "volume variance." This is reviewed in Chapter 13, relating to manufacturing expenses.

THE PRODUCTION BUDGET ILLUSTRATED

When the planning and coordination is completed between the sales and manufacturing executives, and the least-cost combination of sales, produc-

FIG. 10-3 Production Budget

THE MANUFACTURING COMPANY

PRODUCTION BUDGET
For the Plan Year 19XX

Product/Period	Sales Requirements	Add: Ending Finished Goods Inventory	Total Requirements	Deduct: Beginning Finished Goods Inventory	Unit Production Requirements
Product A					
January	70,000	130,000	200,000	130,000	70,000
February	68,000	132,000	200,000	130,000	70,000
March	78,000	124,000	202,000	132,000	70,000
Total Quarter 1	216,000	124,000	340,000	130,000	210,000
Quarter 2	222,000	127,000	349,000	124,000	225,000
" 3	180,000	157,000	337,000	127,000	210,000
" 4	210,000	147,000	357,000	157,000	200,000
Total — Year	828,000	147,000	975,000	130,000	845,000
Product B					
January	40,000	92,000	132,000	87,000	45,000
February	44,000	94,000	138,000	92,000	46,000
March	48,000	94,000	142,000	94,000	48,000
Total Quarter 1	132,000	94,000	226,000	87,000	139,000
Quarter 2	140,000	100,000	240,000	94,000	146,000
" 3	156,000	84,000	240,000	100,000	140,000
" 4	120,000	100,000	220,000	84,000	136,000
Total — Year	548,000	100,000	648,000	87,000	561,000
Product C					

tion, and inventory levels is arrived at, the short-term production budget can be finalized. Usually this must be done on a product (or product group) basis, by appropriate period. Assuming a policy of reasonable flexibility in inventories, and some limited production changes (accounted for by major maintenance) the production plan, in units, may appear as in Figure 10-3.

In this example, production was not permitted to vary more than 8 percent between periods in order to stabilize the work force; the normal inventory level of about two months' sales was permitted to vary to offset the sales decline. This was particularly evident in the fourth quarter for both of the products.

The production budget in this example is expressed in *units* of product. However, ultimately for valuing inventory, determining cash requirements, and financial position, it must be converted to monetary units.

STEPS IN DEVELOPING THE MANUFACTURING BUDGET

Because of the many complexities in developing the production budget, it is best to describe these before outlining the principal steps in establishing the production budget and the related cost budgets. A summary of the steps in the planning and control of manufacturing costs, many of which are discussed in subsequent chapters, includes these actions:

1. Select the period of time, and time intervals, to be used as the basis of the production budget.
2. Determine the physical quantity or volume of product to be manufactured item by item and by time period, to meet sales requirements, provide balanced inventories, and maintain manufacturing costs at acceptable levels.
3. Establish, in substantial detail, *when* the goods are to be manufactured.
4. Resolve *where* the goods are to be produced or subcontracted (which plants).
5. Determine the manufacturing operations required.
6. Establish standards for the manufacture of the products — direct material, direct labor, and overhead — to measure manufacturing efficiency.
7. Translate the production plan into monetary units to establish inventory cost requirements, and to establish total financial requirements, by appropriate time period.
8. Measure actual manufacturing performance against the manufacturing standards.
9. Provide manufacturing management with the data it needs to control costs.
10. Revise the budget and cost standards as required.

11

Direct Labor

INTRODUCTION

Direct or production labor relates to that portion of salaries or wages that can be directly charged to a product or process. Given the trend to automation and the increased use of continuous processing type of manufacture, the distinction between "direct" and "indirect" labor tends to lose its significance. For purposes of planning and control, any factory salaries or wages directly identifiable with a *productive* department will be treated as direct labor. All other labor will be classified as indirect, and is discussed in Chapter 13.

The direct labor budget is not simply a question of determining the manhours and costs of carrying out the production budget. There are some broad social implications. For this reason, among others, the methods used to develop the direct labor budget vary by company and industry.

SOCIAL IMPLICATIONS OF THE LABOR BUDGET

While it may be expected that management will seek to hold its labor costs to a minimum, due consideration must be given to the effect of the program upon the workers. The worker is a human being, not a machine, and as such he has a vital interest in the regularity and security of his employment and in fairness of reward, opportunity for advancement, and favorable working conditions. The workers constitute the most numerous, and therefore the most important, group in the industrial partnership of management, capital, and labor. Their interests should therefore receive paramount consideration. As an individual, the worker is seldom in a position to demand such consideration; and his interests sometimes must be represented through collective bargaining agencies. Management in industry, as now constituted, must largely accept the responsibility for a fair adjustment between the rights of workers, investors, and consumers. The assumption of this responsibility demands far more than just a favorable attitude toward the rights of workers. Good intentions are not sufficient. Management must earnestly, sincerely, and intelligently explore every possibility of sales, production, and financial programs leading to stability and security of employment. Fair and accurate methods of employee reward must be established and continuously refined. The financial integrity of industry must be maintained but, within the limits imposed by this requirement, it must be recognized that the workers' interests are of major importance.

It is the opinion of the author that this responsibility is being widely accepted by American industrial leaders and that upon such recognition depends our chief promise of future economic strength, stability, and growth.

IMPORTANCE OF LABOR PLANNING AND CONTROL

The social obligations and responsibilities of management in developing labor plans are not inconsistent with management's attempt to hold labor costs to a minimum. What good workers want is regularity and security of employment, with reasonable pay and acceptable fringe benefits, such as adequate health insurance, and retirement pay. This objective is not necessarily in conflict with low costs. If production is carelessly planned, with the result that there is an unnecessary amount of spasmodic increasing and decreasing of the labor force, the results may be both unsatisfactory to workers and productive of high costs. Such procedure usually results in idle investment in equipment and materials, poor labor morale, and a frequent lack of necessary training and skill on the part of workers, all of which contribute to high costs.

It must be recognized that consumer demand, which is to some extent beyond the control of management, limits the degree of regularity of employment that can be provided; yet, with due allowance for such limits, much depends upon the degree of care exercised in developing the sales and production programs and the coordination of labor requirements with these programs.

It should be understood that intelligent control of labor cost contributes both to the satisfaction of workers and to low costs. It is better, both for workers and management, to have the job done by 20 workers who are required to meet fair and reasonable standards of performance and who can consequently be paid a reasonable wage than, through laxity of labor control, to require 25 workers whose individual hourly wages must be held to a minimum in order to vie with a more efficient competitor.

In view of the social implications of labor planning and the fact that labor is frequently the largest element of manufacturing cost, the importance of labor budgeting and control is readily apparent.

PURPOSE OF THE LABOR BUDGET

While one of the first objectives of the labor budget is to provide the highest practicable degree of regularity of employment, consideration must also be given to the estimating and control of labor cost. Regularity of employment in itself effects some reduction in labor cost but when carried beyond the point of practicability it may increase other costs. For example, additional sales effort may be required to expand sales volume or to develop new products for slack periods; the cost of carrying inventories and the dangers of obsolescence and price declines must also be considered. A proper balance must be secured.

Certain factors have arisen in recent years to add to the importance of regularity of employment. Merit rating plans have been adopted in many states whereby the unemployment compensation tax rates are based upon the degree of regularity of employment maintained by the taxpayer, with materially lower rates for level employment. The federal Fair Labor Standards Act and various state laws of a similar character make higher wage rates mandatory for overtime work and thereby encourage regularity of work as opposed to spasmodic slack and rush periods. But an overriding need of management is to secure and maintain a reliable cadre of experienced and dependable employees.

Provision for regularity of employment begins not with the labor budget itself, but rather with the sales and production budgets as described in previous chapters. Once these general budgets are established, however, the detailed work of planning for labor requirements and controlling the labor costs becomes the function of the labor budget.

More specifically, the definite purposes of the labor budget are to:

- Ascertain the number and kind of workers and manhours that will be necessary to execute the production program during the budget period, and the time when such workers will be needed.
- Ascertain the labor cost of the production program.
- Determine amount and time of cash disbursements for labor that will be required by the production program.
- Provide suitable bases for the measurement of labor performance and the control of labor costs.

TECHNIQUES USED IN DEVELOPING THE LABOR BUDGET

The labor budget comprises the manhours and related direct labor cost required to carry out the production budget. Each of these two phases are discussed.

Budgeting Labor Hours

The method of estimating the hours of labor that are required to execute the production program depends largely upon the circumstances of production. Where products are uniform and standard labor time allowances have been established for products, it is necessary only to multiply the production called for by the standards to arrive at the standard labor hours required. To this must then be added a percentage of variance from standard which experience has demonstrated to be representative of actual results, or which production executives believe, under the immediate circumstances, is likely to result, in order to arrive at the actual labor hours to be budgeted.

Where the products manufactured are not sufficiently uniform to make the above method feasible but where there is considerable uniformity of operations, the production may be translated into operation requirements. If the operation standards have been established in terms of man- or machine-hours, the quantity of labor required may be ascertained by multiplying the operations by the standards and making reasonable allowance for variances.

Where detailed standards have not been developed or established, the budget can be prepared utilizing estimates, ratios, or other factors. Historical records of past performance should indicate the number of labor hours needed for a given product or operation. Also, records of past experience should reveal the relationship of labor hours to various volume levels of production. Separate ratios should be established for each unit, department, or, in some cases, group of skills. Ratios may also be generated for each class of product.

If no history or past experience is available, the labor hours must be estimated. Industrial engineers in many cases can make realistic estimates by having a thorough understanding of the manufacturing processes. Another technique is to have factory management, foremen, or department heads make their own estimates based on previous experience. With knowledge of the products and manufacturing capability, they can estimate the skills and quantity of labor needed to produce the units of product assigned to them in the production budget. The estimate must then be reviewed, revised, and approved by management. It may also be appropriate to have the production planning and control department, or cost department, analyze the estimates or assist in making the estimates.

In many businesses it is necessary to use several methods of preparing a budget due to the number of products and operations as well as new products introduced each year.

Even in those concerns in which products and operations are highly standardized, and in which there is a continuous program for setting and revising the standards, there usually will be found some work in a transitional state for which dependence must be placed upon foremen's estimates. It is also desirable to check one method against another; thus, past ratios of labor hours to physical quantity of production in each department may serve as a test check on foremen's estimates or on calculations of standard hours required. It should be emphasized that, even where standards are available, it is the expected actual time that is desired for the purpose of the budget.

Time-Phasing Manhours

In preparing the annual planning budget, the manhours estimated must indicate not only the total requirements, but also the time when the skills are needed. It must be time-phased. The labor estimate must be structured to develop labor hours by increment of time — by day, week, month, or by another interval of time within the budget period. This information — hours by skill and time required — is required by the personnel department to assure that the labor is on hand when needed. As in all departments, the personnel department must integrate its hiring efforts into the overall production program. Personnel advertising, recruiting, and hiring must be done well in advance in order to provide time for training of new workers and balancing the labor force between shifts and departments.

Budgeting Labor Costs

Direct Labor. The labor hours required to satisfy the budgeted production program must be translated into total labor costs. The method of determining estimated labor costs depends upon how the hours or quantity of labor was established as well as the payment method used. Where standard labor costs were utilized for the products to be manufactured, it is necessary only to multiply the units of product called for in the production budget by the standard labor costs. To this total must be added a reasonable variance from standards that experience has demonstrated to be representative of actual results. It is necessary, of course, to evaluate the standards periodically to consider any changes, such as increased or decreased labor rates, which may be anticipated to occur during the budget period.

If the labor hours are estimated for each labor skill or classification, and standards are not used, the labor rate for each skill or classification must be determined. Usually, these current labor rates are available from the personnel department and are multiplied by the number of hours required, to obtain the total labor cost. In addition, a factor must be added to the current pay rate to recognize anticipated increases for merit performance or cost of living adjustments. Of course, any exceptional circumstances that may be predicted such as idle time, delays, overtime, use of untrained workers, changes in operations, and new methods should be evaluated and considered. In most companies historical factors have been developed which may be used.

Successful budgeting of labor hours and cost depends to a large degree on the standardization of labor operations and the adequacy of labor records pertaining to historical labor performance and costs.

Indirect Labor. While the foregoing discussion of labor costs pertained primarily to direct labor — wages paid to employees working directly on the product being produced — the same methods may be applied to indirect labor. Labor budgets for service or other indirect departments are based on past experience, anticipated volume of operations, ratios to direct labor, and, in many cases, standards. Production executives should review and analyze the indirect labor budget to ensure its consistency with the budgeted production program.

Obviously, it is necessary to determine the total labor cost by periods of time — days, weeks, months — so that the cash flows can be an input to the financial plan of the company. This necessitates time phasing the labor budget inputs. Labor costs are significant when related to the total costs of operations and, accordingly, must be determined with a high degree of accuracy.

As is discussed in Chapter 13, some companies derive the indirect labor budget as part of the manufacturing overhead. Often it is based on the standard hours of direct labor — as to total amount. The annual planning procedure may or may not extend to the specific skills needed by labor classification, depending on circumstances. The specific requirements for indirect labor may be determined in the weekly or monthly production planning process.

REVISING THE LABOR BUDGET

The preceding commentary relates principally to determining the annual or short-term planning budget. Yet for the shorter periods, the labor budget may need revising. For example, if major changes take place in the salary and wage rates, the budget must be changed in order to provide meaningful control reports and permit the planning of cash needs, among other reasons. Then, too, if major labor performance standards change, as reviewed later, the labor budget must be revised. These guidelines would apply when production can be planned with reasonable certainty over the short run of, for example, six months.

In companies where the production is subject to large individual orders or contract basis, the labor budget must be flexible and adjusted as orders are received. This results in a continuous update of the labor budget. A contract labor budget will be established concurrently with the issuance of the contract work authority to the production department. The purpose of issuing the labor budget at the same time work is authorized is to ensure proper performance measurement. In these situations the budgets are based on the estimated labor, which was included in the contract proposal establishing the price.

To provide effective cost control and performance measurement, budgets should be revised as conditions and circumstances change. In general, labor budgets are modified and revised systematically when:

- Production volume increases or decreases.
- Changes occur in scope of work being performed under a contract.
- Revisions are made to work-flow or sequence of operations.
- Facilities being utilized are modified.
- Production management provides detailed analysis with justification and recommends that a labor budget be revised.
- Organizational changes result in shifting work effort from one department to another.

RESPONSIBILITY FOR THE LABOR BUDGET

For effective planning and control, the labor budget should be developed following organizational lines of authority and responsibility. In the final sense, responsibility for the labor budget rests with the chief manufacturing executive. However, the accumulation of labor costs and related reporting against the budget must be by functional responsibility. This being the case, responsibility for the labor budget rests with the department head or organizational unit manager responsible for performance. These individuals can take the actions necessary to perform within the budgeted amounts and meet the production program budget. Obviously, each next level executive is also responsible for determining that the labor budgets are appropriate under the circumstances. Finally, the chief manufacturing executive is responsible for all production labor costs and should approve the final direct labor budget.

In some instances the labor budget will be prepared by the chief production executive's staff, depending upon the size of the company. However, the labor budget is normally prepared by the controller's organization, the cost accounting, or budget department, based on labor inputs from the operating units. Also, the budget department can be of great assistance in compiling analytical and historical data for use in reviewing the prepared budget. The labor budget must be given a critical review by operating and financial management to ensure that it is consistent with the sales, inventory, and related production budgets, and that it falls within the financial capabilities of the firm.

LABOR BUDGETING PROCEDURES

The procedures to develop the direct labor budget will depend on a great number of factors, including such items as:

- Basic manufacturing process — whether process or job order
- Existence of performance standards
- Organizational structure — whether centralized or decentralized
- Degree of computerization of both labor control and financial reporting
- Dispersion of manufacturing centers — number, locations, and distances
- Methods of labor cost control

Some of the typical procedures are highlighted below.

Illustrative Procedures — Commercial Aircraft Manufacturer

The procedure followed by a commercial aircraft manufacturer is typical of that used by many small- or medium-sized metal working shops:

1. Upon receipt of the production budget, the industrial engineering department estimates the (average) standard manhours for each plane in each month of the budget period, based upon an efficiency or learning curve. This standard is then adjusted, based on past experience, to recognize the overstandard manhours expected.

2. This information, after approval by the works manager, is passed to the budget administrator, who extends the unit data to determine total manhour requirements by month.
3. From the production schedule of spare parts, based on the standard manhours, the data processing department computes the total standard manhours, by months, needed for the production of the spare equipment.
4. The budget department adds allowances for expected overruns, and calculates the labor cost by period.
5. The sum of the two elements constitutes the estimate of direct labor for the budget period, subject to the approval of management.

Illustrative Procedures — Chemical Company Process Plant

The practice followed by a chemical company is illustrative of the approach used in a process plant:

1. By reference to the approved production schedule, the plant level of operation is determined: An 80 percent level of capacity, a 50 percent level, or a 100 percent level. (Each level has a different manpower requirement.) Thus an 80 percent level might be needed for six months, and a 100 percent level for another six months.
2. By reference to the calendar, the number of operating days in each month is established.
3. The standard labor rate per operating hour is multiplied by the number of operating hours in each department to arrive at the total standard labor cost.
4. Based on past experience, a percentage is added to cover probable excess crews.
5. Total estimated labor cost is compared with standard to reveal extent of excess labor costs arising by reason of rates of production. Thus, it might be determined that $10,000 per week of labor cost is incurred for production that should require only $9,000. However, the process is such that shutdowns for short periods are uneconomical.
6. Estimated labor costs are included in the total production budget, which is submitted for approval.

Illustrative Procedure — Project-Type Budget

The procedural instructions concerning a project-type labor budget for a company operating on a project basis is shown in Figure 11-1.

FIG. 11-1   Labor Budget Procedure — Project Type

FUNCTION:

Establish a budget in terms of hours and dollars for each labor element that is required for performance of a task in accordance with the contract.

DESCRIPTION:

Study the contractual and sales order requirements, minutes of negotiation, statement of work, and the cost proposal to gain a clear understanding of the task or tasks to be performed under the contract or purchase order. This is a prerequisite to establishing a challenging but realistically attainable performance target.

PROCEDURE:

1. Labor budgets are prepared and published, and input is sent to data processing on Form NS XXXX, "Project Financial Analysis" or a similar form.

2. Compare hourly labor rates projected at the midpoint of the task with the rates used in the cost proposal. Labor control must be by dollars although hours are used as a measuring device. Realistic rates are to be used for budgeting, which may demand an adjustment of hours.

3. Determine what is a reasonable amount that should be withheld as a reserve. This may amount to a flat 5 or 10 percent of each labor element, or it may be more or less. Circumstances will cause a considerable variation, and judgment must be exercised.

4. Compare forecast bid burden rates for the midpoint of the task or the composite forecast rates, if more than one fiscal period is involved in the period of performance. Realistic rates will be used in the budget. A difference between contract value and forecast bid rates may aid in making possible a larger withhold or may reduce this amount.

5. The method of distribution of a budget for various labor elements varies considerably; therefore, these elements are discussed either singularly or in groups, below, depending upon their characteristics.

   a. *Fabrication — Machine Shop and Sheet Metal.* An approach to measuring this element is by the use of standard hours. The package standard hours will have to be factored upward to establish a realizable budget. This factor, pertinent realization, is a matter of judgment. A guide is performance on a preceding program on the same or a similar product.

      In the event no standards have been established, the hours and dollars negotiated for fabrication is a good approach to a budget.

   b. *Assembly — Mechanical or Electrical.* The comments regarding a., Fabrication, apply. The learning curve technique may be applied when there have been previous production lots of units of identical or similar configuration. It is well to use any available cross-checks to determine the validity of the budget.

   c. *Paint and Process.* This element will usually represent a relatively small percentage of the fabrication and assembly effort. The percentage relationship established in negotiations for paint and process compared with fabrication and assembly may provide a reasonable basis for setting the paint and process budget.

(continued)

FIG. 11-1   Labor Budget Procedure — Project Type (cont'd)

d. *Manufacturing Engineering, Planning and Liaison, Maintenance and Quality Control, Quality Control Tests.* These supporting labor elements represent a fairly high percentage of the combined total of fabrication, processing and assembly. The percentage relationship established in negotiations represents a guide. However, a comparison should be made to historical performance or standards, if available.

e. *Tool Design and Tool Fabrication.* These cost elements are usually bid for the design and manufacture of a definite number of tools. The bid amount less some withhold is one approach to a budget. In some cases, it may be decided after receipt of the contract that manufacturing will be facilitated by providing additional tooling. Obviously, this must be taken into consideration. The added tooling cost will be covered by transfer of budget from fabrication and/or assembly as appropriate. Relate the budgeted hours to the contract specifications and have manufacturing/engineering review for proper relationship.

f. *Shipping Labor.* This element should be based upon the contractual and sales order requirements, and the statement of work — number of shipments, weight, and packaging requirements.

g. *Engineering.* The engineering task must be clearly defined in a statement of work in order for it to be budgeted properly. When engineering liaison to the shop is involved, engineering may represent as little as one or two percent of fabrication, process, and assembly. When the engineering task involves this, plus any combination of the following: design, testing, test witnessing, and/or others, the various elements of the task should be considered separately and budgeted separately. The budget must be prepared based on a detailed breakdown of engineering tasks.

h. *Technical Proposals and Reports, Logistics, Field Service, and Training.* The contract scope of work must be reviewed and each task be budgeted separately. Refer to the amount proposed and negotiated as a guide. Consider the previous performance on similar work effort.

i. *Supervision and Production Control.* These budgets are established by applying approved percentages (see Table B, "Allocated Labor Ratios" [*omitted*]) to the applicable allocation base hours budgeted. Consult the budget department.

j. *Material and Data Services.* This element is allocated. The budget is an approved percentage of the application allocation base hours budgeted. Consult the budget department.

k. *Reproduction.* This element is usually a minor cost item. Budget should be based on estimated number of items to be reproduced, enlarged, and collated. Rates are available for each task from the budget department.

ILLUSTRATIVE DIRECT LABOR BUDGET

The preparation of the annual planning direct labor budget for a company producing many products and having several manufacturing departments is a monstrous computational effort greatly assisted by the use of a computer. In the illustrative procedure, the product unit standard manufacturing hours, by department, has been determined by the industrial engineers. Hence, by product, the total standard manufacturing hours for each department was calculated monthly and quarterly, as illustrated in Figure 11-2 by simple extension. Direct labor costs were determined by department, by product, as shown. (In some companies, the departmental hours might be further subdivided by craft.) It should be noted that provision was made for a wage change in March.

The standard manhours required may be summarized by department, by product, as reflected in Figure 11-3. The exact type of summary will depend on the needs of management. But the direct labor hours by *department* and time phased, illustrated in Figure 11-3, are needed for production planning and scheduling purposes.

The direct labor budget finally is summarized for the entire manufacturing operation, as to both standard hours and cost, as shown in Figure 11-4. Because standard hours cannot usually be attained 100 percent, a planned variance of 1.5 percent to 1 percent has been superimposed to arrive at a tight, but realistic, direct labor hours budget. Cost variances also arise by reason of craft assignments, lost time and other causes, and are reflected in a 2 percent allowance for labor rate variances, shown in Figure 11-4. Again, the exact type of labor budget summary depends on the needs of management.

DIRECT LABOR STANDARDS

Having reviewed the annual labor budget preparation, some more detailed remarks with emphasis on the control phase may be helpful.

The establishment of labor standards is a responsibility of the production department. Production executives or engineers are presumably the best qualified to determine the amount of labor time required to perform a production operation. The method of setting such standards has been extensively covered in the literature of production management and is beyond the scope of this book. Many concerns have created standards departments whose entire efforts are directed to the continuous improvement and refinement of standards. The types of labor standards actually in use vary from general relationships between the number of labor hours used and the unit volume of production down to the exact time allowed for a specific machine or manual operation. In most plants a considerable range in the degree of

FIG. 11-2 Schedule of Direct Labor Hours and Cost, by Product, by Department

THE MANUFACTURING COMPANY

SCHEDULE — DIRECT LABOR HOURS AND COSTS

For the Plan Year 19XX

Month/Dep't	Grand Total Cost*	Product A Production Schedule (Units)	Unit Standard Hours	Total Standard Hours	Average Rate per Hour	Total Cost	Product B Production Schedule (Units)	Unit Standard Hours	Total Standard Hours	Average Rate per Hour	Total Cost
January											
Dep't 1	$ 448,000	20,000	.8	16,000	$7.00	$ 112,000	40,000	.7	28,000	$7.00	$ 196,000
Dep't 2	453,600	20,000	.4	8,000	8.40	67,200	40,000	.9	36,000	8.40	302,400
Dep't 3	348,000	20,000	.3	6,000	6.00	36,000	40,000	.5	20,000	6.00	120,000
Dep't 4	150,000	20,000	.2	4,000	5.00	20,000	40,000	.4	16,000	5.00	80,000
Total	$ 1,399,600	20,000	1.7	34,000	$6.92	$ 235,200	40,000	2.5	100,000	$6.98	$ 698,400
February											
Dep't 1	$ 564,200	22,000	.8	17,600	$7.00	$ 123,200	50,000	.7	35,000	$7.00	$ 245,000
Dep't 2	552,720	22,000	.4	8,800	8.40	73,920	50,000	.9	45,000	8.40	378,000
Dep't 3	431,400	22,000	.3	6,600	6.00	39,600	50,000	.5	25,000	6.00	150,000
Dep't 4	286,500	22,000	.2	4,400	5.00	22,000	50,000	.4	20,000	5.00	100,000
Total	$ 1,834,820	22,000	1.7	37,400	$6.92	$ 258,720	50,000	2.5	125,000	$6.98	$ 873,000
March											
Dep't 1	$ 455,000	25,000	.8	20,000	$7.50	$ 150,000	30,000	.7	21,000	$7.50	$ 157,500
Dep't 2	420,000	25,000	.4	10,000	9.00	90,000	30,000	.9	27,000	9.00	243,000
Dep't 3	341,250	25,000	.3	7,500	6.50	48,750	30,000	.5	15,000	6.50	97,500
Dep't 4	249,300	25,000	.2	5,000	5.40	27,000	30,000	.4	12,000	5.40	64,800
Total	$ 1,465,550	25,000	1.7	42,500	$7.43	$ 315,750	30,000	2.5	75,000	$7.50	$ 562,800
Quarter 1 — Total	$ 4,699,970	67,500	1.7	113,900	$7.11	$ 809,670	120,000	2.5	300,000	$7.11	$2,134,200
Quarter 2 — Total	4,962,480	67,500	1.7	114,750	7.43	852,590	118,500	2.5	296,250	7.50	2,221,880
Quarter 3 — Total	5,002,500	68,800	1.7	116,960	7.43	869,010	121,300	2.5	303,250	7.50	2,274,380
Quarter 4 — Total	5,016,000	67,500	1.7	114,750	7.43	852,590	120,000	2.5	300,000	7.50	2,250,000
Grand Total	$19,680,950	270,800	1.7	460,360	$7.35	$3,383,860	479,800	2.5	1,199,500	$7.40	$8,880,460

* Grand total includes products other than A and B, and detail is not shown.

FIG. 11-3 Summary of Standard Labor Hours

The Manufacturing Company

STANDARD DIRECT LABOR HOURS
For Plan Year 19XX

Period	Grand Total*	Department 1				Department 2			
		Product A	Product B	Product C	Total	Product A	Product B	Product C	Total
January	167,000	16,000	28,000	20,000	64,000	8,000	36,000	10,000	54,000
February	219,600	17,600	35,000	28,000	80,600	8,800	45,000	12,000	65,800
March	172,500	20,000	21,000	24,000	65,000	10,000	27,000	13,000	50,000
Total — First Quarter	559,100	53,600	84,000	72,000	209,600	26,800	108,000	35,000	169,800
Quarter 2	570,400	54,000	83,000	73,000	210,000	27,000	106,700	34,000	167,700
Quarter 3	575,000	55,000	85,000	74,000	214,000	27,500	109,200	35,000	171,700
Quarter 4	570,000	54,000	84,000	73,000	211,000	27,000	107,900	35,000	169,900
Grand Total	2,274,500	216,600	336,000	292,000	844,600	108,300	431,800	139,000	679,100

* Departments 3 and 4 not shown.

FIG. 11-4   Summary Direct Labor Budget

THE MANUFACTURING COMPANY
DIRECT LABOR BUDGET
For Plan Year 19XX

Month	Direct Labor Hours			Gross Labor Cost		
	Standard	Planned Variances	Total	Standard	Allowance for Variances	Total
January	167,000	2,500	169,500	$ 1,299,600	28,000	$ 1,427,600
February	219,600	3,300	222,900	1,334,820	36,700	1,871,520
March	172,500	2,150	174,650	1,465,550	29,300	1,494,850
Total	559,100	7,950	567,050	$ 4,699,970	94,000	$ 4,793,970
April	191,100	1,900	193,000	$ 1,661,730	33,230	$ 1,694,960
May	189,200	1,890	191,090	1,645,280	32,900	1,678,180
June	190,100	1,900	192,000	1,655,470	33,110	1,688,580
Total	570,400	5,690	576,090	$ 4,962,480	99,240	$ 5,061,720
July	190,000	1,900	191,900	$ 1,652,260	33,050	$ 1,685,310
August	195,000	1,950	196,950	1,695,740	33,910	1,729,650
September	190,002	1,900	191,900	1,654,500	33,090	1,687,590
Total	575,000	5,750	580,750	$ 5,002,500	100,050	$ 5,102,550
October	190,000	1,900	191,900	$ 1,672,000	33,440	$ 1,705,440
November	190,000	1,900	191,900	1,672,000	33,440	1,705,440
December	190,000	1,900	191,900	1,672,000	33,440	1,705,440
Total	570,000	5,700	575,700	$ 5,016,000	100,320	$ 5,116,320
Grand Total	2,274,500	25,090	2,299,590	$19,680,950	393,610	$20,074,560

refinement of labor standards is necessary in covering all operations. Obviously, the degree of definiteness of responsibility and certainty of control depends upon the degree of refinement of the standards. Sound judgment based on practical experience is necessary to determine the degree of refinement most profitable.

An example serves to illustrate how the industrial engineers or standards men coordinate their work with that of the accountant. Assume that in the grinding system of a powder plant, the industrial engineers establish the following requirements through time study:

Required crew per shift:

1 Drum Dumper

2 Mill Operators

1 Packer

½ Handler

Makeup of operating hours:	
Actual processing	6.5
Cleaning	.5
Maintenance, conflict, etc.	1.0
Total	8.0
Pounds to be handled per shift (8 hours)	1,600
Pounds per manhour (standard) $\left(\dfrac{1.600}{4.5 \times 8}\right)$	44.4

Upon receipt of the information and after review by the accounting staff, the standard labor cost would be calculated (on standard cost sheets):

Operator	Number	Manhours	Rate per Manhour	Total Cost
First Shift:				
Drum Dumper	1	8	$3.60	$ 28.80
Mill Operator	2	16	3.75	60.00
Packer	1	8	3.50	28.00
Handler	½	4	3.40	13.60
Second–Third Shifts:				
Drum Dumper	2	16	3.65	58.40
Mill Operator	4	32	3.80	121.60
Packer	2	16	3.55	56.80
Handler	1	8	3.45	27.60
Total				$394.80
Direct labor cost per hundredweight ($394.80 ÷ 48)				$ 8.225

The rates applied are those from the union contract. If the agreement called for premium payments on Sunday as such, for example, this would have to be considered.

REVISION OF LABOR PERFORMANCE STANDARDS

Generally, performance standards are not revised until a significant change of method or process occurs. Since standards serve as the basis of control, the accounting staff should be on the alert for changes put into effect in the factory but not reported for standard revision. If the revised process requires more time, the production staff will usually make quite certain that their measuring stick is modified. However, if the new process requires less time, it is understandable that the change might not be reported promptly. Each supervisor naturally desires to make the best possible showing. The prompt reporting of time reductions might be stimulated through periodic review of changes in standard labor hours or costs. In other words, the current labor performance of actual hours compared to standard should be but one measure of performance; another is standard time reductions, which is also measured against a goal for the year.

It should be the responsibility of the budget and standards supervisor to see that the standards are changed as the process changes in order to report true performance. If a wage incentive system is related to these standards, the need for adjusting for process changes is emphasized. An analysis of variances, whether favorable or unfavorable, will often serve to indicate revisions not yet reported.

While standard revisions will often be made for control purposes, it may not be practical or desirable to change product cost standards. The differences may be treated as cost variances until they are of sufficient magnitude to warrant a cost revision.

LABOR VARIANCES AND CAUSES

There is usually little value in comparing the actual labor cost with the budgeted cost. The budget is an estimate of the labor cost justified by an anticipated volume of production. If the actual volume of production is different from that budgeted, the labor cost may be expected to vary in like degree; hence, the difference between actual and budget may be merely an indication that production volume was more or less than anticipated. What is needed to assist production executives in the control of labor is a detailed analysis of the differences between the actual labor cost and what the costs should have been, for the actual volume of production or operations, and the causes of these variances. Where labor standards are available, such analysis can be made; where such standards have not been established, an estimate must be made by production executives as to what the labor cost should have been, or the budget figures must be proportionately increased or decreased to reflect the changes in production. The absence of standards with the consequent dependence upon estimates usually leaves management in some doubt as to whether labor cost variances are the result of careless estimates or careless work.

In general, there are two causes of labor variances. Either the work takes more time than allowed by the standard, or a higher price is paid for labor than called for by the standard. In either case there may or may not be a justification for the variance. Excessive time results from such causes as:

- Inefficient workers
- Wasted time
- Faulty scheduling of work
- Poor supervision
- Defective materials
- Defective tools or equipment
- Idle time
- Excessive number of learners
- Poor working conditions

Excessive rates of pay result from:

- Increases in general scale of wages
- High-priced workers on low-priced work
- Overtime rates
- Hourly rate guarantees

It is apparent that some of these causes of high cost are the fault of the workers, others are the fault of management or supervision, and still others, such as increases in the general scale of wages, may lie beyond the control of either. In any variance from a standard, the dependability of the standard itself must be questioned; once this is assured, responsibility must be definitely placed and immediate action taken, insofar as the factors are controllable, to prevent its continuance.

LABOR REPORTS

Labor is an elusive cost and its waste must be detected and corrected immediately if excessive costs are to be prevented. In those departments and for those workers who are performing at or near standard, no reports are necessary. For those who fall below, reports must be made promptly — often hourly or daily — showing the extent, cause, and responsibility for the failure. Such reports must serve as the basis for immediate corrective action. Summary reports showing the general performance of departments and major divisions should be prepared at less frequent intervals, usually weekly or monthly.

These summary reports should present such information as the following:

- Percentage of actual performance to standard
- Output in units per labor hour and percentage of standard
- Output in units per labor dollar and percentage of standard
- Ratio of indirect labor hours to direct labor hours and percentage of standard
- Ratio of indirect labor cost to direct labor cost and percentage of standard
- Average earnings per man
- Rate of labor turnover and analysis of causes

This type of information should be reported for individual departments and for the business as a whole.

Illustrative Reports

Some operations lend themselves to hourly or daily reporting. Through the use of computers or other means, daily production may be evaluated and promptly reported upon. A simple computer-prepared daily report showing performance by department for the preceding day, and available to the plant superintendent by 7:00 A.M. is illustrated in Figure 11-5. This report can be easily supplemented by a report showing the shift, workers, or job orders, or when the substandard performance occurred. It also may be expanded to show labor costs. Figure 11-6 illustrates a weekly report prepared for foremen, showing below standard performance for individual men.

Exception Reporting

The principle of reporting, for control purposes, only that segment that needs corrective action is applicable to labor costs. An illustrative exception report, as applied to direct labor, is shown in Figure 11-7.

(*text continues on page 11-26*)

FIG. 11-5 Daily Labor Report

HIGHLAND PLANT

DAILY LABOR REPORT

For the Period Ending at 4:00 P.M.   [Date]

Department	Hours		(Over)/Under Standard Hours	Percentage Standard
	Actual	Standard		
Fabricating	4,710	4,820	110	97.7
Sub-assembly	3,812	3,800	(12)	100.0
Assembly	2,920	3,100	180	94.2
Grinding	670	590	(80)	113.6
Polishing	3,120	2,960	(160)	105.4
Painting	2,860	2,860	—	100.0
Packing	1,040	1,000	(40)	104.0
Total	19,132	19,130	(2)	100.0

FIG. 11-6 Weekly Labor Report to Foreman

WEEKLY REPORT TO FOREMAN

Week ending _____   𝒥𝑅𝐻   Foreman 𝐿𝑀𝑊   Supt.

Worker		Percentage of efficiency			Foreman's explanation	Superintendent's notes
No.	Name	This week	Last week	Last month		
621	Willard	72	70		New man on this work should have longer trial	
622	Olman	88	98	97	No explanation, usually does good work	Investigate.
630	Smith	60	101	98	New work on this machine. Worker O.K.	
637	Hyatt	87	87	88	Machine must be over-hauled. Worker O.K.	Report to Maintenance Dept.

FIG. 11-7   Daily Labor Report — Exception Reporting

THE ASSEMBLY CORPORATION
DAILY LABOR REPORT

Date November 19, 19....

Cost Center: Polishing
Foreman: Smith

Operators		Labor Cost		Over/Under Standard	Reasons for Off-Standard Costs
No.	Name	Actual	Standard		
Off Standard					
1620	Smith	$ 14.81	$ 9.10	$ 5.71	Operator inefficiency
1697	Jones	13.98	12.00	1.98	Faulty tools
1722	Loy	12.14	11.72	.42	Fatigue
1732	Carl	15.62	12.99	2.63	Operator inefficiency
1781	Black	16.21	10.84	5.37	Nonstandard material
1798	Symanski	13.87	12.07	1.80	Lack of materials
1801	Deal	19.87	14.77	5.10	Machine breakdown — Overtime ($3.10)
	Total	$106.50	$ 83.49	$ 23.01	
On Standard		822.04	824.19	(2.15)	
	Total	$928.54	$907.68	$ 20.86	

Average percentage of standard   102.3%

Average percentage of standard — last week   103.4%

**FIG. 11-8   Budget Procedure for Indicated Final
Cost — Labor**

FUNCTION:

Determine the estimated total labor cost of performance of the tasks included in a
contract.

DESCRIPTION:

Analyze labor expenditures and work completion to date, and forecast labor
expenditures from the present to completion of the contract. The total of the
cost-to-date plus the estimate of the cost-to-complete is the indicated final cost (IFC).
The analysis is performed at the labor account level. Under the section headed
"Procedures," steps relative to individual labor accounts are outlined.

PROCEDURES:

Establish the cost-to-date of all labor from the weekly cost report or the monthly cost
ledger. The analyst's task is to estimate the hours of effort and the corresponding
dollar cost to complete all unfinished tasks required by contract. The estimate-to-
complete hours will be priced at approved labor rates. The approach varies from
one labor element to another. The following describes some of the tested approaches
to individual labor elements or groups of elements to which a given approach is
common.

    1. *Fabrication and Assembly.* Maximum use of the Manufacturing Detail Cost
and Performance (MADCAP) and the Locater Estimate to Complete (LETC) programs
shall be employed:

        a. *MADCAP.* This is an electronic data processing (EDP) system for
           measuring work-in-process, completion status, and cost performance. The
           entire fabrication and assembly task is input by part number, down to the
           sequence of operation level.

              Time standards are applied to the operations and accumulated to the
           end-item level as a package. As sequences are completed, standard
           hours are earned and matching actual hours are recorded by the
           operator. The ratio of standard hours earned to total package standard
           required is the physical percentage of completion. This index factored for
           learning (an appropriate improvement slope is employed) produces the
           percent of budget earned at that point. Matching budget earned to actual
           recorded costs at the same level denotes performance.

        b. *LETC.* This is an EDP report prepared upon request by Material Control.

              The locator system is examined for standard hours remaining on all
           open fabrication, sub-assembly, or final assembly, and orders at a given
           sales order level.

              Realization factors are applied to the standard hours remaining to
           produce estimated production hours to complete.

If there are no standards established, the estimate may be established by
considering the period of time remaining for completion and by establishing a likely
rate of input by week or by month for the period of remaining activity. The analyst
will need to consider previous rates of input to the program, correlate the input with
progress made in completion of the task, and use this experience to establish an
estimate of the cost to carry the program to completion. This second approach
obviously cannot be as precise and is therefore not as readily supportable as the
standards approach.

(continued)

**FIG. 11-8   Budget Procedure for Indicated Final
Cost — Labor** (cont'd)

2. *Paint and Process.* This element is generally a relatively small part of the overall production cost and can be estimated as a percentage of fabrication and assembly cost. If the fabrication and assembly effort is well underway, it is possible to compare paint and process costs to date with fabrication and assembly costs to date and establish a percentage relationship which can be used for projecting the paint and process cost to complete.

3. *Manufacturing Engineering Planning, Liaison and Maintenance: Quality Assurance for Production and for Engineering (Quality Control Tests).* These support elements combined represent a high percentage of the combined costs of fabrication, process, and assembly. The contract value established for each of them may be expressed as a percentage of the combined amounts of fabrication, process, and assembly. When establishing an indicated final cost, the project budget analyst should consider the following:

   a. The performance to date as a percentage of the production elements mentioned above.

   b. The indicated final cost determined for fabrication, process, and assembly. These support labor elements tend to vary directly with production, so that if production element IFCs are showing an upward trend, it is probable that the support labor elements will increase correspondingly.

   c. Tooling problems will result in a higher than planned expenditure of effort in manufacturing engineering liaison, or maintenance, or both. The project budget analyst, in addition to taking the above factors into consideration, should consider the program time span. There may be a requirement to maintain level-of-effort support in one or more of the above elements.

The project budget analyst must decide whether the trend to date is likely to continue or to increase or decrease. Unresolved problems effecting cost to date must be considered in the Estimate-to-Complete.

4. *Quality Assurance — Receiving.* As a rule, the relationship between receiving inspection and material costs recorded to date will be employed for the Estimate-to-Complete.

5. *Tool Design and Tool Fabrication.* Several estimating yardsticks are available for these accounts.

   a. It may be possible, if the tooling program involves sufficient quantity, to establish an average cost per design and an average cost of fabrication per tool by considering the number of designs and tools complete to date versus the costs recorded for same, as a basis for estimating the cost to bring the tooling program to completion. This approach is best applied to machine-shop tooling where the costs per tool are likely to lie within a narrow range. Where there are a limited number of tools or where the range of tool cost is great, the average approach is unlikely to be satisfactory.

   b. When there are a limited number of tools and/or they range from inexpensive fixtures to expensive test equipment, it is best to confer with tooling supervision to establish the status of tooling completion and compare with costs to date, and use this as a basis for projecting the estimated cost to complete.

6. *Shipping Labor.* Usually an indicated final cost for this element can be established by computing an average cost to date for the shipment of a system or unit, or in the case of spare parts, by knowing the number of pieces to be shipped and the number already shipped. The analyst can establish an average cost per piece to apply to the number of pieces yet to be shipped. An estimate for shipping rejected parts back to the vendor should also be made.

7. *Engineering Labor.* Estimating engineering by statistical means does not produce accurate IFCs. The total engineering function is an aggregate of many different functions. Engineering is organizationally structured so that a given organization performs a discrete function (i.e., Mechanical Engineer, Optical Engineering). The standard way for a budget analyst to obtain an IFC is to request an ETC (Estimate-to-Complete) from the line manager of the organization that has the responsibility for performing a specific function to complete a contract. It is important that the validity of these estimates be assessed by the budget analyst in terms of any or all factual data about the job, such as:

- Schedule
- Master plan
- Drawing count
- Testing cycles
- Manpower constraints

8. *Engineering Supervision and Data Services.* These accounts are allocated. Apply approved forecast rates to year-to-date and estimate-to-complete bases.

9. *Customer Service.* This general heading includes in-plant training, logistics, technical proposals and reports, and field service.

    a. *In-plant Training and Field Service.* The programs that utilize these labor elements usually involve the services of a specific number of personnel for specific time periods and generally pose no great problem in establishing an indicated final cost.

    b. *In-plant Product Support* (*Logistics*). This labor element is difficult to forecast without a precise understanding of the task under a specific contract. The period of performance may extend well beyond the delivery of hardware. The nature of documentation and requirements for maintenance must be known. The indicated final cost established by the analyst should be coordinated with and receive the concurrence of the supervisor of Product Support.

    c. *Technical Proposals and Reports.* The comments in paragraph b., above, are also applicable to this labor element.

Project-Type Labor Reports

Where costs must be planned and controlled on a project basis, such as in an aerospace contract, it becomes necessary to periodically update the estimated labor cost for the contract. Instructions on this procedure are contained in Figure 11-8.

For an illustrative control report on costs handled on a project basis, refer to Chapter 16, on the advertising and sales promotion expense budget.

CONTROL THROUGH PREPLANNING

The use of the control tools previously discussed points out labor inefficiencies *after* they have happened. Another type of control requires a determination as to what should happen and makes plans to assure, to the extent possible, that it does happen. It is forward-looking and preventive. This approach, which embodies budgetary control, can be applied to the control of labor costs. For example, if the manpower requirements for the production program one month hence can be determined, then steps can be taken to make certain that excess labor costs do not arise because too many men are on the payroll. This factor can be controlled; thus, the remaining factors are rate and quality of production and overtime. Overtime costs can be held within limits through the use of authorization slips.

The degree to which this preplanning can take place depends on the industry and particular conditions within the individual business firm. Are business conditions sufficiently stable so that some reasonably accurate planning can be done? Can the sales department indicate with reasonable accuracy what their requirements will be over the short run? An application might be in a machine shop where thousands of parts are made. If production requirements are known, the standard manhours necessary can be calculated and converted to manpower. For example, electronic computers may be utilized to determine standard manhours by department. Where experience reveals that standard efficiency cannot be attained, an allowance would be made for the predicted degree of efficiency. Thus, if 12,320 standard manhours are needed for the planned production, but efficiency of only 80 percent is expected, then 15,400 actual manhours must be scheduled. This requires a crew of 385 men (40 hours per week). Steps should then be taken to assure that only this number is authorized on the payroll. Of course, one must not lose sight of the probable requirements, say, one month ahead.

12

Direct Materials Purchases and Usage

INTRODUCTION

In the typical manufacturing company, the planning and control of operations is intricately mixed with the planning and control of assets and liabilities. Nowhere is this more true than in the planning and control of direct material purchases and usage. In the production budget (see Chapter 10), the basic decisions involve balancing the sales requirements, the production and manufacturing requirements, and the work-in-process/finished goods inventory. In the *materials* area, the business decisions involve balancing (1) the factory requirements for raw materials, (2) the raw materials inventory level, and (3) the purchases of raw material. As part of the operating budget, the purchases and usage of raw material is discussed in detail in this chapter. As a segment of the control of working capital, the planning and control of inventory is discussed in Chapter 21.

FOUR BUDGETS ARE INVOLVED

Direct material, as traditionally defined, includes all material that is an integral part of the finished product and can be traced to the cost of the finished article, such as raw materials and purchased parts or subcontracted production. It does not include material not directly traceable to the finished article; indirect materials, including items such as factory supplies, repair materials, fuel, and lubricating oils, are discussed in conjunction with manufacturing expenses (see Chapter 13).

The planning and control of direct materials technically involves four budgets that are interrelated but planned and controlled separately.

1. *The materials (usage) budget.* This budget specifies the *quantities* of raw materials and purchased parts (and sometimes the related costs) needed to fulfill the production budget by product, by using department, and by the appropriate time period for production.

2. *The purchases budget*. When the materials (usage) budget is known, then the purchases budget can be developed, taking into account the raw material inventory. It identifies the quantities of each direct material to be purchased, the cost, and the time and place of delivery.

3. *The materials inventory budget*. This budget specifies the *quantities* and *cost* of direct materials to be maintained in the inventory. It is the connecting link between the materials (requirements) budget and the purchases budget.

4. *The cost of materials used* (*in production*) *budget*. This budget often represents the transfer from the raw materials and purchased parts inventory to the work-in-process inventory. Under some methods of accounting, such as standard costs, excess price or usage might be charged directly to the cost of goods sold. This budget is dependent on the costs of both the materials purchased and the materials transferred out of the raw materials inventory.

All of these budgets are related to the planning and control of the respective functions. Additionally, the data must be used to develop planned inventory values for use in costing raw material, work-in-process, finished goods, and, of course, cost of goods sold.

THE MATERIALS (USAGE) BUDGET

The purposes of the materials budget include the following:

☐ To provide the quantified data so that the direct materials purchases budget can be determined. These data are used by the purchasing department.

☐ To supply the basic quantity data so that the materials cost element of the finished product can be calculated. (Quantities required will have an influence on the price; and quantities of each material in the finished product are needed to calculate the cost of the finished item.)

☐ To provide an element needed in determining materials inventory levels.

Budgeting the Quantity Needed

The data required to develop the materials budget are as follows:

☐ The volume of finished articles required for the planning period, time-phased, as reflected in the production budget;

☐ The standard quantity of each type of major material required for each finished article, plus allowances for wastage; and

☐ For those materials that must be budgeted in total or in classes, the appropriate production factors (as discussed below).

Budgeting Individual Materials. The standard quantity of each direct material item required for each product is multiplied by the time-phased production of each product to determine the *standard* quantity of each material item for each segment of the planning period. If this standard is quite restrictive, due allowance must be made for spoilage and other usage variances. If standard costs are employed, the process is quite simple. If standard usage is not known, then historical experience, engineering studies, and bills of material must be used to arrive at the unit quantities required.

Budgeting by Groups or Classes. For those items of materials and supplies that cannot be budgeted individually, the budget must be based on general factors of expected production activity, such as total budgeted labor hours, productive hours, standard allowed hours, cost of materials consumed, or cost of goods manufactured. To illustrate, assume that cost of materials consumed (other than basic materials, which are budgeted individually) is budgeted at $1 million, and that past experience demonstrates that these materials and supplies should be held to a rate of turnover of five times per year; then an average inventory of $200,000 should be budgeted. This means that individual items of material could be held in stock approximately 73 days (⅕ of 365 days). This could probably be accomplished by instructing the executives in charge to keep on hand an average of 60 days' supply. While such a plan cannot be applied rigidly to each item, it serves as a useful guide in the control of individual items and prevents the accumulation of excessive inventories.

In the application of this plan, other factors must also be considered. The relationship between the inventory and the selected factor of production activity will vary with the degree of production activity. Thus, a turnover of five times may be satisfactory when materials consumed are at the $1 million level, but it may be necessary to reduce this to four times when the level goes to $750,000. Conversely, it may be desirable to hold it to six times when the level rises to $1.25 million. Moreover, some latitude may be necessitated by the seasonal factor, as it may be necessary to increase the quantities of materials and supplies in certain months in anticipation of seasonal demands. The ratio of inventory to selected production factors at various levels of production activity and in different seasons should be plotted and studied until standard relationships can be established. The entire process can be refined somewhat by establishing different standards for different sections of the materials and supplies inventory.

The plan, once in operation, must be checked closely by monthly comparisons of actual and standard ratios. When the rate of inventory movement falls below the standard, the records of individual items must be studied to detect the slow-moving items.

The Materials Usage Budget Illustrated

For most companies, it is possible to budget each item of direct material. Typical, but simplified, budget schedules are illustrated in Figures 12-1 and 12-2.

Figure 12-1 is a schedule that translates the planned production of each finished article into the required standard raw material components. The schedule has been prepared based on these standard material requirements for each product:

Raw Material Component	Product A	B
1	3	2
2	5	4
3	—	5

Figure 12-2 summarizes the standard raw material requirements by material component and by time period, and makes provision for above-standard usage (and any margin of safety the manufacturing department considers essential). As can be seen from the numerous calculations, the use of the computer adds flexibility and facilitates the job. Manufacturing management can secure the materials budget in any segregation desired. The treatment of materials that must be handled as a class or group is discussed in connection with the purchases budget.

THE MATERIALS PURCHASES BUDGET

The purchases budget is the connection or link between the materials requirements and the materials inventory. The purchases budget indicates the quantity of each type of material to be purchased, the expected cost of the purchases by unit and in total, and the timing of receipt of the materials.

The purchases budget is intimately entwined with inventory policy and the economics involved. Factors to be considered include

- Quantity and timing of production requirements
- Economical ordering quantity
- Volume discounts periodically available
- Storage facilities available
- Cost of storage
- Availability of materials
- Risks in holding inventory including perishability and price risk
- Accuracy of materials budget

FIG. 12-1 Summary of Unit Standard Raw Material Requirements

THE CALIFORNIA MANUFACTURING COMPANY
SCHEDULE OF UNIT STANDARD RAW MATERIAL REQUIREMENTS
For the Planning Year 19XX

Raw Material/Time Period	Product A			Product B			Total Requirements All Products (Units)
	Planned Production	Unit Raw Material Requirements	Total Raw Material Requirements (Units)	Planned Production	Unit Raw Material Requirements	Total Raw Material Requirements (Units)	
Material 1							
January	42,000	3	126,000	75,000	2	150,000	276,000
February	40,000	3	120,000	72,000	2	144,000	264,000
March	43,000	3	129,000	76,000	2	152,000	281,000
Total — Quarter 1	125,000	3	375,000	223,000	2	446,000	821,000
— Quarter 2	130,000	3	390,000	225,000	2	450,000	840,000
— Quarter 3	140,000	3	420,000	225,000	2	450,000	870,000
— Quarter 4	130,000	3	390,000	230,000	2	460,000	850,000
Total — Material 1	525,000	3	1,575,000	903,000	2	1,806,000	3,381,000
Material 2							
January	42,000	5	210,000	75,000	4	300,000	510,000
February	40,000	5	200,000	72,000	4	288,000	488,000
March	43,000	5	215,000	76,000	4	304,000	519,000
Total — Quarter 1	125,000	5	625,000	223,000	4	892,000	1,517,000
— Quarter 2	130,000	5	650,000	225,000	4	900,000	1,550,000
— Quarter 3	140,000	5	700,000	225,000	4	900,000	1,600,000
— Quarter 4	130,000	5	650,000	230,000	4	920,000	1,570,000
Total — Material 2	525,000	5	2,625,000	903,000	4	3,612,000	6,237,000
Material 3							
January				75,000	5	375,000	375,000
February				72,000	5	360,000	360,000
March				76,000	5	380,000	380,000
Total — Quarter 1				223,000	5	1,115,000	1,115,000
— Quarter 2				225,000	5	1,125,000	1,125,000
— Quarter 3				225,000	5	1,125,000	1,125,000
— Quarter 4				230,000	5	1,150,000	1,150,000
Total — Material 3				903,000	5	4,515,000	4,515,000

- Probable price changes for the material
- Cost and capital requirements of financing the inventory

Some of these factors are discussed in Chapter 21 in relation to inventories.

Responsibility for the Purchases Budget

It is perhaps self-evident that responsibility for the purchases budget rests with the purchasing executive. He is, or should be, the most knowledgeable as to sources of material, reliability of vendors, prevailing prices, terms available, and the exposures on the factors just mentioned. In summary, the responsibilities of the purchasing executive include

- Seeing that the required materials are available at the right time and in the proper form, quality, and location as needed by the manufacturing arm
- Purchasing the proper materials at a competitive price
- Balancing total costs of carrying inventory, versus the best terms of acquiring the materials
- Following management policy regarding inventory levels
- Providing, for estimating and planning purposes, the standard unit costs of the materials

Categorizing the Material Items — Illustration

Reference was made in the materials budget section to complications when the material items sometimes are not of sufficient value to budget on an individual basis. Additionally, different companies use different methods to control inventories. For these reasons there is a diversity in exactly how the quantity of materials to be purchased is arrived at. Assume, for illustrative purposes, that the following information is made available as to production requirements, after a review of the production budget:

| | Class | | | |
| | Units | | | Amount |
Period	W	X	Y	Z
January	400	500	Unknown	Unknown
February	300	600	"	"
March	500	400	"	"
Subtotal	1,200	1,500	"	"
2d quarter	1,500	1,200	"	"
3d quarter	1,200	1,500	"	"
4th quarter	1,000	1,700	"	"
Total	4,900	5,900	10,000	$20,000

FIG. 12-2   Summary Materials Budget

THE CALIFORNIA MANUFACTURING COMPANY

MATERIALS BUDGET

Material Components, in Units, by Product, by Department
For the Plan Year 19XX

Item	Individual Unit Requirements	January	February	March	Quarter 1 Total	Quarter 2 Total	Quarter 3 Total	Quarter 4 Total	Yearly Total
					Gross Material Requirements				
PRODUCT A									
Scheduled production (units)		42,000	40,000	43,000	125,000	130,000	140,000	130,000	525,000
Material 1 standard requirements									
Department 21	1	42,000	40,000	43,000	125,000	130,000	140,000	130,000	525,000
Department 22	1	42,000	40,000	43,000	125,000	130,000	140,000	130,000	525,000
Department 23	1	42,000	40,000	43,000	125,000	130,000	140,000	130,000	525,000
Total standard requirements	3	126,000	120,000	129,000	375,000	390,000	420,000	390,000	1,575,000
Provision for variances (1%)		1,260	1,200	1,290	3,750	3,900	4,200	3,900	15,750
Total requirements		127,260	121,200	130,290	378,750	393,900	424,200	393,900	1,590,750
Material 2 standard requirements									
Department 22	3	126,000	120,000	129,000	375,000	390,000	420,000	390,000	1,575,000
Department 23	2	84,000	80,000	86,000	250,000	260,000	280,000	260,000	1,050,000
Total standard requirements	5	210,000	200,000	215,000	625,000	650,000	700,000	650,000	2,625,000
Provision for variances (1%)		2,100	2,000	2,150	6,250	6,500	7,000	6,500	26,250
Total requirements		212,100	202,000	217,150	631,250	656,500	707,000	656,500	2,651,250
PRODUCT B									
Scheduled production (units)		75,000	72,000	76,000	223,000	225,000	225,000	230,000	903,000
Material 1 standard requirements									
Department 23	1	75,000	72,000	76,000	223,000	225,000	225,000	230,000	903,000
Department 24	1	75,000	72,000	76,000	223,000	225,000	225,000	230,000	903,000
Total standard requirements	2	150,000	144,000	152,000	446,000	450,000	450,000	460,000	1,806,000
Provision for variances (1%)		1,500	1,440	1,520	4,460	4,500	4,500	4,600	18,060
Total requirements		151,500	145,440	153,520	450,460	454,500	454,500	464,600	1,824,060

Material 2 standard requirements								
Department 24	150,000	144,000	152,000	446,000	450,000	450,000	460,000	1,806,000
Department 25	75,000	72,000	76,000	223,000	225,000	225,000	230,000	903,000
Department 26	75,000	72,000	76,000	223,000	225,000	225,000	230,000	903,000
Total standard requirements	300,000	288,000	304,000	892,000	900,000	900,000	920,000	3,612,000
Provision for variances (1%)	3,000	2,880	3,040	8,920	9,000	9,000	9,200	36,120
Total requirements	303,000	290,880	307,040	900,920	909,000	909,000	929,200	3,648,120
Material 3 standard requirements								
Department 24	225,000	216,000	228,000	669,000	675,000	675,000	690,000	2,709,000
Department 26	150,000	144,000	152,000	446,000	450,000	450,000	460,000	1,806,000
Total standard requirements	375,000	360,000	380,000	1,115,000	1,125,000	1,125,000	1,150,000	4,515,000
Provision for variances (1%)	3,750	3,600	3,800	11,150	11,250	11,250	11,500	45,150
Total requirements	378,750	363,600	383,800	1,126,150	1,136,250	1,136,250	1,161,500	4,560,150

SUMMARY REQUIREMENTS

Material 1 standard requirements								
Product A	126,000	120,000	129,000	375,000	390,000	420,000	390,000	1,575,000
Product B	150,000	144,000	152,000	446,000	450,000	450,000	460,000	1,806,000
	276,000	264,000	281,000	821,000	840,000	870,000	850,000	3,381,000
Provision for variances	2,760	2,640	2,810	8,210	8,400	8,700	8,500	33,810
Total requirements — 1	278,760	266,640	283,810	829,210	848,400	878,700	858,500	3,414,810
Material 2 standard requirements								
Product A	210,000	200,000	215,000	625,000	650,000	700,000	650,000	2,625,000
Product B	300,000	288,000	304,000	892,000	900,000	900,000	920,000	3,612,000
	510,000	488,000	519,000	1,517,000	1,550,000	1,600,000	1,570,000	6,237,000
Provisions for variances	5,100	4,880	5,190	15,170	15,500	16,000	15,500	62,170
Total requirements — 2	515,100	492,880	524,190	1,532,170	1,565,500	1,616,000	1,585,500	6,299,170
Material 3 standard requirements								
Product B	375,000	360,000	380,000	1,115,000	1,125,000	1,125,000	1,150,000	4,515,000
Provisions for variances	3,750	3,600	3,800	11,150	11,250	11,250	11,500	45,150
Total requirements — 3	378,750	363,600	383,800	1,126,150	1,136,250	1,136,250	1,161,500	4,560,150

The following four groups of products have been assumed:

Class W — Material of high unit value, for which a definite quantity and time program is established in advance, such as for stock items. Also, the material is controlled on a minimum–maximum inventory basis for budget purposes.

Class X — Similar to Class *W* materials, except that *for budget purposes,* minimum–maximum limits are not used.

Class Y — Material items for which definite quantities are established for the budget period, but for which no definite time program is established, such as for special orders on hand.

Class Z — Miscellaneous material items, which are grouped together and *budgeted* only in terms of total dollar purchases for the budget period.

In actual practice, of course, decisions as to production time must be made as to items using *Y* and *Z* classifications. However, the bases described later in this chapter are applicable in planning the production level.

Class W. Where the items are budgeted on a minimum–maximum basis, it usually is necessary to determine the range within which purchases must fall in order to (1) meet production needs and (2) stay within inventory limits. A method of making such a calculation is as follows:

	Units	
	For Minimum Inventory	For Maximum Inventory
January production requirements	400	400
Inventory limit	50	400
Total	450	800
Beginning inventory	200	200
Limit of receipts (purchases)	250	600

Within these limits, the quantity to be purchased is influenced by factors such as unit transportation and handling costs, price considerations, storage space, availability of material, capital requirements, and so forth.

A similar determination is made for each month for each such raw material, and a schedule of receipts and inventory is then prepared as follows:

	Units					
Period	Beginning Inventory	Receipts	Usage	Ending Inventory	Unit Value	Purchases Budget
January	200	400	400	200	$2000	$ 800,000
February	200	400	300	300		800,000
March	300	400	500	200		800,000
Subtotal		1,200	1,200			$2,400,000

| | Units | | | | | |
Period	Beginning Inventory	Receipts	Usage	Ending Inventory	Unit Value	Purchases Budget
2d quarter	200	1,350	1,500	50		$2,700,000
3d quarter	50	1,200	1,200	50		2,400,000
4th quarter	50	1,200	1,000	250		2,400,000
Total		4,950	4,900			$9,900,000

Class X. It is assumed that the Class X materials can be purchased as needed. Since other controls are practical on this type of item, and since no other procurement problems exist, purchases are determined by the production requirements. A simple extension is all that is required to determine dollar value of expected purchases:

Period	Quantity	Unit Price	Total
January	500	$100	$ 50,000
February	600		60,000
March	400		40,000
Subtotal	1,500		$150,000
2d quarter	1,200		120,000
3d quarter	1,500		150,000
4th quarter	1,700		170,000
Total	5,900		$590,000

Class Y. The breakdown of the Class Y items may be assumed to be as follows:

Item	Quantity	Unit Price	Cost
Y-1	1,000	$10.00	$ 10,000
Y-2	2,000	11.00	22,000
Y-3	3,000	12.00	36,000
Y-4	4,000	13.00	52,000
Total	10,000		$120,000

A determination as to time of purchase must be made, even though no definite delivery schedules or so forth have been set by the customer. In this instance, the distribution of the cost and units might be made on the basis of past experience or budgeted production factors, such as budgeted machine hours. The allocation to periods could be made on past experience, as follows:

| Period | Past Experience as to Similar Units Manufactured | Units | | | | | Value (Purchases Budget) |
		Y-1	Y-2	Y-3	Y-4	Total	
January	10%	100	200	300	400	1,000	$ 12,000
February	15	150	300	450	600	1,500	18,000
March	10	100	200	300	400	1,000	12,000
Subtotal	35%	350	700	1,050	1,400	3,500	$ 42,000
2d quarter	30	300	600	900	1,200	3,000	36,000
3d quarter	20	200	400	600	800	2,000	24,000
4th quarter	15	150	300	450	600	1,500	18,000
Total	100%	1,000	2,000	3,000	4,000	10,000	$120,000

The breakdown of units is for the benefit of the purchasing department only, inasmuch as the percentages can be applied against the total cost, and need not apply to individual units. In practice, if there are numerous types of units and if they are of small value, the quantities of each might not be determined in connection with the forecast.

Class Z. Where the materials are grouped, past experience again may be the means of determining estimated expenditures by period of time. Based on production hours, the distribution of Class Z items may be assumed to be as follows (cost of such materials assumed to be $20 per production hour):

Period	Production Hours	Amount
January	870	$ 17,400
February	830	16,600
March	870	17,400
Subtotal	2,570	$ 51,400
2d quarter	2,600	52,000
3d quarter	2,230	44,600
4th quarter	2,600	52,000
Total	10,000	$200,000

When all materials have been grouped, and the requirements have been determined and translated to cost, the materials purchases budget may be summarized, principally for the financial aspects of the planning procedure, as shown in Figure 12-3.

This information is used to provide the input data to record increases to inventory and the increases in accounts payable (see Chapters 21 and 23). With appropriate lag time, and with provision for cash discounts, this infor-

FIG. 12-3 Summarized Purchases Budget

THE SMALL COMPANY

PURCHASES BUDGET

For the Planning Year 19XX

Period	Class of Material				Total Budget
	W	X	Y	Z	
January	$ 800,000	$ 50,000	$ 12,000	$ 17,400	$ 879,400
February	800,000	60,000	18,000	16,600	894,600
March	800,000	40,000	12,000	17,400	869,400
Quarter 1	$2,400,000	$150,000	$ 42,000	$ 51,400	$ 2,643,400
Quarter 2	2,700,000	120,000	36,000	52,000	2,908,000
Quarter 3	2,400,000	150,000	24,000	44,600	2,618,600
Quarter 4	2,400,000	170,000	18,000	52,000	2,640,000
Total	$9,900,000	$590,000	$120,000	$200,000	$10,810,000

mation serves as the basis for the materials segment of cash requirements. (see Chapter 19).

Another Illustrative Purchases Budget

The numerous computations required, and the ease of presenting the data in various ways makes the use of computers cost-effective in many industries. For example, the materials budget or purchases budget may be summarized in the following ways:

- By type of material, in summary form for each item, by time period
- By type of material, segregated quantitatively as to finished product, by time period
- By product line, detailed by type of material component, by time period

Moreover, the purchases budget, through the use of the computer, may be extended to more of the less valuable material components than was formerly feasible. There is, therefore, less need to use somewhat arbitrary business-factor relationships, as discussed with respect to Class Z components. Assuming use of the computer, the bulk of the materials purchases budget for The California Manufacturing Company is prepared from the materials budget (Figure 12-2) as shown in Figures 12-4 and 12-5.

FIG. 12-4 Schedule of Purchases — Major Materials

THE CALIFORNIA MANUFACTURING COMPANY
SCHEDULE OF PURCHASES — MAJOR MATERIALS
For the Plan Year 19XX

Material/Time Period	Units Required for Manufacture(a)	Add: Ending Inventory	Total Units Required	Deduct: Beginning Inventory	Purchase Requirements Quantity	Unit Cost	Total
Material 1							
January	278,760	545,400	824,160	524,160	300,000	$10.00	$ 3,000,000
February	266,640	550,450	817,090	545,400	271,690	10.00	2,716,900
March	283,810	566,260	850,070	550,450	299,620	10.00	2,996,200
Total — Quarter 1	829,210	566,260	1,395,470	524,160	871,310	$10.00	$ 8,713,100
— Quarter 2	848,400	586,100	1,434,500	566,260	868,240	11.00	9,550,640
— Quarter 3	878,700	572,600	1,451,300	586,100	865,200	11.00	9,517,200
— Quarter 4	858,500	550,300	1,408,800	572,600	836,200	11.00	9,198,200
Grand Total	3,414,810	550,300	3,965,110	524,160	3,440,950	$10.75	$ 36,979,140
Material 2							
January	515,100	1,017,070	1,532,170	1,012,170	520,000	$ 5.00	$ 2,600,000
February	492,880	1,040,020	1,532,900	1,017,070	515,830	6.00	3,094,980
March	524,190	1,044,200	1,568,390	1,040,020	528,370	6.00	3,170,220
Total — Quarter 1	1,532,170	1,044,200	2,576,370	1,012,170	1,564,200	$ 5.67	$ 8,865,200
— Quarter 2	1,565,500	1,077,800	2,643,400	1,044,200	1,599,200	6.00	9,595,200
— Quarter 3	1,616,000	1,056,500	2,672,500	1,077,800	1,594,600	7.00	11,162,200
— Quarter 4	1,585,500	1,000,000	2,585,500	1,056,500	1,529,000	7.00	10,703,000
Grand Total	6,299,170	1,000,000	7,299,170	1,012,170	6,287,000	$ 6.41	$ 40,325,600
Material 3							
January	378,750	747,400	1,126,150	720,150	406,000	$12.00	$ 4,872,000
February	363,600	762,100	1,125,700	747,400	378,300	12.00	4,539,600
March	383,800	757,900	1,141,700	762,100	379,600	13.00	4,934,800
Total — Quarter 1	1,126,150	757,900	1,889,050	720,150	1,163,900	$12.33	$ 14,346,400
— Quarter 2	1,136,250	757,900	1,894,150	757,900	1,136,250	13.00	14,771,250
— Quarter 3	1,136,250	774,700	1,910,950	757,900	1,153,000	14.00	16,142,700
— Quarter 4	1,161,500	781,500	1,943,000	774,700	1,163,300	14.00	16,356,200
Grand Total	4,560,150	781,500	5,341,650	720,150	4,621,500	$13.33	$ 61,616,550
Total All Materials							$138,921,290

(a) From Figure 12-2

FIG. 12-5 Summary — Purchases Budget

THE CALIFORNIA MANUFACTURING COMPANY

SUMMARY — PURCHASES BUDGET
For the Plan Year 19XX

Period	Material 1 Quantity	Material 1 Amount	Material 2 Quantity	Material 2 Amount	Material 3 Quantity	Material 3 Amount	Supplies	Total Amount
January	300,000	$ 3,000,000	520,000	$ 2,600,000	406,000	$ 4,872,000	1,700,000	$ 12,172,000
February	271,690	2,716,900	515,830	3,094,980	378,300	4,539,600	1,700,000	12,051,480
March	299,620	2,996,200	528,370	3,170,220	379,600	4,934,800	1,500,000	12,601,220
Total — Quarter 1	871,310	$ 8,713,100	1,564,200	$ 8,865,200	1,163,900	$14,346,400	4,900,000	$ 36,824,700
— Quarter 2	868,240	9,550,640	1,599,200	9,595,200	1,136,250	14,771,250	5,000,000	38,917,090
— Quarter 3	865,200	9,517,200	1,594,600	11,162,200	1,153,050	16,142,700	5,100,000	41,922,100
— Quarter 4	836,200	9,198,200	1,529,000	10,703,000	1,168,300	16,356,200	4,900,000	41,157,400
Total	3,440,950	$36,979,140	6,287,000	$40,325,600	4,621,500	$61,616,550	19,900,000	$158,821,290

Figure 12-4 reflects adjustment of the unit requirements for the beginning and ending inventories and costs of the purchases. Unit price changes during the year are contained in the schedule. Figure 12-5 is the summary of the purchases budget, with provision for the supplies inventory, consisting of thousands of items purchased on a minimum–maximum inventory basis, in dollar amounts only (to permit financial planning only). It is not used as the basis for purchasing supplies. A summary of the purchases budget is useful to executives in that it provides them with the information they need without excess data.

Revision of the Purchases Budget

The discussion to this point has related primarily to the annual planning budget. However, as operations commence during the planning period, events are encountered and conditions exist that require a revision in the planning budget. Therefore, plans must be changed to meet changing conditions. The materials plan, the planned inventory balances, and the purchases plan must be adjusted to produce the optimum results under the circumstances.

Basic control procedures, of course, need not change, although the measurements may. Materials and purchasing controls are discussed later in this chapter.

THE MATERIALS INVENTORY BUDGET

As discussed earlier in this chapter, a comprehensive planning and control system involving materials used in the manufacturing process in reality is composed of four budgets, one of which is the materials inventory budget. This inventory system, together with the work-in-process inventory and finished goods inventory, is reviewed in detail in Chapter 21.

THE COST OF MATERIALS USED (IN PRODUCTION) BUDGET

The last member of the group of four materials-related budgets is the *cost* of materials used budget. This is the cost of the materials planned to be put into production. For most companies, it represents the cost of raw materials and purchased parts and so forth transferred from inventory accounts into work-in-process, although in some cases it may represent the cost of prime items acquired for the manufacturing operations and placed directly into work-in-process. In any event, the *quantities* of materials required are developed in the materials usage budget, and the unit *cost* of the new purchases is made available in the purchases budget. Additionally, the unit costs of materials in the raw materials inventory are known. Based on the inventory valuation method used (such as first-in first-out (FIFO), last-in first-out (LIFO), moving average, weighted average, or specific cost) the quantities required in production must be multiplied by the appropriate cost to arrive at the planning budget for the cost of materials used. An illustrative budget for the cost of materials put into production using the data for The California Manufacturing Company is presented in Figure 12-6. Basically, it is a simple problem in multiplication; but it is necessary to plan and control the inventory levels and develop the planned operating results. In this connection, the specific method of valuing inventory must be recognized in the budget for materials used in production, and the budgeted inventory is required. Figure 12-7 identifies the specific inventory usage on a FIFO basis. Note that at each ending inventory period the quantities on hand are identified by unit price. Accordingly, each usage must be costed on the comparable basis. Again, in companies with several raw material items and finished products, a computer application may be cost effective.

DIRECT MATERIALS — CONTROLS

The preceding discussion has focused on the planning phases of the purchases and usage of materials, whether the annual planning budget or interim revisions. A discussion of the control phase follows. (Materials *inventory* control applications are discussed in Chapter 21.)

Material cost control basically involves the comparison of actual material costs with predetermined standards. These standards may be mere estimates of what the costs should be, but in most instances they are standard costs (see Chapter 8). Often they are the same unit standard costs used in developing the planning budget, as discussed earlier.

The differences between direct material actual costs and direct material standard (flexible budget) costs represent direct material variances. For purposes of analysis and control, these variances must be segregated into direct materials price variances and direct material usage variances. These basic use variances may be further subdivided into major causes such as shrinkage, scrap, and spoilage.

Material Price Variances

As the name implies, the material price variance is the difference between actual unit prices paid for a particular item of material and the expected or

(*text continues on page 12-22*)

FIG. 12-6 Planned Cost of Direct Materials Used In Production

The California Manufacturing Company

PLANNED COST OF DIRECT MATERIALS USED IN PRODUCTION
Plan Year 19XX

Time Period/Material	Product A		
	Units Required	Units Price[a]	Amount
January			
Material 1	127,260	$10.00	$ 1,272,600
" 2	212,100	5.00	1,060,500
" 3	—	—	—
Total			$ 2,333,100
February			
Material 1	121,200	$10.00	$ 1,212,000
" 2	202,000	5.00	1,010,000
" 3	—	—	—
Total			$ 2,222,000
March			
Material 1	130,290	$10.00	$ 1,302,900
" 2	217,150	5.00	1,085,750
" 3	—	—	—
Total			$ 2,388,650
1st Quarter			
Material 1	378,750	$10.00	$ 3,787,500
" 2	631,250	5.00	3,156,250
" 3	—	—	—
Total			$ 6,943,750
2nd Quarter			
Material 1	262,910	$10.00	$ 2,629,100
" 2	130,990	11.00	1,440,890
" 2	656,500	6.00	3,939,000
" 3	—	—	—
" 3	—	—	—
Total			$ 8,008,990
3rd Quarter			
Material 1	424,200	$11.00	$ 4,666,200
" 2	471,580	6.00	4,829,480
" 2	235,420	7.00	1,647,940
" 3	—	—	—
" 3	—	—	—
Total			$ 9,143,620
4th Quarter			
Material 1	393,900	$11.00	$ 4,332,900
" 2	656,500	7.00	4,595,500
" 3	—	—	—
Total			$ 8,928,400
Yearly Total			$33,024,760

(a) See Figure 12-7

Product B			Total	
Units Required	Units Price[a]	Amount	Units	Amount
151,500	$10.00	$ 1,515,000	278,760	$ 2,787,600
303,000	5.00	1,515,000	515,100	2,575,500
378,750	12.00	4,545,000	378,750	4,545,000
		$ 7,575,000		$ 9,908,100
145,440	$10.00	$ 1,454,400	266,640	$ 2,666,400
298,880	5.00	1,454,400	492,880	2,464,400
363,600	12.00	4,363,200	363,600	4,363,200
		$ 7,272,000		$ 9,494,000
153,520	$10.00	$ 1,535,200	283,810	$ 2,838,100
307,040	5.00	1,535,200	524,190	2,620,950
383,800	12.00	4,605,600	383,800	4,605,600
		$ 7,676,000		$ 10,064,650
450,460	$10.00	$ 4,504,600	829,210	$ 8,292,100
900,920	5.00	4,504,600	1,532,170	7,660,850
1,126,150	12.00	13,513,800	1,126,150	13,513,800
		$ 22,523,000		$ 29,466,750
303,350	$10.00	$ 3,033,500	566,260	$ 5,662,600
151,150	11.00	1,662,650	282,140	3,103,540
909,000	6.00	5,454,000	1,565,500	9,393,000
378,300	12.00	4,539,600	378,300	4,539,600
757,950	13.00	9,853,350	757,950	9,853,350
		$ 24,543,100		$ 32,552,090
454,500	$11.00	$ 4,999,500	878,700	$ 9,665,700
606,320	6.00	3,637,920	1,077,000	6,467,400
302,680	7.00	2,118,760	538,100	3,766,700
378,300	12.00	4,539,600	378,300	4,539,600
757,950	13.00	9,853,350	757,950	9,853,350
		$ 25,149,130		$ 34,292,750
464,600	$11.00	$ 5,110,600	858,500	$ 9,443,500
929,000	7.00	6,503,000	1,585,500	11,098,500
1,161,500	14.00	16,261,000	1,161,500	16,261,000
		$ 27,874,600		$ 36,803,000
		$100,089,830		$133,114,590

FIG. 12-7   Planned Monthly Inventory of Direct Materials (Major)

THE CALIFORNIA MANUFACTURING COMPANY

PLANNED INVENTORY OF DIRECT MATERIALS
FIFO Basis
For the Plan Year 19XX

Item	Quantity	Unit Price	Amount
		Material 1	
Beginning inventory	524,160	$10.00	$ 5,241,600
January — Purchases	300,000	10.00	3,000,000
Available	824,160	10.00	8,241,600
Usage	278,760	10.00	2,787,600
Ending inventory	545,400	$10.00	$ 5,454,000
February — Purchases	271,690	$10.00	$ 2,716,900
Available	817,090	10.00	8,170,900
Usage	266,640	10.00	2,666,400
Ending inventory	550,450	$10.00	$ 5,504,500
March — Purchases	299,620	$10.00	$ 2,996,200
Available	850,070	10.00	8,500,700
Usage	283,810	10.00	2,838,100
Ending inventory	566,260	$10.00	$ 5,662,600
2nd Quarter — Purchases	868,240	$11.00	$ 9,550,640
Available	1,434,500		15,213,240
Usage	566,000	10.00	5,662,600
	282,140	11.00	3,103,540
Total usage	848,400		8,766,140
Ending inventory	586,100	11.00	$ 6,447,100
3rd Quarter — Purchases	865,200	$11.00	$ 9,517,200
Available	1,451,300	11.00	15,964,300
Usage			
Total usage	878,700	11.00	9,665,700
Ending inventory	572,600	$11.00	$ 6,298,600
4th Quarter — Purchases	836,200	$11.00	$ 9,198,200
Available	1,408,800	11.00	15,496,800
Usage	858,500	11.00	9,443,500
Ending inventory	550,300	$11.00	$ 6,053,300

Material 2			Material 3		
Quantity	Unit Price	Amount	Quantity	Unit Price	Amount
1,012,170	$5.00	$ 5,060,850	720,150	$12.00	$ 8,641,800
520,000	5.00	2,600,000	406,000	12.00	4,872,000
1,532,170	5.00	7,660,850	1,126,150	12.00	13,513,800
515,100	5.00	2,575,500	378,750	12.00	4,545,000
1,017,070	$5.00	$ 5,085,350	747,400	$12.00	$ 8,968,800
515,830	$6.00	$ 3,094,980	378,300	$12.00	$ 4,539,600
1,532,900		8,180,330	1,125,700	12.00	13,508,400
492,880	5.00	2,464,400	363,600	12.00	4,363,200
524,190	5.00	2,620,950	762,100	$12.00	$ 9,145,200
515,830	6.00	3,094,980			
1,040,020		$ 5,715,930			
528,370	$6.00	$ 3,170,220	379,600	$13.00	$ 4,934,800
1,568,390		8,886,150	1,141,700		14,080,000
524,190	5.00	2,620,950	383,800	12.00	4,605,600
1,044,200	$6.00	$ 6,265,200	378,300	12.00	4,539,600
			379,600	$13.00	4,934,800
			757,900		$ 9,474,400
1,599,200	$6.00	$ 9,595,200	1,136,250	$13.00	$14,771,250
2,643,400	6.00	15,860,400	1,894,150		24,245,650
			378,300	12.00	4,539,600
			757,950	13.00	9,853,350
1,565,500	6.00	9,393,000	1,136,250		14,392,950
1,077,900	$6.00	$ 6,467,400	757,900	$13.00	$ 9,852,700
1,594,600	$7.00	$11,162,200	1,153,050	$14.00	$16,142,700
2,672,500		17,629,600	1,910,950		25,995,400
1,077,900	6.00	6,167,400	757,900	13.00	9,852,700
538,100	7.00	3,766,700	378,350	14.00	5,296,900
1,616,000		10,234,100	1,136,250		15,149,600
1,056,500	$7.00	$ 7,395,500	774,700	$14.00	$10,845,800
1,529,000	$7.00	$10,703,000	1,168,300	$14.00	$16,356,200
2,585,500	7.00	18,098,500	1,943,000	14.00	27,202,000
1,585,500	7.00	11,098,500	1,161,500	14.00	16,261,000
1,000,000	$7.00	$ 7,000,000	781,500	$14.00	$10,941,000

standard unit price. The price variance is usually the responsibility of the purchasing executive, who also usually establishes the standard. It involves a substantial amount of judgment. Prices of materials are influenced by a great many factors, many of them outside the control of the business. Therefore, the variance is of limited use in that it merely compares what was paid with what was expected to be paid.

Causes of price variance may include factors such as

- Unexpected general price rises, as in periods of high inflation.
- Special shipments
- Delivery costs by express rather than by standard freight
- Purchases in smaller quantities than contemplated
- Required use of a more expensive supplier

When price variances develop, analysis may be helpful in pinpointing some areas for improvement. In many cases, the data is informational, only in that there is little the purchasing department could have done.

It is, of course, necessary to separate price variance from all other variances to develop the true usage variances. In most instances this is the responsibility of the manufacturing executive.

Price variances should be tracked because (1) finished product sales prices may quickly reflect the price changes in component materials, and (2) the material cost standards and finished product standard cost should be changed or updated.

The price variances can be identified (a) at the time of purchase by an analysis of purchase orders, or (b) at the time of receipt of goods (receipt of invoices), or (c) at time of usage. Normally, the variance is written off at time of receipt of goods, with a charge to cost of goods sold, and the inventory item is carried at standard cost (or lower of cost or market).

A typical monthly report summarizing material price variances in total, by material classification, is illustrated in Figure 12-8. When the unit standard cost of a major finished product is closely monitored, a report of the type shown in Figure 12-9 is useful.

Material Usage Variances

The material usage variance is the difference between the actual cost of the material used and the standard cost of the quantity that *should* have been used. Usually, any element of price differential has been removed so that material usage normally (but not always) is the responsibility of the manufacturing executive. The usage variance represents the differential of the standard unit cost of the quantity of material actually consumed as compared to the standard cost of the quantity that should have been used to produce the

FIG. 12-8 Summary of Material Price Variances

THE NORRIS MANUFACTURING COMPANY

SUMMARY OF MATERIAL PRICE VARIANCE

(dollars in thousands)

March 19XX and year-to-date

Material Classification	Month			Year-to-Date		
	Standard Cost of Receipts	Price Variance	Percentage to Standard	Standard Cost of Receipts	Price Variance	Percentage to Standard
Sheet steel	$1,420	$35.5	2.50%	$ 5,211	$104.2	2.00%
Steel wire	762	5.3	.70	2,406	24.1	1.00
Sheet aluminum	1,946	21.4	1.10	6,712	100.7	1.50
Copper wire	173	(10.4)	(6.00)	541	2.7	.50
Coatings	111	1.1	1.00	210	3.6	1.70
Insulation	243	5.3	2.20	704	21.1	3.00
Paints	710	(24.9)	(3.50)	1,842	(46.1)	(2.50)
Cleaners	86	1.4	1.60	196	2.0	1.00
Miscellaneous	41	.8	.20	97	.9	.90
Total	$5,492	$35.5	.64%	$17,919	$213.2	1.19%

( ) Favorable variance

FIG. 12-9   Summary of Unit Standard Material Cost Changes

THE ROCKET MFG. CO.

STATEMENT OF UNIT STANDARD MATERIAL COSTS — PRODUCT 4

For the month of May, 19XX

Item	Standard Cost 4/30/XX	Changes Increases	Changes Decreases	Standard Cost 5/31/XX
Motor	$ 3,840.40	$112.00		$ 3,952.40
Sheet aluminum	876.00	—		876.00
Copper tubing	107.50	—	$ 1.40	106.10
Instruments	8,104.70	57.90		8,162.60
Fasteners	12.70	—		12.70
Electronic gear	1,016.10	70.00		1,086.10
Stabilizer	309.10	15.20		324.30
Composites	201.40	—	17.30	184.10
Small steel parts	81.10	—		81.10
Fuel	119.60	—		119.60
Miscellaneous	41.03	—		41.03
Total	$14,709.63	$255.10	$18.70	$14,946.03

---

departmental output. Excess usage, of course, may be reported as the excess *quantity* used, but often the impact is greater if the monetary *cost* is disclosed.

Material usage variance, also identified as material quantity variance or material yield variance, arises from a number of causes, such as

- Improper handling — spoilage or breakage
- Improper processing — use of wrong machine or malfunctioning machine
- Improperly trained employee
- Substandard quality material or wrong specification
- Defective production
- Wrong material

The standard quantity of the materials is commonly derived from the bill of material prepared by the industrial engineer or from another reputable source.

A typical daily report on excess material usage is shown in Figure 12-10 illustrating (1) the quantity variance, (2) the cost variance, and (3) the cause.

FIG. 12-10 Daily Excess Material Usage

THE NEW MACHINE SHOP

EXCESS MATERIAL VARIANCES

Dept. No. 6

Supervisor _____

Date 6/5/19XX

Material Used	Quantity of Finished Production	Actual Quantity Material Used	Standard Quantity	Quantity Variance	Unit Cost	Cost Variance	Comments
R	1,240	1,297	1,240	57	$16.00	$ 912	Careless workmanship
S	630	1,342	1,260	82	7.00	574	Machine 12 needs repair
T	900	2,816	2,700	116	1.00	116	Material quality below standard
U	2,100	2,103	2,100	3	3.00	9	
V	310	610	620	(10)	12.00	(120)	Operator Johnson changed speed
Total						$1,491	

FIG. 12-11   Summary of Excess Material Usage

THE JEWETT COMPANY
MILWAUKEE PLANT

EXCESS MATERIAL USAGE REPORT

Week ended   6/14/19XX

Department	Actual	Standard	Over/Under Standard
Punching	$126,418	$119,430	$ 6,988
Fabrication	119,832	115,510	4,322
Subassembly	112,910	112,100	810
Painting	77,412	78,010	(598)
Processing	62,316	62,716	(400)
Final assembly	98,413	94,312	4,101
Total	$597,301	$582,078	$15,223
Percentage over/under standard			2.62%

A summary report for the day, week, or month might appear as in Figure 12-11. Supporting details for the plan superintendent or departmental foreman would be available.

Note that the material variance reports are essentially using the flexible budget principle to report what materials should have been used for the quantity of acceptable output.

Frequency of the material usage report depends on local circumstances, including the cause and frequency of the excess usage, the manufacturing process and method of control, and the financial impact of the excess loss. It may be an hourly, daily, weekly, or monthly report. The type of report and content are usually dictated by the needs of management.

Other Control Reports

Other comparisons may be reported with the annual planning budget, i.e., planned requirements by material with actual, or planned purchases by material item with actual. However, except in unusual circumstances, such data are of limited use. Useful material control reports require comparison of actual and standard, not plan. Overall comparisons with plan might pinpoint excess uses of cash for inventories, but in general, they are of limited value.

13

Manufacturing Expense

INTRODUCTION

Expressed in terms of specific budgets, the principal manufacturing or production executive is usually responsible for:

1. *The production budget* — Units of product to be manufactured
2. *Functional budgets:*
   - ☐ The materials usage budget — Quantities of direct material required
   - ☐ The material purchases budget — Cost of material purchases
   - ☐ The materials and work-in-process inventory budgets
   - ☐ The direct labor budget
   - ☐ The manufacturing expense budget

The manufacturing expense budget, discussed here, has unique ramifications as to product costs and inventory values.

NATURE OF MANUFACTURING EXPENSE

By traditional definition, manufacturing expenses, also called "manufacturing overhead," are those manufacturing costs that cannot be charged to, or are not identifiable directly with, a specific product, process, or job. A rather heterogeneous group of expenses are represented; but the increased use of more automatic and sophisticated machinery (e.g., robots) and attendant changes in the manufacturing process are making indirect manufacturing expenses a greater element of production costs, to the exclusion of direct labor. As investments in computer-controlled machinery have grown, with increased productivity in most cases, the attention of management has become more focused on such indirect expenses as repairs and maintenance, depreciation, and power.

Typical of the types of expenses included in manufacturing overhead are the following:

- Indirect salaries and wages
- Fringe benefit costs
- Repairs and maintenance
- Power
- Fuel
- Supplies

- Communications
- Rent
- Sales and use taxes
- Excise taxes
- Insurance
- Depreciation

DIFFICULTIES IN THE PLANNING AND CONTROL OF MANUFACTURING EXPENSES

The very nature of manufacturing expenses has rendered the budgeting, or planning and control, of this cost element somewhat more difficult than the other production factors. Several reasons explain why.

In the first place, there are innumerable items of cost, each often of small consequence at the point of application, each originating from different sources, and each requiring different methods and time of control. This inflow of cost, by reason of these characteristics, contributes to the problems of budgeting and control.

The second difficulty arises because responsibility for control is widely distributed throughout the organization. The expenditures of direct material and labor are usually under the immediate supervision of the production foremen and department heads who may be expected to detect the grosser wastes even without the aid of control devices; but the responsibility for burden items is distributed among general executives, service department heads, and producing department heads, no one of whom accepts the full responsibility. For example, the purchasing agent may buy an uneconomical grade of coal, the head of the power department may expend unnecessary amounts for supervision, and the head of the stamping department may waste power; the net result is a high cost of power, the full import of which is not apparent to any one individual. It will not be detected as readily as a comparable waste of raw materials. This aspect makes sound "responsibility accounting" more difficult.

In the third place, the individual items of cost making up this composite called overhead behave in differing ways as the level of plant activity changes. It therefore becomes more painstaking to discover just what total expense is justified by the current volume of production. Quite often, as volume increases in response to seasonal demands or general improvement in business, there is an unjustified liberality in authorizing expenditures and a corresponding failure to reduce them after the demand has passed. The program of budgetary control must give consideration to the necessary expenditures within the range of probable production volume. Standards must be established to measure the cost justified by the actual production volume.

Finally, there is one other aspect of manufacturing expenses, which raises problems as to the *time* of control, and which might demand a somewhat different approach — a broader and forward-looking viewpoint — than that needed in the day-to-day control of direct labor or direct material. That characteristic is this: The manufacturing expense includes numerous long-term cost commitments such as those arising from investment in plant and equipment. It is extremely important that such commitments be subjected to the most careful study and restricted to those that are justified by the long-term outlook for sales of products. The budget is the chief device by which such commitments are controlled. But plans for keeping expenses within bounds must be made long before the depreciation or maintenance charges appear in the monthly financial statement. These latter aspects are discussed in Chapter 25.

RESPONSIBILITY FOR THE MANUFACTURING EXPENSE BUDGET

While responsibility for the planning and control of manufacturing expenses must rest with the production executive, there are special considerations in the establishment of the budgetary control system for manufacturing expenses that flow from the nature of the expense and the use of the cost data. In establishing the expense budget structure:

- The budget should be based on technical data that are sound from a manufacturing viewpoint.
- The manufacturing supervisors, who must implement the production plan and will be held responsible for controlling costs, must be given the opportunity to understand the budget structure and the reasons for it, and to generally express approval as to its fairness.

- The cost departments, cost classifications, and cost allocations must follow acceptable cost accounting standards.

To achieve these conditions will require the cooperative effort of at least three groups. First, the industrial engineers, or process engineers, must supply the necessary technical data in terms of physical units. For example, the following information is typical of facts that are needed for each department, operation, or product, as may be applicable:

1. Crew size or manpower requirements
2. Running rates or time requirements
3. Stages in the process
4. Power requirements
5. Maintenance needs and other down-time data
6. Supplies required
7. Needs from various service departments

Second, this technical data and the related cost figures should be reviewed with the department managers so that the budget base is fully understood and accepted. Third, the determination of the fixed and variable components, and the translation of the technical information in budget allowances, should probably be handled by the accounting group. Depending upon organization structure, this synthesis is best placed in the budget or cost department for several reasons. Much of the required data is outside the engineering orbit: insurance rates and coverage, depreciation bases, tax bases, and so forth. Furthermore, a detailed knowledge of the accounting methods is needed. Finally, all the actual information flows to this same source, so that a single agency is in a better position to coordinate practice and promote uniformity for each department.

The budget department would also use these budgets in making the required periodic plans.

ITEMS NEEDING SPECIAL ATTENTION IN THE MANUFACTURING AREA

Given the special needs of the manufacturing area, there are some topics related to the problem that need explanation:

- Proper departmentalization of expenses
- Allocation of costs to finished product or process
- Service department expenses

- Activity bases
- Impact of "normal activity"
- Cost behavior
- Account classification

When this background knowledge is assimilated, then the basis is set for establishing the manufacturing expense budget structure and the related annual planning budget.

Proper Departmentalization of Expenses

As mentioned in Chapter 5, costs and expenses must be segregated on a "responsibility basis" for cost control; that is, costs should be accumulated by individual responsibility, according to the person who will be held accountable or responsible for the costs incurred. Thus, the costs will be segregated by department. Generally speaking, for control purposes, most costs (other than service department expenses) will not be allocated. However, for product costing and inventory valuation, costs must be known by finished product. Hence, the departmental structure must be so established that product costs can be accurately determined. Exactly how the manufacturing operation will be departmentalized will involve decisions on (1) the extent to which improved product costs will result and (2) how cost control is best achieved.

Normally a cost center is the most minute division of manufacturing operations. It may be established using this criterion:

- One or more of the same or similar machines; or
- A logical grouping of machinery for the performance of a single operation or for a sequence of closely related operations

The proper segregation of operations is essential because of the cost impact and the best method of controlling the activity and related costs. Not all products will be processed in the same department or to the same extent. For example, Product *A* may require the application of expensive machinery in Department 22, while Product *B* may need only a hand operation or processing in an entirely different manner. Proper sequencing of operations by department and proper departmental or cost center segregation are required to determine the proper product costs; proper product costs are essential to establishing sales prices and inventory values.

Allocation of Manufacturing Expenses

Allocation of manufacturing expenses among departments (except certain service department costs) is not necessary or desirable for proper planning and control. However, it is required for product costing. How costs are allocated to final cost objectives, products, or processes is germane to proper planning. It is basic that a proportional relationship exist between the indirect expenses that are allocated and the basis used for such distribution. The costs allocated should be a fair measure of the services or benefits received. In most cases there is an obvious or logical basis for allocating expenses, although in a few instances arbitrary bases may be required. Thus, building depreciation costs or occupancy costs might be allocated on a square-footage basis. Headcount, or payroll costs, could be used for allocating personnel department expense.

It is beyond the scope of this book to delve into the methods of cost allocation. However, it is preferred that the method used in determining the most appropriate cost be simple, but reasonable.

Some of the commonly used bases for allocating indirect manufacturing expense include these:

- Direct labor hours
- Direct labor costs
- Standard machine-hours
- Square feet occupied
- Direct material cost input
- Units of production
- Total prime cost input

Service Department Expenses

A problem faced by those responsible for the planning and control of manufacturing costs relates to the allocation of service department costs. It has a direct bearing on the proper control of expenses and on cost determination. From both the cost control viewpoint and the cost determination viewpoint, it is essential that the distribution be a fair measure of the benefits received or service rendered.

For many indirect or service departments there is a logical method for distributing expenses, whereas an arbitrary basis must be used for others. As examples, power costs may be distributed in proportion to kilowatt hours consumed; maintenance costs may be allocated on the basis of actual manhours used; building costs can be prorated on a square or cubic footage basis; quality control costs may be distributed on a unit of production base. On the other hand, the expense of planning and scheduling or general factory supervision may be arbitrarily distributed on a manhours, payroll dollars, or total processing cost basis in the absence of a better procedure.

From the practical viewpoint, it is preferable to employ as simple a method as possible, even though not theoretically correct. Yet, when large sums are involved, it is perhaps desirable to consider the nature of the indirect expenses as related to plant activity. In those instances where some costs are fixed and others variable, it may be well to allocate these two types of costs on different bases: The fixed may be distributed on a standard or normal activity basis while the variable element can be allocated in proportion to actual activity. Powerhouse costs are a typical example. Since the plant is presumably built to handle normal capacity, the fixed costs of depreciation, taxes, insurance, and supervision could be allocated in proportion to steam consumption at normal capacity. The more variable expenses such as fuel, hourly labor, and repairs may be distributed on the basis of pounds of steam used each month.

It was stated earlier that the method of allocating service department costs has a direct bearing on cost control. This is related to whether actual or standard costs are distributed to departments using the service. From a cost control viewpoint, the service department supervisor should be held responsible for any costs over his budget. The department using the services should be charged at a standard rate for the actual services used, differentiating between the fixed and variable costs, of course. In this manner, the using department can be held fully responsible for excess service costs in that department, since no share of the inefficiencies or wastes of the service department are charged against the productive department. From the cost control viewpoint, the service supervisor is responsible for efficiently operating his department at whatever level of service is required by the using departments, and as measured by the flexible budget applied to the level of activity. The productive departmental supervisors, on the other hand, are responsible for the quantity of service consumed.

In cost determination, it will be necessary to allocate the variances created in the service departments, usually in proportion to the standard costs already distributed. While this may be done for top management, the practice should not apply in cost control applications.

Activity Bases

Many of the manufacturing activities can be planned and controlled using the flexible or variable budgeting principle, but the selection of the proper measure of activity is essential to an effectively operating budgetary control system. As mentioned in Chapter 5, an acceptable activity base should be:

- A rather direct measure of the cost-incurring activity.
- Readily understood and accepted by those directly involved with the department operations and its budget.
- Applied to costs that are unaffected, in the short run, by any factor other than volume.

Poor correlation between the expense levels and the activity bases may be a reflection of either (1) the wrong measure or (2) improper expense control.

Some of the commonly accepted bases for the planning and control of manufacturing expenses include:

1. Producing departments:
   - Standard manhours
   - Standard machine-hours
   - Units of output
   - Direct labor cost
   - Quantity of material moved
   - Value of output
2. Service departments:
   - Power Department — Kilowatt hours delivered
   - Maintenance Department — Direct repair hours used at preset rates
   - Machine Shop — Actual hours consumed at preset rates
   - Purchase Department — Purchase amounts
   - Personnel Department — Head-count or payroll dollars

Impact of "Normal Activity"

In discussing activity levels, another important consideration is the degree of activity selected in setting the cost standards for the manufacturing expenses. While it is not too relevant to the planning or control of the individual departmental indirect manufacturing costs, it does have a bearing on the planned and actual income statement and inventory valuation. The activity level selected, as most accountants know, has a great impact on the "volume variance."

There are three levels on which the unit fixed standard manufacturing expenses may be determined:

1. The anticipated sales volume, or manufacturing, for the year or other planning period when the standards and budgets are to be applied
2. The practical plant capacity, which represents the volume at which the plant could produce, assuming no lack of sales orders
3. The normal, average, or expected production volume over a period of time

If the expected near-term sales volume is used, then all costs would normally be adjusted or changed for each applicable period. Comparability is lost in making cost comparisons, and management does not get the real sense of the impact of manufacturing volume changes on costs. Standard manufacturing costs will be higher in low-volume years, when lower prices may be necessary to secure needed business. Conversely, the standard manufacturing costs will be lower in high-volume periods, where the opportunity of securing increased prices would exist if the facts were known.

Practical plant capacity tends to give the lowest costs and to understate the real costs, since they are reported as lower than the sales volume would warrant. Under this method, there is a continuing unfavorable volume variance and an understatement of inventory costs.

Normal or average plan capacity, defined as "normal activity," is the degree of utilization of the plan that is necessary to meet the average sales demand over the period of a complete business cycle, and thus is sufficient to level out the seasonal and cyclical influences. Such a base permits the stabilization of costs, recognizes the longer-term trends, and makes comparisons more useful. All things considered, "normal activity" would seem to be the most suitable basis for determining unit standard fixed manufacturing expenses.

If only one product is manufactured, then normal capacity may be expressed in terms of the quantity of this one product. If more than one product is made, then a common unit such as productive hours is necessary. If the normal productive hours are known for each department or cost center, the aggregate of all departmental hours will reflect plant capacity. The sum of the fixed manufacturing expenses divided by the productive hours at normal capacity will produce the fixed expense per productive hour.

Cost Behavior

The crux of the solution to effective planning and control of manufacturing expenses is the proper application of the flexible budget principle. This, in turn, depends on the segregation of expenses into their fixed and variable components. How can this be best accomplished? There are three general approaches to the measurement of cost variation with volume:

1. Inspection of the company's chart of accounts and assignment of costs to the fixed or variable category, according to the type of cost represented by each account

2. Statistical analysis of previously recorded costs to determine how costs have actually varied with volume

3. Industrial engineering studies to determine how costs should vary with volume

All three methods may be utilized profitably in a given company, for each has certain areas of application as well as certain weaknesses. Chapter 5 provides substantial detail on how a proper cost segregation can be done by methods 1 or 2. Some limited examples of method 3 are discussed in this chapter.

Several general propositions are relevant to a study of cost behavior. To restate a comment made earlier, costs are not necessarily variable or fixed by inherent nature alone. Rather, these characteristics may be acquired by reason of managerial decisions. For example, management may decide that a given number of key employees constitute an irreducible minimum. However, a year later the opinion may change by reason of changed conditions or otherwise. Likewise, decisions as to accounting practice may effect the segregation. Thus, a unit-of-output method of depreciation might be employed to allocate the cost of equipment to the production. This would be reflected as variable expense behavior in the records. If, however, a straight-line method of depreciation were used, the expense would assume the character of a fixed cost. Of course, it would be a question of fact as to whether time, or usage, or both were the primary determinants of the physical life of the equipment. Finally, the separation of costs into fixed and variable categories cannot be completely accurate. There are always borderline cases. However, these areas of doubt usually can be reduced so as not to affect the validity of the results in planning and control applications.

Account Classification of Manufacturing Expenses

A prerequisite to the most effective budgeting of manufacturing expenses, then, is a proper classification of costs. The incorporation in the books of account of an expense segregation according to variability with volume permits the development of desired relationships in the regular accounting statements. Moreover, such a practice facilitates flexible budgeting. If a company does not wish to fully incorporate the twofold split, a general or approximate breakdown into the fixed and variable groups is possible.

An illustrative chart of accounts wherein fixed and variable expenses are segregated follows.

5100   VARIABLE MANUFACTURING EXPENSES
    5101 — 1   Labor — Hourly — Straight time
    5101 — 2   Labor — Hourly — Bonus
    5101 — 3   Labor — Hourly — Overtime penalty
    5102   Salaries
    5103   Provision for vacation pay
    5104   Payroll taxes
    5105   Workmen's compensation insurance
    5107   Health and accident insurance
    5108   Provision for retirement expense
    5110   Fuel
    5111   Power
    5134   Cartons and containers
    5135 — 1   Repairs — Material
    5135 — 2   Repairs — Outside labor
    5135 — 3   Repairs — Labor and overhead   (*continued*)

5139	Rent
5140	Supplies
5141	Safety supplies
5142	Auto trips
5143	Postage
5144	Samples
5145	Spoilage, salvage, and reclamation expense
5160	Communications
5162	Laundry
5163	Dues and subscriptions
5164	Auto expense
5170	Legal and professional
5180	Taxes — Sales and use
5181	Taxes — Federal transportation
5182	Taxes — Excise
5190	Recreation and welfare expense
5191	Miscellaneous
5192	Royalties

5200   FIXED MANUFACTURING EXPENSES
(General Management Level)

5202 — 1	Salaries — Executive
5204	Payroll taxes
5208	Provision for retirement expense
5239	Rent
5270	Legal and professional
5285	Taxes — Property
5289	Insurance — Property and liability
5295 — 1	Depreciation — Buildings
5295 — 2	Depreciation — Machinery and equipment
5295 — 3	Depreciation — Laboratory equipment
5296 — 1	Amortization — Machinery and equipment
5299	Amortization — Patents

5300   FIXED MANUFACTURING EXPENSES (Production Level)

5301 — 1	Labor — Hourly — Straight time
5301 — 2	Labor — Hourly — Bonus
5301 — 3	Labor — Hourly — Overtime penalty
5302	Salaries
5303	Provision for vacation pay
5304	Payroll taxes
5305	Workmen's compensation insurance
5306	Health and accident insurance
5308	Provision for retirement expense
5311	Power
5335 — 1	Repairs — Material

5335 — 2	Repairs — Outside labor
5335 — 3	Repairs — Labor and overhead
5339	Rent
5340	Supplies
5341	Safety supplies
5342	Auto trips
5343	Postage
5360	Communications
5363	Dues and subscriptions
5380	Taxes — Sales and use
5381	Taxes — Federal transportation
5382	Taxes — Excise
5392	Royalties

Any such classification as the foregoing must, of necessity, be only illustrative, since the question as to whether a particular burden item varies directly with physical volume of production or remains fixed regardless of volume depends upon the nature and methods of operations peculiar to the individual concern. Royalties, for example, are shown as a variable cost but will, in some instances, constitute a fixed cost. On the other hand, depreciation on some items of equipment and amortization of patents may be variable costs.

It will be noted that fixed costs are further classified as to those that are beyond the usual control of production executives and those that are currently fixed by the production executives. Such a classification assists in the ultimate control of the fixed costs.

The chart of accounts shown above segregates manufacturing expenses by type of expense and by fixed and variable characteristics. Of course, this same breakdown must extend to each service department and to each production department in order to place responsibility for excess costs and to secure the total variable and/or fixed expense by the segment being analyzed.

In any particular company, it may or may not be possible to structure the accounts into their fixed or variable category. If not, then the natural expenses, by department, will represent a combination of behaviors, and the budget structure must make provision for the proper allowance.

TYPES OF MANUFACTURING EXPENSE BUDGETS

Now that some of the basic considerations in setting manufacturing expense budgets are behind us, the remaining question might be what type of budget should be used in the planning and control of manufacturing expenses. It is in this area of manufacturing expense that budgeting experience has been the most extensive.

Three types of budgets might be applied to manufacturing overhead. They may be described as

- A fixed budget
- A step budget
- A flexible budget

Business executives *do* have a choice as to the type of budget to be employed, but, as will be seen, one type may be better than the other two in many applications.

As the name implies, a fixed budget is constant in amount for the planning and control period or periods under review. Once the budget has been determined, actual expenses are compared with the predetermined amount. An example of a quarterly fixed budget, in which each monthly budget in the quarter represents one third of the quarterly budget, is shown in Figure 13-1. This budget has the advantage of simplicity, and some reflection of the expected changing production volume during the year is seen in the quarterly budgeted amounts. If, however, the production volume for the month in the second quarter is greater than 13,332 hours, then would the budgeted expense level be realistic? It would be realistic only for the fixed expenses; it would be entirely inapplicable to another expense (e.g., power).

A step budget is a budget prepared for selected different levels, or steps, in operations. In this method, a budget is determined for predetermined activities rates. An example is provided in Figure 13-2. To be sure, the budget for different levels is shown, but (1) several budgets must be calculated, and (2) variations within the segment range are not recognized.

A so-called flexible budget is shown in Figure 13-3 and is the type suggested for many of the manufacturing operations. It is more realistic than the fixed or step budgets because it recognizes the actual level of operations for each time period — whether for planning purposes or control applications. The means of constructing such a budget is fully explained in Chapter 5.

Incidentally, a comparison of the three budgets for an operating level of 12,500 (thousand) hours is shown in Figure 13-4. Since the step budget was set at the midpoint of the activity range (a level of 13,500 hours in the application), the planned hours of 12,500, being below the midpoint, produce an excessive budget. The fixed budget at 12,000 hours is too "tight." The flexible budget provides the fairest answer.

FIG. 13-1 Manufacturing Expense Budget — Fixed Type

The Middle Manufacturing Company
ANNUAL BUDGET — FIXED TYPE
Department 12

Expense	Annual Budget	Quarter 1		Quarter 2		Quarter 3		Quarter 4	
		3 Mos.	1 Mo.	3 Mos.	1 Mo.	3 Mos.	1 Mo.	3 Mos.	1 Mo.
Planned production (hours)	160,000	36,000	12,000	40,000	13,332	44,000	14,667	40,000	13,332
Supervisory salaries	$ 48,000	$ 12,000	$ 4,000	$ 12,000	$ 4,000	$ 12,000	$ 4,000	$ 12,000	$ 4,000
Other salaries	72,000	16,500	5,500	18,000	6,000	19,500	6,500	18,000	6,000
Indirect wages	160,000	36,000	12,000	40,000	13,333	44,000	14,666	40,000	13,333
Fringe benefit costs (30%)	84,000	19,350	6,450	21,000	7,000	22,650	7,550	21,000	7,000
Power	120,000	33,000	11,000	32,000	10,667	26,000	8,667	29,000	9,666
Supplies	12,000	3,000	1,000	3,000	1,000	3,000	1,000	3,000	1,000
Repairs and maintenance	80,000	18,000	6,000	20,000	6,666	22,000	7,333	20,000	6,667
Depreciation	12,000	3,000	1,000	3,000	1,000	3,000	1,000	3,000	1,000
Other	12,000	2,500	833	3,000	1,000	3,500	1,167	3,000	1,000
Total	$600,000	$143,350	$47,783	$152,000	$50,666	$155,650	$51,883	$149,000	$49,666

FIG. 13-2 Manufacturing Expense Budget — Step Type

THE MIDDLE MANUFACTURING COMPANY
ANNUAL BUDGET — STEP TYPE
Department 12

Expense	Annual Budget at Normal Activity Range (hours) 160,000	Monthly Budget at Indicated Activity Range (hours)			
		3,000–5,999	6,000–8,999	9,000–11,999	12,000–14,999
Supervisory salaries	$ 48,000	$ 4,000	$ 4,000	$ 4,000	$ 4,000
Other salaries	72,000	5,400	5,560	5,790	6,800
Indirect wages	160,000	8,910	10,410	11,910	13,410
Fringe benefit costs	84,000	5,490	5,990	6,510	7,260
Power	120,000	6,690	7,810	8,940	10,060
Supplies	12,000	470	650	830	1,010
Repairs and maintenance	80,000	3,350	4,480	5,600	6,730
Depreciation	12,000	1,000	1,000	1,000	1,000
Other	12,000	340	560	790	1,010
Total	$600,000	$35,650	$40,460	$45,370	$51,280

FIG. 13-3 Flexible Budget Type

THE MIDDLE MANUFACTURING COMPANY

ANNUAL BUDGET — FLEXIBLE TYPE

Department 12

Activity Level — 160,000 Hours

Expense	Annual Budget Total	Annual Budget Fixed	Annual Budget Variable	Fixed Amount Per Month	Variable Rate Per Hour[a]
Supervisory salaries	$ 48,000	$ 48,000	$ —	$ 4,000	$ —
Other salaries	72,000	60,000	12,000	5,000	.075
Indirect wages	160,000	80,000	80,000	6,667	.50
Fringe benefit costs	84,000	56,400	27,600	4,700	.1725
Power	120,000	60,000	60,000	5,000	.375
Supplies	12,000	2,400	9,600	200	.06
Repair and maintenance	80,000	20,000	60,000	1,666	.375
Depreciation	12,000	12,000	—	1,000	—
Other	12,000	—	12,000	—	.075
Total	$600,000	$338,800	$261,200	$28,233	$1.6325

(a) Variable amount ÷ 160,000 hours

FIG. 13-4 Comparative Budget Results

THE MIDDLE MANUFACTURING COMPANY

COMPARABLE BUDGET ALLOWANCES
Department 12
For a Month With 12,500-Hour Level

Expense	Fixed Budget[a]	Step Type[b]	Flexible Budget
Supervisory salaries	$ 4,000	$ 4,000	$ 4,000
Other salaries	5,500	6,800	5,938
Indirect wages	12,000	13,410	12,917
Fringe benefit costs	6,450	7,260	6,856
Power	11,000	10,060	9,688
Supplies	1,000	1,010	950
Repairs and maintenance	6,000	6,730	6,353
Depreciation	1,000	1,000	1,000
Other	833	1,010	938
Total	$47,783	$51,280	$48,640

(a) The closest month (Quarter 1) — range of 12,000 hours was used
(b) Step budget range of 12,000 to 14,999 was selected

PRACTICALITY OF FLEXIBLE MANUFACTURING EXPENSE BUDGETS

Generally speaking, the principle of flexibility has been applied more widely in (or at least more numerous attempts have been made to introduce it into) the field of manufacturing expenses than in the other expense areas. As would be expected, some objections have been raised. Therefore, before examining in any more detail the methodology as applied to manufacturing expenses, it is in order to review the more commonly voiced criticisms. The more serious contentions are essentially that

1. The introduction of flexibility is a poor substitute for sound planning.
2. Flexibility is in conflict with the principle of continuous employment.
3. Flexible budgets are not in fact a basis for cost control at the point of application.

Consider, first the argument that flexibility is a poor substitute for sound planning. Chapter 5 is devoted almost exclusively to the application of the flexible principle to each of the planning, coordinating, and controlling functions of a business enterprise. The need for planning has been reiterated. Business must plan, with or without flexible budgets. Unfortunately, no present-day business management, nor indeed any management, is sufficiently clairvoyant to predict the future with certainty, and to control all events so that inexorably the objective is always attained. It is self-evident that when the fortunes of a business turn less favorable than expected, reductions in costs or increases in income must be made, or the business will not long survive. The assumption that flexibility must be introduced at the whim of management because of improper planning is not warranted by the facts.

Another argument relates to continuous employment. Chapter 10 emphasizes the idea that stabilized employment can be achieved to a much greater degree through adequate planning that permits the leveling out of production through the buildup of inventories. However, merely to enforce stabilized employment without regard to the financial condition of the business is to invite disaster. Through merit rating plans, most companies already have an incentive to stabilize employment. Moreover, salaries and wages are not the only costs subject to variability. What about supplies, power, or repairs? Is the principle not applicable here?

FLEXIBILITY AND CONTROL

The argument that flexible budgets cannot be a basis for cost control at the point of application is worthy of more analysis. A typical illustration in support of the impracticality of the flexible budget is the situation where the foreman is told, *after the fact,* that his operating level was 80 percent of normal production volume, and, accordingly that the budget is x dollars. It is stated that he must know in advance what his level of operations will be. Moreover, it is avowed that this front-line supervisor cannot reduce his work crew tomorrow, increase it two days later, and cut back in the following week — all within budget. Severance pay, unemployment insurance, and other costs incident to hiring and terminations are stated to produce an impossible situation.

Granted that the task is difficult and 100 percent flexibility cannot always be attained. Yet, on the basis of experience, there are sufficient means at the disposal of an intelligent management to make the flexible budgeting of manufacturing expenses reasonably effective and rewarding in its application. Some examples are:

1. The top echelon of management can and must advise the operating staff of proposed changes in production levels so as to permit an orderly adjustment in costs. Some companies, as an illustration, on about the twentieth of each

FIG. 13-5   Quarterly Budget Forecast

GENERAL AIRCRAFT CORPORATION
QUARTERLY BUDGET FORECAST

Cleveland Division
Factory Accounting Department

Quarter First
Year 19XX

Classification	Budget Base	Fixed Budget	Variable Rate Per M Units	January Base Units(a)	January Budget Forecast	February Base Units	February Budget Forecast	March Base Units	March Budget Forecast
Direct labor: none									
Total direct labor: none									
Indirect salaries and wages	6	$7,519	28.64	143.6	$11,632	148.7	$11,778	130.7	$11,262
	Total Allowed Direct Labor Hours								
Other departmentalized expense		300	4.50	143.6	946	148.7	969	130.7	888
Total departmentalized expense	XXXX				$12,578		$12,747		$12,150
Dept. performance (Direct Labor and Department Expense)	XXXX	XXX	XXX	143.6	12,578	148.7	12,747	130.7	12,150
Assigned Expense									
656 Office supplies	6	100	.40	143.6	157	148.7	159	130.7	152
657 Postage	6	200	1.20	143.6	372	148.7	378	130.7	357
658 Telegraph	6	200	3.57	143.6	713	148.7	731	130.7	667
664 Property taxes	F	1,750			1,750		1,750		1,750
665 State franchise tax	F	300			300		300		300
668 Other taxes	6	100	1.50	143.6	315	148.7	323	130.7	296
669 Property insurance	6	400	3.00	143.6	631	148.7	646	130.7	792
671 Other insurance	6	200	6.00	143.6	1,062	148.7	1,092	130.7	964
672 Audit fees & expenses	F	450			450		450		450
674 Rent tabulating	F	1,400			1,400		1,400		1,400
688 Depreciation	F	3,620			3,620		3,620		3,620
Total assigned expense					$10,970		$11,049		$10,768
Total expense					$23,548		$23,796		$22,918

(a) Express base units in thousands of hours

Issued Dec. 6, 19XX

month prepare a control budget for the following month setting forth the operating level at which production will be held and the necessary costs. The staff is judged against the budget so established.

Another firm insists that expense levels be held at a level measured by standard labor hours of actual output, but prepares a quarterly forecast to indicate the approximate level of activity and the approximate budget allowances that will be granted. The form of notification to the department manager or foreman is shown in Figure 13-5.

2. As special circumstances arise, appropriate allowances can be granted. For example, a major breakdown that is not the responsibility of the foreman must be handled budgetwise by an allowance equal to actual cost.

3. Multiple-rate budgets may be necessary. As the level of operations, number of shifts, or number of operating days per week varies, a single fixed cost allowance or a single variable rate may be insufficient. Separate rates for the various types of operations may be found necessary — each designed to best measure the performance of the supervisor under the actual conditions experienced.

4. Proper accounting by responsibility might require that severance pay, for example, would not be a departmental charge against Mr. X but would be a cost of his superior. While some such circumstances could be regarded as mere cost transfers, the benefits are that (a) actual expenses are reduced and (b) the method does not penalize a department manager for costs beyond his control. A similar result for this last benefit can be secured through a special budget allowance.

In summary, to make the flexible budget an effective control tool, good communication must exist at all levels in the organization. Moreover, the budget staff must exercise good judgment in the way in which the problem is solved. The psychological benefits of the flexible budget are good because each supervisor is kept "on his toes" if budget adjustments are made as production levels change and he is required to meet the new level. The tie-in of budget performance to an incentive plan makes the control tool even more effective.

THE BUDGET PERIOD

At this point, a question might be raised as to how long the budget period should be for manufacturing expenses. As a general statement, the estimates of expense for planning purposes would cover the same period as the sales budget (i.e., by months or quarters for a twelve-month period in the typical case). Long-range plans, however, will extend over a longer period — perhaps five years.

For control purposes, the question of length of period is of less significance. As will be seen later, the variable manufacturing expense budget is often expressed as a unit budget, and time is not a factor. In the fixed expense category, the budget period is perhaps of less significance than the method selected to apportion charges to fiscal years.

A GENERALIZED BUDGET PROCEDURE

While the exact procedure to be followed in developing and implementing a sound procedure for budgeting manufacturing expenses in a particular company will be influenced by local conditions, the following steps indicate some of the actions that should take place:

1. Arrange for the accumulation of manufacturing expenses on a responsibility basis, giving recognition to the needs of adequate product costing.
2. Ensure that the accounts provide for the grouping of natural expenses in a manner that facilitates control; that is, the individual expense accounts should be sufficiently broken down so that expenses will tend to vary with the same volume factor or must be controlled in the same fashion or point in time. Indirect labor, for example, should not be combined with repair materials in that the latter may be controlled by watching requisitions — before the expense is incurred — and the former may be controlled through manning tables or in relationship to direct labor input.
3. Determine the fixed and variable components of the expenses, preferably on an individual account basis through the use of regression equations or on the basis of the entire departmental expenses. If this principle is not to be employed, then the appropriate method should be selected.
4. To prepare the annual planning budget, apply the departmental flexible budget structure to the expected or planned volume factors by appropriate planning period. Summarize the data for all departmental budgets to arrive at the total annual budget for all manufacturing expenses.
5. For control purposes, assuming the flexible budget is used, apply the budget structure to the experienced volume for the month, or other period, to arrive at the allowable budget.
6. Compare actual expenses, account by account, with the budget; and search out the reasons for the variances. These should be reported to the appropriate manufacturing executive for proper corrective action.

AN ILLUSTRATIVE ANNUAL PLANNING BUDGET

Assuming the proper departmental structure (on a responsibility basis) for planning and control, the desired breakdown of accounts by natural expense, and the departmental budget structure, then the structure would be applied to the factor of variability (standard manhours in the illustration) to determine the annual planning budget for the planning periods. This is illustrated in Figure 13-6 for the fabrication department.

Similar procedures are followed to arrive at the budget for each department, although the activity base may change. Power, for example, might be related to thousands of kilowatts generated. When all departmental budgets have been prepared, they are summarized on a responsibility basis for the entire function. Such a summary is illustrated in Figure 13-7. Please note that where service department expenses are involved (and they usually are) and are charged to the using department, an elimination should be made similar to intercompany eliminations to arrive at the total manufacturing expenses (without duplication). In addition, the manufacturing expenses may be summarized by type of expense to indicate where the changes took place, as compared to the prior year, for example.

INDIRECT LABOR — PLANNING AND CONTROL

Some special comments should be made on indirect labor, inasmuch as it comprises a significant portion of factory manufacturing expenses. In the preceding examples, indirect labor was determined by measuring historical costs against a factor of variability — the factory's standard manhours. In many instances this is practical; but the correlation may not be as clear-cut as desired, and in some cases a competent staff or complement of indirect labor is difficult to attract and retain. Instead of merely correlating total indirect labor costs with factory standard hours, a more analytical approach may be necessary, using the assistance of the industrial engineers. As discussed in Chapter 11, a similar approach to that of direct labor may be necessary and is illustrated now. The detail steps could be these:

1. Based on a study of the specific functions required, the industrial engineers could determine by job code or function the exact manhours required at various activity levels.
2. An activity base could be selected that would represent a fair measure of demand for each function of the indirect labor crew.
3. Estimates could be made determining the portion of the crew that should be treated as fixed, and the variable manhours could be determined.
4. The hours data could be costed, a fixed base determined, and a variable rate arrived at per unit of variability.

An example of this analytical approach in crew analysis and related costing is shown in Figure 13-8.

(*text continues on page 13-28*)

FIG. 13-6 Departmental Annual Planning Budget

THE NEW MANUFACTURING COMPANY
FABRICATION DEPARTMENT
PLANNING BUDGET FOR 19XX

Type of Expense	Mandatory Budget Structure Fixed	Variable[a]	Annual Budget	Quarter 1 January	February	March	Total	Quarter 2	Quarter 3	Quarter 4
Standard manhours (000s)			1,870	150	120	170	440	490	510	430
Supervisory salaries	$ 3,400	—	$ 40,800	$ 3,400	$ 3,400	$ 3,400	$ 10,200	$ 10,200	$ 10,200	$ 10,200
Other salaries	2,100	$ 32.20	85,414	6,930	5,964	7,574	20,468	22,078	22,722	20,146
Indirect wages	14,800	41.70	255,579	21,055	19,804	21,889	62,748	64,833	65,667	62,331
Subtotal	$20,300	$ 73.90	$ 381,793	$31,385	$29,168	$32,863	$ 93,416	$ 97,111	$ 98,589	$ 92,677
Fringe benefits (30%)	$ 6,090	$ 22.17	$ 114,538	$ 9,416	$ 8,750	$ 9,859	$ 28,025	$ 29,133	$ 29,577	$ 27,803
Repairs — Labor and overhead	4,000	14.60	75,302	6,190	5,752	6,482	18,424	19,154	19,446	18,278
Repairs — Outside	3,000	31.40	94,718	7,710	6,768	8,338	22,816	24,386	25,014	22,502
Depreciation	10,000	—	120,000	10,000	10,000	10,000	30,000	30,000	30,000	30,000
Perishable tools	500	20.15	43,681	3,523	2,918	3,925	10,366	11,373	11,777	10,165
Power	5,000	92.30	232,601	18,845	16,076	20,691	55,612	60,227	62,073	54,689
Supplies	2,000	14.70	51,489	4,205	3,764	4,499	12,468	13,203	13,497	12,321
Communications	500	8.50	21,895	1,775	1,520	1,945	5,240	5,665	5,835	5,155
Miscellaneous	500	5.00	15,350	1,250	1,100	1,350	3,700	3,950	4,050	3,650
Total	$51,890	$282.72	$1,151,367	$94,299	$85,816	$99,952	$280,067	$294,202	$299,858	$277,240

(a) Per standard manhours (000s)

FIG. 13-7 Summary Manufacturing Expense Budget

THE NEW MANUFACTURING COMPANY

SUMMARY MANUFACTURING EXPENSE BUDGET

For the Plan Year 19XX

Department	Annual Budget	Quarter 1				Quarter 2	Quarter 3	Quarter 4
		January	February	March	Total			
Standard manhours (000s)(a)	6,500	510	450	540	1,500	1,700	1,800	1,500
General manufacturing	$ 168,000	$ 14,000	$ 14,000	$ 14,000	$ 42,000	$ 42,000	$ 42,000	$ 42,000
Fabrication(b)	1,151,367	94,299	85,816	99,952	280,067	294,202	299,858	277,240
Subassembly	1,274,210	103,430	98,100	105,770	307,300	327,200	332,410	307,300
Final assembly	1,158,040	91,070	90,430	94,650	276,150	296,150	310,400	275,340
Production control	268,510	20,370	19,810	22,460	62,420	68,420	74,810	62,640
Quality control	228,500	17,310	16,790	19,120	53,220	58,100	63,960	53,220
Industrial engineering	239,200	18,100	17,100	21,200	55,300	61,300	67,300	55,300
Purchasing	254,400	21,200	21,200	21,200	63,600	63,600	63,600	63,600
Transportation	208,510	15,370	14,810	17,460	47,640	53,420	59,810	47,640
Maintenance	361,650	28,200	26,430	29,520	84,150	92,500	100,850	84,150
Power	697,800	56,100	48,230	62,100	166,430	180,680	186,200	164,490
Less: Interdepartmental charges(c)	(1,059,450)	(84,300)	(74,660)	(91,620)	(250,580)	(273,180)	(287,050)	(248,640)
Total	$4,950,737	$395,149	$378,056	$414,712	$1,187,917	$1,264,392	$1,314,148	$1,184,280

(a) For information only; not every department uses its standard manhours as the factor of variability.
(b) See Figure 13-6.
(c) Represents the sum of "Power" and "Maintenance" department expenses.

**FIG. 13-8   Budget and Standards Technical Data —
Indirect Labor**

BUDGETS AND STANDARDS TECHNICAL DATA

Account Name Indirect Labor
Account No. 5101
Length of Period Month

Plant Navarre Street
Dept. Tooling
Year 19XX

Normal Work Week: Shifts per day 1
Hours per shift 8
Days per week 5

Operating Range 66% — 100%

Activity Base Standard Direct Labor Hours
Activity Units at Capacity 4,644

TECHNICAL DATA
(men per shift)

Job Code	Description	Requirements at Activity Level			Data at 100% Level	
		66%	80%	100%	Fixed	Variable
110	Cleanup	.5	.3	.5	.5	
111	Trucking	2.0	2.5	3.0		3.0
112	Testing	1.0	1.0	1.5		1.5
113	Preparation	.5	.7	1.0	.5	.5
114	Inspection	2.0	2.5	3.0		3.0
	Total	6.0	7.0	9.0	1.0	8.0

COST DATA

Job Code	Description	Manhours			Rate per Hour	Fixed		Variable		Variable Rate per M Units	
						Manhours	Amount	Manhours	Amount	Manhours	Amount
110	Cleanup	86	86	86	$ 7.00	86	$ 602	—	$	—	$
111	Trucking	344	430	516	9.50	—	—	516	4,902	111.1	$1,055.45
112	Testing	172	172	258	12.00	—	—	258	3,096	55.6	667.20
113	Preparation	86	86	172	8.00	86	688	86	688	18.5	148.00
114	Inspection	344	430	516	14.00	—	—	516	7,224	111.1	1,555.40
85	Union meeting	10	10	10	10.00	10	100	—	—	—	—
86	Physical inventory	10	12	14	10.00	10	100	4	40	.9	9.00
89	Experimental	8	8	8	10.00	—	—	8	80	1.7	17.00
90	Training	10	10	10	5.00	10	50	—	—	—	—
	Total	1,070	1,244	1,590		202	$1,540	1,388	$11,177	298.9	$3,452.05

Supplementary Data and Comments:
1. Calculation of direct labor hours at capacity: a = 27 men per shift; b = 8 hours per shift; c = 5 days per week; d = 4.3 weeks per month = $a \times b \times c \times d$ = 27 × 8 × 5 × 4.3 = 4,644 hours.
2. At a 100% operation, one tester will spend one-half of time on cleanup. At the 66% operation, preparation man will spend alternate days on cleanup.
3. Time for 80-90 codes will be offset by overtime, if needed.

CONTROLLING MANUFACTURING EXPENSES

When the month, or other cost control period is over, then the usual procedure is to compare actual expenses to the budgeted expenses and provide the department manager with the information to the end that he may take any corrective action necessary.

An example of a budget report using the flexible budget principle is shown in Figure 13-9. In this instance, the production department (milling) is charged for certain services used: machine shop, quality control, testing, and the boiler. However, this using department is charged only for actual services received at the standard rates. Excess costs of the service departments, in effect, are not transferred. Incidentally, the illustrative report includes all costs under control of the manager: direct labor, direct material, and manufacturing expenses. While Figure 13-9 represents a direct production department, the same principle would be followed in determining the budget for a service department.

JUDGMENT MUST BE USED

In this chapter, emphasis has been placed on the flexible budget, as contrasted with a fixed budget or step budget, for the best means of planning and controlling manufacturing expenses. This assumption or conclusion is true for most manufacturing expenses; but, depending on local circumstances or practices, departures from a strict application of this principle may be necessary. Thus, judgment should be exercised in selecting that budgeting method that seems to fit the circumstances. The nature and diversity of manufacturing processes, expenses, and procedures must be investigated when special planning and control methods seem warranted.

As an example, consider maintenance and repair expense in a situation where the in-house maintenance department performs all such work. Typical conditions in some such enterprises are discussed in the following paragraphs.

Repair and maintenance expenses represent sizable expenditures in most companies. The cost may aggregate 5 or 10 percent of net sales in some industries, so that savings in this area can be quite significant. Although repair and maintenance expense is typically quite high in most companies, it is also typically not under adequate control. The phrase "adequate control" does not imply a rather low cost level for a particular period: Too little maintenance could prove worse than too much. Experience has demonstrated that too tight a control over these expenses can be expensive over the longer term by reason of interrupted production, higher accident rates, scrap increases, lost machine time, lost manhours, and probably lost customers.

The following conditions are but a few of the problems that complicate the task of controlling maintenance expense:

1. Responsibility is divided, on many phases, between the production and maintenance staffs.
2. Breakdowns and accidents may be quite irregular.
3. It is difficult to judge whether costs are excessive because an acceptable level of expense will vary with the age of equipment, past maintenance practice, operating conditions, and so forth.
4. Major repair jobs must be undertaken at regular intervals, with a resulting fluctuation in total expenditure for maintenance.
5. From the individual work-order viewpoint, many jobs are difficult to estimate as to expected cost or manhours required.

The objective in maintenance cost control is the securing of the lowest possible expenditure over a relatively long period, consistent with the efficient operation of the plant. It may be taken for granted that the responsibility for proper maintenance and reasonable costs will continue as a joint responsibility of the production group and the maintenance department. The foreman may abuse the equipment, or the maintenance crew may do a poor repair job. The machinery may be improperly installed or operated; or the sales requirements may interfere with proper inspections and care. Thus, there are a host of reasons why excess maintenance can occur and why it is difficult to place responsibility clearly. It appears that the most effective answer lies in close teamwork between production and maintenance.

While the following suggestions do not assure control of maintenance costs, they appear to be a step in the right direction.

1. Classify all maintenance costs, both past and future, into two broad groups:
   a. Routine and clearly repetitive items (e.g., the usual oiling, greasing, and preventive maintenance on equipment)
   b. Major repair projects (e.g., the rebuilding of furnace walls, revamping of crane runways, replacement of roof, reconditioning of ventilating systems, or the resurfacing of parking lots)
2. Establish separate budgets for each of the two major classifications:
   a. For the routine, on the basis of the determination of variable and fixed costs, as discussed earlier in this chapter and in Chapter 5. Past experience and engineering estimates of necessary maintenance may be used as guidelines.
   b. For the major projects, by estimates on individual projects of what is needed and at what cost. The survey should cover an extended time span — perhaps five years — so that all costs are considered. (See Chapter 16 for the project budget approach.)
   These costs ought to be included in the product standard costs; and satisfactory methods should be selected for allocating the costs to periods in a

FIG. 13-9 Departmental Budget Report — Production Department

THE METAL FABRICATION COMPANY

DEPARTMENTAL BUDGET REPORT

Dept. Milling #109
Dept. Manager Johnson

Month March, 19XX
Base Units 450,000 Standard Machine Hours

Item	Month Budget Fixed	Variable	Total	Month Actual	Month (Over) or Under Budget	Year to Date Actual	Year to Date (Over) or Under Budget Amount	Year to Date (Over) or Under Budget Percentage
Direct labor	$10,000	$ 450,000	$ 460,000	$ 457,600	$ 2,400	$1,477,900	$ 8,340	.6
Direct material	—	900,000	900,000	967,800	(67,800)(a)	2,756,400	(36,280)	(1.3)
Manufacturing expenses								
Direct:								
Supervision	12,000	27,000	39,000	39,000	—	119,000	1,000	1.0
Salaries — other	2,000	4,500	6,500	6,800	(300)	20,100	(100)	(.5)
Payroll taxes and insurance	2,800	4,500	7,300	7,360	(60)	22,260	140	.5
Supplies	—	36,000	36,000	38,300	(2,300)	110,300	1,700	1.5
Repairs and maintenance	10,000	18,000	28,000	25,600	2,400 (b)	86,100	(100)	—

								Percentage (over) or under budget
Power	1,000	9,000	10,000	10,850	(850)	30,300	700	2.3
Other	2,000	4,500	6,500	6,450	50	19,800	200	1.0
Depreciation	25,000	—	25,000	25,000	—	75,000	—	—
Property taxes	3,000	—	3,000	3,000	—	9,000	—	—
Insurance — property	500	—	500	500	—	1,500	—	—
Total direct expenses	$58,300	$103,500	$161,800	$162,860	($ 1,060)	$493,360	$ 3,540	.7
Allocated services								
Machine shop	$ 6,250	$ 94,500	$ 100,750	$ 102,190	($ 1,440)(c)	$ 313,550	$ (800)	(.2)
Quality control	3,000	45,000	48,000	47,990	10	149,150	(150)	(.1)
Testing	1,000	9,000	10,000	10,100	(100)	31,000	—	—
Boiler	6,000	45,000	51,000	49,340	1,660	159,100	(1,100)	(.7)
Total allocated	$16,250	$ 193,500	$ 209,750	$ 209,620	$ 130	$ 652,800	($ 2,050)	(.3)
Total manufacturing expense	$74,550	$ 297,000	$ 371,550	$ 372,480	$ (930)	$1,146,160	$ 1,490	.1
Total departmental cost	$84,550	$1,647,000	$1,731,550	$1,797,880	($66,330)	$5,380,460	($26,450)	(.5)
Statistical data								
Machine-hours			450,000	452,000	(2,000)	1,412,500	12,500	.8
Direct manhours			112,500	114,400	(1,900)	338,700	(1,200)	.4

(a) Lot 421 declared not salvageable
(b) Preventive maintenance program effective
(c) 380 excess manhours due to machine failure

manner similar to other fixed costs. Perhaps a reserve basis might be found desirable. (Reports on actual expenditures can be made regardless of the accounting treatment.)

3. For the major projects, annually or at other periodic intervals, review the properties and projects to determine that

   a. The estimated cost is reasonable.

   b. All major items have been considered.

   c. The tentative schedule for maintenance is satisfactory.

4. Establish a timetable for each of the projects, and prepare an annual budget for those to be started during the fiscal period. Such budget would be subject to the regular approvals.

5. Secure estimates for each job (if practical), whether major or routine. Compare actual costs with estimates.

6. Test the maintenance expense by such supplementary methods as the following:

   a. In relationship to the cost of the assets — perhaps 5 percent per annum is a fair standard

   b. The ratio of maintenance-crew size to production workers

   c. In relationship to industry experience

REVISION OF THE MANUFACTURING EXPENSE BUDGET

In general, a budget should be revised whenever it no longer serves as a useful planning and control tool. From previous comments, it can be understood that major changes in production levels from those contemplated certainly would require changes in a fixed budget and, in some cases, in the step budget. This fact alone would not require modification of the flexible budget structure, since its construction already provides for its application under conditions of volume change. However, the annual planning budget, which is a budget predicated on a given volume of business, may need updating when prospective volumes are greatly different from those planned. Such revisions may be necessary for determining financial needs, financial results of operations, and generally to coordinate the required accommodations throughout the company.

Of course, it should be recognized that departmental budget structures should be revised when

- There are major changes in the functions or processes of the department.
- Major salary or wage adjustments take place in the compensation structure.
- Major price changes for outside goods and services take place due to inflation or other factors.

14

Cost of Goods Sold

NEED FOR CAREFUL PREPARATION OF THIS BUDGET

Anyone charged with preparing schedules of the cost of goods sold knows it is a detailed and meticulous process and is a major influence in calculating gross income. In fact, if it is determined by persons unfamiliar with the accounting principles employed and the accounting system of the company, then things can, and often do, go astray. For this reason, some brief explanations are necessary.

THE BASIC EQUATION

The accounting principle involved, of course, is the matching of costs with revenue. Therefore, as a first step, the cost of manufacture, or more specifically, the inventory carrying value of the product sold, must be determined, inventory accounts must be reduced or relieved, and the cost-of-goods-sold account must be charged. What is done in the actual accounting of the company must be performed in parallel for the planning process. Hence, if inventories are carried on a first-in, first-out (FIFO) basis, comparable calculations should be made on a budget basis to determine the cost of goods sold.

As a summary, then, the cost of goods sold for a manufacturing company will generally include these elements:

- The "normal" inventory carrying value attached to the specific product sold.
- Items that are expensed as incurred in the manufacturing process, and are not carried into inventory. Where a standard cost system is in operation, for example, variances would be included directly in the cost-of-goods-sold figure, or other nonrecurring costs that should not be a part of the inventory valuation.
- Any adjustments deemed necessary under generally accepted accounting principles, wherein the cost-of-goods-sold category would be the proper disposition (e.g., inventory losses, adjustments to the lower of cost or market).

USE OF COST-OF-GOODS-SOLD DATA

Data on all other items of cost or expense discussed in this text are used for both planning and control purposes. The cost of goods sold, however, is not used for control. It is used primarily as a planning tool to determine gross margin, or gross profit, and *not* as a current control device. This results from the fact that costs are gathered for control purposes as the costs are incurred (i.e., in the purchasing or manufacturing process). Since control action is normally taken at that time, for each element of cost — direct labor, direct material, and manufacturing expense — the cost-of-goods-sold figure (an after-the-fact calculation) need not be used for control of the elements.

STEPS IN PREPARING THE BUDGET

The cost-of-goods-sold budget is, in part, a derivative of the sales budget in that the units of product to be sold must be costed and then other appropriate adjustments made. The few steps in establishing the cost-of-goods-sold budget may be summarized as follows:

1. When the budgeted units of sale have been determined for each product (or group, if applicable), the manufacturing cost of goods sold should be calcu-

lated in the appropriate time period in such detail as is necessary to prepare any desired segment information as to gross margin, etc., by:

- Territory
- Product
- Channel of distribution
- Salesperson

This calculation will be made on the basis of the company inventory, accounting method, and the budgeted manufacturing costs. A type of worksheet, or a computer run, might be somewhat as shown in Figure 14-1, detailing the levels of inventory used. In this example, the accounting method employed in the inventory valuation is the last-in, first-out (LIFO) method.

2. If applicable, the direct charges to cost of goods sold such as variances in manufacturing costs (material variances, labor variances, and manufacturing expenses) should be secured from the manufacturing budget and combined as an identifiable charge in the cost-of-goods-sold budget.

3. Depending on the profit plan, any anticipated write-off chargeable to cost of goods sold and not included in Step 2 above should be accumulated and made part of the budget.

4. The various components for the cost-of-goods-sold budget should be summarized as in Figure 14-2. This is a schedule for one product type only. For product planning, a similar summary would be needed for each product (or grouping). A tabulation of the *trend* of the relationship of the cost of goods sold to sales, as in Figure 14-3, may be helpful.

The Appliance Corporation sells manufactured products and also provides certain services which of course, are not inventoried. In addition, certain charges are made directly to cost of goods sold, in this case, manufacturing research expense. Moreover, it is anticipated that certain write-offs will be required during the plan year. Accordingly, each segment of the estimated or planned cost of goods sold should be summarized, as in Figure 14-4. If applicable, adjustments should be made for estimated sales returns.

The basic point is that various analyses and subanalyses are required to determine the cost-of-goods-sold budget for each profit segment that will be tracked by management. Sales and cost of goods sold, for example, must be developed for each territory, by product, for each salesperson, channel of distribution, method of sale, or size of order analysis. See Chapter 15. An accurate cost-of-goods-sold figure (or direct cost) is necessary to plan sales that will achieve the highest gross margin, or margin after direct costs (see Chapter 6). Hence, the specific segregation of the cost-of-goods-sold elements, while following generally accepted accounting, will depend on the

(*text continues on page 14-8*)

FIG. 14-1 Worksheet for Calculation of Cost of Goods Sold

THE APPLIANCE CORPORATION

CALCULATION OF COST OF GOODS SOLD
By Product and Territory
For Plan Year Ending 12/31/XX

Item	Units	Unit Cost	Total Cost	By Sales Territory					
				Western			Middle West		
				Units	Unit Cost	Total Cost	Units	Unit Cost	Total Cost
PRODUCT A									
January									
Beginning Inventory									
Lot 11	192	$114.30	$ 21,945.60						
Production									
Lot 12	90	115.60	10,404.00						
Sales at Cost (LIFO)									
Lot 12	90	115.60	10,404.00						
Lot 11	43	114.30	4,914.90						
Total	133	$115.18	$ 15,318.90	76	$115.18	$ 8,753.68	57	$115.18	$ 6,565.22
Ending Inventory									
Lot 11	149	114.30	17,030.30						
February									
Production									
Lot 13	220	118.70	23,114.00						
Sales at Cost									
Lot 13	196	118.70	26,265.20	103	118.70	12,226.10	93	118.70	11,039.10
Ending Inventory									
Lot 13	24	118.10	2,848.80						
Lot 11	149	114.30	17,030.70						
Total	173		$ 19,879.50						

PRODUCT B

	Units		Amount		
January					
Beginning Inventory					
Lot 260	490	440.20	215,698.00		
Lot 261	330	446.30	147,279.00		
Total	820	$442.65	$362,977.00	730	328,353.80
Production					449.80
Lot 262	614	452.40	277,773.60		
Total	1,434		$640,750.60		
Sales at Cost					
Lot 262	614	452.40	277,773.60		
Lot 261	330	440.30	147,279.00		116,948.00
Lot 260	46	446.20	20,249.20		
Total	990	$449.80	$445,301.80	260	449.80
Ending Inventory					
Lot 260	444	440.20	195,448.80		

TOTAL ALL PRODUCTION

January		
Beginning Inventory	464,300.00	
Production	312,430.00	
Sales at Cost	491,720.00	348,510.00
Ending Inventory	295,010.00	143,210.00
February		
Production	541,640.00	349,888.00
Sales at Cost	498,300.00	148,412.00
Ending Inventory	$328,350.00	

FIG. 14-2   Cost-of-Goods-Sold Budget — Product *A*

THE APPLIANCE CORPORATION

COST-OF-GOODS-SOLD BUDGET
Product *A* — By Territory
For the Prior Year Ending 12/31/XX

	Total		Western		Middle West	
Period	Units	Amount	Units	Amount	Units	Amount
January	133	$ 15,318	76	$ 8,753	57	$ 6,565
February	196	23,265	103	12,226	93	11,039
March	240	28,560	120	14,280	120	14,280
Total	569	$ 67,143	299	$ 35,259	270	$ 31,884
April	270	$ 32,400	130	$ 15,613	140	$ 16,787
May	220	26,752	140	17,024	80	9,728
June	209	25,477	106	12,921	103	12,556
Total	699	$ 84,629	376	$ 45,558	323	$ 39,071
Third Quarter	520	$ 63,440	260	$ 31,720	260	$ 31,720
Fourth Quarter	440	53,240	271	32,791	169	20,449
Total	2,228	$268,452	1,206	$145,328	1,022	$123,124

FIG. 14-3   Summary — Cost-of-Goods-Sold Budget — Manufactured Product

THE APPLIANCE CORPORATION

SUMMARY — COST-OF-GOODS-SOLD BUDGET
Manufactured Products
For the Plan Year Ending 12/31/XX

			Prior Years	
Period	Total	Percentage Sales	Total	Percentage Sales
January	$ 491,720	64.3	$ 447,400	60.2
February	498,300	65.1	451,200	60.4
March	586,200	65.3	539,110	60.3
April	602,400	66.4	547,600	61.4
May	557,100	66.9	527,440	61.8

Period	Total	Percentage Sales	Prior Years Total	Prior Years Percentage Sales
June	531,800	66.8	509,810	62.0
July	501,400	66.9	498,300	62.3
August	490,060	67.0	471,400	62.4
September	471,370	67.2	442,300	62.7
October	465,390	67.2	429,110	63.2
November	454,200	67.9	412,610	63.7
December	441,820	67.9	407,100	64.1
Total or Average	$6,091,760	66.7	$5,683,380	62.3

FIG. 14-4   Summary — Cost-of-Goods-Sold Budget

THE APPLIANCE CORPORATION

COST-OF-GOODS-SOLD BUDGET

For the Plan Year Ending 12/31/XX

Period	Manufactured Products	Services	Other Direct Charges	Adjustments	Total
January	$ 491,720	$ 112,040	—	—	$ 603,760
February	498,300	116,090	$ 62,430	—	676,820
March	586,200	117,430	41,400	—	745,030
April	602,400	122,060	—	—	724,460
May	557,100	144,070	—	—	701,170
June	531,800	152,100	69,760	$ 42,900	796,560
July	501,400	184,600	24,380	—	680,380
August	490,060	159,200	19,900	—	669,160
September	471,370	154,300	27,430	81,300	764,400
October	465,390	191,600	107,110	—	764,100
November	454,200	201,400	21,500	—	677,100
December	441,820	202,300	20,300	106,300	770,720
Total	$6,091,760[a]	$1,857,190	$394,210	$230,500	$8,573,660

(a) See Figure 14-3.

type of analysis useful by sales management and others for the particular business decision under study. While the concept is simple, the gathering of the information is detailed indeed and must follow the actual accounting contemplated by the company.

The numerous analyses and subanalyses of the cost of goods sold (or direct cost) needed in planning make the cost-of-goods-sold budget a suitable computer application. The cost-of-goods-sold budget should be developed for each sales analysis segment desired, as discussed in Chapter 9.

15

Distribution Costs

"DISTRIBUTION COSTS" DEFINED

In a general sense, "distribution costs" may be defined as the costs incident to all activities from the time the goods are manufactured until they are in the hands of the customer; they are the costs to sell or market. On this basis, distribution costs include a share of the general and administrative expenses, and financial expense that fairly might be allocated to the distribution activities. However, because the concept of responsibility accounting and reporting is used for the budgeting of any costs or expenses, distribution costs as used herein will relate to those expenses usually under the jurisdiction of the marketing or sales executive. Specifically, they include these classifications:

1. *Direct selling expense.* All the direct expenses involved with the solicitation of sales orders: direct expenses of sales persons, branch sales offices, sales service, and the expenses related to the direct management and supervision of the sales effort.

2. *Advertising and sales promotion expense.* Such expenses include the cost of advertising preparation, media time or space, and all direct expenses connected with sales promotion campaigns, market development, and publicity.

3. *Transportation expense*. Costs under this classification relate to outbound transportation charges, transportation of returned goods, and the expense of managing the function.

4. *Warehousing and storage*. This category relates to all the expenses of warehousing, storing, and handling of finished goods or parts properly chargeable against the distribution function.

5. *Market research expense*. Components of market research expense include the expenses of the various projects undertaken to test or secure data on various products, sales markets, or methods of distribution. Additionally, the expenses of administering the department are a part of the costs.

6. *General distribution expense*. This is a catch-all category to cover all expenses under the control of the marketing executive and not otherwise mentioned above.

The classifications of expenses outlined above are typical for a manufacturing company with an extensive marketing activity. For planning purposes, all expenses for which the marketing executive is responsible must be considered. Thus, in a wholesaling or retailing concern, purchasing and merchandising are closely related, and sometimes are performed by the same staff. Whatever functions in a given industry or company are treated as the responsibility of the chief marketing executive are budgeted and controlled along with the other distribution expense.

IMPORTANCE OF DISTRIBUTION COSTS

Many of the subjects discussed in this volume relate to the planning and control of manufacturing costs. Yet, the costs of distribution are significant in a competitive economy. Much of the growth in manufacturing productivity in the United States from the 1950s through the 1970s has been due to marketing efforts which have enabled the mass-produced output of the factories ultimately to reach the consumer.

There is every reason to believe that the 1980s will require a more analytical approach to markets and marketing effort. There are, indeed, some indications that the United States is entering into a decade of slower growth and shorter business cycles. In an article from *The Wall Street Journal* concerning business management in the 1980s, the following statement was presented in the context of a reduced inflation rate[1]:

---

[1] Kenneth H. Bacon, "Managing in the 1980s Won't Be Easy Task," *The Wall Street Journal*, Sept. 20, 1982, p. 1.

Companies are going to have to think harder about how to beat the system. Inflation has bailed out a lot of companies in the past. That's no longer going to be possible. We're in a period of survival, requiring consolidation, cost reduction, and continued efforts to expand markets. The emphasis is going to be on expanding market share even more than increasing rates of return. Companies will assume that higher returns will follow market share.

In operating a business, management long has had to decide what products to sell, to whom they should be sold, how they should be sold — the method, and at what prices. There is now increasing evidence that the rise in competition makes an analysis of possible alternative plans even more imperative. Thus, the planning and control of marketing efforts may receive relatively more attention in this decade than in the last.

PURPOSE OF THE DISTRIBUTION COST BUDGET

The general advantages of business budgeting are reviewed in Part I of this book. It may be useful to restate these benefits as they specifically apply to distribution costs. The purposes or benefits of budgeting distribution costs include these:

- To coordinate the distribution efforts with the sales plan, the production or manufacturing plan, and the financial resources of the enterprise.
- To select the most profitable combination of distribution factors (i.e., volume, prices, sales effort, selling expense).
- To more intelligently direct selling effort.
- To better control distribution costs.

Stated in another way, the task is first to decide how much should be spent to distribute the product, what types of expenditures should be made, and when and where they should be made — all to secure certain sales results. When this marketing effort planning is completed, then the management task is to cause the expenditures to be made as planned, and to monitor the results.

Some comments on each of these budget purposes follow.

Coordination of Distribution Effort

The sales management will often talk about "the marketing plan." This is in reality composed of several parts: (1) the sales plan (see Chapter 9), which relates to the volume and price of products to be sold; (2) the selling effort plan, that is, what activities or actions must be taken to attain the sales plan, and the costs of such effort; and (3) the related support for the sales and selling effort in the nature of advertising and sales promotion (see Chapter 16), and perhaps market research effort. Neither the sales plan nor the marketing effort plan should be developed independently of the other. The selling effort must be planned to sell those products that can be manufactured and sold most profitably. Those products should be promoted that make use of the special advantages of the company and that enable the enterprise to secure an adequate market share.

The objective is to select that combination of selling effort and the particular products that will produce the optimum return over the longer term. Almost any product can be sold if the price is right and the selling effort is intensive enough. Conversely, selling effort and the related expense can be reduced to the point where no sales are made. What is needed is *balance* and *coordination* between sales revenues (the result) and sales effort (the expense).

Somewhere between excessive selling effort and little or no effort must be found the right amount. This principle applies not only to total sales volume, but also to the sales of individual products or groups of products in individual sales territories, and even to individual customers.

As previously stated, the sales budget must be coordinated with the manufacturing or production budget, and all must remain within the financial capability of the enterprise.

Plans must be coordinated to be most effective.

Selection of the Best Combination of Distribution Factors

Were a concern to sell only one product, at one price, to one class of customers, through one channel of distribution, by one selling method, and in a restricted territory, the problem of planning the distribution cost would be comparatively simple and the point of diminishing returns would be established with reasonable certainty; but few, if any, such cases exist. Perhaps certain public utilities most nearly approximate such a situation. Usually, however, there are numerous products, varying prices, numerous classes of customers to whom sales can be made, several channels of distribution employed, various selling methods, a considerable choice of territories, and many other variations. What program of distribution effort will be most profitable in the face of these numerous possibilities?

One of the purposes of budgeting the distribution costs is to compel the sales executives to study the various possibilities early, while there is time for proper investigation and before the money is spent, and thereby to find the combination of distribution factors offering greatest promise of profit.

Directing the Distribution Effort

Generally speaking, the distribution effort should be directed in accordance with market possibilities. The realization of this objective is one of the most important purposes of budgeting distribution costs. Many concerns, upon analyzing the potentialities of their markets and their corresponding distribution effort, have found astonishing misalignment. By intelligent redistribution the profitableness of the effort has been greatly increased.

For example, if there are 1,000 potential buyers in Territory A and 2,000 in Territory B, it would seem logical, other conditions being the same, to direct twice as much effort to Territory B as to Territory A. It is the effort, not the cost, that should be apportioned. It is quite possible that the amount of effort per dollar of cost may vary in the two territories due to such a factor as density of population. Many factors, other than number of buyers, must be considered. For example, buying power and intensity of competition may vary considerably in different territories. The point to be emphasized is that, the more intelligently the effort is distributed, the more profitable will be the results.

The intelligent direction of sales effort is aided in one other way through the use of budgets. When considering how funds are to be spent, the marketing executive must face the question of distribution effort to be expected, as well as the cost of such effort. He must answer such questions as: How many calls should a salesman make per week in a given territory? What should be the cost of a salesman's call? What should the per unit warehousing cost be? A well-conceived budget program may involve the establishment of distribution cost standards to assist in the direction of sales effort.

Controlling the Distribution Costs

The fourth purpose of budgeting distribution costs is that of control. To be sure, the budget process as applied to distribution is, first of all, a matter of coordinating such effort with the sales, production, and financial programs; of selecting the most profitable combination of distribution factors; and further of seeing that the sales effort is intelligently guided. Yet, the budget does offer, in addition, certain measures of control over certain distribution operations and costs.

In the control of manufacturing costs, the typical budget application consists of comparing actual and budgeted or standard costs, and the bringing of continued pressure on actual performance until it is in line with the budget. This can be done in the distribution cost area as regards the more repetitive or routine operations such as warehousing or order handling. By and large, however, a more positive approach is necessary and desirable so as to avoid the injurious curtailment of necessary services. The technique therefore tends to lie in the direction of getting more distribution effort and results for the same money. For example, emphasis might be placed on seeing that the budgeted number of calls are made; and that the budgeted sales per call are attained. These are instances where measures of individual performance are applied. More general indicators, such as percent of selling expenses to sales, may be used as guides in increasing the sales level or in scrutinizing the level of selling expenses.

TYPES OF DISTRIBUTION COST BUDGETS

Having reviewed the purposes of distribution cost budgets, the next question that arises is, "How can these objectives best be secured?" In considering the planning and control of distribution costs, several different kinds of budgets may be involved. Much depends on the type of activity. Within any industry, and indeed, within a single company, various methods or techniques may be used in the planning and control of distribution costs. The key is how rigidly the costs can and should be controlled; and, first, how the cost level should be planned. Knowledge of each function or activity will provide some clues as to the best technique. How closely and quickly should costs be related to sales volume, for example? What method is likely to secure the most cost effective result?

Distribution activities probably are best planned and controlled through one of these budget types:

- Project
- Administrative
- Standardized volume related
- Competitive service

Each of these is explained.

Project-Type Budgets

Some distribution activities are not *directly* and immediately related to a volume factor, such as units handled or units sold. The key word is *directly*, because over a period of time expenditures should be made with the expectation of getting something of value in return that is greater than the cost. But this return may be several months, or even years, away. One example is advertising expense (discussed in Chapter 16); another might be market

FIG. 15-1 Project Budget Report — Market Research Department

MARKET RESEARCH DEPARTMENT
Project Budget Report — Month Ended June 30, 19XX
(in hundreds of dollars)

Project No.	Name	Professional Man-hours	Annual to Date — Actual						Commitments	Estimated Cost to Complete	Indicated Total Cost	Project Budget	Indicated Underrun (Overrun)
			Salaries and Wages			Consultants	Other Expense	Total					
			Professional	Clerical	Total								
Market Potential Studies													
182	Blender "S"	400	$40	$110	$150	$10	$70	$230	$12	$42	$284	$290	6
183	Portable fan	260	31	20	51	—	22	73	4	12	89	90	1
189	Cordless electric knife	1,410	153	160	313	30	110	453	300	700	1,453	1,500	47
190	Cordless electric toothbrush	800	80	40	120	12	60	192	78	20	290	300	10
192	Remote control color adapter	1,030	214	370	584	51	243	878	400	878	2,156	2,150	(6)
	Total	3,900	$518	$700	$1,218	$103	$505	$1,826	$794	$1,652	$4,272	$4,330	$58
Product Acceptance Surveys													
309	New York — "L" Series	170	$15	$80	$95		$22	$117	$30	$100	$247	$250	$3
310	Chicago — "M" Series	220	20	20	40	$ 3	20	63	10	30	103	100	(3)
311	Los Angeles — "R" Series	60	7	5	12	2	6	20	20	40	80	80	—
312	San Francisco — "A" Series	90	11	19	30	—	15	45	20	20	85	80	(5)
315	Boston — "B" Series	110	13	21	34	7	17	58	30	40	128	130	2
	Total	650	$66	$145	$211	$12	$80	$303	$110	$230	$643	$640	($3)
Other Categories													
802	Salesman's time scheduling	100	9	11	20	—	8	28	5	30	63	65	2
803	Product labels	460	37	17	54	—	27	81	10	20	111	115	4
807	Redesign of call report	70	7	2	9	—	4	13	1	14	28	30	2
808	Credit card promotions	350	43	34	77	—	40	117	40	150	307	250	(57)
	Total	980	$96	$64	$160	—	$79	$239	$56	$214	$509	$460	($49)
	Grand Total — Project budgets	5,530	$680	$909	$1,589	$115	$664	$2,368	$960	$2,096	$5,424	$5,430	$6

research. In any event, a project budget approach may be used in those instances where specific activities are planned, expenditures are made, and the hoped-for results are awaited in due course. The emphasis is placed on getting a certain task accomplished, within time and cost constraints considered to be reasonable in terms of the end product — perhaps securing certain market information or a certain sales volume.

The steps for establishing the planning budget, and controlling the expense, are outlined as follows:

1. The general program to meet the sales plan objectives is established.
2. The cost required to complete the individual tasks or projects is estimated by type of expense and by time period.
3. On a responsibility basis, the total project expense is summarized for inclusion in the planning budget of the marketing department.
4. Periodically, as costs are incurred, the project estimated costs are rechecked and updated to compare with the authorized budget. Where necessary, action is taken to keep expenses in line with the budget.
5. In conjunction with the monthly or quarterly budget review, the status of each project is examined. Of course, when the project is completed, the work product is discussed in detail and appropriate market action taken.

The annual planning budget for a department handled on a project basis, sometimes called an appropriation type budget, is included in the overall functional budget (see Figure 15-10). An interim budgetary control report for a project type budget is illustrated in Figure 15-1. In this example, projects for a market research department are shown.

Administrative-Type Budgets

Distribution functions that might best be handled by an administrative type budget are those that are not influenced by the day-to-day sales level in the sense that constant adjustments in the manhours are required; and output cannot be easily quantified. The output often is subjective and relates to the broad planning and management of the activity. Expense levels must be maintained in proper relationship to sales, but this is accomplished over a period of time, such as a year or two, and is handled by planning the total manpower required. The activity is further characterized by the preponderance of "people expense" — payroll expense, fringe benefit costs, travel expense, and communications expenses. There are a limited number of routine and recurring duties associated with the functions. Typical of the expenses to be handled on an administrative type basis would be the expenses for the office of the vice-president in charge of sales.

FIG. 15-2   Distribution Cost Budget — Administrative Type

THE SALES CORPORATION
ANNUAL BUDGET
General Sales Manager
(dollars in thousands)

| | Prior Year | | | Plan Year | | | | Increase |
	Actual 10 mos.	Estimated 2 mos.	Total	1st Quarter	2nd Quarter	Second Half	Total	(Decrease)
Number of staff	7	7	7	7	8	8	8	1
Expenses								
Salaries — Exempt	$124.5	$25.5	$150.0	$ 40.5	$ 40.5	$ 81.0	$162.0	$12.0
Salaries — Other	25.0	7.0	32.0	8.5	11.8	23.6	43.9	11.9
Incentive pay	40.0	—	40.0	50.0	—	50.0	50.0	10.0
Fringe benefit costs	75.8	13.0	88.8	39.6	20.9	41.8	102.3	13.5
Travel	74.2	12.0	86.2	25.0	25.0	50.0	100.0	13.8
Occupancy	20.0	4.0	24.0	7.5	7.5	15.0	30.0	6.0
Entertainment	46.0	10.0	56.0	14.0	15.0	34.0	63.0	7.0
Communications	5.3	1.5	6.8	1.9	2.0	3.5	7.4	.6
Dues and subscriptions	4.0	1.0	5.0	1.0	2.0	2.0	5.0	—
Supplies	8.0	2.0	10.0	3.0	3.0	5.0	11.0	1.0
Depreciation	4.7	1.0	5.7	1.5	1.5	3.0	6.0	.3
Insurance	3.1	.6	3.7	1.0	1.0	2.0	4.0	.3
Miscellaneous	2.0	.2	2.2	.3	.5	1.6	2.4	.2
Total	$432.6	$77.8	$510.4	$193.8	$130.7	$262.5	$587.0	$76.6
Percentage net sales			1.4					1.2

An administrative-type budget might be developed in the following manner. (See also Chapter 18.)

1. The department manager is provided with the actual expenses by type of cost for the recent period, perhaps a 10 or 12 month period. In Figure 15-2, expenses for a 10-month period are provided and the manager is asked to estimate the remaining two months in order to provide a full year comparison with the plan submitted. Included with such data is the head count.

2. With this information in hand, the department executive estimates the staff requirements and expense levels, by type of expense for the planning period — by month or quarter, and for the year. Taken into account in estimating the expenses are the sales and/or activity level expected, the special tasks to be undertaken, the probable change in expenses levels due to inflation, and activity level.

   Instructions or guidelines, of course, are provided by the budget coordinator.

3. Upon completion of the estimate, the plan is reviewed by next level supervisor for changes — either increases or decreases — necessary in the light of business requirements. Normally, the budget officer or controller is consulted for possible input, reasonableness of expense level, and so forth.

   The completed administrative type budget for the distribution activity might appear as in Figure 15-2.

   Such a budget would be consolidated with the other distribution activity plans to arrive at the total marketing budget. (See Figure 15-10).

4. After approval of the entire annual plan and with the onset of the planning year, the department manager is given periodic comparisons of budgeted and actual expenses, as in Figure 15-3. In general, in this type of budget, if staff is kept within authorized limits, and one or two types of expenses are watched, the burden on the marketing executive is minimal.

5. As appropriate, attention should be directed to any problem areas by the cognizant budgeting or accounting officer or the functional executive.

Standardized (Volume-Related) Activity Budgets

Distribution functions for which the standardized activity type of budget may be used for planning and control are those that *should* respond immediately to the activity level for the amount of expenses incurred, and which, by implication, can be measured on a quantitative basis. A great number of the actions are repetitive in nature and may be likened to manufacturing operations. The objective is to keep the costs in line with what they *should be* for the volume of business handled. A good example is the stock handling function in a branch warehouse.

FIG. 15-3   Budget Report

THE SALES CORPORATION

BUDGET REPORT

General Sales Manager

(dollars in thousands)

Month: March 19XX

	Current Month		Year-to-Date	
	Actual	(Over) Under Budget	Actual	(Over) Under Budget
Number of staff	7	—	7	—
Expenses				
Salaries — Exempt	$13.5	—	$ 40.5	$—
Salaries — Other	2.8	—	8.5	—
Incentive pay	—	—	47.0	3.0
Fringe benefit costs	6.5	—	38.4	1.2(a)
Travel	8.0	.6	25.7	(.7)
Occupancy	2.5	—	7.5	—
Entertainment	4.4	.2	13.8	.2
Communications	.6	—	1.8	.1
Dues and subscriptions	—	—	1.0	—
Supplies	.9	.1	2.8	.2
Depreciation	.5	—	1.5	—
Insurance	.3	—	1.0	—
Miscellaneous	.1	—	.3	—
Total	$40.1	$.9	$189.8	$4.0
Percentage net sales	1.1		1.0	

(a) Fringe benefit costs under budget relate solely to incentive pay.

Steps. A summary of the steps involved in setting a budget is as follows:

1. On a responsibility accounting basis, the expenses should be separated by type of expense, so-called natural expenses, for the function: salaries and wages, fringe benefit costs, supplies, fuel, and repairs.
2. The costs should be analyzed and the fixed and variable components determined, as discussed in prior chapters. (See especially Chapter 5.)
3. The annual short term planning budget should be set by the application of the expense structure to the expected volume, for the appropriate time period,

such as month or quarter, as well as for the entire planning period. The planning budget for the period would appear essentially like the description column and the first three quantified columns of Figure 15-4.

4. For control purposes, the expense structure should be applied to the volume actually handled to arrive at the flexible budget; and actual expenses should be compared with this standard. An illustrative budget report is shown in Figure 15-4.

5. Where applicable, that is, where costs are out of line, corrective action should take place.

A Partial Application. The preceding illustration relates to a repetitive function when costs are *directly* related to the business volume, but, as previously mentioned, a basic approach to budgeting distribution costs, for many types of expense, is to secure the most effective results from the expense, i.e., to secure the greatest contribution to profit. The objective is not to attempt to keep expenses at the lowest level. As to *direct selling effort,* the emphasis is not to reduce the number of salesmen, but rather to make them more productive. Hence, in a direct selling department, the sales salaries budget will be established based on the number of persons required to do the job over a period of time. No attempt usually is made to treat the expense as a variable — directly related to the monthly sales volume. However, a type of flexible budget application might be used for control of the field selling expenses. A budgetary control application is shown in Figure 15-5. In this instance, territorial standards have been determined and the salesman has been informed of the expected costs. The budget is based on a planned schedule as follows:

Item	*Basis of Allowance*
Hotel	
Meals	
Laundry and valet	Per diem standard allowance
Entertainment	
Telephone and telegraph	Standard allowance per month
Travel	
Auto	Scheduled miles at standard rate
Railroad	
Pullman	Actual cost, based on trips scheduled
Plane	
Other	Specific authorization

This technique can be more productive in that the allowance relates to the actual operations to be undertaken. It avoids fixed allowances per month

FIG. 15-4   Illustrative Budget Report — Branch Warehouse

The Standard Food Distributing Corp.
San Francisco Terminal

BUDGET REPORT

Month April, 19XX

Dept. _____ Perishables
Dept. Head _____ Roth
Units Handled 800,000

Description	Budget Fixed	Budget Variable	Budget Total	Actual	(Over) or Under Budget	Budget (Adj.)	Actual	(Over) or Under Budget Amount	Percent*
		Current Month					Year-to-Date		
Salaries	$2,000	$ 800	$ 2,800	$ 2,770	$ 30	$ 11,500	$ 11,300	$ 200	—
Wages	1,000	24,000	25,000	24,800	200	102,000	105,300	(3,300)	(3.2%)
Fringe benefits	600	4,960	5,560	5,510	50	22,700	23,320	(620)	—
Subtotal	$3,600	$29,760	$33,360	$33,080	$280	$136,200	$139,920	($3,720)	(2.7%)
Supplies	$ 200	$ 800	$ 1,000	$ 1,240	($240)	$ 4,800	$ 4,680	$ 120	—
Gasoline and oil	340	1,600	1,940	1,860	80	7,360	7,810	(450)	(6.1%)
Repairs — Regular — Labor	120	800	920	950	(30)	3,480	3,220	260	7.5
Repairs — Regular — Material	120	800	920	900	20	3,480	3,100	380	10.9
Repairs — Major — Labor	—	—	—	—	—	12,300	12,000	300	2.4
Repairs — Major — Material	—	—	—	—	—	15,700	16,800	(1,100)	(7.0)
Heat, light, and power	420	200	620	600	20	2,280	2,090	190	8.3
Miscellaneous	60	20	80	80	20	320	310	10	3.1
Depreciation	900	—	900	900	—	3,600	3,600	—	—
Property taxes and insurance	250	—	250	250	—	1,000	1,000	—	—
Total	$6,010	$33,980	$39,990	$39,860	$130	$190,520	$194,530	($4,010)	(2.1%)
Percent					.003				

Comments:
* Only if significant (2 percent or more).
Issued by Budget Dept. 5/10/XX

FIG. 15-5 Budget Report — Field Selling Expense

THE WESTERN CHEMICAL CORPORATION

FIELD SELLING EXPENSES

Budget Report for Month of April

Salesman: Signorelli
Territory: Los Angeles

Description	Unit Allowance	Current Month			Year-to-Date			
		Actual	Budget	(Over) or Under Budget	Actual	Budget	(Over) or Under Budget* Amount	Percent
Days traveled		12	14	2	60	56	(4)	(8.8%)
Field Selling Expenses								
Hotel	$15.00 per diem	$ 210	$ 180	($ 30)	$ 980	$ 900	($ 80)	—
Meals	10.00 per diem	130	120	($ 10)	610	600	—	—
Laundry and valet	2.00 per diem	15	24	9	100	120	—	—
Telephone	.50 per diem	5	6	1	28	30	—	—
Subtotal		$ 360	$ 330	($ 30)	$1,718	$1,650		
Travel:								
Auto	.12 mile	$ 240	$ 250	$ 10	$1,200	$ 1,500	$300	20.0
Plane		600	800	200	2,030	2,100	70	—
Railroad					210	220		
Total travel		$ 840	$1,050	$210	$3,440	$ 3,820		
Conventions	4.00 per diem	$ 130	$ 48	($ 82)	$ 220	$ 240		
Entertainment	1.00 per diem	10	12	2	55	60		
Miscellaneous								
Total expense		$ 1,340	$1,440	$100	$5,433	$ 5,770	$337	5.8%
Statistical Data								
Cost per day traveled		$111.66	$ 110		$90.55	$ 100		
Cost per call		44.67	40		36.22	40		
Gross revenue per call		36,900	35,000		35,000	35,000		

Comments:

* Only if off budget by 5 percent or $50, or more.

Signorelli's trend of expenses and effort to keep within budget is good.

which may be unrelated to the planned activities of any given month. More-over, emphasis is placed on year-to-date performance rather than on that of a single month. It is to be noted that budget plans provide for a certain number of days traveled which is compared with actual. If necessary, the excess cost, if any, can be analyzed by cause, i.e., as between excess units (days traveled) and excess cost per unit. The general guide as to effective-ness is the cumulative percent of total field selling expense to net sales. The method has proven somewhat successful in those activities where the selling is not too analytical, and calls tend to be short.

Competitive Service Activity Budget

One other approach that has found some use in budgetary control is the competitive service type, also called the profit or loss type. The activities budgeted on such a basis are generally of a service nature wherein it is possible to compare the cost of the operation with an independent competi-tive price. For example, building services, warehousing, or printing might be handled in such a manner.

The system may be combined with the standardized activity approach as outlined in the following procedural steps:

1. As in most budgetary control procedures, costs are segregated on a responsi-bility accounting basis, by type of expense.
2. Expenses are analyzed into their fixed and variable components.
3. The competitive prices charged per unit for the services to be rendered are determined.
4. In the annual or short-term planning budget, the service requirements (e.g., units to be handled) are estimated, and
   • Charged to the using activity for the expected volume at the competitive billing prices, and incorporated in the annual plan of the department;
   • Applied to the flexible budget structure to arrive at the allowable annual budget for the performing activity; and
   • Properly treated as to intra-departmental income in the plan consolidation.
5. For control purposes, the actual expenses for the period of the service de-partment are
   • Measured against the flexible budget standard allowance for the volume actually handled, and
   • Also compared to the net billings (sales) to the using activities. Hopefully, a profit results.

An illustrative competitive service control budget report is that in Figure 15-6.

FIG. 15-6   Competitive Service-Type Budget Control Report

THE OLESON COMPANY
TOLEDO WAREHOUSE

COMPARISON OF BUDGETED AND ACTUAL INCOME AND EXPENSE
For the Month of April, 19XX

Description	Actual	Budget	Favorable (Unfavorable)
Net billings to using activities	$106,000	$100,000	$6,000
Operating expenses			
Salaries and wages	$44,500	$43,000	($1,500)
Supplies	11,500	12,000	500
Repairs	16,300	20,000	3,700
Taxes	2,000	2,000	—
Depreciation	3,000	3,000	—
Total	$77,300	$80,000	$2,700
Operating profit	$28,700	$20,000	$8,700
Statistical data			
Units handled			
Month	100,000		
Year-to-date	392,000		

DISTRIBUTION COST ANALYSIS

In establishing the sales plan, Chapter 9 reviews the mathematical/statistical methods and judgmental methods of determining the sales level. However, the point is made that sales analysis is the starting point. A vast quantity of valuable information can be derived from a study and analysis of the company sales records, but, as explained, sales analysis alone is not usually enough. To do the best job requires a joint effort of sales analysis and distribution cost analysis. There must be available data on the effort and cost to perform specific distribution functions and the sales results deriving from such effort and cost.

Distribution cost analysis is broad in its scope. It seeks to study the present method of distribution in comparison with all other possible methods. By implication it is not restricted merely to historical analysis, but may extend to untried processes. Moreover, it must extend to *expected* prices and *expected* costs. It seeks to determine the most effective marketing pattern for the business; it seeks to lay before management the effects of alternative courses of action.

Then too, the cost analysis of market operations need not, and indeed must not, be limited to the company's distribution segment. That might be fatal; it certainly would be short-sighted. In many instances distribution cost analysis must consider the effect on the *total distribution* picture, and not merely the segment with which a given manufacturer might be concerned. The particular company may represent only one step in the distribution process.

One other observation: It is to be noted that generally cost analysis is a forerunner of control. Cost analysis seeks to assist management in selecting the proper policy or method, and control subsequently involves the measurement of the actual performance against certain predetermined goals.

The nature of the distribution cost analysis required naturally varies with the needs of the individual concern; however, the basic analyses commonly found useful are:

1. By the nature of cost items or object of expenditure
2. By functions or functional operations performed
3. By the manner in which the distribution effort is applied

In most concerns it is necessary to apply all methods, at least to some extent, in order to supply marketing executives with the information necessary for the efficient planning, direction, and control of distribution effort.

These types of analyses and their value are described in the following text.

OPERATING MARGIN OR CONTRIBUTION MARGIN?

In performing distribution cost analysis and analysis of the impact of marketing decisions on the company earnings, recognition must be given to the distinction between the operating margin and the contribution margin of the distribution segment being measured and analyzed.[2] To be sure, strategic planning and decision-making must consider the operating profit or margin of the product line or territory. But short-term tactical decisions, i.e., short-term planning, may use the contribution margin as a more appropriate guide for the near-term action.

The contribution margin figure is calculated by deducting from sales income all those costs that would not need to be incurred if the segment being costed were not present. This resultant value is a measure of what the

---

[2] See also Chapter 6.

FIG. 15-7 Statement of Marginal and Operating Income

THE MARTIN COMPANY

STATEMENT OF CONTRIBUTION MARGIN AND OPERATING INCOME
AND EXPENSE BY PRODUCT LINES

For the month ended October 31, 19XX

Description	Total	Products A	B	C
Net sales	$100,000	$50,000	$20,000	$30,000
Less variable cost of sales	43,000	20,000	13,000	10,000
Manufacturing margin	57,000	30,000	7,000	20,000
Less variable distribution costs	20,000	15,000	2,000	3,000
Contribution margin	$ 37,000	$15,000	$ 5,000	$17,000
Less fixed and allocated costs				
Manufacturing	$ 3,000	$ 1,000	$ 1,000	$ 1,000
Selling	5,000	2,000	2,000	1,000
Advertising	5,000	2,000	2,000	1,000
Administrative	2,200	1,000	500	700
Total	$ 15,200	$ 6,000	$ 5,500	$ 3,700
Operating income or (loss)	$ 21,800	$ 9,000	($ 500)	$13,300

segment contributes to the joint or continuing expenses and to overall company profits. The use of such an approach usually precludes the error of discontinuing a unit where the revenues exceed the out-of-pocket costs (but not total costs). As a practical matter, in a distribution cost analysis, it is advantageous to develop the contribution margin, and then to proceed and deduct fixed or joint expenses to arrive at the operating profit or loss of the segment being measured. An illustration where both approaches are combined in a single statement is shown in Figure 15-7. In this instance, the segments being measured are specific products.

Having clarified the two degrees of analysis, the types of distribution cost analysis are discussed in the text following.

ANALYSIS BY TYPE OF EXPENSE

Typically, the first analysis of distribution costs made by a company for planning or control purposes is that by nature of expenditure. Expenses such as salaries and wages, commissions, fringe benefit costs, traveling expense, supplies, and communication expense are usually recorded in separate accounts, and thus may be analyzed fairly easily.

An analysis by type of expense provides some general information of possible use by management. If, for example, traveling expense is recorded in a separate account, it will be possible to compare the expense with previous periods and determine the ratio of the expense to sales volume. Such comparisons and relationships may reveal weaknesses if they are extreme; but they will not reveal the fact that the cost per mile of operating salesmen's automobiles is excessive, or that many calls are being made on customers whose business, actual or potential, cannot possibly justify the traveling expense involved. Again, it is possible by such analysis to ascertain the percentage of advertising cost to sales; but, if this appears excessive, it is not possible to tell what adjustments should be made to effect a satisfactory relationship. Analysis by nature of cost item is sufficient only when there are no problems as to the efficiency of particular distribution operations; or as to what territories to cover, what commodities to sell, and what sales methods to employ. There are few concerns in which these conditions prevail.

By this type of analysis it is possible only to ascertain the cost of the distribution function as a whole. But too many executives know merely how much it costs to *carry on business as a whole,* without knowing the cost of performing specific operations or securing particular results. A sales manager may be told that his selling costs are too high, but such a statement is of no great help in reducing them. Before they can be reduced they must be analyzed to the point where it is known just what operations are too costly or unproductive and who is responsible. An executive cannot base intelligent action on generalities; he must have specific facts.

ANALYSIS BY FUNCTIONS

The analysis of distribution costs by functions and functional operations is particularly valuable for both planning and control purposes. It is also helpful in extending the cost analysis to the application of sales effort, as explained below.

Steps

The steps in making a functional analysis of the distribution activity are suggested in this outline:

1. Determine the functional operations that should be measured, taking care to see that the functions are properly segregated in terms of responsibility accounting. Some illustrative functional distribution operations are these:
   - Salespersons' calls on old or new customers
   - Units handled in warehouse
   - Mailing of samples
   - Invoice postings
   - Days of travel

2. Arrange for a proper expense segregation for the operations to be measured. For *planning* purposes in this connection, allocated expenses may be used to recognize total costs. For *control* purposes, however, generally only direct expenses need be involved. In a branch warehouse activity only the direct expenses of the function need be used for the planning and control of the warehouse expense. But, where total costs are a factor in the decision, then allocated regional sales office expense, or general sales management expense, may be relevant costs.

3. Establish suitable units of measurement. Number of salesperson's calls may be used for measuring selling expense in territories; pounds handled, in a warehouse, may be practical.

4. Determine the unit cost of operation. This is the simple process of dividing the relevant expense by the units of measure.

5. Use the resulting data to take corrective action where warranted.

In planning applications, the above approach will be useful in, for example, determining the expected level of expenses applicable to a product sold within a given territory — when calculating profit by product. In control uses, the method is useful in applying the flexible budget (as previously illustrated).

When the costs of the function in a particular area are known, then comparisons can be made with the costs of other areas; when functional costs are identified, questions can be raised more easily as to whether such costs are too high, and whether or not other alternatives should be studied.

The functional approach to planning and control can be applied to many, although not necessarily all, distribution functions in any given concern.

Functional Cost Analysis as a Control Device

The use of functional analysis as a control device may be made clearer by a simple illustration. Assume, for example, that a certain concern has had the following monthly experience relative to certain distribution functions:

PAST EXPERIENCE

Functional Operation	Functional Unit	Number of Functional Units	Total Cost	Unit Cost
Salespersons' calls on prospects	Salesperson's call	10,000	$40,000	$4.00
Mailing samples	Individual order	5,000	500	.10
Assembling stock for orders	Item assembled	100,000	3,000	.03
Issuing monthly promotional literature	Customer account	5,000	500	.10

Assume next that standard unit costs are established for the above functional activities and that a sales program is developed for a subsequent month as follows:

STANDARD COSTS AND BUDGET

Functional Operation	Budgeted Number of Functional Units	Standard Unit Costs	Budget Total
Salespersons' calls on prospects	12,000	$4.20	$50,400
Mailing samples	6,250	.09	563
Assembling stock for orders	90,000	.03	2,700
Issuing promotional literature	5,250	.097	509

Assume further that the actual results for the month in question are as follows:

ACTUAL RESULTS

Functional Operation	Actual Number of Functional Units	Total Actual Cost	Actual Unit Cost
Salespersons' calls on prospects	12,100	$49,610	$4.10
Mailing samples	5,575	558	.10
Assembling stock for orders	95,000	3,040	.032
Issuing promotional literature	5,025	487	.097

COMPARISON OF BUDGETED AND ACTUAL COSTS
WITH EXPLANATION OF DIFFERENCES

Functional Operation	Total Budgeted Cost	Total Actual Cost	Difference	Explanation of Difference Volume Factor	Efficiency Factor
Salespersons' calls on prospects	$50,400	$49,610	($790)	$420[a]	$1,210[e]
Mailing samples	563	558	(5)	(61)[b]	56[f]
Assembling stock for orders	2,700	3,040	340	150[c]	$190[g]
Issuing promotional literature	509	487	(22)	(22)[d]	None[h]
Total	$54,172	$53,695	($477)	$487	($ 964)

(a) 12,100 − 12,000 = 100 units; 100 × $4.20 = $420.
(b) 6,250 − 5,575 = 675 units; 675 × $0.09 = $61.
(c) 95,000 − 90,000 = 5,000 units; 5,000 × $0.03 = $150.
(d) 5,250 − 5,025 = 225 units; 225 × $0.097 = $22.
(e) $4.20 − $4.10 = $0.10; 12,100 × $0.10 = $1,210.
(f) $0.10 − $0.09 = $0.01; 5,575 × 0.01 = $56.
(g) $0.032 − $0.03 = $0.002; 95,000 × $0.002 = $190.
(h) $0.097 − $0.097 = 0; 5,025 × 0 = 0.

Analysis of Results. The following analysis of results is now possible.

Salespersons' calls. It was planned to make 12,000 calls on customers; actually, 12,100 calls were made. This number of calls should have cost $50,820 (12,100 × $4.20); actually the cost was $49,610; hence, there was an efficiency saving in this activity of $1,210. Actual performance, which resulted in a cost of $4.10 per call, was above the standard of $4.20 per call.

Mailing samples. It was expected that 6,250 sample mailings would be necessary; actually, only 5,575 were made. This number should have cost $502 (5,575 × $0.09); actually the cost was $558; hence, this department caused an efficiency loss of $56. Actual performance, which resulted in a unit cost of $0.10, was below the standard, which called for a unit cost of $0.09.

Assembling stock for orders. It was expected that 90,000 items of stock would be assembled; actually, 95,000 items were assembled. This number should have cost $2,850 (95,000 × $0.03); actually, the cost was $3,040; hence, there was an efficiency loss of $190. Actual performance, which resulted in a unit cost of $0.032, was below standard, which called for a unit cost of $0.03.

Issuing promotional literature. It was expected that 5,250 monthly packets would be prepared and mailed; actually, only 5,025 were sent. This number should have cost $487 (5,025 × $0.097) which was also the actual cost; hence, the performance of this operation was exactly at standard with a unit cost of $0.097.

It should be noted that a comparison of the budget and actual costs in themselves does not give a true picture of the results. The cost of salespersons' calls, for example, is $790 less than budgeted, but the actual savings effected in this activity is $1,210. In the mailing of samples there is a reduction of $5 from the budget, but actually there has been an efficiency loss of $56.

In an analysis such as this, it is usually desirable to include in the costs only the items that are subject to control by those whose performance is being measured.

While the foregoing illustration is extremely simple, it suggests the value of functional analysis as an instrument of cost control. Such procedure is applicable to a considerable amount of the distribution activities.

However, the limitations also should be recognized. Thus, it is possible for the salesperson to make too many calls — all of them too short and consequently ineffectual. The interpretation of functional analyses must be carefully done.

This functional approach is closely related to distribution cost standards, which are discussed in Chapter 8.

ANALYSIS BY MANNER OF APPLICATION

Analysis of distribution costs by type of expense, or by function, provides some useful information, mostly for control purposes, and to a lesser degree for planning purposes. But, as mentioned, the budgeting of distribution activities should focus on securing the optimum results — earnings — from the expenditures made. The key is to properly plan the direction of the distribution effort and this means, in large degree, planning the selling and advertising and sales promotion effort. Distribution effort, even though efficiently exercised, will be unproductive unless given proper direction. It is one thing to have an organization that may efficiently perform some individual functions, and quite another matter to make certain that the performance is so directed and coordinated as to achieve the most fruitful results. Ultimately, it is necessary to extend the cost analysis to a point that reveals the manner in which the distribution effort is being applied. This is necessary in order to relate effort and cost to results obtained, to adjust the effort to sales possibilities, and to balance properly the distribution factors.

The analyses to be made by a particular concern in developing its budget and control procedure depend upon its individual method of organizing and directing sales effort. The analyses most frequently needed are:

- *By territory* — for example, districts, branch areas, sales territories, trade centers, states, counties, or cities.

- *By product* — for example, individual commodities or related groups of commodities.

- *By channel of distribution* — for example, to wholesalers, retailers, or ultimate consumers.

- *By method of sale* — for example, through salesperson, mail order, company stores, house-to-house solicitation, and so forth.

- *By class of customer* — for example, customers with large or small annual purchases.

- *By size of order* — for example, the cost applied to securing, handling, and filling orders of varying size, measured in money.

- *By organization and operating division* — for example, branches, departments, stores, etc.

- *By salesperson* — that is, the cost applied to the work of individual salespersons or groups of salespeople.

- *By method of delivery* — for example, over-the-counter, delivery-on-request, store-door delivery, peddler trucks, etc.

- *By size or number of physical units* — for example, full and broken cases, gross and fractions of a gross, carload and less than carload lots, and so forth.

- *By terms of sale* — for example, cash, short-term credit, or installment.

It should be understood that not all of these analyses are usually necessary in any one concern, and that such analyses as are used need not all be made continuously. Certain of them, such as analysis by channels of distribution, may be found necessary only once a year. Others may be the subject of special studies, to be used only when it is necessary to localize weakness. In some instances it is desirable to make cross-analyses. Thus, sales and costs may be analyzed by territories; the cost of each territory is then further subdivided according to product or size of customer order.

A principal requirement in making useful distribution cost analyses by manner of application is a proper segregation of expenses into three basic categories: direct expenses, semi-direct expenses, and indirect expenses. In addition, for some analyses it is desirable to categorize the expenses as fixed or variable for planning purposes.

Some definitions may be helpful. Direct expenses are those identified with the distribution segment being analyzed, and need no proration or allocation. Thus, in an analysis by territory, the salaries and expenses of the salespeople servicing the territory are direct. However, if an analysis is being made by product, such expenses might be semi-direct or indirect, depending on whether or not a salesperson sells one product or several.

Generally speaking, expenses that are direct in one type of analysis are not in another. The marketing organization structure usually will influence the chart of accounts — responsibility accounting — and therefore the types of analyses for which many of the expenses are direct.

Semi-direct expenses may be defined as those that are related in some rather easily measured way to the distribution segment under analysis. An activity factor of some sort would be a fair gauge of the expense and a means of prorating the expense to the distribution segment. Thus, in an analysis by product, the time spent by the salesperson on each product, or the amount of sales (units or value), could be a reasonable basis on which to allocate direct selling expenses to products in those cases where one person sells several commodities. Basically, the relationship between expense and activity level is rather obvious, and closer, than for so-called indirect expenses. Accordingly, the significance of the cost analysis is greater.

Indirect expenses are those bearing no clear and measurable relationship to the distribution segment being analyzed. Accordingly, any allocation of expenses must be quite arbitrary. As an example, there may be no discernable direct relationship between institutional advertising and the sales of product Y. But in an analysis of product Y, any advertising expense specifically devoted to promoting that product would be direct. And if several products were advertised jointly, then the expense might be considered semi-direct and prorated on a lineage or space basis. Or, there might be no observed direct relationship between the expenses of the chief sales executive and the sale of product S in territory Z. Hence, an arbitrary cost allocation method might be employed — sales, for example. If, on the other hand, the sales executive recorded time spent on each product line, then such a basis might be used for prorating the expense.

Obviously, care must be exercised in interpreting the results of distribution cost analysis. For many decisions, the total costs of distribution for the segment should be known, including the arbitrarily allocated indirect expenses. But for near-term tactical decisions, there will be cases where only direct and semi-direct expenses should be considered. Obviously, the most reliable analyses will be those related to direct expenses — both in the fixed and variable category.

PROCEDURE FOR ANALYSIS BY MANNER OF APPLICATION

While the procedure for making distribution cost analyses may differ somewhat by company as to degree of detail wanted or extent of cost segregation, the commonsense approach, perhaps using the computer for sub-analyses, would be essentially as follows:

1. *Select the distribution cost analysis that is to be made.* This will depend, of course, on the answers being sought: The margin contributed by each product? The profit after direct expense earned in each territory? The margin provided by different size of order? Some analyses will be recurring; others will be special one-time jobs.

2. *Categorize the distribution expense into the appropriate group — direct, semi-direct, and indirect.* This classification will change as to certain expenses, depending on the type of analysis.

3. *Select the bases for expense allocation.* In this connection, it often will be desirable to separate costs into fixed and variable. This data may be needed for planning applications when the planned or budgeted sales or other activity is substantially different from past experience.

4. *Apply the activity base, prepare the analysis, and draw conclusions for the use of the marketing executive (or others).* Several "layers" of profit-volume data typically may be calculated, depending on the segment being analyzed:

   - Sales volume by parts of the segment (e.g., by product)
   - Margins including one or more of (a) gross margin after variable manufacturing expense, or (b) after all manufacturing expense
   - Profit after all direct expenses, or after all variable expenses, and then all direct expenses
   - Income after semi-direct expenses, or selected portions thereof (variable)
   - Income after all indirect expense
   - Net income after taxes

Two types of analyses useful in planning and directing sales effort are described. Chapter 9, on the sales budget, discusses some of the questions raised in planning the marketing activity.

Analysis by Product

Business management constantly must make decisions concerning the marketing of company products. Customer moods and wants change. New competitive products enter the market. Research brings forth products with greatly improved qualities or uses. So, market behavior and market potential change. Questions relating to some phases of marketing are answered by product sales analysis and by market research. But, when questions of return on assets or adequacy of earnings arise, distribution cost analysis is often required to assist in making decisions; that is, product analysis must extend from sales through distribution expenses to contribution margin or net income by product. Product cost analysis is useful in planning when the company can use such information in changing prices. Distribution cost analysis should be made where it is known or suspected that different prod-

FIG. 15-8   Sales and Income Analysis by Product Line

THE CHICAGO CORPORATION

STATEMENT OF INCOME AND EXPENSE BY PRODUCT LINE
For the Year 19XX
(dollars in thousands)

Description	All Products Amount	All Products Percentage Net Sales	R Amount	R Percentage Net Sales	S Amount	S Percentage Net Sales	T Amount	T Percentage Net Sales
Gross Sales	$196,000	108.89	$63,100	105.17	$91,700	114.63	$41,200	103.00
Less: Returns and allowances	16,000	8.89	3,100	5.17	11,700	14.63	1,200	3.00
Net Sales	180,000	100.00	60,000	100.00	80,000	100.00	40,000	100.00
Less: Variable cost of sales	72,000	40.00	26,400	44.00	31,200	39.00	14,400	36.00
Margin after variable manufacturing costs	108,000	60.00	33,600	56.00	48,800	61.00	25,600	64.00
Direct Distribution Costs								
Variable	11,340	6.30	1,180	1.98	7,280	9.10	2,880	7.20
Fixed	26,460	14.70	4,660	7.77	16,560	20.70	5,240	13.10
Semi-Direct Distribution Expense (Variable)	14,220	7.90	4,660	7.77	6,720	8.40	2,840	7.10
Contribution Margin	55,980	31.10	23,100	38.50	18,240	22.80	14,640	36.60
Continuing Costs								
Fixed manufacturing costs	10,440	5.80	3,480	5.80	4,640	5.80	2,320	5.80
Other indirect expenses	12,960	7.20	4,320	7.20	5,760	7.20	2,880	7.20
Total	23,400	13.00	7,800	13.00	10,400	13.00	5,200	13.00
Income before income taxes	32,580	18.10	15,300	25.50	7,840	9.80	9,440	23.60
Less: Income taxes	14,987	8.33	7,038	11.73	3,606	4.50	4,343	10.86
Net income	$ 17,593	9.77	$ 8,262	13.77	$ 4,234	5.30	$ 5,097	12.74

ucts incur varying or dissimilar costs to sell and distribute. In other words, cost analyses should be made where a uniform basis of allocating distribution costs to products, such as net sales, would not be indicative of the real cost of distribution. Some instances where some general basis of cost allocation to product line would be misleading include these:

- Where there are significant differences in the effort needed to make a sale. For example, a small hand-held computer may be sold in five minutes when the customer responds to an advertisement. But the sale of a business computer to a medium-sized firm may require six or so calls over a three-month period. Or, one product may require considerable technical service to the customer while another might need none at all.
- Where there are significant differences in delivery costs. For example, some might require special handling and some might not.
- Where there are differences in method of sale. Obviously the cost of a mail order is quite distinct from that requiring a personal sales visit.
- Where the channels of distribution vary. One product may be sold through wholesalers and another direct to the retail trade — with a greatly different cost to sell.
- Where there are differences in size of order. The unit cost to sell one case of product may vary drastically from the sale of a carload.

First-hand knowledge of the business and the guidance of the sales executive will help determine when an analysis by product will be useful in (1) setting selling prices, and (2) in planning or directing sales effort.

An example of an analysis by product line is presented in Figure 15-8.

Some data to be gleaned from the illustrative analysis (which may have been partially realized by marketing management) to be used in planning the sales effort include these:

- The returns and allowances for Product S are 14.63 percent of net sales. This should be reviewed as to cause, and the condition remedied if feasible.
- The contribution margin of the largest selling line, Product S, is substantially smaller in the absolute, and relative to sales than either lines R or T. Perhaps selling effort on these two more profitable lines should be increased.
- The direct distribution costs of Product line S is 29.80 percent of net sales — more than double that of line R and much greater than the 20.30 percent of line T. The methods need a review as to what expenses, and where, are out of line.

Analysis by Sales Territory

Another common distribution cost analysis relates to sales territories. For our purposes, a sales territory may be defined as any geographical area such

FIG. 15-9   Sales and Income Analysis by Territory

THE US SALES CORPORATION

STATEMENT OF INCOME AND EXPENSE BY TERRITORY

For the Year 19XX

(dollars in thousands)

	Total		Far West		Middle West		Middle Atlantic	
		Percentage Net Sales		Percentage Net Sales		Percentage Net Sales		Percentage Net Sales
Description	Amount		Amount		Amount		Amount	
Gross Sales	$530,300		$164,500		$177,900		$187,900	
Less: Outward freight	46,390		4,290		14,400		27,700	
Returns	4,110		710		1,000		2,400	
Allowances	2,800		1,000		1,200		600	
Total deductions	$ 53,300		$ 6,000		$ 16,600		$ 30,700	
Net Sales	477,000	100.00	158,500	100.00	161,300	100.00	157,200	100.00
Less: Variable cost of sales	190,800	40.00	60,256	38.02	64,520	40.00	66,024	42.00
Margin after variable manufacturing costs	286,200	60.00	98,244	61.98	96,780	60.00	91,176	58.00
Direct Distribution Costs								
Variable	28,620	6.00	10,303	6.50	6,936	4.30	11,381	7.24
Fixed	66,780	14.00	23,934	15.10	19,356	12.00	23,490	14.94
Total	$ 95,400	20.00	$ 34,237	21.60	$ 26,292	16.30	$ 34,871	22.18
Semi-Direct Distribution Costs	47,700	10.00	14,265	9.00	14,517	9.00	18,918	12.03
Contribution Margin	143,100	30.00	49,742	31.38	55,971	34.70	37,387	23.79
Continuing Costs								
Fixed manufacturing	77,751	16.30	24,118	15.22	26,084	16.17	27,549	17.52
All others	27,189	5.70	8,035	5.07	9,020	5.59	10,134	6.45
Total	$104,940	22.00	$ 32,153	20.29	$ 35,104	26.76	$ 37,683	23.97
Income/(loss) before income taxes	38,160	8.00	17,589	11.09	20,867	12.94	(296)	(.18)
Less: Income taxes	17,554	3.68	8,091	5.10	9,599	5.95	(136)	(.08)
Net income or (loss)	$ 20,606	4.32	$ 9,498	5.99	$ 11,268	6.99	($ 160)	(.10)
Other Data								
Sales potential	$790,000		200,000		350,000		$240,000	
Percentage potential captured	60.4%		79.3%		46.1%		65.5%	

as county, city, state, trading area, or sales area used by an enterprise in the planning, directing, and controlling of marketing effort.

Where, or in which territory, a product is sold may have a great bearing on the net income. This arises because there may be vast differences in sales prices and the cost of distribution in dissimilar sales areas. Prices may be quite different in New York City, where competition may force some quite low. But the cost of a sales call in densely populated Manhattan may be quite different than, for example, in rural Nebraska. To be sure, if goods are sold free on board (FOB) factory, the gross margin will be unaffected by delivery costs. But under FOB destination pricing, the delivered price per unit will vary significantly. Because of dissimilar conditions, a business usually can employ distribution cost analysis by sales territory to advantage, especially where a wide geographical area is covered.

An example of an analysis by sales territory is reflected in Figure 15-9.

Once an analysis by territory is made, sales and market planning should recognize these points, or might consider such actions as these:

- While the Middle Atlantic territory shows a slight loss on a full-cost basis, the territory is contributing $37,887,000 towards the continuing and fixed expenses, which would exist whether or not sales were made in the territory.
- Given the high impact of outbound freight, perhaps a change in sales terms or prices should be reviewed for the Middle Atlantic.
- Since the direct distribution expenses in the Middle Atlantic are substantially greater than in the Midwest, the two areas should be compared, and targets for cost reduction examined.
- The same is true for the Far West territory versus the Midwest.

The objective is to locate that best combination of factors so as to increase the margin.

As a general statement, distribution cost analysis by territory searches for any improvements in operations, such as:

- Recasting of sales territory boundaries to reduce selling expenses and secure more coverage.
- Reorganization of the territory to facilitate selling effort in line with the potential.
- Rerouting of salespeople.
- Changing the method of sale or channel of distribution, for example, from personal calls to telephone calls, or from direct sales contacts by the sales force to the use of an agent.
- Changing the product mix to secure a higher margin.
- Changing the emphasis on customers — from those of small potential to large potential.

Other Distribution Cost Analyses

Two illustrative types of distribution cost analysis have been presented —
by product line and by territory. Other literature discusses other reviews
that might prove useful.[3]

IMPROVING DISTRIBUTION EFFECTIVENESS

The purpose of distribution cost analysis as reviewed in this chapter, and a
major purpose of *planning,* is to improve business results. Voluminous analysis and highly sophisticated techniques are not required. Large companies
have found them useful, and affordable. But commonsense applications and
very simple observations often produce excellent results. An old method is
to look for the good performers, see what they do, and attempt to select the
best combination of effort. For example, assume that a simple analysis by a
salesperson provides these condensed financial results for the year in the
two sales territories, each possessing substantially similar potentials and
characteristics:

	Armstrong		Schroeder	
Item	Amount	Percentage of Sales	Amount	Percentage of Sales
Net sales	$40,000,000	100%	$30,000,000	100%
Less cost of sales	24,000,000	60	21,000,000	70
Gross margin	16,000,000	40	9,000,000	30
Less direct marketing expense	12,000,000	30	7,500,000	25
Margin before allocated expenses	4,000,000	10	1,500,000	5
Less allocated expenses*	1,200,000	3	900,000	3
Profit before taxes	$ 2,800,000	7%	$ 600,000	2%

* 3 percent of sales

[3] See, for example, James D. Willson and John B. Campbell, *Controllership, The Work of
the Managerial Accountant* (N.Y.: John Wiley & Sons, Inc. 1981) Chapter 16.

Basically, the sales manager had these observations when he reviewed the figures:

1. Schroeder should have produced sales of $40 million based on the territorial potential.
2. Knowing the customers, he could see no reason why Schroeder's territory should not produce a gross margin of 40 percent — the same as Armstrong's. The customers were in the same industries and served the same markets.
3. Armstrong, although an excellent salesperson, was inclined to spend too much on entertainment.
4. By and large, a direct marketing expense budget of 25 percent of sales was entirely adequate.

Given these statements, the controller prepared the following income statement, using the best performance of each, with substantially better results:

	Armstrong		Schroeder		Best Combination	
	Amount	Percentage of Sales	Amount	Percentage of Sales	Amount	Percentage of Sales
Net sales	$40,000,000	100%	$40,000,000	100%	$80,000,000	100%
Less cost of sales	24,000,000	60	24,000,000	60	48,000,000	60
Gross margin	16,000,000	40	16,000,000	40	32,000,000	40
Less direct marketing expense	10,000,000	25	10,000,000	25	20,000,000	25
Margin before allocated expenses	6,000,000	15	6,000,000	15	12,000,000	15
Less allocated expenses*	1,200,000	3	1,200,000	3	2,400,000	3
Profit before taxes	$ 4,800,000	12%	$ 4,800,000	12%	$ 9,600,000	12%

* 3 percent of sales

This admittedly overly simplified example, using the best combination, reflects an increase in profit before taxes of $6.2 million — a whopping 182 percent. The "best combination" cannot always be established as "the marketing plan." The point is, however, that simple, not complicated, analysis is useful in planning for better marketing results.

FIG. 15-10 Summary Marketing Division Budget

THE WEST COAST CORPORATION
MARKETING DIVISION BUDGET
For the Plan Year Ending 12/31/XX
(dollars in thousands)

Department	Type of Budget	Quarter 1	2	3	4	Total	Prior Year	Increase (Decrease)
Direct selling	Administrative							
East		$ 5,310	$ 5,420	$ 5,440	$ 5,530	$ 21,700	$ 20,840	$ 860
Middle West	"	3,100	3,140	3,190	3,220	12,650	11,060	1,590
Far West	"	5,820	5,910	6,180	6,270	24,180	22,810	1,370
Canada	"	1,700	1,770	1,790	1,820	7,080	6,700	380
Total		$15,930	$16,240	$16,600	$16,840	$ 65,610	$ 61,410	$4,200
Advertising and sales promotion	Project	$ 8,820	$ 9,210	$ 9,400	$ 9,610	$ 37,040	$ 35,100	$1,940
Warehousing	Standard (fixed and variable)							
Camden, N.J.		$ 1,600	$ 1,640	$ 1,730	$ 1,790	$ 6,760	$ 6,300	$ 460
Chicago, Ill.		1,120	1,100	1,210	1,240	4,670	4,400	270
Los Angeles, Cal.		2,630	2,720	2,540	2,560	10,450	10,300	150
Vancouver, B.C.		470	480	460	490	1,900	2,000	(100)
Total		$ 5,820	$ 5,940	$ 5,940	$ 6,080	$ 23,780	$ 23,000	$ 780
Administrative								
General and administrative	Administrative	2,100	2,100	2,100	2,210	8,510	8,300	210
Market research	Project	470	490	490	510	1,960	1,900	60
Customer relations	Administrative	100	100	100	110	410	410	—
Branch offices	Administrative							
New York, N.Y.		$ 340	$ 340	$ 350	$ 360	$ 1,390	$ 1,320	$ 70
Chicago, Ill.	"	220	230	230	230	910	880	30
Los Angeles, Cal.	"	440	440	450	460	1,790	1,700	90
Total		1,000	1,010	1,030	1,050	4,090	3,900	190
Total administrative		3,670	3,700	3,720	3,880	14,970	14,510	460
Grand Total — Division Budget		$34,240	$35,090	$35,660	$36,410	$141,400	$134,020	$7,380
Percentage of net sales						9.6%	9.4%	(.2%)

THE DISTRIBUTION COST BUDGET ILLUSTRATED

The objective in the planning and control of distribution costs has been reviewed, together with the several types of budgets that may be suited to varying kinds of distribution activity. The role of analysis has been covered. When the concepts are applied to the marketing activities, presumably an acceptable and realistic distribution cost budget can be prepared as part of the budgeting process. A summarized planning budget for the marketing division is shown in Figure 15-10. The only difference between the illustration and reality is that the applicable type of budget has been designated for the assistance of the reader.

While the annual plan budget is summarized by quarters, in many cases the monthly financial statements compare actual and plan by month and by year-to-date. If the company contemplates such reporting, then the departmental budgets should be prepared on a monthly basis.

It is to be noted that the marketing division budget is summarized on a departmental basis, i.e., a responsibility basis. Supporting the departmental budget are summaries by type of expense. In this way, comparison of budgets for the two years, by type of expense, will reveal the specific accounts where the increase is anticipated.

It bears repeating that administrative type budgets, for control purposes, will not change monthly by reason of fluctuations in the activity level. Rather, the volume (and profit) factors are considered in setting the total level of expense. What is perhaps important is not *how* the control budget may respond to volume changes, but rather that it does.

BUDGETARY CONTROL REPORTS

In the control phase of budgeting, it is usual practice to compare actual and budgeted expenses (either the fixed budget or flexible budget, as is appropriate), and to take corrective action. Examples of control reports have been presented in earlier sections of this chapter. Actual and budgeted expenses, department by department, and type of expense by type of expense are compared. Additionally, project type budgets are updated as to estimated project cost and compared with the project budget.

16

Advertising and Sales Promotion Expense

"ADVERTISING" AND "SALES PROMOTION" DEFINED

There are several definitions of advertising that contain some common elements, and that, from a purist viewpoint, attempt to make certain distinctions. From the budgeting viewpoint, it is not necessary to unduly refine the meaning. The American Marketing Association (AMA) recommends this definition: "Advertising is any paid form of nonpersonal presentation and promotion of ideas, goods, and services by an identified sponsor.[1] On the other hand, in *Advertising,*[2] this description is provided: "Advertising is controlled, identifiable information and persuasion by means of mass communications media." Inherent in these definitions are these characteristics:

1. Nonpersonal presentations take place; that is, there are no personal face-to-face meetings. Although advertising may complement personal selling, it is done through mass media. The mass media may be the printed word or electronic (TV or radio).
2. The service is a controlled, paid form; it is not free publicity. It provides information or entertainment — presumably in a persuasive form by an identified sponsor. Because the sponsor does pay for the advertising, he can control the content, time, and direction of the information presented.

Thus, the reader or receiver of the message is able to identify both the purpose and the source. He presumably is aware that the purpose is to persuade him to accept the idea or message presented.

The above attributes distinguish advertising from other direct selling efforts. Further, advertising is a distinct function in the distribution effort of a company, and it is usually under the cognizance of an advertising manager who is in charge of a separate department in the marketing organization.

Sales promotion, on the other hand, is a little more difficult to describe. It is supplementary to both personal selling and advertising. It may be continuous, but more typically it is a specific time-limited campaign. Through numerous devices such as cents-off coupons, cash refunds, contests, special price offers, and premiums, sales promotion seeks to motivate and "sell" consumers, salesmen, middle-men, or others. It is a sort of coordinative force which assists, or makes more effective, both advertising and personal selling. It motivates, or induces special effort, by the three principal groups at which different programs may be aimed: the consumer, intermediaries, and company sales people. A sales promotion has been defined by some as a short-term incentive to the consumer or trade to induce purchase of the goods or service; it is usually under the jurisdiction of the advertising manager and is closely coordinated with the advertising programs.

---

[1] Ralph S. Alexander and the Committee on Definitions, *Marketing Definitions* (Chicago, Ill.: American Marketing Association, 1963), p. 9.

[2] John S. Wright et al., *Advertising,* 4th ed. (New York: McGraw-Hill Book Co., 1977), p. 9.

REASONS FOR SEPARATE BUDGET CONSIDERATION

Advertising and sales promotion are significant segments of the total distribution effort. In some avenues of endeavor they are vital — as in retailing. Not only must advertising be coordinated with the sales promotion activities, but it should also be synchronized with the other distribution functions: direct selling, warehousing and handling, and transportation.

Yet, in practice, the advertising and sales promotion budget is usually developed separately from the marketing budget, although they are coordinated. This procedure may arise from a number of considerations, such as those that follow.

Major Financial Outlay

In some industries and companies, advertising and sales promotion expenses by themselves, and certainly together, may constitute a major financial outlay. For example, in 1980, the advertising expenditures of the one hundred leading U.S. national advertisers rose to an estimated $13 billion. Procter & Gamble, the long-time leader, spent $649,624,200, or 5.7 percent of sales; Sears, Roebuck & Co., back in the number two spot, had expenditures of $599,600,000, or 2.4 percent of sales. The extent of advertising expenses in the absolute, and as a percentage of sales, for the one hundred leaders is shown in Figure 16-1.[3] In this listing, advertising expenses as a percentage of sales ranges from 0.3 percent for Mobil Corp. to 79.4 percent for Jeffrey Martin, Inc.

Given expenses of great magnitude, separate consideration would often seem warranted.

Less Direct Impact on Sales

Advertising in many concerns is viewed as having a less immediate and direct impact on sales than do other distribution or marketing efforts. This is particularly true in those circumstances where the program is directed to some long-range objective. Given a rather illusive relationship between advertising and its results, and perhaps the need to exercise more subjective judgment, the top management and board of directors often desire to consider the outlays separately in order to retain a certain amount of flexibility.

---

[3] *Advertising Age Yearbook, 1982* (Chicago, Ill.: Crain Books, 1982), pp. 102–103. Reprinted with permission.

Effectiveness Difficult to Measure

The effectiveness of advertising, at best, is difficult to measure. Rightly or wrongly, for this reason as compared with other expenditures, some managements feel advertising should be treated in a separate review process.

Separately Identified Responsibility

Finally, advertising and sales promotion activities are usually organized in a separate department, or indeed in an outside agency. Hence, following the principle of "responsibility accounting," the cost accumulation should follow the administrative pattern of separate identification.

TYPES OF ADVERTISING AND SALES PROMOTION EXPENSE

As is true with all costs, for both planning and control purposes, costs should be segregated by responsibility, significant type of expense, and perhaps by program, with appropriate subaccounts according to manner of application such as by product, territory, and channel of distribution. A great share of advertising and sales promotion expense consists of production costs of the programs and space costs for the different media. A practical listing of expense accounts might include the following:

1. *Media costs:*
   - □ Broadcast media:
     - Television — National and local spots
     - Radio — Local spots
   - □ Printed media:
     - Publication media — Newspapers and magazines
     - Direct advertising — Direct mail and specialties
   - □ Out-of-home media
     - Outdoor advertising
     - Transit advertising

2. *Administrative expense:*
   - □ Salaries and wages — Supervision
   - □ Fringe benefits — Supervision
   - □ Salaries and wages — Staff
   - □ Fringe benefits — Staff
   - □ Occupancy costs
   - □ Travel and entertainment
   - □ Supplies
   - □ Maintenance
   - □ Automobile expense

FIG. 16-1 1980 Advertising Expenditures of the 100 Leading U.S. Advertisers

	Rank	Company	Advertising	Sales	Advertising as % of Sales
Airlines	53	Trans World Corp.	$ 88,975,000	$ 5,018,281,000	1.8%
	75	UAL, Inc.	60,164,100	5,041,335,000	1.2
	80	Eastern Air Lines	54,100,000	3,452,542,000	1.6
	89	American Airlines	46,315,720	3,820,978,000	1.2
	96	Delta Air Lines	38,700,000	3,280,000,000	1.2
Appliances, TV, Radio	27	RCA Corp.	164,328,300	8,011,300,000	2.1
	29	General Electric Co.	156,196,300	24,959,000,000	0.6
Automobiles	6	General Motors Corp.	316,000,000	57,728,500,000	0.5
	8	Ford Motor Co.	280,000,000	37,085,500,000	0.8
	32	Chrysler Corp.	150,300,000	9,225,300,000	1.6
	54	Toyota Motor Sales U.S.A.	87,628,000	13,422,976,000	0.7
	68	Volkswagen of America	70,000,000	18,390,000,000	0.4
	69	Nissan Motor Corp.	69,865,700	13,510,000,000	0.5
	79	American Honda Motor Co.	54,339,063	7,980,019,000	0.7
	90	American Motors Corp.	45,896,300	2,522,587,000	1.8
	100	Mazda Motors of America	31,097,700	925,000,000	3.4
Chemicals	43	American Cyanamid Co.	125,000,000	3,453,934,000	3.6
	49	DuPont	98,300,000	13,652,000,000	0.7
	65	Union Carbide Corp.	74,311,166	9,994,100,000	0.7
Communications, Entertainment	37	Time, Inc.	141,851,000	2,881,783,000	4.9
	40	CBS, Inc.	132,372,000	4,062,052,000	3.3
	59	Warner Communications	82,326,000	2,059,414,000	4.0
	66	MCA, Inc.	74,000,000	1,297,104,000	5.7
	88	ABC, Inc.	46,764,600	2,280,380,000	2.1
	91	Columbia Pictures	43,000,000	691,800,000	6.2
Drugs	38	Richardson-Vicks	134,000,000	1,211,151,000	11.1
	47	Schering-Plough Corp.	100,000,000	1,740,000,000	5.7
	52	Sterling Drug Co.	89,600,000	1,701,433,000	5.3
	62	SmithKline Corp.	81,438,800	1,771,938,000	4.6
	67	Miles Laboratories	72,987,900	686,117,000	10.6
	70	Squibb Corp.	69,000,000	1,675,780,000	4.1
	85	Pfizer, Inc.	49,712,000	3,029,300,000	1.6
	95	A. H. Robins Co.	41,125,900	432,328,000	9.5
Food	3	General Foods	410,000,000	6,601,300,000	6.2
	14	McDonald's Corp.	206,962,100	6,266,000,000	3.3
	15	Ralston Purina Co.	206,794,860	4,886,000,000	4.2
	19	Esmark, Inc.	189,907,000	2,956,422,000	6.4
	23	Beatrice Foods	175,000,000	8,772,804,000	2.0
	25	General Mills	171,114,790	4,852,400,000	3.5
	33	Nabisco, Inc.	150,000,000	2,588,700,000	5.8
	34	Consolidated Foods Corp.	149,221,000	5,600,000,000	2.7
	35	Norton-Simon, Inc.	149,000,000	3,012,772,000	4.9
	41	Dart & Kraft	128,283,000	9,411,000,000	1.4
	44	Pillsbury Co.	124,025,700	3,301,700,000	3.8
	48	Quaker Oats Co.	99,666,700	2,405,200,000	4.1
	51	Kellogg Co.	95,689,900	2,150,900,000	4.4
	60	Nestle Enterprises	82,000,000	2,400,000,000	3.4
	61	H. J. Heinz Co.	81,900,000	3,568,889,000	2.3
	63	CPC International, Inc.	77,900,000	4,120,300,000	1.9
	76	Campbell Soup Co.	57,997,500	2,900,000,000	2.0
	82	Borden Co.	51,695,700	4,595,795,000	1.1
	84	MortonNorwich	50,212,800	846,601,000	5.9

	Rank	Company	Advertising	Sales	Advertising as % of Sales
Food (cont.)	92	Standard Brands	$ 42,124,000	$ 3,018,466,000	1.4%
	97	Carnation	37,200,000	3,236,222,222	1.1
Gum and Candy	58	Mars, Inc.	83,729,375	976,360,000	8.6
	81	Wm. Wrigley Jr. Co.	51,843,340	557,632,000	9.3
	93	Hershey Foods	41,300,000	1,335,289,000	3.1
Photographic Equipment	57	Eastman Kodak Co.	83,887,700	9,734,303,000	0.9
	86	Polaroid Corp.	49,253,300	1,450,785,000	3.4
Retail Chains	2	Sears, Roebuck & Co.	599,600,000	25,195,000,000	2.4
	5	K Mart Corp.	319,311,000	14,200,000,000	2.2
	45	J. C. Penney Co.	108,000,000	11,353,000,000	0.9
Soaps, Cleansers (and Allied)	1	Procter & Gamble	649,624,200	11,416,000,000	5.7
	13	Colgate-Palmolive Co.	225,000,000	5,130,464,000	9.4
	28	Unilever U.S., Inc.	158,329,100	1,486,660,000	10.6
	64	Clorox Co.	74,554,000	637,433,000	11.7
	83	S. C. Johnson & Son	51,411,600	1,800,000,000	2.9
Soft Drinks	12	PepsiCo, Inc.	233,400,000	5,975,220,000	3.9
	20	Coca-Cola, Inc.	184,185,000	5,912,600,000	3.1
Telephone Service, Equipment	9	American Telephone & Telegraph	259,170,000	50,791,200,000	0.5
	36	International Telephone & Telegraph	143,000,000	18,529,655,000	0.7
Tobacco	4	Philip Morris, Inc.	364,594,700	9,822,300,000	3.7
	7	R. J. Reynolds Industries	298,524,100	10,354,100,000	2.9
	50	B.A.T. Industries	95,757,000	1,475,000,000	6.5
	56	American Brands	85,598,900	6,801,456,000	1.3
	98	Liggett Group	36,000,000	1,076,090,000	3.3
Toiletries, Cosmetics	10	Warner-Lambert Co.	235,202,000	3,479,207,000	6.8
	16	American Home Products Corp.	197,000,000	4,074,095,000	4.8
	17	Bristol-Myers Co.	196,286,400	3,158,300,000	6.2
	31	Gillette Co.	150,981,700	2,315,294,000	6.5
	41	Chesebrough-Pond's	128,316,000	1,377,484,000	9.3
	46	Revlon, Inc.	105,430,400	2,203,324,000	4.8
	77	Beecham Group	56,615,500	2,676,100,000	2.1
	93	Noxell Corp.	41,318,600	204,160,000	20.2
	99	Jeffrey Martin, Inc.	35,708,100	45,000,000	79.4
Wine, Beer, and Liquor	21	Anheuser-Busch	181,278,500	3,822,400,000	4.7
	26	Heublein, Inc.	170,000,000	1,921,879,000	8.8
	30	Seagram Co. Ltd.	152,000,000	2,534,952,000	6.0
	71	Jos. Schlitz Brewing Co.	66,443,700	896,667,000	7.4
	72	Brown-Forman Distillers	65,000,000	768,772,000	8.5
Miscellaneous	11	Gulf & Western Industries	233,800,000	6,885,000,000	3.4
	18	Mobil Corp.	194,816,700	63,726,000,000	0.3
	22	Johnson & Johnson	177,000,000	2,633,600,000	6.7
	24	U.S. Government	172,964,514	—	—
	39	Loews Corp.	132,785,200	4,530,000,000	2.9
	55	Mattel, Inc.	87,100,000	915,690,000	9.5
	73	Greyhound Corp.	63,577,400	4,782,010,000	1.4
	74	American Express Co.	63,000,000	5,504,000,000	1.1
	78	Kimberly-Clark	54,527,900	2,600,300,000	2.1
	87	Levi Strauss & Co.	48,700,000	2,840,800,000	1.7

PURPOSES OF ADVERTISING

Advertising Objectives Support Marketing Objectives

As has been discussed, goals and objectives of a business are in turn supported by objectives and goals of each unit or function. The same is true of advertising. Usually the advertising objectives and the related sales promotion objectives are in support of the broader corporate marketing objective. Thus, a broad marketing objective might be to increase the sales volume in certain highly profitable product lines or areas. The related advertising objective might be to create brand preference for these product lines. The marketing goal, for example, might be to secure 15 percent of the industry sales for the product category by 1984. A corresponding advertising goal might be to attain a 25 percent preference for brand X among its 40 million estimated consumers in that same year.

It is probably well recognized that advertising may reduce direct selling effort and increase sales volume, thus contributing to increased profits. How and when this may be accomplished will depend on the strategy. Hence, the purpose of advertising is germane to planning the activities for the planning period, selecting the programs, and establishing a realistic budget.

Examples of Advertising Goals

Some of the purposes of advertising are to:

- Increase immediate sales
- Maintain prices
- Reduce the cost of other selling efforts
- Educate consumers in the use of products or services or in particular policies
- Establish and maintain trademarks and brands
- Establish new products in the market
- Develop new markets
- Meet competition
- Establish in the minds of consumers a favorable attitude toward, and confidence in, the concern and its products and policies
- Create favorable public opinion and prevent hostile legislation

A given company may have several objectives — some differing by product line or territory — and there will be some overlapping. However, the formulation of the strategy and programs will usually be specific for specific purposes. The more definitely a firm is able to define the advertising (and sales promotion) objectives, the more intelligently can its advertising program be formulated, the effort controlled, and the results measured.

COMPLEXITIES IN MANAGING AND BUDGETING ADVERTISING

Before discussing budget procedures, it might be helpful to gain a sense of some of the imponderables and, indeed, inconsistencies and divergencies in managing the advertising program.

It is a singular fact that, while it is more difficult to budget advertising cost intelligently than perhaps any other important element of distribution cost, yet the budget method was applied to advertising earlier than to other costs. This anomalous situation arose from the fact that early advertising budgets were frequently merely "lump-sum" appropriations that served as maximum limits of expenditure. Little intensive study was directed to the problem as to just how much advertising should be done — when, where, and how — in order to realize the greatest benefit. The answers to these questions can never be secured with absolute certainty. Too much depends upon such factors as future business conditions, competition, new developments in markets and products, and finally, the effectiveness of the advertising itself, to permit exact answers. A large element of judgment will always be necessary. Yet, much analysis of value can be made. While some of these factors are obviously uncontrollable, their past movements can be studied, their relationships and effects noted, and their importance weighed to a degree that will provide at least some basis for intelligent decisions as to advertising expenditures.

Tenuous Relationship of Costs to Results

There is probably no one single item of business cost in which there is greater potential for waste than in advertising. This does not signify that too much is spent for advertising, but rather that the amounts spent are subjected to less rigid tests of probable relation of cost and result than are most cost items. The author has sat in executive conferences where lengthy and heated discussions raged over the desirability of adding a few salesmen at a cost of forty or fifty thousand dollars a year, and then has seen the same executives approve an advertising appropriation of many times that amount merely by noting the fact that it represented some *reasonable* increase over the expenditure of the previous year. No justification for the increase was presented or called for. The impression seemed to exist that the advertising expenditure represented some imponderable element entirely beyond the pale of analytical test. While such an attitude is no longer general among executives, it is still true that advertising expenditures are subjected to less critical tests than most cost items.

Company-to-Company Variations

It is extremely difficult to generalize upon the methods that should be employed in the budgeting of advertising costs, due to the wide variety of circumstances existing in different business establishments. For example, firms vary widely in their practices. Some companies do not have an advertising department within their own organization, but place all responsibility for advertising with a professional agency. Some concerns depend entirely upon their own advertising departments. Still other companies maintain their own departments, which function in cooperation with an advertising agency. In some firms the advertising manager reports to the sales manager, whereby sales and advertising programs are closely correlated; in others the advertising manager is independent and coordination is effected either by conferences or through the chief executive. In some concerns the advertising is largely of an institutional nature; in others it is directed mainly to immediate sales projects. In some corporations advertising is chiefly local, as with the typical department store; in others it is national in scope, as with the manufacturers of automobiles. In some manufacturing concerns expenditures are made directly by the manufacturer; in others the manufacturer contributes to the advertising of jobbers and dealers. In some instances it is comparatively easy to identify the advertising costs with individual products and territories; in others no such definite identification is possible. Finally, a great variety of different media and combinations of media are employed as, for example, newspapers, periodicals, direct mail, outdoor advertising, radio, television, etc.

Given the environment in some corporations, careful analysis — including the assistance of constructive financial review — will contribute to a more effective advertising and sales promotion effort.

STEPS IN DEVELOPING AN ADVERTISING PLAN OR PROGRAM

To be sure, it will chiefly be the advertising executive and not the budget coordinator who will conceive and develop the advertising plan and its related programs. However, some knowledge of the steps necessary in creating an effective plan will provide useful background to the budget executive and financial analysts in understanding the problems of the advertising executive, as well as making more worthwhile any financial analysis (such as comparing contribution margin or gross profit potential on product Y in territory P with the expense of a given campaign in that area).

When a national advertiser undertakes an advertising campaign — the steps necessary in the planning and control of the activity — these steps may be involved:[4]

1. Analyze the market
2. Determine the advertising objectives and goals
3. Establish or apply the requisite budgetary system
4. Develop the advertising strategy:
   - Select the media
   - Create the messages
5. Coordinate the advertising program with the other promotional and marketing methods
6. Evaluate results
7. Where appropriate, take necessary corrective action

Any extensive discussion of market analysis, advertising objectives, advertising strategy, media selection, and related subjects are beyond the scope of this book. Those interested are referred to the many good texts on the subject. However, those facets of planning and control that are of rather immediate interest to financial disciplines are reviewed in the next section.

FINANCIAL ASPECTS OF PLANNING AND CONTROLLING THE ADVERTISING AND SALES PROMOTION BUDGET

The budget director and those other financially oriented executives who have an interest in the advertising and sales promotion budget probably should be knowledgeable about these more or less interrelated aspects of the budget procedure, at a minimum:

- Methods to determine the overall amount to be spent on advertising and sales promotion
- Some of the financial quantitative analyses useful in appraising advertising plans and in the follow-up control
- Minimum financial-type data to be presented for securing budget approval
- Control reports for advertising and sales promotion expense
- Some cost standards for monitoring advertising expense

---

[4] Adapted in part from Wright, et al., *op. cit.*, p. 502.

METHODS OF ESTABLISHING THE BUDGET AMOUNT

Most financial executives would agree that the advertising and sales promotion budget, as with any significant, planned expenditure, should be built and held within the financial capabilities of the company. At the same time, every effort should be made to see that the planned disbursements are as effective as possible.

There are two basic methods of establishing an advertising budget currently in use:

1. The lump-sum appropriation
2. An amount determined by estimating the cost of attaining certain objectives — the "bottom to top" budget procedure

LUMP-SUM APPROPRIATION

Under the lump-sum approach to budgeting, a simple, single appropriation is authorized based on some factor, such as a percentage of sales. Among other reasons, because advertising results are difficult or impossible to measure, some managements feel it is practical to set a general limit and then let the management decide the best way to spend the funds, and how to "split the pie."

Under the plan of making lump-sum appropriations, the total advertising budget may be determined as follows:

- A percentage of the previous year's sales or an average of several years' sales
- A percentage of budgeted sales
- A fixed amount per unit of product
- An amount comparable to or determined by the appropriation of competitors
- An arbitrary increase or decrease over the past year's expenditure.
- A percentage of the net profit of the previous year
- A percentage of net profit for planning year
- A percentage of gross margin of previous year or planning year

Percentage of Sales

Where the advertising appropriation is based upon a percentage of sales, it is quite generally agreed that budgeted sales should be used in preference to sales of the previous year. This at least gives some consideration to changes in sales policies and the expected trend in general business conditions. The percentage used is frequently based on the average of the industry. There are certain advantages to the plan of basing the advertising appropriation on a percentage of budgeted sales. The plan is simple and easily understood by the executive group generally. It automatically controls the advertising expenditure in relation to planned dollar volume. Where a great variety of goods are sold, and where much of the advertising represents joint cost, it is difficult to make appropriations for individual products. With well-established lines, reasonably stable conditions, and considerable past experience as a guide, the results are likely to be similar to those secured by more intensive analysis. On the other hand, the plan is basically weak in that it does not require a critical analysis of definite objectives and the probable cost to attain them. In most concerns the sales program is constantly shifting; new ventures and new projects, new products must be considered; shifts are being made in the emphasis on various types of sales effort. Simply to perpetuate a plan of allotting a percentage of budgeted sales to advertising may result in a disproportionate and misdirected sales effort. Such a plan tends to set a *maximum* rather than a *proper* allowance for advertising.

A modification of this plan is to use a different percentage for the budgeted sales of each class of goods. This method is used to a considerable extent by department and other retail stores. For example, a large furniture store uses a much higher percentage for living room suites than for kitchen specialties.

Fixed Amount per Unit

Some concerns manufacturing or selling a uniform product or only a few products appropriate a given amount of advertising per unit. The plan is used particularly by the manufacturers of specialty goods such as electric sweepers, washing machines, automobiles, and the like. A certain brewery, for example, uses 40 cents per barrel. Exceptions are made when new territory is being developed. Where this plan is used, the appropriation should be based on budgeted unit sales.

This plan lends itself particularly to vertical cooperative advertising. Thus, the manufacturer may appropriate a dollar in advertising for each dollar required of the distributor. The plan, being based on budgeted units, is simple and easily applied. Moreover, it is expressive of at least some relationship between the advertising appropriation and the specific task to be performed. Where there is sufficient past experience to base intelligent judgment on the expenditure necessary to sell the product, this is usually the most satisfactory method for concerns of the type mentioned.

Competitive Actions

One of the most difficult factors to contend with in setting the advertising appropriation is the action of competitors. Some smaller concerns use the plan of "following the leader" on the theory that it may benefit by the more extensive research and study of the large competitor. Concerns of comparable strength may attempt to match the appropriations of their leading rivals, or even to out-advertise them, on the theory that they cannot afford to do otherwise. When this becomes the governing factor in determining appropriations, it is obviously poor marketing strategy. Somewhere the increased advertising meets the law of diminishing returns. Moreover, there are other types of selling effort that must be considered. Company X may increase its advertising appropriations from $10 million to $15.5 million, but its rival, Company Y, may show greater earnings by appropriating an extra $2 million for other types of selling effort or product research, or even by limiting its total sales effort to previous amounts.

There is no denying the fact that advertising appropriations must give some effect to the actions of competitors, but such influence should not be the governing factor. An intensive study of advertising objectives, their relative importance, and their cost-result relationship should ultimately govern the appropriation.

Adjustment of Prior Year's Expenditures

The plans of making an arbitrary increase or decrease in the appropriation over the previous year or of appropriating a percentage of the previous year's profit have little to commend them. They are based upon the assumption that there is no intelligent basis for determining what amount of advertising effort will contribute most to the long-run profit and, consequently, the matter should be determined by such considerations as expected trends in general business, financial position, dividend policy, tax savings, and so forth. This policy is more often used in concerns where there is little direct or immediate effect of advertising upon sales volume. While this policy is still followed by some large and successful concerns, its adherents are becoming fewer.

With regard to the effect of general business conditions on the advertising appropriation, some consideration, of course, should be given to shifting the emphasis as between luxuries, usual convenience goods, and necessities. The general opinion is that luxuries should be emphasized in good times, necessities in bad times, and that usual convenience goods should have the same emphasis at all times.

Percentage of Gross Margin

While a great many companies using a lump-sum appropriation method employ net sales as the base, there may be merit in considering a profit-related approach. Management concern should be with profits and not merely sales. For discussion purposes, attention is focused on gross margin to avoid the impact of tax rate changes or other nonoperating factors and to more closely relate advertising to the margins it should help attain.

There may be several variants of this margin approach, but basically a percentage of advertising expense to product margin is developed. This can be based on overall industry ratios of advertising expense to gross margin,[5] on company experience in total, or by product line. In applying an advertising expense to gross margin strategy, one of two philosophies may be followed: (1) the earnings maintenance approach, or (2) a type of management-by-objective scheme based on potential gross.

The so-called earnings maintenance scheme is based on the concept that a business must maintain gross margins. If a particular firm has higher margins, it has a higher budget to continue, or protect, or to maintain its lead. That is to say, some credit for the higher margins must be given to advertising; and, assuming the use of an industry average gross margin to sales ratio, the higher ratio will permit a higher advertising expense budget to maintain the level of margin.

Another school of thought would base an advertising budget on the potential gross profits available. The potential gross margin for a company, and its advertising budget, is determined as follows:

1. The market potential is multiplied by the advertiser's market share to determine his potential sales.
2. From these potential company sales the potential gross margin is calculated.
3. The potential gross margin is multiplied by the industry average advertising expense to gross margin ratio to calculate the lump-sum budget needed.

This approach has the merit of matching potential profits against the advertising expense level deemed necessary to reach it. Obviously, great judgment and care must be employed, or the advertising funds can be spent and the margins never attained.

Simplicity of Lump-Sum Appropriations

To the extent that the advertising is done for immediate results, the sales budget, or its related gross margins or net profit, must serve as the basis. The

---

[5] See, for example, some ratios by industry published in *Industrial Marketing,* Dec. 1979, p. 54.

advertising executives, with such outside counsel as may be employed, must estimate the cost of the advertising necessary to produce the sales or margins budgeted. It is never possible, even under the most favorable circumstances, to tell exactly the amount of advertising necessary to produce a given sales volume; but, with adequate records of past experience properly analyzed as to cost and results, reasonably close estimates can be made. Department stores and mail order houses are illustrative of the type of concerns in which much of the advertising expenditure is directed to immediate results.

To the extent that the advertising is directed to less immediate results, such as the creation of goodwill, establishment of brands, development of new markets, and so forth, the amounts to be appropriated must be based upon such factors as:

1. *The amount of funds that can be released in any one year.* No matter how attractive the advertising program may appear, it must first be tested by its effect upon the financial position of the company.

2. *The amount necessary to make the program effective.* Small expenditures are sometimes sheer waste, whereas larger expenditures may accomplish desired results.

3. *The general program of future expansion.* Where advertising is largely of an institutional nature, the amount to be expended depends upon the rate of expansion contemplated.

In summary, the lump-sum appropriation method has the advantage of simplicity. There will be instances where the knowledge of top management and its "gut feeling" about the situation — perhaps buttressed by studies showing a long-term relationship between advertising expenditures and sales — make the lump-sum appropriation method an acceptable procedure. However, in many instances, this process lacks the specifics that so often are desirable and available.

ESTIMATED COST OF ATTAINING-THE-OBJECTIVES METHOD

The second general plan of developing an advertising program is to examine carefully the objectives, the detailed methods by which such objectives can be accomplished, and the costs that will be involved. These individual costs are then combined into a total appropriation. This plan involves such detailed considerations as:

- Necessary marketing and advertising research
- Selection of individual advertising projects relative to products and territories
- Selection of detailed advertising methods and media
- Detailed estimates of direct and indirect costs
- Detailed analysis of time when expenditures will be made (i.e., in what month or quarter)
- Research as to effectiveness of methods

It is beyond the scope of this book to consider these detailed steps; this is a specialized task for those trained and experienced in the field of advertising. It must be performed by either the company's own advertising staff, outside advertising agencies, or both. It should be made clear, however, that the advertising departments should not be given a carte blanche appropriation to do with as they please and without reckoning. They should be required to justify their program before the money is appropriated and spent. This can be done by requiring them to define their objectives clearly, to outline the exact methods by which they plan to attain them, and to estimate the cost of each element of the program. In brief, the advertising departments should be compelled to justify their programs before, rather than after, the money is spent, with an understanding that they will be held accountable for the results as planned.

FINANCIAL ANALYSIS FOR PLANNING PURPOSES

There is a phase, however, in which the financial discipline, properly used, can be helpful: This is financial analysis and summary of costs, and, perhaps, related margins.

Types of Costs

As a foundation for both planning and control, the advertising costs must be properly analyzed. The objectives of such analysis are the determination of the cost of specific advertising projects, the cost in individual territories, the cost of particular products or product groups, the cost related to individual customer groups, and perhaps to the expected margins.

To make such analyses, the costs must first be resolved into their direct and indirect elements as pertains to the particular analysis at hand. For example, a concern that extends its advertising effort over a wide area may find it necessary to make a territorial analysis. Direct costs of territories would include:

- Salaries and expense of advertising executives and supervisors within the individual territories
- Clerical salaries and office expense of territorial advertising offices
- Salaries and expense of demonstrators
- Local newspaper space
- Outdoor advertising space (billboards, signs)
- Advertising allowances to customers
- Local contest expenses
- Local contributions
- Property insurance and taxes on advertising equipment and facilities within individual territories
- Insurance and taxes on territorial direct advertising payroll
- Communication, supplies, and general expense of territorial advertising offices

Indirect territorial costs would consist of:

- Advertising administration and overhead such as advertising executives' salaries
- Cost of copy preparation such as copy writing and art work (where copy is widely used)
- Cost of physical production such as printing of catalogs, circulars, and so forth (where used in several territories)
- Direct cost of advertising media of general coverage such as radio time, magazine space

Such indirect costs must be further resolved into individual medium costs and each medium cost then distributed to individual territories. Thus the direct, indirect, and total advertising cost of each territory is ascertained. While the above analysis relates to a sales territory, comparable analyses by product, channel of distribution, method of sale, or other segment may be helpful.

Relating Costs to Expected Benefits

Such analyses, aside from providing a more solid estimate of the cost, should attempt to relate the proposed expenditures to the anticipated benefits. In this vein, much research and effort has been made in attempting to measure advertising effectiveness. Linear programming or mathematical models have been applied in some large corporations, usually with inconclusive results. While business judgment and subjective analysis may continue to bulk large in this function, the financial executive or budget director in cooperation with the advertising manager may be able to "make a stab" at judging the optimum point of a given advertising expenditure through marginal analysis.

Essentially, these estimates or facts will be required:

- The estimate of incremental (additional) units to be sold by successive incremental advertising expenditures

- The unit or total gross profit (or contribution margin under proper circumstances) of the products

- The estimated incremental advertising expense per unit

With such information, some opinion can be formed as to the profitability result of successive amounts of advertising and the effect on income before taxes (or some other appropriate measure) if it is within the financial capability of the firm.

An oversimplified example is shown in this illustration:

Incremental Advertising Expense	Additional Units to Be Sold	Estimated Unit Marginal Profit After all Direct Costs and Before Advertising Expense	Incremental Unit Advertising Cost	Unit Increment or Decrement to Profit	Margin
$ 0	10,000	$ .60	$—	$ .600	$ 6,000
10,000	60,000	.70	.167	.533	31,999
10,000	40,000	.80	.250	.550	22,000
10,000	40,000	.50	.250	.250	10,000
10,000	30,000	.40	.333	.067	2,010
10,000	20,000	.30	.500	(.200)	(4,000)
10,000	10,000	.25	1.000	(.750)	(7,500)

With this type of information, the cumulative or total profit picture may be determined. In the example, based on assumptions, analysis indicates that not more than approximately four incremental blocks of advertising expense (or $40,000) should be spent on that product.

ADVERTISING AND SALES PROMOTION COSTS STANDARDS

Advertising and sales promotion activity is the most difficult of all elements of distribution effort to measure in terms of cost standards. For some advertising and sales promotion activities, accurate and immediate cost standards can be applied; but for others, the cost measurement must be very general in nature and applied to periods of considerable length of time. A manufacturer selling neckties exclusively by direct mail will be able currently to measure its advertising performance with reasonable accuracy by applying a standard cost per unit of product sold, particularly if different standards are established for different territories and seasons. But even here a varying cost per unit sold will reflect changes in general market conditions as well as the factor of advertising performance. When it comes to the establishment and maintenance of trade names, brand consciousness, and dealer and customer goodwill, only general long-run cost measurements can be used. Since the advertising and sales promotion expense of most concerns is relatively large, every possible cost standard that will serve to guide management in the intelligent direction of the effort and measurement of performance must be applied, whether of an immediate or long-run nature.

For control purposes, the advertising costs should be classified as to:

- Advertising administration and overhead
- Preparation of advertising copy
- Physical production of advertising material
- Direct media costs
- Miscellaneous

Advertising Overhead

Administration and overhead cost as a whole may be measured by such standards as:

- Cost per dollar of all direct advertising and sales promotion cost
- Cost per unit of principal medium used, for example, direct mail piece, newspaper inch (where advertising is restricted chiefly to one medium)

The standards may pertain to the advertising administration and overhead as a whole or to those parts of the overhead that pertain to copy preparation, physical production, direct media, or miscellaneous advertising activity. Thus, different cost measurements may be applied as follows:

Administration and Overhead Costs Pertaining to	Cost Measurements
Preparation of advertising copy	• Cost per copy unit prepared
	• Cost per labor hour
	• Cost per dollar expended for copy preparation

Administration and Overhead Costs Pertaining to	Cost Measurements
Physical production of advertising material	• Cost per direct labor hour • Cost per physical unit
Direct media supervision	• Cost per medium unit
Miscellaneous	• Cost per direct medium dollar • Cost per dollar expended for miscellaneous advertising and sales promotion

Copy Preparation

The preparation of advertising copy, including the overhead pertaining thereto, may be measured by such standards as the cost per copy unit (e.g., catalog page, newspaper inch, etc.). Such standards are obviously quantity measurements only and give no effect to quality of output. This must be subjected to the judgment of executives and its effectiveness measured in the long run by sales results.

Physical Production of Advertising Material

The physical production of advertising material, such as printing, and the construction of signs, dealer helps, and so forth, present no particular difficulties. These costs can be measured by standard unit production operations the same as all production costs.

Advertising Media

Ultimately all of the advertising costs, except certain miscellaneous items, should be resolved into individual advertising and sales promotion medium costs. Each medium cost should consist of its advertising copy, its physical production, its direct cost, and its share of the overhead, insofar as these are applicable. Cost standards should then be selected for each medium.

The ideal procedure is to apply both cost and result standards. Thus, in direct mail advertising the standard cost of preparing and mailing a certain type of circular may be $100 per 1,000 pieces; the standard measurement of results expected may be 50 units sold per 1,000 circulars mailed, or $1,000 of sales per 1,000 circulars mailed. Such definite standards can usually be applied currently to individual media costs but seldom to the results. Both types of standards should be applied, however, insofar as practicable. Result standards must frequently apply to longer periods of time.

Advertising and sales promotion media and illustrative standards applicable are as follows:

Media	Standards
Publications of general and national circulation	• Total cost per unit of space • Cost per inquiry received (e.g., when identification coupons are used) • Cost per unit of product sold or per dollar of sales when identifiable
Special publications directed to particular groups, such as business, trade, farm, industrial, technical, professional, religious, class, etc.	• Total cost per unit of space • Cost per inquiry received • Cost per unit of product sold or per dollar of sales to corresponding groups
Miscellaneous publications, including directories, theater programs, house organs, etc.	• Total cost per unit of space • Cost per inquiry received
Newspapers	• Total cost per unit of space • Cost per sales transaction (particularly in department and local retail stores) • Cost per dollar of net or gross sales (where this is the chief medium used)
Direct mail, including circulars, booklets, folders, letters, calendars	• Total cost per unit mailed for each type of direct mail piece used • Cost per dollar of gross or net direct mail sales • Cost per inquiry received
Catalogs	• Total cost per page or standard space unit • Cost per dollar of gross or net catalog sales when identifiable
Outdoor advertising, including billboards, signs, street cards, railroad cards, advertising on trucks	• Total cost per outdoor unit for each type used
TV and radio	• Total cost per unit of time factored by reported or tested coverage • Cost per dollar of net sales of featured items
Store and window displays	• Total cost per unit distributed of store and window cards and displays • Total cost per day of window trimming and display

Media	Standards
Dealer helps, including dealer advertising, sales assistance, and management aid	• Total cost per account sold
Sample distribution	• Total cost per sample distributed
Demonstrations	• Total cost per demonstration
Advertising allowance to dealers	• Cost per dollar of net sales

Miscellaneous Advertising and Sales Promotion Costs

Most concerns have certain advertising and sales promotion expenditures of a miscellaneous nature that cannot be classified with the regular media costs and for which cost standards are not available. The cost control here must be left to the direct supervision of executives. Illustrative of such miscellaneous items are:

- Special exhibits
- Contests
- Public service of employees
- Motion pictures of an educational nature
- Stockholders letters and dividend inserts
- Contributions
- Community welfare
- Pure research

Total Advertising and Sales Promotion Effort

The advertising and sales promotion effort as a whole may be measured by such result standards as:

- Cost per dollar of net sales
- Cost per unit of product sold
- Cost per prospect secured
- Cost per sales transaction

Such standards are very general measures of the results secured from the general advertising and sales promotion cost. Over long-run periods they are valuable and, in some instances, the only measurements that are possible.

Putting the Expenditures Program in Writing

Once the detailed program of expenditures is developed, it should be given definite form in writing. This has the following advantages:

- The advertising department (or agency) is placed on record as to what they propose to accomplish and at what cost.
- The expenditures are timed and can thus be provided for in the financial budget.
- The detailed program, once approved, will serve as a basis for definite control over expenditures.
- Various department heads will know in advance the nature and extent of the advertising assistance they are to receive and when it will be given.

The timing of the advertising expenditures is especially significant. In some instances, as in the promotion of new products, or in the development of new markets or territories, the plans may extend, at least tentatively, for several years in advance. In well-established markets, the program is usually for the fiscal year with a breakdown by months or quarters.

COORDINATING THE ADVERTISING PROGRAM WITH OTHER PROGRAMS

As discussed, advertising is only one of numerous types of selling effort. It should be timed and coordinated with other sales effort to form the most effective results. The entire program of sales effort should then, in turn, be coordinated with the sales, production, and finance plans generally. Elementary as this statement may appear, the lack of such coordination is one of the chief sources of waste in advertising expenditures.

It is frequently desirable to hold a part of the advertising appropriation in reserve to meet unexpected circumstances. This permits the use of special effort where the regular program has failed in its effectiveness or where a sudden change in conditions has altered the sales program. Many such changes arise as a result of unexpected moves on the part of competitors, introduction of new products, or quick changes in general business conditions.

PRESENTING THE PROPOSED ADVERTISING BUDGET

The data to be submitted to the chief executive and, of course, to the board of directors will depend upon past practice, the wishes of the executives, and other special circumstances. And, of course, the marketing or advertising executives may make the presentation. However, under normal circumstances, this minimal information is suggested (along with the samples):

1. The overall sales objective
2. Estimated total cost and relationship to sales projects
3. Comparisons with prior years (perhaps an average of five prior years and each of the preceding three):
   - Sales volume
   - Sales values
   - Advertising costs by medium and function
   - Detail by type of sales promotion (free goods, store displays)
   - Unit advertising costs
4. Cost and profit (or contribution margin) relationships by territory or product
5. Schedules for each product as to names of publications
6. Such other data as the advertising staff think pertinent

In any event, from the financial viewpoint essential information should give aggregates, trends, and relationships at a glance:

- Trend of sales
- Trend of advertising expense
- Costs by media
- Costs by product
- Costs by territory

Graphs and other visual aids often have proved very useful in such presentations.

ACCOUNTING CONTRIBUTION TO SOUND ADVERTISING BUDGETS

In response to this heading, some advertising executives might ask how this is possible. Effective advertising depends, among other things, upon skillful planning; and it is in this phase that a contribution by the accountant can be made. To be sure, he cannot and should not decide whether a given medium should be used, or whether the company should advertise in a certain magazine; that is a decision for the advertising executive. However, he must raise questions of "why" and "how." Thus, if in a cooperative attitude the accountant can review the advertising budget before it is presented for ap-

FIG. 16-2   Actual and Budget Performance — Advertising and Sales Promotion Expense

THE MANUFACTURING COMPANY

STATUS REPORT — ADVERTISING AND SALES PROMOTION BUDGET

As at April 30, 19XX

(in thousands of dollars)

Category	Project Budget	Actual to 4/30/XX Expenditures	Actual to 4/30/XX Commitments	Actual to 4/30/XX Total	Estimated Cost to Complete	Indicated Total Cost	Balance Available for Use or Transfer
Broadcast Media:							
Television							
National	$ 800	$270	$390	$ 660	$120	$ 780	$ 20
Local spots	200	40	60	100	100	200	—
Total	$1,000	$310	$450	$ 760	$220	$ 980	$ 20
Radio — Local	100	20	10	30	40	70	30
Total Broadcast	$1,100	$330	$460	$ 790	$260	$1,050	$ 50
Printed Media:							
Consumer magazines	140	70	20	90	40	130	10
Newspapers	90	20	10	30	20	50	40
Business publications	40	30	10	40	—	40	
Total	$ 270	$120	$ 40	$ 160	$ 60	$ 220	$ 50
Direct mail	180	110	60	170	20	190	(10)
Catalogs	70	60	10	70	—	70	—
Displays and exhibits	80	—	70	70	30	100	(20)
Total Printed Media	$ 600	$290	$180	$ 470	$110	$ 580	$ 20
Advertising Administration	300	100	—	100	200	300	—
Grand Total	$2,000	$720	$640	$1,360	$570	$1,930	$ 70

proval, he can assist the advertising manager. By analytical questions, such as whether the program is directed to those cities or products that offer the most profit, he can bring up points for consideration. Comparisons of estimated cost with expected additional profit should be used and can be provided in support of the program. If the advertising executive can answer the analytical questions raised by the accountant, he can be that much better prepared for the interrogation by the chief executive or board of directors.

In addition to this review of plans *before* expenditures or commitments are made, useful information can be provided as to the status of individual advertising projects. An illustrative monthly report is shown in Figure 16-2. Supporting these project costs may be a tabulated listing of the detailed invoices and requisitions.

Besides the reporting of costs by project, useful comparisons with standard can be made. Moreover, occasional tests of the effectiveness of a program, such as determination of additional sales or operating profit, would represent areas where the accountant's analytical skills can be put to good use.

17

Research and Development Expense

"RESEARCH AND DEVELOPMENT EXPENSE" DEFINED

In a general sense, the budget for research and development (R&D) expense
may be considered as relating to those expenses under the jurisdiction of the
vice-president or director in charge of research and development activities.
Certainly this definition satisfies "responsibility accounting" — the planning and control, and, hence, accumulation, of costs according to those
responsible for the expenditures.

However, to provide more meaningful assistance to the research staff
who must plan and control the R&D activities, it is desirable that the financial executives having a role in the budget procedure possess a somewhat
deeper insight into R&D efforts. For this purpose, costs related to these
activities ought to be more clearly delineated. Perhaps the most authoritative
definition of R&D expense is that provided by the Financial Accounting
Standards Board.[1]

8. For purposes of this Statement, research and development is defined as
follows:

a) *Research* is planned search or critical investigation aimed at discovery of
   new knowledge with the hope that such knowledge will be useful in developing a new product or service (hereinafter "product") or a new process or
   technique (hereinafter "process") or in bringing about a significant improvement to an existing product or process.

---

[1] Statement of Financial Accounting Standards Board No. 2, *Accounting for Research and
Development Costs,* (Oct. 1974) ¶¶ 8, 9. Copyright © by the FASB, High Ridge Park, Stamford,
Connecticut 06905. Copies of the complete document are available from the FASB.

b) *Development* is the translation of research findings or other knowledge into a plan or design for a new product or process or for a significant improvement to an existing product or process whether intended for sale or use. It includes the conceptual formulation, design, and testing of product alternatives, construction of prototypes, and operation of pilot plants. It does not include routine or periodic alterations to existing products, production lines, manufacturing processes, and other ongoing operations even though those alterations may represent improvements and it does not include market research or market testing activities.

9. The following are examples of activities that typically would be included in research and development in accordance with paragraph 8 (unless conducted for others under a contractual arrangement — see paragraph 2) [omitted]:

a) Laboratory research aimed at discovery of new knowledge.

b) Searching for applications of new research findings or other knowledge.

c) Conceptual formulation and design of possible product or process alternatives.

d) Testing in search for or evaluation of product or process alternatives.

e) Modification of the formulation or design of a product or process.

f) Design, construction, and testing of pre-production prototypes and models.

g) Design of tools, jigs, molds, and dies involving new technology.

h) Design, construction, and operation of a pilot plant that is not of a scale economically feasible to the enterprise for commercial production.

i) Engineering activity required to advance the design of a product to the point that it meets specific functional and economic requirements and is ready for manufacture.

While the reader's attention in this chapter is directed to the R&D activities of an entire organization segment (the R&D department), and not to the accounting treatment of the cost (whether expensed, capitalized in inventory, or capitalized in a fixed-asset account), the above definition and listing of R&D activities may be helpful.

POTENTIAL CORPORATE IMPACT OF RESEARCH AND DEVELOPMENT

In the entire gamut of budgeting activities, there will be those areas wherein the effort will be to keep the costs or expenses at the lowest possible level, such as in manufacturing overhead. On the other hand, there will be activities where attention should be focused on making the expenditures as effective as possible, with the function being carried out in the most efficient manner, and assuming a *reasonable* outlay of funds, as contrasted with a minimum of funds. R&D expense probably should be included in the latter category of maintaining a reasonable level of expenditures. Expenses must be held within the financial capabilities of the firm; but an enlightened or far-sighted outlook may be necessary in setting the R&D budget.

There is some empirical evidence to indicate that, over a period of time, earnings tend to increase as more funds are devoted to effective R&D activities. Certainly, current literature would support this contention in the drug, chemical, computer, and electronics industries. Even the currently depressed automobile and steel industries may be suffering from lack of new technology.

In any given company, there may be difficulty, from time to time, in measuring the rate of return to shareholders from research outlays for R&D; but the available data suggests that companies grow and prosper through the development of new and improved products, as well as with continuous efforts at bettering or perfecting the manufacturing process. In today's highly competitive economy, innovation is to be encouraged.

In one way of thinking, R&D outlays are part of the "business regeneration expenses." Such expenditures are essential to the continued growth and prosperity of the company. Some would say R&D expenses are truly an investment, just as much as are expenditures for new, more efficient plants and equipment. The financial executives who assist the research executives in the planning and control of R&D expenses should be aware of the potential impact of the activity on the earnings growth of the company.

AMOUNT SPENT ON RESEARCH AND DEVELOPMENT

Some indication of the importance of industrial R&D expenditures is reflected in *Business Week*'s annual survey for 1981. The 776 companies included in the R&D Scoreboard spent more than $32 billion to develop new products and processes in the recession year 1981.[2] The following table shows the fifteen U.S. companies spending the highest total for R&D.

1.	General Motors	$2,250,000
2.	Ford Motor	1,718,000
3.	AT&T	1,686,000
4.	IBM	1,612,000
5.	Boeing	844,000
6.	General Electric	814,000

---

[2] *Business Week,* July 5, 1982, pp. 54–74.

7.	United Technologies	$ 736,000
8.	DuPont	631,000
9.	Exxon	630,000
10.	Eastman Kodak	615,000
11.	Xerox	526,000
12.	ITT	503,000
13.	Dow Chemical	404,000
14.	Honeywell	369,000
15.	Hewlett-Packard	347,000

A summary by industry of the percentage of sales and percentage of profits spent on R&D, as reported in the survey, is as follows:

Industry Composite	Percentage of Sales	Percentage of Profit
Aerospace	4.8%	141.6%
Appliances	2.0	82.9
Automotive:		
Cars, trucks	3.7	(231.3)
Parts, equipment	2.0	59.9
Building materials	1.2	42.1
Chemicals	2.5	47.1
Conglomerates	2.0	41.4
Containers	0.8	22.4
Drugs	5.3	57.1
Electrical	2.9	48.8
Electronics	3.1	74.3
Food and beverage	0.7	16.3
Fuel	0.5	8.9
Information processing:		
Computers	6.4	72.4
Office equipment	5.0	94.6
Peripherals, services	5.9	94.2
Instruments (measuring, controls)	4.6	87.5
Leisure time	4.4	55.5
Machinery:		
Farm, construction	2.9	61.1
Machine tools, industry, mining	1.9	35.7
Metals and mining	1.1	21.8
Miscellaneous manufacturing	2.0	36.0

(*continued*)

Industry Composite	Percentage of Sales	Percentage of Profit
Oil service and supply	1.8%	16.5%
Paper	0.9	16.4
Personal and home-care products	2.0	33.1
Semiconductors	7.1	174.0
Steel	0.6	10.7
Telecommunications	1.2	10.9
Textiles, apparel	0.4	19.0
Tires, rubber	2.0	70.9
Tobacco	0.5	5.2
All-Industry Composite	2.0%	39.3%

What is interesting is the wide range, as a percentage of sales (from 0.4 to 7.1 percent), and the heavy share of profit (before extraordinary items and discontinued operations) — an all-industry composite of 39.3 percent.

TYPES OF RESEARCH AND DEVELOPMENT EXPENSES

Cost Accumulation

Typical elements of cost associated with R&D activities follow. This listing provides an indication of the types of expenses to be incurred for each of the various organization units associated with the R&D function. The expenses must be accumulated by type of expense and by each department or cost center.

1. *Personnel costs.* Salaries, wages, and fringe benefit costs of those engaged directly in R&D activities. Included are the related costs of:
   □ Department managers and administrative staff
   □ Professional nonadministrative staff
   □ Nonprofessional technical staff
   □ Clerical
   □ Hourly labor
   This group of expenses usually is the largest element of cost.

2. *Cost of materials and supplies.* Included are the cost of such items as:
   □ Expendable equipment with no alternative future use
   □ Chemicals and drugs
   □ Other laboratory supplies
   □ Repair materials and supplies

3. *Cost of intangible services purchased from others.* These costs include:
   - ☐ Purchased research or analysis with no alternative future use other than the project for which purchased
   - ☐ Purchased testing services

4. *Cost of contract services.* Cost of services performed by others in connection with the R&D activities.

5. *Other direct expenses.* Other indirect expenses include:
   - ☐ Travel expenses
   - ☐ Consulting fees
   - ☐ Periodicals and other literature
   - ☐ Dues and memberships
   - ☐ Occupancy costs
   - ☐ Depreciation

6. *Allocated overhead.* In certain circumstances, a share of general administrative expense may be allocated to the R&D activities and should be reflected in the budget and actual expenses.

Allocating Expenses by Project

One other aspect of planning and controlling research and development expense should be recognized. The types or elements of expense may be accumulated by responsibility segments, but each such organizational segment may be working on a selected number of projects. Therefore it is necessary to assign or allocate such expenses to each program benefiting therefrom. As discussed later, the R&D budget probably will be prepared on a project basis, other than the administrative expense element. The principal method of control follow-up will be by program or project.

CORPORATE OBJECTIVES AND THE RESEARCH AND DEVELOPMENT BUDGET

A long-term viewpoint should be taken when planning the R&D budget. Because project or program costs will bulk large, and since such activities cannot effectively be turned on and off, it is rather important that the probable outlay over several years be weighed. It is obvious that the planned R&D activities should be consistent with the long-term corporate purpose or mission. The preferred relationship is illustrated in Figure 17-1. If a corporate objective, for example, is growth in the communications or counter-measure fields, then the research projects undertaken should support and enhance

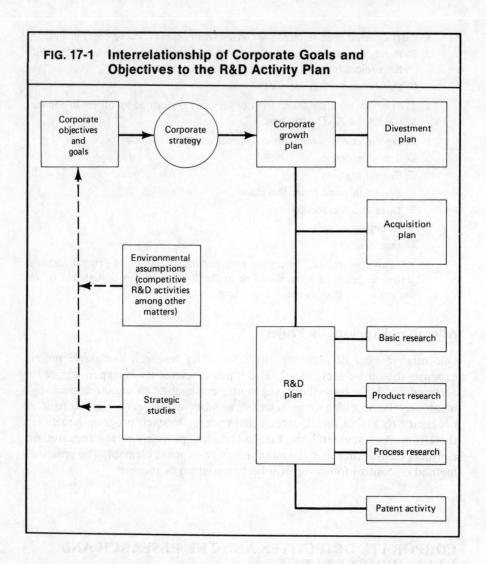

FIG. 17-1 Interrelationship of Corporate Goals and Objectives to the R&D Activity Plan

this objective. If the concern plans on divesting product lines or companies in, for example, the aluminum fabrication business, then it probably makes little economic sense to spend significant sums that would have only a long-run impact on the business prospects.

In summary, if the corporate objective and goal consists of optimizing earnings to the shareholder over a considerable or long-term period of time, as contrasted to maximizing the near-term profits, then the planned R&D budget should reflect such expectations.

OVERALL STEPS IN THE BUDGETING PROCEDURE

With a background as to the scope of R&D activity, its relationship to corporate objectives, and the types of costs that might be incurred, it is now appropriate to discuss the budgetary procedure.

The director of R&D with the assistance of the budget coordinator, usually must give recognition to these steps in planning the budget:

1. Determining the total budget for the planning period, or the planned aggregate expenditures on R&D
2. Establishing departmental budgets
3. Establishing individual project budgets
4. Securing budgetary approval
5. Providing for periodic control reports on commitments and expenditures
6. As applicable, establishing standards and measuring individual functions
7. Providing some periodic evidence as to the effectiveness of research and development

Each, of course, is in fact closely related to the others.

DETERMINING THE TOTAL BUDGET

A basic decision to be made early in the budgeting process is how much, in total, is to be spent on R&D activities. This determination, of course, must be closely related to the number and extent of R&D programs to be undertaken. Why not simply add up the projected cost of the individual programs? The answer is relatively easy. Given the resources — both financial and manpower — the potential programs that might be undertaken by a creative director of R&D is almost limitless. Usually there are always new products or processes to be developed, or improvements to be made in existing ones. Hence, more often than not, it is desirable to set an overall limit on the level of expenditures, giving recognition to the multi-year requirements on some programs.

Constraints

Some of the practical constraints in setting the total amount to be spent include these factors:

- *The financial position of the company.* No matter how worthy the research objectives, the company must be in a position to make the funds available.

- *The amount necessary to make the program effective.* To spend too little may not permit attainment of the desired results.
- *The expansion program.* The future growth plans of the company will influence both the nature and extent of the research program.
- *Competitive activity.* Action of the principal competitors usually will be considered in reviewing any research plans.
- *General economic outlook.* The future prospects, tax burden, and similar factors must be weighed.
- *Availability of manpower with the proper professional background.*

Measurement

With these general considerations in mind, management may select any one of several guideposts to measure the *total* budget:

- A percentage of estimated sales for the next year, or perhaps an average of the next several years
- A percentage of operating profit before research and development expense
- A percentage of net profit
- The expenditures of the preceding year, perhaps adjusted by a flat percentage
- A fixed amount per unit of product sold or estimated to be sold
- A percentage of cash flow for a single year or perhaps the average of several years
- A percentage of investment in capital assets
- The cost of the selected projects and related support activities

To reiterate, an important point to keep in mind is the need of awareness of the longer-term implications of the R&D budget — and not merely a single year.

ESTABLISHMENT OF THE OPERATING BUDGET

The establishment of an overall budget or appropriation merely sets the total limits of expenditure. It becomes necessary to establish (1) the amount for each operating department, which in turn may relate to project costs, and (2) the funds necessary for the supporting services and general administration — the "overhead" or indirect costs.

Indirect Costs

In practice the project budgets may be planned first, and then the required indirect expenses. For ease of discussion, these indirect expenses are reviewed before touching on the project costs.

While project costs, being the direct outlay applicable to specific projects (the "direct labor" and "direct material"), may be controlled by the project leader, it is probably necessary to consider and control these indirect costs on a total requirements basis.

Indirect costs result from the many aids and supporting activities that benefit the overall technical program. Costs may include those related to:

- Departmental administration
- Depreciation of technical facilities and equipment
- Authorship of technical papers
- Preparation of technical proposals
- Library services
- Attendance at technical meetings and seminars

In principle, indirect costs must be held to reasonable *proportions* in relation to the direct costs of the project. Basically, the approach to this expense is similar to that of manufacturing or distribution overhead:

- Definite assignment of responsibility for the budgeted costs
- Establishment of proper amounts, depending on level needed, to support the project activity and direct research effort
- Control by comparison of budget and actual, by responsibility, and by type of expense

Selection of Projects

Project budgets ordinarily will be established after an evaluation of the projects at hand and the work to be done. In this process recognition should be given to the various major groupings of research and development activity; and the segregation of total costs budgeted and expended in each category will have considerable significance as to the direction of the R&D effort. Some illustrative major classifications are as follows:

- Pure, nonprogrammatic, or fundamental research (that which has no immediately commercial value in sight)
- Sales service (projects requested and originated by the sales department)
- Factory service (those projects requested by the factory)

- New product research (on items not in existing lines)
- Product improvement (improvement in the quality and appearance of present products)

The selection of the particular projects to be undertaken during the coming year, or other budget period, is usually first the responsibility of the research director. He probably would meet with his staff and discuss individual ideas proposed for the future program. Several factors would govern the selection, among which might be:

- Anticipated economic gains, perhaps measured by rate of return (discounted cash flow method)
- Availability of qualified personnel
- Prior research by others, either within or without the organization
- Time required for the research
- Relative importance of the subject in relation to present or future plans

The proposed program would be subjected to critical review by management before approval.

In any company with a balanced research program, usually there are more ideas available to exploit through research than there are funds that can be provided. Consequently, it becomes necessary to select certain projects and reject others. In evaluating projects or programs the following observations should be kept in mind:

- Development projects ordinarily should be given a high priority. These are the projects for which successful applications seem most assured. Therefore, in a competitive economy, funds should be allocated initially to such projects, with residual funds, if any, available for exploratory and fundamental research projects.
- The amount to be invested in fundamental research should probably be based on the collective judgment of management and the research director, and not by the financial planners.
- Development projects should be "ranked" or evaluated relative to each other, giving consideration to:
  a. Operating expenses, capital investment, and return, in the light of the best available alternatives and financing;
  b. Time of application, recognizing that the earlier a process or product is used, the greater its value, other things being equal, on a present worth basis; and
  c. Potential licensing income.

Allocation of Funds Among Projects

The question arises not only as to whether or not funds should be spent on a given program, but also what the optimum amount might be. These are finite limits on the degree to which financial measures may be applied in selecting R&D projects, and the extent to which a return on assets test may be used; the intangibles or unknowns are simply too great. There are, however, two quantitative approaches to evaluating potential R&D programs where the financial analyst assisting the director of research might be of some help. These are as follows.

☐ *Models or calculations which measure the expected economic benefits.* Such an approach attempts to quantify the rate of return on the proposed stream of cash outlays, perhaps using the discounted cash flow method.[3]

☐ *Models which index or score selected programs.* Under this approach, each project is scored, according to how it fits certain characteristics. Those projects with the higher scores are selected.[4]

Whether or not such approaches are useful is a matter to be discussed between the financial planner and the research director.

Of course, it would not be prudent to spend significant sums on a development project only to learn the market had disappeared about the time the research was completed; and it would make little business sense to commence a research project if the probable return from the sale of product simply could never approach the gross outlay. In general, the end product of R&D — a product or process — ought to be considered viable only if it

- Provides for recovery of the cost of research,
- Permits recoupment of the cost of working capital and plant investment, and
- Provides an acceptable rate of return on the cash funds required.

Return on Assets. The cost-volume-profit relationship may provide some insight as to the viability of the end product of R&D, albeit with assumptions that are gross estimates.

Assume these facts:

1. Management expects a return of 8 percent on assets employed, after taxes.
2. The expected sales of the newly developed product should approximate $50,000,000.

---

[3] See Chapter 25.

[4] An example of such an approach is published in D. Bruce Merrifield, "How to Select Successful R&D Projects," *Management Review*, Vol. 67, No. 12 (Dec. 1978), pp. 25–39.

3. The expected product gross margin is 20 percent.

4. The required investment, after the research is completed, is as follows:

Working capital	$3,000,000
Plant and equipment	2,000,000
Total	$5,000,000

5. The federal income tax rate is expected to be 40 percent.

The question to be considered, using return on assets as a guide, is, How much R&D (before taxes) can be spent on this product? An indication of the outlay for R&D may be calculated in this manner:

$$ROA = \frac{\text{Net income}}{\text{Total assets}}$$

where:

Net income = Gross margin − R&D − Income tax

Income tax = (Gross margin − R&D) × 40%

Gross margin = Sales × 20%

ROA = 8%

By substitution:

Net income = (Gross margin) − R&D
          − [(Gross margin − R&D) × 40%]

$$ROA = \frac{(\text{Gross margin}) - \text{R\&D} - [(\text{Gross margin} - \text{R\&D}) \times 40\%]}{\text{Total assets}}$$

$$8\% = \frac{(50,000,000 \times 20\%) - \text{R\&D} - [(50,000,000 \times 20\% - \text{R\&D}) \times 40\%]}{5,000,000}$$

Simplify:

$$400 = 10,000 - \text{R\&D} - [(10,000 - \text{R\&D}) \times 40\%]$$
$$-9,600 = -\text{R\&D} - 4,000 + .4 \text{ R\&D}$$
$$.6 \text{ R\&D} = 5,600$$
$$\text{R\&D} = \$9,333,000$$

Proof:

Sales	$50,000,000
Gross margin at 20%	10,000,000
Less research and development	9,333,000
Income before taxes	667,000
Income taxes at 40%	267,000
Net income	400,000
Total assets	$ 5,000,000
ROA ($400,000 ÷ $5,000,000)	8%

Of course, this calculation may be adjusted to an annual basis.

Percentage Return on Net Sales. Sometimes management believes it has a sense of the return on a project needed to be acceptable as judged by the percentage return on net sales.

Assume these facts:

1. The objective is a net return (after taxes) of 10 percent on sales.
2. The expected sales are $40,000,000.
3. The federal income tax rate is estimated to be 40 percent.

How much can be spent on R&D? The estimate can be made in this manner:

$$ROS = \frac{\text{Net income}}{\text{Sales}}$$

where:

Net income = Gross margin − R&D − Income tax

Income tax = (Gross margin − R&D) × 40%

Gross margin = Sales × 20%

ROS = 10%

By substitution:

Net income = (Gross margin) − R&D
− [(Gross margin − R&D) × 40%]

$$ROS = \frac{(\text{Gross margin}) - \text{R\&D} - [(\text{Gross margin} - \text{R\&D}) \times 40\%]}{\text{Sales}}$$

(continued)

$$10\% = \frac{(40,000,000 \times 20\%) - \text{R\&D} - [(40,000,000 \times 20\% - \text{R\&D}) \times 40\%]}{40,000,000}$$

Simplify:

$$40,000,000 = 8,000,000 - \text{R\&D} - [(8,000,000 - \text{R\&D}) \times 40\%]$$
$$-4,000,000 = -\text{R\&D} - 3,200,000 + .4 \text{ R\&D}$$
$$.6 \text{ R\&D} = 800,000$$
$$\text{R\&D} = \underline{1,333,000}$$

Proof:

Sales	$40,000,000
Gross margin (20%)	8,000,000
Less: Research and development expense	1,333,000
Income before taxes	6,667,000
Income taxes at 40%	2,667,000
Net income	$ 4,000,000
ROS ($4,000,000 ÷ $40,000,000)	10%

Of course, the derived answers are rough estimates only.

In addition to the previous kind of analysis, if the assumptions are considered reasonably reliable, the discounted cash flow method of evaluating an investment might be attempted in order to reflect the time value of cash flow.

PRESENTING THE APPROPRIATION REQUEST

Because R&D activities are often so important a factor in company profitability and growth, top management and the board of directors usually pay close attention to the expected program. In fact, frequently the funds to be spent are approved by the board of directors through the mechanics of reviewing an appropriation request and its supporting data.

The director of research makes the board presentation, discussing in some detail each of the major projects. Supporting his request should be an easily understood summary of significant expenses. One type of financial summary is shown in Figure 17-2. The attention of the board and top management is usually focused on the project costs and not on expenditures by types of expenses (e.g., salaries, fringe benefits, and travel expense). A highly summarized appropriation request which, nevertheless, provides estimates of the significant economic factors is illustrated in Figure 17-3.

FIG. 17-2 R&D Budget Summary

THE ELECTRONICS COMPANY
PROPOSED RESEARCH AND DEVELOPMENT BUDGET SUMMARY
For the year ending December 31, 19XX

Budget	Required Staff Additions (Professional)	Proposed for 19XX		Estimated for Present Year
		Total Manhours	Cost (in $000)	Cost (in $000)
PROJECT				
Research				
Laser "4"	8	42,000	$ 372	$ 109
Electronic "5"	12	82,000	902	404
Hydro "A"	2	14,000	140	10
Completed projects	—		—	612
Total research	22	138,000	$ 1,414	$1,145
Development				
Traveling tubes	5	112,000	$ 1,455	$ 964
Electrode modes	24	246,000	3,198	3,050
Electronic gauge	17	81,000	990	1,710
Microwave tester	8	42,000	525	46
Total development	54	481,000	$ 6,168	$5,770
Total project budgets	76	619,000	$ 7,582	$6,915
ADMINISTRATIVE				
General			$ 850	$ 802
Patent efforts			970	1,016
Library			420	401
Research associates			312	409
Total administrative			$ 2,552	$2,628
Grand Total			$10,134	$9,543
Percentage net income — 3-year average			1.1%	1.0%
Percentage net sales — 5-year average			4.5	4.4

FIG. 17-3   Appropriation Request for R&D Budget

A.R. No. _____

THE ELECTRONICS COMPANY

APPROPRIATION REQUEST
Research and Development Department
Year _____

Brief description of major efforts and expected results:

Summary of estimated costs and related data
  Research and development professional manhours   _____

  Total project costs $ _____
    Research
    Development
    Pilot plant
      Total $ _____
  Applicable administrative and general charges   _____

  Total proposed budget   ========

For development projects
  Expected sales — Year 1 $ _____
                        2
                        3
                        4
                        5
      Total   _____
  Estimated gross margin — 5 years $ _____

  Total development expense _ Years $ _____

  Estimated working capital requirements $ _____
  Estimated plant and equipment   _____

      Total capital requirements $ _____

  Estimated return on assets (DCF)   _____ %

                                                          Date

Originated by _____   _____
Approved by
  Director of Research _____   _____
  VP Sales _____   _____
  Controller _____   _____
  Chief Executive Officer _____   _____
  Board of Directors, by _____   _____

CONTROL REPORTS

Once the budget is approved and research efforts are under way, the research director has the task of measuring actual costs, and commitments in some instances, to assure that total outlays are held within budget. A key figure, of course, is manhours expended and needed to complete the task. By the same token, all expenditures and commitments need to be monitored to keep within budget limitations. This report should be the responsibility of the research director's financial assistant, working with the project managers and department heads. A suggested form of report, which indicates the cost to complete as planned for the year, is illustrated in Figure 17-4. While the emphasis may be on project costs, a supplemental report comparing actual and budgeted expenses by department is presented in Figure 17-5. In this organization, the department manager is held accountable for total departmental costs, irrespective of the project worked on. Another report, by type of expense, as illustrated in Figure 17-6, may be helpful in insuring that given types of expense do not get out of line (e.g., consulting fees or travel expenses). While the example shows expenses slightly within budget, in circumstances where expenditures are substantially over budget, the latter reports will indicate what departments and what types of expense were significantly over plan. Of course, each department manager would receive a departmental budget similar to the one illustrated in Figure 17-6, which would pinpoint the over-budget area. Further, such reports by department would be supported by a computer run identifying actual expenditures transaction by transaction. Locating the cause of the over-budget condition would be relatively easy.

CONTROL BY PERFORMANCE STANDARDS

Although budgetary control is a necessary and important criterion in judging the efficiency of research, it cannot and should not be the sole criterion. It is entirely possible to waste funds or to use them inefficiently and still remain within the limits imposed on expenditures. What is needed, therefore, are performance standards. It is true that R&D work is varied and sometimes difficult to predict, but in many instances performance standards have been used to good advantage. These standards do not serve as a substitute for the watchful eye and necessary guidance of the research supervisors, but they can be of assistance in evaluating the quantitative aspects of some phases of the work. Where the activities are numerous, the benefit of close personal supervision by the higher echelon is lost, but reports on performance can give some indication as to effectiveness.

Standards based on performance of other similar activities can be de-

FIG. 17-4 R&D Project Budget Report

THE PLASTIC MANUFACTURING COMPANY

SUMMARY PROJECT STATUS REPORT

For the Month Ended October 31, 19XX

Project	Project No.	Month Manhours	Month Salaries and Wages	Month Other Expense	Month Total	Cumulative to Date Manhours	Cumulative to Date Amount	Purchase Order Commitments	Estimated Cost to Complete Manhours	Estimated Cost to Complete Amount	Indicated Total Cost	Project Budget	Indicated Cost (Over) or Under Budget
New Product Research													
Urea filler	1152	1,223	$ 3,790	$ 2,319	$ 6,109	3,994	$32,110	$ 1,519	500	$ 1,200	$ 34,829	$ 34,500	($ 329)
Automobile wax	1154	173	385	475	860	346	1,634	222	—	—	1,856	1,900	44
Phenolic resin	1159	812	3,420	820	4,240	1,042	6,321	8,301	400	1,200	15,822	16,000	178
Alkyl resin	1160	76	232	120	352	76	352	—	350	1,000	1,352	1,500	148
Total		2,284	$ 7,827	$ 3,734	$11,561	5,458	$40,417	$10,042	1,250	$ 3,400	$ 53,859	$ 53,900	$ 41
Product Improvement													
Wet strength resins	1123	317	$ 702	$ 610	$ 1,312	892	$ 5,420	$ —	300	$ 1,300	$ 6,720	$ 6,800	$ 80
Brightness — pulp	1124	214	427	410	837	612	3,241	160	—	500	3,901	4,000	99
High quality rayon	1125	926	2,980	2,119	5,099	2,107	12,342	920	800	5,200	18,462	18,000	(462)
Cure binder — adhesion	1126	173	350	722	1,072	173	1,072	—	5,000	22,000	23,072	23,000	(72)
Total		1,630	$ 4,459	$ 3,861	$ 8,320	3,784	$22,075	$ 1,080	6,200	$29,000	$ 52,155	$ 51,800	($ 355)
Sales Service													
Paint	1129	173	$ 375	$ 10	$ 385	185	$ 397	$ —	—	$ —	$ 397	$ 1,000	$ 603
Molding compound	1130	865	2,310	2,460	4,770	2,540	16,310	2,400	2,000	7,100	25,810	30,000	4,190
Total		1,038	$ 2,685	$ 2,470	$ 5,155	2,725	$16,707	$ 2,400	2,000	$ 7,100	$ 26,207	$ 31,000	$4,793
Fundamental Research													
Silicone resins	1127	223	$ 415	$ 375	$ 790	315	$ 875	$ —	200	$ 600	$ 1,475	$ 1,500	$ 25
Electronic appliances	1128	519	1,350	727	2,077	921	3,760	—	50	150	3,910	5,000	1,090
Total		742	$ 1,765	$ 1,102	$ 2,867	1,236	$ 4,635	$ —	250	$ 750	$ 5,385	$ 6,500	$1,115
Total Research and Development		5,694	$16,736	$11,167	$27,903	13,203	$83,834	$13,522	9,700	$40,250	$137,606	$143,200	$5,594

FIG. 17-5 Actual and Budgeted R&D Expense by Department

THE JONES COMPANY

TECHNICAL EXPENSES BY DEPARTMENT

For Month Ended October 31, 19XX

(dollars in thousands)

Department Item	Current Month			Year-to-Date		
	Budget	Actual	(Over)/ Under Budget	Budget	Actual	(Over)/ Under Budget
Research						
Synthetics	$ 107	$ 87	$20	$ 860	$ 724	$136
Aluminum	82	82	—	810	807	3
Rubber	12	11	1	100	100	—
Total	$ 201	$ 180	$21	$ 1,770	$ 1,631	$139
Development						
Transportation	$ 601	$ 607	($ 6)	$ 5,840	$ 5,862	($ 22)
Testing	47	46	1	450	446	4
Agricultural	802	797	5	7,890	7,870	20
Military	97	99	(2)	930	927	3
Total	$1,547	$1,549	($ 2)	$15,110	$15,105	$ 5
Other						
Pilot Plant	$ 106	$ 105	$ 1	$ 99	$ 99	—
Library	20	20	—	200	196	$ 4
Patents	41	35	3	408	370	38
General administrative	62	62	(2)	619	626	(7)
Total	$ 229	$ 227	$ 2	$ 1,326	$ 1,291	$ 35
Grand Total	$1,977	$1,956	$21	$18,206	$18,027	$179
Percent (Over)/Under Budget						.98%

Date: _____

FIG. 17-6   Actual and Budget Expense by Type of Expense

THE JONES COMPANY

TECHNICAL EXPENSES SUMMARY BY TYPE OF EXPENSE

For the Month Ended October 31, 19XX

(dollars in thousands)

Items	Current Month			Year-to-Date		
	Budget	Actual	(Over)/ Under Budget	Budget	Actual	(Over)/ Under Budget
Controllable						
Salaries and wages	$1,020	$1,017	$ 3	$ 9,870	$ 9,840	$ 30
Fringe benefits	506	504	2	4,935	4,920	15
Contracted services	89	69	20	910	906	4
Consulting fees	107	117	(10)	500	425	75
Travel expenses	42	40	2	370	390	(20)
Repairs	10	10	—	50	40	10
Supplies	27	29	(2)	180	157	23
Legal	8	7	1	90	87	3
Dues and subscriptions	14	15	(1)	30	27	3
All other	34	28	6	61	25	36
Total	$1,857	$1,836	$21	$16,996	$16,817	$179
Noncontrollable						
Depreciation	$ 10	$ 10	—	$ 100	$ 100	—
Corporate office allocation	110	110	—	1,110	1,110	—
Total	$ 120	$ 120	—	$ 1,210	$ 1,210	—
Grand Total	$1,977	$1,956	$21	$18,206	$18,027	$179

Date: _____

vised. The ingenuity and guidance of the research staff must be used in gathering the data and selecting bases for measurement and the functions to be measured. It is a joint project for both the accountant and the research technician.

Some applications of performance standards are:

- Number of requisitions filled (laboratory supply room)
- Cost per manhour of supplies

- Cost per manhour of total research expense
- Number of tests per month
- Number of formulas developed per man-week
- Number of pages of patent applications written per man-day
- Estimated manhours for function (overall project or part thereof; similar to estimating maintenance or other job orders)
- Cost per patent application
- Pounds of production per manhour (pilot plant)
- Cost per operating hour

OTHER METHODS TO EVALUATE THE EFFECTIVENESS OF RESEARCH

Another question to be answered by management is, Is the research effective? This does not relate to under-budget or over-budget results, or to the efficiency with which segments of the activity seem to be conducted; it relates to the question, What does research do for the company? Is it worthwhile? Does it pay off? Does the long-term benefit from R&D exceed the cost? Is the company earning an acceptable return on the effort?

There is no easy way to measure research effectiveness because many of the factors to be considered are subjective. In the experience of the author, no single method of evaluation has been sufficient; however, to the extent that some measures are applied, these might be considered:

- Evaluation of individual projects as compared to company objectives
- A comparison of economic (or other) results achieved with those originally estimated
- Even though specific net income figures may not be derived, an evaluation or measure of how the decisions or fruits of research and development have been utilized by the company

An approach to estimated net income or return on asset objectives has been reviewed. Aside from this approach, other attempts at measurement that have been made are briefly described below.

Nonprogrammatic Research

For basic, pure, or "nonprogrammatic" research, where no direct objective is evident, measurement is difficult. At best, in some cases subjective values have been assigned to certain qualities, such as the originality of the idea, and a relative value has been determined.

Generally speaking, however, R&D activity is expected to result in:

- A less expensive manufacturing process,
- An improved product, or
- A new product

As projects enter the pilot plant and development stage, it becomes easier to estimate probable costs and return, very often by drawing on the knowledge of the marketing and manufacturing executives. The problem is to value these results and compare them with the cost. The approach can take one of two avenues: The research expense can be compared with the *total* estimated savings or profits, or the expense may be compared against a *standard allowance,* perhaps expressed as a percentage of net sales. Obviously, not every research project undertaken can be expected to show a profit; but over a period of time management can expect a rather high batting average.

New Process or Improved Product

If the fruit of research and development is a new process, the calculation of savings is relatively easy. The cost of the new process is compared with the old, including amortization of obsolete equipment, for an arbitrary number of years or for the life of the process.

Some firms have rules of thumb which, for example, stipulate that new equipment or other expenditures must pay for themselves in two years. If an "index of return" is used, then the measuring stick, which might be 3 percent of net sales, can be applied against the value of all sales for the year or years.

Where an improved product is developed, the worth of R&D is more difficult to measure. Basically, of course, the yardstick is the net profit on the sales secured because of the improvement as compared with the research cost. Or it may be the normally expected research expense (e.g., 3 percent of net sales) on the sales resulting from the improved product as compared with actual expense. If the sales manager cannot estimate this volume realistically, then arbitrary decisions must be made, such as an equivalent of one year's sales. Finally, if a new product is developed, the measure may be the normal net profit over a period of years, or as an index, the normally expected research expense on this sales volume, expressed as a percentage of sales.

A comparative statement incorporating the above suggestions might appear as follows (in thousands of dollars):

Product	Cost Savings or Net Profit (Three Years)	Standard Research Allowance (3% of Net Sales)	Actual Research Expense	Gain or (Loss)
New Soapsaver	$ 3,540	$1,420	$1,560	($ 140)
New Allergon Process	12,400	5,400	1,100	4,300
New Quickmold	8,590	2,140	1,020	1,120
Improved Paintsaver	6,400	840	2,800	(1,960)
Total	$30,930	$9,800	$6,480	$3,320

Common Subjective Indices

In numerous scientific organizations, the research management has wrestled with other indices or rules of thumb in an attempt to evaluate research projects individually or to judge the entire R&D activity. Most of these incorporate subjective or experience factor cutoff points to determine the effectiveness of the activity. Examples of other indices include:

1. *Index of return on R&D expenditures:*

$$\frac{\text{Net income}}{15 \ (\text{R\&D costs})}$$

In this application, the expected net income from the resulting products during their economic lifetime is expected to be at least 15 times the research and development expense.

2. *Index of dollar volume:*

$$\frac{\text{Additional revenue}}{\text{Total revenue}/20}$$

In this test, the R&D project must result in additional annual sales of at least 5 percent.

3. *Index of market share:*

$$\frac{\text{Additional sales}}{\text{Available market}/2}$$

By this measurement, in this particular company a project is considered satisfactory only if one half of the available market is captured.

Another acceptable basis of measuring return on research related to new products would be the discounted cash flow method.

As a general comment, a periodic follow-up comparison of expected savings of earnings as shown on the authorization request should be made with actual realization. Among other advantages, it offers the benefit of keeping estimated earnings more reasonable.

Ultimately, the benefits of R&D will flow from the quality of the decisions made and not from the amount of money spent.

Sound planning and control will involve, among other things, proper follow-up on reviewing such matters as:

- Actual return on asset as compared with estimate
- Reasonableness of project cost and time estimates

But the basic ingredient to the best results will include:

- An environment which permits a search for the greatest opportunities for profitable growth
- Periodic review of the plans and projects to weed out the unproductive or unpromising projects and emphasize the more fruitful ones
- A rather full and free exchange of ideas between research personnel and top management as well as sales and manufacturing management

18

General and Administrative and Other Expenses

FUNCTIONS INVOLVED

The budget for general and administrative expense (G&A expense) relates primarily to the expense of the various top management functions — key activities that determine the company's mission and basic course of action, including overall policy determination, planning, organizing, and control. General administrative activity may include other functions that are not strictly administrative, since they are general in nature and closely related to the functioning of the enterprise as a whole. Departments whose functions involved in a typical business organization may be included as G&A expense are:

- ☐ Office of the chairman of the board
- ☐ Office of the president
- ☐ Financial department:
  - Office of the chief financial officer
  - Treasurer's department:
    - a. Office of the treasurer
    - b. Cash administration
    - c. Retirement fund administration
    - d. Risk management (insurance)
  - Controller's department:
    - a. Office of the controller
    - b. Accounting
    - c. Financial analysis
    - d. Financial planning and control
    - e. Taxes
    - f. Systems and procedures
  - Office of the chief internal auditor
- ☐ Legal department:
  - Office of vice-president — Legal
  - Corporate secretary
  - Litigation
  - Securities and Exchange Commission matters
  - Patents and trademarks

☐ Corporate policy direction function (in a decentralized structure):
- Manufacturing
- Industrial relations
- Public relations
- Marketing
- Strategic planning

It is obvious that the budgets for the chairman of the board and the president should be considered as general and administrative expenses. These offices are concerned with the tasks of determining the specific objectives as well as the overall direction of the enterprise. They are responsible for establishing goals and objectives, allocating resources, and, generally, directing the current operations.

The financial vice-president has overall responsibility for financial policies and procedures, securing necessary funds, making temporary investments, guiding accounting and financial planning activities, ensuring the existence of an adequate system of internal controls, and properly handling insurance and tax matters — all through an appropriate organization, as previously outlined. These activities have to do with the financial well-being of the entire corporation, and generally the costs would be included in the G&A expense category.

Similar comments could be made about the legal department. This organization is responsible for the legal well-being of the corporation: ensuring compliance with applicable laws, making the necessary legal reports and filings, and so forth. It also provides legal counsel across the board to all levels of management. In carrying out these broad legal responsibilities, the costs of the function are included as general and administrative expense.

The preceding are typical functions considered as G&A expenses for most companies. In addition, some businesses have policy-making responsibilities at the top management level. These functions provide overall policy direction in such areas as manufacturing, industrial relations, public relations, marketing, and strategic planning. In these instances, G&A expenses will include the costs relative to these efforts.

In some companies, certain types of services are performed more economically on a centralized basis. These types of costs, however, should not be considered as G&A expenses. The costs should be allocated or charged to the specific business unit that benefits from the service.

TYPES OF EXPENSES

General and administrative expenses are made up of the same types of costs that may be found in a typical manufacturing or marketing operation. Of course, there are also certain types of expenses that are unique to the company as a whole. The usual departmental operating expenses would include:

- Salaries and wages
- Fringe benefits
- Travel
- Dues and subscriptions
- Communications (telephone)
- Depreciation
- Rent
- Training and education
- Repairs and maintenance
- Services
- Utilities
- Computer expenses
- Allocated expenses

In addition to the ordinary or typical expenses incident to the direction of an administrative function, the budget may include expenses not found in the typical operating department. Such expenses may include:

- Executive incentive payments
- Contributions
- Legal fees
- Corporate expenses (registration fees)
- Taxes
- Excess facilities costs
- Gain or loss on disposal of capital assets
- Provision for doubtful accounts
- Cash discounts
- Other income and expense
- Research

The title of this chapter includes "Other Expenses." These are expenses of a nonoperating nature, by some definitions, although the line of demarcation is hazy. Often they are identified separately in the statement of income and expense. Included would be:

- Interest expense
- Amortization of bond discount
- Nonrecurring gains and losses

In some instances, these expenses are included as part of the financial department expenses for budgetary control purposes.

GENERAL APPROACH TO CONTROL OF G&A EXPENSES

Experience shows that there may be a certain laxness in the control of G&A expenses. This results in part from the fact that some of the expenses are unique and are somewhat unpredictable. It makes the budgeting process more difficult and subject to greater variances. It also results from failure to assign the responsibility for control of each cost to a specific executive. There are some types of G&A expenses that are difficult to determine in advance. However, with responsibility for incurrence of cost assigned to a specific executive, some level of expense can be reasonably projected. Cost history, trends, comparisons, or some other factors can be used to develop the most appropriate basis for the budget.

At the outset, it should be recognized that given the involvement with broad policy matters and other longer-term considerations, many of the expenses will not be — and indeed should not be — immediately responsive to changes in sales or manufacturing activity levels. A larger proportion of the expenses will be fixed in nature: fixed at certain levels by management until circumstances dictate otherwise. However, these costs must be controlled or held within reasonable bounds over the longer term.

With inadequate budget controls on G&A expenses, excessive expenditures result. In today's complex business environment, there is an ever-increasing need to plan and control these expenses. In developing the budget, management must be aware of these significant expenditures, use the appropriate budgeting technique, and assign responsibility for each kind of expense to a specific executive.

There are many prerequisites and considerations essential to an acceptable budgeting and control system:

1. An intelligent classification of accounts, which sets forth the expenses in necessary detail.
2. Specific assignment of control responsibility to an individual.
3. A separation of expenses into their fixed and variable components, with a suitable unit of variability, where practical, or, in some instances, use of other budgetary techniques, such as a program approach.
4. A reporting system that provides feedback to management on all variances, with proper interpretation, for appropriate corrective action.

Top management must direct sufficient attention to the planning and control of G&A expenses to ensure that the amount of these types of expenses is appropriate for the level of expected business. In many cases, the expenses can be related to some level of activity such as sales dollars, production manhours, number of employees, net income, number of business units, or a combination of activities. Some of the expenses may be fixed in nature, such as those whose level is determined by the board of directors. In those cases, the task is to provide data and information so that reasonable levels of expense are budgeted and approved by the appropriate management. Of course, the expenditures must be controlled within the authorized limits. When such expenses are determined by the executive office, the problem is to ensure that the facts are developed and presented to the cognizant executives so as to arrive at a prudent level of expense.

DISCUSSION OF SELECTED "UNIQUE" EXPENSES

The techniques used to develop budgets for G&A expenses are similar to those used for budgeting other operating expenses in business. In most cases, some relationship to overall activity, such as production or sales volume, exists. However, some of the "unique" expenses present special problems.

Compensation of Officers and Directors

The compensation of officers and directors consists of salaries, incentive payments, stock bonus awards, and perquisites. These payments are usually determined on a yearly basis in advance and may be subject to a written agreement between the executive and the company. There are no special difficulties of budgeting or control. Usually, such arrangements are approved by the board of directors. Bonus and incentive payments are usually governed by such factors as net income, growth in earnings per share, increase in sales volume, or some other specific objective. The projected amounts can be easily estimated and budgeted by using the relevant factors. Top executives may have perquisites, which may be set forth in an agreement or a policy statement. For example, certain executives may be furnished with company automobiles, country club memberships, reimbursement for spouses' travel, extra insurance, and tax and financial planning services. These types of expenses also can be easily estimated and budgeted in accordance with the corporate policy.

General and Administrative Salaries

The compensation of functional executives and their staffs should be budgeted with their respective departments. Again, no particular budgeting problem should arise. The industrial relations department can provide a list of all employees by department. Any additional or new hires for the year should be listed with full justification and salary rate. Any special salary arrangements should be indicated. The department budget should include a factor for anticipated salary increases, including cost-of-living adjustments, if applicable. Vacation pay and accrual must be considered and recognized in the budgeting process.

Fringe Benefits and Taxes

Factors should be developed for the various fringe benefit programs and taxes related to salaries and wages. As these types of costs are an increasing share of G&A expense, it is important that they be recognized as separate items of expense and be budgeted by department. When salaries and wages are controlled, the fringe benefit costs should follow. The rates can be ascertained from the specific retirement, savings, or benefit programs. In the case of taxes, the rates can be determined from the applicable regulations. The planning budget can then be established by applying the rates of the budgeted salaries. Obviously, the control of payroll taxes must be effected through the control of general and administrative salaries.

Charitable Contributions, Dues, and Subscriptions

Companies have a civic responsibility to contribute to various charitable institutions, civic undertakings, aid to higher education, and similar activities. A policy should be established as to the types of organizations or specific organizations to which contributions will be made. In some concerns, such a list, including amounts, is approved by the board of directors as a special budget item. The responsibility to develop the list, obtain approval, and make the payments should be assigned to a specific executive. It may be appropriate to establish some guidelines for certain charitable organizations in total (so much per employee). Another guideline may be a percentage of net income. The budget would be prepared within the constraints of the policy.

Other Items of Income and Expense

Most concerns recognize all items of activity and establish a budget responsibility to provide for adequate control. Other income items include dividends, interest, royalties, rent, or any type of return on investments. These can usually be estimated for the budget period based on the factors involved in the investment. Purchase discounts may also be included here, but usually would be included in the purchases budget. Other expense items should also be budgeted, even if the estimate does not have much of a factual basis. Responsibility should be assigned for every item of expense. For example, bad-debt expense should be assigned to the executive responsible for collections. The amount can be reasonably estimated based on past experience, as a percentage of sales. Provision must also be made in the budget for estimated losses or gains on sale or disposal of capital assets or other investments.

Interest Expense

The interest expense budget can be readily determined from the cash flow analysis and the level of projected borrowings for the budget period. The financial budget or plan should indicate the source of borrowings and the expected interest rate to be applied to each type of borrowing.

Taxes

Taxes have become one of the most significant items of expense in carrying on a business. Each tax must be considered, estimated, and budgeted for each department responsible, and controlled in total. It is important that the company's tax executive be involved in reviewing each of the budgets for taxes. The tax department should provide guidelines that can be considered in preparing the respective tax estimates. These guidelines should be consistent with the tax planning, particularly as they relate to investment tax credits, foreign tax credits, utilization of net operating losses, and other tax credits and factors.

Excess Facility Costs

The cost of carrying excess or idle facilities may be considered as an item of G&A expense. Responsibility should be assigned for the disposal of excess production capacity or the determination for proper utilization. The carrying costs of insurance, depreciation, maintenance, taxes, and so forth can be significant. A budget should be established for all costs related to retaining used production capacity. Executive management should review critically such budgets to ensure that appropriate decisions are being made and that timely action is taken.

Corporate Expenses

There are various types of corporate expense that must be estimated by the executives assigned responsibility for the cost. Such expenses include professional fees for auditors, lawyers, engineers, economists, and consultants; state and federal capital stock and franchise taxes; stock exchange fees; and business registration and qualification fees and taxes. All of these expenses are easily estimated and a reasonable budget can be established. The control of these expenses is largely a matter of direct executive responsibility.

THE G&A BUDGET ILLUSTRATED

In developing a total budget for general and administrative expenses, management should provide each department head with some general guidelines to be used in preparing each budget. These guidelines should include relevant factors such as estimated sales volume, head count (by department), tax rates, estimated rate for salary increases (if applicable), cost-of-living adjustment factors, expected goals for each department, and any special issues to be considered.

Each department head should participate in the development of his budget. The amounts estimated by type of expense reflect the anticipated level of effort for the department for the budget period. The budget should be reviewed and agreed to by the next higher level executive before submission to the appropriate financial executive for consolidation. When the budget for G&A expenses has been consolidated it should be reviewed and analyzed by the financial executive or budget coordinator. Comments and supporting data should be submitted to the chief executive officer as part of the budget package.

In presenting the budget for executive management approval, comparative information should be provided to permit an intelligent evaluation. Additional analytical data may also be useful in arriving at the appropriate budget levels. Figure 18-1 compares the proposed G&A expense budget to the prior year's expenses by functional responsibility. This is a type of fixed budget often used by larger companies.

Of course, the budget should be detailed by organizational unit within the functional group. For example, Figure 18-2 details the proposed finance department budget by unit. This in turn is supported by an analysis, account by account, as to the reason for the requested increase.

In determining the aggregate amount for the budget of G&A expenses, there are several yardsticks that may be considered, such as:

- Historical relationship to sales
- Comparison to prior years and growth of the company

FIG. 18-1 Summary — General and Administrative Budget

GENERAL AND ADMINISTRATIVE BUDGET FOR 19XX

FUNCTIONAL GROUP SUMMARY

(thousands of dollars)

Group	Prior Year				Proposed Budget		
	Budget	Actual	Over/(Under) Budget Amount	Percentage	Request	Increase/(Decrease) From Prior Year Budget Amount	Percentage
Executive office	$ 8,200	$ 7,700	($ 500)	(6%)	$ 8,500	$ 300	4%
Legal department	3,400	3,300	(100)	(3)	3,500	100	3
Administration and services	5,800	6,200	400	7	7,600	1,800	24
Corporate planning	500	600	100	20	700	200	29
Finance	5,300	4,700	(600)	(11)	5,200	(100)	(2)
Industrial relations	2,800	3,100	300	11	3,700	900	24
Public relations and advertising	3,600	3,400	(200)	6	3,500	(100)	(3)
International marketing	4,900	4,700	(200)	(4)	5,100	200	4
Domestic marketing and technology	5,700	5,400	(300)	(5)	5,300	(400)	(8)
Total	$40,200	$39,100	($1,100)	(3%)	$43,100	$2,900	7%

FIG. 18-2 Finance Department — Budget Summary

GENERAL AND ADMINISTRATIVE BUDGET FOR 19XX

FINANCE DEPARTMENT SUMMARY

(thousands of dollars)

Unit	Prior Year				Proposed Budget		
			Over/(Under) Budget			Increase/(Decrease) From Prior Year Budget	
	Budget	Actual	Amount	Percentage	Request	Amount	Percentage
Vice-president	$ 375	$ 360	($ 15)	(4%)	$ 375	—	—
Controller	1,600	1,260	(340)	(21)	1,500	($100)	(7%)
Treasurer	1,160	940	(220)	(19)	980	(180)	(18)
Tax department	825	850	25	3	910	85	9
Risk management	240	230	(10)	(4)	270	30	11
Internal audit	925	825	(100)	(11)	965	40	4
Business analysis	175	235	60	34	200	25	13
Total	$5,300	$4,700	($600)	(11%)	$5,200	($100)	(2%)

FIG. 18-3   Comparative Analysis Head-Count — General and Administrative Budget

GENERAL AND ADMINISTRATIVE BUDGET FOR 19XX

COMPARATIVE ANALYSIS — HEAD-COUNT

Function	Prior Year				Proposed Budget		
	Budget	Actual	Over/(Under) Budget Number	Percentage	Request	Increase/(Decrease) From Prior Year Budget Number	Percentage
Executive office	37	37	—	—	42	5	14%
Legal department	42	37	(5)	(12%)	34	(8)	(19)
Administration and services	34	37	3	9	37	3	9
Corporate planning	4	4	—	—	5	1	25
Finance	80	77	(3)	(4)	80	—	—
Industrial relations	36	37	1	3	39	3	8
Public relations and advertising	23	23	—	—	26	3	13
International marketing	28	25	(3)	(11)	27	(1)	(4)
Domestic marketing and technology	33	37	4	12	39	6	18
Total	317	314	(3)	(1%)	329	12	4%

- Comparison to other companies and to the industry as a whole.
- Relationship to income before G&A expenses.
- Head-count of general and administrative personnel compared to total head-count for the company.
- Annual compound rate of growth in each of the functions.

In reviewing the proposed budget, a comparative analysis of head-count provides additional insight into the variances, as is illustrated in Figure 18-3.

In examining and evaluating the proposed budget, a comparative analysis of the detail elements of expense may be considered. Figure 18-4 presents an analysis of the entire G&A expense by type of expense. The basic comparison of the proposed budget is with *both* the actual expenses of the prior year and the budget for the prior year. It provides a comparison of actual performance against the requested budget, and identifies the areas of most rapid growth. Schedules of this type are prepared for each department to assist in screening out unnecessary expenses.

APPLICATION OF THE FLEXIBLE BUDGET — SELECTED FINANCIAL DIVISION DEPARTMENT EXPENSES

Clearly, certain of the costs or expenses under the category of G&A can be estimated, based on known factors or contracts, such as interest expense, taxes, and excess facility costs. Also, it is evident that a large segment is not subject to immediate change by reason of month-to-month variations in sales or production, since it deals with policy matters. However, this segment must bear some relationship to sales or income over a longer period; for example, two or three years. An example is salaries paid to officers and directors. Yet, there will be some areas involving mass handling of paperwork that *should* respond to changes in activity. Handling payroll activities is an example — where many of the costs should relate to the size of the payroll. Where it seems there should be a change in expenses by reason of volume, the flexible budget approach should be considered.

If the company is large enough, there will be several departments within the financial division, whose managers can be held responsible for cost control on a fixed and variable basis. Budgets should be prepared in detail for each activity whose head is assigned the authority and responsibility to keep expenses within established budget limits. Some of the departments that may be logical budgetary control units are:

- Vice-president–Finance
- Treasurer
- Controller's office
- General accounting

FIG. 18-4 Expense Summary — General and Administrative Budget

GENERAL AND ADMINISTRATIVE BUDGET FOR 19XX

EXPENSE SUMMARY
(thousands of dollars)

Item of Expense	Prior Year				Proposed Budget		
	Budget	Actual	Over/(Under) Budget Amount	Over/(Under) Budget Percentage	Request	Increase/(Decrease) From Prior Year Budget Amount	Increase/(Decrease) From Prior Year Budget Percentage
Salaries	$12,160	$11,800	($ 360)	(3%)	$14,300	$2,140	18%
Retirement costs	2,720	2,610	(110)	(4)	3,200	480	18
Savings plan	340	330	(10)	(3)	400	60	18
Employee insurance	1,530	1,490	(40)	(3)	1,800	270	18
Payroll taxes	800	780	(20)	(3)	940	140	18
Advertising	2,330	2,120	(210)	(9)	2,070	(260)	(11)
Business conferences	200	180	(20)	(10)	200		
Corporate expenses	850	890	40	5	950	100	12
Communications	1,200	980	(220)	(18)	1,100	(100)	(8)
Computer	2,350	2,440	90	5	2,470	120	5
Contributions	2,150	1,900	(250)	(12)	1,970	(180)	(8)
Depreciation	1,140	1,190	50	4	1,230	90	8
Dues and memberships	420	440	20	5	450	30	7
Employee relations	180	210	30	17	190	10	6
Entertainment	70	90	20	29	80	10	14
Insurance — General	420	460	40	10	440	20	5
Miscellaneous	100	120	20	20	110	10	10
Patent expense	10	10	—		10		
Postage	130	160	30	23	150	20	15
Professional services	3,480	3,340	(140)	(4)	3,280	(200)	(6)
Rent	2,480	2,520	40	2	2,670	190	8
Repairs and maintenance	550	540	(10)	(2)	600	50	9
Services purchased	470	490	20	4	520	50	11
Subscriptions and books	110	110	—		130	20	2
Supplies	1,450	1,460	10	1	1,510	60	4
Taxes, licenses	240	250	10	4	270	30	13
Travel	2,320	2,180	(140)	(6)	2,060	(260)	(11)
Total	$40,200	$39,100	($1,100)	(3%)	$43,100	$2,900	7%

- Cost accounting
- Internal auditing
- Tax
- Budgets and standards
- Standards
- Cash management

- Insurance
- Office administration
- Payroll
- Data processing
- Special analysis

Each department head should be given a voice in setting his budget.

Practical experience will indicate that accounting costs are not all fixed, any more than are purchasing costs or industrial relations costs. However, a relatively larger portion may be fixed. Some simple variable factors should be found that will serve to indicate the expense justified at each level of activity. Thus, standard or actual labor hours in the factory may be used in the payroll department. At any given time, the total budget allowance would be the fixed expense plus an amount per standard labor hour. Other factors of variability might be dollar sales volume, units of sale, or number of transactions.

The budget department should prepare the same reports on the accounting activities as it does on that of others in order that management may be informed of the budget performance. An example of a plant controller's budget report is shown in Figure 18-5. In this case a base allowance has been established to which is added a fluctuating allowance depending on factory productivity. For this month, the added allowance was based on 82.699 thousand standard manhours. In the following month, the additional allowance might be restricted to only 68 units. Such a method of granting allowances does relate accounting costs to the income-producing factor — standard labor hours.

Figure 18-5 also illustrates a practice of assigning to a specific executive the responsibility for expense control of items other than his own departmental expenses. In this case, office supplies, postage, and so forth were not departmentalized in the accounts and the controller was assigned the task of keeping them in line.

CONTROL OF G&A EXPENSES

The control of G&A expenses is handled on the same basis as those of other operating departments, although the share of fixed expenses may be somewhat higher.

Whether on a fixed-type budget, as reviewed earlier, or on a flexible budget, comparisons should be made of actual expenses with the allowed budget, and corrective action taken. A control report using the flexible budget approach is illustrated in Figure 18-5.

FIG. 18-5 Departmental Budget Report — Accounting

GENERAL MANUFACTURING CORPORATION

DEPARTMENTAL BUDGET REPORT

Dept. 9 Accounting
Dept. Head J. Jones

Month March, 19
Units 82.699 Base 6

| Classification | Amount (in dollars) | | Over or under | | Percent realization | | |
| | Allowed | Actual | Current month | Year to date | Current month | Moving average | |
						Previous	Current
DIRECT LABOR							
None							
TOTAL DIRECT LABOR	–	–	–	–	–	–	–
INDIRECT SALARIES AND WAGES							
601 Supervisory salaries		2110					
605 Other salaries		2120					
606 Indirect wages		6214					
607 Janitors and sweepers							
608 Trainees salaries and wages							
609 Idle time							
612 Vacations and holidays		285					
614-16 Overtime premium		26					
Subtotal (1)	10548	10755	(207)	1682	98.1		
OTHER DEPARTMENTALIZED EXPENSES							
618 Special printed forms		524					
619 Travel expense		1					
621 Telephone		124					
622 Books, periodicals, & information services							
623 Memberships							
624 Consultants' fees							
623 Operating supplies		9					
626 Perishable tools							
628 Miscellaneous department expense							
Subtotal	747	658	89	529	113.5		
TOTAL DEPARTMENTALIZED EXPENSE	11295	11413	(118)	2211	99.0		
DEPT. PERFORMANCE (D.L.S. DEPT. EXP.)	11295	11413	(118)	2211	99.0	103.6	107.8
ASSIGNED EXPENSE							
656 Office supplies	133	265	(132)	67	50.2		
657 Postage	299	1020	(721)	(271)	29.3		
658 Telegraph	495	438	57	(51)	113.0		
664 Property taxes	3613	3613	—	285	100.0		
665 State franchise tax	569	283	286	1144	—		
668 Other taxes	633	163	470	842	—		
669 Property insurance (2)(3)	1186	1180	6	(28)	100.5		
671 Other insurance	605	601	4	524	100.7		
672 Audit fees & expenses	350	350	—	—	100.0		
674 Rent computer	1365	1240	125	500	110.1		
688 Depreciation	3410	3431	(21)	(86)	99.4		
TOTAL ASSIGNED EXPENSE	12658	12584	74	2926	100.6		
TOTAL EXPENSE	23953	23997	(44)	5137	99.8		
DIVISION OVERALL PERFORMANCE					99.1	100.1	102.9

(1) Includes special allowance of $72. for C.P.C
(2) Includes special allowance of $146. for HAC-20.
(3) Includes $392. transfer from Cont. Fund.

CONTROL OF MASS CLERICAL COSTS
BY USE OF STANDARDS

In circumstances where there is a handling of vast amounts of paperwork, standards of performance and cost may be useful. Standards may be applied to many office functions just as they have been applied to manufacturing and sales functions. They are not applicable to all accounting activities, nor can the same degree of accuracy be secured as in the factory. But in many offices, the possible cost savings for certain clerical activities are sufficient to justify the effort of establishing the standards.

While the general method of setting standards was discussed in preceding chapters, the application to the measurement of clerical work is outlined as follows:

1. *Preliminary observation and analysis.* This step is fundamental in securing the necessary overall understanding of the problem, and in selecting those areas of activity which may lend themselves to standardization. Also, it assists in eliminating any obviously major weakness in routine.

2. *Selection of functions on which standards are to be set.* Standards should be set only on those activities which are in sufficient volume to justify standards.

3. *Determination of the unit of work.* A unit must be selected in which the standard may be expressed. This will depend on the degree of specialization and the volume of work.

4. *Determination of the best method and setting of the standard.* Time and motion study can be applied to office work, with sufficient allowance being given for fatigue and personal needs.

5. *Testing of the standard.* After the standard has been set, it should be tested to see that it is practical.

6. *Final application.* This involves using the standard, and preparing simple reports which the supervisor and the individual worker can see. It also requires a full explanation to the employee.

Illustrative accounting and clerical functions, which lend themselves to standardization, and the units of work that may be used to measure performance are these:

Function	*Unit of Standard Measurement — Number of:*
Order handling	Orders handled
Mail handling	Pieces handled
Billing	Invoice lines
Check writing	Checks written
Posting	Postings

Function	Unit of Standard Measurement — Number of:
Filing	Pieces filed
Typing	Lines typed
Customer statements	Statements
Order writing	Order lines

In addition to performance standards, unit cost standards can be applied to measure an individual function or overall activity. Thus, applying cost standards to credit and collection functions may involve these functions and units of measurement:

Functional Activity	Unit Cost Standard — Cost per:
Credit investigation and approval	• Sales order • Account sold • Credit sales transaction
Credit correspondence records and files	• Sales order • Letter • Account sold
Preparing invoices	• Invoice line • Item • Invoice • Order line • Order
Entire accounts receivable records, including posting of charges and credits and preparation of customers' statements	• Account • Sales order • Sales transaction
Posting charges	• Invoice • Shipment
Preparing customers' statements	• Statement • Account sold
Posting credits	• Remittance • Account sold
Calculating commissions on cash collected	• Remittance
Making street collections	• Customer • Dollar collected
Window collections	• Collection

PART III

Working Capital Budget

19

Cash and Temporary Investments

INTRODUCTION

Today, increased attention is being paid to proper cash planning. In the context of working capital, cash probably has the greatest flexibility. When surplus cash is available, even for only a day, it can be advantageously invested. The two categories, "Cash and Temporary Investments," or "Cash and Equivalents," which are involved in a more or less continuous interchange, are both discussed in this chapter.

IMPORTANCE OF THE CASH BUDGET

The cash statement is one of the three key financial statements because cash planning is an integral part of sound management. Not only must the business operate within the limit of available funds, but, conversely, the required funds must be made available to implement the planned business activity.

While it may seem unnecessary to define "cash," for our purposes it is intended to describe cash on hand and demand deposits in banks at the close of business on the balance sheet date. The essence of cash is immediate availability as legal tender or purchasing power.

Cash must be available at the right time, in the right place, and at the proper cost. It therefore must be planned, and cannot simply be the residual of the operations planning and resultant levels of inventories, receivables, capital assets, and related liabilities. Proper planning expects an appropriate return from the excess cash, and in most companies this excess cash can be a source of significant income.

Before discussing the purpose of the cash budget, or the techniques of preparing the cash plan, it may be well to review a basic principle. In any given company a certain cash balance is necessary to meet the business needs: to pay obligations promptly, to maintain required compensating balances with commercial banks, and to retain flexibility to transfer funds between operating centers — to name a few. The availability of electronic transfers capability and other devices may reduce the amount of cash needed for operations, but the need should not be set at zero, if only for psychological reasons.

The budget coordinator, through discussions with the financial officers should gain some awareness of what a reasonable cash balance, including cash equivalents, should be. The cash balance may relate to sales, but need not increase in direct proportion. The chief point to be made is that an analysis of proper balances might be considered as a prelude to determining the cash budget.

PURPOSE AND USES OF THE CASH BUDGET

The basic purpose behind the preparation of the cash budget is to plan so that the business will have the necessary cash — whether from the short-term or long-term viewpoint. Further, when excess cash is to be available, budget preparation offers a means of anticipating an opportunity for effective utilization. Aside from these general purposes, some specific uses to which a cash budget may be put are to:

- Point out peaks or seasonal fluctuations in business activity which make larger investments in inventories and receivables necessary.
- Indicate the time and extent of funds needed to meet maturing obligations, tax payments, and dividend or interest payments.
- Assist in planning for growth, including the required funds for plant expansion and working capital.
- Indicate well in advance of needs the extent and duration of funds required from outside sources, and thus permit the securing of more advantageous loans.
- Assist in securing credit from banks, and improve the general credit position of the business, including the maintenance of required compensating balances.
- Determine the extent and probable duration of funds available for investment.
- Plan the reduction of bonded indebtedness or other loans.
- Coordinate the financial needs of the subsidiaries and divisions of the company.
- Permit the company to take advantage of cash discounts and forward purchasing, thereby increasing its earnings.
- Facilitate the making of short-term investments.

CASH BUDGETING METHODS

At least three methods have been developed for constructing a cash plan. While the end product is the planned cash balance, the methods differ chiefly

FIG. 19-1 Statement of Estimated Cash Receipts and Disbursements

THE JOHNSON COMPANY

STATEMENT OF ESTIMATED CASH RECEIPTS AND DISBURSEMENTS

For the Year Ending 12/31/XX

(dollars in thousands)

Item	January	February	March	1st Qtr. Total	December	4th Qtr. Total	Year Total
Cash at beginning of period	$ 2,300	$ 4,000	$ 700	$ 2,300	$ 6,100	$ 5,000	$ 2,300
Cash receipts:							
Regular							
Collections on account	$ 8,400	$ 7,200	$ 9,100	$24,700	$ 7,000	$21,300	$ 96,300
Cash sales	300	100	400	800	100	200	1,900
Dividends	1,400	700	1,400	3,500	800	2,700	12,100
Interest income	700	1,000	600	2,300	1,000	3,200	10,200
Subtotal	$10,800	$ 9,000	$11,500	$31,300	$8,900	$27,400	$120,500
Special							
Sale of fixed assets	3,100	—	—	3,100	—	3,500	6,600
Bank loans	—	—	4,000	4,000	—	2,000	6,000
Sale of subsidiary	2,200	—	—	2,200	—	—	2,200
Total cash receipts	16,100	9,000	15,500	40,600	8,900	29,400	135,300
Total cash available	$18,400	$13,000	$16,200	$42,900	$15,000	$37,900	$137,600
Cash disbursements:							
Accounts payable	$ 3,200	$ 4,000	$ 2,700	$ 9,900	$ 3,100	$ 8,700	$ 24,600
Payrolls — Net	8,600	7,100	8,800	24,500	7,400	22,900	82,400
Dividends on common stock	900	—	—	900	900	900	3,600
Interest expense	—	—	1,000	1,000	100	100	2,200
Capital expenditures	700	300	800	1,800	800	1,100	4,100
Retirement plan	900	800	900	2,600	800	2,200	13,000
Other	100	100	200	400	600	700	1,700
Payments on indebtedness	—	—	—	—	—	—	4,700
Total cash disbursements	14,400	12,300	14,400	41,100	13,700	36,600	136,300
Cash at end of period	$ 4,000	$ 700	$ 1,800	$ 1,800	$ 1,300	$ 1,300	$ 1,300

as to the starting point of the forecast and the detail made available. The three techniques are described as follows:

☐ *Direct Estimate of Cash Receipts and Disbursements.* This is a detailed forecast of each cost element or function involving cash. It is essentially a projection of the cash records. Such a method is commonly used in business and is quite essential to giving a complete picture of the swings or gyrations in both receipts and disbursements. It is particularly applicable to those concerns subject to wide variations in activity. Moreover, it is very useful for controlling cash flow by comparing actual and forecasted performance. A cash forecast prepared on this basis is shown in Figure 19-1.

☐ *Adjusted Net Income Method.* As the name implies, the starting point for this procedure is the estimated income and expense statement. This projected net income is adjusted for all noncash transactions to arrive at the cash income or loss, and is further adjusted for cash transactions that arise because of nonoperating balance sheet changes. A worksheet showing the general method is illustrated in Figure 19-2. This is the "cash flow" approach.

It will be observed that since net income is used, the true extent of the gross cash receipts or disbursements is not known. Where a company must work on rather close cash margins, this method probably will not meet the needs. It is applicable chiefly where sales volume is relatively stable and the out-of-pocket costs are fairly constant in relation to sales.

In line with recent trends, if it serves a useful purpose, this statement may be modified to segregate the cash results from operations, from financing activities, and from investment activities in order to conform to some published formats. Of course, for management uses, the significant transactions are identified in the budgeting process.

☐ *Working Capital Differentials.* By this method the net working capital at the beginning of each month or other period is adjusted by estimated net income and by other receipts and disbursements to arrive at the estimated working capital at the end of each month or other period. From this amount, we deduct the required working capital, excluding cash, and the standard cash balance, to arrive at the amount of cash available for deposit and investment.

Such an approach has been used when standard valuations required for receivables, inventories, and other working capital at various sales volumes have been determined and when the major objective is the reinvestment of surplus funds. This method is not illustrated since the other two methods are more useful, and are to be preferred because they either require a more detailed look at the factors causing cash changes or are more easily prepared from the financial statements normally available in the planning process.

ESTIMATING CASH RECEIPTS

The sources of cash receipts for the typical industrial or commercial firm are well known: collections on account, cash sales, royalties, rent, dividends,

FIG. 19-2 Statement of Cash Sources and Uses

THE JONES COMPANY

STATEMENT OF ESTIMATED CASH SOURCES AND USES

For the Year Ending 12/31/XX

(dollars in thousands)

Item	January	February	March	1st Qtr. Total	December	4th Qtr. Total	Year Total
Sources of Cash							
Net income	$2,460	$2,070	$1,870	$ 6,400	$1,300	$5,200	$21,070
Depreciation	800	800	890	2,490	1,010	2,890	10,280
Deferred taxes	200	800	400	1,400	—	—	3,160
Internal cash generation	3,460	3,670	3,160	10,290	2,310	8,090	34,510
Accounts receivable	700	800	100	1,600	(200)	(700)	2,900
Long-term obligations	4,000	—	—	4,000	—	—	4,000
Total sources	$8,160	$4,470	$3,260	$15,890	$2,110	$7,390	$41,410
Uses of Cash							
Accounts payable and accruals	3,800	2,700	2,100	8,600	(790)	(210)	18,700
Capital expenditures	900	1,020	870	2,790	270	840	6,000
Dividends	—	—	700	700	600	600	2,510
Purchase of treasury shares	—	500	—	500	1,000	1,400	2,900
Purchase of Aloha subsidiary							11,470
Total uses	4,700	4,220	3,670	12,590	4,380	2,630	41,580
Increase (decrease) in Cash & Temporary Investments	$3,460	$ 250	$ (410)	$ 3,300	($2,270)	$4,760	($ 170)
Cash Position at End of Period							
Cash	1,100	1,000	1,010	1,010	970	970	970
Temporary investments	7,600	7,950	7,530	7,530	4,100	4,100	4,100
Total	$8,700	$8,950	$8,540	$ 8,540	$5,070	$4,760	$ 5,070

sale of capital items, sale of investments, and new financing. These items can be predicted with reasonable accuracy. Usually, the most important recurring sources are collections on account and cash sales. Experience and knowledge of trends will indicate what share of total sales probably will be for cash. From the sales plan, then, the total cash sales value can be determined. In a somewhat similar fashion, information can be gleaned from the records to enable the budget officer to make a careful estimate of the timing of collections. Once the experience has been analyzed, the results can be adjusted for trends and applied to the credit sales portrayed in the sales plan.

An example will illustrate the technique. Assume that an analysis of collection experience for June sales revealed the following collection data:

Collections Data	June Credit Sales
June	2.1%
July	85.3
August	8.9
September	2.8
October	.3
Cash discounts	.5
Bad debt losses	.1
Total	100.0%

If next year's sales in June could be expected to fall into the same pattern, then application of the percentages to estimated June credit sales would determine the probable monthly distribution of collections. The same analysis applied to each month of the year would result in a reasonably reliable basis for collection forecasting. The worksheet (June column) for cash collections might look somewhat as follows:

	Description		
Month of Sale	Total	Net Sales	June Collections
February	.4%	$149,500	$ 598
March	1.9	160,300	3,045
April	7.7	290,100	22,338
May	88.3	305,400	269,668
June	2.1	320,000	6,720
Total collections			302,369
Cash discounts (May)	.5	305,400	(1,527)
Losses	.1		(320)
Total			$300,522

Anticipated discounts must be calculated since they enter into the profit and loss forecast.

These experience factors must be modified, not only by trends developed over a period of time, but also by the estimate of general business conditions as reflected in collections, as well as contemplated changes in terms of sale or other credit policies. Refinements in the approach can be made if experience varies widely between geographical territories, types of customers, or channels of distribution. Obviously, the analysis of collections need not be made every month; it is sufficient if the distribution is checked occasionally.

ESTIMATING CASH DISBURSEMENTS

If a complete operating budget is available, the budget officer should have little difficulty in assembling the data into an estimate of cash disbursements. The usual cash disbursements in the typical industrial or commercial firm consist of salaried and hourly payrolls, materials, taxes, dividends, traveling expense, other operating expenses, interest, purchase of equipment, and retirement of stock.

From the labor budget, the manufacturing expense budget, and the various other expense budgets, the total anticipated expense for salaries and wages can be secured. Once this figure is available, the period of cash disbursement can be determined easily, for payrolls must be met on certain dates closely following the time when earned. Reference to a calendar will establish the pay dates. Separate consideration should be given to the tax deductions from the gross pay, since these are not payable at the same time the net payroll is disbursed — unless special bank accounts are established for the tax deductions.

The materials budget will set out the material requirements each month. The more important elements probably should be treated individually — power units or engines, for example. Other items will be grouped together. Only in a few instances is material purchased for cash. However, reference to required inventories and to delivery dates, as well as assistance from the purchasing department, will establish the time allowed for payments. If thirty days are required, then usage of one month can be moved forward for the purpose of estimating cash payments. The effect of cash discounts should be considered in arriving at the estimated disbursements.

The various manufacturing and operating expenses should be considered individually because they are by no means all the same. Some are prepayments or accruals, paid annually, such as property taxes and insurance. Some are noncash items, such as depreciation expense or bad debts.

For a large number of individual small items, such as supplies, telephone and telegraph, and traveling expense, an average time lag may be used.

Cash requirements for capital additions should be determined from the plant budget or other known plans. No particular difficulty presents itself because the needs are relatively fixed and are established by the board of directors or other authority.

Usual practice requires the determination of cash receipts and disbursements exclusive of transactions involving voluntary debt retirements, purchase of treasury stock, or funds from bank loans. Decisions relative to these means of securing or disbursing cash are reached when the cash position is known and policy formulated accordingly.

As a summary comment, each cost-type transaction must be segregated into those elements needed for display in the estimated cash statement. Thus, the payroll element of each function or transaction is summarized for the cash disbursements line item — "Salaries and Wages." It combines the salary and wage element of items such as:

- Inventories
- Selling expenses
- Administrative expense
- Research and development costs

A similar accumulation sheet or computer tape would be made for the accounts payable element of various inventory and expense components. A summary of cash required for raw materials is shown in Figure 19-3.

This schedule is indicative of the vast amount of detail required to prepare the accounts payable — raw materials and purchased parts estimated disbursements. Comparable calculations are required on most accounts payable (and payroll and taxes) items, or for any voluminous transactions.

While Figure 19-3 is prepared on a monthly basis (to arrive at a monthly statement of estimated cash, and statement of financial position), the summaries for certain needs may be on a quarterly basis only.

LENGTH OF CASH PLANNING PERIOD

It is elementary and axiomatic that the period of cash planning must fit the needs of the company. Both short-term and long-term projections or budgets may be necessary and desirable — each serving different purposes. Thus, if cash balances are low, a daily forecast for perhaps a week or month in advance may best serve operating needs. At the other end of the spectrum, for the determination of general financial policy perhaps a 15-year projection

FIG. 19-3   Estimate of Cash Requirements — Raw Materials and Purchased Parts

THE NMM MANUFACTURING COMPANY

ESTIMATE OF CASH REQUIREMENTS FOR RAW MATERIALS AND
PURCHASED PARTS

For the Year Ending 12/31/XX

(dollars in millions)

Month	Beginning Balance — Accounts Payable	Purchases	Total Estimated Liability	Estimated Carry-Forward[a]	Cash Required
January	$16,400	$ 37,300	$ 53,700	$12,400	$ 41,300
February	12,400	27,600	40,000	9,200	30,800
March	9,200	43,100	52,300	14,400	37,900
April	14,400	31,300	45,700	10,400	35,300
May	10,400	39,200	49,600	13,100	36,500
June	13,100	28,700	41,800	9,600	32,200
July	9,600	40,400	50,000	13,500	36,500
August	13,500	39,700	53,200	13,200	40,000
September	13,200	42,600	55,800	14,200	41,600
October	14,200	44,100	58,300	14,700	43,600
November	14,700	48,900	63,600	16,300	47,300
December	16,300	41,500	57,800	13,800	44,000
Total	$16,400	$464,400	$621,800	$13,800	$467,000

(a) Estimated at 33⅓% of monthly purchases

would be almost mandatory. Additionally, the extent of detail needed probably will be somewhat inversely proportionate to the length of the period covered, the larger projections requiring less detail.

A representative report structure covering cash planning of a well-known large corporation is indicated by the following schedule of cash forecasts, plans, or projections.

1. *Short-term:*

   □ *Daily forecast.* This report details by broad category expected receipts and disbursements by days for a period of one week in advance. The format might be similar to the cash receipts and disbursements sections of Figure 19-1, but by days. It serves as a control report for specific planning of short-term investments.

☐ *Weekly forecast.* This report in form is similar to Figure 19-1, but covers by weeks about a six-week period.

☐ *Monthly forecast.* This report is in a receipts and disbursements statement form as in Figure 19-1, indicating by month for the next three months the cash position and the indicated status at the end of the period. As is necessary in connection with short-term loans, a monthly operating format is shown in Figure 19-4.

☐ *Annual.* Such a cash projection, either in receipts and disbursements form (Figure 19-1) or cash-flow form (Figure 19-2), indicates the outlook for the year in advance. It may be revised quarterly as part of the regular budget revision procedure.

2. *Long-range:*

☐ *Annual.* Such a projection, covering a broad-range estimate of sources and disposition of funds, indicates cash activity by years for a period of 5, 10, or 15 years.

This type of cash planning is necessary as a guide in answering these points:

- Extent, duration, and timing of long-term financing
- Timing for liquidation of existing long-term indebtedness
- Funds available for capital expenditures over the period
- Cash availability for cash dividends, and consideration of change in dividend policy
- Funds available or required for new acquisition

THE CASH BUDGET AS RELATED TO OTHER BUDGETS

The emphasis in this chapter has been on the *annual* cash budget, as one of the key financial statements. Other interim cash budgets have been discussed briefly, however. But it can be seen that the annual cash budget is generally dependent on all other budgets: the annual operating budget, the budget for receivables and inventories, and accounts payable. In actual practice, the cash budget is prepared *after* the other plans have been completed. The cash plan cannot be prepared until asset and liability levels are known. The cash balances are, in a sense, a surge tank, the actual cash balances being dependent on the business investment needs. In the planning process, borrowings are assumed if the cash level at any month-end period is insufficient; and excess funds are assumed to be placed in temporary investments.

It can be appreciated that any failure to meet the operating plan will impact on available cash. If sales are below plan, earnings may be less, and the investment in accounts receivable will be lower. Thus, the annual cash budget is part of a coordinated program of sales, cost incurrence, and investments.

FIG. 19-4 Monthly Updating Cash Forecast

COOPER PETROLEUM COMPANY
CONSOLIDATED CASH FORECAST
Year 19XX as of May 1, 19 —
(dollars in thousands)

	Actual — 1/1/XX — 4/30/XX	Forecast May	Forecast June	Forecast July	Forecast Balance of Year	Present View 19 —	Prior Month's View 19 —
Cash Receipts:							
Sales revenue	$216.2	$51.4	$51.0	$52.0	$261.3	$631.9	$611.5
(Increase) or decrease in receivables	3.2	1.6	(.8)	(.6)	(1.4)	2.0	2.1
Estimated taxes collected for government	38.1	10.0	10.1	10.4	49.7	118.3	118.1
Sale of property and facilities	3.2	.7	—	—	1.1	5.0	5.0
"R" inventory liquidation	—	—	—	—	6.0	6.0	6.0
All other receipts	31.8	6.6	9.6	7.0	39.8	94.8	85.1
Total	$292.5	$70.3	$69.9	$68.8	$356.5	$858.0	$827.8
Cash Disbursements:							
Raw material and purchased-product cost	$113.4	$19.0	$23.7	$22.5	$119.6	$298.2	$281.0
Controllable operating expenses	68.8	19.4	19.5	17.2	92.3	217.2	209.6
Tax payments	1.8	1.3	.9	.8	9.8	20.9	20.8
Insurance	1.8	1.1	.1	.1	.6	2.7	3.0
Interest	3.6	.2	.9	.8	3.9	9.4	9.5
Payment of taxes collected for Government	37.8	9.7	10.1	10.1	51.0	118.7	118.5
Purchase of treasury stock	—	.6	1.1	.1	1.2	3.0	3.0
Preferred dividend payments	1.7	—	—	—	.9	3.4	3.4
Carved-out oil sale repayments (incl. interest)	9.2	2.3	2.4	2.3	11.9	28.1	28.1
Debt repayment	18.3	.2	.8	.4	13.3	33.0	33.0
Capital expenditures	29.2	7.4	8.2	7.6	31.4	83.8	85.0
All other disbursements	25.3	4.1	8.6	5.3	26.7	70.0	68.2
Total	317.2	64.3	76.3	68.0	362.6	888.4	863.1
Increase (decrease) cash balance	($ 24.7)	$ 6.0	($ 6.4)	$ .8	($ 6.1)	($ 30.4)	($ 35.3)
Ending Cash Balances:							
Primary	$ 10.5	$11.8	$11.8	$11.8	$ 11.8	$ 11.8	$ 11.8
Field	6.1	6.0	6.0	6.0	6.0	6.0	6.0
Subsidiary	4.1	5.0	5.0	5.0	5.0	5.0	5.0
Temporary investments	29.9	33.8	27.4	28.2	22.1	22.1	17.2
Total	$ 50.6	$56.6	$50.2	$51.0	$ 44.9	$ 44.9	$ 40.0

Because cash is so vital to the business, there usually is a need to update the cash plans quite frequently, possibly monthly, as shown in Figure 19-4. Failure of any part of the plan immediately impacts cash, so that new cash plans are required with the related corrective action — more bank borrowings, restriction on capital expenditures for a time, more intensive collection efforts, and slowing of payments of bills.

In preparing the cash budget, due consideration must be given to electronic transfers of funds, all methods of accelerating cash collections, and slowing payments.

Depending on the financial position of the company, the cash forecast or budget may have a high priority. Many executives prefer to review the cash projection in advance of the financial expression of operating results, and it may, therefore, take the number one spot in a review of expected operations. Much depends, of course, on the relative financial strength and liquidity of the company.

ENFORCING THE CASH BUDGET

In the control phase of budgeting, the usual procedure is to compare actual with plan (or flexible budget, or both) and to take corrective action, where appropriate, to bring actual results in line with plan. Yet, the inability to meet the cash budget usually results from failure to meet other budgets — too much inventory, or slow collections, or lower sales than expected. Hence, the cash budget cannot be enforced independently of the other budgets of which it is the consequence. Therefore, appropriate steps would be as follows:

1. Analyze by responsibility area the causes of not meeting the budget.

2. Advise the responsible parties of the under-plan cash (or temporary investments) condition, due to their individual activities, and suggest what each should do to get back on plan — if he does not already know.

3. Update the current forecast (as in Figure 19-4) to ascertain that sufficient cash will be made available to meet business needs; if not, advise the chief financial officer so that appropriate arrangements may be made.

It often is necessary to "keep tabs" on how cash requirements will be met. A simple weekly cash report is illustrated in Figure 19-5. This provides a guide as to where the company is not meeting the estimate and, therefore, where extra effort may be required.

FIG. 19-5   Comparison of Actual and Estimated Cash Activity

THE HICKS COMPANY

WEEKLY CASH REPORT

For the Week Ended November 16, 19 —

(dollars in thousands)

Description	Actual Week Ended 11/16/XX	Month to Date Actual	Month to Date Estimated
Beginning cash balance	$17,890	$ 32,511	$ 32,510
Cash Receipts			
Government	10,810	18,310	18,000
Wholesale	19,620	67,730	65,500
Retail	8,330	21,100	23,400
Total	38,760	107,140	106,900
Cash Disbursements			
Accounts payable — Expenses	12,330	12,860	12,300
Payrolls	12,660	37,010	36,900
Material purchases	1,890	19,340	14,300
Federal taxes	2,790	8,640	8,920
Capital expenditures	13,370	39,990	40,190
Other	1,060	2,030	2,000
Total	44,100	119,870	114,610
Ending cash balance	$12,550	$ 19,781	$ 24,800
Estimated month-end balance			$ 30,000

IMPROVING CASH ADMINISTRATION

In preparing the cash budget, under normal circumstances, past experience is the chief factor in estimating required cash balances, cash inflows and cash outflows. That is to say, the annual budgeting process usually does not encompass an intensive study of cash administration or cash management. Yet, the budgeting process may stimulate questions about cash procedures. These circumstances may become evident:

- The free cash balances allegedly required for operations may appear to be large as compared to competitive practices, or may increase substantially with a rise in activity level.
- The average days receivables may be appreciably larger than the stated terms of sale (e.g., net 30 days, or 2 percent 10th proximo).

• The time elapsed between writing a check on accounts payable and receipt of the cancelled check might be quite short.

Conditions such as these might encourage a review of procedures to increase the cash available for investment. After all, one of the management tasks is to use the assets wisely to increase the return on assets (ROA), and cash should be no exception. Improved cash administration can do either of two things: (1) release cash for temporary investment, or (2) reduce current bank borrowings or other loans.

One area for review, of course, would be the cash transfers between company segments and the balances maintained: branches, subsidiaries, and divisions. Are electronic transfers used? Are there ways to reduce the number and amount? Are there too many accounts? Are the balances simply too high (as a precaution against over-drafts)?

But the primary way to increase cash utilization probably will be through reduced float — either collection float or disbursement float. It is the collections on account and payments to vendors and suppliers that comprise the greatest movement of cash. *Collection* float may be defined as the funds from checks or other negotiable instruments that are in the process of being collected, but do not represent available cash. It may be estimated by testing or sampling the time from the mailing by the debtor to the time the funds are made available by the banking systems. The *disbursement* float, similarily, may be defined as the funds issued by the company for accounts payable which have not yet been cleared to the corporate bank account, and hence are still technically eligible for use (just as long as funds are available when the check or draft must be redeemed). The amount of the disbursement float may be estimated by sampling the number of days from check issuance to clearance at the drawee bank.

Float can be quite large and is composed principally of these elements:

• Time during which the documents are in the mail for either cash receipts or cash disbursements.

• Internal processing time — being the time required by the company to receive and open the payments, process the documents, and make the deposits in the bank for collection.

• Availability time — being the time required by the bank from receipt of funds until they are made available by the bank.

Collection float might be calculated as follows:

Mail time	2.00 days
Processing time	0.75
Availability time	1.40
Total collection float	4.15 days

(*continued*)

Average monthly collections	$20,000,000
Average daily collection (30 days)	$666,667
Average float (4.15 × $666,667)	$2,766,667
Lost investment income per annum:	
14% × $2,766,667 =	$387,333

Any number of devices have been developed to reduce collection float, such as area concentration banking or regional lock boxes. Disbursement float has been *increased* by the use of banks located in geographically remote areas or at great distances from the payee locale.

In any event, analytical effort on cash procedures may result in improved cash budgeting.

TEMPORARY INVESTMENTS

General Comments

In the practical world, the cash budget is initially developed as "cash and equivalents" in planning the excess cash or cash deficiency in the annual business plan. Once the "cash" balance is determined, from it is deducted the minimum cash needed to operate the business, and the remainder is available for temporary investment. The month-end figures may be used for calculating investment income, although a more precise pattern of interim cash versus close of the month may be developed, similar to the procedure used to estimate cash collections discussed earlier.

In any event, the purpose of the segregation, once it is determined that sufficient cash is available for the business needs, is to determine the income budget. Ordinarily, the treasurer advises what rate might be used for the planning period, and this is applied to the "free cash" balances. With the relatively high return currently being paid on overnight, weekend, or weekly invested funds, excess cash can cumulatively be an important source of income.

Investment Vehicle

In budgeting the expected income, the budget coordinator should inquire into the pattern of investments, and the accounting treatment to be afforded them. If there is some evidence that losses could occur on the existing investments, over and above that to be recognized in the prior year-end closing (perhaps an unusual event), provision should be made.

To be sure, temporary investments should be made in certificates of

FIG. 19-6   Summary — Temporary Investments

THE MAGRAUDY CORPORATION

SHORT-TERM INVESTMENTS
SUMMARY — MATURITIES AND YIELDS
Month of March 19XX
(dollars in thousands)

	Actual	Annual Plan
Aggregate amount invested	$29,416	$28,000
Investment income — Month	225	224
Year-to-date	$ 679	$ 600

	Amount	Percentage
Maturities		
Under 30 days	$14,212	48.3%
1– 3 months	7,610	25.9
3– 6 months	5,400	18.4
6–12 months	2,194	7.4
Total	$29,416	100.0%
Average maturity — Months		2.2%

	Percentage
Yield	
Average yield — 3 months	
Mark to market	9.48%
Book accounting	9.76
Market — 4/1/XX prime paper	
1 month	9.40
3 months	9.50
6 months	9.80

deposit, Treasury bills, commercial paper or other suitable investments. Yet these principles should be considered according to the company needs:

- Safety of principal
- Marketability
- Price stability
- Maturity

But information or judgments can be wrong. Therefore, an examination of the portfolio, past history, and other pertinent factors should be at least briefly considered in arriving at the budget for return on temporary investments.

Budget Reports on Temporary Investments

The amount invested in temporary funds at any time may, in fact, result from the actions — or non-actions — of different responsibility areas. Therefore, a comparison of actual and budgeted investments and yields has less significance than some reports. The emphasis probably should be on maturities, distribution of risk, and actual yield versus going yield.

It is suggested, therefore, that a brief informational report is sufficient. A simple one, which shows budgeted and actual results, but more importantly, provides some indication of performance, is shown in Figure 19-6.

20

Receivables

ELEMENTS OF THE ACCOUNTS RECEIVABLE BUDGET

Accounts receivable and inventories make up the largest segment, by far, of working capital for most U.S. industrial or commercial companies. In the context of budgeting to improve the return on assets, planning and control techniques should apply to these important items.

Accounts receivable that arise in the ordinary, normal course of business are the assets on which budgeting attention is usually focused. Discussion is made easier if these three elements in the accounts receivable budget are treated separately:

1. Accounts receivable arising from customer credit sales
2. The reserve for doubtful accounts, and
3. Other, or miscellaneous, short-term receivables.

ACCOUNTS RECEIVABLE — CUSTOMERS

The accounts receivable budget is the reflection of the sales made on account and the cash collections. Basically, to establish the budget, an entry must be made for each month's budgeted sales and cash collections, just as is done for actual operations:

> *For the sales:*
> Debit: Accounts receivable   XX
> Credit: Sales — Customers   XX
>
> *For the cash collections:*
> Debit: Cash   XX
> Credit: Accounts receivable — Customers   XX
>   Discounts on sales   XX

The method of estimating the cash collections on account is discussed in Chapter 19.

A summary computer printout, or worksheet, for the accounts receivable budget would appear essentially as illustrated in Figure 20-1, "tying into" the sales plan on the one-hand, and the cash budget on the other. The "other adjustments" column represents a periodic writeoff of accounts receivable estimated, based largely on past experience, to be uncollectible.

The cash collection estimate of when each month's sales will be paid is usually based on recent past experience, and may take into account the stage of the business cycle and its impact on collections. A test of the reasonableness of the receivables budget is the planned number of days the accounts are outstanding. The formula, which may be applied on an annual basis, or perhaps on a quarterly basis, is as follows:

$$\frac{\text{Average number of days}}{\text{receivables are outstanding}} = \frac{\text{Average receivables}}{\text{Annual credit sales}} \times 365$$

Applying this formula on an annual basis to the data shown in Figure 20-1 provides this result:

$$\frac{\text{Average receivables}}{\text{Annual credit sales}} = \frac{\$11,075,000}{\$125,560,000} \times 365$$

$$= .088205 \times 365$$

$$= 32.19 \text{ days}$$

The ending receivable balance for each month was used to secure *a weighted average*. Use of the yearly beginning and ending balance would produce a

FIG. 20-1   Printout of Accounts Receivable Budget

THE ILLUSTRATIVE COMPANY

BUILD-UP OF THE ACCOUNTS RECEIVABLE BUDGET
For the Year Ending December 31, 19XX
(dollars in thousands)

Month	Beginning Balance	Sales	Cash Collections	Other Adjustments (Credit)	Ending Balance
January	$12,210	$ 9,400	$ 8,450	—	$13,610
February	13,160	9,900	10,240	—	12,820
March	12,820	10,300	12,560	—	10,560
April	10,560	10,700	11,600	$110	9,550
May	9,550	9,400	9,400	—	9,550
June	9,550	8,760	8,300	—	10,010
July	10,010	9,100	8,960	20	10,130
August	10,130	10,700	10,240	—	10,590
September	10,590	13,430	10,870	—	13,150
October	13,150	12,400	12,510	—	13,043
November	13,040	11,040	13,100	—	10,980
December	10,980	10,800	12,330	80	9,370
Total	$12,210	$125,930	$128,560	$210	$ 9,370

somewhat more favorable picture. In the illustration, the average days the receivables are outstanding calculates to be 32.19 days. This figure should be compared to the nominal terms. If, for example, The Illustrative Company grants credit on net 30 days, then the above planned performance must be judged quite good. If the terms, however, are net 20 days, then a lower accounts receivable budget probably would be in order. If a review of credit and collection procedures with the credit manager and chief financial officer results in a reasonable conclusion that improvement in average days receivables outstanding can be made, then a budget adjustment should be made.

RESERVE FOR DOUBTFUL ACCOUNTS

Most companies that make sales on credit incur bad debt losses. If they do not, it may signify that their credit terms are so stringent that a decrease in sales actually occurs. In any event, in the annual planning process, provision should be made for expected bad debt losses.

As most budget directors know, a provision for uncollectible accounts is usually made in one of two ways. Based on experience, each month a percentage of monthly sales is set aside as a reserve for probable bad accounts. This amount may be determined on an overall basis, by territory, or by product. The second method of establishing the reserve is to periodically analyze the past due accounts and arrive at an estimate of uncollectibles. Bad debt losses may be significant, depending on the industry. Provision should be made in the annual plan for the estimated losses and the method used should largely parallel the one the controller expects to use in the actual accounts. Hence, the operating plan will include a "provision for uncollectible accounts," with the set-up of a corresponding reserve in the statements of planned financial condition. The plan should provide for an estimated write-down of the reserve to parallel the expected actual accounting.

MISCELLANEOUS RECEIVABLES

Quite often, most companies have relatively small amounts due from various sources, including such items as:

- Claims receivable
- Due from officers and employees
- Accounts receivable — Special transactions
- Notes receivable — Miscellaneous

Normally, the account balances are quite small, and remain at a rather constant level. From a budgetary standpoint, it is suggested that plans be checked, and inquiry made, as to any expected transactions of an unusual nature, such as sale of land, idle assets, so that provision is made for such items in the receivables budget, as well as in the cash budget or any other accounts which might be affected. Other income and expense, for example, may be affected.

REDUCING THE RECEIVABLES BUDGET

If the amount invested in accounts receivable is considered excessive, credit terms may be too liberal, the receivables processing cycle too long, or collection procedures simply poor. The receivables budget is constructed using expected credit terms, and existing billing and collection procedures. If the results are unsatisfactory, then review or analysis of these factors may be necessary for a more satisfactory receivables cycle.

The credit manager can examine the credit terms against those of competitors, the corporate credit terms history, and appropriate changes can be made. If the terms appear satisfactory, then a complete review of the procedures from order receipt to cash collections may be appropriate. These actions ought to be analyzed for means to speeding up the entire procedure:

- Process and time involved from receipt of the customer order in the mail room until receipt in the order or sales department, as applicable.
- Time and steps used in processing the order in the order or sales department.
- Credit approval procedure and time required.
- Time and steps required to process the order, after credit approval.
- Shipping department procedure and required time.
- Time and procedure required to transfer shipping documents to the billing department.
- Time and procedure required to prepare the invoice and mail.
- Procedure to expedite collection.
- Procedure and time required to process the payment.

A detailed systems and procedures review may in itself aid in reducing the number of days a receivable is carried.

21

Inventories

INTRODUCTION

This chapter might have been entitled "The Inventory Budget." However, the planning and control of inventories, also called inventory management, involves techniques which may be employed in their own right and, technically, without reference to the budget. However, these same methods may be, indeed often should be, employed in developing the inventory budget. Hence, some of the procedures found useful in inventory management will be reviewed prior to their budget application.

The purpose of this chapter is to identify those major factors involved in inventory management as they impact on the budgeting procedure and the financial well-being of the company.

IMPACT OF INVENTORY

Inventory, as the term is used herein, refers to the stock of goods owned by the enterprise, and evidenced under the "inventory" caption in its statement of financial position. It encompasses the stock on hand of raw materials, purchased parts, work-in-process, finished goods for sale, and merchandise purchased for resale — the tangible current assets which can be seen, weighed, counted, and measured.

The financial impact of inventories on a company may be reflected in at least three ways:

1. A significant amount of resources for a manufacturing or trading concern, as differentiated from a service company, usually must be invested in the various categories of inventory.
2. The method of valuing inventory has a direct influence on the tax liability — both amount and timing — of the enterprise.
3. Inventories have a direct impact on the operating income and net income, resulting from (1) the carrying cost of the inventory; (2) the effect of write-downs or other adjustments; and (3) the method of costing the goods sold.

However, inventories are a necessity in that their ultimate purpose is to assist in meeting customer needs.

PERVADING NATURE OF INVENTORY MANAGEMENT

"Inventory management" to some people might signify solely the maintenance of the appropriate stock levels. However, it should not be viewed this narrowly. It ought to consider these closely related functions:

- Procurement or purchasing
- Transportation
- Receiving and inspection
- Warehousing and stores
- Production or manufacturing

Raw material inventories serve as the link between raw material purchases and the production function. Finished goods inventories are the link between the manufacturing function and marketing. Proper inventory management is a balancing of production needs, marketing requirements, and the financial capabilities of the enterprise. One of the chief purposes of effective inventory management is to find the least cost combination of meeting customer needs. An important objective is to reach a compromise among the three factors just mentioned.

As an example, the purchasing department may wish to acquire goods in large quantities because of special prices. But this alternative should be weighed against the costs, risks, and financial capability of carrying the inventory. Again, the marketing department may wish to carry a large finished goods inventory to meet any conceivable customer demand. But this alternative must be weighed against the consequences of stock outages and the economic cost of carrying a larger stock of finished goods.

Customer needs will influence the sales plan or budget which, in turn, will be a singularly important factor in setting the production budget. But the finished goods inventory is the balancing factor between the most economical way of manufacturing the product and the timing of customer demand. It can be seen that the major planning and control systems of a manufacturing or trading company are closely interrelated with inventory management.

IMPORTANCE OF INVENTORY MANAGEMENT

The emphasis on the importance of inventory planning and control is no mere academic platitude. Inventories are the largest single item among the current assets of many industrial firms, to say nothing of mercantile concerns. Within the experience of many financial executives, the importance of inventory control is vivid — whether because of sizable unfavorable adjustments as a result of physical inventories, whether as a result of heavy losses from obsolescence or market declines, or merely because inventories were allowed to grow to unwieldy sizes with the risk of losses and excess costs. Inventories have frequently been the prime cause of business failure, and it is not without reason that they have been called "the graveyard of American business."

The cost of carrying inventory is high at any time, but especially when inflation is rampant and interest rates are correspondingly in the upper atmosphere. But aside from either the interest charges or the lost "opportunity cost" of investing elsewhere, other costs mount: handling costs, insurance, pilferage, spoilage, shrinkage, deterioration, and obsolescence. The cost of carrying inventory is never less than 10 to 12 percent, and frequently reaches 40 percent, of the total inventory value on an annual basis. Hence, proper planning and control can help achieve considerable profit improvement or cost reduction for the company.

ADVANTAGES OF PROPER INVENTORY MANAGEMENT

Proper planning and control of inventories, together with the necessary integration with other business functions, provides several benefits, including these:

- The investment in inventory and the related costs usually are reduced.
- With the proper composition of inventories on hand, production delays tend

to be averted; and production runs are longer and at a reduced cost because of greater efficiency.

- With planned fluctuations in inventory, production may be leveled out, contributing to stability of employment and increased efficiency.
- Proper planning and control may reduce investments in storage facilities and material handling equipment.
- Losses resulting from theft, pilferage, spoilage, and obsolescence may be reduced.
- Handling and storage costs are likely to be lower.
- Proper planning and control may contribute to advantageous purchases, taking advantage of price movements, or avoidance of loss due to price declines.
- The quality of service to customers, and customer relations, may be improved by avoiding stock outages and providing more rapid deliveries.

Good inventory management does not necessarily contemplate lower inventories. It does include having the right goods at the right place at the right time, and it does include balancing the economics of purchasing, production, and inventory carrying.

KEY COMPONENTS IN AN EFFECTIVE INVENTORY MANAGEMENT SYSTEM

Just as there are essential requirements for a sound budgetary system, so there are components of, or conditions for, a properly operating inventory management system. The system may be simple or complex, but it must be responsive to management needs on an economical basis. It must be adopted to the realities of the environment, but these elements should be present:

- Well-defined inventory policies
- Proper organization, clearly defined authority, and responsibility for inventories
- Competent personnel
- Adequate procedures, including:
  a. Proper classification and identification of inventories
  b. Adequate inventory records
  c. A responsive reporting system
  d. Proper specifications and descriptions
  e. Practical quantitative parameters, such as reorder points and order quantities
- Adequate physical facilities for storage and handling

Most of these requirements are discussed in this chapter.

Inventory Policies

Effective management of a business enterprise, or any elements thereof, is possible only when sound policies are established, communicated to and understood by those directly involved, and adequately enforced.

Among the suggested topics to be covered in an inventory policy statement are:

- The objectives of inventory management
- The basic methods by which inventories will be planned and controlled
- Perhaps specific quantified goals by which management will be measured, such as inventory levels, turnover rates, spoilage and obsolescence limits, and stock outages
- The extent or scope of inventory management

Proper Organization — Responsibility for Inventories

The organization structure should be fitted to the company needs as to both reporting relationship and relationship to other departments. It is essential that it be staffed by competent personnel. The responsibility and authority for inventory management should be clearly defined. The functional outline and job descriptions should spell out the authority and duties of the executives as to inventory management and the corresponding responsibility. Because the particular structure depends on the size and type of business, the industry, and the types of materials and products, only these general observations are worth mentioning.

- Responsibility for those inventories that relate largely to manufacturing (e.g., raw materials, purchased parts, manufacturing supplies, and work-in-process) probably should rest with the chief manufacturing executive. There will be instances, however, where raw materials and purchased parts may be placed in the hands of the purchasing executive, such as where supply factors or market conditions are critical to procurement.
- Responsibility for the finished goods inventory might be placed with the sales executive (although the warehousing and handling would be directed by one of the staff), who is in the best position to sense product sales trends. On the other hand, the sales manager might be responsible only for field warehouse inventory, with finished goods at the factory under the responsibility of the production executive until the goods are shipped.
- Regardless of where responsibility is placed, there must be full and complete coordination between sales and production so that the material purchases and production schedules are consistent with the sales demand and the related inventory requirements.

□ While a single executive may be primarily responsible for all or designated portions of the inventory (i.e., direct materials, work-in-process, or finished goods), other executives will have a certain responsibility for peripheral or related duties. Thus, the facilities manager may have responsibility for the procurement and maintenance of physical warehousing and storage facilities and equipment; the financial officer for providing the necessary funds; the security staff for policing the inventory storage areas for pilferage; and the controller for the inventory pricing and valuation methods. Each respective responsibility should be spelled out in the functional outline or other appropriate documents.

Adequate Systems and Procedures

Adequate systems and procedures relate to a multitude of things necessary for the day-to-day operation of the inventory system. Some of these systems and procedures are discussed below.

Proper Classification and Identification of Inventories. The various major types of inventory each will be influenced by, and will impact upon, the major functions or activities of a business in different ways. Hence, from the broad planning and control standpoint, they must be properly described, designated, and segregated. Additionally, from the day-to-day operating viewpoint, different subcategories may be controlled by a different method by different executives. And the processing and physical handling may be unique in some instances. For these reasons, among others, the inventories should be properly classified.

Typical categories of inventory in a manufacturing company include these:

- Raw material
- Supplies
- Work-in-process
- Finished goods

Depending on the industry, other important classifications might be these:

- Goods on consignment (to others)
- Materials on loan (from others)
- Manufactured product on consignment
- Returnable containers
- Material in the hands of subcontractors

The classifications should fit the needs of the business.

Within these broad categories, a number of subcategories usually will be found necessary for control. An aerospace firm, for example, might have these subcodes for raw materials and purchased parts:

1. Aluminum stock	6. Composites
2. Steel stock	7. Hydraulic components
3. Fabricated parts	8. Castings
4. Standard parts	9. Forgings
5. Electronic parts	10. Machined parts

Proper segregations of work-in-process perhaps by department, or finished goods by type of product, would be typical subcodes.

In addition to the proper classification of inventory, there must be adequate identification of the individual materials or parts or product. Improperly identified materials brought to the production line would cause delays and added cost if it is the wrong item. Moreover, parts and raw materials must meet certain specifications. Hence, part numbering is essential; and a specification file for each material or part is a necessary part of the inventory control system.

Adequate Inventory Records. Inventory planning and control is based on facts, and these in turn may be based on adequate, detailed records on each part. The information must meet the requirements of purchasing, manufacturing, marketing, and even finance. Typical information could include:

• Item description	• Safety stock
• Location	• Quantity on hand
• Receipts	• Quantity on order
• Usage — both historical and prospective	• Quantity in transit
• Standard ordering quantities	• Quantity set aside for specific orders
• Reorder points	• Unit cost
• Minimum-maximum quantities	• Date of physical count

Obviously, exactly what information is needed will depend on the system; but the computer does make vast amounts of information available quickly at a modest cost.

Finally, the point should be made that adequate and accurate data are essential to good inventory management, including budgetary planning and control.

Adequate Reports. It is one thing to have adequate information on hand, but it is quite another thing to use it in the planning and control of inventories. The inventory clerk in the corner may know the item is slow-moving, per the records. But this condition must be reported and acted upon if the information is to be of use.

Accordingly, there must be a responsive reporting system that provides informational or exception control reports on matters such as:

☐ Comparison of actual and planned inventory
☐ Critical out-of-line conditions, including:
  • Turnover experience
  • Obsolete and slow-moving items
  • Imminent shortages
  • Stock outages
  • Open order status
  • Changes in costs

Proper inventory management requires the assistance of proper reporting.

Simplification and Standardization

Yet another facet to consider in proper inventory management is the simplification of the line, and the standardization of materials, parts, and products. Simplification is merely the elimination of what might be described as excess models, types, and sizes. Obviously, the reduction in the variety of items carried should contribute to lower investment in inventories, and perhaps lower purchasing, handling, and manufacturing costs.

Standardization has to do with the establishment of standards in the sense of reducing the types and sizes that are considered standard. The objective, among other things, is to facilitate the interchange of parts in the manufacturing process. With more interchangeability, inventories usually can be reduced.

Adequate Storage and Handling Facilities

The last requisite for an effective inventory management system, and one of the most important, is adequate handling and storage facilities. Policies, procedures, records, and reports are fine. But no system can succeed in the face of an inadequate, ill-equipped, disorganized, and messy warehousing or storage facility. Under these conditions, parts often cannot be located, production is delayed, material is purchased when it is not needed. Again, the wrong part or product will be shipped to a customer. Under the circumstances, losses from obsolescence or excessive inventories or outages might run high. Frankly, perpetual manual records or computer records are usually meaningless under these circumstances. So, adequate, but not elaborate, facilities are a necessity.

VALUATION OF INVENTORIES

It is not within the scope of this book to deal at length with different methods of valuing inventories. However, in periods of high inflation and rapid price changes, the valuation method can significantly effect the company's income tax liability, reported earnings and, of course, the amount of investment in inventories. The method of inventory valuation in those concerns with heavy investment in this current asset can significantly impact the current ratio.

It is perhaps elementary to state the point, but the inventory budget should recognize and incorporate the basis of valuation used by the company. If a firm, for example, uses the first-in, first-out (FIFO) method of inventory valuation, then this principle should be recognized in the budgetary procedure. If it is not practical to do it monthly (and with computers it usually should be), then at least quarterly adjustments can be made (as in the lower of cost or market). Chapter 12 illustrates how the inventory method is used in pricing the material usages budget.

The purpose of valuing inventories, among other reasons, is to properly match costs with revenues in determining the results of operations. Presumably, the chief financial officer, in conjunction with the controller and tax manager, has selected the method that most appropriately reflects the income for the period. The annual business plan should incorporate the same accounting principle as do the actual financial statements.

The reader is referred to the many good books on the subject of inventory valuation. But, as a reminder, here is a listing of some of the more commonly used methods:

- Lower of cost or market
- First-in, first-out (FIFO)
- Last-in, first-out (LIFO)
- Identified or specific cost
- Simple arithmetic or average cost
- Weighted average cost

- Moving average cost
- Monthly average cost
- Base or normal stock method
- Replacement cost
- Standard cost

APPROACH TO INVENTORY PLANNING AND CONTROL

Inventory planning and control basically relates to these three basic questions:

- *What* should the inventory level be?
- *When* should specific materials or products be ordered?
- *How much* of each specific item should be ordered?

No single system of inventory management is necessarily the best for an industry or every company in that industry. Each firm may have differing management styles and differing needs. It well may be that a combination of methods is desirable. A great many factors can influence the decision as to the method of planning and controlling inventories, including:

- Nature of the business
- Nature of the product
- Number of products
- Number of storage locations
- Type of information system or communication system existent between operational centers
- Nature of the distribution (marketing) system and delivery system
- Customer service requirements

But management must be assured in the first instance that the proper raw materials and components are on hand to meet the production needs. This contemplates the proper amount of material of the right kind, at the right place, at the right time, and at the right price. It also should expect in the second instance that the finished goods are available to meet customer needs, either by timely shipment to him, or on the shelves available for him — also of the proper type, in the right amount, at the right place, at the right time, and at an acceptable cost.

Some of the techniques used for planning and control, and in budgeting the inventories, include these devices or processes:

- Inventory turnover rates
- ABC method of inventory management
- Material requirements planning (MRP)
- Reorder point systems:
    - a. Reserve stock system (two-bin system)
    - b. Min-max system
    - c. Reservation systems

    d. Visual check systems

    e. Reorder point — EOQ systems

  • Economical order quantity (EOQ)

It is not within the scope of this book to discuss the many systems that may be considered, or the detail technical points of their operation. The readers are referred to the selected references. But comments are made particularly as they apply to budgetary planning and control.

Use of Inventory Turnover Rates

In the planning and control of inventories, an early question to be resolved involves the level of inventory to be maintained. How much stock should be kept on hand? A great many factors may influence it, and judgment is involved. Some companies use turnover ratios or rates as a standard. In long-range *planning,* for example, where the data is of a somewhat broad and general nature, the investment in inventories may be established for each time period by the use of acceptable turnover rates. Even in the annual short-term planning cycle, turnover rates may be employed. However, more precise methods can be used for the early periods in the planning year or for the entire year. In the *control* area, an executive may be held responsible for keeping specified inventories within the turnover standard. It is common for department-store buyers to operate on a turnover basis. Thus, assume an inventory turn of five times is required and that the planned cost of goods sold is $35 million; then the average inventory should not exceed $7 million ($35,000,000 ÷ 5 turns).

The turnover is calculated by dividing the expected usage factor by the average inventory. It is desirable to measure each segment of inventory (and perhaps by location) by its factor, although overall rates could be used. Specifically, the turnover of the four main categories of inventory would be calculated as follows:

$$\text{Finished goods turnover} = \frac{\text{Cost of goods sold (actual or prospective)}}{\text{Average finished goods inventory}}$$

$$\text{Work-in-process turnover} = \frac{\text{Cost of goods manufactured}}{\text{Average work-in-process inventory}}$$

$$\text{Raw materials turnover} = \frac{\text{Materials and parts placed in production}}{\text{Average raw materials inventory}}$$

$$\text{Supplies turnover} = \frac{\text{Cost of supplies used}}{\text{Average supply inventory}}$$

The quotient or answer is the number of turns. Thus, in the annual planning cycle, if the cost of goods sold is expected to be $100 million, and a standard of four turns has been set, then the average inventory for finished goods would be budgeted at $25 million ($100,000,000 ÷ 4). The turnover rate might also be expressed as the average length of inventory on hand. As an example, a turnover of four times could be called a three-month turn.

Inventory turnover rates differ widely by industry and even company, depending on manufacturing methods and the distribution system. For example, a company that merely assembles purchased parts may have a turnover substantially greater than a vertically integrated manufacturer who must carry raw materials and work-in-process inventory in addition to the parts. By the same token, a company handling finished goods through regional warehouses will have a lower turnover rate than one who operates through a wholesaler. Therefore, the factor that causes different turnover rates should be examined. A low turnover rate may signify an excessive inventory. But a higher turnover may be achieved at the expense of lost sales or higher replacement parts purchase cost. The specific reason for a lower turnover should be analyzed before considering corrective action.

Within a given company, turnover trends can be tracked and improvements encouraged to reach acceptable levels.

ABC Method of Inventory Analysis

Acceptable inventory planning and control well may begin with an analysis of the composition of the items in the inventory. Each type of item in stock has its own characteristics which may influence the method of control. How an item in inventory should be planned for and controlled will depend partially upon its cost or value and the cost of control. For example, if one electric motor costs $50,000, then more attention should be paid to the quantity carried in stock, because of the unit investment and related carrying cost, then the stock of $1.50 chromeplated steel bolts.

One of the most widely recognized inventory management systems is known as the ABC method, or proportional parts system. Although originally developed as a manual system to reduce clerical effort and record keeping, the concept is applicable to computerized systems. Under the method, inventory items are categorized into three classes: A, B, and C, based upon unit value and usage. The annual cost usage is determined by multiplying the annual usage in units times the unit value, and then listing all items in descending order of total cost.

Typically, "A" items may represent but 15 percent of the total parts used, but perhaps 65 to 80 percent of the dollar amount of inventory. These high value items are ordered (whether externally for raw stock, or internally for finished product) on an individual item basis and more or less on the basis of the exact quantity needed for a customer or for manufacturing requirements. There may be a daily, weekly, or monthly review of needs, and a corresponding order of the quantities wanted. Changes in the sales plan normally would be quickly reflected in the inventory level and the purchase volumes.

"B" items, the middle value units, typically represent 15 to 20 percent of the quantity of parts in inventory, and a corresponding proportion of the cost. The "B" units may be ordered in quantities differing from actual need, for economic reasons, such as the economical ordering quantity. Perhaps they are ordered three times a year. By purchasing a larger quantity then currently required, the unit cost might be reduced significantly. As discussed later, setup cost, carrying cost, and so forth must be considered.

"C" items often represent 60 to 75 percent of the parts volume, but only 15 percent or so of the value. These low value items might be handled on a min-max basis.

The principle as applied to the material purchases budget is illustrated in Chapter 12.

The point being made is that this method should be considered in selecting the inventory control method.

Material Requirements Planning

Many manufacturing companies use a technique called material requirements planning (MRP) to plan and schedule the materials and purchased parts needed to build for a specific customer order or for inventory. A simplified version was illustrated in Chapter 12 as related to the "explosion" of the material purchases budget. A bill of material and the master schedule is needed. Given the detailed raw material components in the bill of material required for each finished product, and the master production schedule, together with other data, the MRP system explodes or translates the individual order, time-phased, into the gross material requirements. With the lead time to manufacture and purchase known, the purchases, inventory schedules, and so forth can be prepared. Devices such as this facilitate a rather precise planning for inventory.

Reorder Point Systems

The second basic question to be answered in any inventory management system is, *when* should the item be ordered? This, in turn, relates to the reorder point system used to initiate the purchase of material — the stock replenishment system.

Reorder point systems may be divided into two basic categories: (1)

those based on known material requirements, such as a job shop operation or a fixed production schedule; and (2) those systems where a degree of uncertainty exists about needs. As to those known requirements, the MRP systems just described, combined with specialized techniques such as critical path method (CPM), program evaluation and review technique (PERT) or other methods, can explode the production schedules, recognize the safety stock required, and otherwise determine when the materials are needed. Such techniques can be used to order the materials and to budget the inventories.

The other reorder system involves changing stock levels over a period of time, and reflects an estimated volume level and provision for error through safety stock. The basic formula is

$$\text{Reorder point (ROP)} = L(D) + \text{safety stock}$$

where:

L = Anticipated lead time (in weeks)

D = Estimated demand in units per week

When the stock level reaches the reorder point, a purchase requisition is initiated for additional inventory.

Some of the widely used methods to determine when to reorder include those discussed below.

Reserve Stock Method (Two-Bin System). Simply described, this method physically separates the amount of material equal to the reorder point. This is done by putting the reserve stock in a partitioned bin, separate bin, or bag. When it is necessary to use the reserve stock, a purchase requisition is initiated.

No perpetual inventory is maintained, and specific data about the inventory quantity or usage is not known. Reliance is placed on the stores person to originate the purchase order.

Min-Max System. The minimum-maximum method often is used in conjunction with perpetual or manual inventory records. The minimum quantity is determined in the same fashion as the reorder point. The maximum quantity level is the minimum quantity plus the optimum order lot size. In actual operation, a purchase order requisition is originated when the inventory level reaches minimum. The key to the system effectiveness is the reasonableness or accuracy with which the min-max perimeters are established. This system also can be used in setting inventory budget.

Reservation System. This system, in effect, recognizes the requirements prior to disbursement of the stock, and the available stock as well as the physical stock. The available stock usually is the physical stock on hand, less the open (unfilled) requirements, plus the stock on order. The reorder point is based on the available stock balance rather than the physical balance on hand.

Visual Check System. This system may seem like old times, as when the owner or manager of the general store or very small business checks his stock levels. With his knowledge of the business and sales prospects, he can determine when to reorder. While it may seem highly subjective, it may work in some situations. Obviously, the quality of the decision depends on the judgment of the checker and the frequency of review.

The Reorder Point — EOQ System. The system depends on tables and charts and related equations to determine the reorder point and the economical order quantity (EOQ). Computers and models involving many variables can be employed on an objective basis to make the calculations. In some circumstances, charts and tables may be used to reflect selected levels.

As a general statement, there are a number of methods of determining the reorder point. Those persons involved with the control of inventories and budgets should be familiar with the uses and limitations of each.

Economical Order Quantity

In connection with replenishing inventories, the last of the three questions is, how much material should be ordered? In those instances where the order quantity is based on an analysis of related costs, the quantity ordered often is referred to as the economical order quantity, or EOQ.

A formula has been developed which takes into account the four variables that determine the order quantity: (1) the planned or forecasted annual usage of the item, expressed in units; (2) the variable or out-of-pocket expenses associated with order handling, including both issuance and follow-up; (3) the expense of carrying the inventory for one year; and (4) the variable cost of one unit. The formula may be expressed in this fashion:

$$\text{EOQ} = \sqrt{\frac{2AO}{C}}$$

where:

A = Estimated annual usage of the item

O = Average annual variable expense of handling the order

C = Annual carrying cost of one unit in inventory for one year (insurance, storage, cost of interest or return on capital for the investment, etc.)

To apply the formula, assume these facts:

Planned annual usage in units	10,000
Cost to place and follow up on order	$17.50
Annual cost of carrying one unit in inventory	$2.40

Applying the formula, the EOQ is 382 units calculated as follows:

$$EOQ = \sqrt{\frac{(2)(10,000)(\$17.50)}{\$2.40}}$$

$$= \sqrt{\frac{350,000}{2.40}}$$

$$= \sqrt{145,833}$$

$$= 382 \text{ units}$$

This particular item would be ordered 27 times per year (10,000 ÷ 382).

BUDGETARY CONTROL

The techniques of control through minimum-maximum inventory points, turnover rates, or executive decisions regarding speculation can each be used alone, against all or some segments of the inventory. However, in some companies, the inventories are tied in more closely, more formally, to expected operations. This is accomplished through budgetary control, of which inventory planning is a phase. After all, many of the same considerations necessary in establishing turnover rates or minimum or maximum inventories are required in budgeting the purchases and inventory. Usually, budgetary control tends to get the inventories coordinated more closely with expected usage. This application is discussed in the next few sections.

Budgeting the Materials Inventory

There are basically two methods of developing the inventory budget of raw materials and supplies:

1. Budget each important item separately based upon the production program.
2. Budget materials as a whole or as classes of materials based upon selected production factors.

Practically all concerns must employ both methods to some extent, though one or the other predominates. The former method is always preferable to the extent that it is practicable.

In Chapter 12, the materials budget for both purchases and usage is discussed, and the reader is referred to the subject matter. However, material purchases and usage are intimately linked to the inventory budget for materials. It may be helpful to relate the budgeting of major items of raw materials for the combined aspects by this summary:

The following steps should be taken in budgeting the major individual items of materials and supplies:

1. Determine the physical units of material required for each item of goods which is to be produced during the budget period.
2. Accumulate these into total physical units of each material item required for the entire production program.
3. Determine for each item of material the quantity which should be on hand periodically to provide for the production program with a reasonable margin of safety.
4. Deduct material inventories, which it is expected will be on hand at the beginning of the budget period, to ascertain the total quantities to be purchased.
5. Develop a purchase program which will insure that the quantities will be on hand at the time they are needed. The purchase program must give effect to such factors as economically sized orders, economy of transportation, and margin of safety against delays.
6. Test the resulting budgeted inventories by standard turnover rates.
7. Translate the inventory and purchase requirements into monetary amounts by applying the expected prices of materials to budgeted quantities.

In practice, many difficulties arise in executing the foregoing plan. In fact, it is practicable to apply it only to important items of material which are used regularly and in relatively large quantities. Most manufacturing concerns find that they must carry hundreds or even thousands of different items of materials and supplies to which this plan cannot be practically applied. Moreover, some concerns cannot express their production programs in units of specific products. This is true, for example, where goods are partially or entirely made to customers' specifications. In such cases, it is necessary to look to past experience to ascertain the rate and the regular-

FIG. 21-1   Summary Materials Inventory Budget

THE GENUINE COMPANY

MATERIALS INVENTORY BUDGET
For the Plan Year 19XX
(dollars in thousands)

Month	Beginning Inventory	Purchases	Usage	Ending Inventory
January	$42,610	$ 21,840	$ 21,040	$43,410
February	43,410	20,460	21,500	42,370
March	42,370	22,400	21,910	42,860
Total	$42,610	$ 64,700	$ 64,450	$42,860
April	42,860	21,540	20,870	43,530
May	43,530	20,760	21,600	42,690
June	42,690	21,870	21,930	42,630
Total	$42,860	$ 64,170	$ 64,400	$42,630
July	42,630	22,870	22,450	43,050
August	43,050	24,500	22,670	44,880
September	44,880	22,040	23,100	43,820
Total	$42,630	$ 69,410	$ 68,220	$43,820
October	43,820	18,120	20,160	41,780
November	41,780	17,800	19,700	39,880
December	39,880	18,210	19,000	39,090
Total	$43,820	$ 54,130	$ 58,860	$39,090
Grand Total	$42,610	$252,410	$255,930	$39,090

ity of movement of individual material items and to determine maximum and minimum quantities between which the quantities must be held. This necessitates a program of continuous review of material records as a basis for purchasing, and frequent revision of maximum and minimum limits, to keep the quantities adjusted to current needs.

Chapter 12 reviews the budgeting for the movement into and out of raw materials inventory — regardless of the class of material. But it should be observed that suitable inventory levels must be set. When the policy concerning inventory levels is established and applied, the materials inventory budget may be summarized as shown in Figure 21-1. The entire movement through the inventory is depicted. This is useful in cross-checking or tying in the purchases and usage budgets with the inventory budget to assure all are consistent. It is to be observed that the inventory policy is, roughly speaking, to stock approximately two months of expected usage, or to secure a turnover of six times per year. Computer techniques for records and faster communication systems between plants and vendors assist in maintaining inventories at lower levels.

Additionally, this inventory summary may be supported by appropriate listings by material categories or margin items, showing both units on hand and monetary levels for the designed time period.

The Work-in-Process Inventory Budget

The work-in-process inventory is the buffer between the direct materials inventory and the finished goods inventory. Input of direct labor, materials, and manufacturing expenses is largely controlled by the production budget. (See Chapter 10.) However, for several reasons, the time taken in process, and before transfer to finished goods inventory or directly to the customer, sometimes is excessive. To be sure, it often is economically wise to maintain substantial inventories of only partially finished goods as a means of assuring quick completion of some items in finished stock, and as a means of reducing the finished goods inventory. But given a tendency to accumulate excess work-in-process inventories, this current asset must be planned and controlled.

Some parts, partially assembled items, and items individually identified and stocked as selected centers may be planned and controlled in the same manner as direct materials. Thus, inventory quantities may be set for individual items based on enforcement of the production program; or perhaps based on standard turnover rates or min-max controls.

The inventory may be planned and controlled overall, or by department or cost center, based on standard turnover rates based on planned production. As an illustration, assume the following for a particular department:

1. In process inventory planned for March 1: 300 units (a)
2. Budgeted production for March (in units): 1,600 (b)
3. Standard number of turns (per month): 4 (c)
4. Average unit value per piece: $25

If the standard number of turns is four per month, then the average inventory should be 400 units (1,600 ÷ 4). To provide an average inventory of these 400 units, an ending inventory of 500 is within the limits, calculated in this way using ninth-grade algebra.

$$\frac{300 + X}{2} = 400$$

$$\frac{2(300 + X)}{2} = 2(400)$$

$$300 + X = 800$$

$$X = 500$$

Or, the ending inventory can be calculated using this formula:

$$X = \frac{2b}{c} - a = \frac{2(1,600)}{4} - 300$$

$$= 800 - 300$$

$$= 500 \text{ units}$$

where:
  X = Quantity to be budgeted as ending inventory
  a = Estimated beginning inventory
  b = Budgeted production for the month
  c = Standard monthly turnover rate

If the formula produces a negative quantity, which may result from excessive beginning inventory, then a specific estimate should be made for the department.

Control of work-in-process can be maintained by a continuous review of turnover rates with a special investigation made of excessive segments.

A typical work-in-process budget is summarized in Figure 21-2. Both input and output are shown — though in practice they would be supported by more details of kind of input (such as direct labor, direct material, and manufacturing expenses by department) and specifically priced finished product output.

To save space, the full monthly data is not presented. Note that the summary shows the detail of the input which can be checked against the corresponding operations planning budget. The detail of the transfers to finished goods can be cross-checked to the finished goods inventory plan-

FIG. 21-2 Summary — Work-in-Process Inventory Budget

THE GENUINE COMPANY
SUMMARY OF WORK-IN-PROCESS BUDGET
For the Plan Year 19XX
(dollars in thousands)

Month	Beginning Inventory	Total Direct Material(a)	Total Direct Labor	Total Manufacturing Overhead	Total	Subtotal	Transfers to Finished Goods	Ending Inventory
January	$31,700	$ 21,040	$ 42,300	$ 63,450	$ 126,790	$ 158,490	$ 126,000	$32,490
February	32,490	21,500	43,160	64,740	129,400	161,890	129,890	32,000
March	32,000	21,910	43,960	65,940	131,810	163,810	135,510	28,300
Total								
Quarter 1	$31,700	$ 64,450	$129,420	$194,130	$ 388,000	$ 419,700	$ 391,400	$28,300
Quarter 2	28,300	64,400	131,760	197,640	393,800	422,100	389,600	32,500
Quarter 3	32,500	68,220	137,100	205,650	410,970	443,470	406,270	37,200
Quarter 4	37,200	58,860	129,400	195,100	383,360	420,560	388,560	32,000
Total	$31,700	$255,930	$527,680	$792,520	$1,576,130	$1,607,830	$1,575,830	$32,000

(a) From Figure 21-1

ning budget. The summary also provides a means of reviewing inventory trends and the turnovers.

Budgeting Finished Goods Inventory

Just as the direct materials inventory must be adequate to properly support the production plan or budget, so also the finished goods inventory must support the sales plan or budget. If, for example, it is expected that 10,000 units of finished product X will be sold during the budget period, then the production plan (see Chapter 10) and the finished goods inventory budget must be so determined that the units will be available when required to meet the expected sales demand. Any reasonable inventory policy, of course, will allow a margin of safety for variances in customer demand if the product comes from stock. In this connection, it should be mentioned that a number of computer manufacturers have developed computer software programs which may assist retailers, wholesalers, and manufacturers to maintain a proper assortment of items while balancing two basic and conflicting goals — maximum level of service and minimum inventory investment.

Basically, there are two ways to budget the finished goods inventory: (1) each specific item is budgeted separately; or (2) the inventory must be budgeted in the aggregate or by specific groups — but not by individual item.

Where there is a limited variety or number of the product, and where the unit value is quite high, then budgeting by individual item may be desirable. Under this basis, the sales plan is developed on the basis of sales analyses, expected trends, and so forth (see Chapter 9). On the basis of the sales plan, the production budget and all related budgets are prepared — the direct materials budget, including purchases and usage and inventory; the direct labor budget; the manufacturing expense budget; and the cost of materials used in production budget. The finished goods inventory budget obviously is the sum of the extension of the budgeted quantities on hand times the budgeted cost.

Control over the finished goods inventory normally will be accomplished by enforcement of the sales and production programs. If either departs significantly from the plan, then adjustments must be made to compensate for the variances, and the inventory budgets will require corresponding change. The total finished goods inventory budget, if necessary, can be tested by the use of turnover rates, as earlier discussed.

The advent of the computer and related technology is permitting the development of finished goods inventory budgets by individual item to a greater degree, and involving smaller values. Nevertheless, there are circumstances, and there comes a time, when it simply is not practical or economical to budget by individual item. Under these conditions, finished

---

FIG. 21-3   Summary of Finished Goods Inventory Budget

THE GENUINE COMPANY

SUMMARY OF FINISHED GOODS INVENTORY BUDGET

For the Plan Year 19XX

(dollars in thousands)

Month	Beginning Inventory	Transfers From Work In Process(a)	Transfers to Cost of Goods Sold	Ending Inventory
January	$256,100	126,000	116,700	$265,400
February	265,400	129,890	129,490	265,800
March	265,800	135,510	143,810	257,500
Total				
Quarter 1	$256,100	391,400	390,000	$257,500
Quarter 2	257,500	389,600	376,100	271,000
Quarter 3	271,000	406,270	417,270	260,000
Quarter 4	260,000	388,560	399,460	249,100
Total	$256,100	1,575,830	1,582,830	$249,100

Average number of turns   6.27

(a)   From Figure 21-2

---

goods inventory may be budgeted through establishing turnover rates for the category. These rates may be determined on an overall basis, or perhaps, preferably, by classes of products. Thus, it might be decided that certain auto parts might have a turnover of six times per year, while small appliances warrant a turnover of only four times.

When the sales plan is developed, the finished goods inventory budget is based on these predetermined standards. As the year progresses, the appropriate executives are charged with seeing that the individual classes of goods are so controlled that the overall inventory, or segments, conform to the turnover standards.

Having determined the acceptable inventory level, those in charge of finished goods inventory must use some of the control devices mentioned earlier, such as min-max quantities or reserve stock, to keep the total inventory within budget. Thus, individual items should be checked, keeping track of movement, trend in demand, and expected changes, to the end that adjustments in production plans are made to keep production and inventory levels in line with anticipated sales.

Inventory control cannot be considered purely a routine operation, although many routine functions must be performed. The successful inventory control plan requires the exercise of judgment, a continuous check of sales trends, and records of movement of the individual items.

An illustrative summary of a finished goods inventory budget is shown in Figure 21-3. This reflects the movements in and out of inventory, to be cross-checked against the production plan and the cost of sales budget. The summary reflects monetary aggregates but, where applicable, supporting data will reflect units as well as dollars.

INVENTORY REPORTS

It is through the use of reports that facts or opinions are conveyed to management for its use in the planning and control of inventory. But the facts must be communicated on a timely basis and must be understood if they are to be acted upon. With the advent of the computer and related equipment, data transmission is facilitated — some of it on a real-time basis. The data are stored in the computer and may be retrieved and displayed on a screen or tube at the work station.

Summarizations, analysis, and comparisons quite often are needed, and this is where a responsive reporting system is valuable. The types of reports to be issued for the planning and control of inventories might be said to be limited only by the imagination of the preparer and the cost of gathering and analyzing the data.

A simple listing of some of the inventory reports found useful are these (in no special order):

- General summary of inventory, by category
- Comparison of planned and actual inventory, by inventory category by investment center (Figure 21-4)
- Comparison of inventory activity and commitments as related to requirements
- Inventory turnover by part number (Figure 21-5)
- Stock status report (Figure 21-6)
- Report on physical counts (Figure 21-7)
- Projections of inventory status as selected periods, such as year-end

FIG. 21-4 Comparison of Planned and Actual Inventory

THE PARTS MANUFACTURING COMPANY

COMPARISON OF PLANNED AND ACTUAL INVENTORY

As of March 31, 19XX

(dollars in thousands)

Item	March 31			Indicated Status at 12/31/XX		
	Actual	Plan	(Over) Under Plan	Estimated	Plan	(Over) Under Plan
Eastern Division						
Raw materials	$20,600	$22,600	$2,000	$23,800	$24,800	$1,000
Work-in-process	12,500	12,400	(100)	10,100	10,100	—
Finished goods	16,870	17,300	430	14,200	14,300	100
Total	$49,970	$52,300	$2,330	$48,100	$49,200	$1,100
Western Division						
Raw materials	$12,850	$12,300	($ 550)	$17,400	$17,400	—
Work-in-process	5,200	5,700	500	4,000	4,100	100
Finished goods	9,300	8,900	(400)	10,600	10,700	100
Total	$27,350	26,900	(450)	$32,000	$32,200	$ 200
Canadian Division ($US)						
Finished goods	$ 8,450	$ 8,700	$ 250	$10,200	$10,000	($ 200)
Total	$ 8,450	$ 8,700	$ 250	$10,200	$10,000	($ 200)
Raw materials	$33,450	$34,900	$1,450	$41,200	$42,200	$1,000
Work-in-process	17,700	18,100	400	14,100	14,200	100
Finished goods	34,620	34,900	280	35,000	35,000	—
Grand Total	$85,770	$87,900	$2,130	$90,300	$91,400	$1,100

FIG. 21-5 Inventory Turnover Report

INVENTORY ANALYSIS

Inventory Class	Part Number	Part Name	Month	Day	Year	Number of Transactions	Twelve Months' Usage	Average Inventory	Turnover
142		HARDWARE							
	3298	SCREW	12	10		65	25,440	1,020	25
	3786	SCREW	12	15		32	37,850	3,128	12
	4325	WASHER	10	20		875	102,750	31,427	3
	4326	WASHER	12	10		624	9846,200	824,700	12
	10111	NUT	1	15		1	1	3,100	
	11121	BOLT	12	13		130	48,750	8,107	6
	12032	COTTER PIN	4	11		64	6,547	2,182	3
	13242	SCREW	11	28		770	125,470	10,455	12
	28785	BOLT	10	27		700	95,622	95,675	1
	35435	BOLT	12	3		500	428,720	9,075	48
	43292	NUT	6	15		28	65,280	10,880	6
	47856	WASHER	10	23		139	325,755	13,330	25
	49221	PIN	12	7		270	95,470	8,247	12
	55687	TAPER PIN	12	7		801	428,675	221,525	2
	65493	LOCKWASHER	11	21		765	795,250	400,550	2
	65494	LOCKWASHER	11	9		724	787,343	196,805	4
	65495	LOCKWASHER	10	11		158	60,222	20,074	3
	72187	STUD	7	14		103	30,480	3,810	8
	72195	STUD	8	17		48	32,765	4,096	8
	75148	SCREW	12	2		725	865,420	96,150	9
	90185	BOLT	11	30		415	528,780	52,961	10

FIG. 21-6   Stock Status Summary and Availability Report

STOCK STATUS
SUMMARY

Item Description	Item Code	Issues Year to Date	Last Active Mo	Day	E.O.Q.	Average Unit Cost	Previous Balance	– Issues
SQ SHANK SWIVEL	11202	3825	6	10	250	8 50	250	75
SQ SOCKET RIGID	16102	6775	6	18	300	2 05	1750	1500
EXT SHANK WITH BRK	17203	2445	6	15	350	4 30	575	125
ADJ ADAPTER SQUARE	23702	6518	6	20	375	18 68	1370	243
SQ SOCKET SWIVEL	26302	6682	6	10	250	1 12	175	112
FLAT TOP SWIVEL	33202	6725	5	20	200	1 04	4650	
FLAT TOP SWIVEL	33205	5924	6	05	375	1 06	2257	662
CUSTOM BUILT	35105	6827	6	20	420	34 01	3652	300
RND SPR RING STEM	44104	5525	5	10	300	42	257	
RND SPR RING STEM	44106	4537	6	09	325	50	1022	785
SQ SHANK RIGID	51105	4357	6	19	300	1 50	1572	637
FLAT TOP SWIVEL	53208	6498	6	25	150	2 75	2275	278
FLAT TOP SWIVEL	53209	3752	4	15	200	2 50	1027	
ROUND SOCKET SWIVL	55706	5722	4	25	125	3 42	1975	
BOLT AND NUT SHANK	62110	7712	6	17	175	30	4025	837
CUSTOM BUILT	65112	5428	6	05	175	27 50	2172	250

PERIOD ENDING _____ ACTION

+ Receipts	= On Hand	Minimum Balance	+ On Order	– Requests	= Available	Inactivity	Reorder
100	275	100			275		
	250	500	1000		1250		
	450	100	700	1138	13		*
	1127	200		170	957		
25	88	600		30	54		*
	4650	300			4650	*	
75	1670	100			1670		
420	3772	100	125	160	3737		
	257	200			267	*	
700	937	100			937		
150	1085	200			1085		
	1997	150		400	1597		
	1027	50			1027	*	
	1975	225			1975	*	
	3188	150		500	2688		
	1922	100	400		2322		

FIG. 21-7   Report on Physical Inventory Differences

REPORT ON INVENTORY DIFFERENCES
ROTATING INVENTORY

Date _____

Description	Item Number	Unit	Physical Count	Stores Record Quantity	Physical Over (Short)	Unit Cost	Value Gain	Loss
Batteries	41,213	each	324	324	—	—	—	—
Cable ig., wire — small	77,021	feet	227	207	20	$ .20	$4.00	—
Distributor — "C"	26,110	each	116	120	(4)	4.00	—	$16.00
Spark plug assembly	8,510	each	42	42	—	—	—	—
Pulleys — ½"	91,306	dozen	5	4	1	3.00	3.00	—
Hub caps — 2½	70,010	each	62	64	(2)	1.75	—	3.50
Page Total							$7.00	$19.50

SUMMARY

	Units	Percent
Items Correct	410	90.7
Items Incorrect	42	9.3
Total Counted	452	100.0%
Net Gain or (Loss)		($305.10)

22

Other Current Assets

Part III, Working Capital Budget, discusses the major individual segments of the two components of working capital: namely, the current assets and the current liabilities, where current assets are defined as cash and other assets or resources commonly identified as those that reasonably are expected to be realized in cash or sold or consumed during the normal operating cycle of the business. Because of their individual importance in most companies, the chief components of current assets have each been discussed separately in Chapters 19 through 21. The remaining category, largely represented by prepaid expenses, is briefly reviewed now.

WHAT PREPAID EXPENSES INCLUDE

In authoritative accounting literature, the last category of current assets discussed in defining this general term is "prepaid expenses such as insurance, interest, rents, taxes, unused royalties, current paid advertising service not yet received, and operating supplies."[1] The same source goes on to state that "prepaid expenses are not current assets in the sense that they will be converted into cash but in the sense that, if not paid in advance, they would require the use of current assets during the operating cycle." [2]

Most published financial statements may include other minor miscellaneous assets (e.g., deposits, advances, and claims), which warrant being categorized as current, but the discussion in this chapter is limited to prepaid items. If transactions are contemplated in the planning period that involve any of the miscellaneous assets, they should be reflected in the plan in the manner in which it is expected they will be recorded upon occurrence.

WHY BUDGET THE PREPAID ITEMS?

Since the sum of the prepaid items is quite small on most statements of financial position, why budget them at all? While the author is not disposed to plan and track insignificant items, the true measure of importance of such items probably is not the *balance* in the accounts at the *end* of the year, but rather the impact on the financial statements during the year, and especially the impact on the income statement. This category should be budgeted for the following reasons:

☐ The aggregate of payments for prepaid items during a planning year or years is usually significant and should be identified and included in the cash budget. Cash transactions in the annual plan or strategic plan should also be reflected in the appropriate asset accounts. For example, property taxes and insurance aggregate millions of dollars annually in many companies and should be recognized.

☐ The expense disposition of the prepaid items is significant in most companies, and, if ignored, could represent an important gap in the statement of planned income and expense, especially when actual and plan are compared. The integrity of the income statement practically demands that the prepaid items be properly handled in the planning and control process.

☐ Finally, with the availability of computers and the relative ease of recording the plan transactions, it probably is prudent, as a discipline, to handle the plan accounting in as close a fashion to the actual accounting as is practical. This avoids the temptation to avoid recording other planned transactions, the sum of which might be significant.

---

[1] Paul Grady, *Inventory of Generally Accepted Accounting Principles for Business Enterprises,* Accounting Research Study No. 7 (New York: AICPA, 1965), p. 235.

[2] *Ibid.*, p. 235.

FIG. 22-1 Schedule for Prepaid Taxes

THE APPLIANCE CORPORATION

SCHEDULE FOR PREPAID TAXES
For the Plan Year Ending 12/31/19XX
(dollars in thousands)

Month	Beginning Balance	Additions	Amortization	Other Adjustments	Ending Balance
January	$ 4,230	—	$ 1,410	—	$ 2,820
February	2,820	—	1,410	—	1,410
March	1,410	—	1,410	—	—
April	—	$18,120	1,510	—	16,610
May	16,610	—	1,510	—	15,100
June	15,100	—	1,510	—	13,590
July	13,590	1,812	1,711	—	13,691
August	13,691	—	1,711	—	11,980
September	11,980	—	1,711	—	10,269
October	10,269	—	1,711	—	8,558
November	8,558	—	1,711	($47)	6,800
December	6,800	—	1,700	—	5,100
Total	$ 4,230	$19,932	$19,015	($47)	$ 5,100

THE BUDGETARY METHOD

Each of the categories in the prepaid expense grouping probably warrants budgetary treatment on an individual basis. While prepaid taxes will be used as an example, each account would be handled in a comparable way. The basic principle is to plan each transaction as it is expected to occur: the payment for, or acquisition of, the asset, and the amortization on a sound basis. The planned transactions for prepaid taxes for the annual business plan are illustrated in Figure 22-1.

When all analysis and planning has been completed, a summary budget may be prepared for all prepaid items as in Figure 22-2. This information serves to advise management as to exactly what constitutes the "other current assets" at year end and the transactions planned for the year. Oral or written commentary can explain any unusual expected events, such as the impact of a new operation or the closure of an obsolete plant.

FIG. 22-2   Summary Budget for Other Current Assets

THE APPLIANCE CORPORATION

BUDGET FOR OTHER CURRENT ASSETS
For the Plan Year Ending 12/31/19XX
(dollars in thousands)

Item	Beginning Balance	Additions	Deductions	Ending Balance
Prepaid insurance	$ 6,820	$22,480	$20,212	$ 9,088
Prepaid taxes	4,230	19,932	19,062	5,100
Prepaid interest	2,730	1,000	2,420	1,310
Advance royalties	1,910	—	1,200	710
Prepaid rent	850	200	750	300
Sundry deposits	410	—	—	410
Miscellaneous	40	—	—	40
Total	$16,990	$43,612	$43,644	$16,958

BUDGET REPORTS

In most companies no periodic reports are necessary for the prepaid items or other current assets except as a line item in the monthly statement of financial position. Usually, these assets are not the focus of problems, and control is not difficult. The financial officers should secure occasional analyses of the items as part of their review of the financial statements, but more for the purpose of ascertaining that the proper accounting is being followed rather than controlling the asset.

23

Current Liabilities

CORPORATE LIQUIDITY AND CURRENT LIABILITIES

It is particularly in periods of economic distress, such as the recessions of 1974–1975 or 1981–1982, that the matter of corporate liquidity receives attention. Record business failures, record bankruptcies, and major declines in business activity levels and profit rates, make business management much more aware of the need to properly control liabilities.

The proper management of liabilities enables a company to survive economic storms. In the 1981–1982 recession, firms deeply in debt fared differently than those that reduced debt and guarded corporate liquidity, perhaps at the expense of corporate growth.[1] The management of liabilities starts not when a business is in financial difficulty, but in the planning process, whether the annual budget or the long-range plan is used. The proper level of liabilities and, indeed, the proper *composition* of liabilities, both current and long-term, must be planned. Such planning does not involve merely reviewing the year-end status. It is not sufficient to conclude, in the budgeting process, that the year-end financial position is adequate. Especially in those firms without a top credit rating, it is necessary to watch the *trend* of key indicators (discussed later in this chapter) from month to month to ascertain if a problem is developing and to take steps to prevent it. Moreover, once the budget is approved, proper budgetary control usually requires a check of actual trends of certain indicators to spot problems early. Trends relating to current liabilities are discussed in this chapter, but other signals relating to sales and cost or expense control and to asset management are reviewed in Chapter 24, dealing with working capital.

NATURE OF CURRENT LIABILITIES

From a practical business standpoint, corporate liquidity problems usually surface first in the current liability section of the balance sheet. This is true,

---

[1] *The Wall Street Journal*, April 30, 1982, p. 1.

among other reasons, because companies experience cash deficiencies and incur short-term bank obligations, or typically, because they slow the payment of short-term debt with the consequent reduction in working capital. Accordingly, this chapter concentrates on the planning and control of *current* liabilities.

The current liability section of a typical U.S. company would include these items, albeit in several different groupings or combinations:

- Notes payable
- Long-term debt due within one year
- Accounts payable
- Dividends payable

- Accrued income taxes
- Accrued compensation and related items
- Other current liabilities

In the budgeting process, the budgeting executive is guided by two basic principles:

1. Follow generally accepted accounting practice in the account segregation.
2. Identify or separate for planning purposes the most active and significant current liability accounts from the others.

The first principle should be followed so that management will know the level and content of the current liabilities in the internal statements of financial position. The second principle is practical because the more active accounts will probably be budgeted separately (i.e., accounts payable, accrued compensation), and those of less significance and activity will be grouped for ease in planning (i.e., other current assets and other accrued items).

While a complete discussion of technical accounting definitions or conventions is not within the scope of this book, some general comments may be helpful.

Overall Definition

"Current liabilities" generally are defined as those due to be paid within the operating cycle — usually a one-year period. A related definition includes as current liabilities obligations whose liquidation is expected to require the use of existing current assets or the creation of new current liabilities.

Significant Categories

While the accounting-trained budget coordinator is familiar with the content of the various categories of current liabilities, a few comments about some of the more common balance sheet classifications may be helpful. In any particular company, for internal purposes the segregations used should

- Be critical and must be closely followed for control purposes;
- Lend themselves to a natural grouping in the planning process; this grouping should be consistent with the actual recording procedure (i.e. accounts payable, accrued income taxes, and so forth); and
- Be of major significance and should be disclosed in the published financial statements (i.e., current portion of long-term debt).

Following are some observations on some common categories of current liabilities.

Notes Payable. The short-term notes payable included in current liabilities represent the obligations of the company evidenced by an explicit promise to pay a specified amount at a specified time. Although the category ordinarily represents notes payable to commercial banks, it may include other notes, such as commercial paper. To preserve the credit standing of the company, these obligations should be paid when due. The budgeting process should identify the amount of the payment and the payment date, and provide for the timely liquidation of these obligations. The current portion of long-term debt also should be scheduled and specifically budgeted for timely payment.

Accounts Payable. For the most part, accounts payable represent amounts due to trade creditors for materials and services. As such, the obligation is closely related to the budgeting of inventories and the many categories of expenses throughout the many functional organizations. The charges to inventory accounts and the many expense accounts are offset by the recording of the account payable. This category is one of the largest current liabilities on most balance sheets. Obviously, accounts payable should be maintained on a current basis to preserve the credit standing of the company.

Accrued Expenses. Accrued expenses, or accrued liabilities, represent short-term obligations for which invoices normally are not received from the creditor, but that nevertheless periodically must be accumulated or computed from other source documents. They may be calculated with the passage of time (such as salaries and wages, vacation pay, payroll taxes, retirement expenses, or interest expense) or in accordance with company policy (product warranties, royalties, advertising expense). Normally, an obligation exists when benefits have been received but payment is not yet due. Hence, it is recorded as an accrued expense.

The accrued expense or liabilities category also bulks large on most balance sheets and is periodically recorded from more or less standard journals, each easily identified. Again, the offsets in both budgeting and actual accounting are largely to inventory or expense accounts.

Accrued Income Taxes. In the normal accounting system, taxes based on income, whether federal, state, local, or foreign, are separately calculated periodically based on applicable laws or statutes. Since tax expense is a significant cost for most profitable companies, and because failure to make timely payment can incur heavy penalties, it is usually budgeted as a separate item.

The principal current liabilities for most enterprises are covered by the previous categories. For ease in establishing budgets, it is desirable to group the obligations so as to avoid a morass of individual accounting entries. Where this cannot be done, or where a particular liability must be tracked, then specific provision should be made in the budgeting process. Examples of current liabilities to be provided for in the plan, even if the exact amount is unknown, could include matters in litigation, claims payable, dividends payable, tax assessments, and refunds to customers. The business plan or budget should provide for all known liabilities so that the financial position will be fairly presented. Actual or probable significant liabilities should be distinguished from significant contingent liabilities (as in outlining the plan assumptions to the board of directors). (See Chapter 28.)

NOTES PAYABLE BUDGET

The corporate need for making timely payments on the obligations to commercial banks or other short-term lenders is obvious. The company's credit standing must be maintained so that required funds will be available when needed. Hence, the notes-payable budget should be prepared on a conservative basis, and payment terms should be met.

Whereas the accounts payable and accrued compensation budgets, for example, represent voluminous transactions, for most companies the activity in notes payable is quite limited. The cash budget (see Chapter 19) usually indicates when funds are needed and when cash is available to repay the loan. In some companies, these are specific dates evidenced by short-term notes. In other firms, especially the larger ones, a revolving credit agreement may exist, so that funds may be borrowed daily and paid back with equal

FIG. 23-1   Notes Payable Budget

THE WENDY MANUFACTURING COMPANY

NOTES PAYABLE BUDGET

For the Year Ending December 31, 19XX

(dollars in thousands)

Month	Beginning Balance	Borrowings	Repayments	Ending Balance
January	—	$1,300	—	$1,300
February	$1,300	2,100	—	3,400
March	3,400	3,800	—	7,200
April	7,200	—	—	7,200
May	7,200	—	$ 500	6,700
June	6,700	—	1,100	5,600
July	5,600	—	1,300	4,300
August	4,300	—	2,000	2,300
September	2,300	—	1,000	1,300
October	1,300	—	300	1,000
November	1,000	—	1,000	—
December	—	—	—	—
Total	$ —	$7,200	$7,200	$ —

frequency. In any event, the budget should reflect the expected transactions in accordance with the terms of the agreement. The availability of funds is usually subject to the maintenance of satisfactory ratios, including working capital levels, and an acceptable financial position. This is another reason for careful planning and monitoring of the current liabilities of all types.

Part of the budgeting process includes testing the financial position or operating results, or both, against the requirements of the lenders, as evidenced by the credit agreement or other contract. For example, the percentage of accounts receivable and inventories deemed necessary to support the credit should be checked for adequacy.

When reviewing the annual plan with the banks supplying funds, the expected requirements, time of repayment, and financial tests should be explained. The notes-payable budget schedule for a typical company, with only limited transactions, is illustrated in Figure 23-1.

BUDGETING ACCOUNTS PAYABLE

The budgeting of accounts payable is closely related to the level of business activity. Purchases of raw materials, supplies, and parts, on the one hand, and procurement of operating expense items, or capital assets, on the other, usually reflect existing and expected business volume and profitability. As a matter of fact, receipt of these items creates an entry to accounts payable. In a similar fashion, the requirement to pay for these obligations is an integral part of the cash budget. (See Figures 19-1 and 19-2). A budget for accounts payable, whether manually or computer-maintained, would appear essentially as in Figure 23-2. The specific segregations depend, in part, upon the degree considered necessary for planning and control purposes. Thus, the management system would probably identify the accounts payable incurred for inventory items; the accounts for expense elements might be grouped or split by responsibility function, depending on each individual case.

The additions to accounts payable are the logical offset to the raw material and purchased parts inventory budget or to the various expense budgets. Ordinarily this offsetting presents no problems. The reduction in accounts payable by reason of cash disbursements, however, must recognize the normal payment cycle to the vendors. If a large portion of the accounts payable originates with two or three major vendors, such as for aircraft engines or for steel, it may be desirable to account for such invoices separately and to group the remaining vendors' obligations (which may be in the hundreds or thousands of dollars) and use an average or typical payment period. Thus, assume that invoices from Major Vendor A, accounting for 25 percent of the raw material purchases, are due on 10th proximo (the tenth of the following month), and that other typical payment terms are net, 10 days. A computer prepared or manual worksheet calculating the month-end budget is illustrated in Figure 23-3. If the payments are not synchronized with obligations incurred in the budget process, then the accounts payable balance will soon appear to be incorrect. Note that the more specific the accounts payable calculation (such as for ten major vendors), the greater the computational effort.

ACCRUED COMPENSATION BUDGET

One of the significant costs in most companies is salaries and wages. Because the benefits are incurred in one period but usually paid in another, the costs appear in the accrued expenses category on the balance sheet.

The source of data for the accrued compensation budget is the estimated

FIG. 23-2   Accounts Payable Budget

THE NMM MANUFACTURING COMPANY
ACCOUNTS PAYABLE BUDGET
For the year Ending December 31, 19XX
(dollars in millions)

Item	January	February	March	Total 1st Quarter	Annual
Balance, beginning of month	$47,300	$44,710	$41,510	$ 47,300	$ 47,300
Add					
Purchases — Raw materials	$37,300	$27,600	$43,100	$108,000	$464,400
Purchases — Capital assets	2,600	1,430	3,200	7,230	29,320
Manufacturing expenses	8,100	7,930	8,500	24,530	97,640
Selling expenses	2,400	2,300	2,610	7,310	27,870
R&D expenses	900	850	920	2,670	10,700
Administrative expenses	1,300	1,300	1,300	3,900	16,460
All other	40	30	60	130	460
Total additions	$52,640	$41,440	$59,690	$153,770	$646,850
Deduct					
Payments — Raw materials	$41,300	$30,800	$37,900	$110,000	$467,000
— Operating expenses	11,900	12,000	12,300	36,200	144,900
— Capital assets	2,000	1,800	3,400	7,200	26,300
— Other	30	40	40	110	400
Total deductions	$55,230	$44,640	$53,640	$153,510	$638,600
Balance, end of month	$44,710	$41,510	$47,560	$ 47,560	$ 55,550

FIG. 23-3 Worksheet for Calculation of Accounts Payable Budget

THE ILLUSTRATIVE COMPANY

WORKSHEET FOR CALCULATION OF ACCOUNTS PAYABLE BUDGET

For the Year Ending December 31, 19XX

(dollars in thousands)

Month	Beginning of Month			Costs Incurred			Payments			End of Month		
	Major Vendor A	All Other Vendors	Total	Major Vendor A	All Other Vendors	Total	Major Vendor A[a]	All Other Vendors[b]	Total	Major Vendor A	All Other Vendors	Total
January	$15,300	$32,000	$47,300	$ 9,400	$43,240	$52,640	$15,300	$34,890	$50,190	$ 9,400	$40,350	$49,750
February	9,400	40,350	49,750	10,400	31,040	41,440	9,400	61,050	70,450	10,400	19,740	30,140
March	10,400	19,740	30,140	14,210	45,480	59,690	10,400	50,070	60,470	14,210	15,150	29,360
December	$13,300	$27,480	$40,780	$16,830	$42,600	$59,430	$13,300	$55,890	$69,190	$16,830	$14,190	$31,020

(a) Beginning of month balance
(b) Beginning of month balance plus 66⅔% of current month costs incurred

FIG. 23-4   Accrued Compensation Budget

THE WARE COMPANY

ACCRUED COMPENSATION BUDGET

For the Year Ending December 31, 19XX

(dollars in thousands)

Item	January	February	March	Total 1st Quarter	Annual
Balance, beginning of month	$37,400	$32,890	$33,220	$ 37,400	$ 37,400
Add gross payrolls					
Manufacturing	$49,400	$44,620	$50,260	$144,280	$579,130
Sales	14,310	12,010	14,970	41,290	167,800
R&D	2,670	2,100	2,700	7,470	31,400
Engineering	4,820	4,730	4,910	14,460	59,430
Finance	3,700	3,120	3,740	10,560	44,570
Administration	7,890	7,400	7,930	23,220	94,900
Total additions	$82,790	$73,980	$84,510	$241,280	$977,230
Deduct payments					
Salaries	$42,600	$42,600	$43,400	$128,600	$521,800
Hourly wages	44,700	31,050	34,690	110,440	452,710
Total payments	$87,300	$73,650	$78,090	$239,040	$974,510
Balance, end of month	$32,890	$33,220	$39,640	$ 39,640	$ 40,120

salaries and wages component of the operating budget for each department or function. Based on the number of working days in each month and the manpower requirements, the total expense is determined, with the offset being the accrued salaries and wages account. By the same token, a review of the calendar for each month permits calculation of the payroll cash disbursements for the period (see Chapter 19 on the cash budget) and the residual accrued compensation. Thus, in a typical company, if salaries are paid on the last day of the month, no accrual will exist at month-end. The hourly wage accrual can be calculated on the number of days unpaid. If, in March, there are twenty-three working days, and four days will be unpaid, then the hourly wage accrual, based on weekly payments, will be four twenty-thirds of the estimated monthly wage costs. A typical schedule determining the accrued compensation, whether done by computer or manually, is illustrated in Figure 23-4. Note that the budgeting process is parallel to the actual accounting.

BUDGET FOR ACCRUED INCOME TAXES

For most companies, a significant charge against income, and an important cash disbursement, is the expense for federal, state, and, possibly, foreign income taxes. In the planning or budgeting process, the estimated cost, the expected payments, and the estimated accrual are calculated for *each taxing entity* much as is done in calculating actuals during the accounting period. Basically, the steps are as follows:

1. Determine, for the planning period, the estimated pre-tax book operating income.
2. Make adjustments to the estimated book income for the significant differences between the tax base and book base for each taxing entity (i.e., each state tax, or an average; each foreign entity tax; and the federal tax).
3. Calculate the expected liability (on a conservative basis) using the effective tax rate.
4. Estimate the required cash disbursement, with a knowledge of tax payment dates and constraints in calculating the minimum payment to avoid penalty for underpayment (such as 90 percent of the prior year).
5. Deduct payments from the gross accrued taxes to arrive at the net accrual.

An example of the calculation of budgeted accrued U.S. federal income tax is shown in Figure 23-5.

Once the budget has been determined, cumulative adjustments are made for the year-to-date actual accrual and the estimate to complete for the planning period. In this manner, management is advised of the original

FIG. 23-5 Calculation of Accrued Federal Income Tax Budget

THE LEGGE COMPANY

CALCULATION OF ACCRUED FEDERAL INCOME TAX BUDGET

For the Year Ending December 31, 19XX

(dollars in thousands)

Item	January	February	March	Total 1st Quarter	Annual
Budgeted income before taxes	$3,100	$2,060	$3,700	$8,860	$37,490
Adjustments to tax base					
Nondeductible expenses	$ 460	$ 210	$ 350	$1,020	$ 3,100
Research expense	(140)	(70)	(160)	(370)	(1,100)
Taxable income	$3,420	$2,200	$3,890	$9,510	$39,490
Application of rate (46%)					
Tax liability	$1,573	$1,012	$1,789	$4,374	$18,165
Tax adjustments					
ITC	($ 210)	($ 100)	($ 130)	($ 440)	($ 1,130)
Foreign tax adjustments	(30)	(30)	(30)	(90)	(300)
Estimated liability	$1,333	$ 882	$1,629	$3,844	$16,735
Add					
Accrued tax, BOM	$1,200	$2,533	$3,415	$1,200	$ 1,200
Total	$2,533	$3,415	$5,044	$5,044	$17,935
Deduct					
Payment[1]	—	—	$4,275	$4,275	15,700
Accrued tax, EOM	$2,533	$3,415	$ 769	$ 769	$ 2,235

1 Adjusted for timing differences

budget and updated as to any changes in actual expense and liability as the year progresses.

BUDGETING OTHER CURRENT LIABILITIES

The principles that apply to the method of budgeting the typical, and usually more significant, current liabilities are applicable to the budgeting and accounting for *any* liabilities. If the normal accounting process lends itself to natural segregation, or if specific liabilities should be identifiable and followed, then these categories should be employed in the planning process and the subsequent control procedures. Groupings are used to lessen the accounting burden and avoid unnecessary detail.

SUMMARY BUDGET FOR CURRENT LIABILITIES

A quarterly summary of the current liability budget or plan is shown in Figure 23-6. The summary of individual items facilitates the overall testing of current liabilities. A quarterly statement is helpful in checking the interim status against credit agreements, or simply in illustrating to the commercial bankers or other creditors the status and trend (perhaps when used as a visual aid in an oral presentation).

CONSTRAINTS ON CURRENT LIABILITIES

The preceding portions of this chapter relate principally to the nature and content of current liabilities, the summary components schedules that support the budget, and some methods by which certain budgets are determined. Yet, proper budgeting procedure does not consist simply of determining the account activity, based on operating plans and other asset levels. Rather, the process compares testing the levels with selected standards to assure they (1) are within acceptable perimeters, based on financial judgments and (2) meet the requirements of credit agreements or other contract terms, if applicable. Moreover, as previously stated, these tests are not only of the year-end condition; they also include interim-period checks to see that credit agreement terms are not violated, and to observe the possible development of any adverse trends.

There are several guidelines available to measure the acceptability of current indebtedness levels. Each industry tends to have ratios that are considered acceptable by professionals. For example, Dun & Bradstreet

FIG. 23-6 Summary of Current Liabilities Budget, by Quarter

THE MANUFACTURING COMPANY

SUMMARY OF CURRENT LIABILITY BUDGET

For the Year Ending December 31, 19XX

(dollars in thousands)

Item	Estimated Balance 12/31/XX-1	Planning Year Ending 12/31/XX			
		Quarter Ending			
		1	2	3	4
Notes payable	$ 8,700	$ 8,100	$ 7,400	—	$ 7,500
Current maturities of long-term debt	1,400	1,400	1,400	$ 1,400	1,400
Accounts payable	22,800	18,200	16,500	14,300	19,600
Accrued income taxes	1,900	2,800	3,400	2,100	2,600
Accrued compensation	8,100	7,400	7,300	8,000	8,200
Other accrued items	3,600	3,100	2,900	3,400	3,700
Total	$46,500	$41,000	$38,900	$29,200	$43,000
Selected Ratios					
Current ratio	2.3:1	2.0:1	2.5:1	2.6:1	2.4:1
Quick ratio	0.43:1	0.41:1	0.54:1	0.71:1	0.44:1
Current liabilities/shareholders' equity	0.27:1	0.26:1	0.25:1	0.19:1	0.24:1

periodically issues selective ratios on different lines of business showing the median, upper quartile, and lower quartile for certain operating and balance sheet items. Moreover, bankers, financial analysts, and many company managers use such measuring sticks. It is not uncommon for a company to use ratio analyses in comparing itself with competitors or perhaps industry averages.

Some suggested ratios to measure the acceptability of debt levels, including current liabilities as well as total indebtedness, include the following:

- Current ratio
- Quick ratio
- Minimum net working capital
- Current debt-to-tangible net worth

- Current debt-to-inventory
- Total debt-to-tangible net worth
- Number of days payables on hand (payable turnover)

Ratio analysis may assist in revealing where a company may be out of line as to current liabilities.

Current Ratio

This is calculated by dividing current assets by current liabilities. It is an indication of the company's ability to meet its short-term obligations. The current ratio of the individual company can be compared with industry data to see if it is more or less liquid. Although a traditional ratio is two-to-one with better control of inventory or receivables, an acceptable ratio may be somewhat less. With a two-to-one ratio, however, current assets could shrink in value by 50 percent and still be sufficient to cover current liabilities. Obviously, the higher the ratio, the greater the protection of the current short-term creditors, all other things being equal.

Quick Ratio

Time may be required to sell some current assets, such as inventories or prepaid items. Hence, another ratio that measures the short-term liquidity of a firm is needed. A quick ratio is defined as the relationship of the highly liquid assets — cash, temporary investments, and accounts receivable — to current liabilities. It is also known as the acid test or liquidity ratio and is an indicator of the extent to which the very liquid assets are available to meet the demands of the short-term creditors.

Net Working Capital

Net working capital is defined simply as current assets less current liabilities. Some loan and credit agreements provide that a company must maintain a minimum amount of working capital irrespective of the current ratio. The net amount indicates the amount by which current assets could shrink in value and still be adequate to liquidate the current obligations.

Current Debt (or Total Debt) to Tangible Net Worth

This ratio measures the relationship of the short-term debt (or total debt) to shareholders' equity less any intangibles on the balance sheet.

As is explained in Chapter 27, relating to shareholders' equity, the funds provided by the owners are the primary basis for credit extension. To the extent that the assets are financed by the owners, there is more protection (more assets are available) for the creditors. Hence, measures of indebtedness as related to shareholder equity are important guides to acceptable limits. They can be measured in two ways: (1) as current liabilities related to equity, and (2) as total liabilities measured against equity.

Lenders have minimum requirements for the debt/equity relationship; and prudent financial managements carefully monitor total indebtedness of whatever type to stay within acceptable limits and preserve the credit worthiness of the company. Industry data and ratios of specific companies are available as yardsticks.

Number of Days Payables

Where available, such as from internal statements, number of days payables represents the accounts payable divided by the amount of purchase, multiplied by the days in the period. For example, assume the following:

1. Quarterly end balance of accounts payable $14,610,000
2. Purchases in the period $74,380,000
3. Business days in period   69

Then the number of days payables represented by the balance is:

$$\text{accounts payable} \div \text{purchases}$$

$$= \$14,610,000 \div \$74,380,000$$

$$= .196424 \times \text{number of days (69)}$$

$$= 13.55 \text{ days}$$

If purchases are not available, the cost of goods sold from the published financial statements may be used in a manner similar to purchases to indicate trends. The greater the number of days, compared to normal credit terms, the more a company may be relying on trade creditor financing (and not paying bills currently).

If special terms are arranged with large creditors as an agreed-upon financing method, perhaps such liabilities should be separated from "regular term" creditors. The business plan should be tested at year-end, and at interim periods, such as each quarter, to ascertain that planned current liability level meets bank or other lender requirements and conforms to the management standards. Actual monthly results should be measured against plan, and trends should be reviewed.

WHAT CORRECTIVE ACTION CAN BE TAKEN?

In the budgeting process, whether in the planning or control phase, what can or should be done if the current liabilities appear excessive? Much depends on the specific circumstances, including the period of time in which the current liabilities are excessive, the trend, and the degree of over-commitment.

In the planning phase, which is the period during which *preventive* action can be initiated if required, some of the following corrective actions can be taken.

☐ If the over-limit conditions appear to be temporary or of a seasonal nature, for perhaps three or six months, then any one of several steps can be taken:
  • Lenders can be asked to waive the contract restriction for six months or so, after showing them the temporary nature of the problem, the basically sound overall financial condition, and convincing evidence of the short-term nature of the problem (e.g., inventory buildup or special terms to a major customer).
  • A review of plans can be made with the objective of reducing accounts receivable through special collection efforts, or perhaps a discount incentive to encourage early payment.
  • Planned inventory levels can be reduced by a change in production levels, or partial assembly only, or simply an increased turnover on selected items for which quick delivery can be obtained.
  • Arrangements can be made with suppliers for special terms (noncurrent obligations) or for obtaining goods on a consignment basis.
☐ Where the condition appears more permanent, and may represent an attempt at excessive growth, a basic change in the business plan may be indicated. Among possible solutions, depending on economic conditions, market outlook, and so forth, are these:
  • Seek additional long-term debt, within the perimeter of acceptable financial standards, to permit the reduction of excessive short-term obligations.

- Increase the amount of shareholders' equity, if this is economically feasible and timely.
- If a change in capital structure is not deemed feasible, then consider a less ambitious business plan, such as cutting back on the less profitable sales levels or eliminating product lines or marginal sales territories with the consequent reduction in receivables or inventory requirements (and perhaps capital asset needs).
- Consider plan reductions in those phases that require noncurrent assets (e.g., a reduction in capital expenditures or other long-term investments).
- See what can be done to improve profit margins, for example, by making cost reduction efforts and pricing policy changes.

The point to be made is that quite often liquidity problems begin to surface in the current liability segment of a business plan and arrangements must be made to accommodate or eliminate them.

In the *control* phases of budgeting, the same general procedures apply.

☐ When the *actual* current liabilities are determined each month, the actual results should be

- Tested against the standards established by prudent financial management, such as current ratio or quick ratio, to see if any out-of-line conditions exist.
- Checked against the terms of any or all credit agreements for acceptability or conformance.
- Reviewed during the planning period for adverse trends, such as a constant decrease in the current ratio or in working capital, and the causes of adverse trends.
- Compared against plan, and reasons for departure determined.

If unacceptable relationships exist, then consideration should be given to possible corrective action, just as might be done in the planning phase.

BUDGET OR CONTROL REPORTS

Budget or control reports on current liabilities may be issued weekly, monthly, or quarterly, depending on need. They may relate to current liabilities, as such; more commonly they relate to total liabilities and/or working capital. The more common reports issued for management or creditor requirements, as may be applicable, could include the following:

- Comparison of actual and budgeted amounts, and projected year-end status, and reasons for variances;
- Aging of accounts payable;

- Comparison of actual, and perhaps projected quarterly or year-end status with credit agreement terms and/or management standards;
- Detailed analytical reports required by credit agreements; and
- Special analyses of trends, where unfavorable conditions appear to be developing, with suggested remedies.

24

Working Capital — An Overall Perspective

WHY REVIEW WORKING CAPITAL IN ITS TOTALITY?

Each element of gross working capital, which may be defined collectively as current assets (cash and temporary investments, accounts receivable, inventories, prepaid items, and other current assets), has been discussed individually. In a similar fashion, the current liabilities have been reviewed. These current assets, less the current liabilities, make up what has been described as working capital. A more precise definition might be *net* working capital. So why review these combined two segments of the balance sheet as an entity, when the individual segments have been examined?

There are several reasons. In most companies, especially the small- and medium-sized, the current assets comprise, by far, the majority assets of the business. Furthermore, they bear, or should bear, a direct relationship to the current or anticipated level of business activity. Hence, there should exist an acceptable relationship of these current assets to current liabilities. Moreover, standards of an acceptable relationship of working capital to operating factors exist within each industry. For these reasons it is often desirable to measure the total of these liquid assets net of current liabilities to see if, as a whole, the status is satisfactory. It avoids the problem of "not seeing the forest for the trees." It saves some time in initial analysis. Also, it can be a starting point for a more in-depth review, balance sheet item by item, of the planned or actual condition of the company when such an examination seems warranted.

Other supplemental or supporting reasons for checking the overall liquidity status of a company are as follows:

☐ In long-range planning, there are instances where data or plans are so general or indefinite that the overall working capital measurement is entirely adequate, such as where detailed measurement of individual inventory, receivable, or cash levels is not meaningful or necessary.

☐ In companies that are relatively stable or that have an abundance of working capital, further details or analysis may add little to the planning or control process.

☐ The individual components of working capital may depart from plan to varying degrees, some favorable and some unfavorable, so that the overall impact should be observed and measured.

☐ Some managements may be receptive to a discussion of aggregate working capital to the detriment of its components. A summary approach is helpful in focusing on the immediate status and, later, on the more detailed problem areas if this is warranted.

So there is something to be said for ascertaining that the overall working capital status is or is not satisfactory, and is "balanced" against operations, before doing further analysis.

In many companies, the planning process will proceed first, with the determination of the plan levels for each element of current assets and current liabilities. There the working capital sufficiency would be tested in total before further specific analysis is introduced.

OBJECTIVES IN WORKING CAPITAL MANAGEMENT

The planning and control objectives, and therefore what might be called the management objectives, as applied to each element of the current assets and current liabilities of an enterprise are discussed in the applicable chapters earlier in this text. But considering working capital as a whole, it may be helpful to summarize the more important objectives, with an emphasis on the financial management aspects. It will be seen that proper management of working capital has both financial and operating, and therefore profit, implications.

From the Viewpoint of Financial Management

From the viewpoint of the financial officers, the following would seem to be prudent objectives, many of which are interrelated:

- Maintain the ability to meet current obligations on a timely basis.
- Retain the ability to command adequate lines of short-term bank credit or other appropriate lines on a reasonable cost basis.
- Maintain the quality of the current assets so that they may be converted into cash in a reasonable period of time.
- Maintain a working capital posture that will facilitate the acquisition of long-term debt or equity, if later needed on a reasonably acceptable basis.
- Keep the noncash current assets at as low a level as is consistent with sound operations, so as to maximize cash equivalent balances, and therefore increase income from the short-term investments.
- Maintain the noninterest-bearing current liabilities at levels to maximize cash equivalent balances and related income, but without jeopardizing the short-term credit rating.

From the Operating Viewpoint

From the viewpoint of operations, the following would seem to be the appropriate objectives:

- Permit adequate investment in accounts receivable, through the use of competitive and attractive credit terms and policies, to assist the marketing of the product and/or services.
- Maintain adequate levels of raw materials, supplies, and work-in-process inventories to support economic manufacturing operations giving recognition to cost trade-offs.
- Maintain an adequate inventory of finished goods to facilitate timely shipments to customers.

IMPACT OF WORKING CAPITAL MANAGEMENT

Many companies have well-developed budgeting techniques for the planning and control of *operations,* sales, manufacturing costs, marketing expenses, research and development, general and administrative expenses, and other items of income or expense. Usually they have a reasonably acceptable cash planning procedure, and an adequate, formal capital expenditure program. But little attention is paid to working capital or, indeed, to financial position. The result sometimes is a serious imbalance between operating plans and financial sufficiency.

This condition may arise from any number of conceptions and misconceptions among business managers, including the following:

- ☐ The funds tied up in current assets are not "cast into concrete" as are monies for plant and equipment; and receivable or inventory levels or commitments can be adjusted with relative ease.
- ☐ The levels of specific current assets, being needed for the current operation of the business, should be set by the operating managers at their discretion.
- ☐ The capital budget, representing a significant investment in nonliquid assets, should require board approval; but this review should not extend to current assets, since competitive pressures are a primary determinant of needs — credit terms, territorial coverage, warehousing locations, and so forth.

Assumptions such as the above, most of them unwarranted, have influenced the attitudes of management about control of working capital. Yet management should be made aware of the nature of working capital and the need for proper planning and control. Lack of proper knowledge in this field, on the part of operating and top management, may result in wrong decisions on how to finance a business, on the impact of changes in current asset levels on profitability, and on what can and must be done to maintain an adequate, but not excessive, level of working capital. Such knowledge should not be restricted to the financial arm of the business, even though the financial officers often will make the necessary analysis and do the "selling" of a change in course.

Working capital must be planned and managed just as are other segments of the business. It must be made more productive. Changes in working capital levels may impact a business in two ways: (1) costs involved in carrying working capital and (2) profit impact when levels are changed. In reducing working capital, often it is helpful to use simple arithmetic to dramatize the advantages, especially in times of high interest charges, of reducing net working capital. For example, assume the company

- Expects sales of $2 million,
- Experiences a net profit of 6 percent on sales,
- Carries inventories of $35 million, and
- Borrows funds at 13 percent.

With the planned sales, net income should approximate $12 million (6 percent times $200 million). However, if inventories were reduced by only 10 percent, or $3.5 million, then pretax earnings could increase by $455,000 (13 percent × $3.5 million), assuming borrowed funds were used. With a 40 percent tax rate, net income would increase by $273,000, or 2.3 percent. This $273,000 is the equivalent of additional sales of $4,550,000 ($273,000 ÷ 6 percent). If sales increases are difficult to achieve, this arithmetic may motivate the management to action; and if the company is not borrowing funds to carry inventories, then the cash surplus created by inventory reduction can be advantageously invested in income-producing short-term investments. The point is that maintaining unnecessary working capital entails costs. Working capital should be held to reasonable levels.

Aside from the cost of maintaining working capital, changes in levels, i.e. reductions, can have a profit impact. For example, a decision to reduce accounts receivable levels and related carrying costs by giving less favorable credit terms could result in loss of customers and reduced profitable sales. By the same token, inventory reduction could cause stock outages, impacting production unfavorably or causing the loss of customers, resulting in a reduction in current and future profits. Therefore, in considering working capital, the trade-off between risk and profitability must be considered.

WORKING CAPITAL CYCLE

Often the financial officers must be the teachers or motivators in encouraging management action, whether affecting sales, costs, or asset levels. And

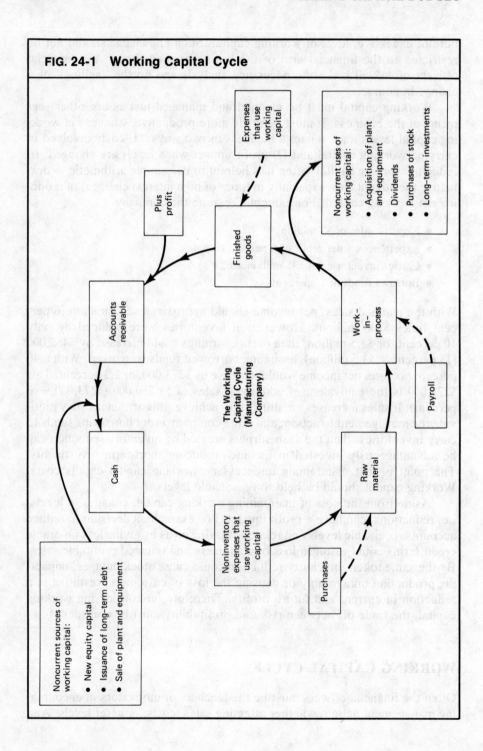

FIG. 24-1 Working Capital Cycle

Expenses that use working capital

Plus profit

Finished goods

Noncurrent uses of working capital:
- Acquisition of plant and equipment
- Dividends
- Purchases of stock
- Long-term investments

Accounts receivable

Work-in-process

The Working Capital Cycle (Manufacturing Company)

Cash

Payroll

Raw material

Noninventory expenses that use working capital

Purchases

Noncurrent sources of working capital:
- New equity capital
- Issuance of long-term debt
- Sale of plant and equipment

even this group is influenced by fads and by popular trends. As an example, emphasis was on *profitability* for much of the 1960s and 1970s. However, financial crises, bank failures, and inability to secure adequate credit is again putting increased emphasis on financial condition or health as an important factor in achieving the profitability objective. It might be said we are returning to the *basics* of financial management; and proper management of working capital is a necessary part of this trend.

In managing working capital it probably is well to recognize the cycle or flow of these current assets and current liabilities. A diagram of the flow is shown in Figure 24-1. Basically, the cycle begins with cash provided by the owners and/or long-term creditors. Cash is then invested in inventories and supplies and services, together with funds provided by suppliers and other short-term creditors. The inventories are sold as finished goods to customers and thereby are converted to accounts receivable. Finally, the receivables are converted into cash. Thus the cycle begins again. The exact length of the cycle depends on many factors, including credit terms demanded by suppliers, the raw material acquisition span, the manufacturing and selling period, and the credit terms granted to customers. However, these two principles are evident:

1. The total amount of net working capital is changed largely by these factors:
   □ Profitability of the business
   □ Decisions made by the owners or long-term creditors as to what funds will be provided for working capital (guided by management)
   □ Sums to be invested, at the discretion of management, in "noncurrent" activities, including:
     • Plant and equipment
     • Dividends to shareholders
     • Long-term investments
     • Purchase of outstanding stock or bonds
2. Management controls the composition of working capital and must keep the various elements (cash, receivables, inventories, accounts payable, accrued items, and so forth) in proper balance with each other, and at an adequate level in the aggregate, depending on the amount of present or prospective activity.

SETTING AN ACCEPTABLE PLAN LEVEL FOR WORKING CAPITAL

Simple logic will indicate that a relationship should exist between the level of business activity, as measured by sales, and the amount of working capital. As a matter of fact, in some industries where working capital is a heavy

FIG. 24-2   Working Capital Ratios and the Business Cycle

Period	Cyclical Phase	Working Capital to Sales Ratio
1960–1966	Relatively normal	30%
1967–1972	Bad times	50
1973–1975	Good times	25
1975 to present	Relatively normal	27

Note: Industry statistics became available in 1970; for previous years, International Mineral & Chemicals data have been used to estimate industry ratios.

consumer of funds, this short-term net asset tends to vary noticeably, inversely with the business cycle. Why? Because recession and the resultant increased competition force extended credit terms with high receivable levels. Conversely, falling sales produce high inventories. In prosperous times, the ratios become more acceptable. A specific example is shown in Figure 24-2 for the fertilizer industry.[1]

This ratio of working capital to sales (or net sales to working capital) is an acceptable guide for monitoring working capital. Dun & Bradstreet, Inc. publishes a ratio, net sales to working capital, by industry; and other industry data are available in most instances. The company may determine its own experience, and make comparisons with acceptable standards.

Ratio analysis can be used to determine the historical relationship. And such a calculation, with appropriate adjustment, may serve as a basis for annual planning. Again, it may be used to calculate the working capital required in conjunction with a new capital investment (see Chapter 25). Suppose the recent experience of a company is as shown in Figure 24-3. Then the average of 24.03 percent, or perhaps a more optimum figure, such as 23 percent, might be used in planning and control. As a matter of fact, the level of working capital may be synthesized from acceptable amounts of the various elements making up working capital.

Of course, regression analysis may be employed to determine a working capital relationship to sales. This can be performed manually by the standard technique explained in most textbooks on statistics. Alternatively, canned or preplanned computer programs may be employed. For the data presented in

[1] Anthony E. Cascino, "How to Make More Productive Use of Working Capital," *Management Review* (May 1979), p. 44.

FIG. 24-3   Ratio of Working Capital to Sales

THE KENDRA COMPANY

RELATIONSHIP OF WORKING CAPITAL TO SALES
(dollars in millions)[a]

Year	Net Sales	Net Working Capital	Percentage of Sales
1	$ 120	$ 29	24.17%
2	130	32	24.62
3	117	27	23.08
4	116	26	22.41
5	140	36	25.71
6	150	39	26.00
7	170	41	24.12
8	175	42	24.00
9	182	44	24.17
10	171	40	23.39
11	154	35	22.73
12	132	30	22.73
Total	$1,757	$421	23.96%
Average	$ 146	$ 35	24.03%

(a) Adjusted for inflation

Figure 24-3, the following equation results, and can be useful in planning working capital levels for the company:

$$y = -1.5522 + .25(x)$$

where:

y = Working capital
x = Annual sales

When an acceptable working capital standard has been developed, and when the analysis of component levels is completed, the company posture might be explained to top management or to the board of directors by a schedule similar to Figure 24-4.

FIG. 24-4   Schedule of Working Capital Requirements

THE JEFFREY COMPANY

SCHEDULE OF WORKING CAPITAL REQUIREMENTS
AT SELECTED SALES LEVELS
(dollars in thousands)

Annual sales volume	$20,000	$40,000	$80,000
Current Assets			
Cash — Fixed	$ 500	$ 500	$ 500
Cash — Fluctuating	500	800	1,400
Total	$ 1,000	$ 1,300	$ 1,900
Receivables	$ 1,800	$ 3,900	$ 6,800
Inventories — Minimum	$ 1,000	$ 1,000	$ 1,000
Inventories — Fluctuating	600	1,400	2,700
Total	$ 1,600	$ 2,400	$ 3,700
Total current assets	$ 4,400	$ 7,600	$12,400
Current Liabilities			
Notes payable	—	$ 1,000	$ 2,000
Accounts payable	$ 1,400	1,800	2,600
Accrued items	900	1,200	1,700
Accrued income taxes	700	900	1,400
Total current liabilities	$ 2,000	$ 4,900	$ 7,700
Total Working Capital Requirements	$ 2,400	$ 2,700	$ 4,700
Current ratio	2.2 : 1	1.55 : 1	1.61 : 1

IMPORTANT SIGNALS IN WORKING CAPITAL MANAGEMENT

One of the purposes of working capital management is to preserve corporate liquidity. This includes the maintenance of adequate cash levels, as discussed in Chapter 19. When it is recognized that an important source of working capital is net income, as explained earlier, then it must be realized that anything interfering with achieving the profit plan can contribute to either a less desirable mix of current assets, or less working capital. Those with experience in business recognize that there are signals which flash unacceptable trends. And when adversity strikes, a gentle stream can become a flood if not controlled early in the period of change. In the monitoring of corporate liquidity, the experienced financial officer knows that signs such as the following are early warnings of unacceptable trends in working capital.

1. *Sales management:*
   - ☐ Declining sales orders
   - ☐ Inability to pass on increased costs (declining gross margins) to customers
2. *Cost and general management:*
   - ☐ Costs or expenses at all levels are increasing above plan, or are not being reduced relative to lower sales revenues
   - ☐ Profit plans not being met
3. *Asset management:*
   - ☐ Increasing accounts receivable
   - ☐ Build-up of inventories
   - ☐ Reduced inventory turns (inventories not being reduced at same rate as sales)
   - ☐ Reduced receivable turnover (collections slowing; receivables not dropping as fast as sales)
   - ☐ Increase in past due accounts
   - ☐ Cash balances declining
   - ☐ Capital expenditures appear unnecessary
4. *Liability management:*
   - ☐ Current ratio decreased
   - ☐ Quick ratio declining
   - ☐ Accounts payable slowed, or levels increased

When signals such as these, and there are others, surface during an operating period (daily or weekly, as well as monthly and quarterly), then plans and controls must be instituted to limit unwarranted asset increases or the wrong mixture of assets, and to maintain adequate working capital or corporate liquidity.

ACTIONS TO PRESERVE WORKING CAPITAL

If adverse trends appear to be developing in the working capital arena, then the severity will be a determinant in what actions should be taken to correct the condition. Many steps to correct out-of-line conditions have been suggested under the appropriate chapter dealing with sales, cost or expenses, and assets or liabilities. Some of these possible steps are:

1. *Sales management:*
   ☐ Deferment of expansion plans — Territory or product
   ☐ Selection of more profitable product sales strategies
   ☐ Reduction in unnecessary expenses
   ☐ Elimination of marginal products or services

2. *Cost or expense control:*
   ☐ More intensive control of overhead of every type
   ☐ Search for more competitive supply sources, or better terms
   ☐ Freezing of new hires, or reduction of personnel
   ☐ Delay in granting wage increases
   ☐ Elimination of nonessential frills or functions, or use of less expensive items

3. *Asset management:*
   ☐ More vigorous collection efforts
   ☐ Reduction in receivable levels
   ☐ Reduction in inventories
   ☐ Reduced capital expenditures
   ☐ Sales of idle or unprofitable assets or businesses
   ☐ Reduction in dividends to shareholders

4. *Liability management:*
   ☐ Increase in outside borrowings (some long term) — perhaps supplier financing
   ☐ Careful monitoring (and delay) of payments (accounts payable)

As can be seen, management of working capital may involve many management functions in diverse ways, and significant trade-offs of liquidity for profitability might be necessary. The point to be made is that working capital must be managed and corporate liquidity and flexibility preserved.

TRACKING WORKING CAPITAL

The calculation and tracking of working capital, and reporting of trends and relationships, usually falls to the controller and his staff. The same principles of reporting discussed in Chapter 2 are applicable in providing data on trends and status of working capital and its components: responsibility reporting, comparative reporting, and interpreted reporting. While data for the entire firm often must be monitored, in a decentralized company, data should be accumulated by profit center responsibility. Methods of reporting and the items pursued will vary by company, depending on management philosophy, management style, and importance of working capital, to name a few. Items to be calculated at least monthly or quarterly, in most instances, are as follows:

- Absolute amount of net working capital, for the period in itself or as a rolling average
- Days sales in net working capital
- Working capital to sales ratio
- Current ratio
- Quick ratio — Cash and cash equivalents and receivables to current debt
- Inventory to current liabilities
- Current liabilities to net worth
- Net working capital to fixed liabilities

Any one of these, or any combination, may be reported in tabular or graphic form in a variety of frequencies and detail, depending on the needs of operating management charged with responsibility for the item being monitored. A tabulation and graph of month-end working capital, the twelve-month moving average, and comparison to the annual business plan, together with day's sales (actual and plan) in net working capital, is reflected in Figure 24-5. Other ratios used in measuring segments of working capital are discussed in the applicable chapters of this book.

PLANNING AND CONTROL REPORTS ON WORKING CAPITAL FOR TOP MANAGEMENT

Reports provided to top management or to a cognizant executive for an overview of working capital may be of two types: planning or control. As used in this context, a planning report is intended to show the results of planned operations on working capital. An example of a report summarizing changes in working capital for the annual plan is shown in Figure 24-6. While this illustration summarizes the yearly changes, it can also indicate planned results by fiscal quarter to coincide with the related statements of financial position and income and expense. Although this exhibit reflects the planned net change in cash, a plan and prior year comparison could be prepared wherein the net figures relate to working capital, and, of course, any changes in each item of the balance sheet (a format somewhat similar in principal to Figure 24-9). Commentary provided with the data shown in Figure 24-6 could (and, in many instances, should) explain the reasons for the changes.

When the year is underway, depending on needs, periodic reports should provide information on the company status. An example of a daily

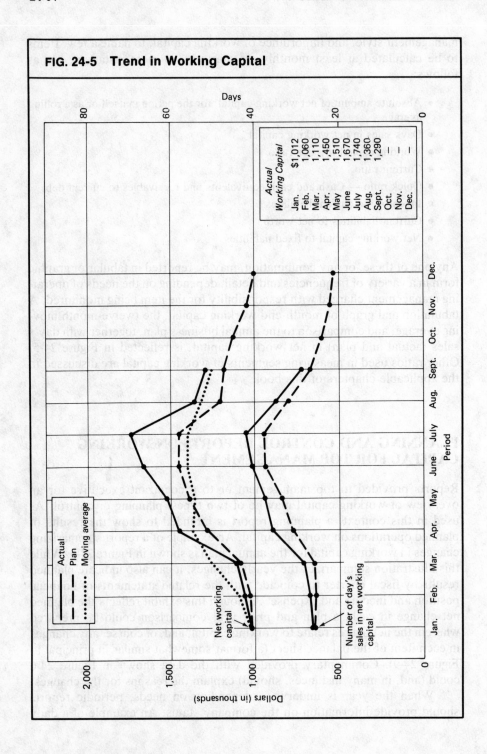

FIG. 24-5   Trend in Working Capital

	Actual Working Capital
Jan.	$1,012
Feb.	1,060
Mar.	1,110
Apr.	1,450
May	1,510
June	1,670
July	1,740
Aug.	1,360
Sept.	1,290
Oct.	—
Nov.	—
Dec.	—

FIG. 24-6 Comparative Statement of Changes in Financial Position

THE DOUGLAS COMPANY

COMPARATIVE STATEMENT OF CHANGES IN FINANCIAL POSITION

For the Plan Year Ending December 31, 19XX

(dollars in thousands)

	19XX	Current Year (Estimated)	Prior Year
Factors increasing cash and cash items:			
Net income	$ 38.3	$31.4	$26.7
Add — Depreciation and amortization	$ 22.1	$20.1	$18.4
— Deferred income taxes	5.7	4.2	7.3
Total internal generation	$ 66.1	$55.7	$52.4
Increase in accounts payable	$ 12.4	$ 4.2	($ 6.2)
Increase in accrued items	9.6	3.6	1.1
Increase in notes payable	7.1	—	—
Increase in long-term obligations	5.0	—	10.0
Total increases	$100.2	$63.5	$57.3
Factors decreasing cash and cash items:			
Increase in accounts receivable	$ 22.9	$14.3	$ 7.8
Additions to property, plant, and equipment	14.6	22.9	27.3
Cash dividends	12.6	11.1	9.1
Increase in inventories	10.2	8.2	7.4
Purchase of common shares	8.4	—	—
Decrease in other prepaid items	1.7	.9	.6
Total decreases	70.4	$57.4	$52.2
Increase in cash and cash items:	$ 29.8	$ 6.1	$ 5.1
Cash and cash items — Beginning of year	97.3	91.2	86.1
Cash and cash items — End of year	$127.1	$97.3	$91.2
Net working capital	$112.2	$98.4	$94.3
Current ratio	2.5:1	2.3:1	2.0:1
Quick ratio	1.8:1	1.7:1	1.5:1
Number of days sales in working capital	27	25	23

report on working capital is shown in Figure 24-7. This is especially appropriate where maintenance of adequate working capital is critical to the operations and the firm is close to insolvency. This report also informs the management of other key operating factors. Daily summarization of cash activity, invoices, and production are the source data.

In a more typical operation, the information is provided monthly, in the same format as the plan, comparing actual and plan, with related key ratios. Figure 24-8 is an example.

Examples of summarized data for the year, as reflected in the annual report to shareholders are contained in Figures 24-9 and 24-10. The former, from the Weyerhaeuser Company 1981 Annual Report, explains the net increase or decrease in working capital.[2] The latter, a report of the Northrop Corporation for 1981, summarizes the changes as reflected in the balance of cash and cash items, as well as in each element of working capital.[3]

COST ALLOCATION AS A MOTIVATING FACTOR

Because of the high cost of carrying current assets, some managements have found it desirable to incorporate working capital objectives into measurements of performance and into incentive compensation results. A given interest rate, or carrying cost, perhaps secured by the company's commercial bank, may be charged against the investment or profit center based on the net working capital level in total or by certain segments. It may be changed as the going prime rate changes. For example, one company assesses the average monthly prime rate cost against the net working capital of each cost center investment to the extent that it does not exceed plan, and prime plus 2 percent for any carrying costs on net working capital above plan. These carrying costs on planned working capital levels are, of course, built into the plan. Given the management objective of reducing inventory levels to a greater degree than receivables, for reasons of risk, another company charges currently the prime interest rate on receivables, and the prime plus 5 percent on inventories. When the compensation received by management is partially influenced by its ability to reduce working capital, the achievements are sometimes astounding when a charge is made for working capital employed. Hence, this is the one segment of total assets over which local or decentralized management can exercise a high degree of control.

---

[2] Reprinted courtesy of the Weyerhaeuser Company.

[3] Reprinted courtesy of the Northrop Corporation.

FIG. 24-7 Daily Conditions Report

THE BUCK CORPORATION
DAILY CONDITIONS REPORT

Date: June 15, 19XX

Working Days this Month: 24
Worked to Date: 11

Working Capital	Beginning Balance	Additions	Deductions	Ending Balance	Past Due
Cash					
Operating funds — Plants	$ 10,000	—	—	$ 10,000	
Security Pacific	742,000	$ 164,100	$ 584,400	321,700	$624,300
Other banks	32,000	5,000	5,000	32,000	10,400
Total	$ 784,000	$ 169,100	$ 589,400	$ 363,700	$634,700
Accounts receivable					
Regular terms	$ 6,830,110	$ 429,000	$ 56,800	$ 7,202,310	
Special terms	2,005,800	381,000	102,300	2,284,500	
Total	$ 8,835,910	$ 810,000	$ 159,100	$ 9,486,810	
Inventories					
Raw materials	$ 1,870,300	$ 124,600	$ 72,610	$ 1,922,290	
Work in process	790,160	144,900	412,000	523,060	
Finished goods	5,820,600	412,000	567,000	5,665,600	
Total	$ 8,481,060	$ 681,500	$1,051,610	$ 8,110,950	
Other current assets	$ 242,000			$ 242,000	
Total current assets	$18,342,970	$1,660,600	$1,800,110	$18,203,460	
Current liabilities					
Notes payable — Security Pacific	$ 3,970,000	—	—	$ 3,970,000	
Notes payable — Other	1,000,000			1,000,000	
Accounts payable	2,427,860	$ 310,000	$ 414,400	2,323,460	
Accrued items	879,900	46,000		925,900	
Accrued income taxes	241,300	40,000	170,000	111,300	
Total current liabilities	$ 8,519,060	$ 396,000	$ 584,400	$ 8,330,660	
Working Capital	$ 9,823,910	$ 264,600	$1,215,710	$ 9,872,800	

Other	Today	Month to Date	Plan to Date	Last Month to Date	Last Year to Date
Sales					
Military	$ 147,000	$1,640,200	$1,620,000	$ 1,020,100	$ 496,300
Commercial	663,000	6,379,800	6,510,000	6,091,500	5,010,000
Total	$ 810,000	$8,020,000	$8,130,000	$ 7,111,600	$5,506,300
Production hours					
Actual	106,300	1,174,200	1,180,000	1,163,400	1,140,700
Standard	99,100	1,149,100	1,156,400	1,150,999	1,104,198
Efficiency	93.2%	97.9%	98.0%	98.8%	96.8%

FIG. 24-8 Comparison of Actual and Planned Changes in Financial Position

THE DOUGLAS COMPANY
STATEMENT OF CHANGES IN FINANCIAL POSITION
For the Six Months Ending June 20, 19XX
(dollars in thousands)

	Actual	Plan	Over (Under) Plan	Comment
Factors increasing cash and cash items:				
Net income	$ 17.4	$ 19.7	($ 2.3)	Slow sales
Add — Depreciation and amortization	7.3	7.1	.2	
— Deferred income taxes	2.1	1.9	.2	
Total internal generation	$ 26.8	$ 28.7	($ 1.9)	
Increase in accounts payable	4.2	6.4	(2.2)	Johnson needed payment
Increase in accrued items	2.7	2.7	—	
Increase in notes payable	5.0	5.0	—	
Total increases	$ 38.7	$ 42.8	($ 4.1)	
Factors decreasing cash and cash items:				
Increase in accounts receivable	$ 19.1	$ 8.6	$10.5	USG receipt late
Additions to plant and equipment	11.3	7.3	4.0	Accelerated program
Cash dividends	6.0	6.0	—	
Increase in inventories	7.9	8.2	(.3)	
Purchase of common shares	7.3	5.0	2.3	Opportunity — Low cost
Other	1.0	1.0	—	
Total decreases	$ 52.6	$ 36.1	$16.5	
Increase (decrease) in cash and cash items	($ 13.9)	$ 6.7	$20.6	
Cash and cash items — Beginning of year	97.3	97.3	—	
Cash and cash items — End of month	$ 83.4	$104.0	$20.6	
Net working capital	$ 84.0	$104.6	$20.6	
Current ratio	2.0:1	2.3:1		
Number of days sales in net working capital	30.6	26.6	4.0	

FIG. 24-9 Statement of Consolidated Changes in Working Capital

For the three years ended December 27, 1981 Dollar amounts in thousands	1981	1980	1979
Working capital was increased by:			
Earnings before extraordinary charges	$ 234,444	$ 321,487	$511,623
Earnings charges not affecting working capital:			
Depreciation, amortization and fee stumpage	372,227	410,761	332,594
Deferred income taxes, net	73,161	118,170	(645)
Working capital provided from operations before extraordinary charges	679,832	850,418	843,572
Extraordinary charges	6,100	43,500	—
Working capital provided from operations	673,732	806,918	843,572
Proceeds from sale of preference shares	161,494	—	—
Proceeds from sale of commercial paper/revolving credit agreement and other bank loans	121,592	—	—
Proceeds from sale of revenue bonds	83,450	104,375	12,810
Market value of treasury common shares and preference shares issued for acquisitions	66,606	7,252	51,478
Property and equipment sales, net	64,977	28,312	13,300
Other transactions, net	(19,900)	28,155	45,121
Working capital increases	1,151,951	975,012	966,281
Working capital was decreased by:			
Expenditures for property and equipment	665,286	680,046	490,981
Expenditures for timber and timberlands, including reforestation	103,065	88,357	113,565
Capital leases, net	12,261	11,014	10,065
Investment in Weyerhaeuser Real Estate Company	12,656	18,825	19,219
Increase in other assets	36,429	130,525	11,076
Payments and other long-term debt changes, net	70,449	19,872	14,945
Cash dividends on preferred, preference and common shares	185,825	174,445	145,237
Purchases of treasury common shares	—	8,661	1,213
Working capital decreases	1,085,971	1,131,745	806,301
Net increase (decrease) in working capital	65,980	(156,733)	159,980
Working capital at beginning of year	508,435	665,168	505,188
Working capital at end of year	$ 574,415	$ 508,435	$665,168
Detail of increases (decreases) in working capital:			
Cash and short-term investments	$ (4,894)	$ (253,482)	$116,217
Receivables	115,043	62,161	37,072
Inventories	(7,928)	15,609	57,926
Prepaid expenses	(7,286)	(17,331)	6,139
Notes payable and current maturities of long-term debt and of capital lease obligations	3,981	6,288	1,495
Accounts payable	24,261	(42,518)	(21,323)
Accrued liabilities	(22,549)	(37,486)	15,714
Accrued income taxes	(34,648)	110,026	(53,260)
Net increase (decrease) in working capital	$ 65,980	$ (156,733)	$159,980

FIG. 24-10 Consolidated Statement of Changes in Financial Position

Year ended December 31	*In millions*	1981	1980	1979	1978	1977
Factors increasing cash and cash items						
Net income		$ 47.9	$ 86.1	$ 90.3	$ 88.4	$ 66.2
Add (deduct) non-cash items						
Deferred income taxes		52.6	(18.3)	84.0	57.3	88.6
Depreciation and amortization		41.0	30.4	26.6	20.5	22.8
Amortization of unvested employee restricted						
award shares		.9				
From operations		142.4	98.2	200.9	166.2	177.6
Increase in progress payments		156.5	225.9	(14.5)	(114.8)	(.8)
Increase in trade accounts payable, accrued employees'						
compensation and other current liabilities		46.0	37.9	(38.9)	59.2	24.0
Increase in long-term obligations		11.2	5.9	2.4	13.8	18.4
Increase in note payable to bank		9.4				
Decrease in other assets		7.7	(.8)	4.4	3.6	.2
Issuance of common stock		2.0	1.6	.7	3.6	9.3
Carrying value of disposals of property,						
plant and equipment		1.9	4.8	5.4	2.0	4.1
		377.1	373.5	160.4	133.6	232.8
Factors decreasing cash and cash items						
Additions to property, plant and equipment		189.7	121.1	70.4	96.6	34.1
Increase in inventoried costs		93.6	267.6	135.3	(53.9)	16.0
Decrease in income taxes payable		65.3	(81.7)	29.4	(27.2)	9.4
Increase in accounts receivable		62.0	(44.9)	(13.9)	63.1	(2.3)
Decrease in advances on contracts		34.0	(85.1)	22.4	35.6	(42.4)
Cash dividends		26.2	25.7	25.6	21.2	16.0
Decrease in long-term obligations		20.8	11.0	.8	9.0	19.0
Increase in prepaid expenses		2.4	(2.0)	.6	.7	1.2
Purchase of shares				1.0		
Principal amount of subordinated debt retired						8.0
		494.0	211.7	271.6	145.1	59.0
Increase (decrease) in cash and cash items		(116.9)	161.8	(111.2)	(11.5)	173.8
Cash and cash items at beginning of year		311.2	149.4	260.6	272.1	98.3
Cash and cash items at end of year		$194.3	$311.2	$149.4	$260.6	$272.1

PART IV

Budgeting for Long-Term Funds

25

Capital, or Plant and Equipment Budget

CAPITAL BUDGETING AND CORPORATE STRATEGY

In the context of capital budgeting as used herein, capital investments refer to those expenditures of a tangible nature for which a future benefit is expected over a prolonged period of time, usually more than one year. In accounting parlance it relates to those expenditures of cash and credit for plant and equipment, or fixed assets, with a useful life of more than one year. Although long-term investments in working capital are discussed in this chapter when related to fixed assets, and though non-current receivables, stock investments, and the like are discussed in this book, the emphasis in this chapter is on land, machinery, and plant and equipment — the fixed-asset category in the balance sheet.

Capital budgeting has long been practiced, sometimes intuitively and

FIG. 25-1 Business Segment Classification

		RELATIVE MARKET SHARE	
		High	**Low**
MARKET SEGMENT GROWTH RATE — **High**		■ Market share growth potential — very high ■ Earnings potential — high ■ Cash — a net user	■ Market share growth potential — high ■ Earnings — relatively low ■ Cash — a net drain
MARKET SEGMENT GROWTH RATE — **Low**		■ Market share growth potential — low ■ Earnings — quite high ■ Cash — a net provider	■ Market share growth potential — low ■ Earnings — low ■ Cash — a net drain

sometimes with sophistication. Often the decisions have been good, or at least good enough. However, in a changing environment, business is becoming more capital-intensive. At the same time, the raising of large amounts of capital is becoming more difficult due to the competition in the marketplace. The result has been pressure for improved techniques and systems. These are more analytical, calling for better documentation on data input, a more systematic investigation, sometimes seeking a broader range of projects being considered, and giving more recognition to the time value of money. These aspects are discussed in this chapter.

Capital investment decisions commit a company to specific courses of action for relatively long periods in the future. More than this, once a decision is made, it usually cannot be easily or quickly changed without a significant loss. Not only is the decision not readily undone, but in most instances, it may also foreclose other profitable decisions because of a limit on the capital resources available, and the manpower to manage it.

It is easy to realize then that the best capital investment decisions must be made in concert with the overall business strategy. Proper capital budgeting procedures consider a spectrum of long-term investment opportunities with the objective of seeing that the projects selected will contribute to achieving the company's goals. In so doing, there may be instances where the most profitable near-term expenditure may not be selected! Thus, long-range strategy must consider both market segment growth and relative market share.[1] The markets for a given corporation may be described as in

---

[1] See the Boston Consulting Group description of cash cows, dogs, etc. H.W. Allen Sweeny and Robert Rachlin, eds., *Handbook of Budgeting* (New York: John Wiley & Sons, Inc., 1981), pp. 32–33.

Figure 25-1. In this example, a product line depicted in the lower right rectangle may represent a low market share, a projected low market growth rate and a net user of cash. Nevertheless, it may provide a near-term higher rate of return on an investment than a project with a high potential market share growth and high earnings. Thus, if a corporation has a "strategic screening test," first, and then an "economics evaluation test," the strategic consideration may cause the project to be eliminated.

In any given instance, the business strategy and the corporation's financial position, meaning adequacy of cash, may result in different capital expenditure decisions than those made by another company. In the context of corporate strategy, certain key questions must be asked in evaluating capital investment decisions, such as:

1. Is the segment of planned expenditure within the area in which the company has certain competitive advantages?
2. Is the segment one in which the firm wishes to increase or to maintain a stream of earnings?
3. Is the proposed project still consistent with the corporate decision on:
   • Foreign competition?
   • Foreign parts and raw material sources?

REASONS FOR MAKING CAPITAL INVESTMENTS

The reasons for making investments in plant and equipment have a bearing on the acceptability of the project, and on the categorization of the capital budget request. The basic reason for capital investment is to increase or at least maintain the profitability and value of the company. A more specific reason for a particular proposal could include one of the following, and, as will be seen, these differing purposes may have an impact on the capital budget analysis, evaluation, and presentation.

1. To permit continued operation of the existing business
2. To meet government pollution control regulations or other regulations
3. To reduce present or prospective manufacturing or distribution costs of existing products by facilitating more efficient use of labor, material, or overhead
4. To improve the quality of existing products
5. To increase sales volume of existing products by increasing manufacturing capacity
6. To expand sales and earnings by adding new products or product lines
7. To diversify through manufacturing and distributing output that which serves a new market or geographical area

GENERAL CAPITAL BUDGETING PROCEDURE

The budgeting or planning and control procedure for capital assets has as its objective the commitment of funds only after careful review and consideration — the planning phase. The control aspect relates to permitting expenditures only for the purpose authorized and in accordance with the planned or actual availability of funds.

In a general sense, a sound budgeting procedure consists of five activities.

1. Searching out or finding attractive investment opportunities
2. Making an economic analysis of the suitability and worth of the projects (at least the major ones)
3. Reaching a decision as to which candidate should be selected
4. Controlling the expenditure of funds within the planned or budgetary limits
5. Conducting a post-audit, in cases of large projects, to compare actual cost and economic benefits with those planned

Each of these basic activities, if properly implemented, requires careful consideration of facilitating procedures.

LOCATING ATTRACTIVE CAPITAL INVESTMENT OPPORTUNITIES
Evaluation of Capital Project Ideas

Some capital expenditures are of a rather routine nature, and generally small in amount, made to maintain the existing level of operations. These expenditures are requested by the operating heads. Examples are requests for new trucks, a new elevator, or modern testing equipment. Our concern in this section is principally with *major* outlays for expansion, cost reduction, or replacement. Usually, special planning, analysis, and approval procedures are required in most companies for relatively large expenditures.

In the real world, especially at capital budgeting time, there is no dearth of proposals. Very often, perhaps most of the time, they are conceived at the profit center level. Each foreman, product manager, plant superintendent, manufacturing vice-president, or marketing vice-president will have ideas. Typically, some will be discussed at the weekly or monthly meeting of managers, and of course, some ideas will originate at the top management level.

A constant flow of good ideas is highly desirable in making capital investment decisions. In fact, without them the best investment decisions will not be made. But the requirement is *good* ideas; for the most extensive review and the most sophisticated analysis will not translate a bad idea into a prudent investment opportunity. To be sure, when there are more ideas than available capital, many good projects must be rejected. Conversely, when there is more capital than ideas presented, revisions or analyses are more likely to be less critical and more cursory. It is far better to have too many good ideas than not enough.

When proposals originate in the profit center, especially when the individual knowledge exposure is rather limited, perhaps to one segment of a product line, a danger is undue emphasis on a narrow phase of the business. For this reason, ideas from *all* elements of the organization should be encouraged and compared. What is needed is a *balanced* listing of possible projects compatible with corporate objectives.

Proper Input Data

When a capital project is suggested and it is thought to be sufficiently interesting to review, adequate data is then required in order to reach a conclusion. Yet, in some companies this is one of the weakest links, even though the evaluation techniques are otherwise quite acceptable. The input data must be reliable, accurate, and, of course, relevant. The author is aware of an oil company that began expanding its chain of service stations. In the quest for specific locations, those responsible for locating sites learned of the acceptable criteria; the economic evaluations, in certain instances, were "worked backwards" (i.e., estimated gallonage to be pumped and estimated price) to present a proposal that appeared to be economically desirable. While the practice was corrected, the fact remains that every effort should be made to secure reliable and unbiased data for decision-making.

Because a capital expenditure is made to secure future economic benefits, a significant amount of information should be made available.

1. *Cash outflow — the cost.* This includes the *initial* cash requirement regardless of accounting treatment (whether expensed or capitalized) estimated according to the time needed. Further, if later outlays are necessary as a logical extension of the original commitment, it should be included as part of the program. It would be imprudent not to recognize the cost of the *total* project (e.g., warehousing space, new outlets). Failure to reveal the total expected cost and the complete plan really necessary, might be viewed as intellectual dishonesty.

   A related aspect of initial cash outflow is the treatment of old equipment in those instances where the new asset replaces it. An incremental basis should be used in the evaluation. To summarize:

□ Provision should be made for salvage value of the old equipment.

□ If there are tax losses on the sale of the old asset, recognition should be given in calculating the net cost.

□ Costs to be incurred that will, for whatever reason, be expensed, should be recognized in the outlay.

The *time* when the funds will be required is essential to sound financial planning so as to assure adequate resources when needed.

Finally, it is usually prudent to provide a contingency, since projects do not always progress as anticipated.

2. *Cash inflow*. The expected net revenues and related cash operating expenses, by time period, should be estimated. These ought to be conservative estimates. It does the company a disservice to overstate anticipated benefits.

3. *Other supporting data*. This may depend on the type of project, but usually information such as the following is necessary:

□ Useful life of the asset.

□ Expected normal and capacity output per year, perhaps in units and dollars.

□ Tax implications. Included are the allowable accelerated cost recovery schedule, investment tax credit, if applicable, and related matters, both federal, state, and local (i.e., property taxes).

□ Financing expenses. These total costs should be known; some may be capitalized and some expensed, but the accounting treatment is irrelevant except as to tax impact.

□ Residual value. This should be estimated for cash recovery (as in the discounted cash flow method).

□ Transferred assets. If some existing assets are to be transferred from other locations, the economic aspects should be reviewed even though no cash acquisition costs are involved (though moving expenses might be).

□ Availability of operating personnel. Sometimes the lack of personnel has proven to be a major obstacle to efficient operations.

□ Inflation factors used in both cash requirements, operating expenses, and product prices — where significant.

The preceding list shows examples of the input necessary to a proper evaluation. Use of the data is covered later in this chapter.

PROJECT EVALUATION METHODS

The extent to which capital expenditures are reviewed, tested, analyzed, and evaluated will depend on several factors, such as the relative size of the expenditure; the financial impact upon a company; the knowledge and sophistication of the management and analysts; perhaps the nature of the industry. For significant expenditures, at least, the proposed outlay should be measured against the future economic benefits. Profitability is only one factor to be considered by the decision-makers, but it is indeed an important one. Given the usual need to compare one project with another, and to eliminate the less desirable, management finds it useful to have a common measuring stick and perhaps to rank proposals in the order of economic worth. While the methods differ in complexity and sophistication, a knowledge of the advantages and disadvantages of each may be helpful.

Some firms will find simple procedures adequate; others, especially capital-intensive ones, will need better tools. Usually these tools include the following elements:

1. An estimate of the expected capital outlay and the amount and timing of future benefits to be received — the cash inflow.
2. A technique for relating future benefits to expected cost — the rate of return on the capital employed.
3. A means of evaluating the risk — a measure of the probability that the estimated results will be within specified perimeters or ranges.

Some of the more common techniques are reviewed in the following text.

Payback Period

The payback technique simply calculates the number of years required to recover the original investment from the cash inflow. The formula may be expressed thus:

$$\text{Payback time in years} = \frac{\text{Initial investment}}{\text{Annual net income} + \text{Depreciation}}$$

Assuming an initial cash outlay of $5,000,000, an average net income of $500,000 per year, and depreciation of $300,000 per year, the payback is calculated as follows:

$$= \frac{\$5,000,000}{\$500,000 + \$300,000}$$

$$= \frac{\$5,000,000}{\$800,000}$$

$$= 6.25 \text{ years}$$

FIG. 25-2   Calculation of Payback Period — Uneven Cash Inflow

Year	Cash Outgo	Cash Inflow	Net Investment (Recovery)
0	$5,000,000	—	$5,000,000
1		$ 700,000	4,300,000
2		1,000,000	3,300,000
3		1,300,000	2,000,000
4		1,600,000	400,000
5		1,200,000	(800,000)

With an average annual cash inflow of $800,000, the investment is recovered in 6.25 years. If the cash inflow (net income plus depreciation) is expected to be uneven, it can be determined as shown in Figure 25-2. The investment is recovered during the fifth year. Of course, investment *recovery* does not necessarily have any bearing on *profitability*. Earnings are determined by the total cash inflow during the life of the project as compared to the cost.

The advantages of the payback method are that

- It is simple to calculate and explain.
- In those cases where cash recovery must be very rapid (i.e., because of poor cash position) it may be useful. A company might find the method of some value where the payback period must be three years or less.
- In instances where the risk of expropriation is high (e.g., mineral rights in certain foreign countries) or if currency devaluation is a consideration, or if capital wastage is predominant, the payback calculation provides some insight as to desirability.
- Although it has drawbacks as a primary indicator of investment desirability, it may be useful as a *supplementary* technique.

The disadvantages of the payback method include

- The technique does not indicate *profitability*. It confuses mere recovery of capital with earnings. The latter is determined by the cash inflow per year and life of project. A project with an economic life of only five years, as in Figure 25-2, has a far different rate of return than a twelve-year project with continuous cash inflows of similar annual amounts and approximately $1 million annually for another seven years.
- Undue emphasis is placed on liquidity. Use of the payback method may tend to encourage projects with a quick payout to the detriment of much more

highly profitable expenditures that have a longer payback period. Liquidity is of concern usually only in periods or circumstances of extremely tight credit or cash availability.

Operators' Method

The operators' method, so described because it is a simple concept often used by manufacturing or engineering personnel or by other personnel not exposed to accounting concepts, is a convenient way of roughly calculating a rate of return on fixed assets. Basically, the technique uses the average cash inflow and relates it to the original investment. Thus, using the payback figures for a constant cash flow:

$$\text{Return on investment} = \frac{\begin{array}{c}\text{Average annual cash inflow}\\ \text{(net income plus depreciation)}\end{array}}{\text{Initial investment}}$$

$$= \frac{\$800,000}{\$5,000,000}$$

$$= 16\%$$

Variations of this method also relate to income before taxes, or net income after taxes, unadjusted for depreciation to the original investment. The method has some limited advantages:

- It is easy to understand, calculate, and communicate.
- If the average cash flow is just that, by implication giving recognition to the life of the item, it offers a rough measure of profitability. Perhaps it could be used where all projects are roughly comparable as to life-span.

The basic disadvantage is that it does not recognize the time-value of money.

Accountants' Method

The accountants' method, so called because it uses the concept of depreciation and average investment, instead of original investment, may be some improvement over the rough approximations of the operators' method. It recognizes that depreciation may be likened to recovered capital and may therefore be invested in other projects. One version of the technique is illustrated in Figure 25-3 under conditions of decreasing profit. Of course, it may be applied to any cash flow pattern.

In Figure 25-3, a capital outlay of $5 million is assumed, with a 10-year life. The rate of return based on the average profit and average investment

FIG. 25-3   Rate of Return — Accountants' Method

ASSET RATE OF RETURN

ACCOUNTANTS' METHOD
Decreasing Profit Pattern

Year	Net Income Before Depreciation	Depreciation	Net Income	Year-end Book Value of Asset	Return of Average Asset Value
0	—	—	—	$ 5,000,000	—
1	$ 1,800,000	$ 500,000	$1,800,000	4,500,000	27.37%
2	2,200,000	500,000	1,700,000	4,000,000	40.00
3	2,000,000	500,000	1,500,000	3,500,000	40.00
4	1,800,000	500,000	1,300,000	3,000,000	40.00
5	1,600,000	500,000	1,100,000	2,500,000	40.00
6	1,300,000	500,000	800,000	2,000,000	35.56
7	900,000	500,000	400,000	1,500,000	22.86
8	700,000	500,000	200,000	1,000,000	16.00
9	600,000	500,000	100,000	500,000	13.33
10	500,000	500,000	—	—	
Total	$13,400,000	$5,000,000	$8,400,000	$27,500,000	
Average	$ 1,340,000	$ 500,000	$ 840,000	$ 2,750,000	

$$\text{Rate of return} = \frac{\text{Net income}}{\text{Average investment}}$$

$$= \frac{\$840,000}{\$2,750,000}$$

$$= 30.55\%$$

(using a straight-line method of depreciation) is 30.55 percent. In actual practice an accelerated depreciation method or cost of recovery most probably would be employed.

Had the earnings before depreciation been flat, that is, the same for each year, there would have been no impact on the rate of return. In other words, over the life of the project the profit patterns makes no difference on the average.

The accountants' method also has several variations in calculating the rate of return on book value. These are as follows:

FIG. 25-4 Comparative Cash Flows and Return on Investment (Asset)

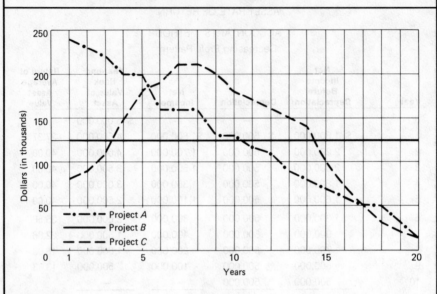

Description	Project A	Project B	Project C
Original investment	$ 500,000	$ 500,000	$ 500,000
Total cash flow	2,500,000	2,500,000	2,500,000
Less depreciation	500,000	500,000	500,000
Net income	$2,000,000	$2,000,000	$2,000,000
Project life (in years)	20	20	20
Average annual income before depreciation (cash flow)	$125,000	$125,000	$125,000
Deduct average depreciation	25,000	25,000	25,000
Average annual net income	$100,000	$100,000	$100,000
Return on original investment	$\frac{\$100,000}{\$500,000} = 20\%$	20%	20%
Return on average investment	$\frac{\$100,000}{\$250,000} = 40\%$	40%	40%
Return calculated by discount cash flow method	42.3%	24.7%	26.0%

1. Average net income, as illustrated in Figure 25-3;
2. Average net income, before depreciation; or
3. Average income before income taxes and depreciation.

This method, too, is relatively easy to use and communicate, certainly to financial people. It does give recognition to the decreasing investment concept. Perhaps it may be employed to compare projects of similar life periods and the same pattern of cash inflows. However, it possesses two disadvantages:

1. It is heavily influenced by the depreciation rate or accelerated cost recovery schedule. A double declining volume depreciation rate, for example, would significantly increase the annual write-off and the rate of return on the much lower resulting investment, as compared to the use of straight-line depreciation.
2. The method fails to recognize the time value of funds. Various projects in the same company in fact may have sharply differing cash flows and therefore a differing economic impact. The importance of the time value of money is discussed in the next section.

Discounted Cash Flow Rate of Return Method

In recognizing the importance of capital expenditures to most business enterprises, much thought has been given over the years to ways of comparing investment opportunities. It is especially difficult in those well-diversified companies with widely different types of investment requirements in, for example, a coal field or a steel-rolling mill. As a consequence of the problem, two methods have been developed that seem far superior in ranking capital projects according to their profitability:

1. The internal rate of return (IRR), also known as the Investor's method, and
2. The net present value (NPV).

Both of these techniques focus attention on the cash flows and specifically take into account the time value of money, i.e., when the fund's inflows are received.

Witness the stream of cash flow (net income plus depreciation) on three capital investments as illustrated in Figure 25-4. All have the same initial investment of $500,000; all have the same economic life of 20 years; all have the same total cash flow of $2,500,000; all have the same average cash flow of $125,000; and each project has the same average annual net income of $100,000. It might be concluded the rate of return on each would be the same, and indeed it is, as calculated by the operators' method or the accountants' method, relating net income to original investment and to the (depreciated) average investment. Yet the stream of each flow is significantly different. Project A provides a heavy cash flow rather immediately, with the amount declining to year 20. Project B provides a constant stream of cash at the same level for the life of the project. Project C reflects a slower build-up of cash to a peak level, but remaining at a high level for a number of years and then declining rather preciptiously. Which is the better investment? Project A is the preferred vehicle, providing a discounted cash flow (DCF) rate of return aggregating 42.3 percent, as compared with Projects B and C. This is true because funds received can be invested and produce further earnings. The earlier they are secured the greater the earnings potential. Thus, the DCF technique adds an important factor of measurement not possessed by the other methods.

Internal Rate of Return. The IRR principle has long been used by bankers in, for example, calculating the split of a monthly mortgage payment between principal and interest. Technically, the IRR on any project is that rate at which the stream of cash inflows, discounted at selected time periods, equals the cost of the project. In other words, it is that constant maximum rate of return that a project could earn throughout the life of the investment and just break even. The rate of return is determined by:

1. Arranging in a time sequence the expected cash flows for both the investment and earnings of the project; then
2. Determining the interest (earnings) rate at which the total project cash flow, discounted from the time it occurs to the present, equals the project investment at the present value.

The principle may best be illustrated by an example. Assume, for instance, that an investment of $110,500 is made, and that, over a six-year period an annual cash inflow of $30,000 is earned. What is the rate of return on the investment? By a trial and error method, and the use of present value tables, a rate of 16 percent is arrived at. The application of the 16 percent discount factor approximates the $110,500 investment as follows:

Year	Annual Cash Flow (a)	16 Percent Discount Factor (b)	Present Value (a) × (b)
1	$30,000	.862	$ 25,860
2	30,000	.743	22,290
3	30,000	.641	19,230
4	30,000	.552	16,560
5	30,000	.475	14,280
6	30,000	.410	12,300
	Net present value		$110,520

The proof of the answer lies in applying a 16 percent earnings factor to the outlay remaining at the beginning of the year, with any balance applied to the year-end outstanding investment in the following fashion.

Year	Cash Flow (s)	16 Percent Return on Outstanding Investment at Beginning of Year (t)	Balance Applicable to Investment "Repayment" (u) = (s) − (t)	Year-end Investment Outstanding (v)
0	—	—	—	$110,500
1	$30,000	$17,600	$12,400	98,100
2	30,000	15,616	14,384	83,716
3	30,000	13,315	16,685	67,031
4	30,000	10,645	19,355	47,676
5	30,000	7,548	22,452	25,224
6	30,000	3,956	26,044	(820)

For the purpose of calculating the IRR on a proposed capital project, assume the following:

1. Estimated project cost:

Depreciable asset	$300,000
Land	100,000
	$400,000

2. Estimated economic life of unit   5 years
3. Depreciation method   200% double declining balance
4. Estimated gross income from sales per year:

First year	$120,000
Second year	100,000
Third year	90,000
Fourth year	70,000
Fifth year	70,000

5. Federal income tax rate   40%
6. At end of five years, land is estimated to be salable at $100,000

What is the IRR?

The net cash flow by time period is derived as in Figure 25-5. Depreciation, being a noncash expense, is added back to arrive at pretax cash in-

FIG. 25-5   Calculation of Cash Flow by Year

PROPOSED CAPITAL INVESTMENT

ESTIMATE OF CASH FLOW

By Years

Year	Gross Investment (a)	Estimated Gross Margin (b)	Depreciation (DDB)* (c)	Taxable Income (b) − (c) (d)	Federal Income Taxes .40 × (d) (e)	Net Cash Flow (a) + (b) + (c) − (e) (f)
0	$400,000	—	—	—	—	($400,000)
1		$120,000	$120,000	—	—	240,000
2		100,000	72,000	$28,000	$11,200	160,800
3		90,000	43,200	46,800	18,720	114,480
4		70,000	25,920	44,080	17,632	78,288
5		70,000	15,550	54,450	21,780	63,770

* Excluding land cost of $100,000

FIG. 25-6 Calculation of Internal Rate of Return Through Trial and Error Approach

Year	Estimated Cash Flow	Discount Applied to Estimated Cash Flow			
		At 28%		At 32%	
		Factor	Amount	Factor	Amount
0	($400,000)	1.000	($400,000)	1.000	($400,000)
1	240,000	.781	187,440	.758	181,920
2	160,800	.610	98,088	.574	92,299
3	114,480	.477	54,607	.435	49,799
4	78,288	.373	29,201	.329	25,757
5	63,770	.291	18,557	.250	15,943
Sales value of land	$100,000	.291	$ 29,100	.250	$ 25,000
			$416,993		$390,718

$$\text{Interpolation} = 28\% + 4\%^* \left(\frac{(\$416,993 - \$400,000)}{\$416,993 - \$390,718} \right)$$

$$= 28\% + 4\% \left(\frac{\$16,993}{\$26,275} \right)$$

$$= 28\% + 4\% \, (.6467)$$

$$= 28\% + 2.59\%$$

$$= 30.59\%$$

* Representing the interval between 28% and 32%

come, and finally the net after tax cash flow. Given the estimated cash flow, an estimated internal rate of return is used, which is applied from present value tables. The aim is to select a rate such that the discounted or present value of the expected cash flows will equal zero. Twenty-eight percent was used as shown in Figure 25-6. Since derived value was greater than the investment, thus indicating a higher rate of return, another high rate, 32 percent, was applied. Finally, to reach the expected rate, an interpolation was made that results in an IRR of 30.59 percent.

In summary, the IRR approach consists of the following specific steps:

1. Ascertain by year the amount of the initial investment (or any subsequent expenditures).
2. Calculate, by years, the net cash inflow, meaning income before taxes plus

depreciation, less income taxes, to arrive at an income after taxes, plus
depreciation.

3. Extend the annual cash flow by a discount rate to arrive at the NPV.
4. Based on the first run at present value, apply other rates until the one closest
   to the investment is arrived at. When necessary, interpolate between the
   nearest discount rates employed to secure a more accurate figure.

The important advantage of the IRR is that it recognizes the time value
of a flow of funds. In times with a significant number of high-yield investments abroad, this is a major consideration.

The disadvantages of the IRR method may be summarized in the following manner:

1. The technique is more complex than the others. (However, the concept and
   methodology can be learned very quickly by most financial analysts.)
2. This evaluation approach takes more time to calculate.
3. There is an implicit assumption that funds can be reinvested at the derived
   rate of return.

On balance, and based on a trial of experience, sophisticated management types have concluded that the IRR method is superior to the operators' method, the accountants' method, and the payback method.

Net Present Value Technique. The IRR method recognizes the time
value of capital, and discounts the stream of cash flow, on a trial-and-error
basis, to arrive at the estimated rate of return. The NPV method of evaluating capital expenditures also considers the time value of money and uses the
discounting technique. The difference between the two methodologies is that
for the NPV a preselected rate is used. It is that rate the company considers
the minimum acceptable rate for making a capital investment. Usually it is a
rate somewhat higher than the cost of capital. (See Chapters 3 and 7.)

If the sum of the present values of the net cash flows exceeds the
present value of the proposed investment, the rate of return exceeds the
target; the true rate of return is higher than the minimum, and the project
meets the earnings requirement. If the NPV is negative, then the expected
rate is below the required earnings rate, and the project fails to meet the test.

The application of the technique is shown in Figure 25-7, where the
NPV is positive, with the sum of $10,500. Hence, the rate of return exceeds
the cut-off rate of 20 percent, and, all other things being equal, the project
should be accepted.

It should be mentioned the NPV method may be supplemented by a
profitability index as illustrated in Figure 25-7. This relates the cash inflows

FIG. 25-7   Application of Net Present Value Method to Proposed Capital Investment

CAPITAL INVESTMENT PROPOSAL

DETERMINATION OF NET PRESENT VALUE

Year	Estimated Cash Flow	Discounting Factor 20% Rate	Present Worth
0	($400,000)	1.000	($400,000)
1	180,000	.833	149,940
2	160,000	.694	111,040
3	100,000	.579	57,900
4	90,000	.482	43,380
5	70,000	.402	28,140
6	60,000	.335	20,100
Net present value			$ 10,500

$$\text{Net present value index} = \frac{\$410,500}{400,000} = 1.026$$

to the present value of the investment, and measures the relative profitability. By this measure, projects with the highest present value probably will have the greatest earning power. The index is another means of ranking capital investment proposals.

INVESTMENT RISK ANALYSIS

The discounted cash flow method of evaluating capital expenditures is, in the opinion of the author, a procedure superior to others. Yet, even knowing an indicated rate of return, and with a full understanding of the assumptions and the intangible factors, the decision-maker does not really have as complete a picture as is now possible. He does not have a reasonable evaluation of the risk factor. Thus while the project shown in Figure 25-6 may indicate a 30.59 percent rate of return as the most likely, a high degree of risk may be involved. As an extreme case, if the best estimate were to be grossly inaccurate — and this occurs many more times than one cares to admit — then the company might come close to bankruptcy. If ways could be found to measure risk, it might be sound business to select a project with a somewhat smaller rate of return but where the probabilities are more favorable.

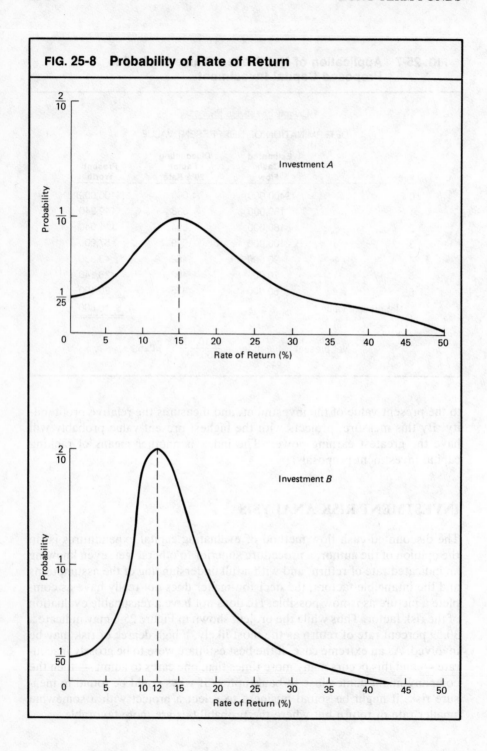

FIG. 25-8   Probability of Rate of Return

Some businessmen think that the "risk factor" is best treated as an intangible to be weighed on a qualitative basis. In other situations, it is handled by the addition of a "risk allowance" to compensate for the inherent danger. Thus, if a cutoff point for capital expenditures is a 20 percent rate of return, perhaps 7 percent is added, making a total of 27 percent return required before consideration — the risk allowance bearing some relationship to the estimate of inherent risk.

There are so many variables involved in capital investments that the decision maker needs to know not merely the most likely value — which is based upon each variable occurring as anticipated, and in itself a most unlikely coincidence — but rather, a *range* of rates of return and the *probability* of each happening. The so-called augmented investors' method may expand the discounted cash flow method by application of probability distribution to the economics of a proposed capital expenditure, recognizing both depreciation and obsolescence. A computer, for example, may be used to generate a frequency curve to represent the proposed project, as in Figure 25-8.

In this example, Investment A indicates a most probable rate of return of 15 percent. However, the chances are 1 out of 10 that this rate will prevail. Also, the chances are 1 in 50 that a 40 percent rate of return can be attained, and that the odds are 9 in 100 that a return of between 10 percent and 15 percent may be gained. Finally, the odds are 1 in 25 that the capital investment will be a total loss.

Quite in contrast, Investment B yields a "most probable rate of return" of 12 percent. However, the chances are 2 out of 10 that such a rate of return may be achieved. Additionally, the probabilities are 9 to 50 that a return of from 9 percent to 12 percent will result. Also, the probability is only 1 out of 50 that the capital investment will be a complete loss. Of course, the odds are negligible that a 40 percent rate of return can be gained.

By thus considering the entire probability graph rather than just the most probable rates of return, the decision-maker may well reach a more realistic conclusion — in this example, that Investment B appears really the more desirable.

In summary, the IRR method, and most other techniques usually used, are intended to provide a one "most likely" rate of return. Yet, the approaches do not make clear the extent of uncertainty or risk. Hence, risk analysis is a valuable adjunct in appraising the capital project.

SENSITIVITY ANALYSIS

A subject closely related to risk analysis is sensitivity analysis. Risk analysis attempts to provide an indication of the probability of attaining certain rates of return. Yet, those involved in making financial analyses of capital expenditures know that the indicated rate of return, and, of course, the probability of reaching selected rates, is highly dependent on the underlying assumptions used in the determination. If certain assumptions, such as the gross margin, are wrong by only a small amount, the rate of return may be materially influenced. Certain other premises, for example, the residual value of the facility, may have little impact, even if substantially in error. It often is a source of surprise how little sway a major change in a given assumption may have on the answer.

Sensitivity analysis essentially is a mathematical technique, such that changes may be made in each or any of the input factors and changes in the calculated results observed. Such knowledge, among other things, can permit the analysts to focus their attention on the important variables. The technique can provide considerable insight to a capital expenditure proposed, and its use is recommended in probing major and critical capital projects. Readers are referred to articles on the subject, particularly when computer applications may be employed in the screening process.

CLASSIFYING AND RANKING PROJECTS

Under normal circumstances, the amount of suggested capital expenditures is far greater than the company's financial resources would permit. This is especially true when an environment to encourage proposals does exist. Further, while profitability will be a major factor in project selection, there will be some instances where it will not be the criterion, for example, where a proposal is inconsistent with corporate strategy. Hence, to simplify the decision-making process, it is suggested that proposals be classified according to basic needs or reasons, and further, that those being made for the measurable economic benefits be ranked in some fashion. A practical method of segregating projects could be something like the following.

1. *Absolutely essential:*
   □ Replacement of exhausted or inoperable facilities, without which the company cannot continue in business.
   □ Installation of equipment demanded by government agencies or laws, such as:
      • Pollution abatement devices
      • Safety controls
      • Items to eliminate health hazards

2. *Highly necessary:*
   ☐ Sufficient parking space for employees
   ☐ Competitive quality control equipment
   ☐ Lighting facilities in profiling area

3. *Economically justified projects:*
   ☐ Plant expansion
   ☐ Cost-saving equipment
   ☐ New product lines, pursuant to corporate goals
   ☐ New facilities close to foreign markets

4. *Miscellaneous:*
   ☐ New facade to improve plant appearance
   ☐ Modernizing cafeteria to aid employee morale
   ☐ Refurbishing community center for public relations purposes

It should be observed that these classifications relate more or less to the perceived urgency of making the expenditures. Some projects must be accomplished to permit operation. Others will contribute indirectly to employee efficiency; some will be justified by the economics; and the last category, when funds are available, will contribute to improved employee/community relations.

For projects whose justification lies in the economic gains expected, some means is deemed necessary to separate the clearly more desirable from the less so. One method is to rank projects in descending order of profitability. Thus, a preliminary screening of profitability rates might produce a schedule such as that illustrated in Figure 25-9. The priority is established by the IRR, but the profitability index also is shown. Possible discrepancies between these two measures are discussed later in this chapter. (See mutually exclusive projects.)

STEPS IN THE CAPITAL BUDGETING PROCESS

Having reviewed some of the issues that arise in the planning of the capital budget, it is now more meaningful to elaborate on the basic budgeting procedure mentioned earlier. Planning the capital budget involves committing the funds only after adequate study, with the careful exercise of executive judgment at the highest level. But the screening process must provide the framework for selecting the essential or economically desirable projects from the others, and support the recommendation with adequate analysis. Having authorized the project, controls must be instituted to keep expenditures

FIG. 25-9   Priority Schedule for Capital Projects

CAPITAL PROJECT RANKING

For the 19XX Capital Budget

Priority	Rate of Return (IRR)	Profitability Index	Description and Location	Estimated Cost
1	34.6%	1.30	New electronics plant — Chicago	$4,870,000
2	30.2	1.21	Modernizing profiler equipment — Los Angeles	3,800,000
3	29.5	1.20	Installing robots– fabrication — El Segundo	8,920,000
4	26.4	1.14	Mechanizing material handling — New York	2,900,000
5	25.0	1.19	Purchase new trucks — Washington	1,410,000
6	25.0	1.10	Renovate warehouse — Chicago	610,000
7	24.3	1.09	Install new point facility — Anaheim	2,460,000
8	21.7	1.01	Replace loading dock — El Cerritos	1,110,000

within the planned amount and time limits. Therefore, from the viewpoint of the budget director, these steps at least should be given some consideration in developing the capital budgeting procedure.

1. For the planning period, *establish* the fund limit or a permissible range for the capital budget, as to both commitments and expenditures. This should be provided to those responsible for formulating the specific budget, the division managers, or appropriate line executives and the financial arm, both in total and for each as to his operation or segment.
2. Through the appropriate channel of organization, and with proper procedures, *encourage* the submission of desirable capital investments. Guidelines should be provided, including cutoff rate of return, and method of calculation, such as DCF for major projects.
3. Provide for a preliminary screening of potential projects.

Perhaps there should be a strategic plan screening to see that the surviving proposals conform to the corporate long-term objectives and goals, and a rough economic or profitability check might be made.

4. When the preliminary screening has been accomplished, the procedure should provide guidelines to:
   - Classify the projects, e.g., according to need, and
   - Specify the detailed method for calculating the economic benefits, including the supporting data that are required.

5. When the proposed capital projects finally are submitted for top management approval, before being presented to the board of directors, the items should be tested by the financial analysts (staff of budget director or controller's staff) for:
   - Validity of underlying nontechnical data,
   - Rate of return, and
   - Conformity to other criteria and compatibility with financial resources, both individual major projects and overall budget.

6. After top management approval, *authority* should be secured from the board of directors. The significant economic and all related data should be presented to the board; and all other information made available upon request.

7. When the board has approved the budget in total, provision should be made for a detailed authorization by the appropriate level of management. At this stage a re-review of the economics and conformance of the detailed plans with the board authorization should be made.

8. When the project commences, appropriate financial and other status reports should be prepared periodically for the responsible management. Such a report might indicate, among other things, expenditures to date, commitments to date, and estimated cost to complete the project.

9. After the project construction or installation is completed, periodic reports should be made on the larger expenditures comparing actual and planned economic benefits (cash flow).

ESTABLISHING THE AMOUNT OF THE CAPITAL BUDGET

There is, to be sure, an interrelationship between the amount of acceptable capital investments and the aggregate sum that may be committed or spent in any planning period. But in most instances, an overall limit must be set by top management. Deciding how much can or should be invested in the aggregate is a complex process, which many pressures or influences may have an impact on. In fact, there will be instances when the "normal" guidelines are set aside because an unusual opportunity exists. Aside from such interactions, some of the factors that impinge on the capital budget, and which the management must consider, include:

- The capital structure of the company
- Internal cash generation, including net income, plus depreciation and amortization, as well as deferred income taxes
- Stage of the business cycle
- Growth prospects of both the industry and the company
- Corporate goals and objectives
- Availability and cost of outside financing
- Rates of return available on capital proposals as compared with objectives or cost of capital
- Share of assets represented by plant and equipment when measured against selected industry ratios, or competitors
- Competitors actions
- Inflation rates and changes in the cost of acquisition
- Age of assets and cost effectiveness

Each of these factors must be weighed in the light of specific circumstances.

The following are some ratio guidelines which may be helpful in assessing the maximum desirable total investment in plant and equipment for a particular company.

1. *Turnover of plant and equipment.* This measures the relation of sales to plant and equipment. Too low a ratio indicates either insufficient sales volume or excessive investment in plant and equipment, or both. Comparisons with the industry mean, median, or mode as published by Dun & Bradstreet might be enlightening.

2. *Ratio of fixed assets to net worth.* Comparisons to competitors and industry data may indicate how much of the net worth is required, for example, to finance fixed assets as opposed to working capital.

For normal capital expenditures, some companies provide for a measure composed of the annual depreciation charge plus one third of earnings. Of the remaining earnings, one third is considered as available for shareholder dividends, and the remaining one third as providing working capital. Finally, the decision must be based on management judgment giving weight to current needs and long-term financial outlook.

TREATMENT OF WORKING CAPITAL

In order to limit comments to plant and equipment expenditures, which is the budget area under review, no examples have been provided regarding the impact of working capital investments. To be sure, some fixed asset expenditures will not impact working capital other than cash expenditures, i.e., pollution control equipment or replacement items. Yet, the fact remains that when business expansion is undertaken, usually the higher sales volume will require investments in receivables and inventory as well as fixed assets. When calculating total financial needs, and the project rates of return, obviously the total fund requirements should be included in the evaluation.

LEASE VS. BUY DECISIONS

Technically, the capital budget should provide for the acquisition of any fixed assets, be they purchased or leased on a long-term, generally noncancellable, contract (as distinguished from an operating lease). The items whether purchased or acquired by long-term lease would be included in the plant and equipment category of assets on the balance sheet.

A corporation may acquire the use of an asset on a rental basis, cancellable at any time. But for long periods of usage, this may be expensive (versus a few days rental of a moving crane). Typically, a company is faced with the question of whether to purchase the equipment or secure its use under a long-term lease. Basically, this is a financing decision in that the lease payments include an interest cost factor, and the payments, in part, are similar to interest and principal payments on indebtedness. The objective, of course, would be to select that method of acquisition which has the least cost, once the decision to make the investment is reached on the basis of profitability.

The IRR techniques may be useful in reaching a lease vs. buy decision. The alternatives may be lease vs. buy, buy and borrow, or outright rental (for short periods). Differences in lease periods, residual values at varying termination dates, and cancellation penalties, to mention a few, are some of the complications to be considered. The reader is referred to some of the excellent publications on leasing to get a better understanding of the opportunities and pitfalls and methods of analysis.

Some managements and financial analysts prefer the NPV method in making a lease vs. buy decision. If the financing cost for funds to purchase the asset is known, the same rate of discount may be applied to the stream of lease payment to arrive at the NPV. Again, other considerations being equal, the alternative with the lower NPV, and hence greater savings, should be selected.

Assuming a corporation may secure the necessary financing to purchase the asset at 15 percent per annum, or 9 percent after taxes, the comparative costs, and present value are illustrated in Figure 25-10. A seven-year economic life (and a purchase price of $800,000) is assumed.

FIG. 25-10 Lease vs. Buy Decision — NPV Calculation

A. LONG-TERM LEASE BASIS

Years	Pre-tax Lease Rental	Tax Savings (40% Tax Rate)	After-tax Lease Cost	Discount Factor (9%)	Net Present Value
1	$ 230,000	$ 92,000	$138,000	.917	$126,546
2	230,000	92,000	135,000	.842	116,196
3	210,000	84,000	126,000	.772	97,272
4	210,000	84,000	126,000	.708	89,208
5	160,000	64,000	96,000	.650	62,400
6	160,000	64,000	96,000	.596	57,216
7	160,000	64,000	96,000	.547	52,512
Total	$1,360,000	$544,000	$816,000		$601,350

B. PURCHASE BASIS

Years	Accelerated Cost Recovery*	Tax Savings (40% Tax Rate)	Discount Factor (9%)	Present Value at 9%
1	$160,000	$ 64,000	.917	$ 58,688
2	160,000	64,000	.842	53,888
3	160,000	64,000	.772	49,408
4	160,000	64,000	.708	45,312
5	160,000	64,000	.650	41,600
6	—	—		—
7	—	—		—
Total	$800,000	$320,000		$248,896

* In lieu of depreciation

The savings by purchase may be summarized as follows:

Present value of purchase price	$800,000
Less: Present value of tax savings if purchased	248,896
Net cost	$551,104
Savings (NPV) by purchase over lease:	
Present value of lease cost	$601,350
Net purchase cost (PV)	551,104
Net savings	$ 50,246

The purchase method represents the least cost method. However, non-financial considerations could influence the decision.

In making lease vs. buy decisions, there are several alternative methods available in calculating the least cost route, and in segregating the invest-ment decision from the financing decision. The reader is referred to the many good sources.[2]

MUTUALLY EXCLUSIVE PROJECTS

In the capital-budgeting process, many projects may be rejected because the profitability rate is not high enough. However, there will be instances when the rate of return is acceptable for any two projects, but the company has insufficient funds for both. One must be eliminated. These are, by definition, mutually exclusive projects because acceptance of one precludes acceptance of the other. What to do? The problem can become more complicated be-cause the IRR method may rank projects in a somewhat different order than the NPV method. This condition may arise for a variety of reasons, but a principal one is the reinvestment rate assumption. As previously discussed, the IRR method assumes that cash inflows are reinvested at the rate of the original investment. On the other hand, the NPV method assumes reinvest-ment at the cost of capital rate (if this is the cutoff rate) or at the investment opportunity rate; the rate that is considered attainable on other projects. Other courses of different relative evaluations are unequal lines and different investment amounts. When the IRR is adequate for each project, and the projects are mutually exclusive, a solution lies in calculating the incremental investment and incremental cash flow on the project with the next higher required investment. Thus, the two mutually exclusive proposals are mea-sured as to differences in cash flow, by years. To this difference is applied the cost of capital on opportunity cost rate. If the incremental rate is higher then the cutoff rate, then the project with the higher value should be selected as illustrated in Figure 25-11, the incremental rate of 18 percent is higher than the cutoff rate of 15 percent, and project Y should be accepted.

COST OF CAPITAL VISITED AGAIN

In Chapter 7, the cost of capital was defined as the rate of return that must be paid to investors to induce them to supply the necessary funds for the

---

[2] See, for example, Richard F. Vancil, ed., *Financial Executives' Handbook* (Homewood, Ill.: Dow Jones-Irwin, Inc., 1970), Chapters 19 and 20.

FIG. 25-11 Measurement of Mutually Exclusive Projects

INCREMENTAL INVESTMENT

MUTUALLY EXCLUSIVE PROJECTS

	Cash Flows		Y − X	Present Value at 18%*	
Year	X	Y	Difference	Factors	Amount
0	($9,000)	($18,000)	($9,000)	$1.00	($9,000)
1	2,700	—	(2,700)	.85	(2,295)
2	2,700	—	(2,700)	.72	(1,944)
3	2,700	8,000	5,300	.61	3,233
4	2,700	8,000	5,300	.52	2,756
5	2,700	8,000	5,300	.44	2,332
6	2,700	8,000	5,300	.37	1,961
7	2,700	8,000	5,300	.31	1,643
8	2,700	8,000	5,300	.27	1,431
					$ 117

* Incremental rate of 18% exceeds cutoff rate of 15%.

company. As explained, it related to the *perceived risk* and the *expected* rate, not the historical experience.

Suffice it to restate here that if long-term commitments are made, such as for capital expenditures, a prudent management must make every effort to secure at least the cost of capital if the firm is to have available the funds, over the long term. That is not to say that there will be no circumstances when projects are undertaken with prospective earnings at less than the cost of capital. It may be advantageous to invest at a lower rate than let funds sit idle. However, if such conditions persist for long periods of time, inevitably the return on shareholders' equity will decline as earnings decline. The common stock will be viewed as less attractive, and the price will trend lower. Consequently, the management may be viewed as not meeting its objectives of maximizing the return to the owners. Hence, the importance of the proper cutoff rate for capital expenditures should not be forgotten.

APPROVAL OF BOARD OF DIRECTORS

In the *long-range planning* process, the required facilities are included in the projected balance-sheet figure and provision is made for necessary funds in the statement of cash sources and uses. The board is then advised of possible needs; but no specific action usually is required.

But in most U.S. companies, once top management has decided how much should be spent on plant and equipment for the *short-term planning* period, a one- to two-year span, the requirements are presented to the board of directors for approval. In fact, where truly large sums will be required, it may be submitted first to the finance committee of the board for concurrence in the proposed source of funding and the wisdom of making the investment. In any event, the guidance and approval of the board is solicited.

The vice-president of facilities or the chief operating officer may make the presentation, but it will have been reviewed and tested by the financial arm. The proposal ordinarily will be summarized in some logical form, with the salient economic facts presented. An example is shown in Figure 25-12. Some features of this figure may be noted:

- The major individual projects are identified.
- The basic reason for the project is given: expansion or replacement.
- The total commitment authority or appropriation required is stated.
- The time period when the actual expenditures would be made, and funds needed, is stipulated.
- The rate of profitability (DCF method) for those projects recommended on an economic basis is set forth.
- Because cost over-runs do occur, the extent of such contingency is disclosed.

Normally the spokesman will be armed with the facts or opinions on each major project, as appropriate: sales expectancy, competitive posture, other risks, and the basis for the cost estimate.

Management must see that the board understands the significant facts or assumptions concerning the project, including the ability of the company to finance the request and the risks. It should be the duty of the chief financial officer or controller to see that the financial aspects are made known and are understood, insofar as possible.

When the board of directors finally does approve the capital budget, it is an approval in principle.

PROJECT APPROPRIATION REQUEST

In many instances, the inclusion of a project in the recommended capital budget signifies that the necessary detailed analysis has been completed by the appropriate parties (engineering staff, marketing staff, financial group, and so forth; however, this is not always the case. Further, the time lapse between the overall budget approval and starting date of the project may

FIG. 25-12   Annual Capital Budget Request

THE TOLEDO COMPANY
ANNUAL CAPITAL BUDGET REQUEST — 19X3
(dollars in thousands)

Description	Appropriations Prior Years	New 1st Quarter	New 2nd Quarter	New Last Half	New 19X3	Return on Investment (DCF)	Total Commitments	Schedule 19X2 and Prior	Schedule 19X3	Schedule 19X4	Schedule Later Years	Total
Expansion and Growth:												
Naphthalene plant	—	—	—	$ 8,650	$ 8,650	22.3	$ 8,650	—	$ 2,130	$ 3,890	$2,630	$ 8,650
Butadiene recovery system	—	—	—	3,100	3,100	19.2	3,100	—	2,200	900	—	3,100
Hydrogen plant	$2,600	—	—	—	—	14.2	2,600	$2,310	290	—	—	2,600
Sulfur recovery system	1,900	—	—	—	—	8.7	1,900	1,500	400	—	—	1,900
Alkylate plant	—	—	$12,300	—	12,300	17.6	12,300	—	6,000	6,300	—	12,300
Isocracker	—	$25,000	—	—	25,000	23.8	25,000	—	6,500	17,300	1,200	25,000
Total expansion	$4,500	$25,000	$12,300	$11,750	$49,050	—	$53,550	$3,810	$17,520	$28,390	$3,830	$53,550
Replacements:												
Absolutely Essential												
Fitzpatrick grinder	$ 590	—	—	—	—	—	$ 590	$ 400	$ 190	—	—	$ 590
Pneumatic tube system	—	$ 390	—	—	$ 390	—	390	—	390	—	—	390
"R" Plant conveyor	—	—	$ 800	—	800	—	800	—	400	$ 400	—	800
Rosin crushers	210	—	—	—	—	—	210	190	20	—	—	210
"X" air pollution catcher	—	—	—	$ 1,020	1,020	—	1,020	—	300	720	—	1,020
Other	20	10	10	30	50	—	70	15	55	—	—	70
Total	$ 820	$ 400	$ 810	$ 1,050	$ 2,260	—	$ 3,080	$ 605	$ 1,355	$ 1,120	—	$ 3,080

FIG. 25-13 Appropriation Request for Capital Expenditure

Competitively Necessary									
"L" quality control lab	$ 300	—	—	—	$ 300	$ 200	$ 100	—	$ 300
Fine screening plant	—	$ 670	670	670	670	—	240	$ 430	670
Color retention process	—	2,300	2,300	2,300	2,300	—	870	1,430	2,300
Other	20	10	20	50	70	10	60	—	70
	$ 320	$ 680	$ 2,320	$ 3,020	$ 3,340	$ 210	$ 1,270	$ 1,860	$ 3,340
Economics Basis									
Urea system	800	800	—	800	800 (20.0)	800	800	—	800
Drum dumpers	—	200	200	200	200 (16.4)	200	200	—	200
Lift trucks	—	—	100	100	100 (12.3)	100	100	—	100
	$ 800	$ 1,000	$ 100	$ 1,100	$ 1,100	$ 1,100	$ 1,100	—	$ 1,100
Other									
Roof — North plant	—	70	70	70	70	—	70	—	70
Toledo landscaping	—	5	15	15	15	—	15	—	15
Miscellaneous	40	5	10	25	65	35	30	—	65
	40	80	25	110	150	35	115	—	150
Total Replacement	$ 1,180	$ 1,225	$ 1,770	$ 3,495	$ 6,490	$ 850	$ 3,840	$ 2,980	$ 7,670
Contingency	300	2,000	700	—	2,700	300	1,000	1,700	3,000
Grand Total	$5,980	$28,225	$14,770	$15,245	$58,240	$4,960	$22,360	$33,070	$64,220

FIG. 25-13   Appropriation Request for Capital Expenditure

AFE No.   605
Date   6/27/

Western   Los Angeles
Division   Plant

This request for authorization of a capital expenditure is made necessary by:
- ☐ Normal replacement
- ☐ Change in manufacturing method
- ☐ Change in quality control requirements
- ☐ Change in styling
- ☒ Cost reduction
- ☐ New business — Product
- ☐ Increased volume of business

Title: Automatic Packaging Equipment

Description and Justification:
Bagomatic to be used in packaging "R" chemical at Smead Avenue warehouse. Cost of container will be reduced by $.50. Present usage 36,000 per year. See attached study on packaging operation.
(Use added sheets if necessary)

Estimated cost		Return on investment	
Materials	$ 800	(Discounted cash flow method)	40.1%
Purchases	21,600		
Labor	—	Pay-out period	2.61 yrs
Total	$22,400	Estimated useful life of equipment	6 yrs
Contingency 5%	1,100	Time to construct	
Total cost	$23,500	Salvage value	$500

Controller's Comments and Recommendations:

		Accounting Dept.	
		No.	Amount
Cash flow appears realistic	Capital Account	19-790	$23,500
Return is above minimum of 16%			
Approval recommended			
	Expense		

Approvals and Authorization:

	Date		
	Approval	Rejection	Reason for Rejection:
Requested by			
Approved by			
Department Head			
Executive Committee			
Board of Directors, per			

cause a change of conditions. Therefore, most capital budgeting procedures require approval of an appropriation request for each capital item, or perhaps even for major repairs.

The authority required for approval of each specific appropriation request usually depends on the relative amount of the request. In small firms, perhaps each one would require the approval of the president. Typically, however, a regular ascending scale of required approvals is provided:

Less than $10,000	Plant Manager
$10,000–$50,000	General Manager
$50,000–$200,000	President or Executive Vice-President
$200,000–$1,000,000	Executive Committee
Over $1,000,000	Board of Directors

An illustrative form is shown in Figure 25-13. This summary sheet contains the pertinent facts and approvals. Requests for large sums, typically, are supported by rather comprehensive facts and figures. It is to be noted that the format shown here provides for the return on investment, calculated on the discounted cash flow basis as well as the payout period. Space is provided for the comments of the controller, including a check against minimum standards established in the company.

Distribution of the approved request serves to initiate the project. If rejected, the originator is advised as to the reasons.

KEEPING EXPENDITURES WITHIN LIMITS — BUDGET REPORTS

Once the request for appropriation has been approved, the next problem is that of keeping expenditures within the limits of the appropriation. In many cases, this is not quite as easy as it sounds. One essential step is the establishment of procedures to accumulate actual costs for comparison at frequent intervals with the authorized amounts. But mere accumulation of actual costs is not enough, for commitments can be made far beyond the bounds of the appropriations. It is usually found necessary, therefore, to maintain a record of commitments and periodically report such information as the following:

- Amount authorized
- Actual costs incurred
- Commitments
- Unencumbered balance
- Estimated cost to complete
- Indicated overrun or underrun

Figure 25-14 is illustrative of this type of report. A commitment register is prepared on the basis of purchase orders issued.

FIG. 25-14   Report on Status of Capital Expenditures Under Appropriation

MONROE MANUFACTURING COMPANY

APPROPRIATION STATUS REPORT

As of August 31, 19___

Appropriation No.	Description	Work Order No.	Amount Appropriated
24	Ottawa Avenue Plant		$ 750,000
	Buildings and equipment	241	
	Site clearance	242	
	Total appropriation 24		
25	Modifications of overhead conveyor		35,000
	Installation Y building	251	
	Others completed as of 7/31		
	Total appropriation 25		
26	Miscellaneous improvements		183,400
	Magnesium pilot line	261	
	Wrapping equipment	262	
	Roll mill — design and install — A.C. plant	263	
	Intercommunication system	264	
	Move hydraulic press and install in Y building	265	
	Design and install air conditioning unit in Y building	266	
	Changes and modifications in paint room	267	
	Buggy scales	268	
	Tote boxes — A.C. plant	269	
	Prepare annealing oven for production use	270	
	Move electric furnaces to A.C. plant	271	
	Lift truck with exide batteries and battery charger	272	
	Purchase and install 100 HP motor in Y building	273	
	Others completed as of 7/31/		
	Total appropriation 26		
29	Aluminum experimental unit		50,000
	Construction of unit	201	
	Total appropriation 29		
	Grand total		$1,018,400

Issued by Accounting Department — September 5, 19___

Actual Completion Date	Original Estimate	Outstanding Commitments	Actual Expenditures to Date	Estimated Cost to Complete	Indicated Total Cost	(Over) or Under Original Estimate
	$670,796.52	$286,672.84	$384,123.68	—	$670,796.52	—
	13,552.86	—	13,552.86		13,552.86	—
	$684,349.38	$286,672.84	$397,676.54	—	$684,349.38	—
	28,353.00	14,533.05	236.39	13,583.56	28,353.00	—
	2,990.00	—	4,615.55		4,645.55	($1,655.55)
	$ 31,343.00	$ 14,533.05	4,881.94	$13,583.56	$ 32,998.55	($1,655.55)
7/31	$ 8,910.00	—	$ 8,551.48	—	$ 8,551.48	$ 353.52
2/28	16,900.00	$ 6.50	14,122.52	—	14,129.02	2,770.98
	11,680.00	8,944.00	154.00	$ 2,582.00	11,680.00	—
	24,974.00	4,794.57	20,179.43		24,974.00	—
5/31	1,155.50	79.15	926.68	—	1,005.83	149.67
	9,725.00	750.00	8,626.84	318.16	9,725.00	—
5/31	30,115.00	29.89	26,664.06	—	26,693.95	3,421.05
	11,275.00	212.20	10,158.39	904.41	11,275.00	—
7/31	3,597.00	340.57	3,198.86	—	3,539.43	57.57
	7,700.00	1,290.03	6,202.29	207.68	7,700.00	—
	3,585.00	2,989.20	—	595.80	3,585.00	—
	30,486.00	21,670.19	2,737.83	6,077.08	30,486.00	—
7/31	4,692.00	424.00	3,701.97	—	4,125.97	566.03
	3,701.00	—	2,482.18	—	2,482.18	1,218.82
	$168,495.50	$ 41,530.30	$107,706.53	$10,716.03	$159,952.86	$8,542.64
	50,000.00	5,533.34	15,385.04	29,081.62	50,000.00	—
	50,000.00	5,533.34	15,385.04	29,081.62	50,000.00	—
	$934,187.88	$348,269.53	$525,650.05	$53,381.21	$927,300.79	$6,887.09

In actual practice, one of the problems is getting all commitments recorded. On occasion, some enterprising young men incur obligations without the necessary paperwork. Sometimes the estimated cost of the article or service is not stated on the purchase order. It requires some persuasion and diligent policing to enforce procedures.

A POST-AUDIT OF CAPITAL PROJECTS

In many companies, a good analysis is made of capital asset proposals, so that a prudent selection is made among the opportunities available and capital expenditures are held within authorized limits. Yet, this may not signify that an acceptable capital budgeting procedure is in place. One of the difficulties lies in the inadequacy of the input data. As mentioned earlier, if the criteria are known, then the presumed input may be "manufactured."

To guard against such a contingency and for the reasons enumerated in the following, it is desirable to systematically audit selected capital projects for a period of time. Actual performance of the economic factors should be measured against the assumptions or expectations. Such an audit may be made of the major capital expenditures after the "shake-down" period, or an arbitrary period after operations start until payback is attained, or for perhaps three years whatever is seemed practical. Such a review may be undertaken by the corporate internal-audit staff, or perhaps by a management-audit team composed of some line managers involved in the operation (but not the original justification group), and some corporate financial or other representatives.

Some of the advantages of such a post-completion audit are:

- It may assist in locating basic weaknesses in the capital-budgeting procedure.
- It serves to hold responsible those estimators who assembled the data for justification of the project (if they are still on the payroll).
- The audit procedure provides a signal as to the importance attached by management to estimates for capital proposals.
- It provides a training ground to estimators and operators on the capital-budgeting procedure.
- The review may permit correction of errors on other current projects, if applicable, before such an opportunity has passed.
- The audit may provide an individual measure of those who are continuously too optimistic or too pessimistic in making estimates.

On balance, a capital-budgeting procedure should provide for an audit of major projects without a reasonable time after completion and for a suitable period.

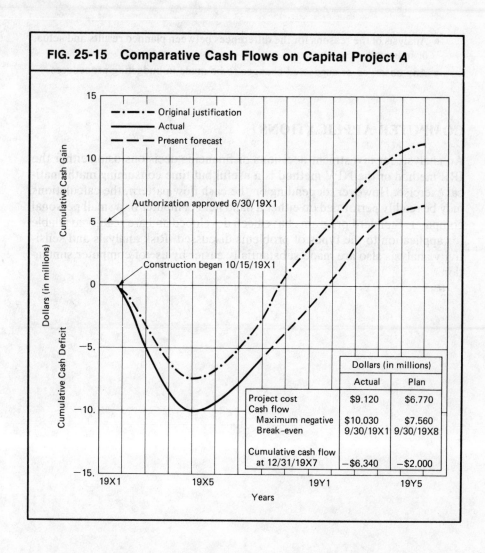

FIG. 25-15   Comparative Cash Flows on Capital Project A

Legend:
- —··— Original justification
- —— Actual
- – – – Present forecast

Authorization approved 6/30/19X1

Construction began 10/15/19X1

	Dollars (in millions)	
	Actual	Plan
Project cost	$9.120	$6.770
Cash flow		
Maximum negative	$10.030	$7.560
Break-even	9/30/19X1	9/30/19X8
Cumulative cash flow at 12/31/19X7	−$6.340	−$2.000

Y-axis: Dollars (in millions) — Cumulative Cash Gain / Cumulative Cash Deficit (15, 10, 5, 0, −5., −10., −15.)

X-axis: Years (19X1, 19X5, 19Y1, 19Y5)

An example of a post-audit report is shown in Figure 25-15. This comparison of cash flow (as planned in the original justification, with actual) should be supplemented with related statistical information, such as

- Actual expenditures vs. planned
- Actual vs. planned completion date
- Anticipated rate of return and presently projected rate
- If applicable, the originally planned payback period vs. the current actual or estimated time
- Anticipated sales — original estimated vs. actual to date and projected

- Analysis of the reasons for the differences between planned results and actual or indicated
- Any observed or suggested changes to be made in budgeting procedures

COMPUTER APPLICATIONS

An analysis for investment decisions or financing decisions using either the IRR method or the NPV method is a useful but time consuming mathematical exercise. However, depending on the cash flow pattern, the calculations may be readily performed on either a hand held computer or a small personal computer. Standard programs have been developed and are readily available for application to the types of problems discussed. Risk analysis and sensitivity analysis also are made substantially easier by use of computer simulations.

26

Long-Term Liabilities

SOURCES OF CORPORATE FUNDS

From an overall viewpoint, the principal sources of corporate funds are
these:

- ☐ *Net internal cash generation* — from earnings, depreciation, and other noncash expenses
- ☐ *Short-term borrowings* — perhaps for seasonal purposes, and basically as
  part of net working capital (see Chapter 24)
- ☐ *Long-term sources*

To be sure, conversion or sale of assets may be another source; but in most
companies it is neither a continuous nor a significant source.

The first two fountains of cash are discussed in Chapter 24. Our attention in this and the next chapter is on long-term sources. Long-term capital is
basically of two types: debt and equity. Equity is discussed in the next
chapter. In this chapter we focus on long-term debt, also referred to in the
financial world as funded debt. For it is to this source, as well as equity, that
a company should be able to turn when it needs significant capital of a
somewhat permanent nature. It is from this source that a company in proper
financial health should be able to secure funds for expansion and to meet
maturing obligations. In a corporation's strategic planning, it is these long-
term sources, and the rules governing them, that management must consider
in determining the proper makeup of its capital structure.

TYPES OF LONG-TERM DEBT

Long-term debt represents a claim by the holder of the instrument against
the company for the payment of principal and interest, or its equivalent,
until the principal is repaid. Technically, long-term liabilities are present
obligations, arising out of past actions or transactions, that are not due to be
paid within the year or within the normal operating cycle, whichever is
longer.[1] Additionally, this section of the balance sheet may contain deferred
credits, representing basically payments received prior to performing the
services or delivering the goods, but which are not to be liquidated within a
year or within the normal operating cycle. The budget officer should be
cognizant of the related accounting under generally accepted accounting
principles (GAAP) so that the planning financial statements are in proper
form.

There are innumerable variations in a long list of debt securities that

---

[1] Paul Grady, *Inventory of Generally Accepted Accounting Principles for Business Enterprises* (New York: AICPA, 1965), p. 284.

seek to secure funds on an acceptable basis. A partial listing of long-term debt sources in these days of "creative financing," fear of high inflation, and capital shortages includes:

1. Secured — Traditional:
   - Mortgage bonds
   - Lease financing
   - Equipment trust certificates
   - Industrial revenue bonds
   - Pollution-control bonds
2. Unsecured — Traditional:
   - Debentures
   - Term bank loans
   - Long-term notes
   - Income debentures
3. Other — Special features:
   - Floating-rate notes
   - Single-payment bonds
   - Zero coupon bonds
   - Deep-discount bonds

Those involved in the budgeting process should be reasonably familiar with the general terms of these various debt instruments so as to avoid unrealistic financial plans. Of course, the specific terms of existing instruments or the probable terms of new indebtedness to be incurred in the planning period should be reflected in the financial plans. These terms could impact cash receipts and payments, composition of the balance sheet, and earnings.

Most readers are familiar with the usual types of long-term obligations, so only a few comments are made below. It should be recognized, however, that there is a vast garden filled with different varieties, each designed to meet a particular financing need. The principal traditional types of long-term liabilities are these:

□ *Bonds.* Essentially, bonds are long-term corporate notes issued under a formal procedure, with a stipulated rate of interest and maturity. They differ from individual notes in that they represent a fractional interest in a group contract called a trust indenture. These bonds may be secured by specific property or by the general credit of the corporation. There are many excellent books on corporate finance that contain more specific terms.[2]

---

[2] See, for example, John F. Childs, *Encyclopedia of Long Term Financing and Capital Management* (Englewood Cliffs, N.J.: Prentice-Hall, Inc., 1976), Chapters 4 and 8.

☐ *Capitalized lease obligations.* Based on certain criteria under recent changes in GAAP, a lease must be classified as a capital lease, and the long-term asset and long-term liability must be placed on the balance sheet. Reference is made to pronouncements of the AICPA on the subject. In any event, the financial planning should recognize the proper accounting for the transaction expected to take place.

☐ *Long-term notes.* Promissory notes may be issued to commercial banks or others for an intermediate (five to seven years) or longer term. They may or may not be supported by liens on selected property. The form is often represented by serial notes with specified interest rates and due dates.

The point to be made, again, is that the financial plans should provide for the type of long-term indebtedness that is expected or planned; the scheduled or expected payments for reduction in such indebtedness should also be a part of the planning document.

OBJECTIVES OF LONG-TERM CAPITAL MANAGEMENT

Proper management of long-term capital is crucial to the strategic plans of the company. In a general sense, the financial officer, through the long-range planning process, must plan for the necessary financing in a manner that serves the corporation and does not unduly constrain it. He must guard against cash insufficiency or insolvency on the one hand (see Chapter 19) and excessive or idle cash on the other. Hence, there is a balance to be weighed: liquidity versus profitability.

In a more specific sense, the proper management of long-term debt should have these objectives:

1. To preserve the company's ability to raise long-term funds at any time, whether the company itself is in poor circumstances (weak or no earnings due to new product development or for other reasons); whether the entire industry is in recession; whether a general economic storm exists (a down cycle); or whether the securities markets are adverse.

2. To so maintain the company's financial health that funds may be secured without an undue straining of credit.

3. To enable the company to raise funds on an acceptable basis, at the lowest cost, so as to enhance the long-term interests of the shareholders.

4. To permit the company to follow a prudent dividend policy (see Chapter 27).

5. To permit the company to be so well regarded that its common stock will command respect from the marketplace far into the future, with an acceptable price-earnings ratio; and the stock will reflect a gradual increase in earnings per share and consequent long-term appreciation.

FIG. 26-1 Debt-Equity Ratios as Related to Return on Equity and Interest Coverage Times

Return on Assets	Debt/ Equity Ratio	Percentage Return on Equity[a]	Times Interest Covered
10%	0	10%	—
10	10 : 90	11	20.0
10	30 : 70	12	6.7
10	50 : 50	15	4.0
10	70 : 30	22	2.9
10	90 : 10	55	2.2

(a) Interest at 5% after taxes

The long-range planning and the annual plan as the first year of the strategic plan should recognize the importance of a proper capital structure and avoidance of excessive debt.

FINANCIAL LEVERAGE

Financial leverage, sometimes called trading on the equity, refers to the relationship of debt to equity. Basically, leverage exists when debt exists; the purpose of financing a company with debt is to increase the return to the shareholder. For example, if an organization can earn 25 percent on its investment and can borrow at 15 percent, the return on the total to the shareholder can be multiplied; this is positive leverage.

Since a basic question is how much long-term debt should be assumed, the statistics shown in Figure 26-1 are interesting.[3] With heavy debt, the return on equity may be substantially increased under favorable conditions. But as the table reflects, interest coverage reduces substantially. Interest charges are only one call on earnings. Others include lease rentals, debt repayment, and dividend to shareholders.

Of course, if earnings are not as expected — less than the interest rate — then it would be negative leverage. The impact of borrowings on a company is illustrated below.

---

[3] From J. Fred Weston and Maurice B. Goudzwaard, eds., *Treasurer's Handbook* (Homewood, Ill.: Dow Jones-Irwin, 1976), p. 644.

FIG. 26-2 Impact of Leverage

COMPANY A

COMPARATIVE RATES OF RETURN

Impact of Leverage

(dollars in millions, except per share)

Item	(A) Before Leverage	(B) Expected Return on Capitalization	(C) Without Leverage (Capacity)	(D) With Leverage Present Capacity	(E) With Leverage New Capacity
Net assets	$140	$210	$140	$210	$210
Capitalization bonds	—	$ 70	—	$ 70	$ 70
Beginning shareholders' equity	$140	140	$140	140	140
Total capitalization	$140	$210	$140	$210	$210
Number of shares outstanding	1,000,000	1,000,000	1,000,000	1,000,000	1,000,000
Sales	$360.0	$597.0	$420.0	$420.0	$500.0
Income before taxes and interest	$71.3	$118.2	$83.2	$83.2	$58.8
Bond interest	—	11.2	—	11.2	11.2
Income before taxes	$71.3	$107.0	$83.2	$72.0	$47.6
Income taxes (47%)	33.5	50.3	39.1	33.8	22.4
Net income	$37.8	$ 56.7	$44.1	$38.2	$25.2
Return on capitalization (net assets)	27.0%	27.0%	31.5%	18.2%	12.0%
Return on beginning shareholders' equity	27.0%	40.5%	31.5%	18.2%	18.0%
Earnings per share	$37.80	$ 56.70	$44.10	$38.20	$25.20
Earnings per share — Percentage increase (decrease) with leverage		50.0%		1.0%	(33.3%)

Assume that Company *A* can earn 27 percent on its fixed assets and net working capital as follows:

Net assets	$140,000,000
Shareholder's equity	$140,000,000
Sales	$360,000,000
Income before taxes	$71,320,750
Income taxes (47%)	33,520,750
Net income	$37,800,000

Return on net assets = ($37.8 million ÷ $140 million) = 27%

Management believes it can expand and continue to earn the same rate. It therefore borrows $70 million in long-term debt at 16 percent interest. The results of favorable and unfavorable leverage are shown in Figure 26-2, as follows:

Column

(A)	Actual earnings before leverage.
(B)	Expected results with income rate on sales continuing, on both present sales and those from the new capacity. A 50 percent increase in earnings is the potential.
(C)	Capacity earnings without expansion or leverage, but earnings rate maintained on sales.
(D)	Same sales levels and margin on sales as (C), but burdened with debt carrying costs. Increase over (A) in sales volume, and pre-tax and interest earnings almost completely offset by carrying costs of debt.
(E)	Leverage, with increased sales, but break in margins. Unfavorable leverage reduces earnings per share by 33⅓ percent.

The principle is "exercise prudence when incurring debt." More than interest coverage should be considered: Stability of earnings is an important factor.

HOW MUCH LONG-TERM DEBT SHOULD BE INCURRED?

Especially when earnings are on the increase, management has a propensity to incur long-term debt. There are several reasons:

☐ Under favorable conditions, as just illustrated, leverage can increase return on shareholders' equity and earnings per share.

□ Under present U.S. tax laws, interest expense is tax deductible.

□ Usually, incurrence of long-term debt for expansion avoids dilution, if the alternative is issuance of more common shares.

□ Typically, management believes the company shares are underpriced; therefore a postponement of common stock financing will result in a more favorable price later, when a higher price-earnings ratio and an increased earnings per share will obtain.

□ Usually management is of the opinion that it can command the present or higher margins on sales and can secure greater sales volume. Therefore, the logical way to expand is with debtor-supplied funds.

□ Management is sensitive to the attitude of many security analysts who dislike dilution — even though such dilution is often temporary until the new facilities or programs are in full operation — when earnings on shareholders' equity and per share increase.

However, the fact is that management must take a long-term view and must be reasonably prudent in its assessment of debt capacity. Some provocative thoughts on the extent of leverage is contained in the *Treasurer's Handbook*.[4]

GUIDANCE ON DEBT CAPACITY

In planning the financial position of the company — whether for the next year or several years down the road — the financial management, including the budget officer, must be aware of the practical limits on corporate debt capacity and should make every effort to see that they are observed in financial planning. Such information is also critical when specific terms are being considered for contemplated new long-term debt. While management must make the final decision of whether or not to assume additional indebtedness and whether the related terms and conditions are suitable, there are several sources that may serve as useful guides, including those discussed below.

Investment Bankers

These middlemen may perform in any one or more of three capacities for a corporation that plans on issuing securities:

• As an underwriter, purchasing the securities for a stipulated price and on a certain date. The firm assumes the market risk of selling them to investors.

---

[4] *Ibid.*, Chapters 30–32.

- As an agent, if the securities are a private placement.
- As a financial adviser, either as such or when acting as underwriter or agent.

The investment bankers may offer opinions on the types of securities in the market, the probable selling price, the acceptable terms in the present market climate, and the suggested time to sell.

Care should be used in selecting a firm that has the knowledge, qualifications, and experience to properly serve the company: adequate staff, proper type of house reputation, integrity, personal equation, and so forth. In any event, an investment banking firm usually is knowledgeable of the marketplace and can provide useful input.

Commercial Bankers

For most companies, the commercial bankers are the ones who supply debtor capital (usually first, and often for the longest period). While much may be in the nature of short-term credits, intermediate- to longer-term funds can also be provided. The rather continuous contacts, with related counseling and advice, often proves the commercial banker to be one of the best sources — the longest lasting and most intimate — of financial information. A bank often has industry specialists, or has access to them, which can be especially useful. Competent men with a good knowledge of the company can act as sounding boards and provide an array of scenarios useful in planning debt strategy.

Institutional Investors

Another useful group are institutional investors; they may be insurance companies, pension and profit-sharing trusts, trust departments of commercial banks, mutual funds and foundations, or representatives of major private interests.

Here, as with investment bankers, much depends on the personal relationship established and the quality of the firm — access to resources, competence of staff, accessibility to knowledgeable lenders, and so forth. Of course, when the investors are hungry to lend funds, the potential sources are more willing to spend time searching out the best ideas.

Competitive Practice

For most public companies, financial statements and credit or loan agreements (filed with the SEC) are available. From such sources and from trade associations or credit agencies, data can be secured to test debt ratios and other credit relationships for specific competitors, other selected companies in the same industry, or for the industry as a whole. These sources may provide some guidance as to what is being or has been done.

Trend Analysis of the Company

Of course, the financial officers should have available extensive data on the company itself. Included are the historical trends of the company as a whole and the individual segments. Trends should be available as to sales levels, operating margins, expense behavior, asset turnover, and debt relationships over the entire business cycle. From this and from plan data, a large number of probable relevant relationships can be determined; these are useful guides in judging debt capacity.

THE OPTIMUM CAPITAL STRUCTURE

The capitalization, or capital structure, of a company is composed of long-term debt and equity capital. In financial planning, a corporation must first decide how much long-term debt it should have. It must establish a financial policy dealing with this matter before it decides specifically what type of security to sell and the timing of any offering. Basically, a corporation must select the optimum capital structure to best serve the long-term interests of both the shareholders and the suppliers of long-term debt capital. In the planning process, a constant effort should be made to move towards this preferred capitalization to meet the objectives that were discussed earlier in this chapter. By maintaining an acceptable capital structure, the company will be reasonably assured of raising the capital at reasonable cost when it needs it, and conversely, will provide a climate in which the suppliers of capital may dispose of their securities in a relatively strong market and under reasonable circumstances — to the extent that a single company can contribute to this condition.

The appropriate capital structure of a specific business enterprise will depend upon many factors — both external and internal. The nature of the business, including the composition of assets and the way in which the company manages them, is one factor. The availability and relative cost of the various segments of long-term capital is another determinant. Securing long-term funds might be seen as an interplay between the business management on the one hand, and the suppliers of both equity funds and debtor funds, on the other.

In planning the appropriate capital structure, which therefore involves the amount of debt deemed appropriate, the financial officer must give weight to management's attitude or degree of conservatism about debt. Management has considerable discretion in selecting a capital structure that tends towards heavy debt versus one that is mostly equity. The decision on debt ratios must reflect the degree to which management is willing to expose the shareholder's equity to additional risk of too much debt for enhanced profit potentials. The penalty for excessive debt in times of adversity is bankruptcy, insolvency, or, at a minimum, a downgrading of the stock and its price.

Just as individuals change, so also does the nature of most industries. Increasing mechanization, international markets, changes in methods of contracting, new products, and changes in competition may all affect a particular company and industry. Cash flows may change; the attitude of investors towards an industry and its earning potential may also change. Hence, the debt tests and methods of financing must be modified from time to time to cope with these changes. The amount of debt to be incurred should be subjected to rigorous financial analysis before it is incurred. The financial structure of the company must retain its flexibility.

STANDARDS FOR DEBT CAPACITY

General Standards

In deciding on the amount of long-term debt to be raised in the annual planning period or changes that must be made for an optimum capital structure in the long-range plan, standards exist that may be used to judge the propriety. Basically, there are two types: (1) capitalization standards and (2) coverage standards. Capitalization standards concern the relationship of the debt to other segments of the balance sheet (e.g., the ratio of long-term debt to equity). Coverage standards usually relate net income and other operating factors to the interest or debt service that must be paid annually. For most companies, plans should be tested against both because tests on one basis may present satisfactory conditions, whereas another might not. Thus, a debt-to-equity test may show a 25 percent ratio, which is ordinarily acceptable. But if the debt must be paid off in three years, instead of thirty, the debt-service coverage may be inadequate to meet the demands of the underwriter.

Earnings coverage ratios seek to measure the total annual sum required for debt service against the earnings available to pay for such service. Obviously, the management wants to be quite certain that, even in times of adversity, there will be sufficient fund flow to meet the obligation. Hence, it is incumbent upon the financial planners to make tests under various scenarios, including the most probable adverse case, to judge the ability of the

FIG. 26-3   Selected Tests of Long-Term Debt Coverage

THE JOHNSON COMPANY
TEST OF DEBT COVERAGE AND RATIOS
(dollars in thousands)

Item	Historical			Plan Years			Worst Case Scenarios	
	19XX	19X1	19X2	19X3	19X4	19X5	20% Drop in Margin	30% Sales Decline and 20% in Margin
Sources of Cash								
Net income	$24,060	$29,310	$32,400	$34,300	$35,200	$39,100	$26,500	$17,200
Depreciation	15,600	17,300	18,100	21,700	22,400	21,700	21,700	21,700
Deferred taxes	10,300	7,400	5,200					
Total internal generation	$49,960	$54,010	$55,700	$56,000	$57,600	$60,800	$48,200	$38,900
Anticipated 19X3 debt offering				50,000				
Revolving credit agreement	12,400	(10,600)	27,600		(19,500)	(10,500)		
Total sources	$62,360	$43,410	$83,300	$106,000	$38,100	$50,300	$48,200	$38,900
Uses of Cash								
Accounts payable	$ 5,100	$ 5,000	$ 600	$ 2,700	$ 2,500	$ 5,000	$ 5,000	
Accrued items	2,700	1,000	800	4,100	2,700	2,800	2,800	
Accounts receivable	12,500	7,670	5,400	8,900	400	4,700	(1,900)	($10,000)
Inventories	7,800	5,200	6,800	10,200	2,100	7,000	7,000	(1,000)
Income taxes (net)	5,200	9,300	12,850	17,600	18,300	9,000	1,000	
Dividends	9,300	10,160	10,540	14,300	15,000	17,000	17,000	17,000
Long-term debt repayment	8,400	7,400	4,400	5,400	6,400	1,400	1,400	1,400
Capital expenditures	17,000	12,700	19,060	40,200	7,500	5,000	5,000	5,000
Total uses	$68,000	$58,430	$60,450	$103,400	$54,900	$51,900	$37,300	$12,400
Increase (decrease) in Cash	($ 5,640)	($15,020)	$22,850	$ 2,600	($16,800)	($ 1,600)	$10,900	$26,500
Selected Data — Coverage								
Net income before interest/interest — times covered	3.86	4.91	4.12	2.99	3.41	4.76	3.54	2.65
Pre-tax income and interest/interest — times covered	6.73	8.82	7.23	4.99	5.82	8.51	6.09	4.30
Longer term debt/equity	45.0%	35.0%	29.0%	49.0%	41.0%	37.0%	39.0%	41.0%
Return on shareholders' equity	18.0%	19.8%	19.3%	18.0%	16.8%	17.0%	12.1%	8.2%

company to meet the debt service. Even in an annual business plan, the proposed financing should be tested against the probable business earnings for the long-term years and in conditions of unexpected adversity before considering it as acceptable for the plan year. In other words, the criterion should not be the single year. The earnings coverage tests deemed appropriate may be similar to the one shown in Figure 26-3.

Specific Standards

By convention, any number of debt ratios are available to test if the plan or proposal is acceptable. Acceptable standards do change, as perceived risk (including rate of inflation) changes. Moreover, the standard will vary by industry. Precisely what is an acceptable ratio can be judged by discussion with the sources mentioned earlier. In any event, some of the more meaningful debt ratios and an indication of approximate "normal" relationships are illustrated below:

Item	Manufacturing Companies	Electric Utilities
1. Capital structure:		
Long-term debt	25%	50%
Equity (preferred and common)	75	50
	100%	100%
2. Number of times fixed charges are earned, before taxes	10	3
3. Cash flow as a percentage of long-term debt	40%	12%
4. Return on shareholders' equity (net after taxes)	16%	12%
5. Return on total capital (net)	13%	9%

Selected Ratios

A more extensive listing of ratios that might be calculated when a specific long-term offering is being considered is shown below. Basically, this is illustrative of information used by a bond rating agency in making its determination. Calculations typically are all made for five historical and five projected years. Data may relate to total debt and senior debt.

1. *Financial Ratios:*
   □ Current assets/long-term debt, including current maturities
   □ Net tangible assets/long-term debt

    ☐ Net property, plant and equipment/long-term debt
    ☐ Long-term debt/total capitalization
    ☐ Long-term debt/tangible shareholders' equity

  2. *Coverage ratios:*
    ☐ Income before rents, interest, and income taxes/rents and interest
    ☐ Income before rentals and lease charges, interest, income taxes and non-cash charges/rentals and lease charges, and interest
    ☐ Income before interest and income tax/interest
    ☐ Net income and interest/interest
    ☐ Net income, lease and rental charges, and interest/lease and rental charges and interest
    ☐ Long-term debt, including capitalized rentals/net income and noncash charges.

  3. *Operating and miscellaneous ratios:*
    ☐ Current assets/current liabilities
    ☐ Current assets/total assets
    ☐ Net sales/current assets
    ☐ Net sales/working capital
    ☐ Net sales/fixed assets
    ☐ Operating margin as percent of sales
    ☐ Net income as percent of sales
    ☐ Net income/shareholders' equity
    ☐ Net income/total capitalization
    ☐ Sales/accounts receivable
    ☐ Sales/inventories

For different industries, different ratios will be more important, and standards will change.

A SUMMARY BUDGET FOR LONG-TERM LIABILITIES

The budget for the long-term liabilities should recognize the anticipated transactions recorded in accordance with GAAP and should test the acceptability against applicable standards. This segment of the annual plan may simply be presented as a part of the statement of financial position, showing the present conditions and the expected plan year-end status. If the items are numerous enough, and if management attention should be directed to special loans or conditions, the long-term liability budget may be summarized, as in Figure 26-4. The schedule shows the principal components of debt, interest rates, and maturities.

FIG. 26-4 Summary of Annual Budget For Long-Term Obligations

THE JONES COMPANY
PLANNED LONG-TERM LIABILITIES
For the Year Ending 12/31/XX
(dollars in thousands)

Issue	Maturity Date	Interest Rates	Estimated Beginning Balance	New Indebtedness	Payments	Planned Ending Balance
Long-Term Debt						
Bank term loans	6/30/89	Floating prime + 2%	$ 37,200	—	$ 5,000	$ 32,200
Proposed mortgage loan	12/31/92	15%	—	$40,000	—	40,000
Mortgage note payable to insurance company	9/30/87	10%	45,600	—	4,560	41,040
Subordinated debentures	12/31/90	14%	21,000	—	6,000	15,000
Convertible subordinated debentures	4/15/84	9%	16,500	—	—	16,500
Other notes payable	5/30/83	10–14%	4,300	1,000	2,300	3,000
Total			$124,600	$41,000	$17,860	$147,740
Other Long-Term Obligations						
Capital lease obligations			$ 45,900	$10,400	$ 3,900	$ 52,400
Accrued warranty costs			12,700	4,100	3,000	13,800
Deferred service income			22,500	—	8,500	14,000
Total			$ 81,100	$14,500	$15,400	$ 80,200
Total Long-Term Obligations			$205,700	$55,500	$33,260	$227,940
Selected Ratios						
Debt to equity ratio			.33			.35
Long-term debt to total capitalization			.25			.23
Times interest charges are covered before taxes			11.3			9.0
Return on shareholders' equity			14.2			14.9

As previously mentioned, adequate tests should be made of expected new financing for a period of several years in the future, with provision for the most adverse conditions reasonably contemplated. A schedule for such a testing is illustrated in Figure 26-3. This type of review is germane to both the annual plan and the long-range plan. If, for example, interest coverage by pretax income plus interest expense of less than eight is unacceptable, perhaps the form of financing should be reconsidered. The company had sufficient coverage only in 19X1; the business plan shows adequate coverage again only by 19X5; and under the adverse scenarios, the coverage standard is not met. If a debt to equity ratio of less than 0.45 to 1 is considered prudent, then perhaps the offering should be delayed another year until sufficient equity is built up; or, a lesser sum should be weighed.

CONTINGENT LIABILITIES

Budgeting usually relates to the direct liabilities of the enterprise; contingent debt may be covered by appropriate footnote to the statement of financial position. However, these two points are made relating to the planning and control of long-term liabilities:

1. If there are reasonable chances that contingent liabilities during the planning period may become direct liabilities, then the probability should be weighed and appropriate provision made as to impact on operating results and financial conditions. The management should be apprised of the judgment.

2. With the rapid changes in certain accounting practices, the financial plan should give recognition to any possible change in GAAP. If, for example, a type of exposure such as unfunded pension liability, now handled as a footnote to the financial statements, might require restatement as a direct liability, the management should be alerted in appropriate oral or written commentary in presenting the business plan. The budget officer and all other financial officers should keep current as to accounting practice changes so that the budgeted and actual financial statements reflect GAAP when appropriate.

BUDGET REPORTS ON LONG-TERM LIABILITIES

For the most part, planning and control reports on long-term liabilities will consist of notes to the statement of financial position, supplemented by special commentary or footnotes when necessary. An example would be appropriate reports to management and creditors when the terms of credit agreements have not been met, or when a default appears imminent and action must be taken.

A suggested list of planning and control reports on long-term liabilities would include:

1. Usual monthly statements of financial condition, comparing budgeted and actual figures
2. Updated projected statements of expected financial position for the year-end, both as part of the current-year interim review and possibly the strategic plan review
3. Reports required by credit agreements, including selected ratios
4. Periodic summaries of contingent liabilities, probability of change, and the profit impact thereof
5. Periodic analyses of "special liabilities" about which management should be informed:
   - Lease obligations
   - Unfunded and vested pension plan liabilities
   - Liabilities of minority-owned companies
   - Liabilities of company health-care plans
   - Liabilities of nonconsolidated subsidiaries
   - Indebtedness payable in foreign currencies

In other words, planning and control reports should be made on any significant aspects of long-term liabilities about which management should be kept informed, but should not inundate management with needless detail or insignificant items.

27

Shareholders' Equity

A WORKING DEFINITION

Simply stated, shareholders' equity is the equity or ownership capital invested by shareholders through either the contribution of assets to the corporation, or the growth in retained earnings. There are a number of rules in the proper accounting for equity capital, which should be recognized in published statements. The basic objective and related principles in accounting for this segment, subject to some change from time to time, are these.[1]

Objective B — Account for the equity capital invested by stockholders through contribution of assets or retained earnings in a meaningful manner on a cumulative basis and as to changes during the period or periods covered. The account structure and presentation in financial statements of a business entity are designed to meet statutory and corporate charter requirements and to portray significant financial relationships.

Principle B-1 — In case there are two or more classes of stock, account for the equity capital invested for each and disclose the rights and preferences to dividends and to principal in liquidation.

Principle B-2 — From a financial viewpoint, the capital invested by stockholders is the corpus of the enterprise and its identity should be fully maintained. Any impairment of invested capital resulting from operating deficits, losses of any nature, dividend distributions in excess of earnings, and treasury stock purchases is accounted for both currently and cumulatively.

Principle B-3 — Capital surplus, however created, should not be used to relieve the income account of the current or future years of charges which would otherwise fall to be made thereagainst. There should be no commingling of retained earnings with invested capital in excess of part of stated values.

Principle B-4 — Retained earnings should represent the cumulative balance of periodic earnings less dividend distributions in cash, property, or stock, plus or minus gains and losses of such magnitude, as not to be properly included in periodic earnings. The entire amount may be presumed to be unrestricted as to dividend distributions unless restrictions are indicated in the financial statements.

Principle B-5 — Retained earnings may be decreased by transfers to invested capital accounts when formal corporate action has, in fact, changed the composition of the equity capital. Accumulated deficit accounts may be eliminated against invested capital accounts through formal action approved by stockholders, which establishes a new base line of accountability.

Principle B-6 — The amount of any revaluation credits should be separately classified in the stockholder's equity section, and it is not available for any type of charge except on reversal of the revaluation.

---

[1] Paul Grady, *Inventory of Generally Accepted Accounting Principles for Business Enterprises, Accounting Research Study No. 7* (New York: AICPA, 1965), pp. 60–61. Copyright © 1965 by the American Institute of Certified Public Accountants, Inc.

Principle B-7 — Disclose status of stock options to employees or others and changes therein during the period or periods covered.

While appropriate detail must be provided in public financial statements, perhaps the only segregation necessary for internal planning and control purposes is that between preferred shares and common shares.

There may be cases where the management wishes the plan statements to follow the prescribed public format, or where the integrity of the retained earnings should be maintained. But, for most internal purposes, the segregation of "equity" or "preferred equity" and "common equity" will be entirely appropriate.

Shareholders' equity is the heart of the capital structure of the company. It provides a margin of safety to protect the creditors of the enterprise. The amount of shareholders' equity is critical in that, without it, in most instances, senior obligations would not be issued. In an appropriate capital structure, as discussed in Chapter 26, the relationship or ratio between senior debt and shareholders' equity is key to sound financing.

LONG-RANGE ASPECTS OF EQUITY PLANNING

In planning the equity budget for a year, several normal, routine, recurring internal transactions must be recognized. But normally, more than planning the recurring action is needed. Most corporations periodically will require an infusion of outside equity capital. This is a key aspect of equity planning; it does not happen suddenly and unexpectedly. Normally, long-range financial planning will establish the approximate amount of external financing that will be required — whether short- or long-term — by a given company, as in Figure 27-1. Then, having decided upon an acceptable capital structure, the financial officers can determine, within broad limits, what types of long-term securities should be sold to maintain an acceptable capital structure. Thus, there are two separate actions in the planning and control of shareholders' equity: (1) to determine or check the relationship annually (at least) of equity capital to long-term debt; and (2) to take steps so that the corporation moves inexorably to the target capital structure. A schedule showing details of such a calculation is presented in Figure 27-2.

The following explains the logic used in the allocation of financing needs, as shown in Figure 27-2, between two types of long-term capital: (1) long-term debt; and (2) shareholders' equity.

1. The management of the company is of the opinion that an acceptable capital structure would be as follows:

FIG. 27-1   Determination of Funds Required

THE ILLUSTRATIVE COMPANY

SCHEDULE OF FINANCING REQUIREMENTS

For the Years 19X1 through 19X5

(dollars in millions)

Item	Current Year (Estimated)	Plan Year 1	2	3	4	5
Funds Required						
Working capital	$22	$25	$26	$ 36	$ 20	$ 1
Long-term debt	10	10	10	10	10	15
Plant and equipment	24	7	24	44	51	20
Investments — Foreign affiliates	—	10	5	12	7	8
Total required	$56	$52	$65	$102	$ 88	$44
Internally Generated Funds						
Net income	$33	$36	$39	$ 40	$ 41	$44
Depreciation and amortization	14	17	23	26	29	35
Miscellaneous	2	1	—	—	(1)	—
Dividends (preferred and common)	(5)	(6)	(8)	(9)	(10)	(12)
Net generation, after dividends	$44	$48	$54	$ 57	$ 59	$67
Financing Required						
Funds — Excess						23
Funds required	12	4	11	45	29	
Funds required (excess) cumulative	$12	$16	$27	$ 72	$101	$78

	Preferred Structure	Minimally Acceptable Structure
Long-term debt	20.0%	25.0%
Shareholders' equity	80.0	75.0
Total	100.0%	100.0%

2. The term loan agreement with the commercial banks permits periodic fluctuations in annual take-downs or pay-backs as long as the indebtedness is liquidated in five years (19X5). Therefore, this source was planned to meet temporary requirements (in 19XX) and relatively minor needs (in 19X1 and 19X2).

FIG. 27-2 Allocation of Long-Term Funds

THE ILLUSTRATIVE COMPANY

LONG-TERM FUND NEEDS
ALLOCATED BETWEEN DEBT AND EQUITY
For the Years 19XX through 19X5
(dollars in millions)

Year	Beginning Balance	Net Income	Dividends	New Issue	Ending Balance	Year-End Percentage of Capitalization*
A. Shareholders' Equity						
19XX (Estimated)	$280	$33	$ 5	—	$308	71.63%
19X1 — plan	308	36	6	—	338	74.45
19X2 — plan	338	39	8	—	369	75.93
19X3 — plan	369	40	9	—	400	72.50
19X4 — plan	400	41	10	30	461	76.50
19X5 — plan	461	44	12	—	493	82.58

	Beginning Funds	Payments	New Funds	Ending Balance	
B. Long-Term Debt					
19XX — Estimated					
Term loan	$ 40	$ 8	$12	$ 44	
Bonds — present	80	2	—	78	
Total	$120	$10	12	$122	28.37%
19X1 — Plan					
Term loan	44	8	4	40	
Bonds — present	78	2		76	
Total	$122	$10	4	$116	25.55
19X2 — Plan					
Term loan	40	8	1	33	
Bonds — present	76	2		74	
Bonds — new issue			10	10	
Total	$116	$10	11	$117	24.07
19X3 — Plan					
Term loan	33	13		20	
Bonds — present	74	2		72	
Bonds — new	10		50	60	
Total	$117	$15	$50	$152	27.50
19X4 — Plan					
Term loan	20	8		12	
Bonds — present	72	2		70	
Bonds — new issue	60	—		60	
Total	$152	$10		$142	23.50
19X5 — Plan					
Term loan	12	12		—	
Bonds — present	70	21		49	
Bonds — new issue	60	5		55	
Total	$142	$38		$104	17.42

* Shareholders' equity percentage plus long-term debt percentage = 100%

FIG. 27-3 Summary of Planned New Security Issues and Resulting Capital Structure

THE ILLUSTRATIVE COMPANY

SUMMARY OF PLANNED NEW FINANCING AND SELECTED SUMMARIES OF CAPITAL STRUCTURE

For the Years 19X1 through 19X5

(dollars in millions)

Item	Beginning Balance 1/1/19X1(a)		Sales of New Securities			Balance 12/31/X4		Balance 12/31/X5	
	Amount	Percent	19X2	19X3	19X4	Amount	Percent	Amount	Percent
Long-Term Debt									
Prime									
Term loans: 12%	$ 44					12		$ —	
Bonds — Existing: 13%	78					70		49	
Bonds — New: 14%	—		10	50	—	60		55	
	122	28.37	10	50	—	142	23.50	104	17.42
Shareholders' Equity	308	71.63			30	461	76.50	493	82.58
Total	$440	100.00	10	50	30	603	100.00	$597	100.00

(a) See Figure 27-2 for detailed payments on long-term debt, take-downs in term loans, and changes in shareholders' equity, by year.

3. Although 19X3 fund needs sends the long-term debt ratio to 27.50 percent of capitalization (above the maximum 25 percent), it is considered acceptable in view of the apparent ability to reach the target rate (20 percent) within about a year, because of increased cash flow and substantial reduction in requirements for one or two years. It is anticipated, however, that automation needs will consume sizable capital sums for another three years, but that the firm could live within the conservative capital structure for the foreseeable future.

Finally, of course, market conditions, extent of needs, and similar considerations will permit the establishment of a practical financing program that will avoid too frequent and too small approaches to the public market. A financing summary that considers these factors is reflected in Figure 27-3. Hence, the year when equity financing will be most appropriate usually will be known before the annual planning cycle is started.

EQUITY GROWTH AS A SOURCE OF CAPITAL

In Chapter 3, it was suggested that a proper profit goal is a stipulated rate of return on shareholders' equity. In thinking about this equity and, indeed, in planning financial policy, there are a number of interesting relationships to consider:

- Relationship of long-term debt to equity
- Rate of growth in equity vs. rate of return on shareholders' equity
- Return on equity (ROE) as related to growth in earnings per share (EPS)

The first relationship is discussed in Chapter 26; and the other two are now reviewed.

If an enterprise is to grow and prosper, usually funds will be needed for working capital, plant, and equipment. The firm may issue new stock, although this action has some disadvantages such as immediate dilution. It also may incur long-term debt within prudent limits. But if the management, for whatever reasons, wishes to use neither type of new funds, then the retained earnings will be the principal source of new capital. But this method is a slow means of accumulating capital. Just how much can equity increase each year? This is germane in setting target rates of return measuring sources of capital and establishing dividend policy.

Although simple in concept, sometimes financial planners forget the principle. The growth in shareholders' equity from internal sources will represent the rate of return on shareholders' equity multiplied by the percentage of earnings retained. It may be presented by a simple formula:

FIG. 27-4 Increase in EPS With a Constant ROE

THE ILLUSTRATIVE COMPANY

ROE VS. GROWTH IN EPS

(dollars in thousands except per share)

Year	Beginning Shareholders' Equity	Net Income	Dividends Paid	Ending Shareholders' Equity	Return on Beginning Equity	Dividend Payout Percentage	Dividends per Share	Earnings per Share	Growth in EPS (%)
19X1	$100,000.00	$10,000.00	$4,000.00	$106,000	10%	40%	$4.00	$10.00	—
19X2	106,000	10,600.00	4,240.00	112,360	10	40	4.24	10.60	6%
19X3	112,360	11,236.00	4,496.00	119,100	10	40	4.50	11.24	6
19X4	119,100	11,910.00	4,764.00	126,246	10	40	4.76	11.91	6
19X5	126,246	12,624.60	5,049.84	133,821	10	40	5.05	12.63	6
19X6	133,821	13,382.10	5,352.84	141,850	10	40	5.35	13.38	6

$$G = R(1 - P)$$

where:

G = Annual percentage growth in shareholders' equity (or earnings)

R = Annual after-tax rate of return on the equity

P = Payout ratio, or the relationship of dividends paid to net income after taxes

If an enterprise can earn 18 percent on its equity, year in and year out, and its payout ratio is 25 percent, then retained earnings (equity) will grow at 13.5 percent, calculated as follows:

$$G = .18(1 - .25)$$
$$= .18(.75)$$
$$= .135$$
$$= 13.5\%$$

If, therefore, the management is of the opinion that the company can grow at 15 percent per year in sales and earnings, and if capital requirements will increase more or less proportionately, then it can surmise that some outside capital may be required if the dividend payout ratio is to remain at 25 percent with resultant internal capital growth of only 13.5 percent.

Sensitivity to growth potential versus rate of return on equity and payout ratio are necessary in fashioning long-range financial plans.

EPS AS RELATED TO ROE

In the planning and control of shareholders' equity, the relationship of the rate of return on such equity to earnings per share should be understood. Even among financial executives, often there is lack of clarity as to just what the rate of return on shareholders' equity has to do with the rate of growth in earnings per share. Fundamentally, the rate of return on shareholders' equity, adjusted for the payout ratio, produces the rate of growth in earnings per share. In reality, it represents the same formula discussed in the preceeding paragraph:

Growth in EPS = ROE × Retention ratio

Thus, as illustrated in Figure 27-4, a constant ROE of 10 percent, with a

FIG. 27-5   ROE vs. EPS

RETURN ON SHAREHOLDERS' EQUITY AS RELATED TO EPS GROWTH

Item	Year 1	2	3	4	5
Beginning book value per share	$33.00	$37.36	$42.29	$47.87	$54.19
Earnings per common share[a]	7.26	8.22	9.30	10.53	11.92
Dividend per share (40% payment)	2.90	3.29	3.72	4.21	4.77
Retained earnings per share	4.36	4.93	5.58	6.32	7.15
Ending book value per share	$37.36	$42.29	$47.87	$54.19	$61.34
Increase in EPS					
Amount		$.96	$1.08	$1.23	$1.39
Percent (rounded)		13.2%	13.2%	13.2%	13.2%
Increase in dividends per share					
Amount		$.39	$.43	$.49	$.56
Percent (rounded)		13.2%	13.2%	13.2%	13.2%

(a)   Estimated rate of 22% on beginning equity

constant payout ratio of 40 percent (i.e., a retention rate of 60 percent), produces an EPS growth rate of 6 percent, as follows:

$$G = \text{ROE} (1 - \text{PR})$$
$$= .10(1 - .40)$$
$$= .10 \times .60$$
$$= .06$$
$$= 6\%$$

(This relationship is also discussed in Chapter 3 in connection with profit goals.)

Knowing the estimated book value per share, rate of return on shareholders' equity, payout ratio, increase in the EPS, both amount and percentage, and dividend per share, the growth rate can be easily calculated. The process is illustrated in Figure 27-5. It is to be noted that a constant payout ratio will result in annual dividend increases in the same percentage as the growth in the EPS.

GROWTH IN EPS

Discussion of the planning and control of shareholders' equity ultimately will include the impact of management actions on the earnings per share. It was pointed out in Chapter 3 that a constant rate of return on shareholders' equity would result in an increase in the EPS. This condition results not from an improvement in efficiency, as often assumed, but from the application of a constant rate to an expanding base (see Figure 27-4) and subsequent division by a constant number of common shares used as the divisor.

Given the current importance attached by the financial community to the growth in the EPS, a review of causes of change may be helpful. All other factors remaining the same, an increase in earnings per common share will result from any one of these actions:

- The retention or plow back of earnings represented by, or resulting from, a constant rate of return on equity
- An increase in the actual rate of return on shareholders' equity
- Use of financial leverage under favorable conditions
- Repurchase of common shares, or otherwise reducing the number of outstanding shares
- Acquisition of a low price-earnings ratio company by one with a higher price earnings (P/E) ratio
- Sale of common stock have the book value of existing shares, assuming the rate of return on shareholders' equity is maintained

Some comments about each are in order:

1. Increased earnings per share as a result of plowing back earnings, given a constant ROE, is healthy and sustainable.
2. An increase in EPS by reason of an actual increase in the overall rate of return on equity also is healthy. But it probably is not sustainable indefinitely, since operating improvements meet diminishing returns. Such an improvement derives from an increased turnover of sales, higher margins, or some combination of each. But these factors cannot increase ad infinitum.
3. Increased leverage is desirable up to a point — where it endangers the company.
4. Repurchase of shares may be a way to increase the return to the owners, but it may be inconsistent with growth potential or expansion if additional equity capital will be needed. However, there will be times when the market price is so low as related to book value, and near-term cash needs can be met internally, that purchase of company shares may be prudent.
5. There is a limit to what allegedly favorable acquisitions of new business by an exchange of stock can be undertaken.

So the prudent and sustained increase in earnings per share will come from the continuous, and occasionally expanding, rate of return on equity. But, since the many factors just mentioned impact shareholders' equity and EPS, the *financial plans* should take them into account.

COST OF CAPITAL

Cost of capital as related to budgeting has been discussed extensively in Chapter 7. To repeat a couple of points made therein, cost of capital is that rate of return that must be paid to investors to induce them to supply the necessary funds. Capital will flow to those markets where the investor expects to receive a rate of return consistent with his perception of the business and financial risks, as well as the comparative return available elsewhere in the marketplace.

Prudent management of shareholders' equity should involve a knowledge of what must be earned on the equity portion of capital in a particular enterprise, as part of the total cost of capital.

The steps in determining cost of capital are summarized again in this sequence:

- Select the appropriate capital structure for the company, with its components of senior obligations, subordinated debt, and common stock equity.
- Determine the appropriate rate of return to investors and the cost of capital for each segment of the capital structure.
- Properly weigh each segment, and calculate the overall cost of capital to the company.

The reader is referred to Chapter 7 for the details on the process.

DIVIDEND POLICY

From the standpoint of business planning and control, and especially as regards the budget for shareholders' equity, dividends have these ramifications:

- For most U.S. corporations, cash dividends declared are the largest single recurring charge against retained earnings.
- Since dividends reduce shareholders' equity, the amount paid may have a direct bearing on the amount of senior capital that may be raised, in view of the relationship of long-term debt to equity.
- Dividend policy will be a factor on the reception of new stock issues.

Under the circumstances, the budget executive should be sensitive to the need for periodically reviewing dividend policy in the context of both the annual business plan and the strategic plan. Some comments on two aspects are made.

DIVIDEND PAYOUT RATIO

A business objective is to optimize the return to the shareholder over the longer term. This return consists of two parts: (1) price appreciation of the stock; and (2) dividend yield. What share of this return is to be paid as a cash dividend, or what should be price appreciation will depend on a great many factors, including: the nature of the industry, the growth prospects of the company (with more cash needed for reinvestment in those corporations offering substantial growth potential), shareholders' expectations, and the financial strength of the enterprise. But the recurring need for capital is a significant factor in establishing dividend policy.

The amount to be paid as a cash dividend may be determined in either of two ways. The most common practice is to measure it as a percentage of earnings. This payout ratio is calculated in this fashion for common stock:

$$\text{Dividend payout ratio} = \frac{\text{Annual dividends paid to common shareholders}}{\text{Annual earnings available for common stock}} \\ \text{(after preferred dividends if any)}$$

As an example:

$$\text{Dividend payout ratio} = \frac{\$8,430,000}{\$21,075,000}$$

$$= .40$$

$$= 40\%$$

Dividends as a Percentage of Book Value

Another less common method is to calculate the dividends per share as a percentage of beginning book value:

$$\text{Dividend payment ratio} = \frac{\text{Annual dividends paid to common shareholders}}{\text{Beginning shareholders' equity}} \\ \text{(book value) applicable to common stock}$$

As an example:

$$\text{Dividend payment ratio} = \frac{\$8,430,000}{\$129,700,000}$$

$$= .065$$

$$= 6.5\%$$

This book has suggested that the primary profit goal of a company should be the rate of return earned on shareholders' equity. If that should be the principal measure, there is a certain logic in using this same base as a factor in calculating dividend payment rates, at least for internal planning purposes. Because earnings do fluctuate, a factor of stability is added, if dividends are related to book value. As was done in the example, an acceptable dividend payout ratio can be selected which would serve corporate purposes over perhaps three or four years. This then can be related to book value. With an increase in book value each year, the dividend would increase. Use of a constant dividend payment rate, as measured against beginning book value, will reflect the change in internal growth from retention and a varying payout rate as the ROE changes. A comparison of the four factors is shown in this tabulation:

Rate of Return on Beginning Book Value	Dividends as a Per-centage of Beginning Book Value	Dividend Payout Ratio	Internal Growth Rate (Retention)
8.0%	6.0%	75.00%	2.0%
10.0	6.0	60.00	4.0
12.0	6.0	50.00	6.0
14.0	6.0	42.85	8.0
16.0	6.0	37.50	10.0
18.0	6.0	33.33	12.0
20.0	6.0	30.00	14.0

Thus, if a 6 percent payment on beginning book value is used, the dividend payout ratio declines as the ROE increases; and the growth rate from retention increases. Normally a lower pay-out ratio is expected as the ROE rises.

From the pragmatic viewpoint, these summary remarks are made as to dividend planning:

- Dividend policy should be viewed over the longer term. The role dividends play in rising capital and in sending messages to the financial community are too important to be guided by short-term tactics.

- As earnings increase, the payout ratio should be reflected in periodic dividend raises.
- Once a dividend paying pattern is set, a dividend reduction should be avoided if at all possible.

Dividend Paying Pattern

Security analysts and investors observe the dividend paying practice and have come to accept it as a pattern for the future payments. Hence, planning should include the pattern that best serves the company over the longer term, and its growth prospects and capital needs. It is preferable that the pattern be continued even if there are periodic and temporary declines in earnings. Of course, a pattern of periodic increases often is to be preferred.

Dividend payment patterns may include any one of these:

- A constant or regular payment each quarter (or monthly)
- A constant pattern with regularly recurring increases — perhaps in the same quarter each year
- A constant or regular quarterly payment, with irregular increases (and perhaps not in the same month of each year)
- Constant or regular payments, with periodic extras so as to avoid committing the company to continuous increases

In summary, we are saying that the dividend pattern should be recognized in the planning process. What should be avoided is an erratic pattern.

OTHER FACTORS IN BUDGETING SHAREHOLDERS' EQUITY

In discussing budgets for shareholders' equity, we have touched upon the importance of the debt-to-equity ratio, and dividend policy. There are other transactions that can impact the amount or form of equity capital. While no detailed remarks are necessary, the financial planners should not overlook these actions, if they are contemplated in the planning period:

- Dividend reinvestment programs
- Stock dividends and stock splits
- Repurchase of common shares

FIG. 27-6   Budget for Shareholders' Equity

THE GEORGE COMPANY

ESTIMATED CHANGES IN SHAREHOLDERS' EQUITY
For the Plan Year 19XX
(dollars in thousands)

Month	Beginning Balance	Net Income	Dividends Declared	Exercise of Options	New Issue	Ending Balance
January	$127,400	1,210				$128,610
February	128,610	1,070		12		129,692
March	129,692	1,320	1,690			129,322
April	129,322	1,360				130,682
May	130.682	1,440		14		132,136
June	132,136	1,530	1,720			131,946
July	131,946	1,340				133,286
August	133,286	1,290		18	25,000	159,594
September	159,594	1,250	1,730			159,114
October	159,114	1,340				160,454
November	160,454	1,460		17		161,931
December	161,931	2,190	2,240			161,881
Total	$127,400	16,800	7,380	61	25,000	$161,881

SUMMARIZING THE BUDGET FOR SHAREHOLDERS' EQUITY

When the expected earnings for the plan year have been established, and decisions have been made as to the other financial transactions that will affect shareholders' equity, then the budget may be set.

The actions which will impact the equity of the company usually include these, although not all will occur in a single year:

- Net income
- Dividends declared
- Purchase of shares
- New issues of stock
- Exercise of stock options
- Special adjustments

The amount and timing of each transaction will be reflected in the budget, essentially as shown in Figure 27-6.

BUDGET REPORTS ON SHAREHOLDERS' EQUITY

In the management of shareholders' equity, the main emphasis is on *planning:*

- Relating the profit goal to shareholders' equity
- Planning the most appropriate capital structure
- Planning the proper dividend policy and disbursement pattern
- Recognizing in the planning process the impact of dividend reinvestment plans, stock options, and related practices

Therefore, once the budget is established, as illustrated in Figure 27-6, there is little need for extensive detailed reports. Perhaps the only appropriate control-type report is a comparison of planned and actual equity levels, as part of a comparative statement of financial position each month-end. If there are significant differences, a suitable explanation should be made. Operating and spending plans should be adjusted where necessary.

PART V

Administrative and Other Aspects of Budgeting

28

Appraising and Presenting the Annual Plan

BUDGETING — A COMMUNICATION PROCESS

Earlier in this book, the budgeting process is defined both as a communication process and as an iterative process. Consider a normal budget review
procedure in a divisionalized company, for example. The division prepares
its plan, and the corporate office budget director and other corporate staff
members meet with the division staff and review it. There is communication
between the division management on how the plan will be accomplished and,
inevitably, some differences of opinion between the corporate staff and the
division staff arise which are resolved after adequate discussion. Typically,
also, testing done by the corporate budget staff indicates conditions that do
not appear satisfactory: a given ratio is not met; the accounts receivable
investment is excessive; inventory turns are too low; the "reserve for con-
tingencies" is too high — even though it is desirable that the plan not be too
optimistic. Quantified test results require discussion and adjustments to the
plan. So there is a continuous give and take, and plans are modified until an
acceptable division plan is developed. It is, of course, important that all
areas of dispute be resolved, that the division general manager and his staff
agree with the proposed final division budget, and that the revised budget be
regarded as fair and attainable.

A comparable review is made of the tentative annual plan or budget in
each division, subsidiary, or segment of the company. In due course, each of
the individual pieces looks satisfactory, and the budget director is ready to
prepare a consolidated plan.

PUTTING THE PIECES TOGETHER

Preceding sections of this book have considered, first, the basic concepts
inherent in a sound budgetary plan; and, second, the application of these
principles to the more significant segments of the operating plan, the cash
plan, the capital budget, and the financial condition of the company. It now

remains to review the system or procedure by which the parts of the puzzle are put together to form a complete and meaningful picture.

There are two aspects to this assembling task: (1) the technical means by which the parts are brought together; and (2) the most informative manner in which the plan or plans should be presented as a communicative device on the proposal and its implications.

METHOD OF PREPARING FINANCIAL STATEMENTS IN THE PLAN

Consider first, the technical procedure by which the summary financial statements are prepared. It is well to remember that the construction of the segments or pieces of the plan follows the same flow of information as do the actual transactions. In other words, the *plan* is *parallel* in structure to the *actual activities*. Hence, from the accounting viewpoint, the plan should be assembled much as if the actual transactions for a month, a quarter, or a year were being recorded.

The simplest method of preparing the estimated statements is by the use of a worksheet or computer program on which is recorded the ending account balances of the prior or beginning period, expected transactions, and adjusted balances. One difficulty is encountered, in that ending balances are not available at the time the estimated statements must be prepared. If, for example, the new budget period covers the six months ending June 30, the estimated statements will be prepared in December before the December 31 account balances are available. For this reason, the transactions for December must also be estimated. A worksheet suitable for this purpose may be constructed with the following sections, each containing debit and credit columns:

- Trial balance November 30, actual
- Estimated transactions for December
- Estimated profit or loss to December 31
- Estimated balance sheet at December 31
- Budgeted transactions for six months ending June 30
- Estimated profit or loss for six months ending June 30
- Estimated balance sheet at June 30

A simplified illustrative form, without explanation of journal entries, is shown in Figure 28-1.

Data for the budgeted transactions are taken from the individual budgets previously prepared. The same method may be used for statements at more frequent intervals. The work should be restricted to approximate figures of even hundreds or thousands of dollars.

FIG. 28-1 Worksheet — Estimated Financial Statements

THE JONES COMPANY

WORKSHEET — ESTIMATED FINANCIAL STATEMENTS

For the Period 19X2

Item	Balance 11/30/X1 Debit	Balance 11/30/X1 Credit	Estimated December Transactions Debit	Estimated December Transactions Credit	Estimated Balance 12/31/X1 Debit	Estimated Balance 12/31/X1 Credit	Planned Transactions Debit	Planned Transactions Credit	Estimated Balance X/XX/X2 Debit	Estimated Balance X/XX/X2 Credit
Cash	$400,000		①277,000	②250,000	$427,000		①1,020,000	②1,170,000	$277,000	
Accounts receivable	300,000		③350,000	①280,000	370,000		③1,200,000	①1,033,000	537,000	
Reserve for doubtful accounts		$10,000				10,000				10,000
Inventories										
Raw materials	300,000		⑧100,000	⑦120,000	280,000		⑧470,000	⑦440,000	310,000	
Finished goods	500,000		⑦250,000	④200,000	550,000		⑦890,000	④700,000	740,000	
Prepayments	50,000			⑦10,000	40,000			⑦30,000	10,000	
Land and buildings	100,000				100,000				100,000	
Machinery and equipment	400,000				400,000				400,000	
Reserve for depreciation		50,000		⑦5,000		55,000		⑦15,000		70,000
Notes payable		50,000				50,000	② 30,000			20,000
Accounts payable		100,000	②100,000	⑧100,000		100,000	②500,000	⑧470,000		280,000
Dividends payable				⑤60,000		60,000	⑨16,000	⑤150,000 ⑨16,000		16,000
Accrued payroll		40,000	②100,000	⑦110,000 ⑤30,000		80,000	②510,000	⑤130,000 ⑦390,000 ⑤15,000		90,000
Accrued taxes		250,000	② 50,000	⑤5,000 ⑥25,000		230,000	②130,000	⑥100,000		215,000
Funded debt		500,000				500,000				500,000
Common stock		800,000				800,000				800,000
Earned surplus		250,000		⑨32,000		282,000				266,000
Sales				③350,000				③1,200,000		
Cost of goods sold			④200,000				④700,000			
Selling expense			⑤50,000				⑤170,000			
Administrative expense			⑤40,000				⑤110,000			
Cash discounts granted			①3,000				①13,000			
Federal income tax			⑥25,000				⑥100,000			
Profit for period			⑨32,000							107,000
Total	$2,050,000	$2,050,000	$1,577,000	$1,577,000	$2,167,000	$2,167,000	$5,859,000	$5,859,000	$2,374,000	$2,374,000

Note: Circled numbers (e.g., ①, ②) represent journal entries.

When a concern has subsidiaries or separate operating divisions, the statements must be prepared for each and consolidated by the same method as employed in making the actual consolidated statements.

EVALUATING THE CONSOLIDATED PLAN

In preparing a consolidated plan, the individual segments appeared reasonable, given the interchange between the division management and the corporate staff, as discussed earlier. It may well have been that the plans for all operating centers met the goals provided to them, but, typically, for good and sufficient reasons, some probably did not. Be that as it may, because each segment in a plan appears reasonable and on target does not mean that the *consolidated* plan is satisfactory. When the overall plan is arrived at, it must be tested to assure that it meets any number of requirements. It is in this process that the budget director, or controller, provides valuable guidance. Thus, if a loan and credit agreement requires a 2-to-1 current ratio, it would be unfortunate if the plan evaluation did not surface a likelihood that such a condition could not be met — with a consequent default in the agreement. If known ahead of time, the condition may be corrected or, if not remedied, perhaps arrangements might be made for a waiver or modification of the requirement well before it is needed.

Therefore, it is suggested that a prudent budgetary program will provide for an overall evaluation against:

1. The terms of any existing (or planned) major contracts — be they credit agreements, supplier contracts, preferred stock agreements, bond indentures, or major customer contracts
2. Predetermined industry goals
3. Industry data
4. Management-developed activities or standards

It is further suggested that tests be made as to interim period status and not merely year-end. While the condition at the close of the planning period might appear satisfactory, perhaps contract covenants will be violated during the year. This probability should be known in advance and acted upon.

What, then, are some of the quantified tests that should be used to evaluate the short-term plan? The various significant contracts should be examined as to covenants and warranties or outright restrictions, and the plan checked against those. However, listed below are a series of checks or comparisons that should be made, most of which represent generally required norms in business, although usual loan and credit agreements may also include certain standards.

1. *Against prior year actual performance:*
   ☐ Sales
   ☐ Gross margin — Amount and percentage of sales
   ☐ Net income — Amount and percentage of sales
   ☐ Net income — Per share
   ☐ Return on assets
   ☐ Return on shareholders' equity
   ☐ Earnings per share
2. *Against management goals, objectives, or targets:*
   ☐ Sales volume:
     • In total (units and monetary)
     • By specific segments
     • As percentage of market
     • Growth rate
   ☐ Net income:
     • In absolute (total)
     • By specific segments
     • As percentage of sales, compared to industry
     • Growth rate
     • Per share, and per share growth rate
   ☐ Return on assets:
     • In total
     • By organization segment
     • Compared to industry norms
   ☐ Return on shareholders' equity:
     • In total
     • Compared to industry norms
     • Compared to selected competitors
   ☐ Gross margin:
     • Percent to total sales
     • By segment, as percentage of sales
     • Trends
     • Compared to industry norms
     • Compared to selected competitors
   ☐ Manpower levels:
     • In total
     • By classification (profession or skill)
     • By age
   ☐ The profit structure
   ☐ The corresponding year of the strategic plan

☐ Specific asset controls:
- Inventory turnover
- Accounts receivable turnover
- Fixed assets turnover

3. *Against other generally accepted norms (in industry) or credit agreements:*
   ☐ Current ratio
   ☐ Quick ratio
   ☐ Working capital
   ☐ Total liabilities to shareholders' equity ratio
   ☐ Long-term debt to shareholders' equity ratio
   ☐ Times interest charges are earned
   ☐ Dividend payout ratio

When the plan is in operation and actual results become known, for both the interim periods and the year, various groups (security analysts, suppliers, and creditors) will check selected results. Hence, the evaluation of the plan should include a review of accepted norms used by various outsiders against expected performance. If unsatisfactory conditions exist, again the condition should be corrected if possible, or a proper explanation provided when it occurs.

The evaluation of the plan should include an appropriate comparison of the quantified measures outlined above. But there is another criterion to which the budget director should be sensitive, and that is *reasonableness*. People tend to be optimistic or pessimistic. What is the track record on meeting the plan, achieving certain marketing goals, or earning results? In the iterative process, and by a review of past performance, the budget officer should form a judgment on the strengths and weaknesses of the consolidated plan (and its segments). Where there are serious doubts, this must be flushed to the surface in presenting the proposed budget.

PRESENTING THE PLAN TO MANAGEMENT — THE OBJECTIVES

When the consolidated annual plan has been reviewed and evaluated, it normally is presented to the chief executive officer and perhaps his key associates: chief operating officer, chief sales executive, and chief financial officer. Occasionally, after such a review, further adjustments are made to the end that the plan is satisfactory to the chief executive officer. In the planning process, this final plan then is submitted to the board of directors for review and approval.

In presenting the plan to the chief executive officer, and then to the board of directors, the basic objective should be to convey the plan's significant aspects so that senior management is aware of what the figures really say. The management should understand the probable outlook for the planning period, the major events or milestones that must take place to achieve it, and the inherent risks. Probably, the group should be sensitive to the best possible performance, as well as the most probable (the plan); and the senior management should comprehend what events could prevent achieving the plan, and the financial consequences of not attaining it.

Senior management should be made aware of these specific points:

- Important assumptions
- Probable sales and earnings compared with the prior year, or several years
- Expected sources and uses of cash in the planning period
- Schedule of major capital expenditures
- Expected financial condition during the planning period and at year-end — with a related appraisal
- Inherent major strengths and weaknesses of the plan
- A summary appraisal of the plan, based on prior performance and corporate objectives (return on shareholders' equity, return on assets, etc.)

Precisely what data should be provided to meet the basic objective of informing senior management depends on such factors as: the industry, the interests of the management, the degree of involvement of management in the business, the financial health of the company, and the extent of detail desired.

A somewhat more detailed outline of what might be included in a presentation of the plan to senior management is as follows:

1. *Basic assumptions:*
   - ☐ Inflation rate
   - ☐ Timing of receipt of major orders
   - ☐ Status of economy
   - ☐ Status of governmental actions
   - ☐ Belligerency status
   - ☐ Tax rates
   - ☐ Interest rates

2. *Highlights of plan.* Major factors making for success should be compared with the prior year, and amount of increase shown. Examples could include:
   - ☐ New orders expected
   - ☐ Sales
   - ☐ Net income — Total, percentage of net sales, and per share

□ Return on assets
□ Return on shareholders' equity
□ New indebtedness required
□ Capital expenditures

3. *Operating results:*
□ Net sales
  - By organizational segments or product lines compared to prior year
  - Reasons for change
□ Gross margin:
  - By organizational segment or product line, or contract compared to prior year
  - Reasons for change — Sales volume versus rate of profit
□ Net income:
  - Overall and by segment, compared to prior year
  - By quarters
  - Relative profitability of segments, perhaps measured as percentage of net sales or as percent return on assets
□ Possible ranges of the above factors — High, probable, and low
□ Key operating statistics in comparative form

4. *Capital budget:*
□ By major project, planned commitments and expenditures by year, and expected ROA.
□ Summary of commitments and expenditures by organizational segment
□ Major projects considered but not included, and reasons why — A *contingent* budget

5. *Planned cash sources and uses:*
□ By calendar quarters, with specific sources and uses shown:
  - Internal generation
  - Borrowings
  - Sale of equity
  - Capital expenditures
  - Income taxes
  - Operations
□ Cash available for temporary investment, by quarters, and income thereon
□ Debt repayment detail

6. *Estimated financial position:*
□ Condensed statement by quarterly periods
□ Reasons for change from past year
□ Significant ratios, and relationship to contract requirements
□ Comments on weak or problem areas

7. *Overall interpretive commentary:*
   - ☐ Acceptability of results, and measures used
   - ☐ Basic risks, or strengths and weaknesses
   - ☐ Reasonableness of plan
   - ☐ Important events (milestones) and probable dates
   - ☐ Comparative industry data

HOW SHOULD THE PLAN BE PRESENTED?

It bears repeating that budgeting is principally a *communication* procedure. In its simplest form, several feasible business plans are considered, and, after proper analysis, the most suitable or optimum plan of action is selected. Then, once the plan is accepted, steps are put in motion to assure that actual results will approach the plan, or improve upon it, to the maximum possible degree. The chief benefit comes, not from preparing a projected statement of income and expense, let us say, but rather principally from a thorough consideration of reasonable alternatives.

Accordingly, to use a maritime figure, the chart of the expected course must be presented to the captain and/or owners. They must be made aware of the speed expected, the shoals to be avoided, the reasons for the course selected, the stops en route (checkpoints), the time and place of arrival, and the expected rewards.

The plan should be presented in that form that gets the best reception and permits the best communication. The author suggests, given its importance, that the plan be presented *orally,* with liberal use of *graphs.* The employment of graphics will quickly demonstrate trends or relationships. An oral presentation, if done concisely, will permit the executives or board members to ask questions that enter their minds. It will enable the speaker to quickly describe a circumstance not easily handled in a written report.

This oral presentation may be supplemented by a written report so that the executives have a record of the plan. Or, for some circumstances, the written report may be the basic presentation, with a period for questions at later meetings.

ILLUSTRATIVE ANNUAL PLAN PRESENTATIONS

While the method of presentation in each company must fit the personalities and requirements, some excerpts from several annual plan presentations are

FIG. 28-2   Highlights of Operating Plan and Financial Condition

EAST COAST PETROLEUM AND CHEMICAL COMPANY CONSOLIDATED

19X3 OPERATING PLAN — HIGHLIGHTS

Income Statement	Actual 19X1	Current Outlook 19X2	Forecast 19X3
Revenue — $M:			
Petroleum product and other revenue	$513,079	$513,777	$497,560
Chemical sales	151,969	161,221	149,130
Total revenue	$665,048	$674,998	$646,690
Consolidated net income before special items	39,474	32,087	31,354
Special items — Sale of properties	4,362	13,011	—
Consolidated net income and special items	$ 43,836	$ 45,098	$ 31,354
Capital extinguishments	61,038	63,445	64,496
Cash flow before special items	100,512	95,532	95,850
Capital Expenditures — $M	76,771	85,288	76,339
Financial Statistics at December 31 (per share based on 12,680,000 common shares at 9/30/X2):			
Net income before special items	$ 2.66	$ 2.12	$ 2.07
Cash flow before special items	7.19	6.83	6.86
Common shareholders' equity	38.65	41.75	43.75
Rate of return, before special items, on:			
Common shareholders' equity	7.9%	5.9%	5.4%
Borrowed and invested capital	5.9	5.1	4.8
Long-term debt (including current portion) — $MM	$255.1	$235.3	$198.5
Operating Statistics (consolidated):			
Refinery input, MB/D*	252.8	248.4	233.9
Sales of refined products, MB/D	246.3	238.7	228.6

* MB/D = Thousands of barrels per day

FIG. 28-3 Illustrative General Premises for Planning Purposes

EAST COAST PETROLEUM AND CHEMICAL COMPANY

GENERAL PREMISES

Year 19X3

Premise	Improvements Over 19X2
1. Debt	15 percent reduction.
2. Crude oil self-sufficiency	5 percent increase.
3. Chemical sales	4 percent increase.
4. Transportation unit costs	3 percent decrease. Calculation is to exclude volumes on which no significant transportation costs are incurred.
5. Refinery unit costs	3 percent decrease, exclusive of effect of noncontrollable and major turnaround costs.
6. Marketing unit costs	Hold even, excluding advertising, sales promotion and training costs. Calculation is to exclude sales such as unbranded and government sales which entail relatively little marketing expense.
7. Refined product unit realizations	2 percent increase.
8. General and administrative expense	2 percent decrease, excluding effect of pension cost changes and general wage increases.
9. Product prices	Same as prior year.
10. Product volumes (petroleum)	3½ percent increase.

shown herein. A review of the entire budget report indicates that the following principal parts have been found essential:

1. Highlights (similar to the annual report highlights; see, for example, Figure 28-2)
2. Interpretative commentary (see below)
3. Summarized premises (Figure 28-3)
4. Summarized comparative statements:
   - Income and expense
   - Capital budget   (*text continues on page 28-16*)

FIG. 28-4 Narrative Accompanying Financial Statements of Medium-Sized Distributor of Liquefied Petroleum Gas

LP GAS INCORPORATED

OPERATING PLAN AND CAPITAL BUDGET

For the Fiscal Year Ending June 30, 19X2

The operating plan, cash flow, and capital budget for LP Gas Incorporated, for its fiscal year ending June 30, 19X2, are summarized herein.

OPERATIONS:

Net income for the next fiscal year is forecast at $807,000, equivalent to $3.08 per common share. As reflected below, this represents an improvement of $129,000 over the latest view for the year ending June 30, 19X1, and an increase of $142,000 over the year ending June 30, 19XX.

Item	19X2 (Plan) Amount	Per- centage	19X1 (Latest View) Amount	Per- centage	19XX (Actual) Amount	Per- centage
Sales Volume (Mbbls)	219,100		223,600		196,600	
$M						
Gross revenue	$14,895	100.0%	$14,309	100.0%	$13,080	100.0%
Cost of sales	7,367	49.5	7,630	53.3	6,895	52.7
Gross profit	$ 7,528	50.5	$ 6,679	46.7	$ 6,185	47.3
Operating, selling & administrative expenses	5,050	33.9	4,535	31.7	4,049	31.0
Depreciation	967	6.5	852	6.0	873	6.7
Operating income	1,511	10.1	1,292	9.0	1,263	9.6
Interest on long-term debt	239	1.6	213	1.5	239	1.8
Other income (net)	(29)	(0.2)	(42)	(0.3)	(46)	(0.4)
Income before tax	1,301	8.7	1,121	7.8	1,070	8.2
Income taxes	494	3.3	443	3.1	405	3.1
Net income after tax	$ 807	5.4%	$ 678	4.7%	$ 665	5.1%
Shares issued at 6/30	262,100		247,990		246,300	
Earnings per share	$3.08		$2.74		$2.70	

(continued)

FIG. 28-4   Narrative Accompanying Financial Statements of Medium-Sized Distributor of Liquefied Petroleum Gas (cont'd)

INCREASE IN INCOME IN 19X2 OVER 19X1:

The forecast increase in income of $129,000 over 19X1 is developed as follows:

	$M
Increase in gross margin due to sales price improvement in the retail class of trade, offset in part by anticipated lower wholesale prices	150
Increase in gross margin due mainly to higher volume in the high margin retail trade, offset in part by lower wholesale volumes	600
Other changes in gross margin (net)	100
Increase in operating expenses due to assumption of expenses of acquired companies	(400)
Other increases (net) principally in wage adjustments of $125,000 and depreciation of $100,000	(270)
Improvement in income before taxes	180
Less: Federal taxes on additional income	(51)
Net change — 19X2 vs. 19X1	129

CASH FLOW:

Cash generated from operations for fiscal 19X2 is expected to total $1,770,000 as compared with an estimated cash flow of $1,528,000 for fiscal 19X1. Cash sources and uses are summarized as follows for fiscal 19X2:

	$M
Sources of Funds	
Cash generated from operations	1,770
Sale of assets	100
Equipment contracts & purchase obligations	468
Changes in working capital and other sources	129
Total sources	2,467
Uses of Funds	
Debt repayment	752
Dividend on common stock	96
Capital expenditures	1,489
Total uses	2,337
Increase in cash balance	130
Estimated year-end cash balance	386

LONG-TERM DEBT:
Long-term debt is projected to decrease $284,000 during the next year as indicated below:

		$M
Estimated balance at 6/30/X1		4,349
Changes 19X1–19X2		
New debt		
Equipment contracts	359	
Purchase obligations	109	468
Repayments		(752)
Net decrease		(284)
Projected balance at 6/30/X2		4,065

Including the projected debt position, the LP Gas debt–equity relationship is reviewed as follows beginning with the year 19XX-2:

| Year Ended | Capitalization ($M) | | |
June 30	Long Term Debt	Equity	Ratio
19XX-2	3,720	4,303	.86 : 1
19XX-1	4,305	4,626	.93 : 1
19XX	4,157	5,203	.80 : 1
19X1 (est.)	4,349	5,788	.75 : 1
19X2 (fcst.)	4,065	6,529	.62 : 1

CAPITAL BUDGET:
The capital expenditures budget of $1,625,000 for fiscal 19X2 is detailed below:

	$M
Summary Authorizations	
Estimated carry-over	$ 492
Current year	1,133
Total	$1,625
Expenditures	
Prior to fiscal 19X2	$ 71
Current year	1,489
Estimated carry-over	65
Total	$1,625

(*continued*)

FIG. 28-4   Narrative Accompanying Financial Statements of Medium-Sized Distributor of Liquefied Petroleum Gas (cont'd)

		$M
Expenditure Detail Replacement and Growth		
Plant additions		
Land	33	
Facilities & equipment	209	$ 242
Customer storage tanks, metering and		
dispensing equipment		499
Transportation equipment		426
Office equipment and other		77
Total		$1,244
Acquisition of independent distributors		381
Grand Total		$1,625

The expenditure authorization of $1,244,000 for replacement and growth provides for normal requirements. The expenditure of $381,000 for the acquisition of independent distributors represents the amount required to close escrow on acquisitions approved prior to June 30, 19X1. Other attractive acquisition opportunities which may develop during the year will be presented to the Board of Directors for budget consideration.

- Cash sources and uses of funds
- Financial position

5. Supporting detail by planning center to be held responsible (division and department)

Interpretative commentary is most essential. An example of a condensed narrative that accompanied the financial statements of a medium-sized distributor of liquefied petroleum gas is reproduced in Figure 28-4. Interpretative commentary is given for the increase in income in 19X2 over 1981, cash flow, long-term debt, and capital budget.

Circumstances may require a much more detailed discussion of the business plan. Another illustration, containing more detail, is that used by a medium-sized appliance manufacturer operating on limited capital, as presented in Figure 28-5. The report in Figure 28-5 has an unusual amount of commentary. In this instance, the chief executive wanted substantial detail in view of a critical situation.

Generally, it is desirable to limit written explanations. It is perhaps best to cover the significant points as concisely as possible. In a sense, as long as the important considerations are conveyed to the reader, it is better to say too little instead of too much.

USE OF VISUAL AIDS

It will bear repeating that a succinct oral presentation, with the use of visual aids, may be a good way to communicate with the board of directors on the annual plan. It facilitates getting the important points quickly to a group of executives who do not spend full time on company affairs, but who have a good sense of the company business. Some illustrative visual aids are presented in Figures 28-6 through 28-17, which follow. While the entire presentation consisted of about thirty slides, the significant results, including group (organization elements) performance, were presented — with ample oral remarks, and many questions from the directors answered — in less than one hour.

SUMMARY

The budget officer or controller has the responsibility of summarizing or consolidating the short-term profit plan, so that the overall results will be known. Such data must be analyzed for reasonableness, conformance to management goals and objectives, and acceptability in the light of general business standards or existing or proposed contract terms. The plan must be evaluated against financial standards considered acceptable by the company financial executives.

It must then be presented to senior management and the board of directors for approval, and in a fashion so that these groups will truly understand the plan and its implications, so that they will perceive what the program is, and how it will be achieved.

FIG. 28-5   Detailed Narrative Accompanying Financial Statements of Medium-Sized Appliance Manufacturer Operating on Limited Capital

ANNUAL PLAN — FISCAL 19XX

CONFIDENTIAL

Mr. O. A. Johnson, President and Chairman
The Midwest Corporation, Inc.

Attached for your information and review are three basic exhibits relating to Fiscal 19XX:

Exhibit A — Statement of Forecasted Income and Expense

Exhibit B — Condensed Comparative Statement of Estimated Financial Condition by Quarterly Periods

Exhibit C — Statement of Estimated Cash Receipts and Disbursements by Months

Exhibit D — Summarized Capital Budget

Supporting these exhibits are several schedules designed to provide additional details as to expectations:

Schedule 1 — Statement of Estimated Income and Expense *by Product Line*

Schedule 2 — Summary of Estimated Gross Sales, in Units and Dollars, by Product Line

Schedule 3 — Detail of Estimated Unit Sales by Private Brand Account

Schedule 4 — Summary of Inventory, Production, and Sales, in Units, of Tornado Lines

It is believed these schedules contain the pertinent details on sales, production, and finished goods inventory.

Although the bulk of the assembling and presentation of the data was done by the Financial Division, this forecast is essentially a cooperative effort. The basic quantitative sales information and selling prices were provided by the Sales Division. The production schedule was prepared by the Materials Division, and each division supplied the basic cost data or expense budget. These were then reviewed, adjusted where necessary in consultation with those involved, and summarized.

Subject to the qualifications contained in these comments, it is my opinion that the data present, on a conservative basis, the estimated income and expense for Fiscal 19XX and the estimated financial condition as of November 30, 19XX.

An explanation of important phases of the forecast are made hereafter.

GENERAL SUMMARY:

Based on the assumptions as explained later, the forecasted net sales for Fiscal 19XX is $34,906,730. This sales volume will produce an estimated net income of $1,330,690, equivalent to 3.81 percent of net sales and 10.7 percent on total capital employed. These earnings, after preferred dividends, are equivalent to $.887 per share of common stock now outstanding (1,400,000 shares). Further, it represents a return of 20.2 percent on the common stock equity at the beginning of the year ($6,150,556).

A condensed summary of income and expenses, by quarters, is shown in Exhibit A [*omitted*].

These figures compare with the two preceding years (XX-1 and XX-2), as follows:

Item	19XX	19XX-1	19XX-2
Net Sales	$34,906,730	$24,430,993	$38,018,762
Net income or (loss):			
Total	$ 1,330,690	($ 566,353)	$ 1,471,278
Percentage of net sales	3.8%	(2.3%)	3.9%
Percentage of common equity	20.2%	(10.0%)	26.3%
Percentage of capital employed	10.7%	(5.4%)	10.2%
Per share of common stock outstanding at the respective year-end	$ .89	($.47)	$1.30

A discussion of the elements of income and expense follows.

STATEMENT OF INCOME AND EXPENSE:

Net Sales. Net sales are based on estimated quantities and prices furnished by the Sales Division, which in some instances have been revised downward for purposes of conservative financial planning.

Details of the gross sales, both units and dollars, are presented in Schedule 2. Based on past experience, these gross sales have been reduced by expected freight-out, cash discounts, allowances, and warranty, in an aggregate amount of $1,896,615. The provision for allowances included therein totals $672,736 and is based on normal experience — not the rather disastrous history of Fiscal 19XX-1.

In terms of evaluating the total sales *volume,* these comments may be helpful:

1. A total of 61,451 Tornado room air conditioners ($11,489,725 gross billings) have been included in the forecast. This represents an increase of over 40 percent above the 1966 level. As stated in the previous forecast, the distributor-dealer pipe lines are clean, and the models have been completely redesigned.

   Based on the excellent reception at the distributor meetings, the movement from distributors to dealers, and the orders received, it is believed the sales level is realistic.

2. Estimated gross billings on Tornado air circulators are 200,000 units, with a dollar volume of $5,716,370. The number of units compares with 109,164 in the 19XX-1 fiscal year and 394,213 units in Fiscal 19XX-2.

(*continued*)

**FIG. 28-5   Detailed Narrative Accompanying Financial
Statements of Medium-Sized Appliance
Manufacturer Operating on Limited Capital** (cont'd)

The introduction of new colors and some new models, an effective early-season sales promotion program, as well as other sales incentives, cause us to feel the sales forecast is conservative.

3. Sales of room air conditioners (units) to private brand accounts, as shown on Schedule 3, are estimated for the forecast to be:

Republic	53,000
Western	3,500
Hotking	7,000
Total	63,500

Firm orders, both filled and unfilled, from Republic now total 46,630 units, with more expected. Western has already given the company firm orders for 4,079 units. Moreover, we orally have been advised they wish 16,600 room units, with an option for an additional 5,000 units. These latter sales are *not* included in the figures.

Firm orders from Hotking total 3,000 units.

4. Sales of central system air conditioners have been included at a level of 23,000 units.

It appears that the sales pattern for these units will be almost as seasonal as that of the room coolers. There is, therefore, quite a concentration of sales in the April–August period.

Since the sale of central units, despite the relatively excellent reception, is in the pioneering stage, it is this part of the sales program which has a less factual basis. Additional comments as to the profit picture for central units are made later.

5. No defense sales are included, although the company is hopeful of securing business in this area. (We are one of three low bidders on a $7,000,000 order for fuel tanks. This award has not yet been made, however.)

6. Parts sales and service are expected to produce gross sales of $825,000. This compares with $982,425 in Fiscal 19XX-1 and $1,497,926 for Fiscal 19XX-2. In view of the expanding service requirements, the gross sales appear reasonable.

A comment is in order concerning the sales *prices* used. For private brand sales, the contract price was the basis of calculations. For Tornado products, the distributor list price was employed to determine gross sales. However, included in allowances, as a deduction from sales, was an amount of $440,700 representing provision for possible price rebates for meeting quotas, etc. (In addition, provision for other promotional costs has been made in the advertising budget.)

To further indicate the low unit selling prices, the following comparison of selected room unit prices for 19XX versus 19XX-1 is interesting:

	Distributor Net	
	19XX	19XX-1
¾ ton Deluxe	$153.45	$173.97
1 ton Deluxe	173.80	216.57
1 ton Custom	214.60	224.97
2 ton Custom	278.60	341.97

The expected annual gross sales of branch offices ($8,148,070) for forecast purposes, were calculated to give a gross margin of only 10 percent above *distributor cost*.

COST AND EXPENSES — 19XX:

Direct material, direct labor, and expenses in all areas have been estimated on the high side in order to present a conservative plan. Comments on the detailed treatment are as follows:

1. Standard *direct material* costs were used for estimating the cost of manufacture. These standards had been adjusted to take into account expected increases in material prices.

   In addition to the standard cost, a surcharge of 2 percent was made to reflect possible excess usage, disappearance, etc. This is higher than comparable 19XX-1 experience — which we expect to improve.

2. Standard *direct labor* costs, which had been increased to reflect recent wage settlements, were used as the basis of calculating labor costs. In addition, amounts varying between 5 and 20 percent were added to reflect labor inefficiency and the effect of change in schedules, start-up, etc.

3. *Expense* levels, whether in manufacturing, engineering, materials division, sales, finance, or general administrative areas were determined on the basis of budgets approved by the Division Head.

   For all manufacturing expenses, a budget overrun of between 3 and 6 percent of total expenses was included to cover special and unanticipated costs.

It is believed these levels are more than ample.

It should be mentioned that the expenses include a provision of $983,050 for tooling, which is a part of the standard cost of sales.

The cost of sales over-standard includes the following excess costs:

Direct material	$ 431,510
Direct labor	148,970
Outside production	18,500
Lack of volume (expense)	549,150
"Manufacturing" expenses	76,900
Other	12,000
Total	$1,237,030

(continued)

FIG. 28-5 Detailed Narrative Accompanying Financial Statements of Medium-Sized Appliance Manufacturer Operating on Limited Capital (cont'd)

It would seem that herein lies an area where substantial improvement over forecast can be made.

A comparison of budgeted selling expenses (including advertising) and general and administrative expenses with 19XX, and in relationship to *total* sales, is as follows:

	19XX		19XX-1	
	Amount	Percentage Net Sales	Amount	Percentage Net Sales
Selling	$2,017,322	5.8%	$1,122,793	4.6%
Advertising	1,130,768	3.2	821,133	3.4
Total selling and advertising	$3,148,090	9.0%	$1,943,926	8.0%
General and administrative	671,170	1.9	723,102	3.0
Total	$3,819,260	10.9%	$2,667,028	11.0%

Selling and advertising expenses represent 15.1 percent and 11.8 percent of *Tornado* net sales for 19XX-1 and 19XX respectively.

As a final overall comment, if operations are in accordance with forecast, the company will have net earnings in every quarter but the fourth.

In summary, it would seem that the cost and expense levels are conservatively figured.

PROFIT BY PRODUCT LINES:

The profit or (loss) before taxes for the year 19XX is split by product lines, as shown below.

	Amount	Percentage Net Sales	Percentage of Total
Tornado room air conditioners	$1,147,810	10.8%	40.5%
Tornado central systems	1,253,630	13.1	44.2
Tornado circulators	119,770	2.3	4.2
Spare parts	43,120	5.4	1.5
Motors	(447,200)	(118.8)	(15.7)
Subtotal	$2,117,130	8.0%	74.7%
Private brands	718,980	8.7	25.3
Defense	—	—	—
Total	$2,836,110	8.2%	100.0%

In calculating this profit before income taxes, all expenses were charged direct which reasonably could be so treated. All other expenses of a joint nature were allocated on a fair basis. The motor loss reflects the lack of volume as a result of relatively low sales level compared to standard.

A comparison of the forecasted *gross profit* with 19XX-1 actual results is interesting:

	Actual — 19XX-1		Estimated — 19XX	
	Amount	Percentage Net Sales	Amount	Percentage Net Sales
Tornado room air conditioners	$ 423,578	5.8%	$2,689,560	26.8%
Tornado central systems	(113,446)	(5.3)	2,397,630	26.0
Tornado circulators	195,662	8.9	973,620	18.5
Spare parts	206,820	31.3	266,120	34.3
Motors	(255,630)	(67.8)	(367,200)	(97.5)
Subtotal	$ 456,984	3.6%	$5,959,730	22.4%
Private brands	902,346	8.0	976,380	11.8
Defense	85,053	25.0	—	—
Total	$1,444,383	5.9%	$6,936,110	19.9%

The heavy dependence profit-wise on central systems is apparent — 34.6 percent of estimated gross profit, or $2,397,630, is expected to be derived from the sale of central systems. If, however, unanticipated obstacles result in sales of, let us say, 13,000 units instead of 23,000, the effect on gross income would be:

Reduction in net sales	$4,171,819
Reduction in variable manufacturing expenses (out-of-pocket)	3,004,029
Estimated reduction in gross profit	$1,167,790

It may well be that the conservative cost and expense levels, plus additional business reasonably expected but not included in the forecast, are sufficient to offset the effect of reduced sales of central units. Despite this, the need for taking steps to assure the meeting of the forecast is apparent.

STATEMENT OF FINANCIAL CONDITION:
The statement of estimated financial condition at quarterly periods is shown in Exhibit B [*omitted*], and the cash flow statement is in Exhibit C [*omitted*].

(continued)

FIG. 28-5   Detailed Narrative Accompanying Financial Statements of Medium-Sized Appliance Manufacturer Operating on Limited Capital (cont'd)

These comments will summarize the principal features:

1. *Cash.* If the income and expenses, and level of inventories, etc., are as anticipated, the company will close the year with cash of $1,497,926 — achieved with substantially less short-term notes payable than at the beginning of the year.

2. *Accounts Receivable.* Accounts receivable are expected to aggregate $1,581,470, which is higher than the November 30, 19XX-1 balance of $735,884. A share of the increase results from expected Fall sales to private brand accounts, from motor sales, and a generally conservative flow of cash receipts from this source.

   It should be mentioned that anticipated cash collections from accounts receivable total $36,430,520. No anticipation discounts for sales by branch offices have been assumed. Should such inducement be offered, some cash can be secured earlier. Cash collections for the corporation are predicted on a 29 percent anticipation under the various dating plans.

   Finally, credit insurance in an aggregate amount of $2,500,000 is added protection on the collection of receivables. On an individual account basis, the expected maximum exposure over insured limits is only $900,000.

3. *Inventories.* It is expected that raw material and work-in-process inventories will be reduced to $2,313,403. This compares favorably with an expected investment of $3,881,205 at November 30, 19XX-1. A principal cause of the reduction is the use of raw materials and components of central air conditioners and fans which were considered excess inventory at November 30, 19XX-1.

   Finished goods inventory will increase slightly, to a level of $4,926,559, reflecting the 18,000 Tornado units produced for stock during the last quarter of 1967.

4. *Short-term Borrowings.* A review of Exhibit A indicates short-term borrowings which reach $10,000,000 at May 31, 19XX, and are completely liquidated in September. This level of anticipated cash borrowings is $3,050,000 higher than that expected in the September 19XX-1 forecast for the year 1967. Contributary causes to this expected increase include (1) a lengthening of credit terms in both the room air conditioner and fan areas to be fully competitive with the industry, (2) establishment of branch offices in the New York — Newark and Baltimore — Washington territories, (3) heavier loss in Fiscal 19XX-1, and resultant less cash receipts from lower sales of central units (principally), and (4) some lengthening of central unit terms to meet distributor needs.

It is believed that the indicated borrowings, which are in excess of present lines of credit, are on the high side. There are several possible avenues by which the borrowings will be reduced, or the term of the borrowings shortened:

- Through additional anticipation payments by distributors or dealers, perhaps stimulated by extra concessions to certain selected accounts.

- Through the possible use of consignment inventories by some of our suppliers.
- By reduced requirements should sales levels be less than expected.
- Through earlier payments, generally, than expected. (In fact, the recoverable income tax has now been received, through personal followup, although the government may take three months to process claims. The receipt was budgeted for May).
- Through the securing of advances from private brand customers.

GENERAL:

In general, the current position at November 30, 19XX would appear to be satisfactory. Working capital during the year is expected to increase by over one million dollars — from $5,229,148 to $6,267,883. The current ratio, likewise, improves from 1.87 to 2.50.

DIVIDENDS:

The regular quarterly dividend payments to the preferred stockholders have been provided for. However, no provision has been made for payment of common stock dividends during the next year. If you and the other directors see fit to follow such a policy, it will mean that approximately 60 percent of the earnings for those three years (19XX-2 thru 19XX) when the corporation was largely publicly owned is retained for use in the business.

PLANT AND EQUIPMENT:

Anticipated expenditures for plant and equipment, including the remaining $160,000 payment on Plant II, approximate $500,000. This compares with a depreciation and amortization provision of $277,800 for the year. Generally, the planned acquisitions will permit significant cost reductions, and a quick recovery of any funds so spent. The major projects and indicated rate of return are shown in Exhibit D [omitted].

THE PROFIT STRUCTURE:

Based on a review of the particular product sales mixture included in the forecast, and on the cost and expense pattern for Fiscal 19XX, we have prepared a graph showing the profit structure of The Midwest Corporation, Inc.

This graph [illustration not shown here] shows that planned costs which are more or less fixed in nature aggregate about $5,250,000 annually. Also, the assumed cost behavior indicates that about twenty-three cents out of every sales dollar will be available to cover such fixed costs. On such a basis, the break-even sales volume for the year will be about $22,600,000 in net sales.

These figures, as you realize, are subject to change, based on management decision as to just what level of expenses will be allowed to stand as fixed (in advertising or tooling, for example). However, the tremendous potential leverage is interesting. If, for instance, the same average profit margin could be secured for additional business, then at a sales level of 16,000,000 standard man-hours in the plant (132,000 average per month), the annual dollar volume would approximate $55,400,000, and net income would approximate $4,200,000. This is just another

(continued)

FIG. 28-5   Detailed Narrative Accompanying Financial Statements of Medium-Sized Appliance Manufacturer Operating on Limited Capital (cont'd)

---

reason to solve the "Fall Problem." (Of course, we probably would be willing to take additional business at lower margins.)

All this is encouraging, but the effect of lower margins cannot be overlooked. If the margins in 19XX on Tornado room units and fans, for example, were to be reduced by only 3 percent, then our gross income would drop by $516,000.

This forecast has been prepared as the formal plan for Fiscal 19XX operations. When, through the combined efforts of you and your associates, this plan is translated into reality, then, indeed, a big step forward has been taken in a highly competitive industry.

If you have any questions, or wish further information, please let us know.

FIG. 28-6   Major Assumptions in Plan

THE ST. LOUIS DEFENSE CORPORATION

ANNUAL BUSINESS PLAN — 19XX

SOME SIGNIFICANT ASSUMPTIONS

(dollars in millions)

A. Contract Acquisitions
   1. Middle East status permits successful conclusion of
       Jordanian order $289
       Iraqi communications $612
   2. Deferment until after 19XX of acquisitions for
       A-69
       A-70
       Iraqi weapons range
       S-29 full scale development

B. High IR&D — Investment Levels
       A-69 Prototype $20
       A-70 $10
       Prelude $29

C. Other
   1. Inflation rate held to 7–9 percent
   2. Wage-price controls — no negative impact
   3. No other adverse government actions
   4. Federal income tax rate — 46 percent plus investment tax credit of $7.1 million
   5. Temporary investment income calculated at 11 percent per annum

FIG. 28-7 Plan Highlights

19XX ANNUAL PLAN HIGHLIGHTS
(dollars in millions, except per share)

	19XX	19XX-1 If	Increase (Decrease) Dollars	Increase (Decrease) Percentage
Contract acquisitions	$2,000.00	$1,153.70	$846.30	73.4%
Backlog	1,658.30	1,187.60	470.70	39.6
Sales	1,500.00	1,824.40	(324.40)	(17.8)
Net income				
— Amount	68.00	88.50	(20.50)	(23.2)
— Percentage of sales	4.53	4.85		
Earnings per share	4.77	6.25	(1.48)	(23.7)
Cash flow from operations	102.00	109.00	(7.00)	(6.4)
Capital expenditures	132.20	96.30	35.90	37.3
Percentage return				
— Assets	7.30	10.60		
— Equity	18.00	27.70		

FIG. 28-8 Sales by Organization Group

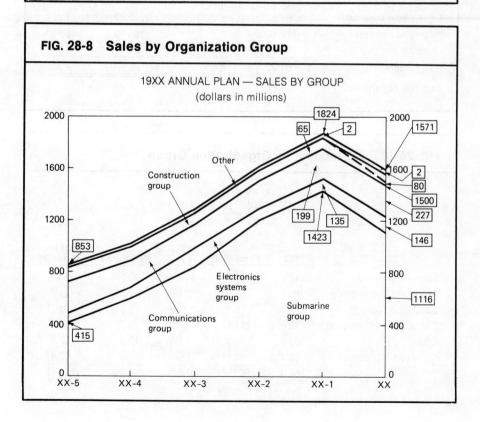

19XX ANNUAL PLAN — SALES BY GROUP
(dollars in millions)

FIG. 28-9   Summary of Income and Expense

19XX ANNUAL PLAN
INCOME AND EXPENSE
(dollars in millions, except per share)

	19XX		19XX-1	
	Amount	Percentage Net Sales	Amount	Percentage Net Sales
Net sales	$1,500.00	100.0%	$1,824.40	100.0%
Cost of sales	1,414,60	94.3	1,684.00	92.3
Operating margin	85.40	5.7	140.40	7.7
Other income				
— Interest	28.00	1.9	31.00	1.7
— Other	2.10	.1	3.30	.2
Interest expense	(3.00)	(.2)	(3.70)	(.2)
Other deductions	—	—	(5.90)	(.3)
Income before taxes	112.50	7.5	165.10	9.1
Income taxes	44.50	3.0	76.60	4.2
Net income	$ 68.00	4.5%	$ 88.50	4.9%
Earnings per share	4.77		6.25	

FIG. 28-10   Net Income by Organization Group

19XX ANNUAL PLAN
NET INCOME BY GROUP
(dollars in millions)

	19XX	Percentage	19XX-1 If	Percentage	Increase (Decrease)
Submarine group	$47.7	70.1%	$82.6	93.3%	($34.9)
Communications group	10.1	14.9	(1.7)	(1.9)	11.8
Construction group	.8	1.1	.9	1.0	(.1)
Electronic systems group	(12.0)	(17.6)	(4.6)	(5.2)	(7.4)
Other	23.8	35.0	11.3	12.8	12.5
Corporate adjustment	(2.4)	(3.5)	—	—	(2.4)
Total	$68.0	100.0%	$88.5	100.0%	($20.5)

FIG. 28-11   Quarterly Results

19XX ANNUAL PLAN
QUARTERLY RESULTS
(dollars in millions, except per share)

| | Quarters | | | | Total |
	1st	2nd	3rd	4th	Year
Net Sales					
19XX	$417.3	$360.3	$358.8	$363.6	$1,500.0
19XX-1 if	434.3	453.0	462.7	474.4	1,824.4
Net Income					
19XX	8.4	18.6	23.4	17.6	68.0
19XX-1 if	19.4	21.5	22.2	25.4	88.5
Earnings Per Weighted Average Share					
19XX	.59	1.31	1.64	1.23	4.77
19XX-1 if	1.38	1.52	1.56	1.79	6.25

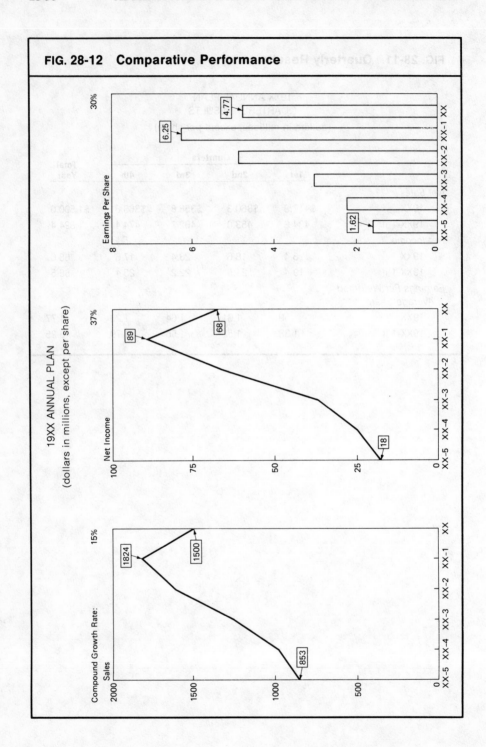

FIG. 28-12   Comparative Performance

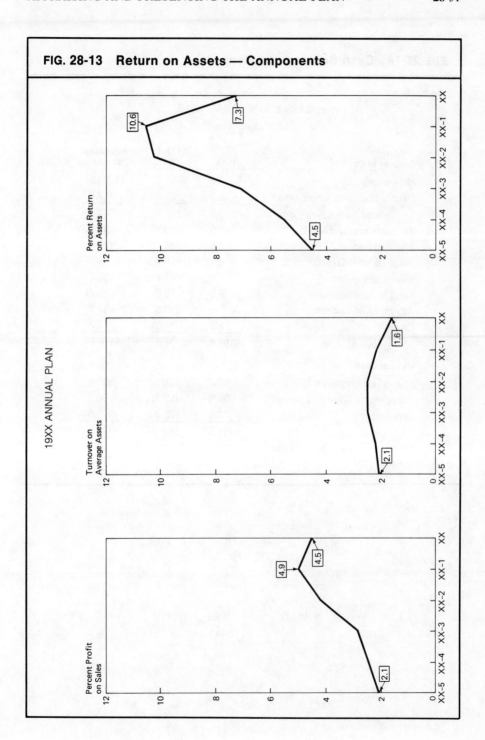

FIG. 28-13   Return on Assets — Components

FIG. 28-14   Cash Sources and Uses

19XX ANNUAL PLAN
CASH SOURCES AND USES
(dollars in millions)

Sources of Cash	19XX	19XX-1 If	Increases (Decreases)
Net income	$ 68.0	$ 88.5	($ 20.5)
Depreciation and amortization	34.0	20.5	13.5
Total from operations	102.0	109.0	(7.0)
Accounts receivable	41.5	(50.4)	91.9
Income taxes	8.8	82.2	(73.4)
Prepaids/other assets	6.1	8.4	(2.3)
Inventories — net	5.0	(64.2)	69.2
Long-term obligations	2.6	10.9	(8.3)
Advances on contracts	.5	(38.6)	39.1
Other	2.3	(5.0)	7.3
Total sources	$168.8	$ 52.3	$116.5
Uses of Cash			
Capital expenditures	$132.2	$96.3	$35.9
Accounts payable and accruals	36.8	(53.7)	90.5
Dividends	22.8	21.3	1.5
Total uses	$191.8	$63.9	$127.9
Decrease in cash and temporary investments	($23.0)	($11.6)	($11.4)

FIG. 28-15 Consolidated Financial Position

19XX ANNUAL PLAN
CONSOLIDATED FINANCIAL POSITION
AT DECEMBER 31
(dollars in millions)

Assets	19XX	19XX-1 If
Current Assets		
Cash	$ 5.0	$ 14.6
Temporary investments	232.5	245.9
Receivables	135.6	177.1
Inventories — Net	197.2	202.2
Prepaid expenses	8.4	12.6
Total	578.7	652.4
Property, plant and equipment	509.7	381.3
Less allowances —		
Depreciation and amortization	194.6	161.9
Net	315.1	219.4
Other Assets	42.6	44.4
Total Assets	$936.4	$916.2

Liabilities and Equity	19XX	19XX-1 If
Current Liabilities		
Accounts payable	$252.0	$288.3
Income taxes (155.4 deferred)	197.3	189.0
Currently matured long-term debt/lease	6.4	4.9
Total	455.7	482.2
Long-Term Obligations		
Senior Debt	15.3	17.6
Other long-term obligations	47.5	44.9
Total	62.8	62.5
Deferred Income Taxes and Credit	17.1	16.7
Equity		
Common stock	14.3	14.2
Additional capital paid	67.6	66.9
Retained earnings	318.9	273.7
Total	400.8	354.8
Total Liabilities and Equity	$936.4	$916.2

FIG. 28-16   Trend of Debt

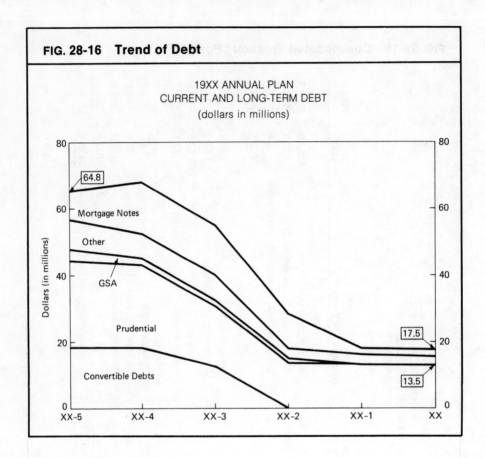

19XX ANNUAL PLAN
CURRENT AND LONG-TERM DEBT
(dollars in millions)

FIG. 28-17   Debt to Equity Ratios

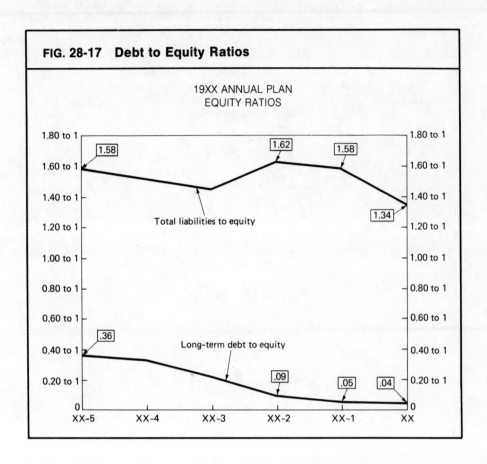

FIG. 28-17   Debt to Equity Ratios

29

Financial Planning Models

INTRODUCTION

The advent of the computer, and the growing use of related computer-based financial planning models, is changing the way in which business decisions are made and business plans are analyzed. To a greater degree than before, financial planning models are playing a more important role in business management because they assist in making better decisions.

It is not necessary that the budget executive, or the financial executive, know all the technical computer jargon, or how to write a computer program. His staff should be informed on such matters. It is important, however, that he have some knowledge of what a financial model is, the capabilities of the computer, and some sense of the modeling process. The purpose of this chapter is to impart some general information on the subject, largely in layman's language.

A DIFFERENT ENVIRONMENT

During the next ten years, business management probably will operate in an environment quite different than that of the 1970s. It well may be that business will face more rapid fluctuation or volatility in business conditions or markets. There may be greater uncertainty and perhaps greater scarcity of resources — both capital and the proper mix of labor. Consequently, the optimum allocation of resources, and the balancing of corporate activities will be even more crucial to the success of the enterprise.

"Coping with change" has been a pervasive business theme recently. In fact, planning and decision-making is largely a matter of managing change. The introduction of the small computer, the extended capabilities of the new equipment, easy access through convenient terminals and time sharing are facilitating the use of computers in the decision-making process.

Given the greater risks and opportunities in commerce and industry, there is a need for faster and better business decisions. To be sure, such decisions probably always have been a combination of what is called hunch (or experience) and analysis, both quantitative and qualitative. But a variety of new approaches are available to assist management; the use of rather

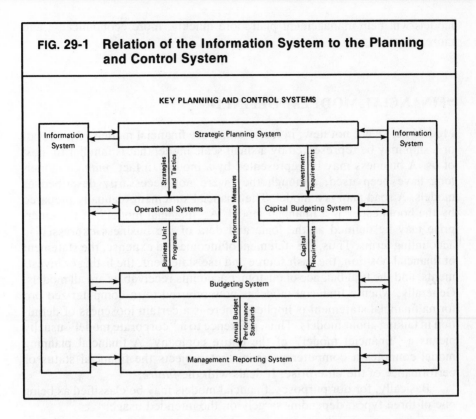

FIG. 29-1   Relation of the Information System to the Planning and Control System

KEY PLANNING AND CONTROL SYSTEMS

simple financial models is one of them. The computer must assemble a great statistical mass, analyze and correlate it, and provide the results to the business manager. He must make assumptions and check computer data against his own experience and intuition. In an iterative process, he must change assumptions and study the impact on the desired answer. This process is greatly facilitated by the use of the computer.

In the current decade, strategic planning probably will be tied in more closely to short-term planning and to continually changing environment. The entire planning system will be better integrated with the budgetary system and the management reporting system, as depicted in Figure 29-1.[1]

Business managers will have to adapt to the changing environment in a much quicker fashion. The proper combination of products, markets, and strategies that best responds to the newer conditions, must be selected so as to produce the optimum operating results and the optimum return on shareholders' equity, long-term factors properly considered. Financial planning

---

[1] From *A Management System For The 1980's* (San Francisco: Arthur D. Little, Inc.), p. 46. Reprinted with permission.

models will help management plan more quickly, more economically, and more effectively.

"FINANCIAL MODELS" DEFINED

Models per se are not new; in fact, neither are financial models. An aircraft or a ship may be represented by a small scale model that is familiar to most of us. A business may be represented by a model. In fact, *manual* models long have been used, although they were not necessarily described as models. A road map is a model. The financial statement manually prepared by the bookkeeper is a financial model. A "financial model" of the enterprise may be defined as the logic and data of the business expressed in accounting terms. Thus, the statement of income and expense, the statement of financial position, the cash source and use statement, the listing of investments, and the trial balance of customer accounts receivables are all models. Generally, when a financial model is now referred to, a computerized pro forma financial statement is implied. There is a certain looseness of definition in talking about models. Thus, reference to a "corporate model" usually means a "financial model" of the entire company. A financial planning model connotes a computer program that projects the financial status or performance of the enterprise. It deals with the *future*.

Basically, for our purposes, financial models may be classified as being one of three types, depending largely on the intended usage:

- Deterministic models
- Probabilistic models
- Optimizing models

Deterministic Models

A deterministic model might be called a one-case or single-dimension model. Based on the assumptions provided, it simulates the corporate operations and provides a set of financial statements that represent the results of the stated assumptions. It answers "what if" questions: "What is the effect on operations if variable costs increase 10 percent?" The assumptions may be changed and another scenario or case may be run, with answers provided for the new set of assumptions. It is this type of model that is most commonly used in business at the present time. The properly designed deterministic type model permits the evaluation of alternative sets of assumptions by simply modifying the parameters, and running the new case.

Often three deterministic projections are made, based on optimistic, pessimistic, or "most likely" sets of assumptions. The result of running three deterministic cases or scenarios is shown in Figure 29-2 relative to pension funding policy.[2]

Probabilistic Models

The probabilistic model provides a range of answers with the associated probabilities of occurrence. For example, it may project the probability of achieving different specified rates of return, or profitability, or the chances of selling $x, y,$ or z quantities. It may be a useful support tool to a deterministic answer. A graph showing how simulation techniques may be used to assess the risk of a range of policies (related to funding in this case) is presented in Figure 29-3.[3]

Optimizing Models

As the name implies, an *optimizing* model calculates the optimal or "best" result by adjusting or substituting the input variables in discrete amounts, testing the results, and selecting the best combinations. Economists have long proposed optimizing models as good strategic or tactical planning tools, and developments in technology have probably laid the groundwork for much more extensive use of such models in planning. Thus, they might be used to select the most profitable combination of sales planning and distribution efforts (see Chapters 9 and 15), or the capital budget projects with the highest rates of return.

THE TIME HORIZON FOR FINANCIAL PLANNING MODELS

In discussing the deterministic models previously reviewed, it is necessary to be familiar with two other terms commonly used in conjunction with modeling: (1) time horizon and (2) time period. The time *horizon* is the time span into the future. Thus, for a forest products company, the strategic plan time horizon may be from 10 to 30 years — the longest time span for which it is practical to plan. The short-term planning model may have a time horizon of one or two years. An operational model may employ a time span of a week or month.

---

[2] Buck Consultants, Inc., "Forecasts — Modeling the Future of the Pension Plan," *For Your Benefit*, No. 68, April 1982, p. 4. Reprinted with permission.

[3] *Ibid.*, p. 5. Reprinted with permission.

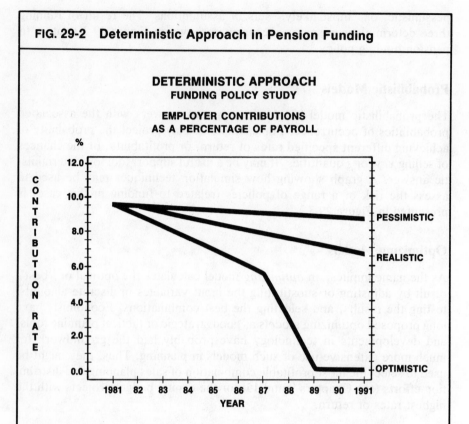

FIG. 29-2   Deterministic Approach in Pension Funding

DETERMINISTIC APPROACH
FUNDING POLICY STUDY

**EMPLOYER CONTRIBUTIONS
AS A PERCENTAGE OF PAYROLL**

The above graph was constructed for a forecasting study where the results were developed using the deterministic approach (that is, without random fluctuation). It shows contribution rates projected over a ten-year period. Three different forecast results are shown, one for each of three economic scenarios — pessimistic, realistic and optimistic.

The purpose of this study was to determine whether the employer would be required to increase contributions as a percentage of payroll over the next ten years under current benefit, funding, and investment policies.

The resulting graph demonstrates that even under the pessimistic scenario, contributions as a percentage of payroll could be expected to decline slightly. Under the optimistic scenario, tax deductible contributions hit zero in 1989. Of course, these results were unique to the conditions existing for this employer and should not be considered typical.

In light of the results of this study, the employer decided to continue its current policies for three more years with the intention of reanalyzing the situation at that time.

FIG. 29-3 Probabilistic Approach in Pension Funding

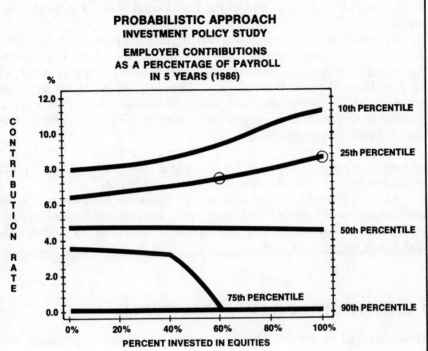

PROBABILISTIC APPROACH
INVESTMENT POLICY STUDY

**EMPLOYER CONTRIBUTIONS
AS A PERCENTAGE OF PAYROLL
IN 5 YEARS (1986)**

The above graph shows how simulation techniques can be used to assess the risk of a range of investment policies.

As shown on the graph, there is a 25 percent chance (25th percentile) that the contribution rate (vertical axis) in five years will be greater than 7.3 percent if plan assets are 60 percent invested in equities (horizontal axis). If plan assets are 100 percent invested in equities, there is a 25 percent chance that the contribution rate would be greater than 8.6 percent.

The graph also indicates that investing anywhere between 60 percent and 100 percent of the plan's assets in equities would result in the 50th percentile line remaining approximately at the 4.6 percent contribution rate level and the 75th percentile line remaining at the 0 percent contribution rate level. Hence, there is little additional reward for increasing the percentage of assets invested in equities above 60 percent.

On the other hand, the risk that higher contributions would be required increases significantly if the percentage of assets invested in equities exceeds 60 percent. Therefore, the employer decided against investing more than 60 percent of the plan's assets in equities.

The term "period" simply refers to the subdivisions of the time horizon. For example, the time period for a long-range plan usually is a year. The plan is reported or presented by years for the time horizon or segments of it. In a short-term plan or budget the time period is either a quarter or a month.

By inference we are indicating that financial models may be classified according to the time horizon used, and the purpose of the calculations. Accordingly, a "strategic" model will cover a time horizon of perhaps 5 years to 10 or 50 years. It usually is well constructed in general terms and relates to both internal data profit rates and product growth rates and to external factors such as gross national product (GNP), U.S. defense strategy, and pollution status.

A "tactical" model usually relates to the one or two year time horizon by months or quarters and is quite detailed (e.g., by specific and not overall) organizational segments. It relates to current conditions.

An "operational" model would be used to monitor such things as actual and standard performance for various departments or cost centers, perhaps by the hour or day; to age customer accounts receivable; or to check the cash status versus daily plan.

THE ANATOMY OF A FINANCIAL MODEL

Those financial executives who use a model, or the output from one, will probably find a brief description of the basic ingredients to be of some value. It may provide some sense of what data can be supplied and what factors should be monitored.

The basic segments or components of a financial model may be categorized in any one of several ways, but this structure seems practical:

- Documentation
- Input assumptions
- Projections or forecasts
- Selected ratios and graphs
- Base case

Each of these components are briefly commented on in the following text.[4]

---

[4] For some alternative classifications and detailed commentary, see Paul L. Kingston, "The Anatomy of a Financial Model," *Managerial Planning* (Nov./Dec. 1977), pp. 1–7.

Documentation

The result of not recording in a systematic manner certain key factors concerning the scenario or case may range from mere inconvenience (e.g., inability to quickly locate the planner or model developer to discuss a technique used) to embarrassment at a major error (e.g., an incorrect or poor assumption). It is highly desirable to reduce to writing and have ready some of the key factors; for example:

1. *Identification of developer:*
   - Name
   - Position
   - Department name and number
   - Telephone number
   - Date of preparation
2. *Basic methodology:*
   - Growth rates assumed
   - Mathematical basis, such as moving average, sum of the digits, and straight line
   - Relationships used, such as receivables to net sales, inventory turns, and profit rate
   - Basis of specific calculations, such as:
     a. Return on equity = Net income × Average shareholders' equity
     b. Earnings per share = Net earnings ÷ Fully diluted shares outstanding at year-end
     c. Debt to equity = Long-term debt at year-end related to shareholders' equity at year-end
3. *Source of input data:*
   - Where did the information come from?
   - Who prepared and approved it?

The judgmental factors especially should be documented. The data are useful in evaluating the output and in considering changes in the assumptions for other case runs.

Input Assumptions

The input assumptions are a key element. Stupid or misleading assumptions produce stupid or misleading answers. It is desirable that the input assumptions:

- Be screened for reasonableness and be related to past experience or known causes for change and degree of change. The key is their "relationship."
- In some important scenarios, be checked with the major executives as to acceptability in the light of known plan changes or environmental circumstances.
- Be recorded, preferably through a computer printout, detailing the key assumptions by time horizon.

Projections or Forecasts

The projections or forecasts are the pro forma displays of a given case. These may be on a screen, hard copy, or both. Several comments about a projection may be made:

- ☐ It should include the key items of interest to the planners and management, especially the latter if they are the principal "customer." Specifically, the "decision lines," those line items by which corporate performance is measured (e.g., net income, earnings per share, and return on equity) are of direct interest to the chief users.
- ☐ Those items of significance, which also may be highly controversial, should be specifically identified (e.g., sales growth rate and absence of regional conflict).
- ☐ The format should be inviting, employing such means as:
  - Eliminating cents or rounding off to thousands of dollars
  - Simple descriptions
  - Adequate spacing
  - Centering
  - Minimizing or eliminating unessential detail

Selected Ratios and Graphs

Quite aside from the usual, although simplified, financial statements, which form the principal output, two other forms of output deserve comment.

"Ratios" are commonly used in the planning and control of the business. They may measure profitability, activity, liquidity, or a host of other attributes in which management is interested, or should monitor. These key ratios should be provided by proper time period in a separate presentation. Typical ratios or relationships could include these:

1. *Profitability:*
   - ☐ Percentage return on sales
   - ☐ Percentage return on assets
   - ☐ Percentage return on shareholders' equity

2. *Indebtedness:*
   ☐ Current ratio
   ☐ Long-term debt to equity
   ☐ Total indebtedness to equity
3. *Other measures:*
   ☐ Accounts receivable turnover
   ☐ Inventory turnover
   ☐ Working capital

Picture representations, in the form of graphs, are another form of computer output. For some executives they communicate ideas much more easily than statistics or tabulations. Hence, this segment should not be overlooked.

The Base Case

Finally, special mention is made of the "base case." Quite often, the first set of assumptions that are run through the computer may produce results that appear unrealistic or unsatisfactory. In any event, assumptions are changed and input data may be modified until, through an iterative process, a reasonable and acceptable answer based on reasonable assumptions has been secured. This base case should be clearly documented because this usually is the foundation for numerous alternative plans. It is essential that the planners and management are knowledgeable as to its content.

A major purpose of a financial model is to assist in developing better plans and to communicate the results of business plans and alternatives to management. These suggestions may be useful for both purposes and in documenting the "footprints."

DEVELOPING A FINANCIAL MODEL

Our review of some key records to be maintained for a planning model and important input/output considerations as to computer capability — items that should be monitored in connection with planning — leads us to try to provide a sense of the steps involved in building a model.

Like any sound procedure, financial modeling should be a planned, systematic approach. It is not a matter of sitting at a terminal and writing a program in one day. On the other hand, it need not be an excessively time-consuming or expensive procedure. The budget or planning officer should be sensitive to the extensive steps necessary in introducing or monitoring the development of an acceptable, i.e., useful, model.

An outline of suggested steps, and a one- or two-sentence commentary on each, is as follows[5]:

1. *The Critical Steps:*

   □ *Define the purpose or objective and scope of the proposed model.* Differing purposes may require a different model construction, i.e., cash maximizing versus inventory control.

   □ *Identify the key issues which must be analyzed.* Defining the key questions to be answered assists in developing a model that is relevant, and is essential in selecting the proper input data.

   □ *Establish the decision-oriented information needs.* The planner should understand the key questions which must be answered in making a planning decision, and the data needed to support it; the information must be gathered, organized, and interpreted.

2. *The Supporting Steps:*

   □ *Develop the report or output specifications.* For each output report, the specific data needed, the line items and time periods, and the level of detail, should be decided upon.

   □ *Develop the calculation and data specifications.* Each line item must be detailed as to method of calculation, preferably in a very simple way. In other words, the system specifications must be analyzed into the specific arithmetic and logic operations needed to solve the problems.

   □ *Select the modeling language.* Out of the numerous software packages, select the most suitable one (each has its difficulties).

   □ *Write the model and test it.* The required steps must be coded into languages and format acceptable to the processor. When the report, calculation, and data specifications have been converted into model language, it should be tested by being debugged and checked for accuracy.

   □ *Analyze and evaluate the key issues.* The financial model facilitates the evaluation of many more alternatives, if developed properly, than would be feasible manually.

   □ *Document the model and train the user.* As mentioned earlier, adequate documenting is essential; and user training is highly desirable.

   □ *Monitor, evaluate, and revise the model when necessary.* Planning is not static, and the model should be updated to reflect changes in plans, assumptions, and techniques.

---

[5] For a detailed discussion of steps in building a computer model to solve specific problems, see Donald H. Sanders, *Computers In Business, An Introduction, Fourth Edition* (New York: McGraw-Hill Book Company, 1979), Chapters 8 through 12, or Donald A. Heckerman, "Financial Modeling: A Powerful Tool For Planning and Decision Support," *Managerial Planning* (Mar./Apr. 1982), pp. 21–25.

FIG. 29-4   Highlights of Long-Range Plan

```
                    1983 - 1989 LONG-RANGE PLAN HIGHLIGHTS
                    (DOLLARS IN THOUSANDS EXCEPT PER SHARE)

                    IF --------------------LONG-RANGE PLAN--------------------
                    1982     1983     1984     1985     1986     1987     1988     1989

ACQUISITIONS
  CUSTOMER          5695533  2594097  2368313  2875324  2227764  2332326  2848131  2086101
  INTRAGROUP          31253    57671    31592    30739    33440    29147    27454    27230
  INTERDIVISION       19548    20996    19280    24700    34100    40550    47500    54100
  INTERCOMPANY          229        0        0        0        0        0        0        0
    TOTAL ACQ       5746557  2672734  2419195  2930763  2295304  2402023  2923085  2167431

SALES BACKLOG
  CUSTOMER          5689890  5678132  5574217  5913354  5703737  5465235  5795572  5379733
  INTRAGROUP          29339    54992    48861    42173    37730    31320    30195    30133
  INTERDIVISION       17302    17748    16668    15795    20012    21129    20946    23363
  INTERCOMPANY           37        5        5        5        5        5        5        5
    TOTAL BACKLOG   5736568  5750877  5639751  5971327  5761484  5517689  5846718  5433234

SALES
  CUSTOMER          2036866  2534655  2472228  2536187  2437381  2570828  2517794  2501940
  INTRAGROUP          29072    32018    37723    37427    37883    35557    28579    27292
  INTERDIVISION       19480    20550    20370    25573    29883    39433    47683    51683
  INTERCOMPANY          328       32        0        0        0        0        0        0
    TOTAL SALES     2085771  2587255  2530321  2599187  2505147  2645818  2594056  2580915


OPERATING MARGIN    -40377   219188   238712   252854   241027   264854   270089   264646
% TO SALES           -1.94     8.47     9.43     9.73     9.62    10.01    10.41    10.25

NET INCOME            5992   148905   170299   190445   202961   234181   249165   262212
% RETURN ON SALES     0.29     5.76     6.73     7.33     8.10     8.85     9.61    10.16

EARNINGS PER SHARE    0.40     9.83    11.22    12.52    13.33    15.36    16.35    17.20

AVERAGE ASSETTS    1302620  1452186  1623481  1874374  2213276  2537530  2752675  3059467
  TURNOVER            1.60     1.78     1.56     1.39     1.13     1.04     0.94     0.84
  % RETURN            0.46    10.25    10.49    10.16     9.17     9.23     9.05     8.57

CAPITAL EXPENDITURES
  PURCHASED ASSET   365183   147504   129995   110452    95535    95896    93647    88206
  CAPITAL LEASES         2        0        0        0        0        0        0        0

TOTAL OTA            81969   100614   102690   109334   111017   116355  1119005   123980
```

In summary, a model is no substitute for the commonsense judgment and experience of the corporate managers. It is a useful tool; however, the tool must provide answers, in everyday English, that are responsive, understood, and reasonably prompt. Only when the product is attractively "wrapped," will knowledgeable businessmen seize the opportunity to use the new capability in making improved strategic and tactical decisions. Finally, as a practical matter, the planning model for the total corporation or major organizational segments must be consistent with the budgetary and accounting system in terms of the operating and financial interrelationships. Basically, the proper accounting system is the framework for building the model.

FIG. 29-5   Long-Range Plan — Balance Sheet

1983 – 1989 LONG-RANGE PLAN HIGHLIGHTS
(DOLLARS IN THOUSANDS)

ASSETS	ACTUAL 1981	IF 1982	1983	1984	1985	1986	1987	1988	1989
CURRENT ASSETS									
CASH	-7135	6400	-26725	-26776	-26963	-26985	-27157	-27178	-27300
TEMP INVESTMENTS	204236	155881	371800	582700	818500	1267500	1479600	1684600	2075700
ACCOUNTS REC	174232	115571	122636	132839	128791	137266	145439	138229	141561
GROSS INVENTORY	810577	1123704	1126450	1227474	1177388	1171346	1101303	1101966	1066158
PROGRESS PYMTS	502989	799833	811809	912187	882019	886390	833048	803654	768688
NET INVENTORY	307588	323871	314641	315287	295369	284956	268255	298312	297470
PREPAID EXP	11197	17285	16460	16711	16790	16856	16926	16966	16985
TTL CURR. ASSETS	690118	619008	798812	1020761	1232487	1679593	1883063	2110929	2504416
PROP PLANT &EQUIP AT COST	666063	1015222	965740	1092358	1199818	1292601	1385549	1475205	1560580
TTL DEPR & AMORT	206831	262256	320262	400149	486151	573962	666401	757991	849178
NET P P & E	459232	752966	645478	692209	713667	718639	719148	717214	711402
N & A RECEIV	8087	8332	8300	8300	8300	0	0	0	0
I/A UNCONSOL	13092	16291	18691	21091	23491	25891	28291	30691	33091
MISC OTH ASSETS	19706	18407	18087	15233	13209	11274	9151	6853	4338
TTL OTH ASSETS	40885	43030	45078	44624	45000	37165	37452	37544	37429
TOTAL ASSETS	1190235	1415004	1489368	1757594	1991154	2435397	2639663	2865687	3253247

LIAB & EQUITY

CURR LIABILITIES									
NOTES PAYABLE	9384	10000	10000	10000	10000	10000	10000	10000	10000
A/P & ACCRUALS	277370	317582	303318	298598	298073	299940	300868	306184	300567
ADVANCES	93123	313062	159332	133055	28105	27379	26838	23487	24877
FED & FOR TAXES	19655	14554	15788	15788	15788	34188	30577	41801	21425
CURRENT DEFERRED	265047	243663	357722	492961	646376	881415	853436	807815	943987
CUR MAT LT OBLIG	2012	2429	2235	2035	2035	35	1000	0	0
TTL CURR LIAB	666591	901290	848395	952437	1000377	1252957	1222719	1189287	1300856
NEW FINANCING	0	0	0	0	0	0	0	0	0
L-T OBLIGATIONS									
LESS CURR MAT									
MORTGAGE & N/P	8000	6000	4000	2000	0	0	0	0	0
CAP LSE OBLIG	2233	2663	1105	1070	1035	1000	0	0	0
ACC PROD SUPPORT	38298	32500	32500	31000	29800	27600	23400	21200	19000
DEFERRED COMP	2177	2630	2302	2667	2999	3370	3818	4203	4587
TOTAL L-T OBLIG	50708	43793	39907	36737	33834	31970	27218	25403	23587
DEFRD INC. TAX	20577	25453	34653	46153	59953	73753	87553	101353	115153
DEFERRED CREDIT	8051	8139	8139	8139	8139	8139	8139	8139	8139
SHAREHOLDERS EQTY									
ADD CAP PAID IN	116202	128061	126857	128566	129900	131186	131198	131198	131198
RETAINED EARNING	403192	392498	527785	686311	865798	1058120	1287904	1534983	1796669
UNVESTED RAS	-28857	-30047	-24161	-18275	-12737	-9094	-5733	-3636	-1746
TTL SHAR EQUITY	490537	490512	630481	796602	982961	1180212	1413369	1662545	1926121
TTL LIAB & EQTY	1190235	1415004	1489368	1757594	1991154	2435397	2639663	2865687	3253247

SENSITIVITY ANALYSIS

In discussing deterministic models, a one-case model, earlier in this chapter, mention was made that a scenario may be run on certain assumptions, then the assumptions would be changed, and another case developed. Figure 29-2 graphed the results of three runs: a pessimistic, an optimistic, and a most likely case. However, quite often, a major change in one assumption will affect the answer very little, whereas a relatively small modification in another assumption may greatly alter the result. This has led to the technique of "sensitivity analysis," a mathematical methodology by which the planner can change one component of the input factors and study the results. Very often, much to the surprise of the solution seekers, a given variable may have no significant effect on the result; consequently, very little attention need be paid to the accuracy or preciseness of the input factor. More attention can be paid to the significant variables. Hence, in a given model, interest rates on indebtedness may be largely ignored, but product mix could have a significant impact on the result.

In working with planning models, it is suggested this aspect be reviewed and applied.

ILLUSTRATIVE FINANCIAL MODEL OUTPUT

It is clear that financial models may be developed for any number of applications, depending on the need. For example, if capital expenditures are of major concern, a model may be built for ranking and comparing alternative proposals. Or, if inventories are a problem, a model on inventory control may be desirable. Figure 29-2 depicts a pension plan application. So there are numerous functions for which a financial model may be constructed.

One of the most useful models relates to the planned operating results, financial position, and related data for the entire enterprise or any organizational segment. Assumptions can be modified, and the resulting changes in earnings or financial position can be quickly ascertained. Figures 29-4 through 29-6 illustrate a typical planning format.

Segments of the long-range plan computer output are shown in Figures 29-4 through Figures 29-6. In the first iteration, the management was interested only in certain operating highlights. These are illustrated in Figure 29-4 for a defense contractor:

- Contract acquisition (new orders)
- Backlog
- Sales (by category)

FIG. 29-6   Analysis of Capital Asset Position

```
                         1983 - 1989 LONG-RANGE PLAN
                  CAPITAL ASSET COMMITMENTS AND EXPENDITURES
                     DEPRECIATION AND AMORTIZATION EXPENSE
                           (DOLLARS IN THOUSANDS)

                   IF    --------------------LONG-RANGE PLAN-------------------
                  1982    1983    1984    1985    1986    1987    1988    1989


COMMITMENTS

LAND & IMPROVEMENTS  605     793     505     153      80     145     118     130
BUILDINGS          28737   28705   11815    7560    4280    4575    4370    2700
MACHINERY & EQUIP. 78726  115376   93392   96602   85450   89666   87799   83426
OTHER                350     500     550     600     650     700     750     800
                  -------------------------------------------------------------
   TOTAL          108418  145374  106262  104915   90460   95086   93037   87056
                  =============================================================


EXPENDITURES

LAND & IMPROVEMENTS 21877    340     813     568      84     126     126     127
BUILDINGS         161210   41249   26085   14748    5095    4651    4430    2980
MACHINERY & EQUIP.180184  105415  102547   94536   89706   90419   88341   84299
OTHER               1914     500     550     600     650     700     750     800
                  -------------------------------------------------------------
   TOTAL          365185  147504  129995  110452   95535   95896   93647   88206
                  =============================================================


DEPRECIATION
 & AMORTIZATION

LAND & IMPROVEMENTS  366     885     839     819     775     725     581     543
BUILDINGS           6552    9554   11033   11144   10940   10761   10376   10085
MACHINERY & EQUIP. 54100   62130   71660   77943   80137   85324   85329   85526
OTHER               3648     350     250     250     250     150     150     150
                  -------------------------------------------------------------
   TOTAL           64666   72919   83782   90156   92102   96960   96436   96304
                  =============================================================
```

- Operating margin, both total and as percentage of sales
- Net income in the aggregate and as a percentage of sales
- Earnings per share
- Return on assets, including average assets and turnover rate

The pro forma balance sheet is presented in Figure 29-5 as a first iteration. (Any new financing is identified.) Supplementing this statement (not shown) is a calculation of selected ratios by years, such as:

- Current ratio
- Quick ratio
- Inventory turnover
- Total debt to equity
- Long term debt to equity

(*text continues on page 29-24*)

FIG. 29-7   Computer Printout of Statement of Planned Income and Expense, by Month

INCOME STATEMENT — PLAN YEAR 1982

	JAN	FEB	MAR	APR	MAY	JUN	JUL	AUG	SEP	OCT	NOV	DEC
FP SALES	6500	6000	6200	6400	6700	6200	6100	6500	6500	6800	6600	6700
TTL CUST SALES	6500	6000	6200	6400	6700	6200	6100	6500	6500	6800	6600	6700
NET SAL - ACCR	0	0	0	0	0	0	0	0	0	0	0	0
NET SAL -CORP ADJ	0	0	0	0	0	0	0	0	0	0	0	0
NET SAL - CORP	6500	6000	6200	6400	6700	6200	6100	6500	6500	6800	6600	-18873
TTL SALES	6500	6000	6200	6400	6700	6200	6100	6500	6500	6800	6600	25573
OP MARG - ACCR	8041	13744	14746	14319	13385	14626	11636	11980	12785	11556	9838	9212
OP MARG-CORP ADJ	-100	-100	-100	-100	-100	-100	-100	-100	-100	-100	-100	-100
OP MARG - CORP	7941	13644	14646	14219	13285	14526	11536	11880	12685	11456	9738	9112
COST OF SALES	-1441	-7644	-8446	-7819	-6585	-8326	-5436	-5380	-6185	-4656	-3138	-2412
OPER MARGIN	6500	6000	6200	6400	6700	6200	6100	6500	6500	6800	6600	6700
G/L DISPO ASSET	0	0	0	0	0	0	0	0	0	0	0	0
INT EARNED-OTH	0	0	0	0	0	0	0	0	0	0	0	0
INT EARNED-TI	1158	391	560	744	949	1476	1941	2101	2082	2224	2590	2826
INT EARNED	1158	391	560	744	949	1476	1941	2101	2082	2224	2590	2826
ROYALTIES	0	0	0	0	0	0	0	0	0	0	0	0
EQTY-NET SUBS	0	0	0	0	0	0	0	0	0	0	0	0
EQTY-NET UNCON	100	100	100	100	100	100	100	100	100	100	100	100
OTH INC-ACCR	0	0	0	0	0	0	0	0	0	0	0	0
OTH INC-CORP ADJ	0	0	0	0	0	0	0	0	0	0	0	0
OTH INC-CORP	125	125	125	125	125	125	125	125	125	125	125	125
DIVIDEND INC	0	0	65	0	0	0	0	0	0	0	0	0
MISC OTH INC	0	0	0	0	0	0	0	0	0	0	0	0
TTL OTH INC	1383	616	850	969	1174	1701	2166	2326	2307	2449	2815	3051
RC INT EXP	78	78	78	78	78	78	78	78	78	78	78	78
INT EXP-CORP OTH	3	3	4	4	4	4	4	4	4	4	4	4
INT EXP-CORP	0	0	0	0	0	0	0	0	0	0	0	0
O/C EST. OF CORP	0	0	0	0	0	0	0	0	0	0	0	0
INT EXP-CORP	81	81	82	82	82	82	82	82	82	82	82	82

	C1	C2	C3	C4	C5	C6	C7	C8	C9	C10	C11	C12
INT EXP-OTHER	0	0	0	0	0	0	0	0	0	0	0	0
NET INT EXPENSE	81	81	82	82	82	82	82	82	82	82	82	82
MIN INT IN SUBS	0	0	0	0	0	0	0	0	0	0	0	0
OTH INC-ACCR	0	0	0	0	0	0	0	0	0	0	0	0
OTH DED-RESV	4	4	4	4	4	4	4	4	4	4	4	6
OTH DED-CORP	4	4	4	4	4	4	4	4	4	4	4	6
MISC OTH DED	85	85	86	86	86	86	86	86	86	86	86	88
TTL OTH DED	9239	14175	15410	15102	14373	16141	13616	14120	14906	13819	12467	12075
INC BEF INC TAX	4515	1849	1182	1848	2242	1788	3152	2879	2455	2242	2970	3182
INVEST TAX CR	0	0	0	0	0	0	0	0	0	0	0	0
PRO TAX-ACCR	3698	6322	6783	6586	6157	6727	5352	5510	5881	5315	4525	4237
PRO TAX-CORP ADJ	-3963	-1650	-876	-1487	-1787	-1090	-2240	-1893	-1479	-1200	-1760	-1864
PRO TAX-CORP												
PROV/NON-DED	4	4	4	4	4	4	4	4	4	4	3	3
FED TAX ON INC	-261	4676	5911	5103	4374	5641	3116	3621	4406	4119	2768	2376
FED TAX YTD	-261	4415	10326	15429	19803	25444	28560	32181	36587	40706	43474	45850
FOR TAX ON INC	0	0	0	0	0	0	0	0	0	0	0	0
PLAN NET INCOME	9500	9500	9500	10000	10500	10500	10500	10500	10500	9700	9700	9700
NET INCOME	9500	9499	9499	9999	9999	10500	10500	10499	10500	9700	9699	9699
NET INCOME-YTD	9500	18999	28498	38497	48496	58996	69496	79995	90495	100195	109894	119593
NET INC - ACCR	4343	7422	7963	7733	7228	7899	6284	6470	6904	6241	5313	4975
NET INC-CORP ADJ	5157	2077	1536	2266	2771	2601	4216	4029	3596	3459	4386	4724
NET INC - CORP	0	0	0	0	0	0	0	0	0	0	0	0
CON ACG-ACCR	0	0	0	0	0	0	0	0	0	0	0	0
CON ACG-CORP ADJ	0	0	0	0	0	0	0	0	0	0	0	0
CON ACG-CORP	0	0	0	0	0	0	0	0	0	0	0	-27711
SA BKLG-ACCR	0	0	0	0	0	0	0	0	0	0	0	0
SA BKLG-CORP ADJ	0	0	0	0	0	0	0	0	0	0	0	-8838
SA BKLG-CORP	-6500	-6000	-6200	-6400	-6700	-6200	-6100	-6500	-6500	-6800	-6600	-25573

FIG. 29-8 Computer Printout of Balance Sheet, by Month

BALANCE SHEET

PLAN YEAR 1982

	JAN	FEB	MAR	APR	MAY	JUN	JUL	AUG	SEP	OCT	NOV	DEC
CASH	35000	35000	35000	35000	35000	35000	35000	35000	35000	35000	35000	35000
TEMP INVEST	32700	45600	66500	82400	107500	187800	200400	219900	226700	248200	269900	295300
ACCTS REC	80000	89000	85000	85000	85000	85000	87500	87500	87500	88000	88000	88500
CONTRCTS IN PROC	57500	59000	55000	56500	57560	58752	55896	55879	57685	57854	58745	59870
LESS: PROG PAY	5400	5200	4300	4200	4500	4600	4750	5780	4320	4680	4500	8750
NET INVENTORY	52100	53800	50700	52300	53060	54152	51146	50099	53365	53174	54245	51120
PRODUCT INVENT	0	0	0	0	0	0	0	0	0	0	0	0
PREPAID EXP	1100	1100	1100	1100	1100	1100	1100	1100	1100	1100	1100	1100
TTL CUR ASSETS	200900	224500	238300	255800	281660	363052	375146	393599	403665	425474	448245	471020
LAND & IMPROV	235750	235750	235750	235750	235750	235750	235750	235750	235750	235750	235750	235750
LND&IMP-CAP LSE	0	0	0	0	0	0	0	0	0	0	0	0
TTL LND & IMP	235750	235750	235750	235750	235750	235750	235750	235750	235750	235750	235750	235750
BUILDINGS	99879	99879	99879	99879	99879	99879	99879	99879	99879	99879	99879	99879
BLDGS-CAP LSE	34679	34679	34679	34679	34679	34679	34679	34679	34679	34679	34679	45780
TTL BLDGS	134558	134558	134558	134558	134558	134558	134558	134558	145659	145659	145659	145659
MACH & EQUIP	74269	76571	79767	82360	84174	87464	89872	92527	100876	106646	107939	109297
M & E-CAP LSE	1386	1386	1386	1386	1386	1386	1386	1386	1386	1386	1386	1386
TTL MACH&EQUIP	75655	77957	81153	83746	85560	88850	91258	93913	102262	108032	109325	110683
LEASEHOLD IMP	25465	25465	25465	25465	25465	25465	25465	25465	25465	25465	25465	25465
LSHLD IMP-CAP LS	0	0	0	0	0	0	0	0	0	0	0	0
TTL LSHLD IMP	25465	25465	25465	25465	25465	25465	25465	25465	25465	25465	25465	25465
CONST IN PROG	107659	107659	107659	107659	107659	107659	107659	107659	107659	107659	107659	107659
TTL PROPERTY	579087	581389	584585	587178	588992	592282	594690	597345	616795	622565	623858	625516
DEPR-LND IMP	4	4	4	4	4	4	4	4	4	4	4	4
AMORT-LND IMP-LS	0	0	0	0	0	0	0	0	0	0	0	0
DEPR-BLDGS	550	580	610	640	670	700	730	760	790	820	850	880
AMOR-BLDGS-LSE	0	0	0	0	0	0	0	0	0	0	0	0
DEPR-MACH&EQUIP	20887	22056	23283	24593	25968	27369	28843	30379	31840	33619	35555	37525
AMOR-M & E-LSE	809	834	859	884	909	934	959	984	1009	1034	1052	1070
AMOR-LSEHLD IMP	310	310	310	310	310	310	310	310	310	310	310	310
AMOR-LSEHLD-LSE	0	0	0	0	0	0	0	0	0	0	0	0
TOT DEPR & AMOR	22560	23784	25066	26431	27861	29317	30846	32437	33953	35787	37771	39789
NET PROPERTY	556527	557605	559519	560747	561131	562965	563844	564908	582842	586778	586087	585427
N & A RECEIVE	8088	8088	8088	8088	8088	8088	8088	8088	8088	8088	8088	8088
I/A: UNCONSOL	13201	13301	13401	13501	13601	13701	13801	13901	14001	14101	14201	14301
I/A: SUBSID	88312	91298	87694	91989	91829	29358	44206	55348	50247	52149	57977	66081
MISC OTH ASSETS	50	50	50	50	50	50	50	50	50	50	50	50
TTL OTH ASSETS	109651	112737	109233	113628	113568	51197	66145	77387	72386	74388	80316	88520
TOTAL ASSETS	867078	894842	907052	930175	956359	977214	1005135	1035894	1058893	1086640	1114648	1144967

Account	1	2	3	4	5	6	7	8	9	10	11	12
NOTES PAYABLE	0	0	0	0	0	0	0	0	0	0	0	0
TRADE ACCTS PAY	2000	2000	2000	2000	2000	2000	2000	2000	2000	2000	2000	2000
OTHER CUR LIAB	19947	20535	16713	16688	16717	16695	16679	16688	16746	16682	16682	16682
ADV ON CONTRACTS	0	0	0	0	0	0	0	0	0	0	0	0
EMPL COMP	6310	3410	3710	4010	4310	4610	4910	5210	5510	5810	6110	6410
TAX PROV-OP CTRS	0	9906	4415	3098	4561	5403	4547	7581	6982	6010	6043	5118
CHG IN DEFERRED	-261	4676	5911	5103	4374	5641	3116	3621	4406	4119	2768	2376
TAX CORP PROV	0	0	0	0	0	0	0	0	0	0	0	0
TAX PAYMENTS	0	0	0	0	0	0	0	0	0	0	0	0
FIT PAY PR BAL	18140	32722	43048	51249	60184	71228	78891	90093	101481	111610	120421	137915
ST TX OP CTRS	816	816	816	816	816	816	816	816	817	817	817	817
STATE TAX PYMTS	0	44	800	446	0	868	0	900	565	1144	885	914
INC TAX-STATE	2767	3346	1158	446	1025	216	795	1374	565	1144	1723	914
INC TAX-FED	18140	32722	43048	51249	60184	71228	78891	90093	101481	111610	120421	137915
INC TAX-FOR	0	0	0	0	0	0	0	0	0	0	0	0
TTL INC TAX	20907	36068	44206	51695	61209	71444	79686	91467	102046	112754	122144	138829
CURRENT DEFERRED	265047	265047	265047	265047	265047	265047	265047	265047	265047	265047	265047	265047
CUR MAT - LTD	2000	2000	2000	2000	2000	2000	2000	2000	2000	2000	2000	2000
CUR MAT-CAP LSE	385	383	379	379	373	371	368	363	365	360	343	333
TTL CUR LIAB	316596	329443	334055	341819	351656	362167	370690	382775	393714	404653	414326	431301
NEW FINANCING												
NOTE PAY- CC	6000	6000	6000	6000	6000	6000	6000	6000	6000	6000	6000	6000
MORTG NOTE PAY	0	0	0	0	0	0	0	0	0	0	0	0
OTH NOTES PAY	0	0	0	0	0	0	0	0	0	0	0	0
TTL SENIOR DEBT	6000	6000	6000	6000	6000	6000	6000	6000	6000	6000	6000	6000
CAP LSE OBLIG	454	424	396	364	336	304	273	243	210	192	171	150
ACCR PROD SUPPORT												
DEF COMPENSATION	2157	2391	2396	2400	2404	2452	2457	2434	2482	2486	2491	2539
TTL L-T OBLIG	8611	8815	8792	8764	8740	8756	8730	8677	8692	8678	8662	8669
DEFRD INC TAXES	20577	20577	20577	20577	20577	20577	20577	20577	20577	20577	20577	20577
DEFERRED CREDIT	8051	8051	8051	8051	8051	8051	8051	8051	8051	8051	8051	8051
ADD PAID IN CAP	116247	116247	116247	116247	116247	116247	116247	116247	116247	116247	116247	116247
RET EARN PRIOR	405053	425853	440566	446994	462381	478752	487887	507311	526038	536890	553712	572063
O.C. NET INCOME	11353	5214	3663	5388	6372	5370	8924	8228	7086	7122	8652	9159
DIVIDENDS	9500	9499	6734	9999	9999	6735	10500	10499	6734	9700	9699	6734
RET EARN CURR	9500	9499	9999	9999	9999	10500	10500	10499	10500	9700	9699	9699
RETAINED EARNGS	425853	440566	446994	462381	478752	487887	507311	526038	536890	553712	572063	584187
UNVESTED RAS	-28857	-28857	-27664	-27664	-27664	-26471	-26471	-26471	-25278	-25278	-25278	-24085
TTL SHAR EQUITY	513243	527956	535577	550964	567335	577663	597087	615814	627859	644681	663032	676349
TTL LIAB & EQTY	867078	894842	907052	930175	956359	977214	1005135	1035894	1058893	1086640	1114648	1144967

FIG. 29-9   Computer Printout of Change in Assumptions Iteration

INCOME STATEMENT – CORPORATE
(DOLLARS IN THOUSANDS)

---PLAN YEAR 1982---

	JAN	FEB	MAR	APR	MAY	JUN	JUL	AUG	SEP	OCT	NOV	DEC
FP SALES	0	0	0	0	0	0	0	0	0	0	0	-18873
TTL CUST SALES	0	0	0	0	0	0	0	0	0	0	0	-18873
NET SAL – ACCR	0	0	0	0	0	0	0	0	0	0	0	-18873
NET SAL-CORP ADJ	0	0	0	0	0	0	0	0	0	0	0	0
NET SAL – CORP	0	0	0	0	0	0	0	0	0	0	0	-18873
TTL SALES	0	0	0	0	0	0	0	0	0	0	0	-18873
OP MARG – ACCR	-8595	-11323	-16353	-11581	-10944	38543	5037	4382	3924	6598	6776	8692
OP MARG-CORP ADJ	-100	-100	-100	-100	-100	-100	-100	-100	-100	-100	-100	-100
OP MARG – CORP	8695	11423	16453	11681	11044	-38443	-4937	-4282	-3824	-6498	-6676	-25465
COST OF SALES	-8695	-11423	-16453	-11681	-11044	38443	4937	4282	3824	6498	6676	6592
OPER MARGIN	0	0	0	0	0	0	0	0	0	0	0	-18873
G/L DISPO ASSET	0	0	0	0	0	0	0	0	0	0	0	0
INT EARNED-OTH	1365	371	65	0	0	0	0	0	0	0	0	0
INT EARNED-TI	0	0	0	0	0	0	0	0	0	0	0	0
INT EARNED	1365	371	65	0	0	0	0	0	0	0	0	0
ROYALTIES	0	0	0	0	0	0	0	0	0	0	0	0
EQTY-NET SUBS	100	100	100	100	100	100	100	100	100	100	100	100
EQTY-NET UNCON	0	0	0	0	0	0	0	0	0	0	0	0
OTH INC-ACCR	0	0	0	0	0	0	0	0	0	0	0	0
OTH INC-CORP ADJ	125	125	125	125	125	125	125	125	125	125	125	125
OTH INC-CORP	125	125	125	125	125	125	125	125	125	125	125	125
DIVIDEND INC	0	0	0	0	0	0	0	0	0	0	0	0
MISC OTH INC	0	0	0	0	0	0	0	0	0	0	0	0
TTL OTH INC	1590	596	290	225	225	225	225	225	225	225	225	225
RC INT EXP	78	233	579	1266	1943	1534	1158	1532	1758	1942	2163	2686
INT EXP-CORP OTH	3	3	4	4	4	4	4	4	4	4	4	4

	1	2	3	4	5	6	7	8	9	10	11	12
O/C EST. OF CORP	0	0	0	0	0	0	0	0	0	0	0	0
INT EXP-CORP	81	236	583	1270	1947	1538	1162	1536	1762	1946	2167	2690
INT EXP-OTHER	0	0	0	0	0	0	0	0	0	0	0	0
NET INT EXPENSE	81	236	583	1270	1947	1538	1162	1536	1762	1946	2167	2690
MIN INT IN SUBS	0	0	0	0	0	0	0	0	0	0	0	0
OTH INC-ACCR	0	0	0	0	0	0	0	0	0	0	0	0
OTH DED-RESV	0	0	0	0	0	0	0	0	0	0	0	0
OTH DED-CORP	4	4	4	4	4	4	4	4	4	4	4	6
MISC OTH DED	4	4	4	4	4	4	4	4	4	4	4	6
TTL OTH DED	85	240	587	1274	1951	1542	1166	1540	1766	1950	2171	2696
INC BEF INC TAX	-7190	-11067	-16750	-12730	-12770	37126	3996	2967	2283	4773	4730	4121
INVEST TAX CR	4515	1849	1182	1848	2242	1788	3152	2879	2455	2242	2970	3182
PRO TAX-ACCR	-3953	-5208	-7522	-5327	-5034	17729	2317	2015	1805	3035	3116	3078
PRO TAX-CORP ADJ	-3869	-1731	-1365	-2376	-3082	-2439	-3630	-3529	-3209	-3081	-3910	-4364
PRO TAX-CORP	0	0	0	0	0	0	0	0	0	0	0	0
PROV/NON-DED	4	4	4	4	4	4	4	4	4	4	3	3
FED TAX ON INC	-7818	-6935	-8883	-7699	-8112	15294	-1309	-1510	-1400	-42	-791	-1283
FED TAX YTD	-7818	-14753	-23636	-31335	-39447	-24153	-25462	-26972	-28372	-28414	-29205	-30488
FOR TAX ON INC	0	0	0	0	0	0	0	0	0	0	0	0
PLAN NET INCOME	628	-4132	-7868	-5031	-4658	21833	5306	4477	3684	4815	5521	5404
NET INCOME	628	-4132	-7867	-5031	-4658	21832	5305	4477	3683	4815	5521	5404
NET INCOME-YTD	628	-3504	-11371	-16402	-21060	772	6077	10554	14237	19052	24573	29977
NET INC - ACCR	-4642	-6115	-8831	-6254	-5910	20814	2720	2367	2119	3563	3660	3614
NET INC-CORP ADJ	5270	1983	984	1223	1252	1018	2585	2110	1564	1252	1861	1790
NET INC - CORP	0	0	0	0	0	0	0	0	0	0	0	0
CON ACQ-ACCR	0	0	0	0	0	0	0	0	0	0	0	0
CON ACQ-CORP ADJ	0	0	0	0	0	0	0	0	0	0	0	0
CON ACQ-CORP	0	0	0	0	0	0	0	0	0	0	0	0
SA BKLG-ACCR	0	0	0	0	0	0	0	0	0	0	0	-27711
SA BKLG-CORP ADJ	0	0	0	0	0	0	0	0	0	0	0	-8838
SA BKLG-CORP	0	0	0	0	0	0	0	0	0	0	0	0

Finally, because of the relatively heavy investment in fixed assets and the significant depreciation charges, the detail of capital asset commitments, expenditures, and depreciation is provided, as reflected in Figure 29-6.

Segments of the annual plan, detailed by months, is shown in Figures 29-7 through 29-8.

Figure 29-7 illustrates the computer model printout of the planned income and expense statement for one organizational segment (corporate office) being reviewed. Similar data are provided for each profit center and the consolidated entity. The expected operating results are identified month by month so as to permit a comparison of actual and planned results, as the year progresses, for each organizational segment and the total company as to both the month and year-to-date. The computer printout represents the considerable working detail needed by the budget coordinator. For managerial purposes, however, the income plan, in total and by segment, is greatly condensed as to line items, and is presented by quarters and yearly total only to avoid providing a mass of detail which simply is not required by the officers and operating managers for decision-making purposes.

Figure 29-8 illustrates the planned monthly financial position, which is analyzed and reviewed for each such time period — for each investment center and the company as a whole. Again, this is a "working balance sheet," which is re-run with combined or condensed line items for each quarter and in total for the plan year for managerial use. Only the significant or important data are presented for management review.

As previously mentioned, planning is an iterative process. In the illustration, a review of the initial assumptions indicated that the interest income rate and the interest expense rate for the plan year (both important as to earnings) were simply too low. Accordingly, these assumptions were changed and a revised scenario was prepared by the computer in less than ten minutes. Figure 29-9 identifies those line items in the statement of planned income and expense that were modified by the changed assumptions. Any line items not changed as a result of the new assumptions were automatically *not* presented. A comparable "line-changes only" balance sheet was produced in the iteration, as well as the revised complete statement of financial position.

30

Specialized Management Uses of Budgeting

INTRODUCTION

From time to time, certain management techniques receive considerable attention and publicity as new approaches in the planning and control of business. Whether they are new or not can be debated. In any event, four processes warrant comment in the context of budgeting. They are

- Zero-base budgeting (ZBB)
- Program planning and budgeting systems (PPBS)
- Management by objectives (MBO)
- Bracket budgeting

It is not within the scope of this chapter to discuss each technique in detail. However, some of the more significant features are highlighted.

COMMENTS ON TRADITIONAL BUDGETING

In reviewing literature dealing with management techniques related to budgeting, a great deal has been written about the pros and cons of the newer systems, such as zero-base budgeting. Some may stress the great benefits of a new system, or, conversely, some are critical of the required higher level of effort. In addition, the literature often emphasizes the shortcomings of the "usual budgeting."

In the experience of the author, there is no system that can substitute for having competent management doing whatever has to be done in the planning and control arena. A good management usually is asking "why," is highly analytical, and seeks to guide the enterprise along an acceptable path to a reasonable objective — regardless of the budgeting system. Be that as it may, some of the newer systems may motivate management to probe operations more deeply, and, accordingly, may be highly desirable.

Many of the listed problems or difficulties of "traditional budgeting" are really a reflection of management sloppiness or lack of concern with the planning process. There is, however, one basic weakness in some of the usual budgeting applications. The process begins with last year's budget levels and adjusts for inflation, new programs, or activities in order to reach ever higher cost or expense levels. Only when the operating results are not as good as expected, or other adversity strikes the enterprise, does the process inquire into the acceptability or necessity of the present level of expenses. Of course, an analytical approach, a so-called tough-minded attitude, can be used in the traditional budgeting. Indeed, some managements *do* question the need for higher expense levels within the perimeters of the usual budgetary review. A new system simply is not necessary when budgets are prepared in a highly analytical or questioning environment.

However, in other cases, these new mechanisms may be motivators for productivity improvement, and those involved with budgetary procedures should be familiar with the basics.

ZERO-BASE BUDGETING

What Is Zero-Base Budgeting?

Zero-base budgeting (ZBB) is a term and technique introduced by Peter Phyrr in 1970. The basic idea, or a substantially similar one, had been used earlier. For example, the U.S. Department of Agriculture began employing a "ground up" budgeting technique in 1962 that included a reevaluation of all programs.[1] Certainly the writings and discussions by Phyrr, combined with the current events, greatly advanced its popularity.

Some sense of the process may be deduced from these comments. Presi-

---

[1] James D. Suver and Ray L. Brown, "Where Does Zero-Base Budgeting Work?" *Harvard Business Review* (Nov./Dec. 1977), p. 76.

dent Jimmy Carter, while Governor of Georgia, explained ZBB in this manner in his January 13, 1972 budget message: "Zero-base budgeting requires every agency in state government to identify each function it performs and the personnel and cost to the taxpayers for performing that function." [2] Another description of the process states this: "Perhaps the essence of zero-base budgeting is simply that an agency provides a defense of its budget request that makes no reference to the level of previous appropriation." [3] All of these definitions have one common theme, namely, that the manager must be able to justify each activity level completely and that no particular degree of activity is automatically assumed to be necessary. Of course, those of us involved with budgeting activity know that the economic climate and trend in earnings for a particular company greatly influences the extent or degree of review and probing in establishing the annual budget. Therefore, tough decisions on the need for a given activity, or the scope of the activity, have taken place when the unfavorable financial outlook and limited capabilities of the firm have demanded it.

Zero-Base Budgeting Procedure

The ZBB approach requires an analysis of management activities and the development of a "decision package," which is discussed later in this volume. However, to be fair, the ZBB procedure should not be regarded as a fixed procedure and a set of forms to be applied rather automatically in a company. Rather, the approach must be adapted to the needs of the user. It may be applied to only selected activities and not to the entire organization. Additionally, the degree of related analysis may vary. The usual steps are outlined as follows:

1. Identify the decision units, that is, the activity to be represented by the "decision package."
2. Develop the decision package for each unit (as will be reviewed in this chapter).
3. Evaluate and rank all the decision packages.
4. Summarize the budgets and prepare the annual profit plan.
5. Modify the accepted decision packages until an acceptable plan emerges and approve the detailed budgets.

Comments on these steps follow.

---

[2] As quoted by George S. Minmier and R. H. Hermanson, "A Look At Zero-Base Budgeting — The Georgia Experience," *Atlanta Economic Review* (July/Aug. 1976), p. 5.

[3] Leonard Merewitz and Stephen H. Sosnick, *The Budget's New Clothes: A Critique of Planning–Programming–Budgeting and Benefit Cost Analysis* (Chicago: Markham, 1971), p. 5.

The Decision Unit

The first step in the ZBB procedure is the selection or identification of the decision unit. The decision units should be discrete segments of the organization for which the activities can be analyzed, with alternative solutions, in a "meaningful" way. One authority identifies four elements in selecting the unit, as follows [4]:

- Size of operation
- Available alternatives
- Organizational level at which meaningful (significant) decisions can be made
- Time constraints

In many cases, the decision unit may correspond with a department or a cost center. However, it may be a function within a cost center. Thus, in the corporate financial department, the functions in the office of the vice-president–finance may be segregated as follows:

1. Treasurer:
   - Management of pension funds
   - Cash management
   - Financing
   - Insurance
2. Controller:
   - Accounting
   - Financial planning
   - Taxes
   - Special analysis
3. Internal Auditing:
   - Financial auditing
   - Data processing audits
   - Operational audits

Perhaps any one cost center, if large enough, may be a decision unit. In any event, it represents a discrete function, with alternatives available concerning the level of operation, and concerning which decisions can be made as to extent or importance of the activity. It may represent a prime function to be performed *now,* or it may represent a *future* oriented function, such as research and development, market development, or a staff (advisory) function.

---

[4] Henry J. Genthner and Joseph L. Hebert, *Automating Zero-Base Budgeting* (New York: Petrocelli Books, Inc., 1977), p. 4.

The decision unit may be an organizational segment, a program, specific projects, or objects of expenditure, such as legal fees and consulting expenses.

Perhaps the most important feature in designating a decision package is size and alternative treatment of the item (i.e., the opportunity to reduce, continue, or discontinue).

THE DECISION PACKAGE

The decision package provides the necessary data concerning each decision unit so that management can review and evaluate the function. Actually, the decision package must be segregated into two or more activity levels, one of which must be *below* the current level so that the alternative impact of reduced activity may be considered.

Data typically put forward for a decision unit will include the following information:

- Purpose or objective of the activity.
- Description of the activity for the level under review. This includes what is being done, the changes contemplated (such as adding six people), and what the result will be.
- The costs and benefits, detailed by type of expense.
- Workload and performance data, such as output, daily work load, and number of machines operated.
- Alternative methods of accomplishing the task, such as subcontracting segments of the work.
- Other levels of effort that could be considered, such as 75 percent of present services (by eliminating certain functions or programs) or 115 percent of the present level (by adding functions).

Presumably, in many departments, such as advertising, the decision could involve:

- Eliminating the function entirely.
- Reducing it.
- Maintaining it at the current level.
- Increasing the activity, if the cost/benefit ratio looked appealing.

Identification of minimum levels does not signify the recommendation of such lower activity. However, it does apprise management of the possible alternatives and the consequences.

AN ILLUSTRATIVE DECISION PACKAGE

A decision package has been defined as a document that describes a discrete activity — whether program, function, or operation — in a manner that permits management to judge and evaluate the activity and compare it with others. An illustrative package is shown in Figure 30-1. However, it is only that — illustrative. The exact format will vary from company to company and even within the organization.

It will be observed that the sample package includes these elements (and presumes a reasonable familiarity of the reviewer with the operation):

1. Certain identifying data:
   - Package name
   - Department number
   - Level of activity
   - Preparation data
   - Preparer
   - Space for ranking
2. Description of the purpose or goals of the activity
3. Certain implementing data:
   - Legal need
   - State of the art
   - Ease of implementation
   - Economic risks
   - Description of the activity contemplated
   - Changes briefly described
   - Resources required, including manpower and cost
   - Consequences of eliminating this package, which is the basic level
   - Other levels of activity — description and cost
   - Economic cost of package versus prior year

Ranking the Decision Packages

Once the decision packages have been completed, management must review them and allocate the limited resources. Essentially it must decide (1) what functions should be accepted and (2) how much should be spent. Very candidly, some decisions will be subjective and some may represent political reality. In any event, it does give management an opportunity to look at the activities and costs, and arrive at a decision as to what can be eliminated, what can continue on a reduced or present level, and what should be expanded.

FIG. 30-1   Illustrative Decision Package

(1) Package Name: Public Relations	(2) Dept. No. 407	(3) Level _1_ of _3_ (Basic)

Page _1_ of _5_	(4) Date: 6/10/19XX	(5) Prepared by: J. J. Johnson	(6) Rank

(7) Description of goals or objectives:

- To secure improved recognition of the company name among the general public.
- To arrange specific institutional advertising programs.
- To coordinate the public relations activities in the profit centers.
- To work closely with Finance, to prepare the annual report to shareholders.
- To prepare the first draft of the chairman's talks to various groups; and to schedule the meetings.

(8) Is Program legally required?   Yes [   ]   No [X]

(9) State of the art   High [   ]   Medium [X]   Low [   ]

(10) Ease of implementation   High [X]   Medium [   ]   Low [   ]

(11) Economic risks   High [   ]   Medium [   ]   Low [X]

(12) Description of activity at this level:

- Staff would consist of 13 members, as follows:

  1 — Vice-President
  1 — Manager: Corporate Affairs
  1 — Manager: Division Affairs
  5 — Staff members for speech writing, coordination and tracking publicity, including 3 in New York office
  1 — Photographer
  1 — Executive secretary
  3 — Secretary-typists
  —
  13
  ==

- Usual activities of preparing drafts of talks by CEO, scheduling appearances and making all arrangements would continue.
- Two series of institutional ads would be issued during year.

- Annual report work would be subcontracted.
- Division public relations would assume more responsibility for product activity.

(13) Changes from current level of activity:

- Staff would be reduced by 10 including 1 manager, 7 staff members, and 2 secretaries.
- Annual report detailed activity would be subcontracted to Jones & Co. with coordination by the Vice-President: Public Relations.
- Review of publicity would be handled by a new agent with little follow-up by corporate staff.
- Supervision or coordination of division public relations activities would be limited to the equivalent of 1 man.

(14) Resources Required:

| | Actual | | | This |
	19X3	19X2	19X1	Level
Total staff	19	21	23	13
Total annual expense ($000)	$3,210	$3,450	$3,700	$2,600
Percentage of prior year				70.3%

(15) Consequences of eliminating this package:

- Not practical. CEO must appear before various groups, including industry meetings, analyst briefings, and customer forums. Lack of coordination of divisions will result in inadequate presentations and inconsistent public statements.
- Alternative is to farm out entire function or have Finance handle talks with financial community and annual report.

(16) Other levels of activity:

	Percent Last Year	Total Cost ($000)	Description
2 of 3	90%	$3,300	Add 3 people for annual report effort and division coordination; no subcontracting.
3 of 3	110	4,070	Continue present activities but add office in London for improved European coverage. Four new staff members.

(continued)

FIG. 30-1   Illustrative Decision Package (cont'd)

(17) Detail of proposed budget ($000):

Expense items	Past Year	This Level
Salaries and wages	$1,560	$ 970
Retirement plan costs	201	120
Payroll taxes and insurance	197	120
Advertising media	630	240
Travel	350	230
Entertainment	70	40
Communications	190	180
Occupancy costs	200	200
Professional services	186	400
Dues and subscriptions	95	80
Depreciation	10	10
General insurance	5	5
Miscellaneous	6	5
Total	$3,700	$2,600

Basically, the procedure may involve reviews of massive data, so that some grouping by a division supervisor of his functions may be necessary. Each manager may rank his own packages and each supervisor may rank the packages of all managers reporting to him. Another alternative is to permit supervision to approve packages up to X percent (such as 80 percent) of the prior year, with higher level packages subject to review by the group executive. Given the vast amount of information generated in some circumstances, a computer application may be warranted.

In any event, top management may set an overall budget for all functions or set specified limits for major groupings, such as finance. When the rankings have been set and agreed upon, the costs involved with the approved packages constitute the new budget.

Obviously, not all functions need be included. Direct labor, supported by productivity standards, for example, may be excluded. However, the procedure might apply to almost all types of expenses.

Some other functions, basically line (as contrasted to staff) activities, for which ZBB might be inappropriate, include:

- Chief executive officer
- Chief operating officer
- Chief marketing officer
- Chief financial officer

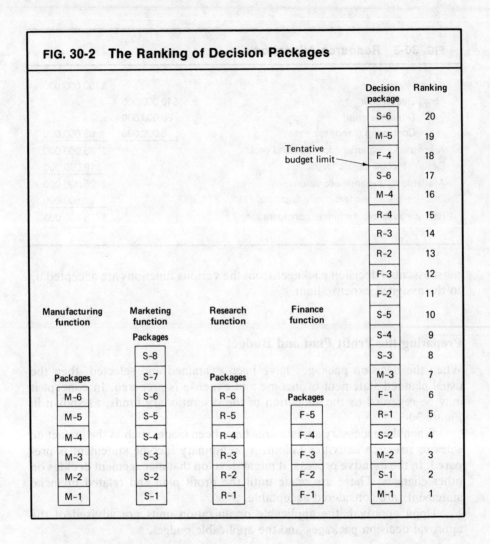

FIG. 30-2   The Ranking of Decision Packages

- Manufacturing — Direct
- Direct marketing (but not staff)
- Warehouses and direct operators

Certain of these activities involve subjective judgment. Others are controlled by output and other standards.

In the selection process, relationships between functions — both horizontal and vertical dependencies — must be considered. Thus, a market research product should not be accepted if the related sales promotional activity is to be dropped.

A sense of the ranking process may be gleaned from Figure 30-2. The

FIG. 30-3   Resource Allocation

Net sales		$100,000,000
Less: Direct labor	$40,000,000	
Direct material	20,000,000	
Continuing (fixed) expense	5,000,000	65,000,000
Available for expense allocation and profit		$ 35,000,000
Desired income before taxes		10,000,000
Available for expense allocation		$ 25,000,000
Decision packages tentatively approved		21,600,000
Balance available for further consideration		$ 3,400,000

most essential decision packages from the various functions are accepted up to the assigned expense limit.

Preparing the Profit Plan and Budget

When the decision packages have been examined and selected, then the usual planned statement of income and expense is prepared. In concept it may be regarded as the allocation of the discretionary funds, as shown in Figure 30-3.

When the necessary adjustments have been made, such as the impact on sales or research activities fallout, a preliminary income statement is prepared. In the iterative process, it might develop that management decides on other changes. These are made until the profit plan and related financial statements are considered acceptable.

Upon approval, the applicable organization units are advised of the approval decision packages and the applicable budget.

Alternatives to Zero-Base Budgeting

The objective of ZBB is to cause a review of the various functions and their need and effectiveness. However, it can be appreciated that top management in a large company probably cannot be familiar with each decision package or function. Moreover, the task of developing the decision package requires considerable time by operating management. Further, the real need for this degree of analysis may relate only to certain selected functions, perhaps ones that have vastly increased in recent years.

If a company does not choose to undertake ZBB, there are two possible alternatives that may provide some of the benefits. Alternative approaches are (1) the use of performance or operational auditing and (2) the sunset concept.

Operational auditing has as its objective the review of the effectiveness and efficiency of particular functions. Hence, in a sense it has the same purpose as ZBB. It may be performed only when deemed necessary, and thus need not be accomplished annually. In addition, it may be done selectively without disrupting the normal planning and control functions. For a real in-depth review of a function the use of an operational audit may be a more cost-effective way. In the practical world, the in-depth reviews, especially at budget time, may leave much to be desired — given the pressure of normal operations.

Such operational audits may be performed by the internal audit staff, a selected management team of various disciplines within the firm, or by the independent accountants.

A useful alternative, especially in governmental operations, is the sunset concept. Basically, the principle is that the "sun will set" on selected activities after a stipulated number of years, perhaps three to seven, if it is not subjected to a review, such as a ZBB type, and is accepted or resurrected.

The basic question as to the application of ZBB in a particular firm depends on (1) the budgeting or profit problems in the company; (2) the availability of time to make the necessary reviews; (3) the availability of staff to truly or meaningfully review the budgets or decision packages; and (4) the receptivity of the organization to the concept.

PROGRAM, PLANNING, AND BUDGETING SYSTEMS

Nature of PPBS

Many knowledgeable professionals have traced zero-base budgeting to the program, planning, and budgeting systems (PPBS) developed by the U.S. Department of Defense in the 1960s.

Be that as it may, PPBS, or simply program budgeting, is used in many businesses, especially in the defense and aircraft industries. Thus, if an enterprise is building several major types of aircraft, each type may be planned and controlled on a program basis. There are many variations and definitions. However, this description is apt: "Essentially it is a management decision-making system that ties together strategic and long-range planning with conventional budgeting and supporting analyses so that an organization can most effectively assign resources to achieve both its short-

and long-range objectives." [5] There is extensive literature on program budgeting for those who wish to pursue the subject in some detail. However, in an overly simplified way, PPBS may be summarized in these statements:

1. Costs and expenses are initially related to programs rather than by types of expenditures. Stated in other terms, expenditures are related to outputs that are tied to objectives and are related much less to inputs in terms of functional costs.
2. The program may be said to relate to its entire life cycle far into the future, not merely on a short-term basis.
3. Each program is subjected to intensive cost-effective analysis. The objective may be to increase the value of the program or to reduce its cost, or both.

In summary, PPBS is program oriented, with a long-range viewpoint that uses cost analysis of several alternative approaches to reach an objective. And the near-term phase is translated into the annual plan.

For those well versed in an analytical approach to planning and control, the relationship between program costs and the object of expenditure may be simply described in the translation shown in Figure 30-4. For cash planning purposes, each year of the long-range plan may be translated into costs or expenditures for each program. Of course, such interpolation is necessary in the early years for annual budgeting. This is not to say that program budgeting is merely the summary of costs or an outlay by program. It is much more; it involves basic planning concepts not necessarily encountered in many companies.

Elements of Program Budgeting

As in any effective management system, program budgeting (PB) must be tailored to fit the management style and needs of the particular enterprise. Though discussion of a generalized procedure may not be necessary, some comments on the key elements or phases may be useful. Many of the writings on PB stress the long-range viewpoint and the analytical aspects of this technique as contrasted to typical budgeting. The more enlightened business firms conduct long-range planning and the related analysis, irrespective of whether so-called program budgeting is used. The annual profit plan or budget is simply a greater detailing, with any necessary modifications, of the first year of the long-range or strategic plan. In fact, the long-range planning

---

[5] H. W. Allen Sweeny and Robert Rachlin, eds., *Handbook of Budgeting* (New York: John Wiley & Sons, Inc., 1981), p. 697.

FIG. 30-4   Summary of Program Budgets, by Type of Expenditure

THE PROGRAM COMPANY

SUMMARY OF PROGRAM BUDGETS, 19XX

By Type of Expenditure

(dollars in thousands)

Cost Category	Yearly Total	Program Fighter Y	Bomber B	Commercial X
Costs and Expenses				
Salaries and wages	$ 221,000	$ 42,000	$ 79,000	$100,000
Fringe benefits	66,300	12,600	23,700	30,000
Materials	452,000	95,000	107,000	250,000
Maintenance	70,000	10,000	20,000	40,000
Occupancy costs	190,000	40,000	70,000	80,000
Depreciation	183,000	22,000	61,000	100,000
Utilities	131,900	37,000	24,900	70,000
Travel	2,800	500	300	2,000
Supplies	5,500	1,000	500	4,000
Miscellaneous	1,500	200	300	1,000
Total	$1,324,000	$260,300	$386,700	$677,000
Assets				
Working capital	$ 272,000	$ 47,000	$ 75,000	$150,000
Plant and equipment	16,000	6,000	5,000	5,000
Total assets	288,000	53,000	80,000	155,000
Grand Total	$1,612,000	$313,300	$466,700	$832,000

and analysis on a major product line, such as television sets, is substantially similar to the PB approach to a type of aircraft. For various reasons, however, the organization structure, such as the use of a program manager, usually is different.

It may be well to comment on a few aspects of PB as commonly expoused, although it does not seem that different from the usual long-range planning and budgeting as practiced by many industrial concerns. Admittedly, in a government environment, the circumstances and requirements may be quite changed. Comments will relate to:

1. *The process phases or segments, as implied by the term PPBS:*
   ☐ Planning
   ☐ Programming
   ☐ Budgeting
2. *Related structural elements:*
   ☐ Supporting analyses of
     ● Issues
     ● Changes
     ● Cost benefit or cost effectiveness
   ☐ *Management information system:*
     ● Multi-year plans
     ● Translation of program costs to elements of expenditure

Process Phases

While there may be some debate about segregating PB into these three specific phases, most literature separates the process into these segments: planning, programming, and budgeting.

Planning. The planning phase, in common parlance, refers to the strategic planning and the related long-range plan.

The strategic plan involves the development of the mission or purpose and the objectives and goals of the enterprise. The basic strengths and weaknesses, among other factors, are determined and the options of the organization are studied in order to arrive at the board objectives.

The long-range plan is then developed, spanning five to 25 years or so, whatever is the *useful* long-range planning period, in order to point the way for the enterprise to reach its goal. In an industrial firm this means developing the sales and marketing plan, the facilities plan, the manufacturing plan, the research and development plan, the financial plan, and the manpower plan all in context of the program structure, with the sources and uses of capital and the operating result of each.

These plans are broad and general in nature, and are usually an iterative process, with options being considered.

Programming. In the long-range planning process just mentioned, major programs or program groupings (or product lines) are determined. Some executives might call *programming* a segment of long-term planning. However, for the PB advocate, programming is the development of more detailed plans for each program. The more specific resource requirements of manpower, materials, and facilities are spelled out in a time-phased plan. However, the detailed expenses by account need not necessarily be determined.

Budgeting. The budgeting phase, in PB jargon, is the detailed translation of the approved programs into the cost and revenue elements and the development of the annual time-phased budget by department and by type of cost (as in Figure 30-4).

The budget, when approved, becomes a commitment of the management and a control device against which to measure actual results, as stressed throughout this book.

Related Structural Elements of PPBS

Some brief comments on some inherent elements in the PPBS scheme of things (or any informed management system) are noted below.

Analyses. An inherent ingredient in planning is proper analysis. This includes the identification and study of critical issues faced by an organization. In strategic planning, it is called issues analysis, and these issues and challenges (threats and opportunities) must be considered again periodically and appropriate action planned to meet them. These analyses, when used in PB, are called special studies.

Throughout the strategic and long-range planning process, the environment changes and new strategies must be developed, or existing strategies and plans modified. Hence, in the annual review of the corporate plan, updating and analysis of the impact of the change are necessary.

Planning involves a weighing of alternatives and the results. An aim is to select the best combination of actions to meet the objectives. Hence, two types of analyses are often made: (1) the cost-benefit analysis that quantifies in monetary terms the inputs and outputs and/or (2) the cost effectiveness analysis that measures not in monetary terms but in quantity of output.

Management Information Systems. An adequate management information system is essential to an effectively operating PB system. Among other features it should:

☐ Provide the necessary data required by management in both planning and control applications.

☐ Permit the translation of program costs or resources, as well as revenues, into the proper account analysis (as in Figure 30-4) and a time phasing of

those data. This includes the construction of required subanalyses by program, by organizational unit, by type of resource, and by account.
□ Facilitate the changing of assumptions and the translation of the revised data into revised financial plans, both short- and long-term.

It is axiomatic that management reports should follow the "responsibility accounting" principle and reflect the organization structure and the related responsibility and authority. Program management groupings in industrial practice do not conform to the usual organization structure. Often, there is, at least in many concerns, a program management organization for each program that overlaps the normal structure. Accordingly, each program manager should be provided with data as relates to the entire program. The usual line department will be provided the data necessary for the planning and control of its segment.

Included in the program data would be the costs and expenses under the manager's cognizance for each type of cost or expense, subdivided by program.

MANAGEMENT BY OBJECTIVES

The Purpose of MBO

Current literature on management by objectives (MBO) characterizes the process in a number of ways — from a form of participative management, to management by contract, to a comprehensive management system. In any event, over the past 25 years, or so, MBO has evolved as a device to improve productivity. As the name implies, the process involves the setting of certain objectives that the individual is expected to attain. It is important that the objective be set in the right way. The ideas behind the management system are twofold: (1) Perhaps the best motivator in the private enterprise system is for the organization to demand the very best in performance of which the individual is capable; and (2) the most acceptable and successful goals or objectives are those set by the individual himself, subject to the overall principles or guidelines that motivate the entire enterprise.

MBO has reached different stages of development in different companies. The manner of setting the objectives is sometimes less, sometimes more, formal in various firms. However, basically they should be set on the basis of discussions or dialogue between persons in different levels of management, and even in different functions, based on verifiable facts. Fundamentally, of course, there must be an appreciation of the worth of the individual, and that recognition is, indeed, a great motivator.

As will be seen, this management technique is one that can be used successfully in planning and controlling the business, as part of the budgeting process.

The Usual MBO Process

In a typical industrial company that employs some variation of the MBO principles, the initial set of objectives is established for the total organization. Some representative objectives, some of which are quantified and some of which are not, might include the following goals (see Chapters 3 and 4):

- Earn 22 percent on shareholders' equity for the year 19XX
- Attain a sales volume of $XXX for the year
- Introduce product Y in territory H
- Secure 22 percent of the market for product type L
- Complete the executive inventory

These objectives are set at a high organizational level, such as by the chief executive officer.

Based on the overall corporate objectives, some key objectives are then set for the top executives. For the senior vice-president–finance, some objectives for the year might be to

- Complete a $100 million financing for the new West Coast facility.
- Arrange export-import financing for the new aircraft.
- Replace the advisors for the pension plan investments.
- Revamp the financial reporting system for board presentations.
- Resolve the federal income tax impass for the years 19XX through 19X5.

In turn, objectives are set for the functional executives reporting to the chief financial officer — objectives that support the corporate objectives and the financial department objectives. Included among the objectives could be specific programs to correct known deficiencies discussed with the lower-level executive.

Arrangements usually include provision for higher executive approval of the objectives and profit improvement program, or correctional programs, which the subordinate executive has established for his staff. Typically, provision also is made for periodic review of progress in meeting the objectives. Often this is done in connection with salary merit increases or before bonus payments.

The entire process may be outlined as in Figure 30-5.

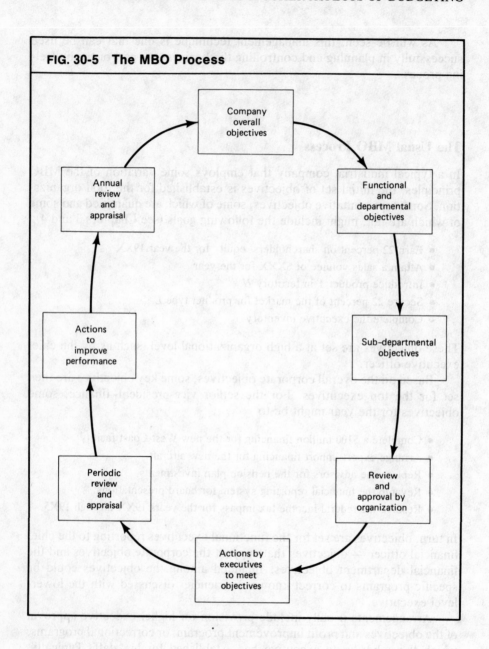

FIG. 30-5   The MBO Process

Some Basic Characteristics of an Objective

A great many corporations use objectives to motivate their people in an effort to improve productivity or to secure a higher rate of return on shareholders' equity or assets, or to accomplish certain other goals. However, experience shows that these objectives, to be successful or useful, must possess certain characteristics. Some are outlined below.

Attainability. Objectives should be attainable and realistic. Objectives should be "tough," i.e., it must take an effort to reach them. Yet they should not be set so high that they represent ideals that never can be reached. To establish goals that cannot be met is demoralizing. Of course, to assign an objective so easy that it is certain of achievement really deprives the individual of a chance to show what he can do.

Comprehension. Objectives should be understood. If the individual who is asked to achieve the objectives does not understand what is expected, then the objectives have lost much of their motivational appeal.

Assignability. Objectives should be assignable. Executives may agree with a stated objective. However, if responsibility cannot be placed on a specific individual to achieve it, or to get it done, then the chances are greatly increased that it simply will not be accomplished. There are times when group objectives may be appropriate. However, the most satisfactory goal is one that can be charged to a specific individual.

Measurability. Preferably, objectives should be measurable. If an objective is not measurable, how will management know it was accomplished? Disagreements well might arise about the degree of accomplishment. Some of the measurable characteristics might relate to:

☐ *Quantity.* This is a typical and usually an easy-to-measure trait. Sales either did or did not reach X amount. Measurements might be in market share, volume, relationship (current ratio), product mix, and in other areas.

☐ *Schedule.* Ordinarily, a time limit is placed on meeting a task. "It should be accomplished by July 1, 19XX." Perhaps milestones are set for specific data as an aid in measuring a difficult or lengthy project.

☐ *Fiscal.* Especially in planning and control, certain fiscal measures could apply. This characteristic might be (considered) a subdivision of quantity as mentioned above. However, certain profit rates, aggregate profit, or return on assets might be established by a specified period. Additionally, expenditures must be kept within given limits, such as capital expenditures or travel expense.

☐ *Quality*. This may be one of the more difficult measurements. Yet, standards of quality are set and can be used as a measure of achievement. There will be instances where the real quality or characteristic is not known for years, as in drug or chemical applications.

How these objectives should be established is of key importance and is treated in the next section.

Setting the Objective

Setting an objective should require discussion and negotiation, as in an implied contract. Otherwise it becomes an edict, and edicts do not necessarily motivate.

MBO represents an evolutionary process. In describing the establishment of objectives, one author comments on a "charter of accountability," which becomes a type of contract between manager and boss. The charter consisted of (1) a statement of job purpose, (2) a listing of objectives, (3) a breakdown of functional responsibilities, and (4) a subseries of performance tools that provide the manager with definitive targets against which to direct efforts.[6] Of course, one of the difficulties in the real world is the one-way street aspect, which often focuses on the obligations of the manager to his boss, but says little about the superior's responsibility. A new book goes somewhat further and stresses the desirability of a contract between each manager and the superior. It states, "The contract represents the manager's commitment to carry out an action program directed towards achieving a set of agreed-upon goals within a prescribed time frame; the quid pro quo on the part of the boss is a commitment to provide the resources, leadership, guidance and support needed to implement the action programs. The two are interdependent and neither is complete without the other." [7] The relationship between the individuals in setting the objectives is critical.

AN ILLUSTRATIVE SET OF OBJECTIVES

In carrying out the budgeting process, the MBO approach can be highly useful in achieving the goals. An illustrative objective listing, arrived at by

---

[6] Phil N. Schneid, "Charter of Accountability for Executives," *Harvard Business Review* (June-July 1965), p. 92.

[7] Charles R. Macdonald, *MBO Can Work! How To Manage By Contract* (New York: McGraw-Hill Book Company, 1982), p. 38.

FIG. 30-6 Annual Objectives for Division Manager

Name _____

Division _____

Position _____

Objective	Weighted Objective	Actual Performance
A. *Major Objectives:*		
1. Achieve a 12% return on assets	25.00	
2. Secure a net income for 19XX of $XXX	20.00	
3. Secure the B Company contract for the major subassemblies	15.00	
	60.00	
B. *Supplementary Objectives:*		
4. Complete all research and development efforts on the new "g" stabilizer, within budget	15.00	
5. Implement the profit improvement program to reduce labor on the m_____ fuselage by 3%	20.00	
6. Complete the installation in the East Complex of the automatic profiler by 10-1-19XX	10.00	
Total	100.00	

Agreed to:

_____
  Manager

Date _____

_____
  V. P. Operations

negotiation between the vice-president of operations and a division manager, and closely related to both budget results and incentive bonus, is illustrated in Figure 30-6. The various objectives were agreed upon between the two executives, including the weighting given to each task. When the year was completed, the manager was graded as to extent of accomplishment, and this was a major influence on incentive payments.

BRACKET BUDGETING

The last specialized technique to be reviewed is bracket budgeting, a fairly recent innovation. The readers are referred to some of the writings of the author and practitioner of the subject.[8] However, a few limited comments are made below.

Nature of Bracket Budgeting

Bracket budgeting may be described as an adjunct to conventional budgeting, which employs sophisticated statistical analyses to assess the probability of achieving a plan or result. It has been described by its developer as a synergistic combination of basic concepts in modeling, simulation, and heuristics that enables management to secure a much better understanding of the plan or other application.[9] The use of probability and sensitivity analysis is discussed in Chapter 25, as it relates to the chances of achieving the planned benefits of capital expenditures and the sensitivity of certain premises or assumptions. Bracket budgeting is a much broader statistical application and covers many more aspects.

When Should Bracket Budgeting Be Considered?

There are many times, to be sure, when the annual plan or budget is not attained. This may be due to circumstances outside the control of business management. However, quite often it results from a plan that is unrealistic in the sense that variables were inadequately considered. In those businesses or segments of a business where there is great uncertainty, a situation that can drastically alter operating results, bracket budgeting may be helpful.

Bracket budgeting can be applied selectively within a company. If a profit center is rather simple, the technique is not needed. Michael W. Curran, the developer, states that the determining factors in the application of bracket budgeting are "uncertainty, complexity, controllability, and commitment." [10] As he says, each of the factors must be evident to a substantial degree in a budget center for the technique to be utilized successfully.

Uncertainty about net earnings must be of sufficient magnitude to concern management. Complexity may be significant if there is a sizable number of variables and the ways in which they could interact that the result is not obvious. Significant controllability exists if there is a range of decision options available to management that can influence earnings. Finally, management must be convinced that bracket budgeting techniques can be genuinely helpful.

---

[8] See, for example, Michael W. Curran, "How Bracket Budgeting Helps Managers Cope With Uncertainty," *Management Review* (Apr. 1975), pp. 4–15, (May 1975), pp. 16–24.

[9] *Op. cit.*, H.W. Allen Sweeny, *Handbook of Budgeting*, Chapter 24.

[10] *Ibid.*, p. 668.

A Tactical Budgeting Model Is Key

If bracket budgeting is to be used, an early step is the development of a simple tactical budgeting model of the budget center to be examined. The model enables management to experiment with different short-term tactics to see, for example, what can be done to improve the profit plan or to modify existing operations in order to improve results and get closer to the plan.

31

Budgeting in Service Organizations

MANUFACTURING AND SERVICE COMPANY BUDGETS COMPARED

Much of the discussion in this book centers on budgeting for manufacturing-type companies: those whose output is represented by a tangible product. To be sure, certain subjects such as the planning and control of direct labor, direct material, manufacturing expense, and inventories (and to an extent, the budgeting of capital assets), have to do rather exclusively with manufacturing. Yet, planning and control for the vast remainder of costs, assets, liabilities, and shareholders' equity applies equally well to service-type companies, whose mission is to provide intangible services instead of physical products. As examples, budgeting for marketing expense, research and development costs, general and administrative expense, cash, receivables, current liabilities, long-term liabilities, and shareholders' equity employs essentially the same techniques, whether in a manufacturing company or a service company.

Budgeting in service companies warrants special comment for several reasons. To begin with, service companies are beginning to account for a much larger share of the gross national product than before.[1] One writer states that in the 1980–1981 time period, 72 percent of all Americans were employed in services; in terms of gross national product, about 65 percent was represented by service. Then, too, many manufacturing companies have entered or are entering the service business in those circumstances where there is a natural or close relationship between its products and the services it offers. For example, some aerospace companies provide not only hardware (product), but also services in connection with maintenance of the product, or training in its use. Construction companies may build facilities for a customer and subsequently, as a service business, provide for repairs and maintenance of those facilities. These hybrid corporations should be, and often are, aware of budgetary techniques in both the product and service areas.

A second reason for singling out service companies is that many managements in this arena seem to feel that budgeting techniques do not apply. Yet, the growth in size and competition in this industrial segment is forcing the adoption of more business-like methods in the planning and control of the business. Survival demands it.

Finally, although many of the basic budgeting techniques in manufacturing or nonmanufacturing businesses are much the same, the point of empha-

---

[1] James Cook, "So, What's Wrong With A Service Economy?" *Forbes* (Aug. 30, 1982), p. 62.

sis may differ. Since salaries and wages, and related fringe benefit costs, are the major element of costs in a service business, more relative effort must be expended in seeing that these human resources are effectively marshalled and controlled. Also, whereas receivables and inventories are two current asset areas for planning and control emphasis in a manufacturing company, most service companies regard only receivables as an important current asset. So emphasis on points of cost control and specific balance sheet items may shift as between the two industrial segments. The fundamental procedures, however, are the same.

THE SAME BASICS

For the growing number of medium-sized to large service companies instituting budgetary systems, the following pattern is observed. It is essentially the same as that discussed earlier in this text.

- A profit goal or target for the company is established by the chief executive officer (CEO).
- Following the principles of responsibility accounting and reporting (see Chapter 2), an annual plan is developed that indicates expected revenues and expenses by organizational segments and in total, and by month.
- The cash budget is established.
- A planned statement of financial position is developed and tested against selected standards.
- Actual performance is measured against plan by specific levels of management position. This involves sales, costs and expenses, assets, liabilities, and shareholders' equity.
- Corrective action is taken as deemed necessary.

Each service industry is organized somewhat differently in recognition of the basic mode of operation required, and the significant features or aspects that must be monitored to achieve the plan. These conditions, varying by industry and company, must be taken into account in developing the planning and control system.

In this chapter, brief descriptions of the planning procedure and the related control mechanisms are provided and discussed for a small- to medium-sized company in each of two service fields: an insurance brokerage company, and a firm of architects and engineers. There are some similarities between the two, despite the different industries.

AN ILLUSTRATIVE INSURANCE BROKERAGE BUSINESS

Nature of the Business

Income in the insurance brokerage business may be generated by

- ☐ Commissions through the sale of insurance policies in various risk fields: property, casualty, and marine; group life insurance and other ordinary life policies; health and medical care.
- ☐ Actuarial fees for the performance of actuarial services, with reference to retirement plans, for example.
- ☐ Fees and/or commissions earned through the installation of various employee benefit systems.
- ☐ Fees or commissions for claims processing services for corporations relating to health and medical plans or other similar types of plans.
- ☐ Fees or commissions earned as an insurance consultant for performing various analytical services related to types of contract clauses regarding insurance matters (e.g., self insurance, excess insurance).

Offsetting this operating income are the necessary operating expenses, a vast share of which relate to personnel: salaries and wages, incentive pay, travel expense, occupancy expense, sales promotion expense, and employee fringe benefit costs, to name a few.

The objectives generally are to generate sufficient income and to maintain personnel levels and related costs within acceptable limits compared to the income expected to be received.

The Budgeting Process

Some comments on the budgetary system recently adopted for an insurance brokerage business are outlined below in conjunction with the instructions issued by the management.

Basically, the planning cycle commences in October of each year, at the field offices; the consolidated plan is completed by top management and submitted to the board of directors at either the December or January meeting. When the plan is approved, the actual results of the prior year are known and are incorporated in the reporting process for comparative purposes. Thereafter, monthly comparisons of actual and planned activity, together with a quarterly updating of the expectations, is prepared.

The general instructions showing the segments of the process are reflected in Figure 31-1.

(*text continues on page 31-8*)

FIG. 31-1   General Financial Planning and Budgeting Instructions — An Insurance Brokerage Business

FINANCIAL PLANNING AND BUDGETING

The role that good planning and budgeting play in the management of a business is best understood when related to the fundamentals of management. The key elements in the management process are:

- Planning
- Execution
- Control

Management must plan its activities in advance, carry out the plan, and institute appropriate techniques of observation and reporting to ensure that any deviations from the plan are properly analyzed and handled.

Budgeting is a *planning* and *control* system, not a financial function performed entirely by accountants or bookkeepers. Also, budgeting is not forecasting — if by that we mean predicting the outcome of events rather than *planning* for a result and exercising *controls* to maximize the chances of achieving that result.

Budgeting is an important component of the management information system. Budgeting (profit planning) is the one basic system that integrates all operational plans to express the financial results and economic performance of the business. This information is the central factor in the company's management information system because the total financial consequences, resulting from the sum of all operating plans, are the final measure of economic performance.

The technique of management by objectives (MBO) is closely related to the budgetary planning and control system. The planning and budgeting system plays a critical role in integrating the establishment of objectives and measurement of performance against these objectives, at specific levels of management position and responsibility.

THE COMPANY'S PLANNING AND BUDGETING PROCESS
The company's planning and budgeting process is comprised of the following components:

- A two-year financial planning cycle — present year projections and the next year's plan.
- A business plan.
- Monthly budgets prepared by each unit, including departmental budgets. (See Section 4 [*omitted*].)
- Quarterly forecasting. (Updating the current year's budget by forecasting the balance of the year on a quarterly basis.)

(*continued*)

FIG. 31-1   General Financial Planning and Budgeting Instructions — An Insurance Brokerage Business (cont'd)

The main component of the planning and budgeting process is the Business Plan. It consists of a short Executive Summary and a condensed Business Plan as outlined below.

EXECUTIVE SUMMARY
The Executive Summary comprises the following:

- Financial highlights
- Management priorities

BUSINESS PLAN
The unit outlines its Business Plan, covering the following areas:

- Production plan
- Operations
- Personnel
- Credit and collection/cash management
- Major expenditures
- Other factors

In December, the Executive Committee reviews the Business Plans submitted and establishes goals for the year. Monthly departmental budgets, reflecting these goals, are then prepared and forwarded to Corporate Finance.

COMPONENTS OF BUSINESS PLAN SUBMITTAL

The outline of the Business Plan shown on the following pages is not necessarily all inclusive. Each unit will include those topics and areas which are relevant to its operation. The Plan should be as concise and condensed as possible, and should include an Executive Summary and Detailed Business Plan as described below.

1. Executive Summary:
   ☐ *Financial highlights:*
   - Compare the present year's projections with the present year's budget. Explain any major variances.
   - Compare next year's plan with the present year's projections, highlighting any major changes.

☐ *Management priorities*. Describe the major management priorities for the next year which the unit must achieve or implement to:
- Meet that year's established objectives.
- Plan future strategy.

2. Detailed Business Plan:

☐ *Production plan*. Discuss the production management plans for the year, covering the following areas:
- Geographic territory coverage
- Target accounts and/or market area for special focus
- Source of business, major lines and classes
- New product sales efforts
- Market conditions — hard/soft
- Impact of competition
- Sales Development Programs, including:
  a. Training and development programs
  b. Utilization of PACE II system
  c. Promotional plans and strategies
- Pricing, e.g., commissions, fees

☐ *Operations*. Comment on the operational setup of the office, including:
- Quality of customer service
- Operating efficiency, including level of productivity
- Adequacy of space/equipment, including plans and programs for facility expansion and upgrading of equipment
- Quality and adequacy of audit and security controls
- Rationale for overall budget

☐ *Personnel*. Indicate personnel requirements, including:
- Type and number of staff needed to meet office's needs
- Personnel training and development programs
- Affirmative Action plans
- Rationale for salary expense

☐ *Credit and collection/cash management*. Comment on the current Accounts Receivable Management performance (including Days Sales Outstanding/Days Payable Outstanding and delinquency) and objectives for the year. Briefly outline management plans and programs in these areas.

(continued)

FIG. 31-1   General Financial Planning and Budgeting Instructions — An Insurance Brokerage Business (cont'd)

☐ *Plans for major expenditures.* Briefly outline plans for any major expenditures. Include:

- Merger/acquisition negotiations. Comment on talks in progress or future possibilities which might enter into the planning process. Indicate specific target companies if known.
- Expansion of space or requirements for new facilities.
- Additional equipment/furniture purchases.
- Promotional activities, including advertising and public relations campaigns.

☐ *Other factors:*

- Summarize local economy, addressing items which will affect the unit. Comment on those assumptions for the future which are to be utilized in the plan.
- Comment on plans to increase utilization of other services for the development of new and/or increased business.
- Pinpoint key/problem offices in region, including a status summary. (Regional management only.)
- Include comments on other factors as appropriate.

3. Planning/Budgeting Input Form (FP-1):

The Planning/Budgeting computer input form is the source document used to enter the figures into the planning system in November. It is used by the offices and corporate departments to enter the annual present year's projections and the next year's plan amounts.

The detailed instructions of what must be included in the business plan are shown in Figures 31-2 and 31-3.

In this service business, it is to be noted that the organizational segments (the profit centers) estimate each category of operating income by its two components: (1) that from the *existing* or established business, and (2) that from *new* business and additional business from existing customers. Thus, property, casualty, and marine (PC&M) planned operating income is estimated by

$$PC\&M = \text{Established plus}$$
$$\text{Additional plus}$$
$$\text{New}$$

Similarly, revenues from group insurance are segregated into planned income from established accounts and income from new accounts. Thus, the additional business that must be secured to support the planned staff is

FIG. 31-2 Components of the Business Plan

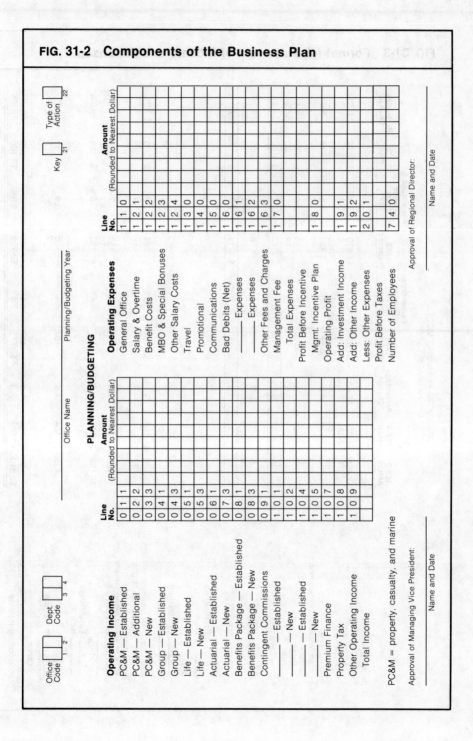

FIG. 31-3 Format for Statement of Income and Expenses

FINANCIAL PLANNING MODEL
OPERATING INCOME

	19X-2 Actual	19X-1 Actual	Percentage Change	19XX Budget	Percentage Change From 19X-1	19XX Projected	Percentage Change From 19X1	Plan	Percentage Change
Operating income									
Property, casualty & marine									
Established	$1,451	$1,678	15.6%	$1,818	8.3%	$1,810	7.9%	$1,970	8.8%
Additional	378	386	2.1	394	2.1	354	8.3–	360	1.7
New	158	165	4.4	178	7.9	165		200	21.2
Subtotal PCM	1,987	2,229	12.2	2,390	7.2	2,329	4.5	2,530	8.6
Human resource management									
Group									
Established	107	118	10.3	130	10.2	134	13.6	160	19.4
New	18	19	5.6	19		19		30	57.9
Total group	$ 125	$ 137	9.6%	$ 149	8.8%	$ 153	11.7%	$ 190	24.2%
Life									
Established	5	6	20.0	6		6		5	16.7–
New	9	9		6	33.3–	5	44.4–	20	300.0
Total life	$ 14	$ 15	7.1%	$ 12	20.0–%	$ 11	26.7–%	$ 25	127.3%
Actuarial Established									
New									
Total actuarial									
Other Established									
New									
Total									
Subtotal human resource management	$ 139	$ 152	9.4%	$ 161	5.9%	$ 164	7.9%	$ 225	37.2%
contingent commissions	46	52	13.0	57	9.6	70	34.6	75	7.1
Other operating income									
Risk analysis management group									
Established	128	142	10.9	155	9.2	153	7.7	160	4.6
New	10	12	20.0	12		10	16.7–	35	250.0
Total	$ 138	$ 156	11.6%	$ 167	8.4%	$ 163	5.8%	$ 195	19.6%
Established								40	
New								40	
Subtotal	138	154	11.6	167	8.4	163	5.8	235	44.2
Premium finance						2		5	150.0
Property tax								20	
Other								10	
Subtotal other operating income	138	154	11.6	167	8.4	165	7.1	270	63.6
Total operating income	$2,310	$2,587	12.0	$2,775	7.3	$2,728	5.5	$3,100	13.6

FINANCIAL PLANNING MODEL
OPERATING EXPENSES THROUGH
PROFIT BEFORE TAX

Operating expenses	19X-2 Actual	19X-1 Actual	Percentage Change	19XX Budget	Percentage Change From 19X-1	19XX Projected	Percentage Change From 19X-1	19X1 Plan	Percentage Change
General office	$ 67	$ 78	16.4%	$ 94	20.5%	$ 90	15.4%	$ 100	11.1%
Salaries									
Salary & overtime	685	767	12.0	860	12.1	830	8.2	1,020	22.9
Benefit costs	151	176	16.6	206	17.0	199	13.1	237	19.1
MBO & special bonuses	30	35	16.7	35		25	28.6–	30	20.0
Other salary costs	12	5	58.3–	9	80.0	5		8	60.0
Total salaries	$ 878	$ 983	12.0%	$1,110	12.9%	$1,059	7.7%	$1,295	22.3%
Travel	44	45	2.3	53	17.8	46	2.2	55	19.6
Promotional	30	31	3.3	35	12.9	28	9.7–	46	64.3
Communications	29	32	10.3	37	15.6	35	9.4	38	8.6
Other fees & charges									
Bad debts (net)	24	40	66.7	12	70.0–	34	15.0–	14	58.8
Expenses	11	5	54.5–	15	200.0	8	60.0	18	125.0
Other				10				20	
Expenses	2	2		2		6	200.0	3	50.0–
Total other fees & charges	37	47	27.0	39	17.0–	48	2.1	55	14.6
Management fee	139	155	11.5	167	7.7	167	7.7	186	11.4
Total operating expenses	$1,224	$1,371	12.0%	$1,535	12.0%	$1,473	7.4%	$1,775	20.5%
Profit before incentive	1,086	1,216	12.0	1,240	2.0	1,255	3.2	1,325	5.6
Management incentive									
Operating profit	1,086	1,216	12.0	1,240	2.0	1,255	3.2	1,325	5.6
Other income (add)									
Investment income									
Other									
Total other income									
Other expenses (less)									
profit before taxes	$1,086	$1,216		$1,240		$1,255		$1,325	

FIG. 31-4   Summarized Income and Expense Plan — Format

FINANCIAL PLANNING MODEL SUMMARY

	19X-2 Actual	19X-1 Actual	Percentage Change	19XX Budget	Percentage Change From 19X-1	19XX Projected	Percentage Change From 19X-1	19X1 Plan	Percentage Change
Total operating income	$ 2,310	$ 2,587	12.0%	$ 2,775	7.3%	$ 2,728	5.5%	$ 3,100	13.6
Total operating expense	1,224	1,371	12.0	1,555	12.0	1,473	7.4	1,775	20.5
Profit before incentive	1,086	1,216	12.0	1,240	2.0	1,255	3.2	1,325	5.6
Management incentive									
Operating profit	1,086	1,216	12.0	1,240	2.0	1,255	3.2	1,325	5.6
Add: Other income									
Less: Other expense									
Profit before taxes	$ 1,086	$ 1,216	12.0%	$ 1,240	2.0%	$ 1,255	3.2%	$ 1,325	5.6%
Statistical data									
Percentage of new PCM to total PCM	8.0%	7.4%		7.4%		7.1%		7.9%	
Percentage of Class 1 PCM to prior year total PCM		84.4		81.6		81.2		84.6	
Percentage of new HRM to total HRM	19.4%	18.4%		15.5%		14.6%		26.7%	
General office ratio	2.9	3.0		3.4		3.3		3.2	
Travel & promotional ratio	3.2	2.9		3.2		3.3		3.3	
Communication ratio	1.3	1.2		1.3		1.3		1.2	
Salary ratio	38.0	38.0		40.0		38.8		41.8	
Operating ratio	53.0	53.0		55.3		54.0		57.3	
Pre-tax profit margin	47.0%	47.0%		44.7%		46.0%		42.7%	
Per employee statistics									
Number of employees at 12–31	41	42	2.4%	45	7.1%	43	2.4%	47	9.3%
Total operating income	$56,341	$61,595	9.3	61,667	.1	63,442	3.0	65,957	4.0
Salaries (including benefits)	21,415	23,405	9.3	24,667	3.4	24,628	5.2	27,553	11.9
Operating profit	$26,488	$28,952	9.3%	$27,556	4.8–%	$29,186	.8%	$28,191	3.4–%

identified, and the detail plans "spell out" how, when, and where the new revenue is to be gathered (the tactics).

Figure 31-4 shows the format for the summarized income and expense segment of the plan. It is to be observed that several key ratios are used to judge the plan, including some that highlight the salary and wage expense:

- Percentage of *new* business to total business for each segment
- Salary ratio
- Selected expense ratios
- Per-employee statistics

The computer input form shown in Figure 31-5 is the source document for the budget figures provided the director of budgets. It is, in fact, an oversized sheet, 18½″ × 13½″, to accommodate monthly and annual figures.

Instructions relative to departmental budgets are presented in Figure 31-6, wherein the two types of departments are identified: (1) *profit centers,* representing a "group of people involved in an activity accountable for income and responsible for related expenses," and (2) *cost centers,* representing a "department which is organized to provide services to other profit and/or cost centers."

The attached exhibits illustrate the *planning* sequence and forms. From the *control* viewpoint, as the year progresses, the usual comparison of plan and actual figures is presented for whatever action is deemed necessary by the management.

AN ILLUSTRATIVE ARCHITECTURAL / ENGINEERING BUSINESS

Nature of the Business

An architectural/engineering firm normally will generate income through designing new buildings or complexes, or modifications thereof, for the owners. It will often provide specifications and blueprints to a general contractor, who will do the actual construction. Sometimes the architectural firm will undertake to do the entire construction job and return over a completed building. In other cases, such a company will "manage" or supervise the construction project for a fee. Technically, architectural/engineering firms may perform a job at specified rates per hour for each grade of professional service. In some cases, a job may be managed for a fixed fee or for a percentage of cost. In other instances, the firm will provide the services on a "turn-key" basis, that is, a fixed price is charged for completion of the building.

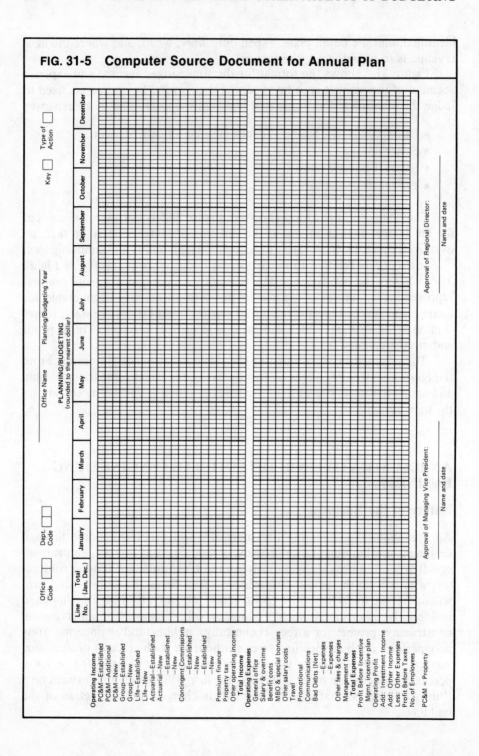

FIG. 31-5 Computer Source Document for Annual Plan

FIG. 31-6 Departmental Budget Instructions

The budget and reporting system allows the office to exercise greater control over its operations through departmental budgeting. Budgets are prepared by department, and operating statements, comparing actual results with budgeted amounts, are produced monthly for each department. Departmental budgeting is recommended, particularly for larger offices, to assist managers with control of their operations on an ongoing basis.

Effective with the 19XX budget, all offices must submit departmental budgets for at least the following minimum breakdown:

- All HRM income and expense
- All other income and expense

Offices submitting budgets for all departments must identify those departments used by HRM.

OFFICE ORGANIZATION:

In order to produce departmental operating statements which provide the office with meaningful information, the office should:

- Prepare an organization chart which defines responsibility and lines of authority.
- Establish departments in accordance with this chart.

Generally, there are two types of departments:

- *Profit Centers.* A department or group of people involved in an activity which is accountable for income and responsible for related expenses. Example: Personal Accounts Department
- *Cost Centers.* A department which is organized to provide services to other profit and/or cost centers. This department accumulates expenses but generates no income. Example: Accounting Department

DEPARTMENTAL BUDGETING AND RESPONSIBILITY REPORTING:

It is recommended that departmental budgeting follow the concept of responsibility reporting, i.e., managers of departments should be held responsible only for those expenditures and income over which they have control. This type of budget will include direct expenses only (primarily salary, travel, and promotional). Indirect expenses (generally allocated among various departments), such as general office and communications expenses, will be budgeted in and charged to a separate "overhead" department. Also, the expense allocation of the various cost centers is excluded from departmental budgets.

Therefore, the budget and actual operating results of a profit center will represent the direct profit contribution of the unit before the addition of office overhead and allocated expenses from the cost center. Cost center budgets and operating results will represent direct departmental expenses only.

While the above is the recommended approach, departmental budgets which include direct and indirect expenses may be prepared. To facilitate this type of budgeting, general indirect expenses, such as general office and communications

(continued)

FIG. 31-6   Departmental Budget Instructions (cont'd)

---

expenses, can be allocated to each department under the "99 Allocation" method. This method is described more fully in the Accounting Manual.

Additionally, cost center expenses can be charged to the profit centers through the establishment of a local office management fee. This local office management fee is added to the corporate management fee of each profit center's budget, and a credit for the total is budgeted in a separate department. This credit eliminates the local office management fee and nets the management fee for the office to 6% (corporate management fee), excluding any regional management fee based on revenues.

The above procedure allows each profit center to budget for its portion of the cost center expenses, and at the same time provides each cost center department with a budget by which its performance can be measured. Additionally, the profit center will be charged only for the budgeted amount of the cost center's expenses, since the local office management fee charged to the profit center will be based on the budgeted amount. Therefore, the profit center will be neither penalized nor rewarded for the variances of any cost center department's expenses.

Ordinarily, jobs are handled on a project or program basis. Thus, the costs are estimated in great detail for the planning phase of the budgeting system. The control phase consists of monitoring the costs against plan, continuously updating the cost to complete the project, including adjustments in costs resulting from owner-directed contract changes (with proper modification of the sales price, if the contract is a fixed-price fee job).

In addition to planning and controlling the job costs, other operating costs must be planned and kept within limits. In general, enough business income must be generated to cover the cost of the personnel force, professional and other, together with related overhead.

Steps in Planning and Control

The budgeting process in a typical architectural/engineering firm may be summarized as follows:

1. A target operating profit or net income is established by the CEO for the planning year. It may be stated as a total amount, representing a percentage return on shareholders' equity, or perhaps as an increase over the prior year. In any event, the completed business plan should reflect this goal — if it can be reasonably attained.

2. Total revenues (sales) are estimated. This is based on two segments:

   a. The revenue expected from existing jobs or contracts in hand is determined. This requires a detailed calculation of expected revenue from each

contract. Each segment, element, or function of the job must be estimated. This often is done by pricing the man-days required on each
function for each job. A sample estimating sheet for architectural services, in the design department, is shown in Figure 31-7.

b. The estimate of sales revenue expected from jobs not yet in hand,
together with a listing of the likely prospects and the contract value of
each, is prepared. Often, the revenue is derived from the company standard operating ratio for its type of business. For example, assume the
target operating profit is $17,800,000, and is expected to be procured as
follows:

Present business	$13,700,000
New business	4,100,000
Target	$17,800,000

If the typical operating margin is 8 percent, then the segment of revenue
from new business must equal $51,250,000 ($4,100,000 ÷ .08).

3. The budgeted costs and expenses by job (or contract) and by department, as
applicable, are determined. The contract sales and direct contract costs are a
point of control. The expenses of the service department are a second point
of control, to be maintained within the limits of the planned or available gross
margin. The principle of responsibility accounting and reporting is followed
in preparing the data.

It is quite usual to estimate jobs using standard rates per hours, which
include related fringe benefit costs, and a profit. Departmental budget "per
diem values" must be coordinated with each contract job. Thus, the planned
total annual man-hours of a department servicing a project (a job) must be
reconciled with the man-hours estimated for each job and in total for the
planned period. Accordingly, the departmental per diem charges making up
the budget for Department 12 in Figure 31-8, will be charged to specific
contract work planned, job by job. A key to effective operations is keeping
the staff fully occupied on chargeable jobs.

Estimated contract job costs, including the per diem charges, are prepared
for each such project, and the project summary becomes a key part of the
plan. See Figure 31-9.

4. When the estimates of costs and expenses are completed, a statement of
estimated income and expenses is prepared and revised until the targeted net
income, or as close as possible, is reached.

5. Upon completion of the operating plan (the statement of income and expense
and related plans), the cash budget and the statement of estimated financial
position can be prepared. Usually, as in most service companies, the accounts receivable will represent the largest single asset, with fixed assets
investment being quite limited (furniture and equipment, mostly). Accordingly, the bulk of the transactions in the balance sheet area will represent

FIG. 31-7 Job Estimate — Design Function

N. ARCHITECTURAL SYSTEMS INC.

JOB ESTIMATE

Contract: S. Engineering Building

Area	Man-Days					Per Division Value
	Partner	Manager	Supervisor	Senior	Junior	
Garage	.5	1.0	3.0	6.0	14.0	$ 4,900
Basement	1.0	2.0	2.0	4.0	12.0	5,000
1st floor	2.0	3.0	4.0	7.0	21.0	8,900
Lobby area	2.0	4.0	3.0	5.0	25.0	9,100
2nd floor	1.0	2.0	3.0	5.0	10.0	5,400
3rd floor	—	—	1.0	2.0	10.0	1,800
4th floor	—	—	1.0	2.0	10.0	1,800
Tennis courts	1.0	.5	1.0	4.0	8.0	3,300
Roof — Other	.5	.5	.5	2.0	5.0	1,400
Site plan	.5	1.0	2.0	2.0	6.0	2,900
Core samplings	—	1.0	1.0	1.0	4.0	1,600
Interior sketches	3.0	6.0	9.0	12.0	12.0	13,800
General review	5.0	7.0	6.0	4.0	5.0	12,900
Total	16.0	28.0	36.5	56.0	142.0	$72,800
Per diem rate	$ 1,000	$ 600	$ 400	$ 200	$ 100	
Total	$16,000	$16,800	$14,600	$11,200	$14,200	

FIG. 31-8 Planned Staff Level, Manhours and Charges

ARCHITECTS AND ENGINEERS, INC.

PLANNED STAFF AND PER DIEM CHARGES

For the Plan Year 19XX

Department No. 12

Name	Total Planned Hours (1)	Non-Working Paid Hours (2)	Available Hours (3) (1) − (2)	Planned Chargeable Time (%) (4)	Chargeable Hours (5) (3) × (4)	Cost Category (6)	Hourly Cost Rate (7)	Total Standard Cost (8) (5) × (7)	Hourly Per Diem Rate (9)	Estimated Billing Value (10) (5) × (9)
A. Johnson	2,080	184	1,896	70%	1,327	1	$70	$ 92,890	$125	$ 165,875
P. Mallory	2,080	184	1,896	70	1,327	1	70	92,890	125	165,875
C. Copper	2,080	184	1,896	80	1,516	2	60	90,960	115	174,340
F. Stevens	2,080	144	1,936	80	1,548	3	55	85,140	110	170,280
J. Powell	2,080	184	1,896	90	1,516	3	55	83,380	110	170,280
S. Rosen	1,620	144	1,936	90	1,742	4	40	69,680	90	156,780
K. Bedford	1,840	144	1,696	90	1,526	4	40	61,040	90	137,340
New hire	1,040	64	976	90	878	4	40	61,040	90	79,020
New hire	1,040	64	976	90	875	5	35	30,730	70	61,460
New hire	520	32	488	90	439	5	35	15,365	70	30,730
Department Total			15,592	81.4%	12,697			$683,115		$1,311,980

FIG. 31-9 Statement of Estimated Revenues and Costs, by Contract

SCHWAB ARCHITECTS & ENGINEERS, INC.

CONTRACT REVENUES AND COSTS

For the Plan Year 19XX

(dollars in thousands)

Jobs	Contract Value	Estimated Revenue 19XX	Estimated Costs 19XX	Estimated Contract Profit or (Loss)	Planned 19XX Gross Profit		Estimated Completion Date
					Amount	Percentage	
BUSINESS IN HAND							
Architectural — Engineering							
Buck Hotel	$ 14,360	$ 12,100	$ 8,470	$ 4,308	$ 3,630	30.0%	7-XX
Carson Center	8,420	6,930	4,850	2,527	2,080	30.0	5-XX
Daring Hospital	6,010	5,420	4,060	1,508	1,360	25.1	3-XX
Foxhill Civic Center	12,100	9,730	6,325	4,234	3,405	35.0	9-XX
Total	$ 40,890	$ 34,180	$23,705	$12,577	$10,475	30.6%	
Construction Management							
Altoona Mall	$ 4,300	$ 2,820	$ 2,250	$ 870	$ 570	20.2%	1-XX
Beck Building	9,107	7,410	6,300	1,364	1,110	15.0	3-XX
Reardon Complex	7,430	3,100	2,900	(400)	200	6.5	2-XX
Welch Shopping Center	11,310	8,120	8,030	90	90	1.1	3-X1
Total	32,147	21,450	19,480	1,924	1,970	9.2	
Total Business in Hand	$ 73,037	$ 55,630	$43,185	$14,501	$12,445	22.4%	
NEW BUSINESS							
Architectural — Engineering							
Grand Central Bldg.	$ 12,470	$ 9,400	$ 6,110	$ 4,360	$ 3,290	35.0%	3-X1
Hyatt — St. Louis	9,800	6,200	3,720	3,920	2,480	40.0	5-X1
Loomis Sayles Office Complex	14,330	10,600	7,740	3,870	2,860	27.0	2-X1
Manhattan Hotel	10,640	7,450	5,520	2,760	1,930	25.9	4-X1
Pfizer Center	24,760	12,720	9,870	5,550	2,850	22.4	6-X3
Total	$ 72,000	$ 46,370	$32,960	$20,460	$13,410	28.9%	
Construction Management							
Newport Center	$ 27,400	$ 12,800	$ 9,220	$ 7,670	$ 3,580	28.0%	4-X3
Penny Warehouse	4,210	1,500	1,350	420	150	10.0	7-X2
Total	31,610	14,300	10,570	8,090	3,730	26.1	
Total New Business	103,610	60,670	43,530	28,550	17,140	28.3	
Grand Total	$176,647	$116,300	$86,715	$43,051	$29,585	25.4%	

cash, accounts receivable, and current liabilities. However, cash sufficiency and quick and current ratios should be reviewed for acceptability.

When the annual plan is deemed satisfactory by the management, it is presented to the board of directors for approval with appropriate written or oral commentary on the significant aspects.

The following key financial statements usually are presented in comparative form:

a. Statement of Estimated Income and Expense

b. Statement of Estimated Sources and Uses of Cash

c. Statement of Estimated Financial Position

The Statement of Planned Income and Expense might be summarized as to gross margin and overhead costs as illustrated in Figure 31-10.

In a business where service contracts are the foundation of the plan, a supporting schedule by contract, substantially as shown in Figure 31-9, will highlight the principal jobs or projects and the revenue and the expected gross profit from each.

6. As the year progresses, the usual comparative statements of actual and planned sales and expenses should be issued on a responsibility basis, as is done in many manufacturing companies with an acceptable budgetary control system.

Normally, supporting the overall financial comparisons is a contract status report, similar in form to Figure 31-11. It is to be noted that the contract status is continually updated so that management is made aware of the status of each project and the expected change in gross profit.

A NEEDED EXPANSION IN SERVICE COMPANY BUDGETING PROCEDURES

Many service companies long have prepared budgets for the departmental expenses, and have tracked these expenses against plan. However, this is not enough. It can be seen that budgetary control should extend to profit centers, where accountability for revenues as well as costs can be placed. Always key, of course, is keeping personnel costs well within the bounds set for planned revenues, so that net income will result. Especially in service companies, where investment in inventories as well as in plant and equipment typically is relatively small, the planning and control techniques should still extend to the statement of financial position, to the end that acceptable current ratios, debt to equity ratios, and other important ratios are maintained.

FIG. 31-10   Statement of Planned Income and Expense

SCHWAB ARCHITECTS & ENGINEERS, INC.

STATEMENT OF PLANNED INCOME AND EXPENSE

For the Year Ending 12/31/XX

(dollars in thousands)

	Last Year	Present Year (Estimated)	Plan 19XX	Increase (Decrease) In Plan
Revenues				
Contracts in hand	$50,217	$ 54,810	$ 55,630	$ 820
New business	47,312	55,700	60,670	4,970
Total	$97,529	$110,510	$116,300	$5,790
Contract costs				
Direct charges — Standard rates	$55,104	$ 59,123	$ 65,036	$5,913
Other direct charges	18,579	23,315	21,137	(2,178)
Project adjustments	430	710	542	(168)
Total	$74,113	$ 83,148	$ 86,715	3,567
Gross profit — Amount	$23,416	$ 27,362	$ 29,585	$2,223
— Percentage sales	24.01%	24.76%	25.43%	.67%
Overhead costs				
Fringe benefits — Projects	$ 5,510	$ 5,976	$ 6,860	$ 884
Promotional	4,277	5,301	4,500	(801)
Training	210	209	360	151
Lost time	1,020	960	650	(310)
Administrative	3,060	3,490	3,800	310
Finance	1,041	1,106	1,200	94
Occupancy	2,437	2,297	2,400	103
Total — Amount	$17,555	$ 19,339	$ 19,770	$ 431
— Percentage sales	18.00%	17.50%	17.00%	(.50%)
Income before taxes	$ 5,861	$ 8,023	$ 9,815	$1,792
Taxes on income	2,755	3,931	4,515	584
Net income — Amount	$ 3,106	$ 4,092	$ 5,300	$1,208
— Percentage sales	3.18%	3.70%	4.56%	.86%

FIG. 31-11 Contract Status Control Report

SCHWAB ARCHITECTS AND ENGINEERS, INC.

CONTRACT STATUS REPORT

For The Four Months Ended 4/30/XX

(dollars in thousands)

Customer	Estimated Final Contract Value	Cost Incurred			Indicated Final Contract Profit (Loss)		Current Year-Gross Margin		
		Incurred To Date	To Be Incurred	Indicated Final	Total	Change From Prior Report	Booked	To Be Booked	Indicated Final
Buck Hospital	$ 14,370	$ 9,760	$ 292	$ 10,052	$ 4,318	$ 10	$ 3,535	$ 105	$ 3,640
Carson Center	8,420	5,783	110	5,893	2,527	—	2,040	40	2,080
Daring Hospital	6,010	4,502	—	4,502	1,508	—	1,360	—	1,360
Foxhill Civic Center	12,300	5,880	2,120	8,000	4,300	66	1,520	1,951	3,471
Altoona Mall	4,300	3,430	—	3,430	870	—	570	—	570
Beck Building	9,150	7,780	—	7,780	1,370	6	1,118	—	1,118
Reardon Complex	7,430	7,830	—	7,830	(400)	—	200	—	200
Welch Shopping Center	11,500	6,510	4,800	11,310	190	100	30	60	90
Grand Central Bldg.	12,470	6,120	1,990	8,110	4,360	—	1,840	1,450	3,290
Hyatt St. Louis	9,800	5,520	360	5,880	3,920	—	2,240	240	2,480
Loomis Sayles Office Complex	14,350	6,470	4,000	10,470	3,880	10	1,040	1,830	2,870
Manhattan Hotel	10,640	5,600	2,280	7,880	2,760	—	640	1,290	1,930
Pfizer Center	24,800	5,800	13,420	19,220	5,580	30	950	1,910	2,860
Newport Center	27,400	2,340	18,110	20,450	6,950	(720)	790	2,070	2,860
Penny Warehouse	4,200	330	3,445	3,775	425	5	30	125	155
Stockton Hotel (new and unplanned)	12,700	6,220	4,890	11,110	1,590	1,590	500	400	900
Total	$189,840	$89,875	$55,817	$145,692	$44,148	$1,097	$18,403	$11,471	$29,874

32

Profit Improvement Programs and the Budget

WHAT IS A PROFIT IMPROVEMENT PROGRAM?

What is a profit improvement program (PIP)? It may be defined as an organized effort to review internal operations with the objective of securing increased efficiency and economy. Some might call it a cost reduction program, although, technically, the scope might in fact extend to margin improvement brought about by product redesign and a higher selling price. However, the sphere of emphasis is usually located in internal operations. Decisions can be made on changing methods so as to improve profits or to increase a return on assets without undue concern for their acceptability by persons outside of the organization. Further, in most instances the subject matter would involve middle management without obtaining the concurrence of top management, in that company policy, objectives, markets, products, or major facilities usually need not be modified. However, if opportunities arise that would involve top management and related policy matters, then they should be considered.

WHY ARE PROFIT IMPROVEMENT
PROGRAMS NEEDED?

If a company has adopted, and is effectively implementing, a sound planning and control system, such as budgetary control or use of standards as discussed in this text, then why should a separate formal effort be required to improve efficiency, to reduce costs, or to increase net income? The fact is that most companies will find it necessary to periodically introduce a PIP. This is entirely consistent with good management practices and is, indeed, good budgetary control. For many reasons, costs do get out of line. In a time of growth, organizations and functions are deemed desirable that, in times of adversity, in "lean" periods, simply appear unnecessary. Even though flexible budgeting, and the planning of costs to stay well within revenue levels, may be a part of management's philosophy, there are many instances when costs do get out of line. That is to say, they are not reduced as much as might be prudent. After all, many budgets are set on past experience, without considering the real need for a given activity. So, when companies experience severe volume changes, major product changes, great seasonality, and declining margins, a periodic reappraisal of operations may be necessary. Some managements plan on drastic pruning or major cost reduction efforts in every recession, or in every few years. The fact is that management's concern with day-to-day operations does not permit a review to reduce costs unless a formal effort is undertaken. Operations periodically must be adapted, through special studies, to changing conditions.

STEPS IN A PROFIT IMPROVEMENT PROGRAM

How a PIP should be initiated in a particular firm will depend on the specific circumstances: the urgency or extent of the need, the management style, the organization's structure, and the status of other planning and control techniques, to name a few. In those cases where a history of reasonably acceptable controls exists, where the company is largely decentralized, and where management (and especially the financial arm) has some sense of where excess costs exist, or where trends are poor, and where no permanent group is available to undertake cost reduction efforts on a full-time basis, these steps are suggested as a means of motivating the managers:

1. Establish some profit improvement objectives for the profit center, or division or subsidiary.
2. Identify some priority study areas, those that may have the greatest potential for yield or improvement.
3. Schedule and plan the reviews.
4. Select the participants, using a task force approach.
5. Conduct the review.
6. Discuss with the appropriate level of management the tentative recommendations.
7. Where appropriate, conduct greater in-depth analyses in order to be certain about the cost savings, impact, and practicality of the recommendations.
8. Implement the approved recommendations.
9. Monitor progress in reaching the objectives.

Obviously, some of these steps are interrelated, and comments on several facets are made below.

Setting Objectives

By review of competitive data and past expense trends in the various functions, a sense of cost growth can be secured. For this purpose, of course, it is the *controllable* costs that should govern. By compiling the trend of such expenses, and perhaps a head-count of the functions over a period of three or four years, it can be determined *where* the areas of greatest costs exist. The extent of cost growth also can be determined. On this basis, a target or goal for cost reduction in each area or function can be set and accumulated, in order to arrive at an objective for the profit center.

Identifying Priority Areas

Knowledge about the nature of operations and the business, together with a rather quick perusal of the levels of costs being incurred, will provide some sense of the potential of the functions for cost reduction. While all areas may be asked for *some* reductions, priorities should be set for achieving the maximum reductions in the shortest period of time. To this end, the priority schedule should consider these factors:

- Magnitude of potential improvement
- Relative ease of accomplishment
- Need or importance of the function itself
- Transferability of improvements to other functions/units/areas

The end product should be an inventory of possible studies for each function or unit and a cost reduction or profit improvement objective.

Scheduling the Reviews

Usually overall profit center or company goals are established, together with individual departmental goals. Then, each team sets target dates for the component reviews each will make. A sample of a division schedule illustrating the rapid pace of operations (it is not a long, drawn-out affair) is shown in Figure 32-1. A more complete schedule for an entire division, which provides the detailed profit improvement goals, the working days deemed necessary, team composition, and the schedule for starting each study and submitting a report, is illustrated in Figure 32-2.

Selecting the Participants

The composition of the team is critical to the success in meeting the profit improvement objective. Usually, the team members should be designated by the management of the division or department to be reviewed. This enlists management's support, since the study is theirs. The manager, in selecting the team members, also designates the study area, sets the improvement goals, and places responsibility for results.

Key components of the profit improvement team include the following.

☐ The *team leader* for each study — who must train the team and direct the study.

FIG. 32-1   Division Profit Improvement Study Schedule

THE JOHNSEN COMPANY
ELECTRICAL DIVISION

PROFIT IMPROVEMENT SCHEDULE

Function	Responsibility	Timetable
Establish division goals	Division General Manager	July 10
Approve division goals	Chairman	July — 2nd week
Establish department goals		July 21
Select first division team		July 26
Orient first division team		August 2
Schedule study by first division team	Division General Manager	August 2
Select second division team		August 9
Orient second division team		August 14
Schedule study of second division team		August 14
Review recommendations of first division team		August 22
Commence implementing recommendations of first division team	Department Manager	September 1

□ A *program coordinator* from perhaps both the corporate office and the division headquarters — who can provide ideas as to actions by other teams, or other divisions; can secure analytical information; and can summarize results and report on progress. A position description of a program coordinator for a chemical company, taken from the profit improvement manual, is presented in Figure 32-3.

□ The *proper mix* of members, in order to secure varied and broad viewpoints. A team may normally be composed of three to six people, including:
   • One from the area being studied
   • One from the financial discipline and who knows the procedures and significance of the data
   • A functional specialist
   • Others from other areas scheduled for study (cross fertilization), or areas in some way affecting or affected by the department under study

FIG. 32-2   Program Schedule for the Division

SAMPLE PROGRAM SCHEDULE

Area Studied	Total Controllable Expenses in Area Studied ($000)	Profit Improvement Goal per Year ($000)	Goal as Percent of Total	Proposed Timing			Proposed Manpower Assignments	
				Start Study	Estimated Working Days	Report Submitted	Team Leader	Team Members
A	$ 1,000	$ 150	15%	February 1	50	April 12	ABC	DEF, GHI, JKL
B	1,500	200	15	April 12	35	June 1	MNO	PQR, STU, VWX
C	500	125	25	April 12	35	June 1		
D	100	20	20	May 25	30	July 2		
E	500	75	15	June 7	30	July 16		
F	500	75	15	July 6	30	August 13		
G	2,000	300	15	August 2	30	September 10		
H	300	45	15	August 30	35	October 15		
I	700	140	20	September 13	30	October 15		
J	4,000	400	10	October 18	40	December 10		
Totals	$11,100	$1,530	14%					

FIG. 32-3   Position Description — PIP Coordinator

BASIC FUNCTION:
The PIP coordinator is primarily responsible for planning and supervising profit improvement studies within his department. In addition, he is responsible for guiding the implementation of study recommendations to ensure that identified savings opportunities are realized.

SPECIFIC DUTIES AND WORKING RELATIONSHIPS:
Within approved limits of authority and company policy, the PIP coordinator is responsible to the department manager for carrying out the duties and relationships set forth below:

1. Recommends studies to be undertaken based on an evaluation of savings potential, overall value to Chemicon and the ease with which savings can be achieved. Assigns priorities to studies using the stated criteria.

2. Works with the department manager to set ambitious savings goals for each study.

3. Selects and trains study team members, with particular emphasis on those who can contribute materially to the study effort, can help to implement the team's recommendations, and can benefit from the experience.
   a. Indoctrinates team members in the purpose and objectives of the PIP program and the specific study.
   b. Provides specific training in fact-finding, analysis and other study techniques.

4. Assists the team in writing the preliminary study plan, ensuring that the plan is sound and that all relevant tasks are included.
   a. Ensures that the plan is targeted toward the study objectives and that a reasonable timetable has been established for conducting the study.
   b. Reviews the plan with appropriate supervisory personnel to ensure its completeness and feasibility.

5. Monitors the fact-finding phase of all PIP studies to ensure that the team develops adequate, useful, and accurate information. Reviews sources of information to ensure that supervisors and other appropriate personnel are contacted.

6. Reviews the team's work planning and scheduling summary sheet to ensure that all ideas are being considered and that all savings opportunities have been identified. Helps the team to develop a sound analytical approach.

7. Reviews an outline of the team's report to ensure that it is accurate and complete.
   a. Analyzes recommendations to ensure that they are practical and that they will meet the savings objectives.
   b. Ensures that the report contains an action plan which includes specific responsibility assignments and time schedules.
   c. Ensures that recommendations are supported by adequate controls.

8. Assists the team in preparing a study abstract and an edited summary sheet to serve as an index for the working papers.

(continued)

FIG. 32-3   Position Description — PIP Coordinator (cont'd)

9. Reviews a final draft of the report with department management to secure concurrence with recommendations and action plan. Negotiates modifications as required.

10. Assists line supervisors in the implementation of recommendations.
    a. Checks periodically with responsible supervisors at all levels to be sure that implementation schedules are being met.
    b. Reviews implementation problems with appropriate managers to seek satisfactory solutions.
    c. Maintains a current file of working papers to assist in solving implementation problems.

11. Publishes periodic progress reports on all PIP study activities for appropriate management personnel.
    a. Issues a monthly savings summary to the department manager, comparing savings achieved against savings identified.
    b. Issues a program progress summary at the completion of each study.
    c. Releases a biannual report of the studies scheduled during the next 12 months.

12. Maintains close working relationships with team leaders and coordinates activities of various study teams within the department.

13. Provides liaison between department management and study teams. Participates in all observer sessions.

14. Maintains contact with his counterparts in other departments by exchanging project abstracts and other pertinent data.

Planning the Review

When the task force has been selected, the study must be planned and scheduled. As in any review of this type, these steps are important:

☐ All members of the team should be familiarized with the study area
☐ Study plans should be prepared for both preliminary and final phases, including:
  • Objectives
  • Analytical methods to be used
  • Specific tasks to be undertaken
  • Target dates for various milestones of the study and for completion
  • Analysis of results
  • Implementation plans

☐ The project should be discussed in detail with the employees of the department to be reviewed in order to:
  - Dispel apprehensions (showing need to grow, new programs possible, and other factors)
  - Exchange ideas and information
  - Secure cooperation, or at least absence of a critical attitude

Conducting the Review

In a cost reduction type of study, the usual procedure is as follows:

1. Gather the facts:
   - Secure specific information to permit the drawing of sound conclusions
   - Eliminate redundant fact-finding
   - Minimize the necessary facts, i.e., gather the basics, and tend to avoid insignificant details
   - Document the data
2. Identify and select the more important profit improvement alternatives
3. Investigate those selected, including discussion with employees
4. Test the recommendations
5. Prepare a brief report, and review recommendations with management

Implementing and Monitoring the Improvements

The departmental management should initiate the improvements using appropriate priorities and a schedule.

The coordinator might be the person best suited to monitor and report progress. He could also suggest similar implementation in other areas.

Some of these follow-up aspects are discussed in later chapters.

REPORTING PROGRESS

Any number of ways may be used to report progress in profit improvement programs. Two graphic methods are illustrated in Figures 32-4 and 32-5. Figure 32-4 charts the target and actual identified savings for a particular unit. Each individual study is included in the target savings, and each is tracked and charted, when completed. Figure 32-5 is a summary chart, showing, by month, the total accumulated actual versus targeted savings for all studies of the division or subsidiary.

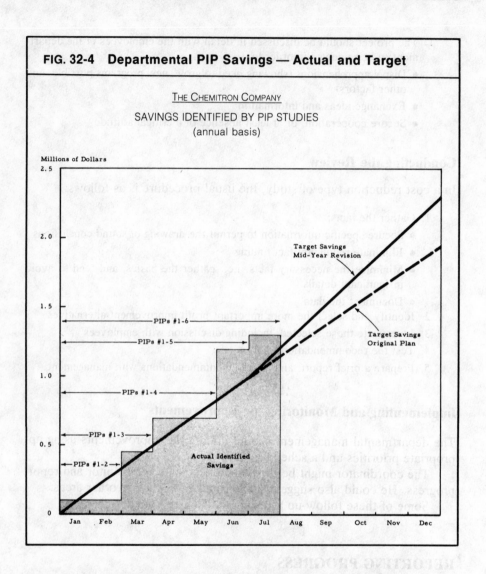

FIG. 32-4   Departmental PIP Savings — Actual and Target

THE CHEMITRON COMPANY

SAVINGS IDENTIFIED BY PIP STUDIES
(annual basis)

AREAS FOR PROFIT IMPROVEMENT

It has been stated that PIPs deal mostly with internal operations, so that the impact on product, market, or customer usually is nil. It also has been mentioned that most changes are in the sphere of middle management. This means that company policies and objectives are not directly affected. Consequently, most specific actions do not concern top management, although this echelon has a responsibility in setting divisional and other objectives for the study. What types of changes would this involve? To be sure, each company

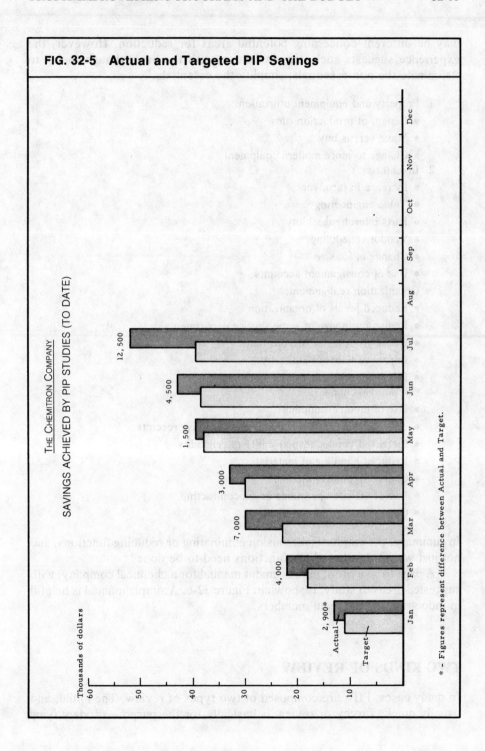

FIG. 32-5   Actual and Targeted PIP Savings

THE CHEMITRON COMPANY

SAVINGS ACHIEVED BY PIP STUDIES (TO DATE)

* - Figures represent difference between Actual and Target.

may be different concerning potential areas for reduction. However, the experience suggests such items as these, with the basic thought being to "eliminate the non-essentials; simplify the essentials."

1. Property and equipment utilization:
   - Length of production runs
   - Make versus buy
   - Change to more modern equipment
2. Inventories:
   - Increase in turnover
   - Value engineering
   - Parts interchangeability
   - Vendor scheduling
   - Change in lot size
   - Use of consignment accounts
3. Organization realignment:
   - Reduced levels of organization
   - Reduction in size of some service departments
   - Better grouping of responsibilities
   - Improved limits of authority
   - Elimination or substitution of functions
4. Operational changes:
   - Use of invoice sampling
   - Test checking or inspection of merchandise receipts
   - Increased vendor responsibility or reliability
   - Reduced handling of materials
   - Change in control methods
   - Use of off-site operations or subcontracting
   - Change in type of material

In summary, the emphasis often is on eliminating or reducing functions, and not just working faster. What functions need to be done?

A page from a profit improvement manual for a chemical company, with suggested areas to study, is shown in Figure 32-6. A simple manual is helpful in indoctrinating the team members.

TWO KINDS OF REVIEW

In many cases, PIPs are composed of two types of review. The initial, and usually quick, survey or review is basically for the purpose of identifying

FIG. 32-6   Guidelines From a Profit Improvement Manual

POSSIBLE AREAS FOR
PROFIT IMPROVEMENT STUDIES

OPERATIONS PROFIT IMPROVEMENT:

1. *Direct and indirect labor.* Improve profits by changing work assignments, methods, equipment, location, instrumentation, or standards of performance and supervision.

2. *Design and purchase.* Improve profits by changing materials, product design, vendors, usage, proportion of materials obtained outside, quality of tolerances, or forecasting of requirements.

3. *Transportation and distribution.* Improve profits by changing methods of transportation, plant location, location of storage facilities, market coverage, products handled, or types of independent distribution agencies.

4. *Operations clerical costs.* Improve profits by changing the types and numbers of reports prepared, methods and procedures, equipment, work load assignments, or performance measurement systems in:
   - Purchasing
   - Receiving

ASSET MANAGEMENT PROFIT IMPROVEMENT:

1. *Cash management.* Improve profits by changing investment policies, internal control procedures, or method of handling receipts and disbursements.

2. *Utilization of fixed assets.* Increase return on assets by making changes in the number, location, and quality of facilities, level of operations (one shift versus two shifts), process improvements, etc.

3. *Inventory.* Increase return on assets by changing amount of product inventoried; number, scope, or location of warehousing and storage facilities; forecasting and scheduling procedures; or distribution channels.

4. *Accounting clerical costs.* Improve profits by changing the types and numbers of reports prepared, methods and procedures, equipment, work load assignments, or performance measurement systems in:
   - Accounts receivable
   - Credit and collection
   - Inventory record keeping
   - Accounts payable
   - Timekeeping, payroll, and labor cost distribution

ORGANIZATIONAL REALIGNMENTS:

Improve profits by changing authority limits, number and composition of organizational units, number of organizational levels, or the grouping of responsibilities.

No unit or function within the entire organization should be exempt from study, nor should any policy, either formal or time-honored, be immune from challenge under this program.

the magnitude of potential profit improvement in the item or specific function. Where it is of a relatively simple nature and quite evident, this survey may be all that is required. The fact-finding in this instance may identify the extent of cost increase, the throughput, the delays encountered, the actions that increase costs, and other factors. The cost impact of the suggested change can be quickly calculated, and impediments to the modification can be measured or identified.

However, if the suggested change is more complex, then a "feasibility study" is necessary. Such a study gathers facts not only on the feasibility, but on the interrelated economics, e.g., changes deemed necessary in other parts of the operation. The key to a successful PIP is not only management support, but also adequate studies that air the problems and the complete ramifications of the change.

WHAT IS THE BEST ORGANIZATION STRUCTURE?

A "team approach" and a temporary organization structure have been suggested. Indeed, in many small- or medium-size companies, this is probably the best approach. It recognizes that the continued maintenance of a profit improvement organization may be costly and, in fact, that the effort "loses steam" after a time. Hence, it may be desirable to organize a short-term effort every three or four years, to secure the benefits, and then to disband for a time until a new cycle is deemed necessary.

However, in some organizations, a small permanent group may be desirable, to serve as a core staff for the periodic "bursts." This might be regarded as a compromise between a large, permanent department and none at all. It would provide some key staff members as leaders in the periodic drives, and might save time in preparing for the next effort. A limited number of industrial engineers and cost analysts might continuously find enough projects for value analysis and other tasks in order to pay their way.

MESHING THE PIP WITH THE BUDGET

When the PIP recommendations have been made and implementation has been underway, one further step remains. This step is to adjust the departmental budget for the expected reduction in costs. This is, in a sense, the test of the permanency of the improvements. Line management presumably has agreed with the change and is implementing it. The department manager supposedly understands the relationship of the PIP to the departmental objectives and to the divisional and/or company objectives. These objectives or goals should, of course, be reflected in a reduced departmental budget.

There will be times when it is prudent to allow the department to operate on the "old" budget for a time and produce favorable budget variances. This has the advantage of showing the impact of the good cost reduction efforts and serves as a motivational device, especially when directly related to incentive compensation. Perhaps the budget adjustment could be incorporated in the next annual budget, if the current year is well along.

There are two ways of adjusting the budget. One is a direct reduction in the expense level. The other is a "line item" or identified reduction provision in allowed expenses. If the budget is adjusted during the year, the "identified" lower budget item is perhaps to be preferred. It shows the cumulative reduction in costs. For example, suppose the original monthly budget for the maintenance department supplies account is $10,000, plus $1.50 per manhour, and the cost reduction results in a 50 percent lower variable cost. The segment of the budget report relating to supplies could read as follows, assuming a variability factor of 12,000 manhours.

	Actual	Budget	Over (Under) Budget
Supplies	$17,400	$19,000[a]	($1,600)

(a) $10,000 + $.75 (12,000)

Or, the budget reduction could be continuously identified in this manner:

	Actual	Budget	Over (Under) Budget
Supplies	$17,400	$28,000[b]	($10,600)
" −PIP adjustment	—	(9,000)[c]	9,000
			($ 1,600)

(b) $10,000 + $1.50 (12,000)
(c) − ($.75) 12,000

INCENTIVE APPLICATIONS

Profit improvement plans sometimes can be made even more effective by attaching incentive pay awards. This may be done at a management level or at the lower operating level. There are at least three levels where this approach has had favorable results:

☐ For top and division management, based on a percentage of the income before income taxes. Depending on the level of company income, and the return to the shareholders, incentive compensation can be paid on (a) the profit level and/or (b) the increase in profit from year to year.

☐ For middle management or department managers, an incentive award bogey may be set depending on the extent to which certain PIP objectives are achieved in the management area.

☐ For all of the members of a department, perhaps awards can be made dependent on cost savings over a specified period — perhaps after one year.

33

The Budget Manual

NATURE OF A MANUAL

A manual may be described as an orderly presentation of directives, instructions, or facts concerning a given activity or repeated procedure. A number of large and small business firms operate a successful budgetary program without the use of a budget manual as such; instead, instructions may be given orally or by letter. Moreover, even when budget manuals are used, there is a great range in content. Be that as it may, it is the experience of the author that the gains resulting from the use of complete written instructions more than offset the time and effort required in their preparation. Certainly it would seem that if planning is beneficial to business generally, then the same might be said of the planned budgetary procedure itself.

BENEFITS OF A BUDGET MANUAL

The more important advantages of making a manual of budgetary procedure available may be cited as follows:

- Clearly defines authority and responsibility in budget matters.
- Promotes standardization and simplification in that presumably the best procedures for developing the budget or plan are stipulated, and a uniform or standard format for presenting the plan is identified.
- Serves to help in coordinating effort by identifying what procedures should be followed and by whom.
- Provides a convenient reference for guidance when questions of procedures, format, or responsibility arise.
- Permits better supervision in that the time of supervisors is conserved to the extent that explanations are covered in the manual.
- Assists in the training of new employees and in transfer of duties because many phases of the job have been reduced to writing.
- Assists in "selling" the budget by explaining the advantages of the procedure.

CONTENTS OF THE BUDGET MANUAL

The contents of a budget manual should be tailored to fit the needs of the specific organization in which it is to be used, and may vary considerably. Moreover, in addition to the general budget manual, there may be one for branches, distributors, agents, and dealers.

The contents of a typical budget manual are outlined as follows:

- General statement of the objectives of the budget procedure
- Designation of central authority for the budget and responsibility for the preparation and enforcement of it
- Authority, duties, and responsibility of major and functional executives with reference to the budget procedure

- Instructions for divisional, departmental, and minor executives in the preparation, review, and revision of estimates
- Statement of length of periods for the various budgets
- Time schedule for budget preparation
- Interdepartmental budget relations
- Procedure for initial budget approval
- Procedure for budget revisions
- Budget reports
- Corrective action
- Special instructions for budget staff, with respect to human relations problems, administration, and so forth
- Most recent budget premises
- Post-audit (capital expenditures, and so forth)

An illustrative page from a budget manual which gives a general picture of the operating budget procedure is shown in Figure 33-1. The manual is in loose-leaf form to facilitate revision. A page from the capital budget procedure of the same company, indicating the preliminary review steps, is set out in Figure 33-2.

PREPARING THE MANUAL

To be of maximum value, a budget manual must be used by those for whom it is intended. Moreover, such use probably will be encouraged if the manual is prepared as a cooperative undertaking. While the primary responsibility for its origination will rest with the budget supervisor, and while a large part may relate to strictly accounting phases, the suggestions and comments of the operating departments should be secured, with particular reference to the operating responsibilities and procedure. For example, the views of the sales manager should be obtained with respect to the best channel or method for arriving at a realistic sales forecast or budget. A simple but effective procedure is as follows:

- The budget supervisor should prepare a general outline of the manual.
- The necessary research and review of the basic data should be made.
- Rough drafts of each procedure should be prepared by the budget department, assisted by the systems and procedures staff, if available.
- These drafts should be circulated among those *directly* involved, so as to secure suggestions and viewpoints. (That is, the *sales* budget procedure would be routed to the proper *sales* group, but need not be circulated among the research staff, and vice versa.)

FIG. 33-1   Page From Budget Manual — Operating Plan Procedure

RICHLAND OIL COMPANY
AND SUBSIDIARIES

FINANCIAL MANUAL — FINANCIAL PLANNING & CONTROLS

SUBJECT: Operating Plan Procedure

I. GENERAL:

1. The operating plan represents the forward programming of operations revenues and expenses based upon the allocated capital funds and approved premises. The plan should represent the most profitable course of action that is practical to follow. It is also a basis against which to measure performance.

2. The operating plan shall consist of:

   a. Operating programs, which are the basis for financial forecasts, and represent a coordinated pattern of the physical activities and volumes of all departments. These include estimated physical volumes for the sale of refined products, raw materials and the production, purchase, transportation, manufacture and storage of such raw materials and refined products.

   b. A net income forecast of revenues and expenses based on the projected operating programs. The plan of expenses will include all programmed expenses for which limits are indicated by the president.

3. The operating plan will be prepared annually and revised each quarter for the remaining period of the year. (At such time as procedures have been sufficiently refined, the plan will cover the succeeding twelve month period, that is, a "rolling" plan). To do this uniformly and relate comparisons to the proper revision, the plan will have the following two segments, with an intermediate estimate.

   a. *Original Plan* — prepared annually for the year ahead, broken down by quarters. First quarter will be further broken down by months. Additional monthly breakdown for all quarters should follow shortly after approval so that comparison of actual performance may be made each month in the consolidated report to management and the Board of Directors.

   b. *Current Plan* — prepared for each quarter of the year detailed by months for the quarter being planned and by quarters for the remainder of the year.

Effective: 11/1/___   Revision Number: ___   Page 1 of ___   Policy Number: FPC-3

- Revised drafts should be prepared to incorporate as many suggestions as practical, and to reconcile any conflicting viewpoints.
- Final drafts should be approved by the general executives, or division heads, as may be applicable.
- A distribution list should be established.
- The manual should be duplicated and distributed.
- Provision should be made for periodic revision.

FIG. 33-2 Page From Budget Manual — Capital Budget Procedure

RICHLAND OIL COMPANY
AND SUBSIDIARIES

FINANCIAL MANUAL — FINANCIAL PLANNING & CONTROLS

SUBJECT: Capital Budget Procedure

In addition to the recommended budget, each division presentation will include a listing of contingent capital projects for management consideration if and when funds can be made available. This listing should present an inventory of desirable capital items with satisfactory rate of return which might be required or should be considered within the succeeding four years except for wells. The contingent list of production wells will consist of a reasonable selection from the well inventory. These inventories of future desirable projects must, of course, give recognition to mandatory or necessary projects which might be imminent.

II. PROCEDURE — ANNUAL REVIEW:

1. *Availability and Preliminary Allocation of Funds*

    a. In consultation with the divisions, the Corporate Financial Planning and Controls will prepare a broadly stated forecast (on "best guess" basis without detailed departmental review) of cash generated from operations, as well as an estimate of expenditures required in the budget year for capital appropriations approved in prior year. From these data the Finance Vice-President will have developed a preliminary estimate of cash flow and funds available for capital expenditures in the budget year. The Finance Vice-President will also make available for review by the President a summary of capital expenditures, by division and function, for the three years immediately prior to the budget year and such other information considered necessary.

    b. The President will make a tentative allocation, by division and function, of the estimated funds available for capital expenditures in the budget year. Historically, as the year's operations unfold unforeseen investment opportunities or other capital requirements arise. To meet these situations as they arise the annual budget will provide an unallocated budget amount which will be under the direct control of the President.

    c. The Finance Vice-President will advise the divisions of the tentative allocations.

2. *Capital Budget*

    a. The original capital budget will be prepared on an annual basis.

Policy Number: FPC-2   Page ___ of ___   Revision Number: ___   Effective: 11/1/___

A PRACTICAL PROCEDURE

A particularly important section of the budget manual, and one which deserves special comment, is the one outlining the duties and responsibilities of those who participate in the budget program. Assuming that the executives, both major and minor, are "sold" on the budget as a useful management tool, then it is essential that each be able quickly to refer to an understandable source reference as to specifically what his part is in the plan. Therefore, this section of the manual needs careful analysis and preparation to be certain that responsibility is correctly placed. Moreover, it is desirable that a definite program be established covering every aspect of the budget procedure. Such a program should be described in considerable detail, usually outlining the who, what, how, and when of the operation.

Several methods or techniques may be used in preparing the responsibility and procedural phases of the manual. Essentially, the differences lie in the method of presentation. Of course, in a particular application, differences may exist as to the degree of detail included. Three suggestions are as follows:

1. Prepare a *summary* chart, showing by type of budget and by executive or department the responsibility of each.
2. Prepare a listing or chart for *each budget* only (that is, sales budget, or production budget, and so forth) indicating the procedure to be followed by each executive or department.
3. Prepare an outline by *individual area of responsibility* showing the various duties expected of that executive as to each budget.

An example of a summary chart is shown in Figure 33-3, although the descriptions are considerably abbreviated. Even though plans 2 or 3 in the list mentioned are used, this chart has the advantage of giving the entire picture instead of only a part. It permits each executive to secure an overall picture of how various functions are coordinated. It can, therefore, serve as a summary, and be supported by other listings as to the more detailed phases of the plan.

A simple checklist which outlines the responsibilities of various executives with respect to a single budget — in this case the materials budget — is illustrated in Figure 33-4. This checklist has the advantage of indicating on a single page the diverse duties regarding one budget. It may be useful as a cross-reference tool.

Perhaps most executives prefer to have stated in one spot *all* of their duties regarding a given function. As presented in Figure 33-5, the general sales manager can review his entire responsibility as regards each phase of budgeting.

FIG. 33-3 Chart of Budget Procedure

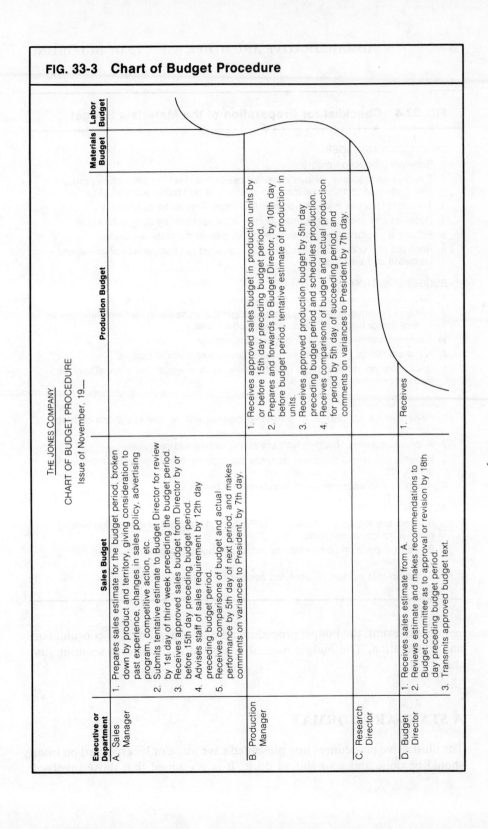

THE JONES COMPANY
CHART OF BUDGET PROCEDURE
Issue of November, 19___

Executive or Department	Sales Budget	Production Budget	Materials Budget	Labor Budget
A. Sales Manager	1. Prepares sales estimate for the budget period, broken down by product and territory, giving consideration to past experience, changes in sales policy, advertising program, competitive action, etc. 2. Submits tentative estimate to Budget Director for review by 1st day of third week preceding the budget period. 3. Receives approved sales budget from Director by or before 15th day preceding budget period. 4. Advises staff of sales requirement by 12th day preceding budget period. 5. Receives comparisons of budget and actual performance by 5th day of next period, and makes comments on variances to President, by 7th day.			
B. Production Manager		1. Receives approved sales budget in production units by or before 15th day preceding budget period. 2. Prepares and forwards to Budget Director, by 10th day before budget period, tentative estimate of production in units. 3. Receives approved production budget by 5th day preceding budget period and schedules production. 4. Receives comparisons of budget and actual production for period by 5th day of succeeding period, and comments on variances to President by 7th day.		
C. Research Director	1. Receives sales estimate from A.			
D. Budget Director	1. Receives sales estimate from A. 2. Reviews estimate and makes recommendations to Budget committee as to approval or revision by 18th day preceding budget period. 3. Transmits approved budget text.	1. Receives		

FIG. 33-4   Checklist for Preparation of the Materials Budget

PRODUCTION MANAGER:
1. Receives production program.
2. Prepares estimates of various materials needed to meet the production program, giving consideration to raw material inventory at beginning and end of period.
3. Transmits tentative materials budget to Budget Director for approval.
4. Receives and executes materials budget after approval by Budget Director.
5. Follows a similar procedure as regards revision of the materials budget.
6. Receives and takes corrective action, as required, on comparison of actual and budgeted performance.

BUDGET DIRECTOR:
1. Receives tentative materials budget from the Production Manager.
2. Presents tentative material budget to Budget Committee with recommendations as to revisions or approval, including supporting data.
3. Transmits approved budget to Production Manager.
4. Follows a similar procedure as regards revision of material budget.
5. Reviews comparative budget reports, makes recommendations, if necessary, and follows corrective action taken.

BUDGET COMMITTEE:
1. Reviews materials budget as presented together with recommendations of Budget Director.
2. Approves materials budget, with any revisions deemed necessary.
3. Reviews actual and budgeted performance together with comments on corrective action, etc.
4. Approves necessary revisions in subsequent period.

ACCOUNTING DEPARTMENT:
1. Renders any requested assistance to Production Manager in connection with original budget or revisions.
2. Prepares reports on comparison of actual and budgeted performance, including commitments.
3. Assists in making special analyses needed by Budget Director.

In any event, the budget procedure requires a great deal of coordination and cooperation. The budget manual can be of assistance in securing just that.

A STANDARD FORMAT

The illustrative procedures just presented have more or less focused on *what* should be done and *who* should do it. It is presumed that those involved

FIG. 33-5   Budget Duties and Responsibilities — General Sales Manager — Page From Budget Manual

Type of Budget	Action to Be Taken	When Annually	When Monthly
SALES BUDGET	1. Provides product sales managers with sales history, and related data, and requests sales estimates in physical quantities by product line, and by territory from product sales managers.	3 months before budget period.	2 weeks before budget period.
	2. Also requests unit price data.	"	"
	3. Reviews sales estimates of product sales managers for reasonableness and unfavorable trends. Gives consideration to past sales experience, price policies, advertising and sales promotion policy, general business conditions, competitive situation, etc.	2 months before budget period.	6 business days before budget period.
	4. Submits tentative sales budget to Budget Director for approval.	6 weeks before budget period.	4 business days before budget period.
	5. Accepts approved sales budget and transmits to product sales managers.	2 weeks before budget period.	2 days before budget period.
	6. Receives comparison of actual and budgeted sales performance from Budget Director.		6th working day of next period.
	7. Explains reasons for variances and corrective action taken.		9th working day of next period.
ADVERTISING EXPENSE BUDGET	1. Requests advertising manager to prepare overall estimate of advertising expenditures, including detailed projects.	3 months before budget period.	
	2. Receives proposal and reviews.	2 months before budget period.	
	3. Transmits tentative budget to Budget Director for approval.	6 weeks before budget period.	(continued)

**FIG. 33-5   Budget Duties and Responsibilities —
General Sales Manager — Page From
Budget Manual** (cont'd)

Type of Budget	Action to Be Taken	When Annually	Monthly
	4. Receives approved advertising budget.	1 month before budget period.	
	5. Advises Advertising Manager of program.	"	
	6. Receives reports on budget and actual expenditures.		5th working day following period.
	7. Submits comments and corrective action statement on any significant departure from budget.		10th working day, etc.
	8. Requests budget revision.	As needed	
SELLING EXPENSE BUDGET	1. Provides department managers with history of cost experience, plans for next year, etc.	2 months before budget period.	
	2. Requests selling expense budgets.	"	
	3. Reviews subject budgets, checks reasonableness of expense, correlation with sales program, etc.	6 weeks before budget period.	
	4. Passes expense budgets to Budget Director for approval.	6 weeks less 2 days before budget period.	
	5. Receives approved budgets and advises department managers of results.	2 weeks before budget period.	
	6. Receives comparison of departmental budget performance with actual.		15th day after end of month
	7. Secures comments from managers and reports on variances.		20th day after end of month.
	8. Requests budget adjustments when applicable.	As needed	

know *how* to develop or revise the budget. However, in medium- to larger-size companies, if guidance is not provided, additionally, on the manner of presentation, then a variety of formats are developed, which makes any consolidation of financial statements much more difficult. Moreover, items on information often are omitted. Consequently, it is highly desirable to provide specific instructions on how the data are to be *presented,* even down to the line items.

Instructions on the format for presenting the annual business plan for a decentralized high-technology company are shown in Figure 33-6.[1] Some comments on the procedure may be informative:

- The budget manual is a section of the corporate finance manual because, among other reasons, the corporate financial staff are chiefly responsible for coordinating the budget or short-term planning effort. At each division, the chief financial officer is responsible for preparing the division "package."

- The procedure is oriented to computer application, through a well-known software program called Foresight, as explained in Section III. Accordingly, to facilitate consolidation, the format and strict adherence standard transaction recording is a "must."

- While the format that will be seen and studied by division and corporate management is shown, there also are instructions on the computer format and the detailed monthly data, which is used only by the accounting departments involved in the consolidation and preparation of the data for computer application and monthly financial reports.

REVISION OF THE MANUAL

If a company has invested the resources to develop a budgeting manual, then it is highly desirable that it be kept up-to-date to recognize changes in organization, new and improved procedures, and policy changes. Generally, a periodic review should be made to eliminate out-dated or needless procedures, and to ensure consistency. Responsibility for revisions and updating should be placed with a particular organization, such as a systems and procedures department, or perhaps the budgeting or finance department.

(*text continues on page 33-46*)

---

[1] Reprinted by permission of the Northrop Corporation.

FIG. 33-6   Annual Business Plan Guidelines

I. POLICY:

   A. Each operating center will submit, on an annual basis, a complete, detailed, business plan. The business plan will encompass forecasts of sales, costs, income, financial position, cash requirements, overhead technical activity, and facility and manpower requirements.

   B. The business plan, when approved by the cognizant operating manager, shall be submitted to the Corporate Office for review and approval in the manner set forth in Section IV, below.

II. DEFINITIONS:

   A. *Firm Sales* are those forecast to be made under contracts on hand at the time the annual forecast is prepared.

   B. *Programmed Sales* are those forecast to be made for products or services which are known to be included in the customer's programmed procurement plans for Northrop.

   C. *Potential Sales* represent an estimate of forecast sales, over and above firm and programmed sales, expected to result from award of contracts or subcontracts in applicable business areas, out of the total national and international market potential.

   D. *Contract Acquisitions* are the dollar value of contracts and subcontracts to be received during the period involved. They are represented by the receipt of formal notification from the customer authorizing work.

   E. *Business Areas/Industry Segments* represent the various broad product/services classifications toward which efforts are directed and which are compatible with approved long-range plans. These are: Aircraft, Electronics and Communications, Construction and Services.

   F. *Overhead of Technical Activity* is the cost of the effort of time-reporting technical personnel and the material, supplies, and services required for the performance of management authorized technical effort not directly chargeable to a contract. Such technical effort shall include independent research and development, bidding and proposal activity; and other noncontractual effort in support of marketing. Included are systems and concept formulation effort applicable to both categories.

   G. *A Program or Project* is a group of related tasks, purchase orders, or contracts which pertain to a specific end item, system, or service within a business area.

   H. For marketing administrative purposes, a *Major Marketing Program or Project* is one designated by the operating manager, or one that will generate one million dollars in sales (billings or input to work-in-process) within a year after contract acquisition, or an annual level of five million dollars in sales in the third year after contact acquisition, or an annual level of twenty-five million dollars in the fifth year.

   I. *Other Major Projects* are those that meet one or more of the following criteria:

     1. Require a new capital acquisition of over $25,000.

2. Entail use of, or support by, facilities or manpower of another division.

3. Represent a departure from the product areas of an approved overhead technical activity program.

4. Involve an estimated expenditure not chargeable to a contract, in excess of $100,000.

5. Any program that an operating center wishes to identify as major for purposes of visibility and control in planning and operations.

J. *A Capital Asset Project* (as distinguished from a product/service project) is a facility acquisition or a collection of individual items logically associated to accomplish or support an identifiable objective associated with a product/service or other definitive effort.

K. *Follow-On Business* represents new contracts or orders which would be a continuation of work presently in-house. *New Business* consists of all new contracts or orders not included under the category of follow-on business.

L. *Backlog* represents value of contract acquisitions not yet recorded as sales on the books of account.

M. *Sales and Cost Analysis Codes*. The codes defined in CFM No. 4-401 are to be used as applicable on the exhibits required by this CFM.

III. PROCEDURE:

A. The business plan is to provide the data specified in the attached formats so that comparisons with actual operations can be made on a consistent basis and the plan may be readily combined into a Consolidated Corporate Business Plan. Consolidations are performed by Corporate Accounting by use of FORESIGHT. To ensure integrity of published consolidated financial statements and reports, strict compliance with established classifications and uniformity in the treatment of transactions is a necessity. However, each operating center may amplify the formats and provide additional data for its own purposes, so long as the minimum data requirements specified herein are provided.

B. Two sets of forms will be provided for the presentation of business plans:

1. *Summary Presentation*. The exhibits to this CFM contain the formats for the summary presentation of the division or subsidiary business plan. The summary presentation formats require only the annual data for the two plan years. Summarization of the monthly detail by quarters and totals for the two years will be computed by Corporate Accounting. It is, of course, imperative that the submittal of the monthly data agree with the summary data for each year. Exhibit A-1 [*omitted*] provides for appropriate comments explaining significant changes and the assumptions used in the preparation of the plan.

2. *Revision to Actuals for Current Year*. Indicated finals for sales backlog, property, and intercompany accounts for the current year-end will be adjusted by Corporate Accounting to actual year-end amounts sometime in February following conclusion of audit. (Planned intercompany balances will be adjusted for differences.)

(continued)

FIG. 33-6   **Annual Business Plan Guidelines** (cont'd)

3. *Monthly Detail.* All operating centers have FORESIGHT capabilities and are required to submit monthly detail and current year indicated finals (as indicated in Section III.D. of this CFM) via the FORESIGHT overflow system currently in use.

C. The Summary Presentation Section of the plan shall consist of the following exhibits:

Summary Exhibit	Title	Form No.
S-A	Financial Highlights	150-10
S-A-1	Narrative Analysis	150-13
S-B	Statement of Income and Expense	150-11(S)
S-B-1	Cost of Sales	150-12(S)
S-B-1A	Statistical Data	150-12A(S)
S-D-1A	Planned Acquisitions, Backlog, Sales and Operating Margin (first plan year)	150-15A(S)
S-D-1B	Planned Acquisitions, Backlog, Sales and Operating Margin (second plan year)	150-15B(S)
S-D-2	Industry Segment Data	150-16
S-G-A	Capital Asset Budget (first plan year)	150-20A(S)
S-G-B	Capital Asset Budget (second plan year)	150-20B(S)
S-H	Balance Sheet	150-17(S)
S-I	Property, Plant, and Equipment Summary of Transactions	150-21(S)
S-J	Overhead Technical Activity	150-22(S)

D. The monthly detail exhibit section of the plan is to be submitted as follows: (NOTE: In order to establish the relationship between the business plan and the management reports as defined in CFM No. 4-301, the same exhibit designations are used.)

Exhibit	Title	Form No.	Monthly Detail Exhibits Required
B	Statement of Income and Expense	150-11	Yes
B-1	Cost of Sales	150-12	Yes
D-1	Planned Backlog Beginning of Year	150-15A	No
D-2	Planned Acquisitions	150-15B	Yes
D-3	Planned Sales	150-15C	Yes
D-4	Planned Operating Margin	150-15D	No
D-5	Industry Segment Data — Quarterly (Noncumulative)	150-18	No
G-1	Capital Asset Budget	150-20A	Yes
H-1	Balance Sheet — Assets	150-17A	Yes
H-2	Balance Sheet — Liabilities	150-17B	Yes
I	Property, Plant, & Equipment — Summary of Transactions	150-21	Yes
J	Overhead Technical Activity	150-22	Yes

Note: All entries on those exhibits related to sales, cost of sales, income, expenses, or acquisition information shall be stated for the month indicated and *not* appear as cumulative information.

E. In addition to the submittal of the above business data, each operating center will submit an overhead technical activity plan separately. Instructions and the forms to be submitted are covered by CPD No. 44.

IV. PLANNING TIME SCHEDULE. The time schedule for the business plan is as follows:

A. Assumptions and guidelines, profit guidelines, and Corporate expense allocations issued to operating centers. — 31 August

B. Complete business plan (including monthly detail) submitted by operating centers. — 31 October

C. Business plan reviewed and approved by Corporate Office. — 15 December

D. Corporate Business Plan consolidated and approved by Corporate Office. — 6 January

E. Corporate Business Plan reviewed and approved by the Northrop Board of Directors. — 3rd Wednesday of January

V. DISTRIBUTION:

A. Fifteen copies of the summary business plan and one copy of the monthly detail are to be submitted to the Corporate Vice President and Controller.

B. Data submitted should be classified as Northrop Private unless a higher classification is deemed necessary.

[Exhibits start on next page.]

FIG. 33-6   Annual Business Plan Guidelines (cont'd)

Exhibit S-A, Financial Highlights

GENERAL INSTRUCTIONS — SUMMARY EXHIBIT S-A

(Form 150-10)

Contract acquisitions, sales and sales backlog are to reflect customer, intercompany, interdivision, and intragroup activity. Each Division and Subsidiary is responsible for assuring that planned intercompany, interdivision, and intragroup business to be acquired from another operating center represents the amount that the prime operating center has established as sales value for the performing operating center.

Form 150-10

Division, Subsidiary or Operating Center

BUSINESS PLAN — FISCAL YEARS 19__ and 19__

FINANCIAL HIGHLIGHTS

(dollars in thousands)

	Indicated Final Current Year	Business Plan 19__	19__
Contract acquisitions — Customer			
Contract acquisitions — Inter/Intracompany			
Sales backlog — Customer			
Sales backlog — Inter/Intracompany			
Total Sales			
Operating margin			
Percentage operating margin to sales			
Net income			
Percentage return on sales			
Average assets employed			
Turnover on average assets			
Percentage return on average assets employed			
Capital expenditures			
Investment tax credit			
Overhead technical activity — Burdened — Unburdened			
Research and development Under contract Company sponsored (non-OTA)			

Form 150-13   **Exhibit S-A-1, Narrative Analysis**

Business Plan Fiscal Years 19___ and 19___
NARRATIVE ANALYSIS OF PLAN

INSTRUCTIONS

GENERAL:

This analysis is prepared by the Chief Financial Officer of each operating center, as a summary of the major changes in the current business plan compared with operations for the previous year or years.

The analysis should concentrate on an explanation of the assumptions used in the current business plan in order to provide an understanding of the adequacy of the guidelines of standards used. For example, list the key program decisions, both external and internal, that are assumed for the plan years.

The format of this report is optional. However, it is suggested that the subject matter be grouped in accordance with the captions listed below and that the factors listed under each caption should be covered whenever applicable.

FOREIGN BUSINESS:

Provide a description of any additions or changes in foreign investments or foreign joint ventures anticipated during the planning period. Also describe any change in foreign licensing activity.

SALES AND CONTRACT ACQUISITIONS:

Identify the major contracts or factors that account for the change between the past year and the current business plan for contract acquisitions and for sales. List dates and amounts for all major contract acquisitions in the plan years.

OVERHEADS:

For each category of overhead, identify the major factors that have caused any change in total dollar amount from the past year to the current business year. (Comments on changes in direct costs may be made here, or under the Operating Margin section.)

OPERATING MARGIN:

In terms of dollars, state the assumptions used for those business areas (or other grouping used for control purposes) in which major changes are forecast from the past year to the current business plan. Relate the operating margin dollars to goals for the operating center.

For operating margin percents, state the assumptions used for each business area in the current business plan. Relate the percentages to goals for the operating center.

BALANCE SHEET AND TURNOVER RATIOS:

Identify major increases in investment for each asset category as to the business areas causing the increase.

State the assumptions used in estimating the investment required for each business area; these are the assumptions governing the turnover ratios. Relate the turnover ratios of the plan to goals for the operating center.

INVENTORIES NOT COVERED BY CONTRACT:

Identify the programs or products for which management risk investments in inventories are planned, including dollar amounts of planned investments.

(continued)

FIG. 33-6   Annual Business Plan Guidelines (cont'd)

INSTRUCTIONS

1. Each division and subsidiary is responsible for assuring that intercompany, interdivision, and intragroup sales are in agreement with the appropriate division or subsidiary. (See Exhibit B-2A for listing of operating center Groups.)

2. Federal Taxes on Income are to be computed at the guideline tax rates issued by the Corporate Office, excluding any adjustments or credits.

Exhibit B, Statement of Income and Expense

Page 1 of 2

Form 150-11
Business Plan — Fiscal Years 19__ and 19__

(Division, Subsidiary, or Operating Center)

STATEMENT OF INCOME AND EXPENSE
(dollars in thousands)

	(Ref)	October 19__ 1F	January	February	March	April	May	June
Sales								
Customers Sales								
Fixed Price	CH 102							
Cost-Plus-Fee	CH 103							
Total Customer Sales								
Intragroup sales	CH 107							
Interdivision sales	CH 107.5							
Intercompany sales	CH 107.8							
Total Sales	(D-3)							
Cost of Sales	(D-1)							
Operating Margin	(D-4)							
Other Income								
Gain/loss on disposal of assets	CH 123							
Interest earned	CH 125							
Royalties	CH 127							
Miscellaneous	CH 135							
Total Other Income								

Form 150-11 (cont'd)

Business Plan — Fiscal Years 19___ and 19___

(Division, Subsidiary, or Operating Center)

STATEMENT OF INCOME AND EXPENSE

(dollars in thousands)

Page 2 of 2

(Ref)	October 19___ IF	January	February	March	April	May	June
Other Deductions							
Interest expense — Corporate (1)	CH 142						
Interest expense — Other	CH 143 2						
Miscellaneous	CH 148						
Total Other Deductions							
Income Before Income Taxes							
Federal and Foreign Income Taxes							
Federal income taxes	CH 150						
Foreign income taxes	CH 161						
Net Income (H-2)							

(1) Enter amount for October 1980 IF only. Plan should be zero.

(continued)

FIG. 33-6   Annual Business Plan Guidelines (cont'd)

Exhibit B-1, Cost of Sales

INSTRUCTIONS

1. The amount shown for Research and Development under Indirect Costs should agree with the total Research and Development shown on Exhibit J.

2. Corporate allocation is the total allocated by the Corporate Office.

Form 150-12
Business Plan — Fiscal Years 19___ and 19___

(Division, Subsidiary or Operating Center)

COST OF SALES
(dollars in thousands)

	(Ref)	October 19___ 1F	January	February	March	April	May	June
Cost Incurred								
Direct Costs								
Labor	CH 204							
Fringe benefits	CH 205							
Material	CH 206							
Subcontracts and outside production	CH 207							
Intragroup purchases	CH 207.5							
Interdivision purchases	CH 207.7							
Intercompany purchases	CH 207.9							
Other	CH 208							
Total Direct Costs								
Indirect Costs								
Manufacturing and engineering	CH 212							
Material	CH 213							
General and administrative	CH 214							
Research and development:								
IR&D	CH 214.5							
Company Sponsored R&D	CH 214.6							
Total R&D								
Other indirect costs	CH 215.5							
Total Indirect Costs								
Corporate allocation	CH 218							
Total Costs Incurred								
(Increase) Decrease in inventories	CH 220							
Total Cost of Sales	(B)							

Form 150-15(S)

Summary Exhibit S-D-1A (First Plan Year), Planned Acquisitions, Backlog, Sales, and Operating Margin

(Division, Subsidiary or Operating Center)
Business Plan Fiscal Year 19___
PLANNED ACQUISITIONS, BACKLOG, SALES
AND OPERATING MARGIN
(dollars in thousands)

By Major Program Within Business Area	Type	Business Plan FY				
		Beginning Backlog	Contract Acquisitions	Total Sales	Ending Backlog	Operating Margin on Sales

(continued)

FIG. 33-6   **Annual Business Plan Guidelines** (cont'd)

Form 150-15(S)

Summary Exhibit S-D-1B (Second Plan Year), Planned Acquisitions, Backlog, Sales, and Operating Margin

(Division, Subsidiary or Operating Center)
Business Plan Fiscal Year 19___
PLANNED ACQUISITIONS, BACKLOG, SALES
AND OPERATING MARGIN
(dollars in thousands)

By Major Program Within Business Area	Type	Beginning Backlog	Contract Acquisitions	Total Sales	Ending Backlog	Operating Margin on Sales
			Business Plan FY			

Form 150-20(S)

Summary Exhibit S-G-A, Capital Asset Budget (First Plan Year)

(Division, Subsidiary or Operating Center)

BUSINESS PLAN — FISCAL YEAR 19____

CAPITAL ASSET BUDGET

(dollars in thousands)

Capital Asset Project	Commitments						Expenditures				
	Prior Year Carry Forward	New Commitments		Total Amount Available	On Prior Years' Commitments		Current Year Authorization		Total Fiscal Year	Commitment Carry Forward to Future Years
		Firm	Programmed				Firm	Programmed		
A. Capital Additions										
B. Capital Leases										

(continued)

FIG. 33-6 Annual Business Plan Guidelines (cont'd)

Form 150-20(S)

Summary Exhibit S-G-B, Capital Asset Budget (Second Plan Year)

(Division, Subsidiary or Operating Center)

BUSINESS PLAN — FISCAL YEAR 19____

CAPITAL ASSET BUDGET

(dollars in thousands)

Capital Asset Project	Commitments					Expenditures				
	Prior Year Carry Forward	New Commitments		Total Amount Available	On Prior Years' Commitments	Current Year Authorization		Total Fiscal Year	Commitment Carry Forward to Future Years
		Firm	Programmed			Firm	Programmed		
A. Capital Additions									
B. Capital Leases									

Summary Exhibit S-B, Statement of Income and Expense

Form 150-11(S)

(Division, Subsidiary or Operating Center)

Business Plan — Fiscal Years 19___ and 19___

STATEMENT OF INCOME AND EXPENSE

(dollars in thousands)

	Current Year Indicated Final	Business Plan 19___	Business Plan 19___
Sales			
Customer sales			
Fixed price			
Cost plus-fee			
Total Customer Sales			
Intragroup sales			
Interdivision sales			
Intercompany sales			
Total Sales			
Cost of Sales			
Operating Margin			
Other Income			
Gain/(loss) on disposal of assets			
Interest earned			
Royalties			
Miscellaneous			
Total Other Income			
Other Deductions			
Interest expense — Corporate			
Interest expense — Other			
Miscellaneous			
Total Other Deductions			
Income Before Income Taxes			
Federal and Foreign Income Taxes			
Federal income taxes			
Foreign income taxes			
Net Income			

(*continued*)

FIG. 33-6   Annual Business Plan Guidelines (cont'd)

Summary Exhibit S-B-1, Cost of Sales

Form 150-12(S)

(Division, Subsidiary or Operating Center)

Business Plan — Fiscal Years 19__ and 19__

COST OF SALES

(dollars in thousands)

Cost of Sales	Indicated Final Cur. Yr.	Business Plan	
		19__	19__
COSTS INCURRED			
Direct Costs			
Labor			
Fringe benefits			
Material			
Subcontracts and outside production			
Inter/intracompany purchases			
Other			
Total Direct Costs			
Indirect costs			
Manufacturing and engineering			
Material			
General and administrative			
Research and development:			
IR&D			
Company-Sponsored R&D (non-OTA)			
Other indirect costs			
Total Indirect Costs			
Corporate Allocation (Total)			
Total Costs Incurred			
(Increase) Decrease in Inventories			
Total Cost of Sales (To Exhibit B)			
General and Administrative Expenses charged to Cost of Sales			

Summary Exhibit S-B-1A, Statistical Data

Form 150-12A(S)

(Division, Subsidiary or Operating Center)

Business Plan — Fiscal Years 19___ and 19___
STATISTICAL DATA

Statistical Data	Indicated Final Cur. Yr.	Business Plan	
		19___	19___
Burden Rates			
Factory			
Engineering			
Materiel			
Administrative			
Head-count — Equivalent People			
Hourly			
Salary			
Off-site local hires			
Total Head-count			
Gross Payroll Analysis (dollars in 000's)			
Hourly			
Salary			
Off-site local hires			
Total Gross Payroll			

(*continued*)

FIG. 33-6 Annual Business Plan Guidelines (cont'd)

Form 150-16

Summary Exhibit S-D-2, Industry Segment Data

(Division, Subsidiary or Operating Center)

Business Plan — Fiscal Years 19___ and 19.___

INDUSTRY SEGMENT DATA

(dollars in thousands)

INSTRUCTIONS

1. Quarterly data should not be cumulative.
2. Operating profit is to be computed per definition in CFM No. 4-301, Exhibit D-1.

	First Quarter	Second Quarter	Third Quarter	Fourth Quarter	Total Year	First Quarter	Second Quarter	Third Quarter	Fourth Quarter	Total Year
	19__					19__				
Customer Acquisitions										
Aircraft										
Electronics/Communications										
Construction										
Services										
Total Acquisitions										
Customer Backlog										
Aircraft										
Electronics/Communications										
Construction										
Services										
Total Backlog										
Customer Sales										
Aircraft										
Electronics/Communications										
Construction										
Services										
Total Sales										
Operating Profit										
Aircraft										
Electronics/Communications										
Construction										
Services										
Total Operating Profit										

Exhibit D-1, Planned Backlog Beginning of the Year

INSTRUCTIONS

1. The planned backlog as of January 1 of the first plan year should be entered on each designated line of the schedule.
2. The January 1 backlog amount will be corrected to actual by Corporate Accounting after final year-end amounts are determined

Form 150-15A

Business Plan — Fiscal Years 19___ and 19___

(Division, Subsidiary or Operating Center)

PLANNED BACKLOG
(dollars in thousands)

January 1
19___

By Major Program Within Product Area	
Ending Backlog	
Total major programs	
Other customer backlog	
Subtotal	CH 183 COL 0
Intercompany backlog	CH 184 8 COL 0
Interdivision backlog	CH 184 5 COL 0
Intragroup backlog	CH 184 COL 0
Total	

(continued)

FIG. 33-6 Annual Business Plan Guidelines (cont'd)

Exhibit D-2, Planned Acquisitions

INSTRUCTIONS

1. The planned requisitions for each plan year should be entered on each designated line of the schedule.

2. Information regarding regulations recorded near year-end that will affect these planned amounts significantly may be revised in accordance with the guideline memorandum.

Form 150-15B
Business Plan — Fiscal Years 19___ and 19___

(Division, Subsidiary or Operating Center)

PLANNED ACQUISITIONS
(dollars in thousands)

By Major Program Within Product Area	January	February	March	April	May	June
Acquisitions						
Total major programs						
Other customer acquisitions						
Subtotal CH 180						
Intercompany acquisitions CH 181.8						
Interdivision acquisitions CH 181.5						
Intragroup acquisitions CH 181						
Total						

Exhibit D-3, Planned Sales

INSTRUCTIONS

The planned sales for the plan year should be entered on each designated line of the schedule.

Form 150-15C

Business Plan — Fiscal Years 19__ and 19__

(Division, Subsidiary or Operating Center)

PLANNED SALES
(dollars in thousands)

By Major Program Within Product Area	(Ref)	January	February	March	April	May	June
Sales							
Total major programs							
Other customer sales							
Subtotal							
Intercompany sales							
Interdivision sales							
Intragroup sales							
Total							

(continued)

FIG. 33-6   Annual Business Plan Guidelines (cont'd)

Exhibit D-4, Planned Operating Margin

INSTRUCTIONS

The planned operating margins for each plan year should be entered on each designated line of the schedule.

(Division, Subsidiary or Operating Center)

Form 150-15D

Business Plan — Fiscal Years 19___ and 19___

PLANNED OPERATING MARGIN
(dollars in thousands)

By Major Program Within Product Area	(Ref)	Total Year 19___	
Operating Margin			
Total major programs			
Other customer operating margin			
Subtotal			
Intercompany operating margin			
Interdivision operating margin			
Intragroup operating margin			
Total			

Exhibit D-5, Industry Segment Data — Quarterly (Noncumulative)

Form 150-18
Business Plan — Fiscal Years 19___ and 19___

(Division, Subsidiary or Operating Center)

INDUSTRY SEGMENT SUMMARY
(dollars in thousands)

		October 19__ IF	January	February	March	April	May	June
Customer Acquisitions								
Aircraft	CH 551		XXXXXXXXX	XXXXXXXXX	XXXXXXXXX	XXXXXXXXX	XXXXXXXXX	
Electronics/Communications	CH 552		XXXXXXXXX	XXXXXXXXX	XXXXXXXXX	XXXXXXXXX	XXXXXXXXX	
Construction	CH 553		XXXXXXXXX	XXXXXXXXX	XXXXXXXXX	XXXXXXXXX	XXXXXXXXX	
Services	CH 554		XXXXXXXXX	XXXXXXXXX	XXXXXXXXX	XXXXXXXXX	XXXXXXXXX	
Total Customer Acquisitions								
Customer Backlog								
Aircraft	CH 561		XXXXXXXXX	XXXXXXXXX	XXXXXXXXX	XXXXXXXXX	XXXXXXXXX	
Electronics/Communications	CH 562		XXXXXXXXX	XXXXXXXXX	XXXXXXXXX	XXXXXXXXX	XXXXXXXXX	
Construction	CH 563		XXXXXXXXX	XXXXXXXXX	XXXXXXXXX	XXXXXXXXX	XXXXXXXXX	
Services	CH 564		XXXXXXXXX	XXXXXXXXX	XXXXXXXXX	XXXXXXXXX	XXXXXXXXX	
Total Customer Backlog								
Customer Sales								
Aircraft	CH 571		XXXXXXXXX	XXXXXXXXX	XXXXXXXXX	XXXXXXXXX	XXXXXXXXX	
Electronics/Communications	CH 572		XXXXXXXXX	XXXXXXXXX	XXXXXXXXX	XXXXXXXXX	XXXXXXXXX	
Construction	CH 573		XXXXXXXXX	XXXXXXXXX	XXXXXXXXX	XXXXXXXXX	XXXXX XXXX	
Services	CH 574		XXXXXXXXX	XXXXXXXXX	XXXXXXXXX	XXXXXXXXX	XXXXXXXXX	
Total Customer Sales								
Operating Profit								
Aircraft	CH 581		XXXXXXXXX	XXXXXXXXX	XXXXXXXXX	XXXXXXXXX	XXXXXXXXX	
Electronics/Communications	CH 582		XXXXXXXXX	XXXXXXXXX	XXXXXXXXX	XXXXXXXXX	XXXXXXXXX	
Construction	CH 583		XXXXXXXXX	XXXXXXXXX	XXXXXXXXX	XXXXXXXXX	XXXXXXXXX	
Services	CH 584		XXXXXXXXX	XXXXXXXXX	XXXXXXXXX	XXXXXXXXX	XXXXXXXXX	
Total Operating Profit								

(continued)

FIG. 33-6   Annual Business Plan Guidelines (cont'd)

Exhibit G-1, Capital Asset Budget

Form 150-20A

Business Plan — Fiscal Years 19___ and 19___

(Division, Subsidiary or Operating Center)

CAPITAL ASSET BUDGET
(dollars in thousands)

	(Ref)	January	February	March	April	May	June
Capital Additions							
New Commitments							
Firm							
Programmed and Potential							
Total							
Expenditures							
Prior year carryover							
Current Authorization							
Firm							
Programmed and Potential							
Total	(1)						
Capital Leases							
New Commitments							
Firm							
Programmed and Potential							
Total							
Capitalization							
Prior year carryover							
Current Authorization							
Firm							
Programmed and Potential							
Total							

INSTRUCTIONS — EXHIBIT G-1
Form 150-20A

1. *Capital Additions* shall be listed by each capital asset project being proposed in the budget that has a total cost of $100,000 or more. Capital projects less than $100,000 may be combined.

2. *Capital Asset Project* is a facility acquisition or a collection of individual items logically associated to accomplish or support an identifiable objective (not to be confused with product/service project).

3. *Commitments*

   a. The budget for firm capital addition will include prior years' uncommitted authorizations only when *re-approved* for current year's commitment. Firm is defined as those capital asset additions which have been approved at the Corporate level without any restrictions.

   b. Programmed commitments are commitments that will be approved at Corporate level during the fiscal year.

4. *Expenditures*

   a. On *prior years' commitments* reflect current year's expenditures on commitments made in prior years.

   b. *Carry forward to future years* indicates the anticipated commitments outstanding at fiscal year's end which will be an expenditure in future years.

(continued)

FIG. 33-6 Annual Business Plan Guidelines (cont'd)

Exhibit H-1, Balance Sheet — Assets

Page 1 of 2

Form 150-17A

Business Plan — Fiscal Years 19___ and 19___

(Division, Subsidiary or Operating Center)

BALANCE SHEET
(dollars in thousands)

Assets	(Ref)	October 19__ IF	January	February	March	April	May	June
Current Assets								
Cash	CH 304							
Temporary investments	CH 306							
Accounts receivable	CH 312							
Contracts in process	CH 316							
Progress payments (positive amount)	CH 317							
Net in process								
Product inventories	CH 319							
Prepaid expenses	CH 324							
Total Current Assets								
Property, Plant and Equipment								
Land & improvements — purchased	CH 331							
— capital leases	CH 331.5							
Buildings — purchased	CH 333							
— capital leases	CH 333.5							
Machinery & equipment — purchased	CH 335							
— capital leases	CH 335.5							
Leasehold improvements — purchased	CH 337							
— capital leases	CH 337.5							
Construction in progress	CH 340							
Total Property	(1)							

Form 150-17A (cont'd)
Business Plan — Fiscal Years 19___ and 19___

(Division, Subsidiary or Operating Center)
BALANCE SHEET
(dollars in thousands)

Page 2 of 2

Assets (cont'd)		October 19__ 1F	January	February	March	April	May	June
Allowances for Depreciation & Amortization								
Depr. — Land improvements	CH 341							
Amort. — Land improvements — cap. lses	CH 341.5							
Depr. — Buildings	CH 343							
Amort. — Buildings — cap. lses	CH 343.5							
Depr. — Machinery & equipment	CH 345							
Amort. — Machinery & equipment — cap. lses	CH 345.5							
Amort. — Leasehold improvements	CH 347							
Amort. — Leasehold improv. — cap. lses	CH 347.5							
Total Depreciation & Amortization (1)								
Net Property								
Other Assets								
Equipment leased to others — cost	CH 351.2							
Less allowance for depreciation	CH 351.5							
Notes and accounts receivable	CH 352							
Investment & advances to unconsolidated affiliates	CH 364							
Miscellaneous	CH 390							
Total Other Assets								
Total Assets	CH 399 COL 0							

(continued)

FIG. 33-6 Annual Business Plan Guidelines (cont'd)

Exhibit H-2, Balance Sheet — Liabilities

(Division, Subsidiary or Operating Center)

BALANCE SHEET
(dollars in thousands)

Page 1 of 2

Form 160-17B
Business Plan — Fiscal Years 19__ and 19__

		October 19__ IF	January	February	March	April	May	June
Liabilities and equity								
Current Liabilities								
Notes payable	CH 403							
Trade accounts payable	CH 405							
Other current liabilities	CH 408							
Advances on contracts	CH 410							
Employees' compensation	CH 413							
Income taxes — state	CH 415							
Income taxes — federal	CH 416							
Income taxes — foreign	CH 417							
Current maturities, long-term debt	CH 426							
Current maturities, capital leases	CH 426.5							
Total Current Liabilities								
Long-term Obligations, less current								
Mortgage notes payable	CH 435.2							
Foreign notes payable	CH 443							
Other notes payable	CH 444							
Capital lease obligations	CH 445							
Accrued product support	CH 459							
Total Long-term Obligations								

Form 160-17B (cont'd)
Business Plan — Fiscal Years 19___ and 19___

(Division, Subsidiary or Operating Center)
BALANCE SHEET
(dollars in thousands)

Page 2 of 2

Liabilities and Equity (cont'd)	(Ref)	October 19___ IF	January	February	March	April	May	June
INTERCOMPANY TRANSACTIONS (SUB/DIV)	CH 467.2							
Intercompany Accounts — Subsidiary								
Due corporate — prior years	CH 467.3							
Due corporate — 19___ (current year)	CH 467.4							
Cash transfers — 19___ (current year)	CH 467.6							
Total Intercompany Accounts								
Division Equity								
Division investment	CH 474.1							
Due corporate — 19___ (current year)	CH 474.2							
Cash transfers — 19___ (current year)	CH 474.4							
Earnings — current year	(B)							
Total Division Equity								
Subsidiary Equity								
Common stock	CH 480							
Additional capital paid-in	CH 482							
Earnings — prior years	CH 484							
Earnings — current year	(B)							
Total Subsidiary Equity								
Total Liabilities and Equity								

(continued)

FIG. 33-6   Annual Business Plan Guidelines (cont'd)

Summary Exhibit S-H, Balance Sheet

Form 150-17S
Page 1 of 2

(Division, Subsidiary or Operating Center)

Business Plan — Fiscal Years 19__ and 19__
BALANCE SHEET
(dollars in thousands)

	Indicated Final	Business Plan 19__	19__
Assets			
Current Assets			
Cash			
Temporary investments			
Accounts receivable			
Contracts in process			
Less progress payments			
Net in process			
Product inventories			
Prepaid expenses			
Total Current Assets			
Property, Plant and Equipment			
Land and land improvements			
Buildings			
Machinery and other equipment			
Leasehold improvements			
Construction in progress			
Total at Cost			
Less allowances for depr. and amort.			
Total Property — Net			
Other assets			
Equipment leased to others — at cost			
Less allowance for depreciation			
Notes and accounts receivable			
Investments and advances — Unconsolidated			
Miscellaneous			
Total Other Assets			
Total Assets			

Form 150-17S (cont'd)
Page 2 of 2   BALANCE SHEET
                                     (dollars in thousands)

Liabilities and Equity	Indicated Final	Business Plan 19__	Business Plan 19__
Current Liabilities			
Notes payable			
Trade accounts payable			
Other current liabilities			
Advances on contracts			
Employees' compensation			
Taxes other than Income			
Income taxes — State			
Income taxes — Foreign			
Current maturities of long-term debt			
Current maturities of capital leases			
Total Current Liabilities			
Long-Term Obligations less current maturities			
Mortgage notes payable			
Foreign notes payable			
Other notes payable			
Capital lease obligations			
Accrued product support			
Total Long-Term Obligations			
Intercompany Accounts — Subsidiary			
Intercompany transactions			
Due corporate — Prior years			
Due corporate — 19__ (current year)			
Cash Transfers — 19__ (current year)			
Total Intercompany Accounts			
Division Equity			
Division investment			
Due corporate — 19__ (current year)			
Cash transfers — 19__ (current year)			
Earnings — Current year			
Total Division Equity			
Subsidiary Equity			
Common stock			
Additional capital paid in			
Earnings — Prior years			
Earnings — Current year			
Total Subsidiary Equity			
Total Liabilities and Equity			

(continued)

FIG. 33-6   Annual Business Plan Guidelines (cont'd)

Summary Exhibit S-1, Property, Plant, and Equipment
Form 150-21(S)
_____

(Division, Subsidiary or Operating Center)

Business Plan — Fiscal Years 19___ and 19___
PROPERTY, PLANT, AND EQUIPMENT

SUMMARY OF TRANSACTIONS

(dollars in thousands)

Property Plant, and Equipment	Indicated Final	Business Plan	
		19___	19___
Purchased Property, Plant, and Equipment			
A. Cost — Beginning balance			
Additions			
Subtotal			
Transfers in (out)			
Retirements			
Ending balance			
B. Allowances for depreciation & amortization — Beginning balance			
Additions			
Subtotal			
Transfers in (out)			
Retirements			
Ending balance			
Capital Leases			
A. Property — Beginning balance			
Additions			
Subtotal			
Transfers in (out)			
Retirements			
Ending Balance			
B. Amortization — Beginning balance			
Additions			
Subtotal			
Transfers in (out)			
Retirements			
Ending Balance			

Summary Exhibit S-J, Overhead Technical Activity
Form 150-22(S)

(Division, Subsidiary or Operating Center)

Business Plan — Fiscal Years 19___ and 19___
OVERHEAD TECHNICAL ACTIVITY

	Indicated Final Cur. Yr.	Business Plan	
		19___	19___
Independent research			
Independent development			
Subtotal			
Burden application			
Total IR & D (A)			
Bidding and proposal activity			
Burden application			
Total B & P			
Other technical activity			
Total OTA			
R & D performed under contract (B)			
Company sponsored R & D (C)			
Total R & D (A) + (B) + (C)			
Statistical Data			
Percent to total sales of:			
Total IR & D			
Bidding and proposal activity			
Subtotal			
Other technical activity			
Total OTA			
Percent of costs incurred of:			
Total IR & D			
Bidding and proposal activity			
Subtotal			
Other technical activity			
Total OTA			

(continued)

FIG. 33-6   Annual Business Plan Guidelines (cont'd)

Exhibit I, Property, Plant and Equipment — Summary of Transactions

(Division, Subsidiary or Operating Center)

PROPERTY, PLANT AND EQUIPMENT SUMMARY
(dollars in thousands)

Form 150-21
Business Plan — Fiscal Years 19___ and 19___

	(Ref)	October 19___ 1F	January	February	March	April	May	June
Purchased Property, Plant & Equipment								
Beginning balance	CH 11.5 COL 0	X X X X X X X	X X X X X X X	X X X X X X X	X X X X X X X	X X X X X X X	X X X X X X X	X X X X X X X
Additions (G)	CH 10							
Transfers	CH 10.5							
Retirements	CH 11							
Ending balance — cost		X X X X X X X	X X X X X X X	X X X X X X X	X X X X X X X	X X X X X X X	X X X X X X X	X X X X X X X
Depreciation allowance — beginning	CH 13.5 COL 0							
Additions	CH 12							
Transfers	CH 12.5							
Retirements	CH 13							
Ending depreciation allowance		X X X X X X X	X X X X X X X	X X X X X X X	X X X X X X X	X X X X X X X	X X X X X X X	X X X X X X X
Capital Leases								
Beginning balance	CH 16.5 COL 0	X X X X X X X	X X X X X X X	X X X X X X X	X X X X X X X	X X X X X X X	X X X X X X X	X X X X X X X
Additions (G)	CH 15							
Transfers	CH 15.5							
Retirements	CH 16							
Ending balance capital leases		X X X X X X X	X X X X X X X	X X X X X X X	X X X X X X X	X X X X X X X	X X X X X X X	X X X X X X X
Amortization beginning balance	CH 19.5 COL 0							
Additions	CH 18							
Transfers	CH 18.5							
Retirements	CH 19							
Ending balance amortization								
Gross Property, Plant & Equipment (H-1)								
Total Depreciation & Amortization (H-1)								
Net Property, Plant & Equipment								

Exhibit J, Overhead Technical Activity

Form 150-21
Business Plan — Fiscal Years 19___ and 19___

(Division, Subsidiary or Operating Center)

OVERHEAD TECHNICAL ACTIVITY

		October 19__ IF	January	February	March	April	May	June
Independent research	CH 20							
Independent development	CH 20.5							
Subtotal								
Burden application	CH 21.5							
Total IR & D								
Bid and proposal	CH 23							
Burden application	CH 23.5							
Total Bid and Proposal								
Total Overhead Technical Activity								
R&D Performed Under Contract	CH 28							
Company Sponsored R&D (non-OTA)	CH 20.5							
Total R&D								

In revising a budget manual, these time-proven suggestions are made:

- All revisions should be handled on a systematic, scheduled basis. Do not leave them to chance, or "when we get to it."
- Any changes should be coordinated with all affected units.
- Typically, the users will forward suggestions for change, however, regardless of the need for a specific change, *all* the procedures should be periodically reviewed for currency and applicability.
- Preferably, the revision should indicate the date of revisions, and the issue it supersedes (See Figure 33-6).
- It is often helpful to indicate, such as by an asterisk, the segment that has been modified.
- The procedure issuing organization should maintain in its files, for a reasonable time, the background for the change — the reasons why, who suggested it, and so forth.
- Finally, and most important, manual changes do cost money. Therefore, the need to make the change should be considered carefully.

34

Scheduling the Budget or Profit Plan

INTRODUCTION

To some it may seem unnecessary to discuss a schedule for the preparation and review of the departmental budgets or the annual profit plan, yet the fact remains that without some guidance or rules, the budgets often will not be submitted in a timely fashion, and consequently the entire planning process is slowed down considerably by unacceptable lapses.

The extent of formality in scheduling the budgeting process will depend on a number of factors, among which are these:

- Size of the company
- Degree of discipline existent within the enterprise
- Perceived priority of importance of the budgeting process
- Personality and management style of the budget coordinator

What is necessary in one set of circumstances will not be required in another. In most instances, a timetable or schedule should be established and adhered to. The method of follow-up and the degree of formality must be selected by those responsible for the success of the budgeting process.

In the experience of the author, a simple means has proved quite adequate in the medium-sized to large organizations with which he has been associated. However, the reader should be aware of the range of methods available. These include:

- Use of simple due-date schedules
- Simple scheduling charts
- Gantt-type charts
- Critical path method (CPM)
- Program evaluation and review technique (PERT)

SIMPLE DUE-DATE SCHEDULE

Some limited type of scheduling effort is necessary if all the required steps are to be accomplished, including the gathering of the data, the preferred detailed review and analysis, and the submission to top management for final review and approval.

In many companies, a simple schedule of due dates is issued for receipt of the various documents, or completion of specified actions. Thus, in a manufacturing company with decentralized operations and each profit center responsible for both the preparation and achievement of its annual plan, the schedule from the corporate office is issued as part of the guidelines (see Chapter 4) with the critical due dates as follows:

Steps	Completion Date
Submission to the corporate office (Controller's Department) of the complete business plan, (including monthly detail)	September 30, 19XX
Review and analysis of business plans by corporate staff (finance, marketing, manufacturing, personnel, and research)	October 25, 19XX
Consolidation and appraisal by finance	November 10, 19XX
Review with CEO and senior officers	November 20, 19XX
Review and approval by Board of Directors	December 12, 19XX

Comparable, but perhaps more detailed, schedules are issued at the division headquarters for submission and review of departmental plans and budgets before forwarding to the corporate office.

Follow-up by the corporate office is limited to occasional phone calls to the division finance officer (the division financial officer is the coordinator) to ascertain that the division timetable is being met. Once the plans are received in the corporate office, frequent personal contact is sufficient monitoring of the progress. Obviously, in these cases, the coordinators at both the divisions and the corporate office are knowledgeable as to the time required for each step.

SIMPLE SCHEDULING CHARTS

Some budget coordinators construct a simple line chart, which details the various specific steps necessary in preparing and approving an annual plan, departmental budgets, or whatever segment of the budgeting process deserves monitoring. The starting dates and completion dates are graphed as horizontal bar charts. The chart serves to clarify the necessary steps and is a useful reminder to make necessary follow-up phone calls. It may or may not be updated by hand notations as to the status of the project. In a sense, it is a simple hand-prepared version of the Gantt chart.

GANTT CHARTS

Technically, as most engineers know, a Gantt chart is a device originated by the late Henry L. Gantt to graphically plan work, and on the same record, to identify the degree of accomplishment. While there are several versions, one adaptable to budget scheduling is illustrated in Figure 34-1. For our purposes, the technique for developing the annual plan in a division of a manufacturing company is described below.

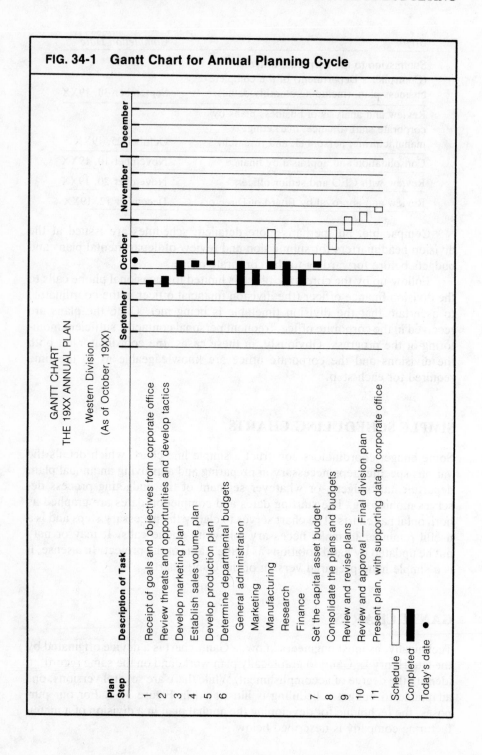

FIG. 34-1   Gantt Chart for Annual Planning Cycle

Identification of Budget Steps

The required detail budget or planning steps are identified. For our example, the steps, which are numbered and identified in the Gantt chart, are as follows:

1. Receiving the goals and objectives from the corporate office
2. Reviewing the threats and opportunities to the business, and developing sales tactics
3. Developing the marketing plan
4. Establishing the sales estimate or volume plan
5. Developing the production plan
6. Determining the individual departmental cost and expense budgets:
   - General administration
   - Marketing
   - Research
   - Finance
7. Setting the tentative capital asset budget
8. Consolidating the plans and budgets
9. Reviewing the plans and budgets, making necessary adjustments, and testing the plans on an iterative basis
10. Reviewing the final plan, and approving it at the top division level
11. Forwarding the approved plan, with analyses, assumptions, and general comments to the corporate office

Depiction of Tasks by Horizontal Bars on the Chart

The individual tasks are depicted on the chart by horizontal bars. The top line, the calendar, identifies time. The length of the horizontal bar represents the time taken to perform the task, and the starting and completion dates.

- As a task is being completed, the progress is identified on the bar by coloring or blacking in the bar graph.
- A movable point at the top of the graph shows the present time.
- Telephone calls can be made to check progress and chart it.

It is obvious that, on this basis, the budget coordinator has a picture of the entire scheduling effort, the relationship of one task to the other in time span, and the status of each task that is under progress, provided the schedule is manually kept up-to-date.

Each budget coordinator has to decide whether this type of effort is practical in scheduling budgets; but the Gantt chart has been effective in many scheduling situations.

There are, of course, some shortcomings, which may or may not be important, in budget-scheduling applications:

- The Gantt chart does not, or does not easily, relate tasks; there is no simple way to relate the impact of delay in one task to other tasks (except through the personal knowledge of the coordinator).
- The Gantt chart does not identify the sequence of *critical tasks*, which determine the overall time span (i.e., those tasks which, if completed on time, assure completion of the entire project as scheduled).

CRITICAL PATH METHOD/PROGRAM EVALUATION AND REVIEW TECHNIQUE

In the late '50s and early '60s, several techniques were developed to assist in the planning and controlling of complex activities. Among these are the program evaluation and review technique (PERT) and the critical path method (CPM). These techniques, and several derivatives, are alike in that they involve the determination of a path or route through a sequence of operations. A simplified version of CPM is emphasized in this discussion since it is used for planning and scheduling in the construction area and since the budgeting process is not complicated.

Under either method, the development of a program could require these steps:

1. Creating the network
2. Estimating the time requirements
3. Developing the critical path and slack paths
4. Establishing the initial schedule
5. Adjusting the schedule to meet time constraints by reallocating resources (manpower) from slack areas to critical areas.

Creating the Network

The network is a graphic description of the flow or work indicating all of the activities and events that must be accomplished to reach the project objective, and showing the sequence in which they must be done. The network must be comprehensive and include all significant interdependencies and interactions required to perform all the work packages in the program.

By definition, an *event* is a specific definable achievement, in a project plan, recognizable at a particular instant in time, such as either the beginning or the end of an activity. It does not consume time or resources. It is usually

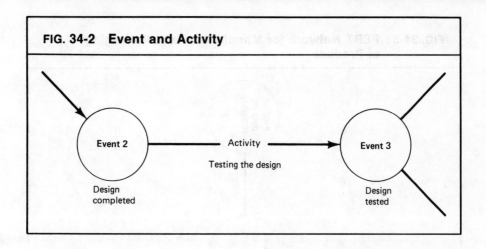

FIG. 34-2 Event and Activity

represented by a circle in a network. An example would be "product testing completed" or "budget completed."

An *activity* represents a process or a task to be done to reach the objective. It is depicted on a network by an arrow that links two successive events.

Thus, in a network, an event and an activity are graphically represented as in Figure 34-2. Note that Event 3 cannot be completed until Event 2 has first taken place.

A complete network for manufacturing and packaging a product might appear as in Figure 34-3. This is a very simple example rather than a complex budget network with many steps or events. Note that a "dummy activity" (the dotted line) is used to indicate that a given activity (such as completing the container) must be finished before subsequent activity can be completed, even though the product is not directly involved. It does not involve an expenditure of resources, but it may be a time constraint.

Estimating the Activity Time Requirements

When the network showing the sequence of activities and events has been completed, the next step is estimating the time required for each activity. In the PERT technique, a total of three estimates must be made of the time to complete the activity: (1) the optimistic, (2) the pessimistic, and (3) the most likely. These are weighted (unequally) in a formula to determine the expected time. In the CPM technique, only the single best estimate of completion time is required. It is obvious, of course, that the CPM method is valuable based primarily on the validity of the time estimates (aside from the benefit of charting the activity sequence).

FIG. 34-3　PERT Network for Manufacture and Packaging of Product

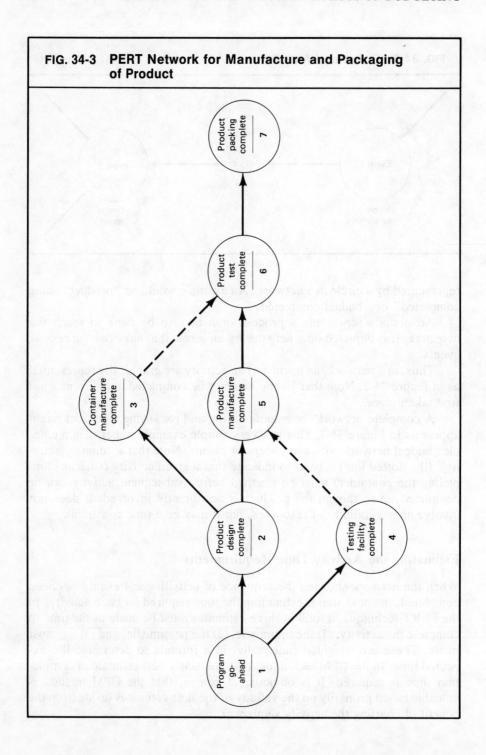

Technically, the time estimating may be done in a forward manner, i.e., beginning with the first event (as illustrated in Figure 34-3). However, the reverse, or backward method could be used, starting from the end objective and working back to the first event. In such a case, the events should be numbered backward.

Initially, the time estimates are made without any constraint, representing the best estimate. The time units, such as days or weeks, are inserted at the center of the activity arrow, as shown in Figure 34-4. Note that in this example, which is the sequence from Figure 34-3, the event is numbered and is without description in order to simplify the process. The time estimates should represent the elapsed time required to complete the activity with normal manpower levels and regular hours. In other words, there were no time constraints. Time estimates in Figure 34-4 are in days.

CRITICAL PATH AND SLACK PATH ANALYSIS

In these instances, where scheduling must be done in detail or must be adjusted, the first step in critical path and slack analysis is to determine the *earliest* time at which an event may be expected to occur. The earliest event time is determined by starting with the first event and, working forward to the objective, answering the question, What is the earliest this event may occur while satisfying all constraints? In practice, these earliest time events are indicated by numbers enclosed in rectangles at the left of each event. This is illustrated in Figure 34-5. The process of adding activity time forward through the network is continued until the objective is reached. In the example, 112 days are required.

Note that the earliest time in which event 5 can occur is 40 hours, since it must wait for event 4, which requires the 40 hours to be completed. If such a constraint did not exist, the earliest time for event 5 would have been 32 hours (24 plus 8).

The "latest event time" is calculated by beginning with the last event and working backwards through the network, answering the question, What is the latest this event can occur and yet complete the project on schedule? Assuming 112 hours are satisfactory, the time for each activity can be subtracted, starting with the last and working back through the network. The latest times are shown in a small circle to the right of the event in Figure 34-5. Thus, the latest time for event 6 is 88 hours before the scheduled completion time (112 minus 24).

Before any schedule can be adjusted, the *critical path* must be determined. This is the longest path from the commencement to the completion of

FIG. 34-4   PERT Network With Time Estimate

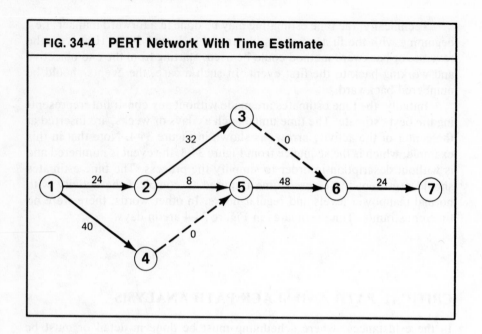

FIG. 34-5   PERT Network With Earliest and Latest Event Time

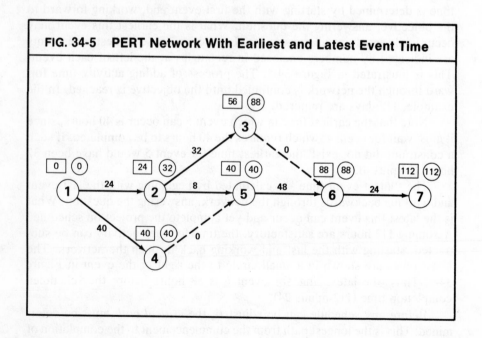

FIG. 34-6 Calculation of Slack

Activity	Duration	Earliest Complete	Latest Complete	Slack
1–2	24	24	32	8
1–4	40	40	40	0
2–3	32	56	88	32
2–5	8	32	40	8
3–6	0	56	88	32
4–5	0	40	40	0
5–6	48	88	88	0
6–7	24	112	112	0

FIG. 34-7 Calculation of Critical Path

Activity	Duration	Earliest Complete	Latest Complete	Slack
1–4	40	40	40	0
4–5	0	40	40	0
5–6	48	88	88	0
6–7	24	112	112	0
1–2	24	24	32	8
2–5	8	32	40	8
2–3	32	56	88	32
3–6	0	56	88	32

the project. It is the path of activities having either the least positive or the most negative slack. Slack is defined as the difference between the earliest and the latest completion time for each activity. The amount of slack associated with each activity in our example is identified in Figure 34-6, arranged by activity number. Figure 34-7 contains the identical data, but arranged in sequence of ascending slack, or the critical path. The critical path, as can be seen, goes from 1–4, to 4–5, to 5–6, to 6–7.

FIG. 34-8   Definition of PERT Activities, Events, Sequence, and Time Requirements — Centralized Manufacturing Company

Description of Activity	Arc	Completed Event Designation	Preliminary Time Estimated (Days)*
Establish the corporate goals and objectives for the plan year	1–2	2	10
Review threats and opportunities and development tactics	2–3	3	5
Develop the marketing plan	3–4	4	10
Determine the sales volume plan (units and dollars, by product, by territory)	4–5	5	5
Develop the finished inventory budget	5–6	6	5
Develop the production plan (by product and department, etc.)	6–7	7	10
Determine the raw materials usages budget	7–8	8	5
Determine the materials purchases budget	8–9	9	5
Establish the raw materials inventory plan	9–10	10	5
Establish the direct labor plan	10–11	11	14
Develop the capital budget (fixed assets)	11–12	12	10
Establish the departmental expense budgets:			
■ Manufacturing	11–13	13	14
■ Marketing	13–14	14	10
■ Research and development	14–15	15	7
■ Finance	15–16	16	5
■ General and Administrative	16–17	17	3
Prepare the statement of income and expense	17–18	18	2
Develop the working capital budget	18–19	19	3
Develop the cash budget (sources and uses of cash)	19–20	20	3
Prepare the statement of financial position	20–21	21	2
Test the plan, by reference to ROE, ROA, EPS, asset turnover, current ratio, percentage of net income, credit agreements, etc.	21–22	22	3
Revise the plan, as necessary	22–23	23	4
Submit plan for approval by CEO	23–24	24	2
Secure plan approval by the board of directors	24–25	25	2

*Actual, without recognizing simultaneous operations.

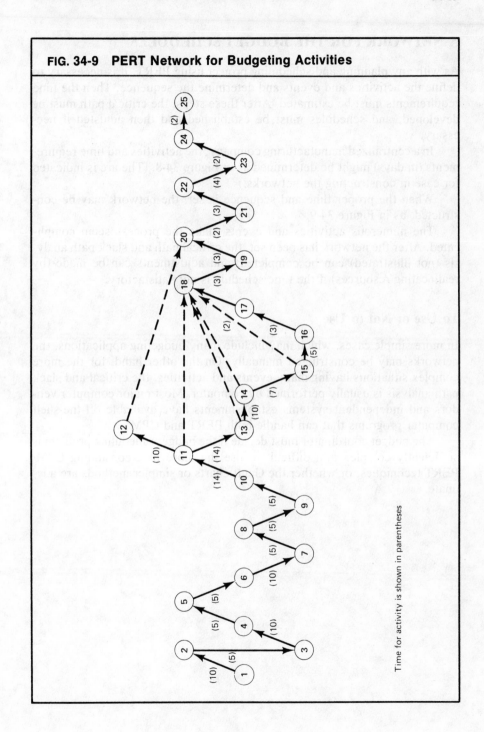

FIG. 34-9   **PERT Network for Budgeting Activities**

Time for activity is shown in parentheses

A NETWORK FOR THE BUDGET SCHEDULES

As with any planning and scheduling project using PERT, it is necessary to define the activities and events and determine the sequence. Then the time requirements must be estimated. After these steps, the critical path must be developed, and schedules must be established and then adjusted if necessary.

In a centralized manufacturing company, the activities and time requirements (in days) might be determined as in Figure 34-8. (The arc is indicated for ease in constructing the networks.)

When the proper time and sequence is set, the network may be constructed, as in Figure 34-9.

The numerous activities and events make the process seem complicated. After the network has been set, the critical path and slack path analysis (not illustrated) can be completed, and adjustments can be made (by reallocating resources) if the time schedule is not satisfactory.

To Use or Not to Use

In more simple cases, which may include many budgeting applications, the networks may be constructed manually. On the other hand, for the more complex situations having many events and activities, the critical and slack path analysis is usually performed by computer. Most major computer vendors and independent systems establishments have available off-the-shelf computer programs that can handle both PERT and CPM.

The budget coordinator must decide if the budget scheduling problem is sufficiently complex and difficult to use the more time-consuming CPM/PERT techniques, or whether the Gantt charts or simpler methods are adequate.

35

Human Relations in Budgeting

BUDGETS AND PEOPLE

For a great many years, business management has developed and refined tools for the more efficient operation of the oftentimes complex business organization. The chief financial, accounting, or budget executive has played an important part in this evolution, which has included standard costs, quality control, production planning and scheduling, and statistical analyses, as well as budgeting. However, those who have had to work with budgets know that, because of problems in human relations, the most effective utilization of the tool quite often has not been realized. Indeed, some believe that over the longer run, the budget may generate forces that tend to *decrease* efficiency by reason of the human problem.

Because the budget is, among other things, a device to control costs through *people,* the author is of the opinion that increased emphasis must be given to the human relations aspects of the subject. In fact, this human phase of budgeting must be ranked as of equal importance with the technical aspects when it comes to achieving full budgeting effectiveness.

SOME CONFLICTING ROLES IN BUDGETING

The frustration, conflicts, or people problems engendered in the budgetary planning and control process may be variously described as boss–worker strife, top management versus lower management differences, or interdepartmental conflict, and so on. These are symptoms that may be related to two basic conflicting roles:

1. The planning function versus the motivating role
2. The control function versus the individual evaluation process

A brief explanation may clarify this. From a management standpoint, the annual plan should represent the most probable or most likely result of operations. It is based on the most likely sales, costs, and expenses. If the plan is unduly conservative or pessimistic, then the company people are not called upon to exert substantial effort, full potential is not realized, resources are not as productive as is possible, and business opportunities may be lost. On the other hand, if the plan is too optimistic and therefore is not achieved, management and insiders who know the plan, such as the company bankers, are disappointed and, often, the required capital or funds are not forthcoming.

From the manager's viewpoint, experience will reflect that often, unexpected obstacles will be encountered that do not permit attaining budget. Then, too, some know that any plan submitted will be "upped" by higher management. Therefore, the tendency is to submit a plan with hidden "reserves" or slack, for the manager knows he must meet or beat the plan. Such a "loose" budget is not a motivating plan and does not require the best efforts of all.

Of course, this slack may or may not be found. One possible solution is to set motivating budgets at the lower echelons, that is, to set tight but attainable budgets at the lower levels, and to provide an identified reserve or contingency at the high levels so that the final product represents the most probable results. The manager of the profit center, but not necessarily his subordinates, should know what this "kitty" is. This approach may reduce the conflict between a motivating plan and a realistic plan. It runs the risk, however, of causing some managers to conclude that there are two budgets: a tough one for him, and an easy one for his boss. This possible stumbling block can, for the most part, be offset by explaining the budget process and the reasons for choosing a particular type of budgeting (as discussed below), and by developing confidence in the fairness of the budget process.

Another major conflict in roles involves the evaluation process. As the reader knows, the control phase of budgeting compares actual result with plan, and attempts to encourage corrective action so that actual will be brought in line with plan. Yet even when responsibility accounting is followed, or flexible budgeting is used, there will be circumstances beyond the control of the individual that cause him to miss budget. It may not be fair to compare actual with some fixed plan, or even flexible plan. It may be found desirable to remove the effect of circumstances over which he had no control. Knowledge that the budget process involves this feature is valuable in getting an effective system. These points are discussed more fully in the next sections.

MOTIVATION — THE ESSENTIAL FOR BUDGETING

When we talk about budgets and people, we are really talking about motivation. No management tool can be used to maximum effectiveness without this ingredient. Further, when we consider the impact of budgets on people, we should not be thinking of only the control aspects, as is quite often the case. Motivation is related to the entire budgeting procedure from planned to actual performance. In fact, there is no better way to encourage the growth and development of managerial talent than by requiring the planning function to be an essential job element.

In this many-faceted game of business budgeting, there are four essential people-oriented phases which should be examined if a thorough review is desired:

1. Orientation or educational phases of introducing the budgetary procedure into a company.
2. Salesmanship, or leadership, or teaching ability of the budget director and his staff.
3. A proper planning environment in which business alternatives are studied and analyzed.
4. Proper application of control techniques in the budgetary process.

ORIENTATION FOR SOUND BUDGETARY CONTROL

If a planning and control procedure is considered worthwhile, then it is a truism that preparation for the installation should be adequate. Time devoted to this educational aspect will ordinarily prove quite rewarding. The management involved with the budget, and particularly the middle management, must have a clear understanding of the budgetary procedure. Since this middle echelon is often compartmentalized, the author suggests a threefold explanation on the "whys" and "hows" of budgeting:

1. The *broad picture,* encompasses the entire business, and enables all levels of management to understand how planning and controls interrelate.

    This orientation includes a description of company objectives and goals and the reasons therefor. Such a phase may be handled by the president, finance vice-president, or budget director.

2. An in-depth discussion of the budget from the *operational viewpoint* of the function involved.

    For example, the manufacturing vice-president may review the budget from the standpoint of manufacturing activities: the relationship between the manufacturing and service departments under his cognizance, interdepartmental coordination, and so forth.

3. Finally, each *individual* supervisor should be counseled by his superior (and maybe a member of the budget staff) as to *his* preparation for the budgetary procedure: how the planning and control method can help him, what he must do, and perhaps some suggestions on how it must be done.

Other aspects of a people-oriented approach to business planning and control are discussed below.

HUMAN PROBLEMS AND BUDGETS

Perhaps because accountants, in many instances, have done a poor selling job on budgets, there is some evidence of a negative reaction to this type of control — a reaction which indicates the budget is sometimes poorly used as a pressure tool in an attempt to increase efficiency. Illustrative are the following tentative conclusions regarding the human relations problems and budgets as applied to certain factory operations, which are as valid today as they were some thirty years ago.

1. Budget pressure tends to unite the employees against management and tends to place the factory supervisor under tension. This tension may lead to inefficiency, aggression, and perhaps a complete breakdown on the part of the supervisor.
2. The finance staff can obtain feelings of success only by finding fault with factory people. These feelings of failure among factory supervisors lead to too many human relations problems.
3. The use of budgets as "needlers" by top management tends to make the factory supervisors see the problems of only their own department. The supervisors are not concerned with the other people's problems. They are not "plant-centered" in outlook.
4. Supervisors use budgets as a way of expressing their own patterns of leadership. When these patterns result in people getting hurt, the budget, in itself a neutral thing, often gets blamed.

These conclusions are certainly evidence of the need for a better approach to the human side of the budget; and the basic question is, What can be done to make the budget a better tool?

It will be observed that most of these negative aspects arise from the control application. However, this is not the only problem area; improvements ought to be effected in the planning side as well.

"COOPERATION" — A KEY WORD

Throughout this volume the author has stressed the need for cooperation. It will bear repeating, again and again, that the first prerequisite in effective budgeting is a *willingness* on the part of each echelon of management to participate in the preparation of a budget, and to be judged against it. The budget must not be viewed as a pressure tool, but as a challenge, a goal, an objective, that can be attained and surpassed. This *positive* thinking must be encouraged and stimulated continually in all areas of management. It is no mere "once a year" procedure, although the planning phases may be emphasized somewhat more during the preparation of the annual forecast.

It should be clearly understood that the decisions reflected in the budget are largely those of operating management and not the financial or budget executive. To be sure, the overall production or sales objectives of the plant cannot be set by the members of an individual department. This is a top-level decision. But the manner in which the goals are to be accomplished should rest upon the interested cooperation of the affected employees. The financial or budget executive does not make those decisions. He may counsel the operating management, and act as a coordinator, but the decisions are the responsibility of operating management. In other words, top management should make certain that real participation, and not half-hearted acquiescence, is the manner in which decisions are reached as to proper budgets. Too often the budget director talks in highly technical terms that the operating staff does not understand. Under such circumstances, any participation by the operating staff, particularly in the lower echelon of management, is purely superficial. Properly used, a budget can and should be a stimulus to improved efficiency. Those who must do the actual controlling will find ways and means of achieving savings that the front office could not even imagine.

COOPERATION IN MAKING BUDGET ESTIMATES

It is easy to talk in general terms about cooperation between the operating group and the budget staff. What is more to the point are some specific suggestions. Consider, first, the preparation of the original budget, or the making of revisions, an area which requires cooperation. This is a time when the budget supervisor or budget representative has much to gain by listening more and talking less. In early meetings, particularly when the budget is new, there is often considerable apprehension as to the purpose of the meeting. Letting the operating man express his ideas will aid in establishing mutual confidence. Moreover, by careful listening, the budget manager will very often secure information about future events that is not obtainable elsewhere. Further, he will learn to know the supervisor better and thus lay the foundation for future participation.

Since the operating heads and foremen are not trained accountants, they will need considerable help in making calculations. The accountant should render every bit of assistance that he can. He will have available data on past experience and will be able to detect efforts to secure a higher budget basis than is necessary. The budget manager should, of course, realize the limitation of past-experience figures. To this end, the foremen or other representatives should be encouraged to express openly and freely their opinions based on their intimate knowledge of their own departments.

Hostility to a thing is often caused by lack of understanding. It therefore behooves the budget manager to avoid technical accounting jargon, and dispel any mystery about the budgeting process. When this is done, a big step forward is taken in securing willing cooperation.

COOPERATION IN REVIEWING ACTUAL PERFORMANCE

The full use of the budget depends on spotting unfavorable trends and taking corrective action so as to avoid a recurrence. In this operating and control area, also, cooperation is necessary. By and large, department supervisors and foremen take pride in the efficient operation of their departments. They usually want to do a good job, and will accept all reasonable help.

Some of this assistance can be given in the utilization of the budget report. It is perhaps too much to expect any supervisor to make the most use of the budget report unaided. Very often, much analysis must be made to determine the reason for the variation. This calls for "operation teamwork" wherein the efforts of the accountant, the engineer, the department supervisor, and sometimes others, should be combined to secure the best solution to the operating variance. When the department supervisor feels he can call for the help of these co-workers in making his part of the program a success, it is then that the dynamic nature of budgetary control shows itself.

In this area of human relations, one of the primary criticisms directed against budget reports is that they show results but not reasons. This subject is discussed in Chapter 2 and in the report section of each chapter, where applicable. However, it should be mentioned here that insofar as practical, explanations as to the cause of variances, as viewed by the operating staff as well as the accounting staff, should be included. The reasons for the excesses or unfavorable variances should be shown.

While the reasons for the variances should be disclosed, of equal importance is the removal of over-budget conditions as to costs, or under-budget conditions as to revenue or income, which clearly are not the responsibility of the supervisors. This can be accomplished (but also disclosed) by adding to the budget allowance a provision to cover the noncontrollable action. Thus, if salaries and wages of the payroll department are higher by $2,300 because of overtime caused by a plan "snafu," then a "plus-in" should be given — but should be identified so as to reconcile with the regular or original plan. A sample excerpt from a departmental budget report might look like this:

	Actual	Budget	Better (Worse) than Budget
Salaries	$24,600	$24,500	$(100)
Wages	39,800	39,600[a]	(200)
Supplies	7,400	6,800	600
Total	$71,800	$70,900	$ 300

(a)   Budget plus-in of $2300 resulting from overtime work in assembly.

ILLUSTRATIVE SPECIAL ANALYSES

A few words are in order as to the special analyses the budget staff may be asked to secure in assisting the operating supervisors. Fundamentally, these analyses are usually a breakdown of costs, which of necessity are grouped in the budget report. Such studies may take many forms; but the principle to be observed is to make a presentation in the language of the department supervisor. A sample type of analysis is shown in Figure 35-1. In this instance, the department supervisor is provided with the details of the excess manhours by occupation. He will review them and see what can be done. Very often computer reports may be used; but many times it is helpful to add some personal comments and to make the figures seem more "friendly." Comparable analyses may be made of other cost elements, such as supplies and indirect labor.

PATIENCE IS NEEDED

Despite the talk of cooperation, there are some capable controllers or budget directors who feel that budget preparation, and sometimes budget reporting, is largely a one-man job, and that time is wasted in gathering widespread suggestions and passing them through innumerable conferences, some of which, it must be admitted, are fruitless.

There is always a temptation to eliminate certain steps. Often the budget director feels that if he can sit down in an intimate conference with each of the major functional executives, and possibly with the chief division heads or branch managers, he can develop the detailed plans and avoid so many steps. This method is quicker and more direct and there can be no question about its successful application in some cases. As a general rule, however, the better results come from a continuous cultivating of the entire executive group from top to bottom.

FIG. 35-1 A Simple Budget Analysis

THE JOHNSON CHEMICAL COMPANY

BUDGET REPORT

Month May   Dept. 20

Summary	Actual	Budget	Better (Worse) Than Budget
Materials	$69,300	$67,100	($2,200)
Operating Labor	10,400	8,300	(2,100)
Direct Overhead	6,400	6,470	70
Total	$86,100	$81,870	($4,230)
Manhours	3,100	2,740	360

Analysis — Significant Items Only

Material

   Resin: 30,000 lbs. excess usage $2,140

Operating Labor

		Manhours		Over Budget	
Code		Actual	Budget	Manhours	Cost
7	Mixing Tank Operator	510	270	240	$1,200
12	Screener	230	170	60	300
13	Union Time	100	10	90	360
19	General Utility	110	50	60	200
	All other over budget	12	—	12	40
	Sub-total	962	500	462	$2,100
	Satisfactory	2,138	2,240		
	Total	3,100	2,740		

Comments

   Considering the exceedingly humid weather, Dept. 20 performed relatively better than most.

   Excess material usage reports indicate that the 30,000 lbs. of excess resin result from contamination by phenol. An attempt to recover will be made.

   Let's discuss with the engineers excess labor hours in mixing and screening and general utility. Perhaps process specifications must be modified. These excess costs total $1,700 out of a total excess of $2,100.

   Excess union time was due to safety work under discussion.

While the financial vice-president or some designated official must actively direct the budget procedure, the chief executive must supply the executive force necessary to compel the execution of the procedure.

USE OF WORKSHEETS AS AIDS

Budget worksheets deserve comment when considering the human relations problems of budgeting. They can be of great assistance in maintaining good communications. If the operating staff is actually to participate, it should have the benefit of past experience. Standardized worksheets are a useful means of indicating the type of information needed. Moreover, they usually facilitate the summarization of data as received from the various branches or departments.

The form and content of budget worksheets will, of course, depend upon the individual circumstances. However, the following information has been found useful:

1. Present budget, perhaps segregated as between fixed and variable allowances.
2. Level of activity contemplated.
3. Year-to-date experience, that is, actual versus budget.
4. Notes on any known future changes in cost levels.

An illustrative worksheet is presented in Figure 35-2 showing the data in connection with a general superintendent's department. It is to be observed that provision is made for approval and comments by the superintendent, as well as his supervisor. While such worksheets can be mailed with an explanatory letter requesting the budget information, there are advantages to having it personally delivered by a budget representative and supplemented with oral comments and suggestions.

INCENTIVES AND THE BUDGET

Yet another aspect of the human side of budgeting has to do with the use of incentives. The additional appeal or motivation to meet or exceed the budget which greater monetary reward might bring is not to be overlooked. To be sure, the adoption of an incentive system will bring with it some more problems. For example, there will be areas in which fair budgets will be difficult to set, and there will be times when the conscientious supervisor

FIG. 35-2 Sample Budget Estimate Sheet

The Northern Company
Budget Worksheet for 19X2

Department: Superintendent – Rawlings Plant

A/C No	Item	Present Unit Budget		19X1 Expenses through 10/31/X1		(Over) Under Budget	Monthly Fixed	Requested Budget 19X2		Comments
		Fixed (per Month)	Variable (per M Standard Manhours)	Actual	Budget			Variable (per M Standard Manhours)	Aggregate for Manhours	
801	Supervisory Salaries	3000	15.00	36,000	37,500	1500				
802	Wages – Other	800	5.00	10,600	10,500	(100)				
803	Salaries – Clerical	650	3.00	8,000	8,000	–				
805	Overtime Premium	–	5.00	1,200	2,500	1,300				
806	Union Time – General	100	1.00	800	1,500	700				
807	Fringe Benefits	900	4.70	10,670	11,350	680				
901	Supplies	50	.40	840	700	(140)				
903	Repairs	50	.30	730	650	(80)				
905	Travel Expense	100	.50	1,890	1,250	(640)				
909	Telephone and Telegraph	50	.10	570	550	(20)				
910	Subscriptions	40	–	400	400	–				
915	Miscellaneous	50	–	490	500	10				
	Total	5790	35.00	72,790	75,400	3210				

Budget Premises

(1) Standard Manhours to 10/31/X1 500,000
(2) Estimated Standard Manhours 19X2 700,000
(3) Fringe Benefits to increase by 5% in 19X2
(4) Merit Increases in 19X2 should approximate 5%

Approvals, etc.

Budget Prepared by:

Approved:
Works Mgr.
Controller
V.P. Mfg.

will feel his reward was unfair as compared with a fellow worker's reward. Yet, in few instances would this same man vote to eliminate the incentive plan. It is the author's experience that fair administration of an incentive plan as applied to budget performance will stimulate additional effort and effectiveness.

ORGANIZING PROPERLY FOR THE BUDGET

Another prerequisite to effective budgeting, and still a part of the human relations phase, is sound organization structure. Duties and responsibilities must be clearly defined, not only as to the budget department itself, but also throughout the entire organization. In fact, weaknesses in this area will be revealed as the budget is developed. This problem is discussed in detail in Chapter 2, and the human side should not be overlooked.

THE BUDGET STAFF

One of the "people aspects" in effective budgeting relates to the budget staff itself. Perhaps the same qualities needed in any management position are those that should be possessed by the budget director and his key staff. Aside from the technical knowledge required, these people should be good communicators, have highly analytical minds, and should have the ability to communicate in the language of the operating people, that is, in nonaccounting terms. It seems obvious also that they should be knowledgeable as to company operations, departmental operations, company and departmental organization, corporate goals, and the effect of specific functions on projects, to name a few desirable qualities.

INSTALLATION OF THE BUDGET

The work involved in the development of a complete budget program should not be underestimated. It is a slow and laborious process. It is seldom, indeed, that it can be worked out and installed as a single unit. Much groundwork must be laid, and much educational effort is necessary. The best procedure is to begin in a small way, usually in one department, and gradually extend the procedure to the company as a whole. In one sense, the work is never finished, as the constant change in business methods requires a continuous revision in the budget and control procedure.

Several points should be stressed in the work of installation. In the first place, there must be an adequate background of information. This involves such matters as complete analysis of past sales, market research, distribution and production cost standards, and detailed records of inventories and plant items. If these are not available, their provision becomes the starting point of the work of budgeting and control procedure. Next, there must be definite lines of authority and responsibility. Finally, the organization must be educated to the merits of budget procedure. Executives, both major and minor, resent dictatorial force. While they may follow orders, they will do so with little initiative and enthusiasm unless they are convinced the plan has merit. All of this requires time and emphasizes the necessity of proceeding slowly. It is usually best to start the work with certain cost items that are readily controllable, as it is in these items that the value of budgeting is most quickly apparent to the organization.

As a final point, note that a budget program need not be complete to be useful. Many concerns have extended their budgeting procedure to only certain departments or operations and have found the results to be extremely valuable.

The work of initial installation of the budget procedure may be directed by the budget director or some other internal officer backed by proper executive authority, or it may be directed by outside consultants. The financial executive has the advantage of more intimate and detailed knowledge of the business, while the consultant is less subject to bias and prejudice and may have the advantage of wider experience. Except in large concerns, where a specialized staff can be employed, the best results usually come from the combined efforts of the controller and a *qualified* consultant. In any event, the major work of maintaining satisfactory budget procedure will fall upon the chief accounting officer and his staff.

A CHECKLIST GUIDE TO IMPROVED BUDGETING

Increased competition and greater internationalism, combined with a more volatile economic environment, is causing management to re-examine its planning and control systems, which means greater emphasis on budgeting, the short-term planning and control vehicle. Technological changes, including both computerization and improved communication devices, are accelerating the amount and pace of analysis related to the budgeting process; but the increased technical applications are making the human aspects of budgeting and administration of the planning and control procedures even

(*text continues on page 35-19*)

FIG. 35-3   Checklist for Improved Budgeting

A. ORGANIZATIONAL MATTERS

DO

1. Do have a functional outline or job description that specifies the budget responsibility of the division department or sectional manager.

2. Do have an organization chart which identifies the functional units, and to which the budget reporting structure conforms.

3. Do assign budget responsibility for *each* component of the assets, liabilities, net worth, revenue or sales, cost or expense elements of the financial statements. The assignee should have the authority to control the item as to amount and timing of increment or decrement.

4. Do stress that responsibility for budgets and performance rests with the department heads and not the budget officer. The budget officer should be regarded as a coordinator and adviser to the operating heads, not as a line executive to whom the department heads report.

5. Do have a properly organized, adequately staffed, practical budget group, made up of people who understand the operations and who can assist the department heads in budget procedures, budget preparation, and interpretation of the budget report.

DON'T

1. Don't force a budget on a department head; let him develop his own budget within the guidelines.

2. Don't place basic budget systems responsibility and authority in those who are apt to be subjective rather than objective.

3. Don't act as though responsibility for meeting budget is the responsibility of the budget officer. It is a function of the department head.

4. Don't fail to have a definite plan for administration of both the planning and controlling phases of the budget.

5. Don't neglect to revise budgets when it is essential.

B. POLICY MATTERS

DO

1. Do issue an understandable, simple policy statement that indicates the purpose and importance of the budgeting, or planning and control, procedures, and the intent of management to use the systems effectively.

DON'T

1. Don't attempt to implement a budgetary control system without the active support of the chief executive

DO	DON'T
2. Do indicate that the chief executive officer supports the system, will issue major directives, will review and approve an acceptable plan, and will judge executives against budget performance, among other factors.	2. In most circumstances, don't issue major budget policy directives except under the signature, or with the express approval, of the CEO.
3. Do indicate the corporate objectives and how the budget will assist in meeting them.	3. Don't neglect any attempt to get budget policy matters changed if they are wrong (through discussions with the appropriate top executives).

C. ADMINISTRATIVE MATTERS

DO	DON'T
1. Where practical, do relate budget performance to incentive pay, as one factor for consideration.	1. Don't attempt to install a budgetary system that is too elaborate or detailed.
2. Do arrange educational meetings to discuss the methods used in establishing department budgets, their purpose, and the procedure for measuring performance.	2. Don't assume that the department heads will understand the need for budgets and the budgetary procedure without an adequate explanation.
3. Do continuously sell or promote the value of sound, practical planning and control procedures.	3. Don't use outworn techniques in making budget changes. Employ the computer and other more technical devices if practical.
4. Do provide simple, written guidelines on budget preparation and use. As necessary, supplement written instructions with verbal aids.	4. Don't overlook the usefulness of a competent operations-knowledgeable budget coordinator to act as liason between the finance department and the operating heads.
5. Do make certain that the chart of accounts permits accumulation of data by responsibility and that it follows the organization structure so that budgeted and actual performance are comparable and relate to the department managers' responsibility and authority.	5. Don't forget to keep the budget manual up-to-date; and don't neglect to simplify procedures, when necessary.
6. Do help the responsible departmental executive to develop a realistic budget, giving	6. Don't forget to tailor the budget procedure to the needs and personalities of the company. A

(continued)

FIG. 35-3   Checklist for Improved Budgeting (cont'd)

DO	DON'T
recognition to the conditions under which he will be working. Tough but attainable with effort is the desired level of difficulty.	ready-made plan in a book may be just a good starting point.

D. THE PLANNING PHASE OF BUDGETING

DO	DON'T
1. Do make sure the budget instructions are understood.	1. Don't issue instructions that only an accountant can comprehend.
2. Do provide all reasonably available data the department manager can use in preparing the budget (e.g., past performance data, properly analyzed).	2. Don't wait for the department manager to ask you for past performance data, or other information useful in preparing his annual budget.
3. Where appropriate, do assist the chief executive in setting the proper profit planning objectives, i.e., return on equity, or assets, which are the foundation for the business plan.	3. Don't use the guidelines or objectives promulgated for the plan if you think they are grossly in error.
4. Do the necessary research and analysis before providing data for operating objectives (e.g., sales levels).	4. Don't forget that analysis and review is necessary to establish a fair budget.
5. Do make sure that every principal function or activity is covered by a realistic budget.	5. Don't exclude some departments from the budgetary procedure because the operation "can't be planned or controlled."
6. Do classify all costs and expenses into the appropriate categories of fixed, semi-variable, and variable. Do be sure the department manager understands the method of calculating the budget, and that he generally concurs.	6. Don't fail to help those department managers who don't seem to know how to determine or set a budget.
7. Do prepare appropriate operating margin or contribution margin analyses to assist the sales executive in selecting the proper combinations as related to sales effort.	7. Don't forget to praise those managers who do a good planning job.
8. Do suggest lines that should be discontinued or instances where prices should be raised (or reduced).	8. Don't neglect to get business plans revised when they no longer serve a useful purpose.

DO	DON'T
9. Do attempt to see that the final sales budget is realistic but attainable with effort.	9. Don't fail to consider a "rolling budget" when the planning system is operating quite well.
10. Do see that production budgets are properly related to the sales budget, after considering inventory, and labor policy.	10. Don't forget the relationship of the annual budget or business plan to the strategic plan.
11. Do see that the corporate business plan, or overall plan, is properly supported by the detailed budget plans for each department or function.	11. Don't forget that the capital budgeting procedures should "rank" projects, and recognize the time value of money.
12. Do see that practical and proper techniques are available to test or formulate support for the plan (e.g., discounted cash flow).	12. Don't forget the benefits of reviewing the annual business plan with your commercial bankers.
13. Do make certain that the capital budget supports the operating budget.	13. Don't neglect the benefits of reviewing the annual plan in person with the appropriate management levels.
14. Do make sure the business plan for operations is within the cash resource or financial capability of the company.	14. Don't forget to provide a realistic appraisal of the business plans to the top management.
15. Do see that the sales plan realistically recognizes such matters as: seasonality; cyclical trends; competitive actions; general business conditions; advertising and sales; promotion plans; and new product development.	15. Don't fail to remember there are a lot of factors besides past performance in setting a good budget. Don't forget changes in conditions.
16. Do communicate to top management the key and critical, assumptions underlying the annual business plan.	16. Don't fail to remember there are many facets to good planning that are not immediately reflected in the financials (e.g., sound personnel planning).
17. Do provide some alternative scenarios to the "most probable" business plans, and its segments (i.e., optimistic scenario and pessimistic scenario).	17. Don't forget to test and evaluate the budget and to revise it if necessary before releasing it.
	18. Don't forget that sound planning doesn't solve all business problems; it is only a beginning.

(continued)

FIG. 35-3   Checklist for Improved Budgeting (cont'd)

E. THE CONTROL PHASE OF BUDGETING

DO	DON'T
1. Do issue budget reports that follow these reporting principles: responsibility reporting; summarized reporting; exception reporting; comparative reporting; and interpreted reporting.	1. Don't issue reports full of unimportant details. Concentrate on the essential.
2. Do make sure that all significant budget variances are correctly explained.	2. Don't issue reports showing major budget variances without making a full and correct explanation.
3. Do report what corrective action has been taken by the department manager, if practical.	3. Don't issue reports just to show how poor performance has been.
4. Do issue reports on a timely basis.	4. Don't issue reports so late they are useless.
5. Do use the newer practical techniques for providing useful data, including computer reports and real time information.	5. Don't use outworn and accounting-oriented formats. Speak the language of the reader. Make the report attention getting; action motivating.
6. Do use more or less standardized formats, if practical.	6. Don't issue business plans and reports that only an accountant would understand.
7. Do provide suggestions for improvement in procedures or operations to the department manager.	7. Don't just issue a budget report and let the operating manager do all the thinking about what changes are necessary to meet the budget.
8. Do attempt to make all budget reports reflect fair and reasonable comparisons, such as by the use of variable budgets.	8. Don't issue a budget report that does not measure performances fairly.
9. Do review the budget results with the department needs on a regular basis.	9. Don't think it is up to the department head to get in touch with you if he has questions about the budget reports. Ask him if you can explain anything or provide more information.
10. Do listen for improvements in the budget reporting system.	10. Don't forget to praise good performance — orally to the employee's boss and in the budget report itself.

DO	DON'T
11. Do analyze operations for improvements and trends and relationships.	11. Don't set control budgets that are unattainable or unrealistic.
12. Do consider issuing comparative reports showing relative performance to develop a competitive spirit or attitude.	
13. Do use graphic techniques and similar devices to get the story across.	
14. Do issue budget reports that compare not only operating results, but also asset and liability levels: actual vs. plan; actual cash receipts and disbursements vs. plan; and corrective action needed.	

more important. To assist the budget coordinator or officer in introducing and administering an effective budgetary system, a checklist of "dos and don'ts," largely from the viewpoint of the top budget official, is presented in Figure 35-3. Although it must be adapted to the management style of a particular company, it contains some useful suggestions for the human relations aspects, as well as some technical points.

Index

[*Chapter numbers are boldface and are followed by a bullet; lightface numbers after the bullet refer to pages within the chapter.*]

A

ABC method, inventory analysis, **21**·13–14

Accountants' method, capital budget evaluation, **25**·10–11, 13

Accounting advertising budget, **16**·25–27

Accounting department expense, standards, **18**·17–18

Accounts manufacturing expense classification, **13**·11–13
standards, incorporation, **8**·16

Accounts payable budget, **23**·4–9

Accounts receivable budget elements, **20**·1
general discussion, **20**·1–5
illustrated, **20**·2–3

Accrued expense budget, **23**·4–5, 7, 10

Accrued income tax budget, **23**·5, 10–12

Activity, defined (PERT), **34**·6–7

Activity measures accounting department, **18**·17–18
costs, **5**·7–8
distribution costs, **15**·11–13, 21–24
manufacturing expense, **13**·8–9

Administrative expense standards, **8**·12–13

Administrative-type budget distribution costs, **15**·9–11
general and administrative expenses, **18**·9–13

Advertising
See also Sales promotion

defined, **16**·2–3
purposes of, **16**·8

Advertising budget
See also Advertising expense; Advertising expense budget
accounting, **16**·25–27
competitive actions, **16**·14
complexities, **16**·9–10
determining amount, **16**·12–17
lump-sum appropriation, **16**·9, 12–16
separate (from marketing), **16**·4–5
steps in preparing, **16**·10–19

Advertising costs
direct, **16**·17–18
indirect, **16**·17–18

Advertising expenditures, **16**·4, 6–7

Advertising expense
budget procedure, **16**·11–12
costs, types, **16**·5, 17–18
magnitude, **16**·4, 6–7
measuring benefits, **16**·18–19
standards, **16**·19–24

Advertising expense budget
establishing amount, **16**·12–17
illustrated, **16**·24–27
lump-sum appropriation, **16**·9, 12–16

Advertising and sales promotion expense budget, **16**·1–27

Advertising program
coordinating, **16**·24
steps, **16**·10–11

Analysis
ABC method, **21**·13–14
advertising budget, **16**·17–19
contribution margin, **15**·18–19
cost of goods sold, **14**·3, 8

I-1

[Chapter numbers are boldface and are followed by a bullet; lightface numbers after the bullet refer to pages within the chapter.]

[Chapter numbers are boldface and are followed by a bullet; lightface numbers after the bullet refer to pages within the chapter.]

[Chapter numbers are boldface and are followed by a bullet; lightface numbers after the bullet refer to pages within the chapter.]

[Chapter numbers are boldface and are followed by a bullet; lightface numbers after the bullet refer to pages within the chapter.]

L

[Chapter numbers are boldface and are followed by a bullet; lightface numbers after the bullet refer to pages within the chapter.]

*[Chapter numbers are boldface and are followed by a bullet; lightface
numbers after the bullet refer to pages within the chapter.]*

[Chapter numbers are boldface and are followed by a bullet; lightface numbers after the bullet refer to pages within the chapter.]

[Chapter numbers are boldface and are followed by a bullet; lightface numbers after the bullet refer to pages within the chapter.]

[Chapter numbers are boldface and are followed by a bullet; lightface numbers after the bullet refer to pages within the chapter.]

[Chapter numbers are boldface and are followed by a bullet; lightface numbers after the bullet refer to pages within the chapter.]

[Chapter numbers are boldface and are followed by a bullet; lightface numbers after the bullet refer to pages within the chapter.]